D0847348

Dictionary of Literary Biography

Dictionary of Literary Biography Documentary Series

Dictionary of Literary Biography Yearbooks

1980 edited by Karen L. Rood, Jean W. Ross, and Richard Ziegfeld (1981)

1981 edited by Karen L. Rood, Jean W. Ross, and Richard Ziegfeld (1982)

1982 edited by Richard Ziegfeld; associate editors: Jean W. Ross and Lynne C. Zeigler (1983)

1983 edited by Mary Bruccoli and Jean W. Ross; associate editor Richard Ziegfeld (1984)

1984 edited by Jean W. Ross (1985)

1985 edited by Jean W. Ross (1986)

1986 edited by J. M. Brook (1987)

1987 edited by J. M. Brook (1988)

1988 edited by J. M. Brook (1989)

1989 edited by J. M. Brook (1990)

1990 edited by James W. Hipp (1991)

1991 edited by James W. Hipp (1992)

1992 edited by James W. Hipp (1993)

1993 edited by James W. Hipp, contributing editor George Garrett (1994)

1994 edited by James W. Hipp, contributing editor George Garrett (1995)

1995 edited by James W. Hipp, contributing editor George Garrett (1996)

1996 edited by Samuel W. Bruce and L. Kay Webster, contributing editor George Garrett (1997)

1997 edited by Matthew J. Bruccoli and George Garrett, with the assistance of L. Kay Webster (1998)

1998 edited by Matthew J. Bruccoli, contributing editor George Garrett, with the assistance of D. W. Thomas (1999)

1999 edited by Matthew J. Bruccoli, contributing editor George Garrett, with the assistance of D. W. Thomas (2000)

2000 edited by Matthew J. Bruccoli, contributing editor George Garrett, with the assistance of George Parker Anderson (2001)

2001 edited by Matthew J. Bruccoli, contributing editor George Garrett, with the assistance of George Parker Anderson (2002)

Concise Series

Concise Dictionary of American Literary Biography, 7 volumes (1988–1999): *The New Consciousness, 1941–1968; Colonization to the American Renaissance, 1640–1865; Realism, Naturalism, and Local Color, 1865–1917; The Twenties, 1917–1929; The Age of Maturity, 1929–1941; Broadening Views, 1968–1988; Supplement: Modern Writers, 1900–1998.*

Concise Dictionary of British Literary Biography, 8 volumes (1991–1992): *Writers of the Middle Ages and Renaissance Before 1660; Writers of the Restoration and Eighteenth Century, 1660–1789; Writers of the Romantic Period, 1789–1832; Victorian Writers, 1832–1890; Late-Victorian and Edwardian Writers, 1890–1914; Modern Writers, 1914–1945; Writers After World War II, 1945–1960; Contemporary Writers, 1960 to Present.*

Concise Dictionary of World Literary Biography, 10 volumes projected (1999–): *Ancient Greek and Roman Writers; German Writers; African, Caribbean, and Latin American Writers; South Slavic and Eastern European Writers.*

Dictionary of Literary Biography® • Volume Two Hundred Sixty-Two

British Philosophers, 1800–2000

Dictionary of Literary Biography® • Volume Two Hundred Sixty-Two

British Philosophers, 1800–2000

Edited by
Philip B. Dematteis
Saint Leo University

Peter S. Fosl
Transylvania University

and

Leemon B. McHenry
Loyola Marymount University and *California State University, Northridge*

A Bruccoli Clark Layman Book

GALE®

THOMSON
™
GALE

Detroit • New York • San Diego • San Francisco • Cleveland • New Haven, Conn. • Waterville, Maine • London • Munich

Dictionary of Literary Biography
British Philosophers,
1800–2000

LIBRARY OF CONGRESS CATALOGING-IN-PUBLICATION DATA

British philosophers, 1800–2000 / edited by Philip B. Dematteis, Peter S. Fosl, and Leemon B. McHenry.
    p. cm.—(Dictionary of Literary Biography; v. 262)
"A Bruccoli Clark Layman book."
    Includes bibliographical references and index.
    ISBN 0-7876-6006-X (alk. paper)
    1. Philosophers—Great Britian.
    2. Philosophy, Modern. I. Dematteis, Philip Breed.
    II. Fosl, Peter S. III. McHenry, Leemon B., 1950– IV. Series.

B72 .B693 2002
192—dc21

2002007416

Printed in the United States of America
10 9 8 7 6 5 4 3 2 1

In memory of our brothers

David Kell Dematteis

Tommy Patrick McHenry

Contents

Plan of the Series

The advisory board, the editors, and the publisher of the *Dictionary of Literary Biography* are joined in endorsing Mark Twain's declaration. The literature of a nation provides an inexhaustible resource of permanent worth. Our purpose is to make literature and its creators better understood and more accessible to students and the reading public, while satisfying the needs of teachers and researchers.

To meet these requirements, *literary biography* has been construed in terms of the author's achievement. The most important thing about a writer is his writing. Accordingly, the entries in *DLB* are career biographies, tracing the development of the author's canon and the evolution of his reputation.

The purpose of *DLB* is not only to provide reliable information in a usable format but also to place the figures in the larger perspective of literary history and to offer appraisals of their accomplishments by qualified scholars.

The publication plan for *DLB* resulted from two years of preparation. The project was proposed to Bruccoli Clark by Frederick G. Ruffner, president of the Gale Research Company, in November 1975. After specimen entries were prepared and typeset, an advisory board was formed to refine the entry format and develop the series rationale. In meetings held during 1976, the publisher, series editors, and advisory board approved the scheme for a comprehensive biographical dictionary of persons who contributed to literature. Editorial work on the first volume began in January 1977, and it was published in 1978. In order to make *DLB* more than a dictionary and to compile volumes that individually have claim to status as literary history, it was decided to organize volumes by topic, period, or

genre. Each of these freestanding volumes provides a biographical-bibliographical guide and overview for a particular area of literature. We are convinced that this organization—as opposed to a single alphabet method—constitutes a valuable innovation in the presentation of reference material. The volume plan necessarily requires many decisions for the placement and treatment of authors. Certain figures will be included in separate volumes, but with different entries emphasizing the aspect of his career appropriate to each volume. Ernest Hemingway, for example, is represented in *American Writers in Paris, 1920–1939* by an entry focusing on his expatriate apprenticeship; he is also in *American Novelists, 1910–1945* with an entry surveying his entire career, as well as in *American Short-Story Writers, 1910–1945, Second Series* with an entry concentrating on his short fiction. Each volume includes a cumulative index of the subject authors and articles.

Since 1981 the series has been further augmented by the *DLB Yearbooks*, which update published entries, add new entries to keep the *DLB* current with contemporary activity, and provide articles on literary history. There have also been nineteen *DLB Documentary Series* volumes which provide illustrations, facsimiles, and biographical and critical source materials for figures, works, or groups judged to have particular interest for students. In 1999 the *Documentary Series* was incorporated into the *DLB* volume numbering system beginning with *DLB 210: Ernest Hemingway.*

We define literature as the *intellectual commerce of a nation:* not merely as belles lettres but as that ample and complex process by which ideas are generated, shaped, and transmitted. *DLB* entries are not limited to "creative writers" but extend to other figures who in their time and in their way influenced the mind of a people. Thus the series encompasses historians, journalists, publishers, book collectors, and screenwriters. By this means readers of *DLB* may be aided to perceive literature not as cult scripture in the keeping of intellectual high priests but firmly positioned at the center of a nation's life.

DLB includes the major writers appropriate to each volume and those standing in the ranks behind them. Scholarly and critical counsel has been sought in deciding which minor figures to include and how full their entries should be. Wherever possible, useful references are made to figures who do not warrant separate entries.

Each *DLB* volume has an expert volume editor responsible for planning the volume, selecting the figures for inclusion, and assigning the entries. Volume editors are also responsible for preparing, where appropriate, appendices surveying the major periodicals and literary and intellectual movements for their volumes, as well as lists of further readings. Work on the series as a whole is coordinated at the Bruccoli Clark Layman editorial center in Columbia, South Carolina, where the editorial staff is responsible for accuracy and utility of the published volumes.

One feature that distinguishes *DLB* is the illustration policy—its concern with the iconography of literature. Just as an author is influenced by his surroundings, so is the reader's understanding of the author enhanced by a knowledge of his environment. Therefore *DLB* volumes include not only drawings, paintings, and photographs of authors, often depicting them at various stages in their careers, but also illustrations of their families and places where they lived. Title pages are regularly reproduced in facsimile along with dust jackets for modern authors. The dust jackets are a special feature of *DLB* because they often document better than anything else the way in which an author's work was perceived in its own time. Specimens of the writers' manuscripts and letters are included when feasible.

Samuel Johnson rightly decreed that "The chief glory of every people arises from its authors." The purpose of the *Dictionary of Literary Biography* is to compile literary history in the surest way available to us—by accurate and comprehensive treatment of the lives and work of those who contributed to it.

The *DLB* Advisory Board

Introduction

British philosophers who were active between 1500 and 1799–the period covered by *DLB 252*–engaged with philosophical topics and used methods that were both different from and continuous with those that were taken up by British philosophers of the next two centuries. The earlier philosophers were involved with wresting philosophy loose from the medieval and Renaissance traditions, formulating new forms of ethics and politics, clarifying and assessing the principles on which modern science is based, and reconceiving the relationship of the human to the divine. They struggled with what later came to be known as empiricism, rationalism, naturalism, natural theology, and liberalism.

Empiricism is characteristic of philosophies that wish to discipline or limit thought by tethering it to some notion of direct human experience. Naturalism is characteristic of philosophies that explain various phenomena by appealing only to features of the natural world–typically, the world as it is observed through human sensation and conceived as behaving as a causal order. Despite the criticism of mechanistic, rationalistic philosophy levied by Romantic thinkers in the late eighteenth and early nineteenth centuries, these powerful currents continued at the center of British philosophical thought through the nineteenth and twentieth centuries. But in a critical response to empiricism and naturalism, British philosophers of this period also developed complex reinterpretations of the project begun by the German idealists, a significant branch of British philosophy that many accounts of its history neglect.

Among empirical and naturalistic philosophers must be counted John Stuart Mill (1806–1873) and Henry Sidgwick (1838–1900), who developed, following David Hume and Joseph Butler in the 1700s, what has perhaps become the most important moral theory of the last two centuries: utilitarianism. Maintaining simply that natural human happiness is the goal of moral life, that happiness must be considered collectively, and that conditions of greater or lesser happiness can be empirically determined, utilitarian theorists sundered moral theory from metaphysical speculation, logical analyses of ideas, and religious dogma. Instead, they tied it to the findings of empirical social science and psychology. John Austin (1790–1859) extended utilitarian insights into the new field of analytical legal theory.

In the wake of the French Revolution and the American War of Independence, and imbued with Enlightenment optimism in the powers of goodwilled rationality to perfect human society, utopian societies and revolutionary thinkers sprang up in Britain and the United States. In New Lanark, Scotland, utilitarians founded a community devoted to social reform, while others influenced by utilitarianism formed the Agapemone cult of free love in Somerset. More-radical thinkers such as the poet Percy Bysshe Shelley and his father-in-law, the political philosopher William Godwin (1756–1836), sought out a more anarchistic vision.

In an effort to examine and hone the methods and assumptions of experimental natural science, William Whewell (1794–1866) deepened the theory of induction. John Stuart Mill's powerful *System of Logic* (1843) followed him in this project, redefining the inductive scientific methods promoted more than two hundred years earlier by Francis Bacon to give them rigor, clarity, and logical sophistication.

After Charles Darwin's *On the Origin of the Species by Means of Natural Selection: Or, The Preservation of Favoured Races in the Struggle for Life* rocked the intellectual world in 1859, naturalistic philosophers of the Victorian era incorporated his insights into social theory and ethics–especially utilitarian ethics. They also used Darwin's theory as a lens through which to reassess the methods and presumptions of inductive science. Herbert Spencer (1820–1903) set out an evolutionary account of cognition and, in what became known as social Darwinism, deployed Darwin's principle of natural selection to explain human society and to prescribe how it ought to be ordered so as to promote and acknowledge those he regarded as the fittest of humankind. Though often criticized as little more than ideological apologetics for capitalist cruelty and neglect of the poor and downtrodden, Spencer's controversial ideas were highly influential on both sides of the Atlantic–not only on philosophers but also on social critics and scientists and in legal circles. In 1902 he was nominated for the Nobel Prize in literature. Spencer's investigations seem to have been prescient, for evolutionary accounts of the social and moral dimensions of human life have again become prominent in the discipline of sociobiology.

Important and powerful though they were, naturalism and empiricism could not escape criticism. The Common Sense school, though in its own way extremely naturalistic, presented a compelling rebuke to eighteenth-century skepticism and the skeptical tendencies of naturalism. Building on the eighteenth-century work of Aberdeen's Thomas Reid, Sir William Hamilton (1788–1856), in important articles of the early 1830s, helped to carry the Common Sense school into the nineteenth century.

The Common Sense reproach was not the only rejoinder to the naturalistic current. Naturalism also generated a critical reply from philosophers influenced by the German idealist Georg Wilhelm Friedrich Hegel who became known as the British idealists and whose doctrines came to dominate British philosophy by the end of the century. In part because of the Hegelian emphasis on the historical development of thought and being, the nineteenth century became an age of intense historical inquiry in Europe. One of the shining lights of Britain's philosophical-historian community, R. L. Nettleship (1846–1892), produced seminal work that enormously advanced the understanding of ancient philosophy in both scope and detail. But the rise of idealism and historical philosophy heralded more than the advent of new philosophical movements; it also marked a shift in Britain's philosophical center of gravity. Nearly all of these important philosophers were university professors; most of their immediate predecessors had not held academic positions. The rise of these professors signaled the reassertion of British universities in the philosophical life of the United Kingdom—a position that they had lost in the turbulent 1500s.

The most important idealists were not the original group but those who followed them—most significantly, the University of Oxford's T. H. Green (1836–1882), Edward Caird (1835–1908), F. H. Bradley (1846–1924), and Bernard Bosanquet (1848–1923). Maintaining that reality is the object of an absolute, eternal, and all-comprehending consciousness, Green argued that knowledge can be understood only as the system of objective relations that this consciousness grasps. Green advanced trenchant criticisms of empiricism in the introduction to his and T. H. Grose's influential four-volume edition of *The Philosophical Works of David Hume* (1874–1875). The introduction was meant to demonstrate the superiority of idealism to empirical, evolutionary naturalism, as well as to utilitarianism—and for many it did so. Green's text also, however, resurrected interest in Hume's philosophical corpus, which had largely been eclipsed by his histories and essays.

Because of this renewal of interest in Hume, Green's efforts were largely self-subverting. The Humean text against which he hoped to leverage his own philosophical ambitions in the end surpassed his own. Indeed, since Green's time, and with the help of commentaries such as the influential 1905 article in *Mind,* "The Naturalism of Hume," by Norman Kemp Smith of the University of Edinburgh, the recognition of Hume's central importance in Anglo-American philosophy has continued unabated. Green's friend Caird undertook a synthesizing path. Struggling to perfect the German philosopher Immanuel Kant's insights into perception and reason, Caird attempted to reconcile idealism, Christianity, utilitarianism, and evolutionary theory in his Gifford Lectures, published as *The Evolution of Religion* (1893).

Bradley's *Appearance and Reality* (1893), like Green's work, presented a critique of discursive thinking and common sense. Beneath ordinary reason and experience, according to Bradley, lies the subverbal; above it stands absolute experience, which transcends the individual mind and the pervasive contradictions and limitations of ordinary consciousness. Bradley's disciple Bosanquet, who left Oxford to engage in adult education and social work in London and ended up at the University of St. Andrews in Scotland, followed his teacher in this critical speculation and developed lines of political thought broached by earlier idealists in his *The Philosophical Theory of the State* (1899). Bosanquet articulated an organicist theory of the state that, like many interpretations of Hegel's political philosophy, subordinated the individual to the collective enterprise of government.

Dissatisfaction with such subordination provoked the generation of a different branch of idealism, whose aim was to sustain the importance of individual consciousness and persons. Among these "personal idealists" may be counted J. M. E. McTaggart (1866–1925) and James Ward (1843–1925).

In the twentieth century British philosophy manifested both continuity with and rejection of its nineteenth-century traditions. While its activity was intense and important, British idealism of the nineteenth century was not enduring. Although the idealistic tradition on the European continent engendered waves of phenomenology, existentialism, and post-structuralism, and although idealistic tendencies remained influential in the philosophy of language as well as in new movements in the sociology of knowledge, British idealism largely foundered in the twentieth century as a more realistic and empirical spirit once again achieved ascendancy in the philosophical centers of Great Britain and Ireland.

Twentieth-century British philosophers became the world's leaders—later, together with many Americans—in perfecting and clarifying the philosophical foundations of logic, natural science, and social science. Among the classics of this literature is *Principia Mathematica* (1910-1913), by Bertrand Russell (1872-1970) and Alfred North Whitehead (1861-1947)—its title inspired by Sir Isaac Newton's *Philosophiae naturalis principia mathematica* (1687). Russell and Whitehead attempted to show how mathematics can in large measure be reduced to logic. In engaging in such projects, British philosophers differed from their Continental counterparts, who developed critical and ideological assessments of the sciences. For the British, science appeared benign, valuable, and, indeed, noble. The British rejected what they found to be the vague and ultimately senseless excesses of the idealist and Continental traditions. In doing so they produced two powerful movements that redefined philosophy not only in Britain but also in much of the rest of the world: logical positivism and analytic philosophy.

Logical positivism was by no means a strictly British phenomenon. The discussion group led by Moritz Schlick (1882-1936) that became known as the Vienna Circle (*Weiner Kreis*) also produced a postivistic backlash against idealism. Among the most influential British thinkers of the positivist movement was A. J. Ayer (1910-1989), whose *Language, Truth, and Logic* (1936) recruited generations of new philosophers with its devastating claim that statements are only meaningful when a method exists to verify them through public, human experience. Karl Popper (1902-1994) responded to criticisms of Ayer's "verification principle" and other developments in the philosophy of science and language by arguing for "falsification" as the engine of philosophical legitimacy and advance.

Controversy both outside and inside this philosophical avant garde was intense. For example, while defending the idea that philosophy comprises genuine intellectual problems before the Cambridge Moral Science Club in 1946, Popper provoked the nearly violent wrath of perhaps the most important thinker to issue from these early-twentieth-century movements in logic and criticism: Ludwig Wittgenstein (1889-1951).

Wittgenstein was the son of one of Europe's wealthiest industrialists and cultural patrons. As a result, his early years were spent at the heart of fin de siècle Vienna's vibrant intellectual world, a cultural scene populated by figures such as Gustav Klimt, Johannes Brahms, and Gustav Mahler. Wittgenstein's own genius was recognized by Russell, who drew Wittgenstein to Cambridge's scientifically renowned Trinity College. Later, however, his influence would be most acutely felt at the more humanistic University of Oxford. With the help of Frank P. Ramsey (1903-1930), Russell arranged for Wittgenstein's profoundly influential *Tractatus Logico-Philosophicus,* some of which had been written while Wittgenstein served in the Austrian army in World War I, to be published in 1921.

Wittgenstein, like Russell, had become fascinated with language and advanced the powerful thesis that many philosophical problems can be resolved—or, better, *dis*solved—through a proper understanding of the way language makes meaning possible and allows people to make true claims about themselves and the world. Philosophical investigation of these concerns yielded stunning critiques of metaphysics, as well as new ways to produce clarity and rigor in philosophical and scientific theory. Analytic philosopher Gilbert Ryle (1900-1976) described the approach in 1932: "I conclude, then, that there is, after all a sense in which we can properly inquire and even say 'what it really means to say so and so.' For we can ask what is the real form of the fact recorded when this is concealed or disguised and not duly exhibited by the expression in question. And we can often succeed in stating this fact in a new form of words which does exhibit what this is and what philosophical analysis is, and that this is the sole and whole function of philosophy."

Whether such analysis of meaning is "the sole and whole function of philosophy" became a matter of intense debate. Such was the case not least of all in ethics, where much of the twentieth century was spent not inquiring about the constitutive elements of a good life or a right action or a good person, but, rather, in attempting to determine how, and even whether, ethical language can be meaningful at all. This project became known as "metaethics." Indeed, for many of the logical positivists, much of what composes ethical discourse is simply an expression of emotion without cognitive meaning.

One of those who came to contrary conclusions was G. E. Moore, who, though he shared the positivists' rejection of idealism, argued for the irreducibility of the moral features of the world. He especially opposed attempts to explain morality in terms of natural phenomena. Later, R. M. Hare (1919-2002), through what he called "prescriptivism" and a modified utilitarianism, moved analytic ethics away from positivism without challenging naturalism by laying out sophisticated theories of the meaning and structure of ethical language—for example, how prescriptive statements differ meaningfully from those that are purely descriptive.

While Russell went on to address specific problems in logic, philosophy of language, and progressive politics, Wittgenstein grew to believe, like the analytic ethicists, that the positivist program was fundamentally flawed—or, at least, limited. He came to think that a new approach was needed to meaning; the relationship between thought, language, and the world; and what constitutes a "healthy human understanding." In his *Philosophical Investigations* (1953) he sought to bring philosophical thought back to the "ordinary" by abandoning the "picture theory" of the *Tractatus Logico-Philosophicus,* which described a correspondence between words and facts, in favor of a theory of what he famously called "language games" and "forms of life."

This so-called later Wittgenstein, nevertheless, preserved from his earlier thought the conviction that many purported philosophical problems, such as the mind/body problem and the problem of skepticism, are actually not problems at all but simply confusions rooted in the misuse of language. He suggested that the proper aim of philosophy is not to determine truths but, in his own memorable phrase, to "let the fly out of the fly bottle." Subsequent British philosophers such as J. L. Austin (1911–1960), Wittgenstein's literary executor and translator G. E. M. Anscombe (1919–2001), P. F. Strawson (1919–), and Michael Dummett (1925–) used Wittgenstein's insights not only to refine the understanding of language, truth, and meaning but also to explore topics in psychology, science, epistemology, and the history of philosophy.

As the twentieth century advanced, the philosophy of mind joined the philosophy of language as a major concern of British philosophers, and in the work of many of them the lines separating psychology, neuroscience, linguistics, and philosophy became blurred. Among these philosophers Derek Parfit (1942–) of Oxford, Timothy L. S. Sprigge (1932–) of the University of Edinburgh, and Scottish-born J. J. C. Smart (1920–) of Adelaide University in Australia stand out. Parfit's reductionist view of the self in his influential *Reasons and Persons* (1984) has helped redefine what it means to have a mind and personal identity. Sprigge's controversial antireductionist renderings of the complexities of consciousness and his arguments for panpsychism echo the idealist tradition and have sustained currents counter to the mainstream. By contrast, Smart has advanced the materialistic thesis that mental states are identical to definable brain states.

Philosopher of history R. G. Collingwood (1889–1943) agreed with the later Wittgenstein that thoughts, words, and deeds can only be understood by situating them in the context in which they occur. Hence, in dealing with a figure from the past, historians must try to work their way inside that figure's world, imagination, or forms of life. For Collingwood this insistence on particularity and context implies that historical thinking cannot yield general scientific laws, but he held that it is, nevertheless, crucially important and has been too much neglected by British intellectual culture.

Looking at the state of British philosophy at the end of the twentieth century and the beginning of the twenty-first, it seems that Collingwood may finally be heard. Although much of British philosophical culture remains dominated by the concerns established by analytic philosophy, one also finds a kind of waywardness—or, perhaps better, an interest in experimentation—with a wider variety of philosophical pursuits, including those originating in the United States and continental Europe. British philosophy seems more committed than ever to advancing work in cognitive science, philosophy of mind, philosophy of language, logic, and epistemology. But it also exhibits new interest in poststructuralism from France, hermeneutics and phenomenology from Germany, ethics, aesthetics, the sociology of knowledge, and the history of philosophy.

These wanderings suggest a period of transformation and self-reflection. Perhaps just as the abstruse analysis of scholasticism yielded in the Renaissance and early modernity to both new sciences and humanistic thought, so the exhaustion of the analytic paradigm will find new direction in both new scientific developments (perhaps in genetics and neuroscience) and in historical, political, and humanistic work. Perhaps just as the Channel tunnel and the European Union have altered British travel, finance, and politics, so new intellectual movements and new technologies will bridge the gulf separating British and Continental philosophy.

—Peter S. Fosl

Acknowledgments

This book was produced by Bruccoli Clark Layman, Inc. Karen L. Rood is senior editor. Philip B. Dematteis was the in-house editor.

Production manager is Philip B. Dematteis.

Administrative support was provided by Ann M. Cheschi, Carol A. Cheschi, and Amber L. Coker.

Accountant is Ann-Marie Holland.

Copyediting supervisor is Sally R. Evans. The copyediting staff includes Phyllis A. Avant, Brenda Carol Blanton, Caryl Brown, Melissa D. Hinton, Philip I. Jones, Rebecca Mayo, Nancy E. Smith, and Elizabeth Jo Ann Sumner.

Editorial associates are Michael S. Allen, Michael S. Martin, and Catherine M. Polit.

Permissions editor is Amber L. Coker.

Prevetter is Nicole A. La Rocque.

Database manager is José A. Juarez.

Layout and graphics supervisor is Janet E. Hill. The graphics staff includes Zoe R. Cook and Sydney E. Hammock.

Office manager is Kathy Lawler Merlette.

Photography supervisor is Paul Talbot. Photography editor is Scott Nemzek.

Digital photographic copy work was performed by Joseph M. Bruccoli.

Systems manager is Marie L. Parker.

Typesetting supervisor is Kathleen M. Flanagan. The typesetting staff includes Patricia Marie Flanagan,

Mark J. McEwan, and Pamela D. Norton. Freelance typesetter is Wanda Adams.

Walter W. Ross did library research. He was assisted by Jo Cottingham and the following librarians at the Thomas Cooper Library of the University of South Carolina: circulation department head Tucker Taylor; reference department head Virginia W. Weathers; reference department staff Brette Barron, Marilee Birchfield, Paul Cammarata, Gary Geer, Michael Macan, Tom Marcil, Rose Marshall, and Sharon Verba; interlibrary loan department head John Brunswick; and interlibrary loan staff Robert Arndt, Hayden Battle, Alex Byrne, Jo Cottingham, Bill Fetty, Marna Hostetler, and Nelson Rivera.

British Philosophers,
1800–2000

Dictionary of Literary Biography

G. E. M. Anscombe

(18 March 1919 – 5 January 2001)

George W. Shields
Kentucky State University

BOOKS: *The Justice of the Present War Examined,* by
Anscombe and Norman Daniel (Oxford, 1939);
Mr. Truman's Degree (Oxford, 1957);
Intention (Oxford: Blackwell, 1957; Ithaca, N.Y.: Cornell
University Press, 1963);
An Introduction to Wittgenstein's Tractatus (London:
Hutchinson, 1959; New York: Harper & Row,
1959);
Nuclear Weapons and Christian Conscience, by Anscombe
and others, edited by Walter Stein (London: Mer-
lin, 1961); republished as *Nuclear Weapons: A Cath-
olic Response* (London: Burns & Oates, 1963);
Three Philosophers, by Anscombe and Peter T. Geach
(Oxford: Blackwell, 1961);
*Problems of Authority: The Papers Read at an Anglo-French
Symposium,* edited by J. M. Todd (Baltimore: Heli-
con, 1962);
New Essays on Plato and Aristotle, by Anscombe and oth-
ers, edited by Renford Bambrough (London:
Routledge & Kegan Paul, 1965; New York:
Humanities Press, 1965);
Causality and Determination: An Inaugural Lecture (London:
Cambridge University Press, 1971);
On Transubstantiation (London: Catholic Truth Society,
1974);
Practical Reason: Papers and Discussions, by Anscombe and
others, edited by Stephan Körner (Oxford: Black-
well, 1974; New Haven: Yale University Press,
1974);
Times, Beginnings and Causes, Henriette Hertz Trust
Annual Philosophical Lectures, 1974 (London:
Oxford University Press for the British Academy,
1975);
Contraception and Chastity (London: Catholic Truth Soci-
ety, 1975);

G. E. M. Anscombe (photograph by Mary Gustafson)

The Collected Philosophical Papers of G. E. M. Anscombe
(Oxford: Blackwell, 1981; Minneapolis: University of Minnesota Press, 1981)—comprises volume

1, *From Parmenides to Wittgenstein;* volume 2, *Metaphysics and the Philosophy of Mind;* and volume 3, *Ethics, Religion, and Politics.*

OTHER: Ludwig Wittgenstein, *Philosophical Investigations,* edited by Anscombe and Rush Rhees, translated by Anscombe (Oxford: Blackwell, 1953);

René Descartes, *Philosophical Writings: A Selection,* translated by Anscombe and Peter T. Geach (London & Edinburgh: Nelson, 1954; revised, 1970);

Wittgenstein, *Remarks on the Foundations of Mathematics,* edited by Anscombe, Rhees, and Georg Henrik von Wright, translated by Anscombe (Oxford: Blackwell, 1956);

Wittgenstein, *Notebooks, 1914–1916,* edited by Anscombe and von Wright, translated by Anscombe (Oxford: Blackwell, 1961);

Plato, *The Sophist and The Statesman,* translated by A. E. Taylor, edited by Anscombe and Raymond Klibansky (London & New York: Nelson, 1961);

Wittgenstein, *Zettel,* edited by Anscombe and von Wright, translated by Anscombe (Oxford: Blackwell, 1967);

Wittgenstein, *On Certainty,* edited by Anscombe and von Wright, translated by Anscombe and Denis Paul (Oxford: Blackwell, 1969);

"On the Form of Wittgenstein's Writing," in *Contemporary Philosophy: A Survey,* volume 3, edited by Klibansky (Florence, Italy: La Nouva Italia, 1969), pp. 373–378;

"Modern Moral Philosophy," in *The Is-Ought Question: A Collection of Papers on the Central Problems in Moral Philosophy,* edited by W. D. Hudson (London: Macmillan, 1969), pp. 175–195;

H. D. Lewis, ed., *Contemporary British Philosophy: Personal Statements, Fourth Series,* contribution by Anscombe (London: Allen & Unwin, 1976);

Wittgenstein, *Remarks on Colour,* edited by Anscombe, translated by Linda L. McAlister and Margarete Schättle (Oxford: Blackwell, 1977; Berkeley: University of California Press, 1977);

Wittgenstein, *Remarks on the Philosophy of Psychology,* 2 volumes, edited by Anscombe and von Wright, translated by Anscombe (Chicago: University of Chicago Press, 1980);

"A Theory of Language?" in *Perspectives on the Philosophy of Wittgenstein,* edited by Irving Block (Cambridge, Mass.: MIT Press, 1981), pp. 148–158;

"The Causation of Action," in *Knowledge and Mind: Philosophical Essays,* edited by Carl Ginet (New York: Oxford University Press, 1983), pp. 174–190;

"Von Wright on Practical Reason," in *The Philosophy of Georg Henrik von Wright,* edited by Lewis E. Hahn

and Paul Arthur Schilpp, The Library of Living Philosophers, volume 19 (La Salle, Ill.: Open Court, 1989), pp. 377–404;

"Knowledge and Meaning," in *A Wittgenstein Symposium,* edited by Josep-Maria Terricabras (Amsterdam: Rodopi, 1993), pp. 29–35;

"The Origin of Plato's Theory of Forms," in *Modern Thinkers and Ancient Thinkers,* edited by R. W. Sharples (Boulder, Colo.: Westview Press, 1993);

"Murder and the Morality of Euthanasia," in *Euthanasia, Clinical Practice and the Law,* edited by Luke Gormally (Indianapolis: Hackett, 1994), pp. 37–50;

"Practical Inference," in *Virtues and Reasons: Philippa Foot and Moral Theory,* edited by Rosalind Hursthouse (Oxford & New York: Clarendon Press, 1995);

"Die Wahrheit 'Thun'" and "Paganism, Superstition, and Philosophy," in *Menschenwurde: Metaphysics und Ethik,* edited by Mariano Crespo (Heidelberg: Carl Winter University, 1998), pp. 57–60, 93–105;

"Making True," in *Logic, Cause, and Action: Essays in Honour of Elizabeth Anscombe,* edited by Roger Teichman, Royal Institute of Philosophy, supplement 46 (Cambridge & New York: Cambridge University Press, 2000), pp. 1–8.

SELECTED PERIODICAL PUBLICATIONS–
UNCOLLECTED: "Chisholm on Action," *Grazer Philosophische Studien,* 7/8 (1979): 205–213;

"Commentary II: On Harris' Ethical Problems in the Management of Severely Handicapped Children," *Journal of Medical Ethics,* 9 (Summer 1981): 122–123;

"Prolegomenon to a Pursuit of the Definition of Murder: The Illegal and the Unlawful," *Etyka,* 19 (1981): 77–82;

"Medalist's Address: Action, Intention, and 'Double Effect,'" *Proceedings of the American Catholic Philosophical Association,* 56 (1982): 12–25;

"Symposium: Sins of Omission: The Non-Treatment of Controls in Clinical Trials, II," *Aristotelian Society Supplements,* 57 (1983): 223–227;

"Were You a Zygote?" *Philosophy,* 18 (1984): 111–116;

"Existence and Truth," *Proceedings of the Aristotelian Society,* 88 (1987–1988): 1–12;

"Elements y escencias," *Anu Filosof,* 22 (1989): 9–16;

"Wittgenstein: Whose Philosopher?" *Philosophy,* 28 (1990): 1–10;

"Why Have Children?" *Proceedings of the American Catholic Philosophical Association,* 63 (1990): 48–53;

"Russell or Anselm?" *Philosophical Quarterly,* 43 (1993): 500–504;

"On Wisdom," *Acta Philosophica,* 1 (1993): 127–133;

"Cambridge Philosophers II: Ludwig Wittgenstein," *Philosophy,* 70 (1995): 395–407.

G. E. M. Anscombe was a wide-ranging analytic philosopher of the first rank, a close student and translator of major works of Ludwig Wittgenstein, and a Roman Catholic social activist and apologist. She was known for her keen and penetrating interrogations of that which is taken for granted by many other philosophers; according to John M. Dolan, A. J. Ayer once said that she was the only philosopher he could think of who had made truly original contributions to philosophy on the basis of reflections on Wittgenstein, and W. V. O. Quine of Harvard University expressed the opinion that Anscombe's extraordinary book *Intention* (1957) was no less than the single most important philosophical work on the concept of action since Aristotle. She is widely credited with founding the discipline of analytic philosophy of action with *Intention;* with coining the now familiar expression *consequentialism* in ethics; and with moving contemporary moral philosophy toward revisiting Aristotle and the tradition of inquiry into the virtues. Anscombe was also a critically discerning apologist for the Catholic positions on abortion, sexuality, euthanasia, and the traditional theoretical notion of "double effect"—the claim that an act is morally acceptable if it is intended for its good effect, even though it also has an unintended, though foreseen, bad effect. Applying her analytic skills to natural theology, she defended St. Anselm's "ontological argument" for the existence of God against Immanuel Kant's and Bertrand Russell's well-known objections.

Born on 18 March 1919 in Limerick, Ireland, to Alan Wells Anscombe, a British army officer who later became master of sciences at Dulwich College, and Gertrude Elizabeth Anscombe, Gertrude Elizabeth Margaret Anscombe was their only daughter; she had two older brothers. She excelled academically at the Sydenham secondary school and in 1937 was awarded a scholarship to St. Hugh's College of the University of Oxford. There she took what is often regarded as Oxford's most rigorous course of study, the *Literae Humaniores* or "Greats," which involves the study of Greek and Latin literature, Greco-Roman history, and ancient and modern philosophy. She converted to Catholicism during her first year at Oxford. In 1938 she met Peter T. Geach, a student three years her senior and also a convert. Assured by friends that she was "reliably Catholic," Geach pursued and won Anscombe's affections; he also became her philosophical mentor. In a 1939 pamphlet, *The Justice of the Present War Examined,* Anscombe and a fellow Oxford student, Norman Daniel, argued from a Catholic point of view that it was immoral for Britain to demand uncondi-

tional surrender by the Germans in World War II, because such a demand would inevitably result in the killing of innocent civilians.

In 1941 Anscombe graduated with a bachelor's degree, earning first-class honors. On 26 December of that year she and Geach were married. Anscombe and Geach went on to became one of the famous couples of British academe, holding distinguished university posts, publishing prodigiously both separately and in collaboration, and traveling all over the world; they also raised four daughters and three sons. Despite their close relationship, however, Anscombe disliked being called "Mrs. Geach"; she preferred and became known within professional philosophical circles as "Miss Anscombe" (her friends called her "Elizabeth").

After their marriage the Geaches moved to Cambridge, where Anscombe had a research scholarship at Newnham, the women's college of the University of Cambridge. At Cambridge she became the student of Wittgenstein, one of the most original and influential philosophers of the twentieth century and a central figure in the analytic philosophical tradition. In a manner reminiscent of the peripatetic practices of Aristotle's Lyceum, Anscombe and a few other students who were under Wittgenstein's tutelage would often stroll with him for hours in the gardens of Trinity College, engrossed in deep philosophical conversation. Wittgenstein regarded Anscombe with great affection; he jokingly referred to her as "the old man," in part because of her penchant for wearing trousers and coats or jackets (she also smoked cigars). Wittgenstein named her one of his literary executors and sent her to Vienna in 1949–1950 to polish her German and learn the nuances of his Austrian dialect. Wittgenstein remained an important influence throughout her career, although she disagreed with him on several issues. Her background in ancient Greek philosophy, with a special interest in Aristotle, as well as her knowledge of the whole of the history of philosophy enabled her to demonstrate the power of Wittgenstein's techniques and ideas in application to a host of celebrated philosophical issues and thinkers.

Anscombe's Newnham College research fellowship expired in 1946, but she was soon named a research fellow at Oxford's Somerville College. Her association with Somerville as research fellow, and later as fellow, lasted some twenty-four years and was one of the most productive periods in her career. During this period Anscombe's skill at public debate became evident. In a famous 1948 encounter she presented a stunning critique of the third chapter of C. S. Lewis's *Miracles: A Preliminary Study* (1947), arguing that confusion in his use of language had prevented him from showing that naturalism is self-refuting. Lewis rewrote

INTENTION

by

G. E. M. ANSCOMBE

*Lecturer in Philosophy and
Research Fellow in Somerville College*

CORNELL UNIVERSITY PRESS

ITHACA   NEW YORK

1963

*Title page for the U.S. edition of Anscombe's 1957 book that
many critics consider the single most important philosophical
work on the concept of action since the writings of Aristotle
(University of Tennessee, Knoxville)*

editing and translating this material from the German shortly after Wittgenstein's death. The first posthumous book to appear was the work that is most closely associated with the "later" or "post-*Tractatus*" Wittgenstein, *Philosophical Investigations* (1953); Anscombe translated it and served with Rhees as co-editor. She was also co-editor, translator, or both of Wittgenstein's *Remarks on the Foundations of Mathematics* (1956), *Notebooks, 1914–1916* (1961), *Zettel* (1967), *On Certainty* (1969), *Remarks on Colour* (1977), and *Remarks on the Philosophy of Psychology* (1980).

In the 1957 pamphlet *Mr. Truman's Degree* Anscombe protests Oxford University's decision to give former U.S. president Harry S Truman an honorary degree, arguing that the atomic bombing of Hiroshima and Nagasaki, which he ordered, involved the deliberate killing of thousands of innocent noncombatants. She rejects the argument that the bombings prevented an Allied invasion of Japan, which would have entailed the deaths of thousands of Allied and Japanese soldiers, the massacre of the Allied prisoners of war, and the killing of a large number of civilians by "ordinary" bombing: "Choosing to kill the innocent as a means to your ends is always murder." In *Intention*, published the same year, she identifies such reasoning as "consequentialism," a perspective that she regards as morally catastrophic. According to Anscombe, intentions, not consequences, count for morality.

Intention is universally regarded as the seminal work in the philosophy of action, a discipline that examines the logic, semantics, and concepts employed in articulating human actions and their connections with mental events. Anscombe analyzes the concept of intention into three types or modalities: intentional actions that have already been performed, the intention with which an action is performed, and the expression of an intention to perform an action in the future. She argues that an action is intentional if and only if one can appropriately answer the question "Why?" in regard to the action. "Why?" does not apply to an action of which the agent is unaware, an action of which the agent is aware only by having observed it, or to an action of which the agent cannot give an account or explanation without speculating or using some observation that he or she does not have. If a "Why?" can be applied to an action falling outside these cases, then the action is intentional. Cases of "mental causality," such as gasping at having knocked over a teacup or being startled by the buzzing of a wasp nearby, may also be excluded from application of a "Why?" explanation in the proper sense; but the tests to be applied are more complicated than in the first three cases. Using the "later" Wittgenstein's concept of "variant descriptions," Anscombe says that the

the chapter for the next edition. Some have claimed that Lewis was so humiliated and shaken by the experience that he turned away from theology to devotional writing and the Narnia children's books. Anscombe denied that Lewis was angst-ridden about the incident, pointing out that the two dined together quite cheerfully only a few weeks later. She regarded Lewis's rethinking of his argument in *Miracles* as an act of intellectual integrity.

Wittgenstein died in 1951. The *Tractatus Logico-Philosophicus* (1921) was the only book he published during his lifetime; his literary remains included twelve thousand manuscript pages and eight thousand typescript pages that he had not regarded as refined enough for publication. Anscombe and his other literary executors, Rush Rhees and Georg Henrik von Wright, began

same action can be intentional under some descriptions but not under others: for example, in Sophocles' *Oedipus Rex* Oedipus intentionally makes love to Jocasta described as his wife but unintentionally makes love to Jocasta described as his mother.

Anscombe resists assimilating reasons to causes, a perspective championed by "causalists" such as the American philosopher Donald Davidson. For the causalists, an action, to be intentional, must be caused by an antecedent reason, which they construe as a mental event. In Anscombe's view, reasons for actions need not be causes of actions. She argues that talk about intention need not refer to any antecedent mental event and that, in fact, often no such antecedent event exists. As Rosalind Hursthouse observes in her essay "Intention," included in *Intention and Intentionality: Essays in Honour of G. E. M. Anscombe* (1979), a chief advantage of Anscombe's view is that it avoids the problem that any reason given to explain why one performed action x instead of action y at a certain time could also be used as an explanation for doing y. For example, if one desires to write an essay on analytic philosophy of action, one would be doing so intentionally; but even though performing this action might involve first getting Davidson's essay "Actions, Reasons, and Causes" (1963), then obtaining Anscombe's *Intention,* and then procuring a pen and paper, one would not necessarily have all of these actions in mind at the time of forming the intention to write the essay. That is, no specific mental events are causally explanatory of just this sequence of action. While causalists have suggested solutions to the problem, in Anscombe's philosophy it does not even arise.

A further widely recognized contribution of *Intention* is its discussion of "practical knowledge." Anscombe says that modern philosophy is blind to what the ancient and medieval traditions understood about the distinction between contemplative and practical knowledge. For modern philosophers, knowledge is "something that is judged as such by being in accordance with the facts. The facts, reality, are prior, and dictate what is to be said, if it is knowledge." But one who holds this position conflates two kinds of knowledge—contemplative knowledge, which is based in observation, and practical knowledge, which is based in intention—and then, in the midst of acting, incoherently seeks an object of factual, contemplative knowledge "as if there were a . . . special sort of seeing eye." Anscombe argues that Aristotle's "practical syllogisms" have been misunderstood, because they have been too closely assimilated to the model of "proof" syllogisms. She shows that the order of descriptions employed by an agent who reasons from a desired goal to a means for achieving that goal is the reverse of the order of descrip-

tions of an action produced when one puts the appropriate question "Why?" to the action.

Just as *Intention* inaugurated the philosophy of action, Anscombe's 1958 essay "Modern Moral Philosophy," originally published in the journal *Philosophy* and included in the third volume of *The Collected Philosophical Papers of G. E. M. Anscombe* (1981), can be seen as launching the contemporary turn toward "virtue ethics." Modern moral philosophy, she argues, has been characterized by two fundamental preoccupations that are fatal to the practice of the discipline. First, since Kant, moral philosophers have been involved in a quest to articulate the properly moral sense of the terms "ought" and "obligation"; the "moral point of view" is seen as essentially the envisaging of one's duties or obligations. But this standpoint presupposes the notion of a divine lawgiver: an obligation is always an obligation *to someone.* Such a presupposition is no longer possible in a modern pluralistic and secular society. The only hope for revival of genuine moral philosophy in a secular world is a return to Aristotle's primary preoccupations with the virtues, human character, and *eudaimonia,* or human flourishing. Such a return requires a renewal of inquiry into philosophy of action and philosophy of mind—precisely her concerns in *Intention.*

Second, British moral philosophy since Henry Sidgwick has suffered from a shallow philosophical psychology and has issued in a corrupted moral standpoint Anscombe deems "consequentialism." Consequentialists hold that intentions are not essentially connected with ascriptions of moral responsibility and that actions are right or wrong according to the consequences that follow from them. This view entails, Anscombe says, that both moral responsibility and the rightness or wrongness of actions are, ultimately, arbitrary; but morality is properly the sphere of the intentional and the absolute. Thus, as she argued at many junctures in her career and supported practically by engaging in public protests, the taking of innocent life, whether in war or in aborting a fetus, is always wrong—no matter how beneficial the social or personal "consequences" of doing so might be.

An outpouring of articles, both defending and criticizing Anscombe, followed the appearance of "Modern Moral Philosophy." Jonathan Bennett is particularly noted for his vigorous attack on Anscombe's moral "absolutism" in his 1966 article "Whatever the Consequences."

Anscombe's *An Introduction to Wittgenstein's* Tractatus (1959) was one of the first important efforts to make the *Tractatus Logico-Philosophicus*—an enigmatic work consisting of a series of propositions organized according to an intricate numbering scheme intended to show their logical relationships to each other—accessible to a gen-

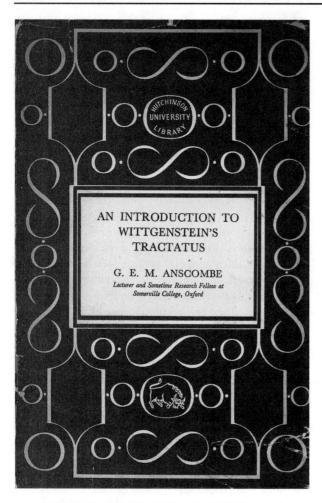

Dust jacket for Anscombe's 1959 work, the first book-length study of Ludwig Wittgenstein's groundbreaking Tractatus Logico-Philosophicus *(Bruccoli Clark Layman Archives)*

eral audience; it was the first book-length study of the *Tractatus* in English. In the *Tractatus* Wittgenstein claims that the world can be analyzed into simple objects, properties, and relations, which combine to make up "states of affairs"; these states of affairs can be expressed in "elementary propositions," which provide "pictures" or "models" of states of affairs. Throughout the *Tractatus* Wittgenstein is concerned to differentiate what can from what cannot be said in propositional language. Since he asserts that "das Mystiche" (the mystical), as well as the "substantial self" and other traditional metaphysical notions, cannot be said or properly asserted in propositional language, logical positivists such as Moritz Schlick and Rudolf Carnap read him as affirming their own doctrines that elementary propositions are analyzable into and verified by units of sense experience (or "sense-data") and that metaphysics can be "eliminated" as cognitively meaningless.

Anscombe's work begins a new tradition of interpretation of the *Tractatus* that resists the positivist

reading. She points out that Wittgenstein never explicitly uses the positivist language of "observation" or "sense-data" in talking about propositions. Moreover, positivist examples of elementary propositions are not elementary in Wittgenstein's sense. Furthermore, the positivist A. J. Ayer's interpretation of Wittgenstein's view—that the mystical is "all nonsense" because there is nothing there for anyone to attempt to say—"cannot be the right interpretation." For Wittgenstein, the mystical cannot be "pictured" in propositions; and since propositions are, according to Wittgenstein, the bearers of sense, the mystical is, strictly speaking, "senseless." But he does not mean that the mystical is unreal: he says explicitly in proposition 6.522 that the mystical makes itself "manifest."

Anscombe also attempts to clarify Wittgenstein's difficult concept of negation. She says that for Wittgenstein, "the picturing-proposition has two poles"—positive and negative—"and in each sense it represents what may perfectly well be true." Whether a proposition is true in its positive or negative pole is a contingent matter. The "two poles" interpretation of the proposition helps to make sense of how Wittgenstein can hold consistently that, first, the world is the sum of existent states of affairs; second, that reality includes both positive and negative facts; and third, that "the world" and "reality" are equivalent. These three claims are inconsistent only if one regards propositions as only positive in nature.

Anscombe also stakes out an important position on the interpretation of the notions of objects, relations, and properties in the *Tractatus*. She argues that the most coherent way to read the propositions under the crucial rubric of 2.02 is to say that, for Wittgenstein, objects alone are concrete particulars; they have properties and relations, but properties and relations themselves are not particulars. This controversial perspective has been debated by such scholars as Irving Copi, James Griffin, and Erik Stenius.

Anscombe reassessed the traditional Catholic moral doctrine of "double effect" in the essay "War and Murder," which was first published in a 1961 collection titled *Nuclear Weapons and Christian Conscience* and republished in volume three of her *Collected Papers*. She argues that the denial of the principle of double effect "has been the corruption of non-Catholic thought, and its abuse the corruption of Catholic thought." On the one hand, she says, the principle is essential to ethics, because the distinction between intended and merely foreseen consequences is required for the adjudication of a variety of moral situations. For instance, the distinction would be applied in the case of a physician who prescribes a pain-relieving drug to a suffering terminal patient, even though the physician foresees that "the drug may very well kill the patient if the illness does not do so first." In such a case, relief of suffering, not death, is intended. On the other hand, she points out, the principle has been much abused since the seventeenth-century introduction of Cartesian psychology, with its notion that the "direction of intention" is controlled at will. The device of directing intention can be used to justify virtually any action or refusal to act, including violations of the strict prohibition within Christian ethics of direct killing of the innocent. So, for example, "The devout Catholic bomber secures by a 'direction of intention' that any shedding of innocent blood that occurs is 'accidental.'" This device, she says, makes nonsense of any genuinely Christian ethic that demands the prohibition of certain behaviors because they are intrinsically wrong.

In 1967 Anscombe was elected a fellow of the British Academy. In 1970 she was appointed to the chair of philosophy at Cambridge, the post that Wittgenstein had held. In her inaugural address, published as *Causality and Determination: An Inaugural Lecture* (1971), she is sharply critical of standard forms of strong determinism (the view that all events are necessitated by prior causes); in particular, she attacks the pervasive assumption that "if an effect occurs in one case and a similar effect does not occur in an apparently similar case, there must be a relevant further difference." In addition to suffering from a variety of conceptual difficulties, this assumption incurs the high cost of being incompatible with freedom of the will. Moreover, she argues, even if an event cannot be explained in terms of antecedent physical causes, it may be explicable in alternative, nonphysical ways. Thus, causation should not be conflated with determination.

Unwavering in her view that neither individuals nor states have the moral authority to take innocent life, Anscombe was deeply involved in the antiabortion movement in Britain. In the 1970s her nonviolent protests against the practice resulted in two arrests and the threat of a third; two of her children, More and Tamsin, were also arrested. Anscombe also protested against the Vietnam War.

In her paper "'Whatever Has a Beginning of Existence Must Have a Cause': Hume's Argument Exposed," originally published in *Analysis* in 1974 and included in the first volume of *The Collected Philosophical Papers of G. E. M. Anscombe,* Anscombe argues against a classic argument in support of the notion that an event could occur without a cause; it has played a role in discussions of theistic arguments and their appeal to a principle of causality. If David Hume is correct that successful counterexamples can be brought against the assertion that "whatever has a beginning of existence must have a cause," then any cosmological argument

for the existence of God (that is, an argument from observed effects to God as the necessary cause) is undermined. Anscombe puts Hume's argument, which occurs in book 1 of his *A Treatise of Human Nature* (1739), under close scrutiny. She concludes that Hume is asserting that, if it is possible to imagine something coming into existence without a cause, then it is possible in reality for something to come into existence without a cause. Therefore, Hume says, "'tis impossible to demonstrate the necessity of a cause." Anscombe says of Hume's argument:

> The trouble about it is that it is very unconvincing. For if I say I can imagine a rabbit coming into being without a parent rabbit, well and good: I imagine a rabbit coming into being, and our observing that there is no parent rabbit about. But what am I to imagine if I imagine a rabbit coming into being without a cause? Well, I just imagine a rabbit appearing. That this *is* the imagination of a rabbit coming into being, and without a cause is nothing but, as it were, the *title* of the picture. Indeed I can form an image and give my picture that title. But from my being able to do *that,* nothing whatever follows about what is possible to suppose "without contradiction or absurdity" as holding in reality.

Hume's "argument," then, amounts to a non sequitur. Consequently, a natural theologian is free to presuppose the principle that *ex nihilo nihil fit* (from nothing, nothing comes) when pursuing a cosmological argument for God's existence.

In her bold and much-discussed essay "The First Person," originally presented as a Wolfson College Lecture in 1974 and included in the second volume of *The Collected Philosophical Papers of G. E. M. Anscombe,* Anscombe says that people are often misled into thinking that "I" functions like a proper name and that, since proper names are regarded as referring expressions, "I" should be regarded as a referring expression. But, she points out, "I" is not a proper name and does not refer. In fact, self-awareness involves no object of the awareness—there is no entity, no "person" or "self," of which the self is aware. If "I" did refer, and if self-awareness did have the self as its object, the situation would be that of René Descartes's "Ego" that is certain only of its own existence. As Wittgenstein says in the *Tractatus,* if the self were an object of self-awareness, it would be as if the eye itself were included within the visual field seen by the eye.

Anscombe's commentaries on Wittgenstein have become the subject of critical discussion and exploration in their own right. Perhaps her most important and original essay on the "later" Wittgenstein of the *Philosophical Investigations* is "The Question of Linguistic Idealism," first published in *Acta Philo-*

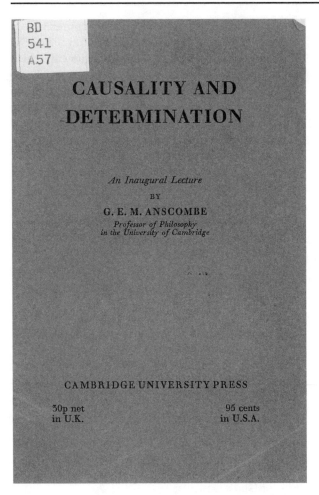

Cover for the published version (1971) of the address in which Anscombe attacks the theory that all events, including human actions, are completely determined by preceding causes (Joyner Library, East Carolina University)

sophica Fennica in 1976 and included in the first volume of *The Collected Philosophical Papers of G. E. M. Anscombe.* The title of the piece is striking in light of the fact that many close students of Wittgenstein, such as Norman Malcolm, have declared that the later Wittgenstein shows no disposition toward any kind of idealism. Anscombe calls the reader's attention to proposition 371 of *Philosophical Investigations,* "Essence is expressed by grammar," which she interprets as meaning that some essences, at least, are created in the linguistic acts of expressing them. "Linguistic idealism" is the view that some realities or truths are created by linguistic activities; thus, insofar as Wittgenstein accepted this view, he was a linguistic idealist. The term *idealist* is appropriate in this context, she says, since the view shares with the idealist philosophical tradition the notion that a socially or culturally conditioned subject creates its entities of discourse and knowledge.

Anscombe contends, however, that Wittgenstein was a linguistic idealist only in certain respects, and that a realist account of objects also enters into his view. She argues that in "Essence is expressed by grammar" *grammar* is to be taken in the specific Wittgensteinian sense of the "rules or routines of our linguistic practices" and that such practices are always connected with nonlinguistic actions. She says that for Wittgenstein, two kinds of entities depend on linguistic practices: concepts and social practices. People create concepts by their linguistic practices, since the objects that they organize or classify by the concepts do not dictate the criteria for application of the concepts. One does not arrive at, say, the concept *dog* simply by encountering dogs; the concept is given to one through socially learned linguistic practices. The objects to which the concepts apply, however, are, in most cases, not human constructions–dogs, for example, are entities independent of human social conventions and linguistic practices. Thus, the situation includes a "realist" component. Anscombe labels the view that concepts are socially-linguistically constructed, but their objects are not, "partial idealism."

But, Anscombe says, for Wittgenstein linguistic idealism is complete or absolute in regard to entities whose existence is constituted by linguistic acts, such as ceremonies, etiquette, games, promises, rights, and rules. While such "social entities" may involve objects that are not of human creation, the entities themselves depend on linguistic practices. Thus, a right to a parcel of land involves an object–the land– but the right itself is constituted by social agreement and linguistic practices. Since games come under the rubric of complete idealism, and since the notion of "language games" is a prominent feature of the *Philosophical Investigations,* it would seem that Anscombe's interpretive thrust toward linguistic idealism cuts to the core of the later Wittgenstein's philosophy. David Bloor maintains that Anscombe's interpretation brings a large measure of coherence to the *Philosophical Investigations* by connecting Wittgenstein's notion of language games with his account of ostensive definitions, his use of paradigms, and many other items.

Anscombe received the Research Prize of the Alexander von Humboldt Stiftung in 1983 and the Aquinas Medal of the American Catholic Philosophers Association in 1984. She retired from her professorship at Cambridge in 1986. The following year she received an honorary doctorate from the University of Notre Dame. Her interest in medical ethics led her to join Mayo Clinic physician Hymie Gordon and philosopher John M. Dolan in founding the University of Minnesota's Program in Human Rights and

Medicine in 1988. In 1989 the Catholic University of Louvain awarded her another honorary degree.

While Anscombe never claimed that she could demonstrate that Anselm's famous argument for the existence of God is valid, she argues in "Russell or Anselm?" (1993) that the argument has been misunderstood and is not guilty of the fallacies that certain celebrated objections claim. Anselm's argument in the *Proslogion* is not, she says, an "ontological argument" (the term is Kant's) that "derives a *thing's* being greater from its *existence in reality's* being greater than existence only in the mind." Anscombe points to Anselm's reply to his first critic, the monk Gaunilo of Tours, in which Anselm's notion of "what is greater" (*quod maius est*) is clarified as "that which cannot have a beginning or ending." Anselm's claim, then, is that a coherent *thought* of a greatest conceivable being must include "that which is not capable of not existing"; the bearing of "greatest" does not turn on a mere comparison of existing "outside the mind" with existing "in the mind." Moreover, Anselm's "that than which nothing greater can be thought" (*quo maius cogitari nequit*) is best described as an "intentional comparative" and not as a Russellian "definite description." Any criticisms of Anselm based on the assumption that *quo maius cogitari nequit* is a definite description, she concludes, are entirely off the mark.

Though she had suffered from heart disease since her sixties, and though she never completely recovered from an injury she received in an automobile accident in 1996, Anscombe continued to be active in scholarly circles. In 1999 Pope John Paul II awarded her the Pro Ecclesia et Pontifice Medal. She died on 5 January 2001, with her husband and four of their children saying the rosary at her bedside. Alluding to her best-known work, Dolan notes in his tribute to her in the journal *First Things* that "Her last intentional act was kissing Peter Geach."

Cora Diamond says in the preface to *Intention and Intentionality*:

If there is anything that characterizes Elizabeth Anscombe's philosophical writings it is the capacity to be struck by questions. She has made new questions for philosophy: has taken familiar and unquestioned assumptions and shown how far from being obvious they are. Philosophy as she does it is fresh; her arguments take unexpected turns and make unexpected connections, and show always how much there is that had not been seen before.

References:

Jonathan Bennett, "Whatever the Consequences," *Analysis,* 26 (1966): 83–102;

David Bloor, "The Question of Linguistic Idealism Revisited," in *The Cambridge Companion to Wittgenstein,* edited by Hans Sluga and David G. Stern (Cambridge: Cambridge University Press, 1996), pp. 354–382;

Irving Copi and R. W. Beard, eds., *Essays on Wittgenstein's* Tractatus (New York: Macmillan, 1966);

Donald Davidson, "Intending," in *Philosophy of History and Action,* edited by Y. Yovel (Dordrecht, Netherlands: Reidl, 1978), pp. 83–102;

Cora Diamond and Jenny Teichman, eds., *Intention and Intentionality: Essays in Honour of G. E. M. Anscombe* (Ithaca, N.Y.: Cornell University Press, 1979);

John M. Dolan, "G. E. M. Anscombe: Living the Truth," *First Things: The Journal of Religion and Public Life,* 113 (May 2001): 11–13;

Philippa Foot, "Abortion and the Doctrine of Double Effect," in her *Virtues and Vices and Other Essays in Moral Philosophy* (Berkeley: University of California Press, 1978), pp. 5–15;

Luke Gormally, ed., *Moral Truth and Moral Tradition: Essays in Honour of Peter Geach and Elizabeth Anscombe* (Blackrock, Ireland: Four Courts Press, 1994);

James Griffin, *Wittgenstein's Logical Atomism* (Seattle: University of Washington Press, 1969);

J. G. Haber, ed., *Absolutism and Its Consequentialist Critics* (Lanham, Md.: University Press of America, 1994);

Duncan Richter, *Ethics after Anscombe: Post "Modern Moral Philosophy,"* Library of Ethics and Applied Philosophy, volume 5 (Dordrecht, Netherlands: Kluwer Academic, 2000);

Roger Teichman, ed., *Logic, Cause, and Action: Essays in Honour of Elizabeth Anscombe* (Cambridge: Cambridge University Press, 2000).

J. L. Austin

(26 March 1911 – 8 February 1960)

Nick Fotion
Emory University

BOOKS: *Philosophical Papers* (Oxford: Oxford University Press, 1961; New York: Oxford University Press, 1979);

How to Do Things with Words: The William James Lectures Delivered in Harvard University in 1955, edited by J. O. Urmson (Oxford: Clarendon Press, 1962; Cambridge, Mass.: Harvard University Press, 1962);

Sense and Sensibilia, edited by G. J. Warnock (Oxford: Clarendon Press, 1962; New York: Oxford University Press, 1964).

OTHER: Gottlob Frege, *The Foundations of Arithmetic: A Logico-Mathematical Enquiry into the Concept of Number,* translated by Austin (Oxford: Blackwell, 1950).

J. L. Austin

J. L. Austin was a leader of the "ordinary language" school of philosophy, which dominated Anglo-American philosophy for about twenty-five years after World War II. This movement, also known as the Oxford School, continues to wield some influence, albeit much diminished, even today. Its followers argued that it is important to attend to how language works, since language is the carrier of thought. Thus, if everyday language makes a distinction between "commanding" and "asking," one can assume that there is a reason for the distinction; the philosopher's job is to identify the basis of the distinction by engaging in language analysis. This activity involves answering a series of questions, such as: Are "commanding" and "asking" similar to one another because, when used in sentences, they represent attempts to direct someone's behavior? Does a command presuppose that the one issuing it is a social superior? Can feelings be commanded? Can one be asked to change one's feelings? What limits are there to the kinds of things one can be commanded or asked to do?

In ordinary-language philosophy, analysis proceeds on two levels. If the analysis is used to help deal with distinctions that contribute to a better understanding of, or solution to, philosophical problems, it is labeled "linguistic philosophy." If the analysis focuses on under-standing how language works in itself, apart from any application to philosophical problems, it is called "philosophy of language." Austin engaged in both kinds of analysis.

One of the five children of Geoffrey Langshaw Austin and Mary Bowes-Wilson Austin, John Langshaw Austin was born in Lancaster on 26 March 1911. His father served in the army during World War I and, after the war, became secretary of St. Leonard's School in St. Andrews, Scotland.

Austin was educated at Shrewsbury School. In 1929 he received a scholarship in classics to Balliol College of the University of Oxford. At Oxford he gradually became interested in philosophy. He won the Gaisford Prize in 1931; that same year he received a first class in honor moderations. In 1933 he received a first in *litterae humaniores* and a fellowship at All Souls College, where he lectured on Plato, Aristotle, Gottfried Wilhelm Leibniz, and Immanuel Kant. In 1935 he became a fellow of and philosophy tutor at Magdalen College.

During these years logical positivism was a prominent movement in British philosophy; members of the movement included A. J. Ayer, Gustav Bergmann, Rudolf Carnap, Moritz Schlick, and Friedrich Waismann. Austin admired the positivists for their attacks on the pretensions and speculative tendencies of philosophy, but he was suspicious of their infatuation with science and their tendency to make sweeping claims about its nature; even in these early years Austin was more comfortable in dealing with philosophical problems in a careful, step-by-step fashion.

With the outbreak of World War II Austin accepted a commission in the British Army Intelligence Corps. In 1941 he married Jean Coutts; they had two sons and two daughters. Austin's superiors in the Intelligence Corps recognized his concern for detail and systematic way of viewing events, and they gave him important responsibilities. In 1944 he was transferred to the Supreme Headquarters of the Allied Expeditionary Force. Prior to the D-Day invasion of 6 June 1944 he was assigned to pull together information about German coastal defenses in France; after the invasion he helped monitor the launching sites of the German V rockets that were raining terror on the British Isles. He was promoted to lieutenant colonel and received the Order of the British Empire, the French Croix de Guerre, and an appointment from the United States as an Officer of the Legion of Merit.

Austin left the army and returned to Oxford in late 1945. His military experiences had taught him the importance of teamwork, and he decided that a team approach was the best way to pursue problems in philosophy. He would be the leader, but all on the team—both students and colleagues—would help in solving, or at least clarifying, philosophical problems, which would be addressed individually and dealt with one step at a time. His preference for a team approach, coupled with his detailed analytic method, may explain why Austin's publishing record is so modest: before the war he had published only one article, "Are There *a priori* Concepts?" in *Proceedings of the Aristotelian Society* in 1939. Philosophical problems, for him, were far too difficult for one to suppose that a bit of thinking by an individual philosopher would result in enough understanding to justify rushing into print.

Nonetheless—though cautiously—he began publishing. One of his first postwar articles, "Other Minds,"

appeared in the *Proceedings of the Aristotelian Society* in 1946; like all of his other articles, it is collected in his posthumous *Philosophical Papers* (1961). It signals a notable change in his philosophical concerns, from the history of philosophy to contemporary philosophy, but his philosophical style has not changed. In "Other Minds" he asks whether one knows that other people have minds and whether and how one knows that they have experiences such as anger and hate. Does one really know these things or does one merely believe that one does? To answer these questions Austin focuses on what it means to know and to believe something. He looks at specific claims to knowledge, such as when someone says, "That was a mockingbird," and someone else asks, "How do you know?" Austin observes that the question is ambiguous: it can mean "How are you in a position to know?" or "What features does that bird have that tell you it is a mockingbird?" The first question is also ambiguous: it can mean "How did you come to know about these birds?" or "Were you in a good position to identify that particular bird, even granting that you know about mockingbirds?" The complete answer the claimant to knowledge could give to the challenge that he or she does not know would, of necessity, be complicated: "Yes, I studied ornithology in college, and, in fact, I saw that bird up close for almost a minute. And the light was good, I was well rested and not on drugs or anything of the sort. Further, I was so close to it that I could see its black and white body and wings, see how big it was, and hear it sing in ways that only mockingbirds can."

On Austin's account, having knowledge of things, events, processes, and so forth is not a matter of having some special intuition or power. One grants that others have knowledge when they meet certain standards, such as whether they have the training to say the things they say. The case is much the same in regard to knowledge of other minds. One knows that someone is angry by coming to know as much about that person as possible, by carefully observing his or her behavior, and by identifying certain responses, such as a flushed face and a rise in the pitch of the voice. To be sure, problems arise in knowing about other people's minds: they can lie, saying that they are angry when they are not; and one can be confused as to whether one is observing anger or some other emotion, such as fear. But though the task of identifying the mental states of others is more difficult than identifying birds, it is not impossible; everyone does it all the time.

In another article, "Truth," published in the *Proceedings of the Aristotelian Society* in 1950, Austin continues to deal with philosophical problems by looking at the way language works. The question he asks is not the Socratic "What is truth?" but "How is 'true' used in our natural language?" His answer is that "truth" and "true"

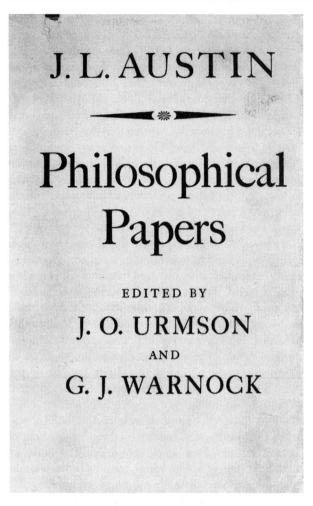

J. L. AUSTIN

Philosophical Papers

EDITED BY

J. O. URMSON

AND

G. J. WARNOCK

Dust jacket for the 1961 collection of Austin's articles
(Bruccoli Clark Layman Archives)

do not refer to an object, quality, or relation; rather, they qualify statements. In part, they confirm or reaffirm what has already been said, as when someone says, "What you say is true." But they assert as well as confirm, as in "It is true that Bill sold his car yesterday." Austin notes that "true" and its correlative, "false," do not apply to all the things one might want to say: "performative utterances," such as "I promise to help you," are meaningful but are neither true nor false. That is, when someone makes a promise, it is not appropriate to respond by saying, "What you said is true," while it is appropriate to respond in that way to someone who says, "The car was sold yesterday."

In 1950 Austin translated Gottlob Frege's *Grundlagen der Arithmetik: Eine logisch mathematische Untersuchung über den Begriff der Zahl* (1884) as *The Foundations of Arithmetic: A Logico-Mathematical Enquiry into the Concept of Number*. In 1952 he was named White's Professor of Moral Philosophy at Oxford and a fellow of Corpus Christi

College. He was also appointed as a delegate to the Oxford University Press.

In "A Plea for Excuses," his famous 1956 presidential address to the Aristotelian Society, Austin states his position in regard to ordinary language: "Our common stock of words embodies all the distinctions men have found worth drawing, and the connexions they have found worth making, in the life-times of many generations," and those distinctions and connections are probably better than "any that you or I are likely to think up in our arm-chairs of an afternoon." What ordinary people say, then, should be the "begin-all" of philosophical investigation but not necessarily the "end-all": the philosopher might ultimately be forced to create a technical vocabulary in dealing with certain problems.

In "A Plea for Excuses" Austin is concerned with identifying the conditions that absolve, and those that fail to absolve, one from blame for one's actions. Using examples not only from ordinary language but also from the specialized languages of law and psychology, he begins by distinguishing between justification, which denies that the action in question was wrong, and excuse, which admits that the action was wrong but denies that the person blamed for the action was, in fact, responsible for it. Mary will be excused for not getting to work on time if she is physically or mentally incapacitated, is dealing with a major emergency, is being coerced into staying away, or is delayed by heavy traffic; she will not be excused if she fails to arrive on time because she is negligent or because she does not care. But it is not that simple. Coercion, for example, can be a matter of degree. If only a small amount of coercion is exerted, it is difficult to tell whether Mary is excused or not.

Most of the other articles Austin published before his premature death on 8 February 1960 deal with linguistic philosophy. The same is true of *Sense and Sensibilia* (1962), compiled by G. J. Warnock from lecture notes Austin made from just after World War II into the 1950s. Austin had modified them each year but had never organized them into publishable form.

The subject of *Sense and Sensibilia* is the sense-data theory. The theory has a long history—it is, he says, "at least as old as Heraclitus," the pre-Socratic philosopher who lived around 500 B.C.—but Austin attends mainly to the version presented by Ayer in *The Foundations of Empirical Knowledge* (1940). Ayer says that the universe is divided into material objects and mental states. He then asks whether people know, perceive, or sense those material objects. No doubt ordinary people would say that they do: they say, "We see tables, chairs, and people sitting in these chairs," and they mean what they say. But Ayer reminds his readers that things appear different to different people under different conditions: a coin looks elliptical from one angle but round from another; a stick looks bent when it is partially submerged in water but straight when it is removed from the water; and an object may look red when one is under the influence of a drug but green when the effects of the drugs wear off. Some color-blind people do not see red objects, while others do. And under the influence of alcohol some people see pink elephants and hear strange sounds, while their sober companions do not. But these experiences, Ayer claims, are not all that different from any other kind of experience. There are no qualitative differences that would lead one to suppose that some of these experiences involve the perception merely of mental phenomena, or "sense-data," while others involve the perception of material objects. "Normal" perception, then, must also be of sense-data. Therefore, all the objects of perception are sense-data. Thus, if one knows anything about material objects, that knowledge must come to one by means of sense-data.

The sense-data theory was seen by its proponents as having a great advantage over other theories of perception because it restored certainty to perception. If one were perceiving objects in the material world, error would enter in sooner or later. The stick in the water and the "wet" highway seen at a distance turn out on closer inspection to be optical illusions, but sense-data are exactly what they seem to be. The pink elephant might not be real in the material sense, but it is real in the sense of something experienced. Because error evidently cannot enter into experiences of sense-data, sense-data became for Ayer and his allies the foundation on which to build a solid theory of knowledge.

Examining the sense-data theory with his linguistic eye, Austin sees it as a mass of verbal fallacies. He attacks the theory in the same piecemeal way he deciphered enemy communications during World War II: part of a message was decoded, then another part, and eventually the decoding process was complete. In the same spirit, Austin looks at various uses of perceptual language. When a speaker says, "It looks like an airplane," the sense-data theorist would claim that what is being said is "I am having an airplane-like sense experience." Austin says, on the contrary, that when ordinary speakers say, "It looks like an airplane," they mean that they are looking at an object in the sky—not at sense-data. But because the object is at a distance and fog is present, they speak cautiously. "Looks" does not report the existence of sense-data; it does not report the existence of anything. It is a word that in some contexts is used to signal that the speaker is talking in a guarded way about things in the material world.

Austin "deciphers" another part of the sense-data theory by reminding the reader that there is a difference between illusions and delusions—delusions involve believing in the existence of things that do not exist—and

then pointing out that sense-data theorists speak loosely about these matters. For example, when discussing the bent-stick-in-water illusion, they carelessly turn the example into one of a delusion. The stick is straight but looks bent, Austin says, but there is no question as to whether the stick exists; the pink elephant is a delusion, but the bent stick is not. If one carelessly slides into talking about the bent stick in the water as a delusion, one is tempted to think of the stick as unreal; what then becomes real is bent-stick sense-data. Careless talk leads to bad theories.

Austin continues in this critical vein throughout *Sense and Sensibilia,* engaging in language analysis and using the results to point out the mistakes of the sense-data theorists. One mistake they are especially prone to make is to invent entities—such as sense-data—in which nobody but philosophers believes. Ayer and his colleagues start by asking the perfectly legitimate question "What does X perceive?" Pondering this question, they realize that X (that is, any person) perceives many different things, but these things fall into two classes. X perceives (or thinks he or she perceives) material objects and mental phenomena (sense-data, "qualia," and so forth). Ayer concludes that "perceives" must have two distinct meanings and, after presenting his skeptical arguments, comes to prefer the latter.

Austin replies that the sense-data theorists have already made a fundamental linguistic mistake: just because X perceives many different things does not mean that perception has different meanings; it has only one. X perceives buildings, cars, people, dogs, rainbows, rivers, moving trains, the wind, the rain, television programs, and so on, and perceives them in different ways: a car can be observed from the front or the side, in sunlight or at night, up close or at a distance, from outside or inside, and so on. But in none of these examples is X perceiving something hidden within his or her mind, such as a cluster of sense-data; instead, X is perceiving ordinary things "out there" in the world, one after another, in various ways.

One consequence of Austin's stance is that no perception, and no knowledge based on perception, is "incorrigible": that is, all knowledge claims are subject to error. It is true that some claims are more reliable than others: when one observes things up close and carefully and is well rested and sober, one can claim to know about them. But possessing knowledge does not mean having information that cannot possibly be wrong; it means having the best information that humans are capable of gathering.

Not satisfied with this kind of knowledge, Ayer and his allies invent sense-data. Sense-data *are* incorrigible—one cannot doubt that one is having the experience one is having at a given moment—and because they are, they provide a foundation for everything else that is

J. L. AUSTIN

❊

How to do
things
with Words

*The William James Lectures
delivered in Harvard University
in 1955*

EDITED BY

J. O. URMSON

*Dust jacket for Austin's major work on the philosophy of
language, published posthumously in 1962
(Bruccoli Clark Layman Archives)*

known; abstract theoretical statements in the sciences, for example, must ultimately be grounded in sense-data if they are to be accepted as true. Austin's reply to these claims is that Ayer and his allies are chasing a will-o'-the-wisp: the concept of a sense-datum is a philosopher's dream based on one linguistic error after another. It is best to forget about it.

Austin's attack on the sense-data theory is an example of linguistic philosophy: he uses insights into language to deal with a philosophical issue. Believing that language deserves attention for itself, apart from its usefulness in helping to solve philosophical problems, Austin and other philosophers in the analytic movement also engaged in philosophy of language. In the early 1950s Austin gave a series of lectures on this topic at Oxford under the title "Words and Deeds"; he used the same material for the William James Lectures he delivered at Harvard University in 1955. The James lectures were edited by J. O. Urmson and published as *How to Do*

Things with Words (1962). It constitutes Austin's major contribution to the philosophy of language.

In *How to Do Things with Words* Austin criticizes a view of language that was held by many philosophers, but especially by those who were trying to ally philosophy more closely with the physical sciences. Although he does not name them, he clearly has in mind the logical positivists. Their view of language was most famously expressed by Ayer when he said that sentences are meaningful if and only if they can be assessed as being true or false. Sentences such as "There are four people in that room," "There are living organisms on the planet Venus," and "Electrons exist" are meaningful, because one can specify, at least in principle, a procedure for determining their truth or falsity. Sentences such as "The Good Angel lives in heaven" and "I promise to help you tomorrow" are meaningless, because their truth or falsity cannot be tested even in principle. Such sentences are neither true nor false.

Austin begins his attack on this view by presenting a series of counterexamples. When Susan says, "I promise to help you tomorrow," why is that not meaningful? Ordinary people think it is. What about a ceremony at which an official says, "I name this ship *Queen Elizabeth*"? Or when Susan says, "I give and bequeath my watch to my brother"? Again, ordinary people seem to understand what is being said. But a more important consideration, Austin argues, is that these utterances follow rules of language–that is, they meet certain standards–and so they are meaningful. For example, a convention or practice exists in the society for making promises. If someone said, "I bromise to help you tomorrow," the utterance would be meaningless, since there is no convention for bromising. A promise must meet other standards, as well: the right person must make the promise at the right time and in the right way. Bill cannot promise to let Richard borrow Susan's car. He might say, "I promise to let you borrow her car"; but unless he had received authority from Susan to make promises for her, his attempt at promising fails–or, as Austin puts it, it is void. Susan herself might fail to make a promise if she begins, "I promise . . ." but then is startled by a loud noise and forgets what she was doing.

As with promising, there are rules for naming ships and for giving away property; conventions for doing these things must be in place, and the right people must do them at the right time and do them correctly and completely. Not just anyone can name a ship the *Queen Elizabeth;* the ship is properly named only when the person assigned to do the job, perhaps the queen herself, says and does the right things (for example, breaks the champagne bottle on the bow of the ship) at the right time.

Austin points out that there are many meaningful uses of language that do not satisfy the logical positivists' standards of truth and falsity. One can order people around, ask them for favors, congratulate them, express condolences, greet them, make bets with them, hire and fire them, declare war on them, and so on. All of these uses are performatives, since they represent what one *does* with language: one *makes* promises, *gives* orders, *congratulates* winners, and *makes* bets.

Having shown that language is meaningful far beyond the bounds of the logical positivist view, however, Austin finds that he has created a problem for himself. He does not deny, of course, that true and false sentences, which he calls "constatives," are meaningful. The problem is that the meaningfulness of constatives appears to be so utterly different from and unrelated to that of performatives that it is impossible to present a unified account of language.

After a few false starts, Austin claims that he has succeeded in putting language back together by looking more carefully at how constatives work. He points out that the constative "The door is open" is similar to the performative "Close the door" in that, first, in both utterances the speaker is saying or expressing something; in Austin's terminology, both are "locutionary" acts. Second, in both utterances the speaker is doing something in making the utterance: in the one case making the statement that the door is open, in the other case directing the hearer to close the door. Austin calls doing something in making an utterance an "illocutionary act." Finally, both utterances, if successful, have effects on the hearer: one results in the hearer believing something about the door, the other in the hearer doing something about it. Thus, they are "perlocutionary acts." In certain contexts, both utterances could have the same illocutionary and perlocutionary force: that is, "The door is open" could be a command to close the door. Both "The door is open" and "Close the door" also have rules that govern their use. In regard to the former, the rules include the speaker being in a position to observe the fact reported and being sober at the time; in regard to the latter, the rules include the speaker being the social superior of the hearer, what is ordered being an act that is within the capability of the hearer, and what is ordered being a future–perhaps immediate future–act. Constatives, then, have the same structure as performatives; therefore, Austin concludes, they, too, should be viewed as performatives.

Austin classifies performatives into five major kinds. "Verdictives" are judicial acts. Certain verbs are associated with these acts, such as "acquit," "rule," "find" (as in "I find you guilty"), "rank," "diagnose," and "describe." "Exercitives" are legislative or executive acts that involve making decisions in favor of or against actions of a certain kind. The verbs associated with these acts include "appoint," "dismiss," "resign," "excommunicate," "name," "order," "sentence," "declare open" (as in "I declare this meeting open") and "nominate." "Commissives" are acts that impose burdens on the speaker. They are associated with verbs such as "promise," "vow," and "swear." "Behabitives" are concerned with the speaker's reactions to the fortunes and misfortunes of others and express the speaker's attitude toward what others have done or will do or what might happen to them. Some of the many verbs associated with behabitives are "apologize," "thank," "condole," "welcome," "toast," and "congratulate." The final group, "expositives," comprises most of the performatives that were formerly classed as constatives. Verbs under this heading include "affirm," "deny," "report," "ask," "tell," "state," "swear," and "describe."

In a career cut short by his early death, J. L. Austin made three major contributions to philosophy. First, he demonstrated by his example how analytic philosophy should be done: by looking at the details of how language works and drawing conclusions cautiously and tentatively. He convinced many philosophers, even those who are not part of the analytic tradition, that philosophy at least has to start with language analysis, even if it does not end there. Second, using the analytic tools he honed over the years, he severely damaged the credibility of the sense-data theory. Third, and most important, he contributed the performative, or speech act, theory of language, which shows that speech acts can only be understood by viewing them not in isolation but in the context in which they are employed.

References:

Joseph J. DiGiovanna, *Linguistic Phenomenology: Philosophical Method of J. L. Austin* (New York, Bern, Frankfurt am Main & Paris: Peter Lang, 1989);

K. T. Fann, ed., *Symposium on J. L. Austin* (London: Routledge & Kegan Paul, 1969);

Keith Graham, *J. L. Austin: A Critique of Ordinary Language Philosophy* (Hassocks: Harvester Press, 1977);

Barry Smith, "Towards a History of Speech Act Theory," in *Speech Acts, Meaning, and Intentions,* edited by Armin Burkhart (Berlin & New York: De Gruyter, 1990), pp. 29–61;

Savas L. Tsohatzidis, ed., *Foundations of Speech Act Theory: Philosophical and Linguistic Perspectives* (London & New York: Routledge, 1994);

G. J. Warnock, *J. L. Austin* (London & New York: Routledge, 1989);

Warnock, ed., *Essays on J. L. Austin* (Oxford: Clarendon Press, 1973).

John Austin

(3 March 1790 – 17 December 1859)

Richard Hartzman

BOOKS: *The Province of Jurisprudence Determined: An Outline of a Course of Lectures of General Jurisprudence or the Philosophy of Positive Law* (London: Murray, 1832); enlarged, 3 volumes, edited by Sarah Austin (1861–1863)—comprises volume 1, *The Province of Jurisprudence Determined, Second Edition: Being the First Part of a Series of Lectures on Jurisprudence, or, The Philosophy of Positive Law;* volumes 2 and 3, *Lectures on Jurisprudence: Being the Sequel to "The Province of Jurisprudence Determined." To Which are Added Notes and Fragments. Now First Published From the Original Manuscripts;*

A Plea for the Constitution (London: Murray, 1859).

Editions: *Lectures on Jurisprudence; or, The Philosophy of Positive Law,* fifth edition, revised and edited by Robert Campbell (London: Murray, 1885);

The Province of Jurisprudence Determined, and The Uses of the Study of Jurisprudence, introduction by H. L. A. Hart (London: Weidenfeld & Nicolson, 1954; New York: Noonday Press, 1954);

The Province of Jurisprudence Determined, edited by Wilfred E. Rumble (Cambridge & New York: Cambridge University Press, 1995).

SELECTED PERIODICAL PUBLICATIONS–
UNCOLLECTED: "Disposition of Property by Will–Primogeniture," *Westminster Review,* 2 (1824): 503–553;

"Joint Stock Companies," *Parliamentary History and Review* (1826): 709–727;

"Review of Friedrich List's *Das Nationale System der Politsche Oekonomie,*" *Edinburgh Review,* 75 (1842): 515–556;

"Centralization," *Edinburgh Review,* 85 (1847): 221–258.

John Austin is widely recognized as the father of English jurisprudence. Building on the work of his friend and mentor Jeremy Bentham, he founded the discipline of analytic jurisprudence and the philosophy of legal positivism. Analytic jurisprudence is the logical elucidation of the concepts of *law* and *legal system* and of

fundamental legal concepts such as *right* and *duty;* with the exception of Bentham, no one in England before Austin had engaged in such a systematic and theoretical investigation into the nature and foundation of law. Legal positivism (not to be confused with philosophical or logical positivism) is the view that law in the proper sense of the term is limited to "positive," or actually existing, law—that is, law laid down by competent political authorities. The roots of legal positivism can be seen in the works of philosophers such as Thomas Hobbes, but the theory was first given a conceptual foundation by Austin and Bentham. Although jurisprudential studies on the European Continent were far in advance of those in England in Austin's day, legal positivism and analytical jurisprudence were unknown on the Continent.

Austin is best known for his command theory of law, his controversial perspective on the nature of sovereignty, and his insistence on the separation of law and morality. His work marks a break from the traditions of historical jurisprudence, which studies the development and evolution of the law, and of natural-law theory, which holds that law, to be valid and binding, must conform to the standards of morality.

Austin's work and thought, however, go beyond analytic jurisprudence and legal positivism. He was a lifelong and thoroughgoing utilitarian—that is, he believed that the rightness of an action depended on its tendency to promote the greatest happiness of the greatest number. He presented a lucid analysis of the concepts of act, will, volition, desire, and intent and applied them in a manner that still offers a penetrating, if incomplete, understanding of the basis of criminal and tort liability. He pioneered in the explication of the logic of judicial decision making and wrote with perspicuity on the nature and value of judicial legislation. He struggled, albeit unsuccessfully, to develop a coherent and scientific map of advanced legal systems. He also contributed to the political thought of his day by attacking the institution of primogeniture, calling for limited liability for corporations, defending free trade against the protectionists, arguing for a hierarchically organized political structure, and upholding traditional British constitutionalism in opposition to democratic reforms.

Nevertheless, Austin's reputation was secured only when his widow brought out, between 1861 and 1863, a second edition of the only book he published during his lifetime, *The Province of Jurisprudence Determined: An Outline of a Course of Lectures of General Jurisprudence or the Philosophy of Positive Law* (1832), along with two volumes of previously unpublished material. Because of Sarah Austin's determination and belief in her husband's greatness, John Austin's work became the engine behind the development of English legal theory.

The first of the seven children of Jonathan and Anne Austin, Austin was born on 3 March 1790 in Ipswich. His mother, the daughter of a yeoman farmer, was well educated, religious, and melancholic in disposition. His father, a miller and corn merchant who profited greatly from the Napoleonic Wars, was the first in his family to acquire wealth. Although he had little education, Jonathan Austin had a precise mind and disliked exaggeration—characteristics shared by his eldest son. He was determined to provide better educational opportunities for his children, several of whom achieved considerable success.

It is not clear whether John Austin attended school or was tutored at home. In any case, in a burst of anti-Napoleonic enthusiasm inflamed by the almost continuous wars with France during his childhood and the presence of the military garrison at Ipswich, he enlisted in the army when he was seventeen. Starting out as an ensign and later promoted to lieutenant, Austin saw virtually no military action and fell into a state of boredom and indolence. Realizing that he was unsuited for a military career, he resigned in 1812 and returned to Ipswich.

Displaying the diffident, vacillating, overly sensitive, and perfectionist personality that hampered his striving for success during his lifetime, Austin was plagued for the next two years with indecision about what he should do next. He finally decided on the profession of law and in late 1814 began reading for the bar at the Inner Temple in London. His announced goal, even at this early stage, was "to study and elucidate the principles of law," according to a letter collected in Janet Ross's *The Fourth Generation: Reminiscences* (1912).

Formal legal education was nonexistent at that time. Instruction in the law was oriented toward practice, rather than theoretical grounding, and was acquired through undirected reading and discussion and by observation in chambers, a law office, or the courts. Austin's legal apprenticeship included work in the chambers of an equity draftsman—a preparer of pleadings for proceedings in courts of equity. According to an 1817 letter from Austin to Sarah Taylor, his work with the equity draftsman developed the "taste for perspicuity and precision" that led both to the clarity and to the often tiresome and dry detail of his writing.

During his period of vacillation Austin had met Sarah Taylor. Shortly after commencing his legal studies Austin proposed to her in a letter that is notable more for its legalistic and moralistically serious tone than for its expression of passion. Despite misgivings about Austin's prospects, Sarah's parents gave their blessing. The couple began an engagement that lasted through Austin's legal education and apprenticeship; they were married in August 1819, one year after he was called to the bar.

Born into a family with a tradition of two hundred years of public service in religion and politics, Sally—as Sarah was known in her younger years—was a good match for a serious young man with a potential for extraordinary achievement. She shared her husband's middle-class origins, good looks, intelligence, and ability. During their long engagement she joined him in reading the works of such thinkers as Tacitus, Francis Bacon, John Locke, Adam Smith, and Bentham. There were significant differences in their characters, however: while John was insecure, overly perfectionistic, humorless, and subject to "feverish attacks" and lengthy bouts of lethargy and despondency, his wife was self-confident, ambitious, and gregarious. She became an able translator of German works into English, a skill she used to help support her family.

Shortly before their marriage Austin had been introduced to Bentham, whose work he had long admired; when the newlyweds took up residence in Queen Square Place in London, they became neighbors both of Bentham and of Bentham's principal disciple, the philosopher James Mill. The Austin home soon became a meeting place for the Benthamite circle. A particularly close relationship developed between the Austins and Mill's son, John Stuart Mill. John Stuart took vacations with the Austins and, though fifteen years older, served as a playmate for their only child, Lucy, who was born in 1821. James Mill engaged Austin to tutor John Stuart in law; the precocious John Stuart, in turn, influenced Austin's understanding of logic, an understanding that played a role in Austin's analytic jurisprudence.

Bentham, who was seventy when the Austins moved to Queen Square Place, was one of England's most important political and legal philosophers, the founder of utilitarianism, and a radical social reformer. He believed that the human condition could be improved by the development of a science of legislation based on the "principle of utility," or the principle of "the greatest happiness of the greatest number." This science of legislation, which he called censorial jurisprudence, was to determine what the law ought to be, in contrast to expository jurisprudence, the study of what the law is.

James Mill worked to put Bentham's ideas into practice in the fields of law, government, and economics. He had a deep influence on David Ricardo's economic theories, and Austin considered his *Elements of Political Economy* (1821) the model of what a work of social science should be.

Sarah Austin presided over a drawing-room salon that attracted intellectual luminaries such as Thomas Carlyle and George Grote. While John Austin was imbibing the radical politics of Bentham and developing his reputation as a master conversationalist, however, his law career was going none too well. He regarded the legal profession as "venal and fee-gathering," according to Lotte and Joseph Hamburger's *Troubled Lives: John and Sarah Austin* (1985). He took a position as a conveyancer and later became an equity draftsman. He also traveled on the Norfolk circuit but gave up his one case when he became tongue-tied. This anxiety about speaking in public, in contrast to his conversational brilliance in an intimate setting, contributed to his lack of success as a lecturer in subsequent years. He gave up the practice of law in 1825.

Austin's real interest lay in political and legal philosophy. His first published article, "Disposition of Property by Will-Primogeniture" (1824), demonstrates this interest, as well as his early adherence to the reformist politics that he later rejected. The article appeared in the *Westminster Review,* the journal founded by Bentham that same year. Austin contends that the tradition whereby the firstborn son inherits all or most of his parents' estate has negative economic consequences, including the concentration of landed wealth in the hands of a few, the creation of "aristocratical ascendancy and aristocratical misgovernment," and exploitation of the people. The radical spirit of Austin's early utilitarianism is expressed in his argument that the "greatest happiness" principle requires the equal distribution of wealth through inheritance:

> That the more there is for all, the more may fall to each, is clear; and it is not less indisputable (however it may be disputed) that a portion of wealth, if distributed amongst a given number with an approach to equality, will give a greater sum of happiness, than if the bulk of it be heaped on one or a few of the number, and the residue be shared by the rest in such pittances as will barely afford a subsistence. So far, therefore, as happiness is the effect of wealth, those institutions and customs are most to be praised, which most conciliate

augmentation in the quantity of wealth with equality in the distribution of it. These ends, perhaps, are conciliated amongst the middling class in England as far as they can be.

In his second article, "Joint Stock Companies" (1826), Austin develops a farsighted critique of the rule that provided for the unlimited liability of partners or shareholders in business ventures. Although it is now generally accepted that limiting the liability of corporate stockholders to the amount of their investment in the enterprise promotes economic progress, England did not institute statutory changes to limit liability until 1844. Austin's article criticizes unlimited liability as a deterrent to investors and the public. He calls the rule "needless and pernicious": needless because creditors would have sufficient information to make sound decisions on lending if companies were properly registered; pernicious because a cautious person would not invest in a joint-stock company for fear that he might lose not only his investment but his personal assets.

In 1826 Austin was appointed professor of jurisprudence and the law of nations at the newly founded University of London and began the only philosophically productive period of his life. His appointment apparently came through his Benthamite associations: Grote and James Mill were members of the governing council of the university.

The University of London—now known as University College London—was established to provide opportunities for students who could not attend Oxford or Cambridge and to teach subjects that were neglected at those schools, including professional courses in law and medicine. The decision to offer a course in jurisprudence was a significant innovation and a prime example of the influence of Benthamite progressivism; neither Oxford nor Cambridge had such courses.

Though he was known in his circle as a profound legal thinker, Austin had never taught. To prepare his lectures, which were to begin in the Michaelmas term of 1828, he decided to go to Germany for six months to familiarize himself with the writings of German jurists and to look for models of academic jurisprudence that were lacking in England. The Austins moved to Germany in 1826 or 1827. By fall 1827 they had settled in Bonn, the home of a newly founded university with distinguished faculty members such as B. G. Niebuhr, author of *The Roman History* (1827), and Wilhelm von Schlegel. According to Sarah Austin's preface to *The Province of Jurisprudence Determined,* the Austins quickly developed a fondness for the townspeople's "respect for knowledge, love of art, freedom of thought, and simplicity of habits."

Austin returned to England in the winter of 1828 less enamored of progressive causes than when he had left. He had come to view the Prussian monarchy and bureaucracy as superior to English representative democracy, had developed a dislike for the "general meanness of English life," and had acquired an interest in "the poetic and contemplative."

Delayed because of an illness until 1829, Austin's course began auspiciously with thirty-two students, including John Stuart Mill, but attendance rapidly dwindled. No students showed up for the first lecture in the November 1830 term, and attendance thereafter was no more than six or seven students.

In 1832, at his wife's urging, Austin published *The Province of Jurisprudence Determined*. The book is based on the first ten lectures of his course but is divided into six lectures to conform to the structure of the material. The first sentence lays out his philosophical position and begins the definitional task of the work: "The matter of jurisprudence is positive law; law, simply and strictly so called; or law set by political superiors to political inferiors." A law in the most general sense is "a rule laid down for the guidance of an intelligent being by an intelligent being having power over him." The intelligent beings who lay down laws are God and the political ruler, or sovereign; the body of rules set by God constitutes the divine law, while rules set by the sovereign make up the positive law.

Separated from both divine law and positive law is the realm of "positive morality." Positive morality is divided into rules set by men but not by political superiors and rules set and enforced by mere opinion and sentiment. The first category includes rules set by parents for children and by masters for slaves, which Austin calls "laws in the proper sense"; the second, "laws in the improper sense of the term," include international and constitutional law, etiquette, and fashion. Finally, Austin classifies the "laws of nature"–of physics, chemistry, and biology–as laws only in a metaphorical sense: "For where *intelligence* is not, or where it is too bounded to take the name of *reason,* and, therefore, is too bounded to conceive the purpose of a law, there is not the *will* which law can work on, or which duty can incite or restrain."

Austin's classification scheme flows from his analytical definition of law as command–the central concept of his philosophy of law and, in his words, "the *key* to the sciences of jurisprudence and morals." The term *command* denotes a wish or desire, conceived by a rational being, that another rational being shall do or forbear doing; an evil to proceed from the former and to be incurred by the latter, in case the latter does not comply with the wish; or an expression of the wish by words or other signs. Divine laws are the commands of God; positive laws are the commands of the sovereign; and positive morality consists of the commands of human beings in their private capacity (law in the proper sense of the term) and the sentiments of an indeterminate body of persons, that is, public opinion (law in the improper sense of the term). The liability to evil in case a command is not obeyed gives rise to *duty,* which is the obligation to obey; the evil to be visited on those who disobey is the *sanction,* or the enforcement of obedience.

The second, third, and fourth lectures focus on divine law. Divine law is divided into two parts: the law as revealed in the word of God, and the unrevealed law, which is determined by the principle of utility. The principle of utility, or greatest happiness principle, serves for Austin as the guide to the divine law: "the laws of God, which are not revealed or promulgated, must be gathered by man from the goodness of God, and from the tendencies of human actions. In other words, the benevolence of God, with the principle of general utility, is our only index or guide to his unrevealed law."

The practical impossibility of individuals calculating all of the consequences of each of their proposed actions on a utilitarian basis leads Austin to suggest that an intellectual elite be charged with inquiring into the unrevealed law on the basis of the principle of utility and disseminating the rules that most likely constitute the divine law. Such a college of moral workers would slowly lift the veil of prejudice and move humankind toward moral perfectibility. The public at large and even legislators would slowly learn to trust this elite group, which would have to be insulated from class and other interests. One source of this growing trust would be universal education: the multitudes would be taught the principles by which they could judge the work of the intellectual moral elite. Foremost among these principles would be respect for private property and capital:

> Without *capital,* and the arts which depend upon capital, the reward of labour would be far scantier than it is; and capital, with the arts which depend upon it, are creatures of the institution of property. The institution is good for the many, as well as for the few. The poor are not stripped by it of the produce of their labour; but it gives them a part in the employment of wealth which it calls into being. In effect, though not in law, the labourers are co-proprietors with the capitalists who hire their labour. The reward which they get for their labour is principally drawn from *capital;* and they are not less interested than the legal owners in protecting the fund from invasion.

Austin's defense of private property shows that although he maintained his Benthamite belief in progress–through the vehicles of science and utilitarianism humanity would move toward moral perfectibility–he had abandoned his conviction that a more equal distribution of wealth was desirable. He also abandoned his belief in democratic suffrage. By the time he gave the lectures, in other words, Austin was no longer a radical Benthamite.

The fifth lecture is on the nature of positive morality. Austin's view that international law is not law in the proper sense but, rather, positive morality, is the logical outcome of his definition of positive law as the command of the sovereign. A rule of international law does not come from a person or body of persons sovereign over those being commanded.

The sixth–and by far the longest–lecture is on the nature of positive law. After the concept of command, that of sovereignty is most important for Austin's enterprise of demarcating the varieties of law. Sovereignty is inseparably connected to the concept of an independent political society; as a consequence, in Austin's account positive law exists only in such a society. Independent political societies are distinguished from independent natural societies–families and primitive tribes, confederations of independent political societies, and subordinate political societies–by the presence of a sovereign. The sovereign is the person or body of persons that is habitually obeyed by the bulk of the members of the society but does not habitually obey any other human superior. Those who obey the sovereign are the subjects.

Austin divides the forms of government into two basic types: monarchical, or rule by one, and aristocratic, or rule by more than one. The latter category includes limited monarchies, such as that of England in the nineteenth century, and democracies, whether participatory or representative.

A distinctive and controversial feature of Austin's concept of sovereignty is its relation to law. The sovereign is the sole source of positive law; only the sovereign can issue commands that are legally binding. Since the sovereign has no superior, the sovereign is not subject to the law. The sovereign's imposition of a law on itself would be meaningless, as it could repeal that "law" at will. Thus, constitutional law is relegated to the realm of positive morality, having only the force of public opinion. The laws that sovereigns affect to impose on themselves are merely principles or maxims that they are not legally obliged to follow. In aristocratic societies (including democracies) the superiority of the sovereign to the law extends only to the sovereign body as a whole, not to its members acting in their individual capacities.

Austin stretches the concept of the sovereign to include the electorate. Hence, for England in the nineteenth century the sovereign was the Crown, the members of the House of Lords, and the electors of the House of Commons. For the United States the sovereign body is a complex aggregate of state and federal components and at the federal level extends to those who are empowered to amend the Constitution. Today, with universal suffrage, the sovereign would include the entire adult citizenry. In the American system the government is subordinate to the sovereign, and Austin allows that constitutional law is legally binding on the government.

Austin's concept of positive law as the command of the sovereign forms the basis for the sharp distinction between law and morality, a central feature of the school of legal positivism. In the older tradition of natural law, an unjust or immoral law is no law at all. For Austin and subsequent legal positivists, a law promulgated by the sovereign, or by authorities to whom the sovereign has delegated the power to promulgate law, is legally binding on the members of the society, whether or not it is unjust or immoral. He distinguishes between justice in the legal and the moral senses: justice in the legal sense means conformity to the laws of the sovereign, that is, to positive law; justice in the moral sense means conformity to the laws of God.

Austin does not, however, rule out disobedience to the positive law if it is found to be morally unjust. The decision should be based on the principle of utility: would disobedience to the law increase the sum of happiness in society? Austin deplores what he considers the confused thinking of the natural-law theorists. Acceptance of the view that a morally unjust law is not legally binding would lead to anarchism, he thinks, as each individual would believe that he or she could decide in his or her own conscience which laws are legally binding and which are not.

An important aspect of Austin's view of positive law concerns the pronouncements of subordinate officials, especially the judiciary. The English common-law tradition was based on judge-made law; the statutory promulgations of Parliament were the exception, not the rule. But since the judiciary is not the sovereign, how could judge-made law be the command of the sovereign? Austin answers:

> Now when customs are turned into legal rules by decisions of subject judges, the legal rules which emerge from the customs are *tacit* commands of the sovereign legislature. The state, which is able to abolish, permits its ministers to enforce them: and it, therefore, signifies its pleasure, by that its voluntary acquiescence, "that they shall serve as a law to the governed."

Having completed the task of delimiting the domains of jurisprudence and positive law, Austin is occupied in the remainder of *The Province of Jurisprudence Determined* with an inquiry into a variety of aspects of positive law. These materials, which are of continuing interest and use to legal scholars and theorists despite the fact that Austin never fully developed them, demonstrate both Austin's effort to place jurisprudence on a scientific footing and his efforts to apply utilitarian principles to structural elements of the positive law.

The primary reasons for Austin's failure as a teacher were the primitive state of legal education at the time, the practical orientation of most law students, and the abstract character of jurisprudence–a subject that does not attract many students in law school even today. According to the preface to the fifth edition of *Lectures on Jurisprudence; or, The Philosophy of Positive Law* (1885), this failure was the "real and irremediable calamity of his life–the blow from which he never recovered." He lamented that he "was born out of time and place": "I ought to have been a schoolman of the twelfth century–or a German professor."

Despite his disappointment, Austin continued to teach at the University of London until 1833. In 1834 he was asked to give a series of lectures on jurisprudence at the Inner Temple; but, as at the university, the initial interest soon waned, and he concluded that completing the series would not serve any purpose. He did no further work in jurisprudence, the field he most loved, nor did he produce anything more of an intellectual nature or engage in any other gainful employment during the remainder of his lifetime. Attempts that he did make were aborted by repeated bouts of his neurasthenic illnesses.

No longer able to afford to live in London after Austin's failure as a teacher, the family moved to Boulogne, France, in 1835. In 1836 they moved to Malta when Austin was appointed a colonial commissioner for the island but returned to London in 1838 after the commission was recalled. In 1844 the Austins moved to Germany, where they stayed in Carlsbad, Dresden, and Berlin. Later that year they moved to Paris. During the first year after their arrival in Paris, Austin was elected a corresponding member of the Academy of Moral and Political Sciences of the Institut de France. Sarah again created a popular salon that was attended by many political and intellectual personages, among them the historian and statesman François-Pierre-Guillaume Guizot.

The conservative Austins were deeply alarmed by the revolutionary fervor of Paris in 1848 and returned to England in March of that year. After staying for a while at Queen Square Place, where their daughter–who had married Sir Alexander Duff Gordon in 1840–had followed in her mother's footsteps by establishing a salon, the Austins settled in Weybridge. There Austin finally found tranquillity in reading, walking, meditating, and cultivating his garden. After a seven-week illness, he died on 17 December 1859.

The republication by Sarah Austin of an enlarged three-volume edition of *The Province of Jurisprudence Determined* in the early 1860s could not have come at a more auspicious time to secure her husband's reputation. For-

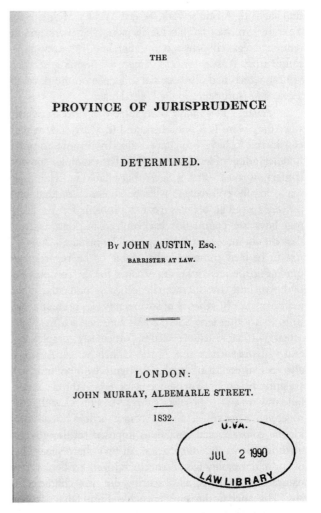

THE

PROVINCE OF JURISPRUDENCE

DETERMINED.

By JOHN AUSTIN, Esq.
BARRISTER AT LAW.

LONDON:
JOHN MURRAY, ALBEMARLE STREET.
1832.

Dust jacket for the only book by John Austin published during his lifetime (Arthur J. Morris Law Library, University of Virginia)

mal legal education was finally taking root in England, creating a need for materials on jurisprudence, and the only texts available were Austin's. The only other major English jurist of the time was Bentham, but his most significant writings in the field were not published until well into the twentieth century. As a result, Austin's works became the de facto standard, providing several generations of English legal scholars and lawyers with their basic grounding in jurisprudence. The legal positivism that he spawned became the dominant school of legal philosophy of the twentieth century.

In the United States, Austin's influence was more diffuse. He was read avidly by Oliver Wendell Holmes Jr., the renowned Supreme Court justice, who agreed with him that laws should be made by legislative bodies, not by courts, and that the spheres of law and morality should be kept separate. Christopher Columbus Langdell, nineteenth-century Harvard law professor and founder of the case method of teaching in American law schools, was familiar with Austin's work, as was Wesley Hohfeld, the Yale law professor famous for his pioneering work on fundamental legal concepts. John Chipman Gray drew inspiration from Austin for *The Nature and Sources of the Law* (1909), which had a substantial influence on the development of jurisprudence in the United States.

Austin's ideas have been subject to heavy criticism since they were first published, and they are now widely considered to have been superseded by a more complex understanding of legal phenomena. For example, "power-conferring rules"—that is, laws that enable individuals to make legally enforceable wills or contracts or that give powers to public officials—pose a problem for his claim that laws are commands backed by sanctions, because they do not impose duties supported by penalties. Austin's notion of tacit commands has come to be regarded as unrealistic, because it fails to account for the complexities of lawmaking by subordinate officials, particularly the judiciary. Austin's theory of sovereignty has been attacked from many quarters. Some critics consider it a misrepresentation of most actual societies, particularly complex federal systems such as that of the United States. Austin is also seen as confusing legal sovereignty with political sovereignty: sovereignty in democracies rests in the electorate, but laws are enacted by legislatures. And his view that the sovereign is not subject to legal restraints does not account for the constitutional limitations imposed on the government in many modern societies. Austin's sharp separation of law and morality has also been criticized, particularly by natural-law theorists, as obscuring the true character of law. His analytic jurisprudence has been faulted as an inappropriate abstract inquiry divorced from the social context and function of the law.

Despite the criticisms, Austin's work has remained a central starting point for modern positivist analyses of the law. Hans Kelsen, the most important of the twentieth-century Continental positivists, saw "no essential difference" between his own pure theory of law and Austin's analytic jurisprudence: "Where they differ, they do so because the pure theory of law tries to carry on the method of analytical jurisprudence more consistently than Austin and his followers." H. L. A. Hart, the leading twentieth-century English legal philosopher, styled his version of legal positivism "a fresh start." Nevertheless, Hart felt compelled to devote three chapters of his central jurisprudential work, *The Concept of Law* (1961), to a critique of Austin's command theory of law and concept of sovereignty. Likewise, the first two chapters of Joseph Raz's positivist work *The Concept of a Legal System: An Introduction to the Theory of a Legal System* (1980) comprise a sustained criticism of Austin's main ideas.

The role given to Austin by outstanding twentieth-century legal positivists as an example of a flawed though important approach to understanding the nature of law led to renewed interest in him in the 1980s. During that decade three books were published on Austin, including the first comprehensive biography of Austin and his wife. In addition, a spate of law-review articles have explored his ideas. This interest was capped in 1995 by the publication of a new edition of *The Province of Jurisprudence Determined*.

Austin's systematic, uncompromising, and deep analysis leaves a powerful impression and remains an important entryway into the field of jurisprudence for both the layperson and the legal scholar. Sir Henry Sumner Maine, the leading nineteenth-century English exponent of historical jurisprudence and a sharp critic of Austin, said that his writings produce a "clearing of the brain," sweeping away confused and muddled ideas about the nature of law. John Austin ranks among the important figures in the pantheon of legal philosophy, and his work continues to be worthy of study.

Biographies:

Janet Ross, *Three Generations of Englishwomen: Memoirs and Correspondences of Mrs. John Taylor, Mrs. Sarah Austin, and Lady Duff Gordon,* 2 volumes (London: Murray, 1888);

Ross, *The Fourth Generation: Reminiscences* (New York: Scribners, 1912);

Lotte and Joseph Hamburger, *Troubled Lives: John and Sarah Austin* (Toronto & Buffalo: University of Toronto Press, 1985).

References:

James Bryce, *Studies in History and Jurisprudence,* volume 2 (New York: Oxford University Press, 1901), pp. 89–97, 127, 180–184;

Roger Cotterrell, *The Politics of Jurisprudence: A Critical Introduction to Legal Philosophy* (Philadelphia: University of Pennsylvania Press, 1992), pp. 52–82;

John Chipman Gray, *The Nature and Sources of the Law* (New York: Macmillan, 1927);

H. L. A. Hart, *The Concept of Law* (London: Oxford University Press, 1961), pp. 1–48;

Hart, "John Austin," in *International Encyclopedia of the Social Sciences,* edited by David L. Sills, volume 1 (New York: Macmillan, 1968), pp. 472–473;

Hart, "Positivism and the Separation of Law and Morals," *Harvard Law Review,* 71 (1958): 593–629;

M. H. Hoeflich, "John Austin and Joseph Story: Two Nineteenth Century Perspectives on the Utility of the Civil Law for the Common Lawyer," *American Journal of Legal History,* 29 (1985): 36–77;

Hoeflich, "Law and Geometry: Legal Science from Leibniz to Langdell," *American Journal of Legal History,* 30 (1986): 95–121;

Hans Kelsen, *General Theory of Law and State,* translated by Anders Wedberg (Cambridge, Mass.: Harvard University Press, 1945), pp. 30–32, 62–64, 71–74, 94–95, 127–128;

Kelsen, "The Pure Theory of Law and Analytical Jurisprudence," *Harvard Law Review,* 55 (1941): 44–70;

Albert Kocourek, "The Century of Analytic Jurisprudence since John Austin," in *Law: A Century of Progress, 1835–1935: Contributions in Celebration of the 100th Anniversary of the Founding of the School of Law of New York University,* 3 volumes, edited by Alison Reppy (New York: New York University, 1937), II: 195–230;

Sir Henry Sumner Maine, *Lectures on the Early History of Institutions* (New York: Holt, 1888), pp. 342–400;

John Stuart Mill, "Austin's Lectures on Jurisprudence," and "Austin on Jurisprudence," in his *Essays on Equality, Law, and Education,* edited by J. M. Robson, *Collected Works of John Stuart Mill,* volume 21 (Toronto & Buffalo: University of Toronto Press, 1984), pp. 51–60, 167–205;

Robert N. Moles, *Definition and Rule in Legal Theory: A Reassessment of H. L. A. Hart and the Positivist Tradition* (Oxford: Blackwell, 1987);

Moles, "Hart's Critique of Austin," *Northern Ireland Legal Quarterly,* 36 (1985): 283–313;

Moles, "John Austin Reconsidered," *Northern Ireland Legal Quarterly,* 36 (1985): 193–221;

W. L. Morison, *John Austin* (Stanford, Cal.: Stanford University Press, 1982);

Morison, "Some Myths about Positivism," *Yale Law Journal,* 68 (1958): 212–233;

Herbert Morris, "Verbal Disputes and the Legal Philosophy of John Austin," *UCLA Law Review,* 7 (1959): 27–56;

Gustav Radbruch, "Anglo-American Jurisprudence through Continental Eyes," *Law Quarterly Review,* 52 (1936): 530–545;

Joseph Raz, *The Concept of a Legal System: An Introduction to the Theory of a Legal System* (Oxford: Clarendon Press, 1980), pp. 5–43;

Eira Ruben, "John Austin's Political Pamphlets 1824–1859," in *Perspectives in Jurisprudence,* edited by Elspeth Attwooll (Glasgow: University of Glasgow Press, 1977), pp. 20–41;

Wilfrid E. Rumble, "Austin in the Classroom: Why Were His Courses in Jurisprudence Unpopular?" *Legal History,* 17 (1996): 17–39;

Rumble, "John Austin and his Nineteenth Century Critics: The Case of Sir Henry Sumner Maine," *Northern Ireland Legal Quarterly,* 39 (1988): 119–149;

Rumble, "The Legal Positivism of John Austin and the Realist Movement in American Jurisprudence," *Cornell Law Review,* 66 (1981): 986–1031;

Rumble, "Nineteenth-century Perceptions of John Austin: Utilitarianism and the Reviews of The Province of Jurisprudence Determined," *Utilitas,* 3 (1991): 199–216;

Rumble, *The Thought of John Austin: Jurisprudence, Colonial Reform and the British Constitution* (London: Athlone, 1985);

Andrea B. Schwarz, "John Austin and the German Jurisprudence of His Time," *Politica,* 1 (1934): 178–199;

John E. Stannard, "A Tale of Four Codes: John Austin and the Criminal Law," *Northern Ireland Legal Quarterly,* 41 (1990): 293–314;

Julius Stone, *Legal System and Lawyers' Reasonings* (Stanford, Cal.: Stanford University Press, 1946), pp. 62–92;

Stone, *The Province and Function of Law: Law as Logic, Justice and Social Control. A Study in Jurisprudence* (Sydney: Associated General Publications, 1946), pp. 55–73;

Samuel E. Stumpf, "Austin's Theory of the Separation of Law and Morals," *Vanderbilt Law Review,* 14 (1960): 117–149.

A. J. Ayer

(29 October 1910 – 27 June 1989)

Ian Morton
Liverpool John Moores University

BOOKS: *Language, Truth and Logic* (London: Gollancz, 1936; London & New York: Oxford University Press, 1936; revised edition, London: Gollancz, 1946; New York: Dover, 1946);

The Foundations of Empirical Knowledge (London & New York: Macmillan, 1940);

Thinking and Meaning: Inaugural Lecture (London: Lewis, 1947);

Philosophical Essays (London: Macmillan, 1954; New York: St. Martin's Press, 1954);

Studies in Communication, Contributed to the Communication Research Centre, University College, London, by Ayer and others (London: Secker & Warburg, 1955);

The Revolution in Philosophy, by Ayer and others (London: Macmillan, 1956; New York: St. Martin's Press, 1956);

The Problem of Knowledge (London: Macmillan, 1956; New York: St. Martin's Press, 1956);

Philosophy and Language: An Inaugural Lecture Delivered before the University of Oxford on 3 November 1960 (Oxford: Clarendon Press, 1960);

The Concept of a Person and Other Essays (London: Macmillan, 1963; New York: St. Martin's Press, 1963);

Man as a Subject for Science: Delivered on 7 February 1964 at the London School of Economics and Political Science, Auguste Comte Memorial Lecture, no. 6 (London: Athlone, 1964);

Philosophy and Politics, Eleanor Rathbone Memorial Lecture, no. 16 (Liverpool: Liverpool University Press, 1967);

The Origins of Pragmatism: Studies in the Philosophy of Charles Sanders Peirce and William James (London: Macmillan, 1968; San Francisco: Cooper, 1968);

Metaphysics and Common Sense (London: Macmillan, 1969; San Francisco: Cooper, 1970);

Russell and Moore: The Analytical Heritage (London: Macmillan, 1971; Cambridge, Mass.: Harvard University Press, 1971);

Probability and Evidence (London: Macmillan, 1972; New York: Columbia University Press, 1972);

A. J. Ayer (photograph by Geoff Howard)

Russell (London: Fontana/Collins, 1972; New York: Viking, 1972);

The Central Questions of Philosophy (London: Weidenfeld & Nicholson, 1973; New York: Holt, Rinehart & Winston, 1974);

Part of My Life: The Memoirs of a Philosopher (London: Collins, 1977; New York: Harcourt Brace Jovanovich, 1977);

Hume (Oxford & New York: Oxford University Press, 1980; New York: Hill & Wang, 1980);

Contemporary Philosophy, Fourth Leggett Lecture, University of Surrey, 1980 (Guildford: University of Surrey, 1980);

Philosophy in the Twentieth Century (London: Weidenfeld & Nicholson, 1982; New York: Random House, 1982);

More of My Life (London: Collins, 1984; Oxford & New York: Oxford University Press, 1985);

Freedom and Morality and Other Essays (Oxford: Clarendon Press, 1984; New York: Oxford University Press, 1984);

Wittgenstein (London: Weidenfeld & Nicholson, 1985; New York: Random, 1985);

Voltaire (London: Weidenfeld & Nicholson, 1986; New York: Random House, 1986);

The Meaning of Life, Conway Memorial Lecture, no. 64 (London: South Place Ethical Society, 1988); enlarged as *The Meaning of Life and Other Essays,* edited by Ted Honderich (London: Weidenfeld & Nicholson, 1990; New York: Scribners, 1990);

Thomas Paine (London: Secker & Warburg, 1988; New York: Atheneum, 1988).

OTHER: *British Empirical Philosophers: Locke, Berkeley, Hume, Reid and J. S. Mill,* edited by Ayer and Raymond Winch (London: Routledge & Kegan Paul, 1952; New York: Simon & Schuster, 1968);

Logical Positivism, edited by Ayer (Glencoe, Ill.: Free Press, 1959; London: Allen & Unwin, 1959);

George Unwin, ed., *What I Believe,* contribution by Ayer (London: Allen & Unwin, 1966);

"An Appraisal of Bertrand Russell's Philosophy," in *Bertrand Russell: Philosopher of the Century. Essays in His Honour,* edited by Ralph Schoenman (London: Allen & Unwin, 1967), pp. 167–178;

The Humanist Outlook, edited by Ayer (London: Pemberton in association with Barrie & Rockliff, 1968);

"Replies," in *Perception and Identity: Essays Presented to A. J. Ayer, with His Replies to Them,* edited by G. F. MacDonald (London: Macmillan, 1979; Ithaca, N. Y.: Cornell University Press, 1979), pp. 277–333;

A Dictionary of Philosophical Quotations, edited by Ayer and Jane O'Grady (Oxford & Cambridge, Mass.: Blackwell, 1992);

"My Mental Development," "Still More of My Life," and replies to critics, in *The Philosophy of A. J. Ayer,* edited by Lewis E. Hahn, Library of Living Philosophers, volume 21 (La Salle, Ill.: Open Court, 1992), pp. 3–53, 105–107, 125–128, 149–156, 175–177, 198–200, 220–224, 237–242, 271–278, 301–307, 326–328, 341–345, 367–373, 387–392, 402–405, 425–428, 455–465, 478–488, 509–515, 542–544, 570–575, 598–607.

A. J. Ayer is the best-known British philosopher of the generation that followed Bertrand Russell. At age twenty-four Ayer published *Language, Truth and Logic* (1936), a vigorous polemical attack on views he dismisses as "metaphysical." The opening sentence declares that "The traditional disputes of philosophy are, for the most part, as unwarranted as they are unfruitful," and the rest of the work is similarly iconoclastic. The book made Ayer's name and influenced the course of philosophical debate for decades. It has been translated into at least fourteen other languages, making his views known worldwide. A later book, *The Problem of Knowledge* (1956), also became a classic text. Ayer was the last in a line of distinguished British empiricists: his philosophical approach and interests are in the tradition of John Locke, George Berkeley, David Hume, John Stuart Mill, and Russell. It is a measure of Ayer's standing that his name is usually added to this list.

Alfred Jules "Freddie" Ayer was born in Abbey Road, St. John's Wood, north London, on 29 October 1910. His father, Jules Louis Cyprien Ayer, whose parents were Swiss Calvinists, was secretary to Alfred Rothschild, a director of the Bank of England. Ayer's mother, Reine Citröen Ayer, was of Dutch Jewish descent; her relatives had wide commercial interests, which included founding the Citröen car company in France. At seven Ayer was sent to Ascham St. Vincent's, a preparatory school on the south coast of England. The purpose of the rather austere education offered by such institutions was to prepare boys for entrance to one of the better English public schools, so the academic emphasis was on Latin, mathematics, history, and English, rather than on the sciences. Ayer does not appear to have enjoyed his time at Ascham; on a television program in 1980 he compared it to a Nazi concentration camp, describing it as "a little Belsen."

In the summer of 1923 Ayer took the examination for a scholarship to Eton; he was not expected to receive one, but the practice would be useful for a more serious attempt later. In the event, Ayer came in third out of forty-six entrants and won a King's Scholarship. In 1928 he won a scholarship to Christ Church College of the University of Oxford to read classics, which included philosophy. Ayer later described the dominant tone of Oxford philosophy at that time as surly, unadventurous, narrow, and dogmatic, but he was fortunate that one of his tutors was Gilbert Ryle, who later published the influential *The Concept of Mind* (1949). Ryle had wide interests, including the work of Russell, G. E. Moore, and Ludwig Wittgenstein at the University of Cambridge. Ryle read Wittgenstein's *Tractatus Logico-Philosophicus* (1922) during his final year at Oxford; he also read the works of Hume. Hume and Russell became the two most important influences on Ayer's philosophical development. On 25 November 1932 Ayer married Grace Isabel Renée Lees.

Shortly after graduating from Oxford in 1932, Ayer went to Vienna at Ryle's suggestion to attend the fortnightly meetings of a group of prominent mathematicians, scientists, logicians, and philosophers led by Moritz Schlick, Rudolph Carnap, and Otto Neurath. Ayer was one of only two visitors ever to sit in on meetings of the group (the other was the American philosopher and logician W. V. O. Quine). The Vienna Circle, as it came to be known, was strongly influenced by contemporary developments in physics, the foundations of mathematics, and formal logic. Its main purpose was to develop a role for philosophical discussion that would include analysis of the logic of science and its relation to ordinary observation and confirm the empirical sciences—construed as endlessly refined common-sense inquiry—as the sole source of what one can properly be said to know. The uncompromising empiricism of the Vienna Circle, which became known as "logical positivism," accorded perfectly with the philosophical views Ayer had found—or thought he had found—in the works of Hume, Russell, and Wittgenstein.

Early in 1933, after four months in Vienna, Ayer returned to Oxford. Having failed to endear himself to several senior academics at Christ Church, he was unable to secure a permanent post and faced an uncertain future. At the end of the year he started to write Language, Truth and Logic, which was in effect and perhaps in purpose the English-language manifesto of logical positivism, although Ayer preferred to call his position "logical empiricism." The book was published to mixed reviews in 1936, creating wide interest and debate. Although Ayer's treatment of ethics and theology caused much hostility, the wider onslaught on "metaphysics" was the philosophically distinctive aspect of the book.

The main weapon Ayer employs in his attack on metaphysics is the claim that every cognitively meaningful declarative sentence—that is, every sentence that expresses a proposition—is either necessarily true or verifiable by sense experience. Formulating this criterion of meaningfulness requires drawing an exclusive and exhaustive distinction between sentences that express empirically testable propositions, such as "The cat is on the mat," "Paris is the capital of France," and the propositions of the physical sciences, on the one hand, and sentences that express necessarily true propositions—that is, propositions that are true in any circumstances—on the other hand. The most obvious examples of the latter are found in mathematics and logic—"2+2=4," "Every statement is either true or false"—but the category also includes ordinary-language statements such as "All bachelors are unmarried adult males" and "A vixen is a female fox."

In the nineteenth century John Stuart Mill had argued that the truths of mathematics and logic are not in fact necessary but are thoroughly confirmed empirical generalizations. No one has ever found an instance in which, say, adding three coins to two coins does not yield five coins; the many observations are generalized to yield the conclusion that the result will hold in all cases. This approach, however, seems to misrepresent the relationship between mathematics and experience: if a child adds two drops of water to three drops of water and creates one puddle, the truth of the equation "2+3=5" in not called into question. Nor does it seem possible to conceive of a Martian mathematics in which the symbols "2," "3," "6," "+," and "=" are given the same interpretation as in Earth mathematics but somehow yield "2+3=6" as a true proposition on Mars.

If Mill's account fails, then empiricism needs another way of defusing the threat that the a priori truths of mathematics and logic pose to the claim that everything one can properly be said to know derives from sense experience. Ayer's approach in Language, Truth and Logic is to accept the necessity of such propositions but to argue that they are analytic—that is, tautologous. This tactic allows the logical empiricist to accept the propositions of mathematics as true, and even as necessarily true, but to argue that their truth rests not on apprehending some nonsensory realm of eternal mathematical verities but on decisions about how symbols are to be used. As Ayer puts it in the preface to Language, Truth and Logic, the reason such "propositions cannot be confuted in experience is that they do not make any assertion about the empirical world, but simply record our determination to use symbols in a certain fashion."

This claim is known as the conventionalist account of necessary truth: it is as if there had been a meeting at which it was decided that the symbol "bachelor" and the symbols "unmarried adult male" were to be equivalent in meaning, as were the symbols "vixen" and "female fox." Given those decisions, it is necessarily true that "A bachelor is an unmarried adult male" and "A vixen is a female fox," but the truths are analytic; the predicate terms of the expressions merely analyze or make explicit what is already "contained in" the subject terms. The statements do not assert that there actually are any bachelors, adult males, vixens, or foxes; they are true, but they are devoid of factual content. Their necessity arises from a contingent decision about the use of symbols—contingent because the choice could have been, for example, to define "bachelor" as synonymous with "female fox."

In *Language, Truth and Logic* Ayer deploys a criterion, the verification principle, to undermine a variety of claims about supposed "realities" of which one has no sensory experience: "We say that a sentence is factually significant to any given person, if and only if, he knows how to verify the proposition which it purports to express—that is, if he knows what observations would lead him, under certain conditions, to accept the proposition as being true, or reject it as being false." If a philosopher asserts that all sensory experience is mere illusion and that beyond the illusion lies a forever-inaccessible "reality," Ayer will first ask whether the statement asserting this state of affairs is a necessary truth; plainly, it is not. He will then ask whether the claim is empirically verifiable or refutable; equally plainly, it is not, since the statement itself rejects every sensory experience as illusory. Since the seeming proposition cannot be accommodated in either category, Ayer dismisses it as "metaphysical" and, therefore, meaningless. He does not mean that the seeming assertion is false; rather, it is, according to Ayer's criterion, literally nonsense and so not a candidate for truth or falsity. If one is told that there is a transcendent God, or a realm of absolute moral truths that is not part of the physical universe, or immaterial minds or souls that do not occupy space, it might appear that one is being presented with grammatically well-formed statements that are either true or false, even though they might be impossible to confirm or disprove. Ayer rejects this assumption: if the seeming statements are neither analytic nor observationally verifiable, they are meaningless—they have no literal or cognitive significance. To say that a seeming statement or proposition has no cognitive content is to say that it cannot form part of a belief system, for to "believe" such a proposition is to believe nothing. Ayer does not deny that using such sentences might offer consolation or be in some ways evocative, but he insists that they have no literal meaning: they are, strictly speaking, "senseless" or "non-sense."

Ayer distinguishes between practical verifiability and verifiability in principle. In 1900 it was not practically possible to verify the proposition that there are mountains on the far side of the moon, but there was no difficulty in understanding what observations would settle the matter. Thus, the proposition was verifiable in principle. More important is the distinction between "strong" and "weak" verification. "Strong" verification would require that to be meaningful a proposition must be conclusively established as true or false. But if meaningfulness depends on strong verification, one encounters problems with many law-like

Ayer in his twenties (photograph © Estate of A. J. Ayer)

generalizations in the sciences: it does not seem possible, even in principle, to verify conclusively Sir Isaac Newton's law of universal gravitation, which asserts that every body in the universe attracts every other body. In the face of this difficulty Ayer argues for a weaker sense of verification that rejects conclusiveness or certainty in favor of probability. Thus, the criterion of factual significance of a proposition is the possibility of making observations relevant to its truth or falsity: "Let us call a proposition which records an actual or possible observation an experiential proposition. Then we may say that it is the mark of a genuine factual proposition . . . that some experiential propositions can be derived from it in conjunction with certain other premises without being deducible from those other premises alone."

Critics have pointed out, however, that this criterion is inadequate. For example, given any perfectly respectable factual proposition O, such as "These trousers are gray" and any nonsensical proposition N, such as "The impossible Absolute is lazy," one can construct the valid argument "If N, then O; N; therefore, O" ("If the impossible Absolute is lazy, then these trousers are gray; the impossible Absolute is lazy; therefore, these trousers are gray,"). Thus, an experiential proposition, O, has been deduced from "If N, then O" and "N." Since one cannot validly deduce "O" from "If N, then O" alone, "N" satisfies Ayer's criterion of factual significance; but it is nonsense.

Despite a considerable philosophical output, Ayer wrote relatively little about ethics. His most important discussion of the topic is in *Language, Truth and Logic,* and it develops in part from applying the verification principle. The sentence "Stealing is wrong" appears to express a proposition that many people take to be true, but it does not fall into either of the categories of meaningful statement Ayer allows. If "stealing" means "taking without the owner's consent and in breach of the law of the land," then "Stealing is wrong" is not analytic. Nor can the wrongness of stealing be verified observationally. One can, it is true, readily verify its typical effects, such as causing distress to the victim. But then the wrongness of stealing would depend on the truth of "Causing distress to innocent people is wrong," and the same problem would arise there. The rightness and wrongness of actions are not properties that can be observed. Thus, since "Stealing is wrong" is neither analytic nor empirically testable, then by Ayer's criterion it must be meaningless. Persuaded by verificationism, one might easily eschew all further talk of transcendent metaphysical "realities"; but it is less easy to see how one could abandon as meaningless all moral precepts and judgments. Such judgments seem to play an important role in directing people's lives; but if they are meaningless, how can they do so? Ayer's answer is that moral utterances do not report observations but express the speaker's approval or disapproval and are intended to inspire similar feelings in the hearer. The factual content in the sentence "You acted wrongly in stealing that money" is exhausted by the assertion "you stole money"; there is no further empirically verifiable content in the disapproving remark "You acted wrongly." The function of moral utterances, then, is to express feelings and to arouse feelings in others that might prompt them to act in certain ways.

Ayer's claim that the meanings of ethical words are the feelings they express or the responses they are calculated to provoke is known as the emotivist analysis of ethical language. A strength of emotivism is that it explains the link between moral judgment and action: moral judgments are taken to be expressions of emotions, and emotions, by their nature, dispose one to act. A common objection to emotivism is that commitments based on emotions must be fickle or capricious, unsuited to the serious business of grounding morality. But this objection misrepresents many deep and stable emotional commitments—for example, parental love. A more serious difficulty for

emotivism is that sentences such as "stealing is wrong" seem to retain their meaning even when not being used to make moral pronouncements. In the conditional "If stealing is wrong, then thieves should be punished" the proposition "stealing is wrong" does not appear to report or express an emotional response; yet, it still has meaning. During his long philosophical career Ayer modified many of his views, but he held to the emotivist analysis. The debate over its adequacy continues.

Ayer and his wife had a daughter, Valerie Jane, in 1936. Ayer was active in Labour Party politics throughout the 1930s and served as chairman of the Soho branch of the Westminster division. In 1937 he was a Labour candidate in the local council elections. In 1939 the Ayers had a son, Julian David.

Although Ayer could have remained in his academic post, at the outbreak of World War II in 1939 he enlisted in the Welsh Guards, one of the more prestigious regiments in the British Army. After officer training at the Royal Military College at Sandhurst, Ayer was offered a job as an interrogator. He spent the rest of the war in military intelligence, eventually transferring to the secret Special Operations Executive, which ran resistance activities behind enemy lines. Ayer did not see combat; he was sent to New York and to Accra before returning to Britain to monitor and report on French Resistance groups. During a posting to Paris at the end of the war Ayer met writers and intellectuals such as Albert Camus, George Orwell, André Malraux, and Maurice Merleau-Ponty. The experience led him to write several articles on existentialism.

The Ayers were divorced in 1940. Ayer left the army in 1945 and returned to Oxford as fellow and dean of Wadham College. In 1946 he was offered the Grote Professorship of the Philosophy of Mind and Logic at University College London. The philosophy department at University College was then in decline, and over the next few years Ayer, leading by example both as an outstanding teacher and an effective administrator, reinvigorated it. In his obituary of Ayer that he read at the International Institute of Philosophy in California on 1 September 1989, the Oxford philosopher David F. Pears said, "In London he achieved a miracle, resurrecting a moribund department and putting it in competition with Oxford and Cambridge."

In 1946 the second edition of *Language, Truth and Logic* was published, with a lengthy new introduction in which Ayer concedes some of the shortcomings of his original discussion and offers corrections. In particular, he admits the deficiencies of the formulation of the verification principle in the first edition and provides an amendment of it. The purpose of the amendment is to meet the objection that the original criterion of meaningfulness allows meaning to any indicative sentence whatsoever. To avoid this problem Ayer introduces the term "observation-statement" to designate a statement that "records an actual or possible observation." A statement is "directly verifiable" if it is "either itself an observation-statement, or is such that in conjunction with one or more observation-statements it entails at least one observation-statement which is not deducible from these other premises alone." Thus, a statement such as "The impossible Absolute is lazy" is not directly verifiable, for it does not record an actual or possible observation, and so it cannot be an observation-statement. Nor is the conditional "If the impossible Absolute is lazy, then these trousers are gray" directly verifiable, for the conditional itself is not an observation-statement, as it would have to be to play the required role as a premise in entailing an observation-statement. That is, in the argument "If N, then O; N; therefore, O," N in the second premise cannot be directly verifiable unless "If N, then O" is an observation-statement, which it is not.

Ayer goes on to define "indirect verifiability": a "statement is indirectly verifiable if it satisfies the following conditions: first, that in conjunction with certain other premises it entails one or more directly verifiable statements which are not deducible from these other premises alone; and, secondly, that these other premises do not include any statement that is not either analytic or directly verifiable, or capable of being independently established as indirectly verifiable." His intention is to exclude nonsense propositions as not indirectly verifiable. He proposes that a statement that is not analytic has literal meaning if it is either directly or indirectly verifiable, as he has defined those terms.

Ayer's revision is, however, also vulnerable to counterexamples. Reviewing the second edition in the *Journal of Symbolic Logic* in 1949, Alonzo Church showed that Ayer's modified criterion still admits as factually significant any arbitrarily chosen nonsense statement. If $O1$, $O2$, and $O3$ are any three observation-statements that are logically independent in the sense that none of them, taken on its own, entails any of the others, and N is any nonsense statement, then a statement S can formed as "Either (not-$O1$ and $O2$) or (not-N and $O3$)." If this statement is made the first premise of a deductive argument, and "$O1$" is added as the second premise, these premises together entail $O3$. Thus, the statement S is directly verifiable, because, when conjoined with the observation-statement $O1$, it entails an observation-statement, $O3$, that is logically independent of $O1$ and so is not entailed by $O1$ alone. But if S

is directly verifiable, then the nonsense statement N can be shown to be indirectly verifiable: if S is retained as the first premise, and N is made the second premise, then these two premises entail $O2$. But $O2$ is an observation-statement and so, by Ayer's definition, is directly verifiable. It follows that N entails a directly verifiable statement, $O2$, when conjoined with a directly verifiable premise, S, which does not entail $O2$ on its own; so the nonsense statement N satisfies Ayer's conditions for being an indirectly verifiable and, therefore, literally meaningful statement. Ayer accepted Church's objection; he discusses it briefly in *The Central Questions of Philosophy* (1973).

Many criticisms have been made of the verification principle, but the failure to find a formulation that excludes "nonsensical" or "metaphysical" statements is the most severe difficulty. No completely satisfactory version of the principle has yet been offered, and few philosophers today declare themselves verificationists in the positivist mold; but a verificationist impulse, at least, continues to influence contemporary philosophy.

In 1956 Ayer published what many philosophers consider his finest book, *The Problem of Knowledge;* Ayer himself thought that it was better than *Language, Truth and Logic.* Though he established his reputation with his robust positivism, Ayer's major philosophical contributions have been to epistemology, or theory of knowledge. The puzzles Ayer addresses in *The Problem of Knowledge* are the central epistemological issues: the nature of knowledge, the threat of skepticism, the quest for certainty, perception and knowledge of the physical world, the trustworthiness of memory, and knowledge of other minds. Traditionally, the main questions in epistemology are "What is knowledge?" and "What may we properly be said to know?" The first question is usually understood as calling for an analysis of the conditions in which it is proper to claim knowledge of some proposition, the second as requiring a response to radical skepticism about the possibility of knowledge.

In *The Problem of Knowledge* Ayer argues that a subject, S, knows a proposition, p, if and only if p is true; S is sure that p is true; and S has the right to be sure that p is true. The first condition is required because one cannot "know" falsehoods. The second condition is required because one does not claim to "know" what one doubts. The third condition—the "justification condition"—is required because having a belief that happens, by accident or lucky guess, to be true is not "knowledge." If S satisfies all these conditions, then S knows p. The three conditions are severally necessary and jointly sufficient.

*Ayer, mathematician and historian Jacob Bronowski, dramatist Robert Bolt, biographer and historian
Allan Bullock, and moderator Norman Fisher in a 1961 episode of the television
program* The Brains Trust *(photograph © BBC)*

In 1963, however, Edmund Gettier raised an example that fails to count as knowledge even though all three conditions are met. Smith has good grounds for believing that Jones owns a Ford; on the basis of that belief alone, Smith forms a belief in the disjunction (either-or statement) "Either Jones owns a Ford, or Brown is in Barcelona." As it turns out, however, despite Smith's evidence, Jones does not own a Ford–but, by chance, Brown *is* in Barcelona. Since, in logic, a disjunction is true if at least one of the disjuncts is true, the disjunction "Either Jones owns a Ford, or Brown is in Barcelona" is true. The evidence justifies Smith's belief in the proposition "Jones owns a Ford" and, therefore, his belief in the disjunction "Either Jones owns a Ford, or Brown is in Barcelona," which is legitimately inferred from "Jones owns a Ford"; and the disjunction is true. Gettier argues that while Smith has a justified true belief in the disjunction, he does not *know* it; so Ayer's analysis is mistaken. Ayer thought that an improved statement of the justification condition would show that counterexamples such as Gettier's depend on unjustified beliefs and would not seriously threaten his original analysis.

In *The Problem of Knowledge* and in an earlier work, *The Foundations of Empirical Knowledge* (1940), Ayer addresses the "problem of the external world": that is, the problem of showing that sensory experience is a reliable guide to the way the world is and even to whether the world exists at all. In *Language, Truth and Logic* Ayer had argued that material things are "logical constructions" out of "sense-contents," which are the immediate data of experience. Ayer's central contention is set out in the second edition of *Language, Truth and Logic:* "we know that it must be possible to define material things in terms of sense-contents, because it is only by the occurrence of certain sense-contents that the existence of any material thing can ever be in the least degree verified." Verification of the occurrence and the nature of one's own sense-contents, or "sense-data," as they are usually called, is not regarded as presenting a problem, even though one might sometimes misdescribe them. Material things are taken to be logical constructions out of sets of actual and possible sense-data, much in the way that "the average family" is a logical construction out of facts about large numbers of actual families. Statements asserting the independent reality of material objects are meaningful only insofar as those statements can be translated into statements about sense-data. This position is known as "linguistic phenomenalism." Some philosophers think that the fact that no one has ever succeeded in satisfactorily translating a material-object statement into a set of statements about sense-data is a conclusive objection to the position. In *The Foundations of Empirical Knowledge* Ayer concedes that there is no prospect of replacing a material-object statement with a finite set of sense-data statements, but he argues that this situation shows only that the language used to talk about material objects is inherently vague, not that phenomenalism is false.

In *The Problem of Knowledge* Ayer revises the phenomenalism of his earlier works and treats assertions about the physical world as a theory that, though justified by being grounded in sensory data, is richer than the sensory basis from which it is developed. The theory derives its meaning from its relationship to sense-experience, but statements about material objects are no longer regarded as replaceable by statements about sense-data.

A distinctive feature of *The Problem of Knowledge* is Ayer's handling of the threat radical skepticism poses to everyday beliefs in the existence of the physical world, in the existence and experiences of minds other than one's own, and that the future will generally resemble the past. Typically, the radical skeptic opens a logical gap between the evidence available for a knowledge claim and what is said to be known on the basis of that evidence. The point is often illustrated by referring to the seventeenth-century French philosopher René Descartes's hypothesis of an evil demon whose whole purpose is to cause one to have delusive experiences; Ayer rejects this supposed possibility as meaningless, because it is unverifiable. The modern equivalent is that one is a disembodied brain floating in a vat and hooked up to a supercomputer that produces what seem to be sensory experiences by electrically stimulating the neurons. How can one know that this situation is not one's current state? Ayer concedes that the skeptic is right in claiming that there is a logical gap that cannot be closed by either deductive or inductive inferences from the evidence, but he argues that this fact should not condemn one's ordinary ways of acquiring beliefs. The belief in an ordered physical world is the best available explanation of the experiences one has. One can still analyze the ways in which one distinguishes reliable from unreliable perceptions, or reliably attributes mental states to others, or makes reliable predictions. That certainty is never achieved in such judgments is inevitable: the skeptic is right, but only because the standard of proof demanded is impossibly high: "if there cannot be a proof, it is not

sensible to demand one. The sceptic's problems are insoluble because they are fictitious."

At about the time *The Problem of Knowledge* was published, Ayer was invited to appear on *The Brains Trust,* a television program on which a panel of intellectuals discussed viewers' questions. Ayer's clarity and quick-wittedness were admirably suited to the format, and the program led to many other television appearances over the next two decades. He broadcast on topics ranging from atheism to football and became nationally known.

In 1959 Ayer was elected Wykeham Professor of Logic at the University of Oxford, with a fellowship at New College. During his tenure in the professorship he wrote prolifically. He also continued to be involved in Labour Party politics and took a prominent part in various causes and campaigns. On 15 July 1960 he married the American journalist Alberta Constance "Dee" Champman Wells; they had a son, Nicholas Hugh. In the 1960s he chaired the Homosexual Law Reform Society, remarking that "as a notorious heterosexual"–he was married four times, including one remarriage, and had many girlfriends while single and married–"I could never be accused of feathering my own nest." Many of his more important articles are collected in *The Concept of a Person and Other Essays* (1963) and *Metaphysics and Common Sense* (1969). His books include *The Origins of Pragmatism: Studies in the Philosophy of Charles Sanders Peirce and William James* (1968), *Russell and Moore: The Analytical Heritage* (1971), the well-received introduction *Russell* (1972), and *Probability and Evidence* (1972). In 1970 he was knighted in recognition of his contribution to philosophy.

In *Probability and Evidence* Ayer seeks to rebut several responses to Hume's discussion of the problem of induction, which he calls "one of the most brilliant examples of philosophical reasoning there has ever been." Hume says that human beings have a natural propensity to generalize observed patterns, but reason cannot establish that these generalizations are valid. In a relatively technical discussion Ayer argues that modern responses to Hume fail because they covertly rely on the question-begging assumption of the uniformity of nature. Although Ayer often cites Hume approvingly–he even says that many of the most radical doctrines of logical empiricism are to be found in Hume's writings in the eighteenth century–an important difference exists between the philosophies of the two men. While much of Ayer's work aims to show why it is reasonable or rational to hold certain beliefs, Hume is skeptical of the claims of reason to be the source or justification of the most significant beliefs held by human beings. According to Hume, beliefs in the independent existence of material objects, in a self that retains its identity over time, and in the uniformity of nature are consequences of the ways in which the mind, particularly the faculty of the imagination, happens to deal with experiences.

The Central Questions of Philosophy, Ayer's most important later book, draws together his thinking on the issues that preoccupied him during his long career. A principal concern is the problem of knowledge of the "external" world. As is so often the case in Ayer's discussions of perception, his starting point is the idea that judgments such as "This is a table" are made on the basis of a single fleeting visual experience, which cannot guarantee that the supposed object of perception is tangible as well as visible, is visible to other perceivers, or continues to exist when it is not being perceived. Ayer argues that insofar as the judgment "This is a table" makes those commitments, it involves an unconscious inference, because the judgment claims more than is entailed by any "strict account" of the experience on which it is based. The judgment is, then, an interpretation that goes beyond the evidence. Ayer concludes that the "naive realist" account of perception as a noninferential, unanalyzable, direct awareness of physical objects is mistaken. If any sort of realism is to be preserved, it must explain how ordinary perceptual judgments can properly go beyond the evidence on which they are based. Ayer offers what he calls "sophisticated realism." The sophistication lies in the steps by which, starting from the contents of the stream of sensory experiences, or "percepts," one "constructs" the concepts of temporal precedence, spatial relations, numerical identity (that an object perceived at various times is one and the same thing throughout), persisting thing, causal relations, and unperceived existence. The derivations of what Ayer calls "visuo-tactual continuants"–space and movement, the relations between tactile space and visual space, and the observer's concept of his or her own body–are developed in detail. While a solitary observer will not get far beyond distinguishing his or her own experiences from the things experienced, sounds and marks–that is, spoken and written words–originating with others can be interpreted as signs that corroborate and elaborate on the individual's account of the world and its contents: "The making of the public-private distinction then goes together with the acquisition of self-consciousness and the attribution of consciousness to others." Thus, the observer forms a conception of visuo-tactual continuants as independently existing physical things and as causally responsible for some of his or her experiences.

In the final stages of construction of the observer's worldview, theory predominates over perception. Once the theory of the physical world–which is simply the common-sense view–has reached this stage, it "takes command in the sense that it determines what there is." Thus, although percepts are the epistemological starting point in developing the conception of the physical world, their significance in ordinary thinking is vastly diminished once the theory has evolved. The theory provides a realist conception of the physical world as existing independently of the experiences of observers, while also providing the best explanation of the nature and course of those experiences. But it is not reducible to those experiences, because within the theory the existence of physical things is a matter of objective fact.

In this discussion Ayer is not offering a contribution to psychology–that is, he is not trying to explain how the human mind actually reaches its belief in the existence of an external world–but is attempting to set out the logic of the construction of the common-sense realist view of the world starting from a neutral or "strict" description of sensory experience. John Foster says of this argument: "His characterization of the steps by which the realist physical theory evolves from its sensory origins is philosophical writing of the highest calibre, in which analytical rigour and constructive artistry are perfectly blended."

The year before he retired from his chair at Oxford, Ayer published the first volume of his autobiography, *Part of My Life: The Memoirs of a Philosopher* (1977). It is a highly readable account of the years before he took the Grote professorship at University College London in 1947. The second volume, *More of My Life,* appeared in 1984. Of these books Ayer wrote in an unpublished typescript (circa 1984), "To the best of my ability I wrote nothing but the truth, but I did not tell the whole truth." Many of the gaps are filled in in Rogers's *A. J. Ayer: A Life* (1999).

Ayer's retirement did not lead to any lessening in his philosophical work. From 1978 to 1983 he was a fellow of Wolfson College at Oxford. He continued to lecture, particularly in North America, and to write. A short book on Hume (1980) was followed by *Philosophy in the Twentieth Century* (1982), which was enthusiastically reviewed. His second marriage ended in divorce in 1982; the following year he married Vanessa Mary Addison Salmon Lawson. A further collection of Ayer's articles, *Freedom and Morality and Other Essays,* appeared in 1984. Ayer's third wife died in 1985. In *Wittgenstein* (1985) Ayer critically engages several ideas of a philosopher he admired but with whom he largely disagreed. Two more studies of individual thinkers followed: *Voltaire* in 1986 and *Thomas Paine* in 1988. In 1989 Ayer and his second wife, Dee, were remarried.

A. J. Ayer was a fellow of the British Academy, an honorary fellow of Wadham College, an honorary member of the American Academy of Arts and Sciences, and Chevalier of the Légion d'Honneur. His death on 27 June 1989 was marked by national front-page press coverage and television reports, attesting to the breadth of his reputation. A posthumous collection of articles and lectures was edited by Ted Honderich as *The Meaning of Life and Other Essays* (1990). Among twentieth-century British philosophers Ayer is widely ranked second only to Russell. In his review of Rogers's biography of Ayer in *The National Review* (29 January 2001) the philosopher Simon Blackburn said that Ayer wrote "some of the most beautiful, lucid, philosophical prose since Hume."

Interviews:

Bryan Magee, "Conversation with A. J. Ayer," in his *Modern British Philosophy* (London: Secker & Warburg, 1971), pp. 48–65;

Magee, "Logical Positivism and Its Legacy," in his *Men of Ideas* (Oxford: Oxford University Press, 1978), pp. 94–109;

Magee, "Frege, Russell, and Modern Logic," in his *The Great Philosophers* (London: BBC Books, 1987), pp. 298–318.

Biography:

Ben Rogers, *A. J. Ayer: A Life* (London: Chatto & Windus, 1999; New York: Grove, 1999).

References:

John Foster, *Ayer* (London & Boston: Routledge & Kegan Paul, 1985);

Edmund L. Gettier, "Is Justified True Belief Knowledge?" *Analysis,* 23 (1963): 121–123;

Barry Gower, ed., *Logical Positivism in Perspective: Essays on Language, Truth and Logic* (London: Croom Helm, 1987);

A. Phillips Griffiths, ed., *A. J. Ayer Memorial Essays,* Royal Institute of Philosophy Supplement, volume 30 (Cambridge & New York: Cambridge University Press, 1991);

Lewis E. Hahn, ed., *The Philosophy of A. J. Ayer,* Library of Living Philosophers, volume 21 (La Salle, Ill.: Open Court, 1992);

G. F. MacDonald, ed., *Perception and Identity: Essays Presented to A. J. Ayer, with His Replies to Them* (London: Macmillan, 1979; Ithaca, N.Y.: Cornell University Press, 1979);

MacDonald and Crispin Wright, eds., *Fact, Science and Morality: Essays on A. J. Ayer's* Language, Truth and Logic (Oxford & New York: Blackwell, 1986).

Bernard Bosanquet

(14 July 1848 – 8 February 1923)

William Sweet
St. Francis Xavier University

BOOKS: *Knowledge and Reality: A Criticism of Mr. F. H. Bradley's "Principles of Logic"* (London: Kegan Paul, Trench, 1885);

Logic, or the Morphology of Knowledge, 2 volumes (Oxford: Clarendon Press, 1888; revised, 1911);

Essays and Addresses (London: Swan Sonnenschein, 1889; New York: Scribners, 1889);

"In Darkest England" on the Wrong Track (London: Swan Sonnenschein, 1891);

A History of Aesthetic (London: Swan Sonnenschein / New York: Macmillan, 1892; revised edition, London: Allen & Unwin, 1904);

Some Thoughts on the Transition from Paganism to Christianity: A Lecture Given before the London Ethical Society (London: Co-operative Printing Society, 1892);

The Civilization of Christendom, and Other Studies (London: Swan Sonnenschein / New York: Macmillan, 1893);

The Essentials of Logic: Being Ten Lectures on Judgement and Inference (London & New York: Macmillan, 1895);

A Companion to Plato's Republic *for English Readers: Being a Commentary Adapted to Davies and Vaughan's Translation* (London: Rivington, Percival, 1895; New York: Macmillan, 1895);

Psychology of the Moral Self (London & New York: Macmillan, 1897);

The Philosophical Theory of the State (London & New York: Macmillan, 1899; revised, 1910; revised again, 1920; revised again, 1923);

The Social Criterion: Or, How to Judge of Proposed Social Reforms. A Paper Read before the Edinburgh Charity Organisation Society, November 15, 1907 (Edinburgh & London: Blackwood, 1907);

Truth and Coherence (Glasgow: MacLehose, 1911);

The Principle of Individuality and Value: The Gifford Lectures for 1911 Delivered in Edinburgh University (London: Macmillan, 1912);

The Value and Destiny of the Individual: The Gifford Lectures for 1912 Delivered in Edinburgh University (London: Macmillan, 1913);

Bernard Bosanquet

The Distinction between Mind and Its Objects: The Adamson Lecture for 1913 (Manchester: Manchester University Press, 1913);

Three Lectures on Aesthetic (London: Macmillan, 1915);

Social and International Ideals: Being Studies in Patriotism (London: Macmillan, 1917);

Some Suggestions in Ethics (London: Macmillan, 1918; enlarged, 1919);

Croce's Aesthetic (London: Published for the British Academy by H. Milford, Oxford University Press, 1919; Norwood, Pa.: Norwood Editions, 1975);

Zoar: A Book of Verse, by Bosanquet and Helen Bosanquet (Oxford: Blackwell, 1919);

Implication and Linear Inference (London: Macmillan, 1920);

What Religion Is (London: Macmillan, 1920; Westport, Conn.: Greenwood Press, 1979);

The Meeting of Extremes in Contemporary Philosophy (London: Macmillan, 1921);

Three Chapters on the Nature of Mind (London: Macmillan, 1923);

Science and Philosophy and Other Essays by the Late Bernard Bosanquet, edited by J. H. Muirhead and R. C. Bosanquet (London: Allen & Unwin, 1927; New York: Macmillan, 1927).

Editions and Collections: *Three Lectures on Aesthetic,* edited by Ralph Ross (Indianapolis: Bobbs-Merrill, 1963);

The Collected Works of Bernard Bosanquet, 20 volumes, edited by William Sweet (Bristol: Thoemmes Press, 1999);

The Philosophical Theory of the State and Related Essays, edited by Sweet and Gerald F. Gaus (South Bend, Ind.: St. Augustine's Press, 2001);

Essays in Philosophy and Social Policy, 1880–1922, 3 volumes, edited by Sweet (Bristol: Thoemmes Press, forthcoming, 2003).

OTHER: G. F. Schömann, *Athenian Constitutional History, as Represented in Grote's* History of Greece, *Critically Examined,* translated by Bosanquet (Oxford & London: Parker, 1878);

"Logic as the Science of Knowledge," in *Essays in Philosophical Criticism,* edited by Andrew Seth and R. B. Haldane (London: Longmans, Green, 1883), pp. 67–101;

Hermann Lotze, *Logic, in Three Books: Of Thought, of Investigation, and of Knowledge,* edited by Bosanquet, Lotze's System of Philosophy, part 1 (Oxford: Clarendon Press, 1884);

Lotze, *Metaphysic, in Three Books: Ontology, Cosmology, and Psychology,* edited and translated by Bosanquet, Lotze's System of Philosophy, part 2 (Oxford: Clarendon Press, 1884);

Georg Wilhelm Friedrich Hegel, *The Introduction to Hegel's Philosophy of Fine Art,* edited and translated by Bosanquet (London: Kegan Paul, Trench, 1886)–includes Bosanquet's introduction, "On the True Conception of Another World";

Albert Schäffle, *The Quintessence of Socialism,* edited by Bosanquet (London: Swan Sonnenschein, 1889; New York: Scribners, 1898);

Schäffle, *The Impossibility of Social Democracy: Being a Supplement to "The Quintessence of Socialism,"* translated by Amy Constance Morant, preface by Bosanquet (London: Swan Sonnenschein / New York: Scribners, 1892);

"The Duties of Citizenship," "Character in Its Bearing on Social Causation," "Socialism and Natural Selection," "The Principle of Private Property," and "The Reality of the General Will," in *Aspects of the Social Problem,* edited by Bosanquet (London & New York: Macmillan: 1895), pp. 1–27, 103–117, 289–307, 308–318, 319–322;

Plato, *The Education of the Young in "The Republic" of Plato,* edited and translated by Bosanquet (Cambridge: Cambridge University Press, 1900);

"The History of Philosophy," in *Germany in the Nineteenth Century, Second Series,* edited by C. H. Herford (Manchester: Manchester University Press, 1915; New York: Longmans, Green, 1915), pp. 187–215;

"Do Finite Individuals Possess a Substantive or an Adjectival Mode of Being?" by Bosanquet, Andrew Seth Pringle-Pattison, G. F. Stout, and Haldane, in *Life and Finite Individuality: Two Symposia,* edited by H. Wildon Carr (London: Williams & Norgate, 1918), pp. 75–102, 179–194;

"Life and Philosophy," in *Contemporary British Philosophy: Personal Statements. First Series,* edited by J. H. Muirhead (London: Allen & Unwin, 1924; New York: Macmillan, 1924), pp. 51–74.

SELECTED PERIODICAL PUBLICATIONS–
UNCOLLECTED: "The Meaning of Teleology," *Proceedings of the British Academy,* 2 (1905–1906): 235–245;

"The Relation of Coherence to Immediacy and Specific Purpose," *Philosophical Review,* 26 (1917): 259–273.

Bernard Bosanquet was one of the leading philosophers and political thinkers in the English-speaking world in the late nineteenth and early twentieth centuries, an important figure in social reform in Britain, and one of the principal exponents, along with F. H. Bradley, of "Absolute Idealism." Though influenced by the German thinkers Immanuel Kant and Georg Wilhelm Friedrich Hegel, Bosanquet's writings also reflect the interest in classical Greek thought that permeated intellectual life in Britain in the mid 1800s. In his work one finds a familiarity with other philosophers outside of the English-speaking world besides Kant and Hegel, such as Emile Durkheim, Edmund Husserl, Benedetto Croce, and Giovanni Gentile.

The breadth of Bosanquet's interests is obvious from the range of topics treated in his books and essays. He made significant contributions to logic, metaphysics, political philosophy, social and public policy, aesthetics, and social work. He was not only a prolific author–

writing or editing some twenty books and more than two hundred articles and reviews—but also a central personality in the Charity Organisation Society (COS), the London Ethical Society, and the London School of Ethics and Social Philosophy. His familiarity with economics and social welfare provided him with a broad base from which to engage in exchanges with social activists such as Sidney and Beatrice Webb and General William Booth, the founder of the Salvation Army.

He received honorary doctorates from the universities of Glasgow, Durham, Birmingham, and St. Andrews and in 1907 was elected to the British Academy. His obituary in *The Times* (London) called him "the central figure of British philosophy for an entire generation." Although his contribution to philosophy was long overshadowed by those of his colleague Bradley and his teacher T. H. Green, since the 1970s there has been a renewed interest in his philosophical work and, particularly, his political thought.

Bernard Bosanquet was born on 14 July 1848 at Rock Hall, near Alnwick, Northumberland, the youngest of four sons of the Reverend Robert William Bosanquet and his second wife, Caroline MacDowall Bosanquet. His half brother, Charles, became one of the founders and the first secretary of the COS; his brother Day was an admiral in the Royal Navy and governor of South Australia; and another brother, Holford, a mathematician, physicist, and lawyer, was elected to the Royal Society and was a fellow of St. John's College, Oxford.

Bosanquet studied at Harrow from 1862 to 1866, then entered Balliol College of Oxford University. At Oxford he fell under the influence of the "new" German philosophy of Kant and Hegel, as interpreted by Edward Caird, Benjamin Jowett, and, particularly, Green. Reacting to the then-dominant empiricism and materialism represented by Jeremy Bentham, John Stuart Mill, and Alexander Bain, Green and Caird held that reality is not ultimately material but is best understood as existing at the level of human consciousness.

Bosanquet took first-class honors in classical moderations in 1868 and in litterae humaniores in 1870. On graduating he was elected, in preference to Bradley, to a fellowship of University College, Oxford. For the next eleven years he taught the history of logic and the history of moral philosophy. His only published work during this time was a translation of G. F. Schömann's *Athenian Constitutional History, as Represented in Grote's* History of Greece, *Critically Examined* (1878).

Bosanquet received a small inheritance after his father died in 1880, and the following year he moved to London. His first major philosophical work was in logic. In 1883 he published "Logic as the Science of Knowledge" in the collection *Essays in Philosophical Criti-*

cism, edited by Andrew Seth (later Pringle-Pattison) and R. B. Haldane; his edition of two volumes of the work of the German philosopher Hermann Lotze (1884)—a project initially undertaken by Green—was followed by his own *Knowledge and Reality: A Criticism of Mr. F. H. Bradley's "Principles of Logic"* (1885) and *Logic, or the Morphology of Knowledge* (1888).

Bosanquet's studies in logic show a strong influence of the work of Hegel; indeed, Bosanquet criticized Bradley for not following Hegel's lead. Yet, he saw his own approach to logic as following in the tradition of Plato and Aristotle, who by his account considered logic to be "the science of knowledge" and not simply "the science of thought." In "Logic as the Science of Knowledge" he explains that logic is concerned not just with classifying judgments (or propositions) and evaluating inferences (or arguments) but with knowledge and truth. Judgments are expressed in sentences, and the sentence, not the word, is "the real unit of language." Judgments and inferences are "organic members within the intellectual whole," and the "form" of knowledge cannot be separated from its subject matter. Metaphysics, the branch of philosophy that inquires into the nature of reality, is inseparable from logic, because reality is "composed of contents determined by systematic combination in a *single* coherent structure," and in logic "the whole world" is "presented to us in the shape of a continuous judgement." Knowledge requires correspondence between thought and fact, but the correspondence can only be judged after the facts are organized into the systems that constitute the various sciences. To say that a judgment is "true," then, one must master the system in which the judgment is included; "and then we shall perceive how unintelligible that part of our world . . . would become if we denied that judgement." In short, "truth and reality are to be looked for in the whole of experience, taken as a system." Bosanquet's theory of truth is, then, more accurately described as a coherence theory than as a correspondence theory.

Bosanquet argues that the truth of judgments cannot be separated from the validity of inferences, because an inference is nothing more than a judgment whose ground or reason is explicitly set forth; a judgment is, therefore, really a conclusion of an argument. He sees the so-called laws of thought, such as the principles of noncontradiction and excluded middle, as "abstractions which express with more or less felicity the nature of that experience whose systematic working is the warrant of their truth." Acknowledging the essential incompleteness of ideas and the fact that ideas pass into one another, Bosanquet favors a dialectical logic, whereby "experience forces thought along certain lines from partial to more complete notions." The goal is, again, coherence. Bosanquet's emphasis on human reason as seeking to understand the "whole" or the "totality of relations" is indicative of his "rationalistic" tendencies, as compared to what has been called Bradley's "metaphysics of feeling."

Bosanquet sees induction and deduction as closely related. His account of induction depends on a distinction between the "verification" and the "establishment" of a hypothesis: in induction a hypothesis is "verified by the agreement of its deduced conclusion with observed facts"; it is established only "in proportion as we are convinced that the verified results could not be deduced from any other principle." In Bosanquet's view, then, "every verified result is . . . a confirmation of any principles from which it is deducible." Certainty, moreover, is not just a property of conclusions based on the truth of the premises; it is the "systematic union" between conclusions and premises that gives certainty to both. Bosanquet's work in logic is one of his major contributions to philosophy, and it influenced such later thinkers as Errol Harris, in his *Nature, Mind and Modern Science* (1954), and Nicholas Rescher, in his *Conceptual Idealism* (1973).

Bosanquet retained an interest in logic throughout his life, but by the mid 1880s his interests had broadened significantly. Half of his time was devoted to philosophical work. In 1885 he joined the Aristotelian Society, founded in 1880; he was elected its vice president in 1888 and served as the second president of the organization from 1894 to 1898. The remainder of his time was devoted to what he called "social work." In 1885 he joined the COS and soon became closely associated with its activities. He became vice chairman of the Chelsea COS the year of his joining, and from 1898 until his death he was a member of the council of the COS, serving as vice chairman from 1901 to 1915 and as chairman in 1916–1917. He also served on the administration committee of the COS for eighteen years and was chairman of the executive council of the COS-sponsored School of Sociology and Social Economics from 1903 until its incorporation into the London School of Economics in 1912.

In the late 1880s Bosanquet began to write extensively on aesthetics and social philosophy. Informed by several visits to Italy and Germany, his work on aesthetics was, within the idealist tradition, unmatched until that of R. G. Collingwood appeared in the 1920s and 1930s. While influenced by Aristotle and Hegel, Bosanquet was critical of both. He published, with his own introduction, a translation of *The Introduction to Hegel's Philosophy of Fine Art* (1886) and several articles on aesthetics, principally in the *Proceedings of the Aristotelian Society*. These works led up to *A History of Aesthetic* (1892), the first such work in English. *A History of Aesthetic* ana-

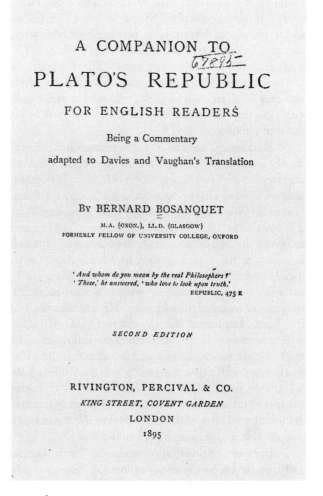

Title page for Bosanquet's analysis of the dialogue in which Plato describes the ideal state (Thomas Cooper Library, University of South Carolina)

lyzes the growth of aesthetic consciousness from classical Greece, when art was regarded as imitative, to the end of the nineteenth century, when it was recognized as primarily symbolic. For Bosanquet, art is an "embodiment of feeling" and refers to much more than what are called the "fine arts." He was deeply interested in the theories of John Ruskin and William Morris on "home art" and craft, and he saw the work of the Home Industries Association as having an important educational character.

Beginning in 1888 Bosanquet wrote a series of articles on social policy and economic and social reform, many of which were published in the *Charity Organisation Review*. This pattern of writing on popular issues, primarily for an audience of those engaged in practical social work, while also pursuing technical philosophical investigations, continued—with a hiatus from 1900 to 1907—for the rest of Bosanquet's life. His *Essays and Addresses* (1889), in which he advances an "ideal of modern life" that he calls "Christian Helle-nism," is almost evenly divided between articles on social reform and texts of a philosophical character, though all are directed at a nonacademic audience. The book includes his important essay "The Kingdom of God on Earth," which summarizes his religious views and puts forth an analysis of the relationship of the individual to the community that he later developed in his political philosophy.

Bosanquet's interest in social reform and political theory led him to supervise translations of the German philosopher and economist Albert Schäffle's *The Quintessence of Socialism* (1889), to write a preface to a translation of Schäffle's *The Impossibility of Social Democracy: Being a Supplement to "The Quintessence of Socialism,"* (1892), and to contribute five of the seventeen essays (one of which is in two parts) of a collection he edited, *Aspects of the Social Problem* (1895). His goal in the latter volume is to combine theoretical analysis with empirical investigation in the realm of social policy. His contributions to the book emphasize the development of character, which, he claims, largely determines the influence of the environment on the individual. He insists that the social worker, to be effective, must enter into the "minds, habits, and feelings" of the people he or she is trying to assist. Other important issues dealt with in his essays include the relation of the individual to the community and the role and responsibilities of the state.

Bosanquet's practical concerns also led during the 1890s to his becoming involved in adult education. He gave occasional lectures for the COS and participated in the programs of the School of Sociology and Social Philosophy; the London Ethical Society, founded in 1886; and the London School of Ethics and Social Philosophy, which existed from 1897 to 1900. Many of his publications, such as *The Essentials of Logic: Being Ten Lectures on Judgement and Inference* (1895), *A Companion to Plato's* Republic *for English Readers: Being a Commentary Adapted to Davies and Vaughan's Translation* (1895), *Psychology of the Moral Self* (1897), and *The Philosophical Theory of the State* (1899), were based on or written to accompany these university extension courses. Bosanquet was a popular lecturer, though he was demanding of his students and—as his wife later wrote—"had not naturally the born expositor's gift." Bosanquet also reviewed philosophical books for the *Manchester Guardian* and the *Pall Mall Gazette* and served as an examiner for the Indian Civil Service.

In 1895 Bosanquet married Helen Dendy, a social worker who was also active in the COS. The policies of the society, and of the Bosanquets in particular, have often been unjustly described as conservative and reflective of Victorian moralism; John Herman Randall Jr. called Bernard Bosanquet "the 'ideal' expression of the Tory *noblesse oblige* of the Disraeli–Joseph Chamberlain–Unionist tradition." One of the major disagreements between the Bosanquets and the Fabian Socialists Sidney and Beatrice Webb–Helen Bosanquet served with Beatrice Webb on the Royal Commission on the Poor Laws from 1905 to 1909–was over the importance of developing individual character and whether government action to alleviate poverty would help or, as the Bosanquets thought, impede such development. The differences between the couples were more theoretical than practical, however. Bernard Bosanquet was an active Liberal and in the 1910s supported the Labour Party. He held that there should be no a priori limitation on state action to promote social well-being, and he was in favor of worker ownership of factories.

By the late 1890s Bosanquet turned his attention to political philosophy and its underlying logical, psychological, and metaphysical presuppositions. In a series of lectures given at the London Ethical Society and published as *Psychology of the Moral Self* Bosanquet defines psychology as the study of "psychical events . . . or the facts experienced within a soul, together with their laws or ways of happening." He opposes the associationist psychology of empiricists such as David Hume, Mill, and Bain, according to which thinking consists of atomistic perceptions linked together by mental habits produced by the repeated conjunction of such perceptions. He describes the "soul," or mind, as "a growth of material, more like a process of crystallization, the material moulding itself according to its own affinities and cohesions." The mind is not a thing in its own right, opposed to the body, nor is it reducible to the functioning of the brain. Instead, according to Bosanquet, it is the "ideal aspect of" the body. Here, too, Bosanquet thinks that "we come back to the conception of Plato and Aristotle at their best."

The Bosanquets moved to Caterham in 1897 and to Oxshott, Surrey, in 1899. In the latter year Bosanquet published *The Philosophical Theory of the State,* the work for which he is probably best known. In it Bosanquet challenges the views of the major nineteenth-century thinkers Bentham, Mill, and Spencer, whom he accuses of giving too cursory an account of political and social life. Drawing on a new understanding of the Greek classical notion of "nature" and on Kant's emphasis on the importance of the development of the moral person, Bosanquet seeks an alternative to empiricist accounts of political obligation. He insists that the state has a positive role in human freedom, and he adapts Jean-Jacques Rousseau's concept of the "general will" and Hegel's notion of the state as an organism to argue that one's rights and duties are based on one's "station" or function in society. For Bosanquet the purpose of the state is "the hindrance of hindrances" to human development.

He argues that the state, like all institutions, is best understood as an "ethical idea" existing at the level of consciousness rather than as a material entity. Under present conditions, he says, the authority of the nation-state must be absolute, because social life requires coordination of the activities of individuals and institutions; but he also says that as the notion of humanity becomes dominant in human consciousness, the chances of effective international institutions and laws greatly increase, and in his later work Bosanquet is sympathetic to the establishment of the League of Nations. His ideas on international relations are developed in the second (1910) and third (1920) editions of *The Philosophical Theory of the State* and in the essays "The Function of the State in Promoting the Unity of Mankind" and "The Wisdom of Naaman's Servants" in his *Social and International Ideals: Being Studies in Patriotism* (1917). The majority of the essays in the latter volume are, however, concerned with issues related to charity and social work—a reminder that, for Bosanquet, political philosophy must not be purely theoretical but grounded in practice.

Leonard T. Hobhouse attacked *The Philosophical Theory of the State* in his *The Metaphysical Theory of the State* (1918), contending that Bosanquet's ideas are little more than an extrapolation of Hegel's and that the notion of the "real will" on the basis of which Bosanquet defends the legitimacy of the state does not make sense and only serves to legitimate the status quo. Other critics faulted Bosanquet for overlooking the problem of competing obligations within the state. Bosanquet addressed some of the criticisms in essays and in the second and third editions of *The Philosophical Theory of the State*. His specific reaction to Hobhouse's critique, however, was not generous: in a letter of 26 January 1919 to a former student at Oxford, W. E. Plater, he wrote: "I don't think I shall read his book—I don't feel I learn much from him, and books are expensive since the war began; and time is not cheap." Hobhouse's attempt to assimilate Bosanquet's views to Hegel's was an oversimplification; while Bosanquet was influenced by Hegel, his work also reflects insights from classical Greek philosophy. This influence is evident from *A Companion to Plato's* Republic *for English Readers,* where he traces the notion of "station" to Plato's concept of *ergon* (function). Nevertheless, Hobhouse's opinion was influential, and it was frequently the source for later critiques, such as that found in Herbert Marcuse's *Reason and Revolution: Hegel and the Rise of Social Theory* (1941).

In 1903 Bosanquet returned to academic life as professor of moral philosophy at the University of St. Andrews in Scotland. He did not discover until later that his election to the position had initially been

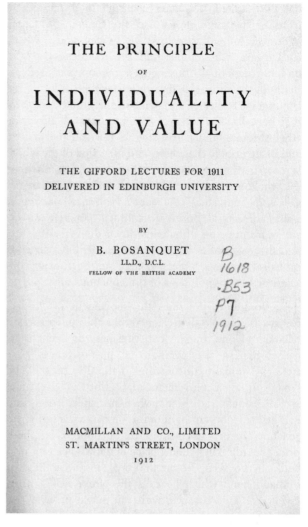

THE PRINCIPLE

OF

INDIVIDUALITY
AND VALUE

THE GIFFORD LECTURES FOR 1911
DELIVERED IN EDINBURGH UNIVERSITY

BY

B. BOSANQUET
LL.D., D.C.L.
FELLOW OF THE BRITISH ACADEMY

MACMILLAN AND CO., LIMITED
ST. MARTIN'S STREET, LONDON
1912

Title page for the first of two volumes in which Bosanquet elaborates his metaphysics of absolute idealism (Thomas Cooper Library, University of South Carolina)

opposed by lecturers in the Divinity School who were concerned about the unorthodoxy of his religious views. Bosanquet's lectures were popular and well attended, but he left St. Andrews in 1908; his health was poor, and his wife's health was suffering from the strain of her service on the Royal Commission on the Poor Laws. Also, he had been planning since 1898 to undertake a major work on metaphysics, but at St. Andrews his time was largely taken up by administrative duties and teaching. The Bosanquets retired to Oxshott, though both continued to write and remained active in COS work.

Bosanquet's metaphysical views were elaborated in the two series of Gifford Lectures he delivered at the University of Edinburgh in 1911 and 1912 and published as *The Principle of Individuality and Value* (1912) and *The Value and Destiny of the Individual* (1913). His position has been called "absolute idealism" to distinguish it from the "personal idealism" of Pringle-Pattison, James Ward, Hastings Rashdall, W. R. Sorley, and J. M. E. McTaggart, who emphasized the uniqueness of the human individual. Bosanquet's metaphysics reflects many of the principles that characterized his logic. For Bosanquet, reality is a system of interconnected parts that he calls "the whole," "positive individuality," or "the Absolute." Each part has its full and real nature and value only in the whole, and the value of the whole is more than the sum of the values of its parts. Because the whole is self-contained and self-sufficient, Bosanquet calls it an "individual." But since it is all-encompassing, it is also a universal; Bosanquet calls it a "concrete universal." This principle of individuality is the basis of value, and the value of a particular person or thing depends on its relation to a larger whole. Thus, persons or consciousnesses are not items of fundamental value.

Bosanquet describes the movement or "nisus" toward the whole that characterizes the universe as a teleological one, but no consciousness or agent is its cause; human and even divine purposiveness arise from an initially unconscious natural process. The "mainspring of movement and effort in the finite world" is "contradiction": when principles come into conflict, a process of harmonization occurs as terms are redefined or new distinctions are introduced, and both principles ultimately find a place in the whole. This process can be seen, Bosanquet says, in the individual human being, which he calls the "finite self": when "what we are" conflicts with our sense of what we should be and then is "harmonised with this higher self, . . . the self is at its best and fullest, and the sense of it, in a way, strongest, when the not self is most expanded." To develop, the self must pass out of itself; but in doing so, it regains itself. In this connection Bosanquet frequently cites Johann Wolfgang von Goethe's phrase "stirb und werde" (die to live).

Bosanquet's metaphysics is not dualistic: he regards the "mind as a perfection and cooperation of the adaptations and acquisitions stored in the body," as "the significance and interpretation" of the body, not as separate from the body. This relationship of the physical and the mental applies to all conscious beings. Thus, finite individuals are not separate and isolated from one another, as the personal idealists held; no hard barrier marks off the being of one from those of the rest. Rather than a mind/body dualism, Bosanquet argues that there is a "multiplicism" in experience. Bosanquet, however, rejects panpsychism—the view that consciousness pervades the universe. He argues, instead, that nature becomes complete in human consciousness, through which it arrives at the Absolute.

The second series of Gifford Lectures focuses on the finite individual. Bosanquet says that insofar as one can speak of the universe having a purpose, that purpose is "the moulding of souls." The life of the finite soul or mind is an adventure that involves suffering. It suffers because it finds itself in a moral world of claims and counterclaims—that is, a world of conflicting duties. But conflict, like contradiction, is necessary for progress. Evil is necessary for the development of the corresponding good, and the existence of both evil and good is evidence of the "evolution" of the finite spirit toward perfection. But no finite good can satisfy a being, and so there is a movement beyond the finite. The soul is driven to "self-recognition" in what Bosanquet calls religious consciousness. In religion the finite self recognizes its own true nature, which involves self-surrender and an unselfish devotion to interests beyond itself. Religious consciousness is the conviction that one belongs to a reality in which everything about which one really cares is permanent and secure. The destiny of the finite self, therefore, is to recognize itself as an element of the Absolute.

Bosanquet gives no clear statement about a life after death, but he says that the desire for survival is really the desire to safeguard what one ultimately cares about in the universe—something that is seen as more important than the self. The "religious attitude" is one wherein the finite being "accepts his worth . . . as lying solely in all that promotes his identification with the greatness of the universe."

Bosanquet later developed several of the points presented in the Gifford Lectures in *The Distinction between Mind and Its Objects: The Adamson Lecture for 1913* (1913). He attacks the "new realism" of Ralph Barton Perry, W. P. Montague, and E. B. Holt for cutting the mind off from physical reality, though he is more sympathetic to the realism of Samuel Alexander. For Bosanquet, "there can be no concrete whole, but a whole centering in mind"; the objects of mind and the mind itself are continuous with each other and reciprocally related.

In a discussion with Pringle-Pattison, Haldane, and G. F. Stout titled "Do Finite Individuals Possess a Substantive or an Adjectival Mode of Being?" published in *Proceedings of the Aristotelian Society* (1917–1918) and republished in *Life and Finite Individuality: Two Symposia* (1918) Bosanquet addresses the criticism that his metaphysics is inconsistent with the basic value of the human person. He denies that finite selves are "necessarily eternal or everlasting units" or "differentiations of the absolute" but asserts that they characterize the world "as permanent qualifications." He rejects the view that the self is independent, self-existent, and a principle of value in itself, but he notes that one cannot have states of consciousness, which are valuable, apart from individuals.

Bosanquet develops his aesthetic theory in *Three Lectures on Aesthetic* (1915). For Bosanquet, a work of art is "an appearance presented to us through perception or imagination." The work and the feelings it evokes conform to one another, so that when one imaginatively contemplates an art object, one is "able *to live in it as an embodiment of our feeling.*" The aesthetic experience itself is not purely affective or mental, but involves the whole person, "body-and-mind." Bosanquet claims that no true work of art can be ugly, although there are cases of what he calls "difficult"–as opposed to "facile"–beauty, in which a combination of some feature of the object and some defect in the observer, such as a lack of education, imagination, or effort, may prevent the observer from appreciating the beauty of the object. Bosanquet thinks that through the contemplation of an individual art object one may be led to an intuition of the Absolute. Thus, art provides access to the Absolute through "feeling." The relevance of Bosanquet's aesthetic theory to his philosophy as a whole has not generally been appreciated; it is noteworthy that his most direct statement of his philosophical method and his commitment to coherence is given in *Three Lectures on Aesthetic:* "I only know in philosophy one method, and that is to expand *all* the relevant facts, taken together, into ideas which approve themselves to thought as exhaustive and self-consistent."

Some of the ethical implications of the ideas presented in the Gifford Lectures are worked out in Bosanquet's *Some Suggestions in Ethics* (1918). Intended for "ordinary thoughtful persons who are interested in reflecting upon morality," the essays not only provide a general account of the nature of ethical value but also address issues that bear on Bosanquet's philosophy of law, particularly on his retributive theory of punishment. Consistent with his political philosophy, Bosanquet's emphasis is on the morality of "my station and its duties": what one ought to do is determined by one's role or function in social life. He distinguishes his view from altruism, holding that self-sacrifice is valuable not because it helps others but because it advances a good that goes beyond both the self and others.

Addressing the charge that Absolute Idealism entails that evil is not real and that everything will turn out for the best independently of human effort, Bosanquet says that evil is not a positive quality but something that is out of place or "too narrow" and that it "can be overcome . . . now and here" by being "turned" to good. He also says that though values are not facts, they are qualities of systems of facts; therefore, ignorance of values is connected with a culpable ignorance

SOME SUGGESTIONS
IN ETHICS

BY

BERNARD BOSANQUET
D.C.L., LL.D.
FELLOW OF THE BRITISH ACADEMY

MACMILLAN AND CO., LIMITED
ST. MARTIN'S STREET, LONDON
1918

Title page for Bosanquet's volume that aimed to serve "ordinary persons who are interested in reflecting on morality" (Thomas Cooper Library, University of South Carolina)

of facts. Education will, Bosanquet thinks, go some way in solving this problem.

The "moral will" is not only a social will but one's "real" will. Individuals have to "create themselves"–mold themselves into persons–through their individual efforts, but this molding cannot be achieved by each person alone. The state has an essential role in the perfection of human personality, but voluntary or nonstate organizations are also important.

Bosanquet's ethics are teleological (goal-oriented) but not consequentialist (that is, they do not make the rightness or wrongness of an act depend entirely on its results). The motive and intention of the agent are important in assessing the morality of an act, but so is the success of the act in achieving its purpose. No "moral code" exists from which one can deduce one's moral duties; one must endeavor to "respond adequately to the situation."

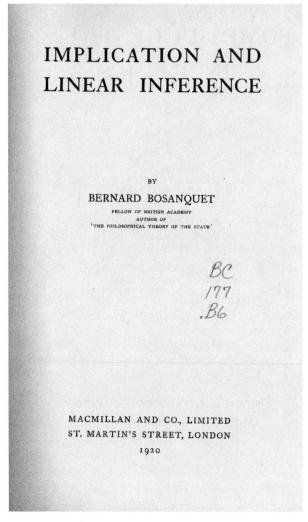

IMPLICATION AND
LINEAR INFERENCE

BY

BERNARD BOSANQUET

FELLOW OF BRITISH ACADEMY
AUTHOR OF
'THE PHILOSOPHICAL THEORY OF THE STATE'

BC
177
.B6

MACMILLAN AND CO., LIMITED
ST. MARTIN'S STREET, LONDON
1920

*Title page for the work in which Bosanquet argues that
standard formal logic is only a limited form of inference
that must be supplemented by intuition (Thomas
Cooper Library, University of South Carolina)*

Though he wrote essays on religion almost from the beginning of his philosophical career, Bosanquet's most extensive treatment of the topic is *What Religion Is* (1920). According to Bosanquet, religious dogma is distinct from religious faith: dogma is the product of an intellectualization, usually by an authority, of a simple religious experience, while faith is "that set of objects, habits, and convictions, whatever it might prove to be," that one "would rather die for than abandon, or at least would feel himself excommunicated from humanity if he did abandon." Particular religious beliefs are often "disguised" metaphysical or ethical propositions, and their truth is something that "evolves."

Religious belief, Bosanquet argues, is about the present world, not a future one. While he challenges such particular beliefs as the personality of God and the existence of an afterlife, he holds that religious faith in general should be treated with respect because it is a nisus toward the Absolute. Bosanquet was sympathetic to the humanistic demythologizing of religion pioneered by David Strauss and Ferdinand Bauer, but he denied that he was an agnostic, and in 1889–1890 he had led a class of working people in reading the New Testament.

Toward the end of his life Bosanquet returned to his early concern with logic. His opponents were no longer the same, however; now he saw his work being challenged by the "new" logic of Gottlob Frege, as developed by Bertrand Russell and Alfred North Whitehead. This new logic was, in Bosanquet's view, no more successful than the old, for it continued to separate judgment from inference and to emphasize "linear" over "systematic" implication. In *Implication and Linear Inference* (1920) he defines inference as "every process by which knowledge extends itself." Standard formal logic—what Bosanquet calls "linear inference"–is only a limited form of inference. Logical principles are the expression of the movement of the mind. Inference is not deductive (from general principles to particular conclusions) or inductive (from "instances" or "sense data" to general principles) but "systematic": it proceeds from within a whole or system that is already recognized as such. Intuition or insight involves looking at an object that is intrinsically systematic and discerning its constitutive terms and relations. Once one has insight into the system, where each part supports every other, one has "necessity"–one sees why it is what it is; "contingency" means not seeing the system. How should conflicts of "insight" be settled? Bosanquet acknowledges that there is no neutral or external test by which truth can be determined; a claim to truth is supported by exhibiting all the evidence that compels the acceptance of a given conclusion.

Bosanquet's last major work to be published during his lifetime was *The Meeting of Extremes in Contemporary Philosophy* (1921). The title reveals Bosanquet's characteristic desire to show the relationships between various schools of thought rather than to dwell on their differences. He returns to an issue that he had addressed in *The Distinction between Mind and Its Objects*: the relationship between realism and idealism (the latter position is represented here by Croce and Gentile). Bosanquet argues that as each side seeks a complete view, it is compelled to adopt positions that are characteristic of its "opponent." He maintains that only a "speculative attitude" can overcome the opposition between realism and idealism.

As Bosanquet's health declined, he and his wife decided to live closer to family and friends. The couple moved back to London in October 1922; Bosanquet died on 8 February 1923. His widow edited the manuscript on which he had been working at the time of his death and published it as *Three Chapters on the Nature of Mind* (1923). In this fragment of what was intended as a much longer work Bosanquet insists that circumstances and history have to be taken into account if one wishes to understand a person and calls Russell's *The Analysis of Mind* (1921) "too narrow"–though he claims that he and Russell agree on many points. Helen Dendy Bosanquet also wrote *Bernard Bosanquet: A Short Account of His Life* (1924). In 1927 J. H. Muirhead and Bosanquet's nephew, R. C. Bosanquet, published the collection *Science and Philosophy and Other Essays by the Late Bernard Bosanquet*. Muirhead also edited a volume of correspondence, *Bernard Bosanquet and His Friends: Letters Illustrating the Sources and the Development of His Philosophical Opinions* (1935).

At the time of his death Bosanquet was, according to Randall, "the most popular and the most influential of the English idealists." An entire issue of *The Philosophical Review* was devoted to studies of his work. He had made significant contributions to many of the major intellectual debates of his time, and he continued to be a central figure in philosophical discussion even after idealism was challenged by logical empiricism in the early twentieth century. Even as idealism declined, Bosanquet was far from a marginal figure. He had exchanges with Russell; he was one of the examiners of G. E. Moore's 1898 Trinity College fellowship dissertation; and the Austrian-born philosopher Ludwig Wittgenstein acknowledged to Moore in 1914 that much of his own (unsuccessful) Cambridge B.A. dissertation was "cribbed" from Bosanquet's logic. Bosanquet was also one of the earliest figures in the Anglo-American world to engage the work of Croce, Gentile, and Husserl.

Within a few years of his death, however, interest in Bosanquet's work waned, and of the idealists, Bradley and, in political theory, Green are now much better known than Bosanquet. Several factors may account for this situation. First, the works that made Bosanquet so well known in his own time–his popular essays and the books and articles that came out of his university extension courses–appeared to later generations to be overly dependent on contemporary concerns and lacking in logical rigor. There is justice in this view: some of the concepts central to Bosanquet's philosophy are not clearly defined, and Bosanquet was an indifferent literary stylist. While insightful and wide-ranging, much of his work betrays the looseness that one tends to find in texts based on lectures prepared for general audiences or for classes. As his wife says in her biography, "his thought is sometimes difficult to follow owing to the absence of the emphasis and intonation which, in the lecture room, made his meaning clear at once." Even his early work on logic was remarked on in a letter by his teacher, R. L. Nettleship, for its "stiffness." But

these stylistic criticisms may stem from Bosanquet's refusal to sever logical analysis from the experience it was trying to describe.

Second, Bosanquet's association with the majority report of the Royal Commission on the Poor Laws led many to see him as a Victorian conservative whose emphasis on the importance of individual character or social life blinded him to alleged conservative systemic discrimination characteristic of the laissez-faire economic system in Britain. Finally, as the recognition of the importance of pluralism and international politics increased, Bosanquet was regarded by many as a champion of the absolute authority of the nation-state. As Stefan Collini notes, until the 1920s an "attack on the neo-Hegelian theory of the state became almost a *rite de passage* for the budding social scientist." The criticisms of Bosanquet's political philosophy by such writers as Hobhouse, Harold Laski, R. M. MacIver, G. D. H. Cole, and C. E. M. Joad have been so influential that they are still generally held to be conclusive. Nevertheless, interest in Bernard Bosanquet's philosophical and social thought increased in the final decades of the twentieth century, and his ideas are experiencing a renaissance in the work of some contemporary liberal theorists.

Letters:

Bernard Bosanquet and His Friends: Letters Illustrating the Sources and the Development of His Philosophical Opinions, edited by J. H. Muirhead (London: Allen & Unwin, 1935);

Muirhead, "Bernard Bosanquet and His Friends," *Mind,* new series 45 (1936): 125–127;

Benedetto Croce, "Lettere di Bernardo Bosanquet," *La Critica,* 34 (1936): 225–231;

R. M. MacIver, *Politics and Society,* edited by D. Spitz (New York: Atherton, 1969), pp. 238–240, 242–244.

Bibliographies:

Peter P. Nicholson, "A Bibliography of the Writings of Bernard Bosanquet (1848–1923)," *Idealistic Studies,* 8 (1978): 261–280;

William Sweet, "Bibliography," in *Essays in Philosophy and Social Policy, 1880–1922,* by Bosanquet, edited by Sweet, volume 1 (Bristol: Thoemmes Press, forthcoming, 2003), pp. lxi–xcvii.

Biography:

Helen Dendy Bosanquet, *Bernard Bosanquet: A Short Account of His Life* (London: Macmillan, 1924).

References:

James Bradley, "Hegel in Britain: A Brief History of British Commentary and Attitudes," *Heythrop Journal,* 20 (1979): 1–24, 163–182;

Matt Carter, "Ball, Bosanquet and the Legacy of T. H. Green," *History of Political Thought,* 20, no. 4 (1999): 674–694;

Stefan Collini, "Hobhouse, Bosanquet and the State: Philosophical Idealism and Political Argument in England, 1880–1918," *Past and Present,* 72 (1976): 86–111;

G. Watts Cunningham, *The Idealist Argument in Recent British and American Philosophy* (New York: Century, 1933);

Sandra den Otter, *British Idealism and Social Explanation: A Study in Late Victorian Thought* (Oxford: Clarendon Press, 1996);

Gerald Gaus, "Green, Bosanquet and the Philosophy of Coherence," in *Routledge History of Philosophy,* volume 7: *The Nineteenth Century,* edited by C. L. Ten (London & New York: Routledge, 1994), pp. 408–436;

Leonard T. Hobhouse, *The Metaphysical Theory of the State* (London: Allen & Unwin / New York: Macmillan, 1918);

François Houang, *De l'humanisme à l'absolutisme: L'évolution de la pensée religieuse du néo-hégélien anglais Bernard Bosanquet* (Paris: Vrin, 1954);

Berel Lang, "Bosanquet's Aesthetic: A History and Philosophy of the Symbol," *Journal of Aesthetics and Art Criticism,* 26 (1968): 377–387;

Herbert Marcuse, *Reason and Revolution: Hegel and the Rise of Social Theory* (Oxford: Oxford University Press, 1941, Boston: Beacon, 1960);

A. M. McBriar, *An Edwardian Mixed Doubles: The Bosanquets versus the Webbs. A Study in British Social Policy* (Oxford & New York: Oxford University Press, 1987);

A. J. M. Milne, *The Social Philosophy of English Idealism* (London: Allen & Unwin, 1962);

Silvio Morigi, "Bosanquet, Temple and Collingwood: 'penetrative imagination' and 'essential symbol' in Aesthetic and Religious Experience," *Bradley Studies,* 7, no. 2 (2001): 214–230;

John Morrow, "Community, Class, and Bosanquet's 'New State,'" *History of Political Thought,* 21, no. 3 (2000): 485–499;

Peter P. Nicholson, *The Political Philosophy of the British Idealists: Selected Studies,* (Cambridge: Cambridge University Press, 1990);

Bertil Pfannenstill, *Bernard Bosanquet's Philosophy of the State: A Historical and Systematical Study* (Lund, Sweden: Ohlsson, 1936);

Igor Primoratz, "The Word 'Liberty' on the Chains of Galley-Slaves: Bosanquet's Theory of the General Will," *History of Political Thought,* 15 (1994): 249–267;

John Herman Randall Jr., "Idealistic Social Philosophy and Bernard Bosanquet," in his *The Career of Philosophy,* volume 3 (New York: Columbia University Press, 1977), pp. 97–130;

Bertrand Russell, C. Delisle Burns, and G. D. H. Cole, "The Nature of the State in Its External Relations," *Proceedings of the Aristotelian Society,* new series 16 (1915–1916): 290–310;

William Sweet, "'Absolute Idealism' and Finite Individuality," *Indian Philosophical Quarterly,* 24, no. 4 (1997): 431–462;

Sweet, "Bernard Bosanquet and the Nature of Religious Belief," in *Anglo-American Idealism, 1865–1927,* edited by W. J. Mander (Westport, Conn.: Greenwood Press, 2000), pp. 123–139;

Sweet, "F. H. Bradley and Bernard Bosanquet," in *Philosophy after F. H. Bradley,* edited by James Bradley (Bristol: Thoemmes Press, 1996), pp. 31–56;

Sweet, *Idealism and Rights* (Lanham, Md.: University Press of America, 1996);

Sweet, "Social Policy and Bosanquet's Moral Philosophy," *Collingwood Studies,* 6 (1999): 127–146;

Sweet, "Was Bosanquet a Hegelian?" *Bulletin of the Hegel Society of Great Britain,* no. 31 (1995): 39–60;

Adam Ulam, *The Philosophical Foundations of English Socialism* (Cambridge, Mass.: Harvard University Press, 1951);

Andrew Vincent and Raymond Plant, *Philosophy, Politics and Citizenship: The Life and Thought of the British Idealists* (Oxford: Blackwell, 1984).

Papers:

Bernard Bosanquet's papers, along with his wife's, are in the library of the University of Newcastle-upon-Tyne.

F. H. Bradley

(30 January 1846 – 18 September 1924)

Gisella Gisolo
University of Florence, Italy

BOOKS: *The Presuppositions of Critical History* (Oxford: Parker, 1874);

Ethical Studies (London: King, 1876; New York: Stechert, 1904; revised and enlarged edition, Oxford: Clarendon Press, 1927);

Mr. Sidgwick's Hedonism: An Examination of the Main Argument of "The Methods of Ethics" (London: King, 1877);

The Principles of Logic (London: Kegan Paul, Trench, 1883; New York: Stechert, 1912; revised and enlarged edition, 2 volumes, London: Oxford University Press, H. Milford, 1922);

Appearance and Reality: A Metaphysical Essay, Muirhead Library of Philosophy (London: Swan Sonnenschein / New York: Macmillan, 1893; revised and enlarged, 1897);

Essays on Truth and Reality (Oxford: Clarendon Press, 1914);

Aphorisms (Oxford: Clarendon Press, 1930);

Collected Essays, 2 volumes (Oxford: Clarendon Press, 1935; Freeport, N.Y.: Books for Libraries, 1968);

Collected Works of F. H. Bradley, 12 volumes, edited by Carol A. Keene and W. J. Mander (Bristol: Thoemmes Press, 1999).

Editions and Collections: *The Presuppositions of Critical History,* edited by Lionel Rubinoff (Chicago: Quadrangle, 1968);

The Presuppositions of Critical History; and, Aphorisms, edited by Guy Stock (Bristol: Thoemmes Press, 1993);

Writings on Logic and Metaphysics, edited by Stock and James W. Allard (Oxford & New York: Clarendon Press, 1994).

F. H. Bradley was regarded by many of his contemporaries as the only great philosopher England had produced since David Hume. Despite his reputation as the most original, acute, and theoretically vigorous of the British idealists, however, his philosophical influence barely survived his death. He was attacked by his fellow idealists both in Britain and the United States: although Bernard Bosanquet described Bradley's

F. H. Bradley

Appearance and Reality: A Metaphysical Essay (1893) as "a gospel among all modern philosophical books," he criticized Bradley's denial of an ultimate coincidence between thought and reality and of the constructive function of contradiction; J. M. E. McTaggart claimed that Bradley failed to attach sufficient metaphysical value to the finite self; G. F. Stout criticized his theory of relations and his characterization of the category of appearance; and Josiah Royce objected that Bradley's definition of the infinite depended too heavily on traditional philosophy. The most devastating criticisms, however, came from outside idealistic circles. G. E.

Moore and Bertrand Russell popularized an account of Bradley's philosophy that verged on caricature. Russell had adhered to idealism after reading the writings of Bradley and Bosanquet while a student at Cambridge, but he deserted the idealist camp after becoming acquainted with the work of Gottlob Frege and Giuseppe Peano in the philosophy of mathematics and started a public war against what he considered a version of Hegelianism. In *Language, Truth, and Logic* (1936) the logical positivist A. J. Ayer uses passages taken at random from *Appearance and Reality* to show how metaphysicians' remarks are devoid of any cognitive significance. By the 1930s Bradley's philosophical approach and literary style—a style that T. S. Eliot claimed to be perfectly suited to the author's philosophical style—seemed to belong to a lost intellectual world. After World War II, Bradley's valuable contributions to logic, epistemology, philosophy of language, and philosophical psychology began to be acknowledged. His discussion of the nature of relations, together with his critiques of associationism, logical atomism, and the correspondence theory of truth, have been recognized as being of great interest. Above all, since the 1960s it has been appreciated that metaphysics, which constitutes the heart of Bradley's philosophy, is not at odds with the "special" sciences but is methodologically and logically prior to those sciences and, therefore, of fundamental importance to them. This understanding has opened a myriad of interpretative perspectives on his writings and led to something of a Bradley renaissance.

The fourth child of Charles Bradley, a prominent Evangelical preacher, and his second wife, Emma Linton Bradley, Francis Herbert Bradley was born on 30 January 1846 in Clapham, Surrey, which is now part of Greater London. Although a tyrant at home, Charles Bradley was the leading figure of a humanitarian evangelical group known as the "Clapham Sect," which included several important political and military figures among its members. George Granville Bradley, one of F. H. Bradley's half brothers, became headmaster of University College, Oxford, in 1870 and subsequently dean of Westminster Abbey; his younger brother Andrew Cecil Bradley held professorships in literature and poetry at the universities of Liverpool, Glasgow, and Oxford and became one of the most distinguished Shakespearean critics of his day.

Bradley was educated at Cheltenham College from 1856 to 1861 and at Marlborough College, where his half brother George was headmaster, from 1861 to 1863. His philosophical interests were comparatively precocious, since he is said to have read at least part of Immanuel Kant's *Kritik der reinen Vernunft* (1781; translated as *Critique of Pure Reason,* 1855) while he was still in public school. Bradley left Marlborough College in

1863, owing to a bout with typhoid fever and then pneumonia. In 1865 he entered University College of Oxford University. He obtained a first in Classical Moderations in 1867, though two years later he only placed in the second class in *Literae Humaniores.* A later admirer of Bradley, the philosopher A. E. Taylor, suggests in "Francis Herbert Bradley, 1846–1924" that this reversal may have come about because of the incapacity of the examiners, who were dogmatically devoted to positivism, to understand Bradley's seminal philosophical views.

After several failed attempts to obtain a fellowship, Bradley received one at Merton College, Oxford, in 1870. The fellowship required no teaching and could be terminated only if Bradley married. In 1871 he suffered a severe inflammation of the kidneys, an illness from which he seems never to have fully recovered.

Bradley was never able to marry the woman who was the greatest attachment of his life, the unidentified "E. R." to whom almost all of his books are dedicated. She was an American who lived in France and seems to have spent some of her winters at the resorts on the English coast and the Riviera to which Bradley's illness periodically forced him to retire. He apparently sketched out his system of metaphysics in a series of letters to her that she destroyed. Because he never married, Bradley was able to remain at Merton College for the rest of his life. There he indulged in what was at once his favorite game and his only weakness: practicing his pistol-shooting skills, of which he was proud, against stray cats, which he greatly disliked, on the college grounds at night.

Bradley's writing style reflects his temperament, a mixture of irascibility and charm. A highly cultivated and stimulating conversationalist, he was much admired but also somewhat feared within his narrow circle of friends. He was intolerant of pacifism and of any form of generalized humanitarian sentiment. His metaphysical views, however, reveal a deeply religious nature tinged with mysticism. Unlike his fellow British idealists Bosanquet and T. H. Green, who were active social reformers, Bradley was politically conservative—at times even reactionary. Nonetheless, he defended absolute freedom of inquiry and expression.

Bradley's first book, the pamphlet *The Presuppositions of Critical History,* appeared in 1874. Despite the overly ornate and rhetorical style, which at times obscures his arguments, Bradley's approach to the question of truth in history is novel. For Bradley, only direct testimony—explicit descriptions of what is said to have occurred—constitutes historical evidence; geological, archaeological, or linguistic "evidence" is to be ignored. The fundamental presupposition of historical research is that of the uniformity of nature: everything happens according to the law of causal connection. Thus, supposedly miraculous events are not the subject matter of history. This assumption is common to historiography and natural science, which agree that "a fact which asserts itself as (loosely speaking) without a cause, or without a consequence, is no fact at all." An essential difference between the two fields, however, is that the historian cannot accept as probably true any testimony to the occurrence of phenomena that bear no analogy to the historian's own experience. Another difference is that while the objects studied by natural science are of interest only insofar as they illustrate universal and abstract relations, history is concerned with events that are unique, perishable, and unrepeatable. History is interested in the individual not for its own sake, however, but as embodying the whole story of humankind–that is, as realizing in every single moment one of the necessary steps of that progression of humanity that constitutes the goal of history. For Bradley, history is inconceivable without the notion of the progress of the human spirit toward ever higher and more comprehensive stages of self-consciousness. This idea hints at Bradley's later metaphysical concept of the Absolute. Anticipating R. G. Collingwood's philosophy of history, Bradley says that historical "facts" are not passively "discovered" but are actively "constituted" in the mind of the historian. Grasping the past as it actually unfolded is impossible, since the historian's viewpoint is necessarily different from that of the original actors; the past can be reconstructed only in the light of present cognitive and normative standards.

Henry Sidgwick's *The Methods of Ethics* was published in 1874. The book was extremely popular and contributed to the consolidation of the utilitarian school within British moral philosophy. Utilitarianism was widely accepted as the touchstone of enlightened thinking on social and political matters in England; its main living representatives at the time, besides Sidgwick, were Matthew Arnold, Frederick Harrison, and Herbert Spencer. Bradley's *Ethical Studies,* which includes a still-classic critique of utilitarianism, appeared in 1876 against this background.

Ethical Studies has been deemed the most "Hegelian" of Bradley's works, though such a description applies more to its dialectical method than to its doctrinal content. Bradley's method in it is to show that the one-sidedness of various rival ethical theories has to be overcome in a higher synthesis. As the task of *The Presuppositions of Critical History* was to inquire into the assumptions of historiography, the objective of *Ethical Studies* is to clear away the psychological and metaphysical preconceptions of then-current ethical theories and spell out the presuppositions of common-sense morality: that people are responsible for their actions, that

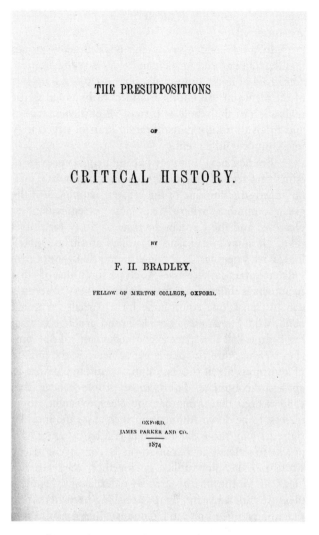

THE PRESUPPOSITIONS

OF

CRITICAL HISTORY.

BY

F. H. BRADLEY,

FELLOW OF MERTON COLLEGE, OXFORD.

OXFORD,
JAMES PARKER AND CO.
1874

Title page for Bradley's first book, in which he argues that only direct testimony constitutes historical evidence (University of Dundee)

virtue is intrinsically good, and that a gap always exists between what people do and what they ought to do. The first condition for the meaningfulness of the ordinary notion of responsibility is "selfsameness," that is, the identity through time of the moral agent as a being capable of rational and free choices. Such a view contrasts with the psychological associationism typical of empiricism, according to which the concept of "personal identity" is barely more than a word. Another condition is that the agent must be free; that is, that his or her choices must not be necessitated or determined. But if determinism is incompatible with the conditions of moral responsibility implicitly presupposed by ordinary people, its opposite, the doctrine of indeterminism, or free will, fares no better. A person cannot legitimately be held morally responsible for an action unless it proceeds from him or her as an effect proceeds from a cause. Yet, according to indeterminism, human actions are uncaused.

In the second essay in the book Bradley argues that the ultimate end for human beings is self-realization, conceived of not hedonistically but rather as the pursuit of the ideal self. All efforts are necessarily aimed at the realization of the whole self, since all particular wishes and motivations are parts of larger ends in which they find complete fulfillment.

Bradley next analyzes two influential theories of ethics that seem diametrically opposed: hedonistic utilitarianism—the doctrine of the greatest happiness of the greatest number, where "happiness" is equivalent to pleasure; and the Kantian doctrine of "duty for duty's sake." Bradley's criticisms of utilitarianism are manifold. First, happiness is a vague notion that cannot provide any practical directives; each person's idea of what happiness is differs from that of almost every other person. At most, one could hope for a partial agreement about what happiness is not. A second problem is what has been called the "paradox of hedonism": if one pursues pleasure directly, one never achieves it; the pursuit of a virtuous life, if successful, may result in pleasure as an accompaniment. Third, most people believe that some actions that bring them no pleasure ought, nonetheless, to be done. Although in such cases the morally right act may serve the utilitarian end by bringing happiness to others, this connection is contingent. Even when morality and utility go together, they are not identical, for they are inspired by different aims. Fourth, pleasures are transient, mere "perishing particulars," so that at any given point in life one has the pleasures one has been able to obtain; yet, there are more pleasures to come if only one can get them, so now one aims at these pleasures, and so on ad infinitum. Thus, one is never in possession of all of the pleasures one desires, and so one is never satisfied. Such a series has no end except in death—and in death one is, presumably, still not happy. A more sophisticated utilitarianism, such as that of John Stuart Mill, which introduces qualitative differences among pleasures, requires some standard other than the mere amount of pleasure and is, therefore, not consistent with the definition of hedonism, which is "pleasure for pleasure's sake alone." Nor can it explain the ground on which different pleasures should be ranked. Nevertheless, for all its defects, utilitarianism is correct in seeing morality as essentially subservient to human needs and the moral life as a realm in which a person may find happiness and fulfillment.

Kantian morality is based on the principle of the "good will." Among the distinguishing features of the good will are the closely connected characteristics of universality and formality. The universal and formal will acts in a concrete world, engaging in a never-ending con-flict with the empirical self, with all its particular states, good and bad desires, passions and aversions, pleasures and pains. And this conflict between the formal and the sensuous self, the universality of the higher self and the idiosyncrasies of the lower one, the realm of the "ought" and that of the "is," constitutes a precondition of morality, as the Kantian ethics emphasizes so well. For the will to be universal and formal, however, it must have no particular object. But to will, one must will something definite; to will in general is a fiction, a "psychological monster." The more general an agent's will, the greater the role played by chance in the agent's actions: "If I run out into the street to kill a man, chance decides who it is I kill. So with duty. If I intend to do duty generally, chance decides what duty I do; for what falls outside the preconceived intent is chance, and here everything falls outside saving the bare form." Thus, the doctrine of duty for duty's sake must be superseded by a more comprehensive theory that, while keeping the value of universality to which the Kantian account aspires, will be capable of filling the abstract formulas of duty with empirical content.

The doctrine that Bradley calls "My Station and its Duties" is a synthesis of hedonism and Kantianism and corresponds in its general lines to the ethical theory of the German idealist philosopher Georg Wilhelm Friedrich Hegel. According to this doctrine, the self to be realized is the self of the social organism to which individuals belong. This organism is a system or an organic unity, not an abstract entity, since it is vitally connected to the individuals of which it is composed and is nothing without them; its self-realization is attainable only through the self-realization of each of them. It

> is a concrete universal, because it not only is above but is within and throughout its details, and is so far only as they are. It is the life that can live only in and by them, as they are dead unless within it; it is the whole soul which lives so far as the body lives, which makes the body a living body, and which without the body is as unreal an abstraction as the body without it. It is an organism and a moral organism; and it is conscious self-realization, because only by the will of its self-conscious members can the moral organism give itself reality.

The "moral organism" is more than a metaphor; the social whole constitutes a real entity, and the individuals who compose it have no reality outside of it. Social units such as the family and the state are not mere logical constructs out of the human beings who participate in them, as individualism mistakenly holds. Morality is fixed in the law, institutions, social usages, moral opinions, and feelings. The individual's moral duties are dictated by the place in the social organization to which the individual belongs. If one wants to be moral and to realize oneself, one must will one's station and its duties.

Bradley, however, finds the doctrine of "My Station and its Duties" insufficient and argues that it, too, must be surmounted. While, on the one hand, it is true that the moral law demands the perfect identification of the individual will with the ideally good and universal will, on the other hand, the essence of morality seems to be a continuous overcoming of the lower self—a striving that presupposes that the individual will can never be completely identified with the ideally good will. Accordingly, morality is an endless process toward the attainment of an ideal world; but in such an ideal world the process would be impossible. Morality, it seems, seeks to transcend itself into a still higher dimension, a supraethical sphere—that is, into religion. It is in religion that one reaches the end of one's striving and finally fulfills the demand of morality that one realize oneself as an infinite whole. The dialectical movement of Bradley's *Ethical Studies* finally reaches an end with the exposition of a metaphysics of the self as a being that can be itself only by transcending itself, and with the transposition of the ethical issue into a religious one. Thus, Bradley hints at the necessity of a religious inquiry, though without actually undertaking it.

The reception of *Ethical Studies* was not enthusiastic, and the book soon went out of print. In a review in the journal *Mind*, Sidgwick dismissed it as a "vehemently propagandist" work presenting "always rather superficial and sometimes even unintelligent" analyses of opposing ethical views. Bradley refused for more than forty years to allow it to be reprinted. In *Appearance and Reality*, published in 1893, he said that it "in the main, still expresses my opinions" and "would have been reprinted" had he "not desired to re-write it."

Bradley continued to write on moral issues for a few years after the publication of *Ethical Studies*. In addition to the polemical pamphlet *Mr. Sidgwick's Hedonism: An Examination of the Main Argument of "The Methods of Ethics"* (1877), he contributed a few articles to *Mind* on topics such as self-sacrifice and malevolence.

As *Ethical Studies* had utilitarianism as its polemical target, Bradley's *The Principles of Logic* (1883) was mainly directed against the other cornerstone of the English empiricist tradition: psychologism. "In England at all events we have lived too long in the psychological attitude . . . we have as good as forgotten the way in which logic uses ideas," he says near the beginning of the book. Psychologism was also the doctrine against which the German logician Frege was fighting in those same years—Frege's *Grundlagen des Aritmetik* (Foundations of Arithmetic) was published in 1884. Despite the many—though for the most part only recently noticed—

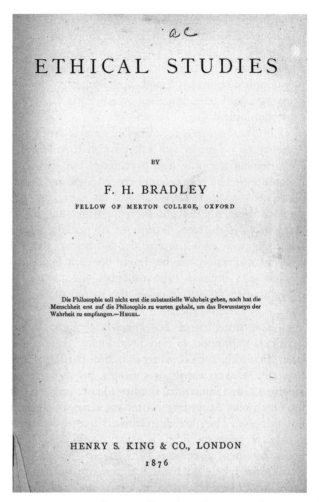

ETHICAL STUDIES

BY

F. H. BRADLEY
FELLOW OF MERTON COLLEGE, OXFORD

Die Philosophie soll nicht erst die substantielle Wahrheit geben, noch hat die Menschheit erst auf die Philosophie zu warten gehabt, um das Bewusstseyn der Wahrheit zu empfangen.—HEGEL.

HENRY S. KING & CO., LONDON
1876

Title page for Bradley's second book, in which he criticizes utilitarianism and presents a common-sense theory of morality (Amherst College Library)

analogies between the two authors, including the influence exercised on both by the philosophy of Rudolf Hermann Lotze, their common acceptance of what would be called today a "contextual principle" of meaning, and their emphasis on separating the grammatical from the logical form of judgments or propositions, Bradley's pioneering contributions to the clarification of some basic notions in logic and the philosophy of language have largely been overlooked. Part of the reason for the lack of modern attention to these contributions is his opposition in principle to the formalization of reasoning as an undue abstraction that detaches inference from actual knowledge, since this stance possesses a greater affinity with the old Hegelian logic than with the more modern mainstream of symbolic logic. Also, some of his contributions are known mainly through the selective intermediation of Russell, who heavily criticized Bradley's logical doctrines in his published writings—despite the admiration he continued to profess privately for the man who had been one of his first philosophical mentors. In 1922, for instance, on receiving the second edition of *The Principles of Logic,* Russell wrote to Bradley: "Your *Logic* was very nearly the first philosophical book that I read carefully, nearly twenty years ago; and the admiration which I felt for it has never diminished."

In *The Principles of Logic* Bradley's aim is to develop a theory of judgment and inference that avoids any entanglement not only with psychology but also with metaphysics. The relationship between logic and metaphysics, however, remained one of the most complex points in Bradley's thought. Near the beginning of *The Principles of Logic* he says, "I confess I am not sure where Logic begins or ends"; toward the end he says that no clear-cut distinction can be drawn between logic and metaphysics, because logic describes the nature of thought, metaphysics describes the nature of reality, and the two realms ultimately coincide.

The structure of *The Principles of Logic* reveals Bradley's opposition to traditional logic: whereas the latter divided its subject matter into three parts, dealing, respectively, with words or concepts, propositions or judgments, and inferences, Bradley focuses only on the last two topics. According to Bradley, ideas are nothing but symbols. They are differentiated from other psychological phenomena, such as sensations and emotions, by their possession of meaning. Meaning is characterized by two main features: artificiality and generality. The meaning of an idea is not an inherent property of it but is arbitrarily assigned; this view contradicts the empiricist assertion of a "natural" correlation among ideas, words, and objects. The generality of a symbol does not arise, as claimed by the empiricist doctrine of associationism, from noting the resemblance of many particulars to each other; on the contrary, the perception of the resemblance of particulars implies that one is already acquainted with a universal that relates them. Bradley's doctrine of the concrete universal, sketched in *Ethical Studies,* locates the relation of universal to particular not in resemblance but in "identity-in-difference": all instances of the same universal, insofar as they belong to the same system or organic unity, are identical to one another. This theory eliminates the problem faced by empiricism of explaining the psychological genesis of universals or the transition from particular to general thought. There is no stage of thought at which the mind has to deal solely with particulars, since universals are necessarily employed from the beginning in judgments about reality.

Logic, as opposed to psychology, is not concerned with mental acts as such but with their truth or falsity. Only the content of a judgment can be true or false. A judgment, according to Bradley, is not the conjunction or separation of the ideas that constitute the subject and predicate, as in empiricism, but "the act which refers an ideal content" to "a reality beyond the act." Ideal content is universal, while the mental event by which it is expressed is unique and datable. An ideal content is related to a mental event in the same way as the meaning of a word is related to the printed or uttered word (this distinction is similar to the more recent one between "type" and "token"). Judgments are referential in character: that is, they refer to a reality beyond the mental. A judgment is true or false in virtue of the relationship of its ideal content to reality. The referential character of judgments does not, however, entail a correspondence theory of truth: thought is always abstract and general, while reality is always concrete and particular, so a one-to-one correspondence between judgment and fact would be impossible. The meaning obtained by abstracting the ideal content of a judgment from the corresponding mental act must be seen as a whole that refers to reality in its complexity, rather than as a combination of separate elements of meaning put together by adding each of them to the others.

In rejecting the atomistic conception of thought put forth by empiricism, Bradley is driven to reject the notion of a particular judgment of fact, that is, of a grammatical structure, usually of the subject-predicate form, where empiricism held that the encounter between thought and reality takes place. To prove this point he analyzes the "singular judgment," which purports to deal strictly with particulars. He divides singular judgments into analytic judgments of sense, such as "I have a toothache" or "That bough is broken," which make assertions about what is directly perceived, and synthetic judgments of sense, such as "This road leads to London" or "Tomorrow there will be a full moon," which describe some portion of space and time that, though not immediately perceived, is within the bounds of possible experience. A singular judgment purports to attribute a property to a particular object; to do so, the judgment must single out or designate the object in question. But according to Bradley, a judgment cannot designate or refer to something in a unique and unambiguous way. If a descriptive expression is used to single out a referent, no matter how precise or specific or elaborate it may be, it could in principle be applied to many other objects besides the one the describer has in mind. A second possibility would be to use demonstratives, such as "this," "mine," or "here." But all demonstratives are universals: anything can be "this" and "here." Finally, the use of a proper name cannot secure uniqueness of reference, since proper names are disguised general terms. Bradley's analysis anticipates Russell's theory of descriptions, according to which grammatical names are replaceable by equivalent quantified general sentences.

Although the ideal content of a judgment always fails to denote any particular real thing, it must, nonetheless, denote something real if the judgment is true. The only real thing that is not a particular piece of reality is reality as a whole. Reality as a whole is, thus, the implied logical subject of all judgments, and the logical form of all judgments is not "S is P" but "Reality is such that S is P." If, for example, someone asserts that this leaf is green, he or she is not making an assertion about a particular aspect of some isolated thing but, rather, is asserting that the universe is such that this leaf is green. And this leaf's being green is a particular fact only because reality is what it is. For Bradley, there is only one single complex fact: the state of reality as a whole.

From the time of Aristotle in the fourth century B.C., logicians had held that all simple judgments or propositions, regardless of their explicit grammatical structure, can, on analysis, be shown to possess a common form: through the "copula"—some conjugation of the verb "to be"—the predicate can be shown to assert something about the subject. Bradley says that his analysis of analytic and synthetic judgments of sense shows this view to be mere superstition: both kinds of judgment claim to be able to map reality by means of a conjunction of atomic facts; but such mapping is impossible; hence, these judgments are, ultimately, false.

The only way to make these kinds of judgment somehow true—though not literally so—is to interpret them as being hypothetical, or conditional, in character. (This view of the logical form of sentences as hypothetical, which Bradley acknowledges inheriting from Johann Friedrick Herbart, was, in turn, inherited from Bradley by Russell, as the latter admits in his famous 1905 article "On Denoting"). Factual judgments must be considered "ideal experiments" in which one attempts to assess the relationship that supposedly holds among ideas and to evaluate how each idea points to the others. Each idea becomes, then, an attribute or adjective of the true subject of all judgments: the whole of reality. Consequently, the only truth that is available does not concern the degree of correspondence between judgments and facts but the degree of internal coherence among ideas that, far from being freely entertained by the mind, are forced on the individual by reality itself. This attention to internal coherence, by itself, is not sufficient to classify Bradley's view as a coherence theory of truth, as opposed to a correspondence theory. He believed in the ability of ideas—as compound mental contents, not as separate logical atoms—to capture something of the real character of their objects and thus, in a sense, to correspond to

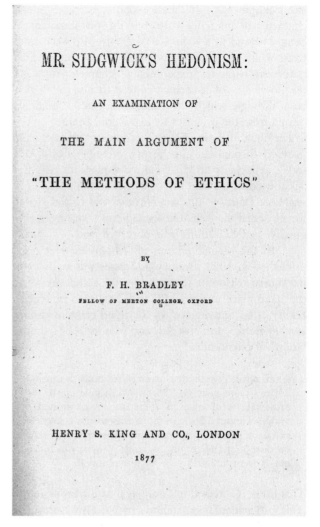

Title page for Bradley's polemical pamphlet directed against the ethical theory of the Cambridge philosopher Henry Sidgwick (Yale University Library)

reality. In the search for truth the web of predicates obtained through the repetition of ideal experiments undergoes expansion, striving to reach the same scope as that of the subject, reality. Insofar as there is a difference between the subject and the predicate, the judgment is imperfect; the predicate must be expanded until there is nothing in the subject that is not in the predicate. Completing this process, however, would lead to the paradoxical result that thought would be as individual and particular as reality and, hence, would no longer be an abstraction but would be reality itself. The identity of thought and reality is always aimed at but never achieved.

Bradley's view of the hypothetical character of judgments underpins his account of the nature of inference, which occupies the second and third parts of *The Principles of Logic*. According to Bradley, an inference, like a judgment, is an "ideal experiment." The "ideal" character of inference rules out the possibility of its being reduced to a sequence of empirical observations from which a general conclusion can be inferred by induction, while its "experimental" character rules out the possibility of its being reduced to a set of logical laws through which the conclusion can be infallibly drawn from the premises by deduction. Bradley's view is a critique of the traditional accounts of inference put forward throughout the history of logic, from Aristotle's syllogisms to Mill's inductive methods. Bradley acknowledges his debt to William Whewell's *On the Philosophy of Discovery: Chapters Historical and Critical* (1860) for its denial that scientific hypotheses result from progressive generalizations from observed facts.

In the second edition of *The Principles of Logic*, published in 1922, Bradley addresses the inability of inferential reasoning to reproduce the actual processes that take place in the world and, hence, to be true to reality. The "movement" of the mind remains discursive, symbolic, and abstract, and so it must be a "mutilation" of phenomena:

> it can never give us that tissue of relations, it can not portray those entangled fibres, which give life to the presentations of sense. It offers instead an unshaded outline without a background, a remote and colourless extract of ideas, a preparation which everywhere rests on dissection and recalls the knife, a result which can not, if events are reality, be aught but unreal.

This claim is directed not only against the reduction of reality to scientific generalizations but also against the Hegelian notions that logical categories reveal the essence of reality and that dialectic is the logical means through which the intertwining of thought and reality is actualized. For Bradley, the identity of the rational and the real is not automatically given, as it is for Hegel, because while reality and thought are not ultimately separate, reality is more than just thought. If, however, reality is interpreted not just as a system of spatial and temporal events but as a metaphysical whole, there might be a sense in which inferential thought could claim to be a transcription of it, since thought is itself a part of the whole of reality. At this point, Bradley's reflections on logic come to an end. He had expressly set out to write on the subject without getting entangled with metaphysics, but this goal turned out to be almost impossible to achieve.

Before venturing into metaphysics itself, Bradley thought it was necessary to undertake some preliminary inquiries into psychology. The separation of logic from psychology on which he insisted did not mean that the latter was a second-rank subject; the distinction was meant to emphasize the methodological differences between the two disciplines. Bradley's attempt to free traditional parts of philosophy, such as logic, ethics, and ontology, from psychologism was, at the same time, an attempt to return to psychology its own specificity and independence. Hence, from 1886 to 1888 he wrote several essays on the nature of attention, association, memory, and volition, which were published in *Mind* and collected with many other papers in the posthumous *Collected Essays* (1935). The 1888 essay "Reality and Thought" marks the beginning of the working up of Bradley's main metaphysical work, published in 1893 as *Appearance and Reality*.

In *Appearance and Reality* the originality of Bradley's philosophical temperament emerges in its fullness, revealing a mixture of skepticism inherited from the British empiricist tradition and the metaphysical commitments and mystical leanings typical of Platonism and idealism. Bradley's skepticism comes to the surface not only in his method but also in his anti-intellectualism. Although he defines metaphysics as the quest for a truth in which the intellect can find the rest and contentment at which it naturally aims, Bradley recognizes that such a quest is based on a fundamental human instinct that answers a basic need. As he says in his famous remark in the preface to the work, "Metaphysics is the finding of bad reasons for what we believe upon instinct; but to find these reasons is no less an instinct." This quest has its starting point in experience, which is the basic datum of philosophy: one can never get in touch with reality except through the immediacy of "this" and "that." The real must be felt in order to be real to the individual.

The kind of experience to which Bradley refers includes anything of which the individual is aware, such as sensations, feelings, volitions, emotions, desires, and thoughts. It is an immediate whole that "contains diversity" but "is not parted by relations"; it is a state prior to all division of self and "not-self," concept and object, or knowledge and existence. In the act of beginning to think such immediate experience is transcended, but it is never lost; it remains the foundation of all subsequent thinking.

There is a reciprocal relationship between Bradley's metaphysical theories and his logical doctrines. For instance, his view of ideas or meaning entails his metaphysical holism, and his denial of metaphysical plurality implies the logical form of the judgment as true of reality in general, not of various subjects. Above all, Bradley's criticism of the subject-predicate grammar entails an attack on the metaphysical correlate of it: the model of a thing and its qualities, or what Bradley calls the "Substantive and Adjective" schema. This attack is launched in the first part of *Appearance and Reality*, "Appearance," which is a skeptical critique in which both common-sense concepts such as relation, space and time, thing, self, movement, and cause and philosophical ones such as thing-in-itself and the primary/secondary quality distinction are analyzed, found to be self-contradictory, and degraded to the status of mere appearances.

Bradley starts with the question of what it means to speak of a thing and its qualities. What does it mean, for example, to say of a lump of sugar that it is sweet, white, and hard? The *is* cannot mean that the thing is identical with its qualities: a lump of sugar has a unity that goes beyond a mere enumeration of qualities and a particularity that is more than just the sum of abstract properties. Replacing *is* with *have* is no better, since saying that the sugar possesses those qualities suggests that the sugar is something separate from them; but taking away the qualities leaves nothing that can be called sugar. Bradley sums up the situation as the "old dilemma" of predication: "If you predicate what is different, you ascribe to the subject what it is *not;* and if you predicate what is *not* different, you say nothing at all." A middle way might be to say that a thing is a group of qualities that stand in certain relations to one another. But the pluralistic worldview against which Bradley is fighting involves not just a multiplicity of separate subjects individuated by their differing properties but also a system of relations among the subjects and among the properties of each subject. Bradley had already dealt with relations in *The Principles of Logic,* and the topic can be considered a constant of his thought—indeed, as lying at its core. He treated the issue in an appendix to the second edition of *Appearance and Reality* (1897), in a series of papers written in response to Russell, and in a long essay that he left unfinished at the time of his death but that was published in his *Collected Essays.* Bradley's arguments against the reality of relations have captured the attention of philosophers for many years and are still the most widely known aspect of his metaphysics.

In the famous chapter of *Appearance and Reality* titled "Relation and Quality" Bradley seeks to prove, through a combination of four arguments, that qualities and relations are both mere appearances. It is impossible, he begins, to find qualities without relations: wherever there is more than one quality, they are related at least by identity, similarity, or difference, if not by any of the many other possible relations. But the coexistence of qualities with relations is also impossible, since every quality must not only exist but must also be in relation to something else—that is, it must possess two aspects. Since these two aspects must be related within the quality, they themselves will each have two aspects. These aspects must, in turn, be related, and so forth, in an infinite regress. Conversely, there could be no relations without qualities, for such relations would be false

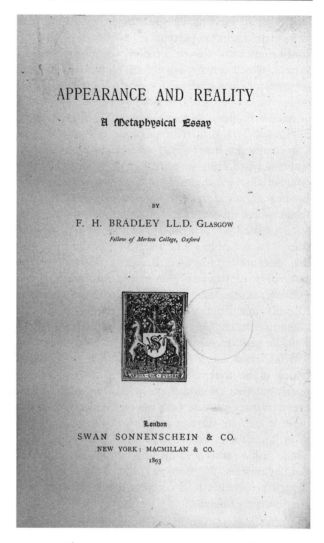

APPEARANCE AND REALITY

A Metaphysical Essay

BY

F. H. BRADLEY LL.D. GLASGOW
Fellow of Merton College, Oxford

London
SWAN SONNENSCHEIN & CO.
NEW YORK: MACMILLAN & CO.
1893

Title page for Bradley's major work, in which he presents his metaphysics of absolute idealism (Beaman Library, Lipscomb University)

abstractions with no guaranteed correspondents outside the mind. (This argument counters the realist view of relations, according to which a relation must be conceivable without its terms, and it was later used by Bradley to support his criticisms of Russell's realism.) Finally, the coexistence of relations with qualities is impossible, because, again, any attempt to relate two or more qualities with each other would lead to an endless regress. From these arguments Bradley concludes that "a relational way of thought—any one that moves by the machinery of terms and relations—must give appearance, and not truth. It is a makeshift, a device, a mere practical compromise, most necessary, but in the end most indefensible."

Bradley's thesis of the unreality of relations as developed in *Appearance and Reality* became a hotly debated point. The objections to his view held either that relations have to be taken as an irreducible and immediate datum of perceptual experience or that his conclusions were absurd. Bradley's later work on the subject, which centers around the notions of internal (or intrinsic) and external (or extrinsic) relations, was no less fiercely opposed. In Bradley's view a relation is internal if it affects its terms, external if it leaves them unaffected. That is, a relational property *P* possessed by some entity *A* is internal if *A* would have been different had it not had *P,* or–another way of making the same point–if anything that did not have *P* could not be *A*. Bradley argues that there cannot be purely external relations, because in such a relation the terms are arbitrarily related to each other; but that cannot be true, since there must always be a reason why this thing and that one appear together. Bradley's rejection of the externality of relations should not mislead one into thinking, as sometimes has been done (most notably by Russell), that Bradley advocated a theory of internal relations. Purely internal relations are untenable, as well, he says, for an internal relation is so bound up with its terms that it coincides with them and, hence, ceases to be a separate element–in other words, a purely internal relation is not a relation at all. Thus, every relation must be both internal and external; but the two kinds of relation are mutually exclusive. Relations are, therefore, contradictory and impossible. Thus, in his earlier and his later writings on relations Bradley argues for one and the same conclusion, though he couches it in different terms: that relations are ultimately unreal.

In *Appearance and Reality* Bradley goes on to argue that the contradictions implicit in both the everyday and the scientific concepts of space, time, movement, causation, activity, and the self show that these objects cannot be ultimately real but only more or less adequate appearances of reality. For example, any given space must consist of parts that are themselves spaces; if space were merely a relation, it would be a relation of relations, which is absurd. On the other hand, space *must* be a relation, for it is infinitely differentiated internally, consisting of parts that in turn consist of parts, and so on indefinitely; these differentiations, however, are nothing but relations. A similar case is made with respect to time: on the one hand, time must be a relation–the relation between "before" and "after"; on the other hand, it cannot be a relation, for if time is a relation between units that have no duration, then the whole of time has no duration, which is absurd. But if the relations between units have a duration, then the alleged units dissolve into relations, and time collapses into an infinite regress of relations. With respect to time, Bradley ventures the hypothesis of the possibility of a plurality of time series whose direction may vary,

so that an event which in a given series is past may be yet to come in a different series–with the inevitable corollary that there may exist a multiplicity of causal relations holding true of a corresponding multiplicity of possible worlds. Traditional idealism may accept the relegation of the spatio-temporal world of external objects to the sphere of appearances, but Bradley's absolute idealism goes further, asserting that even the knowing subject is unable to serve as a foundation for reality. The notion of the self, whether analyzed in a phenomenalistic or in a realistic way, gives rise to insoluble puzzles and hence, according to Bradley, is unreal.

In the second part of *Appearance and Reality,* "Reality," Bradley constructs his positive metaphysics. If being self-contradictory reduces things to appearances, then one of the essential characteristics of reality must be that it is noncontradictory. The logical foundation of Bradley's characterization of reality rests on his view of negation. He rejects as impossible what he calls "bare negation," which would mean that a negative judgment "not-*p*" could be true independently of its relation to any affirmative judgment other than "*p*," the one it explicitly denies. Bradley, on the contrary, holds that since thought is to be construed as predicated of reality as a whole, as he showed in *The Principles of Logic,* for any true negative judgment "not-*p*" there must be a true affirmative judgment "*q*" that provides both the positive ground, or truth-condition, of "not-*p*," as well as the falsity-condition of "*p*." Although the positive grounds of many true negative judgments will remain unknown, any true negation must have a positive ground. The conclusion is that the ultimate reality must be a consistent, harmonious whole that can never contradict itself.

Such reality must have two essential features. First, it cannot be externally related to human consciousness; therefore, all parts of reality must be, in principle, open to possible experience or knowledge. Nor, for the same reason, can any appearance be external to reality. Thus, to call something an appearance is not to deny that it exists: "what appears, for that sole reason, most indubitably *is*." Therefore, reality must embrace all diverse and conflicting phenomena, although it transforms them into a harmonious unity in which no contradictions remain. Reality is the totality of its appearances, not an additional entity behind or beyond them. Second, reality cannot comprise a plurality of independent, self-subsistent entities, because it would have to be possible for those individuals to exist and to be known without reference to each other. The universe would then be less than a totally comprehensive and logically consistent system. Hence, reality, or the Absolute, must be unitary; its differences exist harmoniously within one whole, exhausting all that there is.

To give content to this formal outline of the Absolute, Bradley characterizes it as being of the nature of experience, broadly conceived of as including thought, perception, sensation, will, and desire. The Absolute is an infinite sentient experience that differentiates itself into a myriad of "finite centres of experience," *loci* from within which all beings' immediate cognitive contact with reality takes place. Experience, that is, must be "attached" to some actual sentient being. These beings, however, cannot be identified with human beings, since in that case nothing would exist that is not actually being thought of by someone.

The primitive experience described at the beginning of *Appearance and Reality,* after being transformed into discursive thought and, hence, pervaded with contradictions, is recovered at a higher level and without contradictions by the Absolute. Therefore, the Absolute is spiritual, inasmuch as spirit can be defined as "a unity of the manifold in which the externality of the manifold has utterly ceased." Even the human mind can achieve some unification of the manifold, but within the mind the mutual externality of all elements of the manifold can never utterly cease. Accordingly, the human mind is only imperfectly spiritual. But to describe the Absolute as spiritual does not imply that it is a conscious personal self. Inasmuch as the Absolute is the totality of all appearances, it must include within itself all the aspects of selfhood and personality, but it transforms and transcends them into a comprehensive and all-embracing whole. Nor does the description of the Absolute as spiritual lead to a view of a material universe animated by a sort of world-soul, for there is no reality outside of spirit itself.

Bradley devotes a chapter of *Appearance and Reality* to what he calls "the main thesis of this work": the relationship between thought and reality. Appealing to the theory of judgment put forward in *The Principles of Logic,* he says that there are two components in all that there is that can be distinguished but never separated: existence and content. Thought strives to unify those elements by way of judgments; but if the subject and the predicate of every judgment were identified, the predicative function itself would collapse, and thought, which by its nature is discursive and relational, would cease to exist. Hence, thought could realize the Bradleyan ideal of identity-in-difference only by self-extinction—a situation analogous to that of morality as depicted in *Ethical Studies.* Of course, finite beings cannot know what such an experience would be like; all they can know is that by the increasingly systematic exercise of relational thought the Absolute can achieve its own increasing harmony and satisfaction.

The problem then arises as to how error and evil, which are elements of disorder and inconsistency, can

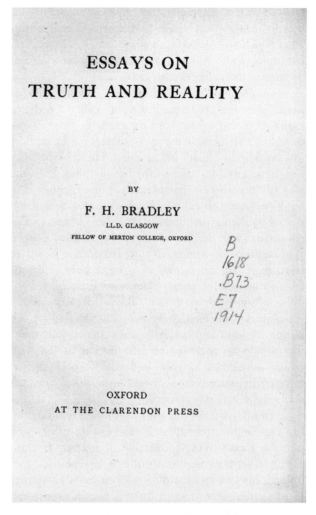

ESSAYS ON
TRUTH AND REALITY

BY

F. H. BRADLEY
LL.D. GLASGOW
FELLOW OF MERTON COLLEGE, OXFORD

OXFORD
AT THE CLARENDON PRESS

Title page for Bradley's 1914 collection of his articles on philosophical psychology, epistemology, and moral philosophy (Thomas Cooper Library, University of South Carolina)

exist within the harmonious and consistent whole that is the Absolute. Bradley answers that those apparently negative features may, once adequately transformed, contribute to the harmony of the whole. Although he is not able to explain how this transformation happens, it is permissible to believe in its existence because of its possibility and necessity. Evil, for instance, is a precondition of morality, since morality consists in an endless overcoming of the lower self, as Bradley claimed in *Ethical Studies.* In regard to error, Bradley's view follows from his theory of the degrees of truth, for which he acknowledges a debt to Hegel: not all appearances are equally one-sided and unreal; some are less far removed from the all-inclusiveness and self-consistency of the Absolute and must undergo a less radical transformation to be comprehended within it. A continuum of degrees exists between complete truth and absolute error. Truth and error are entangled with each other; human beings always have to deal with partial truths, all of which are infected with some degree of error. Partial truths can be ranked in a hierarchy by the criteria of coherence and comprehensiveness.

In *The Principles of Logic* Bradley had claimed that not all ideas need to be predicated on reality in order to exist; some can be held, so to speak, in front of the mind without being used in a judgment—that is, they can lay idle or "float" in the mind. He now modifies this view: any idea entertained by the mind, even the idea of "nothingness," is necessarily used, either consciously or unconsciously. Reality cannot be encompassed by the narrow limits of what lies in "continuous connection with my felt waking body"; it must exist in a multiplicity of worlds. In addition to the world of facts, there are the worlds of science, duty, religious faith, imagination, poetry, desire, dream, and even those of madness, error, and illusion. Reality, or the Absolute, is wide enough for every idea to find a place in one world or another. As a consequence, judgments that would be regarded as false insofar as they are treated as referring to reality in the narrowest sense are, in fact, true, since there is always some world to which they can be veritably referred.

Bradley's theory of truth was much criticized by his contemporaries. Russell, for example, charged that the theory was self-refuting: if nothing is completely true, then neither Bradley's metaphysics nor, indeed, his theory of truth itself can be wholly true. In particular, according to Russell, the coherence criterion runs into the difficulty that there may be many possible systems of judgments, all of them coherent. Any judgment could then be proved true merely by picking a self-coherent system with which that judgment coheres. Bradley responded to critics' objections by developing and clarifying his theory of truth in the essays "On Floating Ideas and the Imaginary" (1906), "On Truth and Coherence" (1909), and "On My Real World" (1914), which are collected in *Essays on Truth and Reality* (1914).

The theory of the degrees of truth is, according to Bradley, at the same time a theory of the degrees of reality; this claim is a corollary of his view that there is no fundamental distinction of subject matter between logic and metaphysics. Bradley does not mean that the Absolute has degrees of perfection, for it is totally perfect; the hierarchy of perfection belongs to the world of appearance. To mitigate the implied dualism between reality and appearance Bradley sketches a scheme in which reality itself allows for degrees, from the lower stage of lifeless matter, where sheer contradiction prevails, to the highest stage of the perfection of the Absolute. Morality is one of the intermediate stages, since it includes a fundamental contradiction between "is" and "ought." Ultimate reality cannot be found in aesthetic experience, either: art brings pleasure, which affects the self, whereas the Absolute is more comprehensive than mere selfhood. The next level is religion, but the religious consciousness reveals itself to be self-contradictory: on the one hand, religion looks at God as the one true reality, thus conceiving of him as infinite; on the other hand, it conceives of God as distinct from the multiplicity of creatures and, thus, as limited—that is, finite. Like morality and art, religion belongs to the sphere of appearance; and, just as morality has to be transcended, so religion has to pass into the metaphysics of the Absolute: "If you identify the Absolute with God, that is not the God of religion," Bradley claims in *Appearance and Reality*. "Short of the Absolute God cannot rest, and having reached that goal, he is lost and religion with him."

In 1893 Bradley and William James engaged in a controversy in the pages of *Mind* on the subject of resemblance and identity; Bradley's contributions were republished in *Collected Essays*. James claimed that although it might be possible to interpret the resemblances between compound objects as instances of partial identity, in that such objects are identical with respect to some attribute and different with respect to some other attribute, with simple objects, such as an ascending series of musical notes, that view of resemblance cannot hold. Since simple objects can be characterized by a single attribute, there is no common ground from which they can share either an identity or a diversity of relations with anything else. For James, however, all instances of compound resemblance are ultimately based on simple resemblance. Hence, resemblance as such cannot be based on identity.

Bradley responds that there can be no relation of resemblance between two simple objects, since such things would have just one property in common and would then be indiscernible—thus, they would be not two objects but one. Furthermore, identity and difference are inseparable and complementary aspects of a complex whole; the notion that a supposedly absolute identity does not allow for difference is illusory. For any two objects there is always an aspect in which they are the same and an aspect in which they are different, and neither of those aspects is anything complete in itself. What lies at the heart of resemblance is some respect in which the resembling things are alike, some universal that makes a comparison between them possible and meaningful. Identity is a basic notion, and the degrees of resemblance have to be explained by reference to it. As for James's example of a musical scale, such a series is based on an increasing or decreasing amount of something that is the same in all the notes.

Bradley's view of identity had played a key role in his philosophy since the *Ethical Studies*, in which he held that the notion of the essence of a person undergoing a process of differentiation while remaining identical with itself is fundamental to morality and religion. Moreover, causation, the laws of nature, and inference are all based on the notion of the same thing acting in the same way over time.

The topic of memory, together with other subjects in philosophical psychology, epistemology, and moral philosophy, occupied Bradley after 1894 in a series of review articles published in *Mind* and included in *Essays on Truth and Reality* and *Collected Essays*. One of the articles, "The Contrary and the Disparate" (1896), was added as an appendix to the second edition of *Appearance and Reality*. Here Bradley identifies the basic flaw in thought as its inability to treat relations as other than solid things. Thought could grasp the fluid passing of each element of reality into the others only by conjugating them without identifying them, or by distinguishing them without separating them.

Bradley was elected to membership in the Royal Danish Academy in 1921 and the Italian Accademia dei Lincei in 1922 and was awarded an honorary fellowship of the British Academy in 1923. In 1924 King George V conferred on him the Order of Merit; he was the first philosopher to receive the honor. Bradley died on 18 September 1924 of blood poisoning. He was buried in Holywell Cemetery in Oxford.

Bradley's philosophy has inspired sharply polarized interpretations as to both the main targets of his attacks and the major influences on his thought. While some see his principal enemies as the British schools of empiricism and utilitarianism, others identify his main opponents as idealists of the Kantian or Hegelian stripe. Some have tried to portray Bradley as the heir to the Cambridge Platonism movement, while others have linked him to the very German idealism that other critics have claimed he was attacking. Russell charged that Bradley was not an original philosopher but a follower of Hegel, but other critics have maintained that he cannot be considered a Hegelian because for Hegel reason is capable of penetrating the inner life of the Absolute by means of dialectical reasoning, while for Bradley the human mind is unable to attain any adequate grasp of the Absolute. Although Bradley acknowledges his debt to Hegel, in *The Principles of Logic* he says:

Assuredly I think him a great philosopher; but I never could have called myself a Hegelian, partly because I cannot say that I have mastered his system, and partly because I could not accept what seems his main princi-

ple. . . . I have no wish to conceal how much I owe to his writings; but I will leave it to those who can judge better than myself, to fix the limits within which I have followed him.

In fact, whereas Hegel was a pure rationalist, Bradley combined skepticism and systematization. His three major books have skeptical conclusions that either cast doubt on what has been argued for with apparent confidence throughout the preceding text or hint at some inquiry still to come. Bradley prefaces *The Principles of Logic* by saying: "We want no system-making or systems home-grown or imported. . . . What we want at present is to clear the ground, so that English Philosophy, if it rises, may be not choked by prejudice. The ground cannot be cleared without a critical, or, if you prefer, a skeptical study of first principles." It is, however, impossible to deny that Bradley's philosophy is full of system-building: in *Appearance and Reality* he characterizes metaphysics as "the effort to comprehend the universe, not simply piecemeal or by fragments, but somehow as a whole," and his philosophizing is pervaded by just such an effort. Ultimately, no partisan divisions can do justice to the complex subtlety and originality of his thought, which combines many influences and affinities.

Bibliography:

Richard Ingardia, *Bradley: A Research Bibliography* (Bowling Green, Ohio: Philosophy Documentation Center, 1991).

References:

Bernard Bosanquet, *Knowledge and Reality: A Criticism of Mr. F. H. Bradley's "The Principles of Logic"* (London: Kegan Paul, Trench, 1885);

Bradley Studies: The Journal of the Bradley Society, 1– (1995–);

James Bradley, ed., *Philosophy after F. H. Bradley: A Collection of Essays* (Bristol: Thoemmes Press, 1996);

Charles A. Campbell, *Scepticism and Construction: Bradley's Sceptical Principle as the Basis of Constructive Philosophy* (London: Allen & Unwin, 1931);

Stewart Candlish, "The Truth about F. H. Bradley," *Mind*, 98 (1989): 331–348;

Ralph Withington Church, *Bradley's Dialectic* (London: Allen & Unwin, 1942);

M. J. Cresswell, "Reality as Experience in F. H. Bradley," *Australasian Journal of Philosophy*, 55 (1977): 169–188;

David Crossley, "Holism, Individuation, and Internal Relations," *Journal of the History of Philosophy*, 15 (1977): 183–194;

John De Marneffe, *La preuve de l'Absolu chez Bradley: Analyse et critique de la méthode* (Paris: Beauchesne, 1961);

T. S. Eliot, *Knowledge and Experience in the Philosophy of F. H. Bradley* (London & New York: Faber & Faber, 1964);

Ralph-Peter Hortsmann, *Ontologie und Relationen* (Königstein: Athenaeum, 1984);

William James, "Bradley or Bergson," *Journal of Philosophy,* 7 (1910): 29–33;

James, *A Pluralistic Universe: Hibbert Lectures at Manchester College on the Present Situation in Philosophy* (New York & London: Longmans, Green, 1909), pp. 25–42;

Rudolf Kagey, "F. H. Bradley's Logic," dissertation, Columbia University, 1931;

William F. Lofthouse, *F. H. Bradley,* Philosopher's Library, no. 1 (London: Epworth, 1949);

Philip MacEwen, ed., *Ethics, Metaphysics and Religion in the Thought of F. H. Bradley,* Studies in the History of Philosophy, no. 42 (Lewiston, N.Y.: Edwin Mellen Press, 1996);

Donald MacNiven, *Bradley's Moral Psychology,* Studies in the History of Philosophy, volume 3 (Lewiston, N.Y.: Edwin Mellen Press, 1987);

W. J. Mander, *An Introduction to Bradley's Metaphysics* (Oxford: Clarendon Press, 1994);

Mander, ed., *Perspectives on the Logic and Metaphysics of F. H. Bradley* (Bristol: Thoemmes Press, 1996);

Anthony Manser, *Bradley's Logic* (Oxford: Blackwell, 1983);

Manser and Guy Stock, eds., *The Philosophy of F. H. Bradley* (Oxford: Clarendon Press, 1984);

Leemon B. McHenry, *Whitehead and Bradley: A Comparative Analysis* (Albany: State University of New York Press, 1992);

G. E. Moore, "The Conception of Reality" and "External and Internal Relations," in his *Philosophical Studies* (London: Kegan Paul, Trench, Trübner, 1922), pp. 197–219, 276–309;

Moore, *Some Main Problems of Philosophy* (London: Allen & Unwin, 1953), pp. 201–233, 288–305;

J. H. Muirhead, *The Platonic Tradition in Anglo-Saxon Philosophy: Studies in the History of Idealism in England and America* (London: Allen & Unwin / New York: Macmillan, 1931), pp. 219–304;

Geoffrey Reginald Gilchrist Mure, "F. H. Bradley: Towards a Portrait," *Encounter,* 88 (1961): 28–35;

John Passmore, "Russell and Bradley," in *Contemporary Philosophy in Australia,* edited by Robert Brown and C. D. Rollins (London: Allen & Unwin, 1969; New York: Humanities Press, 1969), pp. 21–30;

Sushill Kumar Saxena, *Studies in the Metaphysics of Bradley* (London: Allen & Unwin, 1967);

Torgny T. Segerstedt, *Value and Reality in Bradley's Philosophy* (Lund, Sweden: A.-B. Gleerupska Universitetsbokhandeln, 1934);

Timothy L. S. Sprigge, *James and Bradley: American Truth and British Reality* (Chicago: Open Court, 1993), pp. 257–583;

Stock, ed., *Appearance versus Reality: New Essays on Bradley's Metaphysics* (Oxford: Clarendon Press, 1998);

A. E. Taylor, "F. H. Bradley," *Mind,* 34 (1925): 1–12;

Taylor, "Francis Herbert Bradley, 1846–1924," *Proceedings of the British Academy,* 11 (1924–1925): 458–468;

Garrett L. Vander Veer, *Bradley's Metaphysics and the Self* (New Haven & London: Yale University Press, 1970);

Richard Wollheim, *F. H. Bradley* (Harmondsworth, U.K.: Penguin, 1959).

Papers:
F. H. Bradley's unpublished papers, notebooks, and letters received are at Merton College, Oxford. Correspondence between Bradley and Bertrand Russell from 1901 to 1922 is in the Bertrand Russell Archives at McMaster University, Ontario, Canada. Letters from Bradley to William James are in the Houghton Library at Harvard University. The John Rylands Library at the University of Manchester has Bradley's letters to Samuel Alexander.

Edward Caird

(23 March 1835 – 1 November 1908)

Colin Tyler
University of Hull

BOOKS: *Ethical Philosophy: An Introductory Lecture Delivered in the Common Hall of Glasgow College on November 6, 1866* (Glasgow: MacLehose, 1866);

A Critical Account of the Philosophy of Kant: With an Historical Introduction (Glasgow: MacLehose, 1877; London & New York: Macmillan, 1877);

The Problem of Philosophy at the Present Time: An Introductory Address Delivered to the Philosophical Society of the University of Edinburgh (Glasgow: MacLehose, 1881);

Hegel, edited by William Knight, Philosophical Classics for English Readers, no. 7 (Edinburgh & London: Blackwood, 1883; Philadelphia: Lippincott, 1883);

The Social Philosophy and Religion of Comte (Glasgow: MacLehose, 1885; New York: Macmillan, 1885);

The Moral Aspect of the Economical Problem: Presidential Address to the Ethical Society. January 10, 1887 (London: Sonnenschein, Lowrey, 1888);

The Critical Philosophy of Immanuel Kant, 2 volumes (Glasgow: MacLehose, 1889);

Essays on Literature and Philosophy, 2 volumes (Glasgow: MacLehose, 1892; New York: Macmillan, 1892);

The Evolution of Religion: The Gifford Lectures Delivered before the University of St. Andrews in Sessions 1890–91 and 1891–92, 2 volumes (Glasgow: MacLehose, 1893; New York: Macmillan, 1893);

Address on Plato's Republic *as the Earliest Educational Treatise* (Bangor, Wales: Printed and sold by Jarvis & Foster, 1894);

Individualism and Socialism: Being the Inaugural Address to the Civic Society of Glasgow (Glasgow: MacLehose, 1897);

The Evolution of Theology in the Greek Philosophers: The Gifford Lectures Delivered in the University of Glasgow in Sessions 1900–1 and 1901–2, 2 volumes (Glasgow: MacLehose, 1904; New York: Macmillan, 1904);

Lay Sermons and Addresses: Delivered in the Hall of Balliol College, Oxford (Glasgow: MacLehose, 1907);

The Collected Works of Edward Caird, edited by Colin Tyler, 12 volumes (Bristol: Thoemmes, 1999).

Edward Caird

OTHER: Andrew Seth and Richard B. Haldane, eds., *Essays in Philosophical Criticism,* preface by Caird (London: Longmans, Green, 1883);

William Wallace, *Lectures and Essays on Natural Theology and Ethics,* edited by Caird (Oxford: Clarendon Press, 1898);

John Caird, *The Fundamental Ideas of Christianity,* 2 volumes, edited by Caird (Glasgow: MacLehose, 1899);

T. H. Green, *Prolegomena to Ethics,* fifth edition, edited by A. C. Bradley, preface by Caird (Oxford: Clarendon Press, 1906).

Edward Caird was a central figure in the development of British idealism and in the propagation of the study of Immanuel Kant and Georg Wilhelm Friedrich Hegel in Great Britain and the United States. His books on Kant were central texts in their field for decades and are still influential today, and he wrote one of the best short introductions in English to the philosophy of Hegel. He also made significant contributions to the philosophy of religion. Together with Benjamin Jowett and T. H. Green, he played a decisive role in breaking the hold, at least temporarily, of empiricism and associationism over the Universities of Oxford and Glasgow. "To this radical change and reorientation," Rudolf Metz observes in *A Hundred Years of British Philosophy* (1938), "there is no parallel in the entire history of British thought." Moreover, Caird, Green, and Jowett, along with Bernard Bosanquet and David Ritchie, helped to end the influence of Herbert Spencer's social Darwinism and to foster a more interventionist conception of the state through their influence on the "new liberalism" exemplified by L. T. Hobhouse.

Caird remained a central figure in the British idealist movement for many years after Jowett's disillusionment with Hegel. Although the emergence of figures such as Bosanquet and F. H. Bradley lessened the impact of Green's early death, Caird made probably the most significant contribution to the teaching of idealism during the crucial period from 1882 to 1908. He maintained important contacts with Ritchie, Henry Jones, John H. Muirhead, and William Wallace, as well as many other Glasgow and Oxford undergraduates who later became leading figures in the late-Victorian and Edwardian elite as civil servants, church leaders, and prime ministers. Metz notes that no "philosophical teacher of the time sowed so much enthusiasm, and received so much admiration and respect as Edward Caird."

Caird was born on 23 March 1835 in Greenock, Scotland, to John Caird, a partner in an engineering firm, and Janet Caird (née Young). He had four older brothers and two younger brothers, one of whom died in childhood. After his father died in 1838, his mother, unable to raise the six boys by herself, sent Edward to live with his aunt Jane Caird, who maintained the deeply religious environment that had surrounded him since his birth. This

upbringing had a particularly strong effect on Edward and his elder brother John, who became principal of the University of Glasgow and a central figure in the development of Scottish religious life and theology in the late nineteenth century.

Caird was educated at Greenock Academy before entering the University of Glasgow in 1850. At the university he studied arts and divinity–sporadically, because of ill health–until the end of the 1856–1857 session, winning several prizes in Latin and Greek. According to his biographers Jones and Muirhead, he became "the philosopher in chief" of a group of fellow students that included John Nichol. This group rallied around many of the causes that Caird championed throughout the remainder of his life, such as the extension of the franchise, equal rights for women, and labor reform.

Poor health forced Caird to return to live with his aunt from late 1856 until the spring of 1857. During this time he attended St. Mary's College of the University of St. Andrews, where he studied Hebrew, church history, and divinity. He then briefly abandoned all formal study because of his health and moved in with his brother John, who was then a minister in Errol, Perthshire. He returned to the University of Glasgow later in 1857 to continue his studies in divinity.

On 13 October 1860 Caird, having been elected to the Snell Exhibition (a scholarship), moved to Balliol College, Oxford. His fellow students respected his philosophical ability and depth, although they saw him as somewhat grave, shy, and unconventional. He became close to Green through their membership in the Old Mortality Club, created by Nichol in 1857 for the discussion of literature and science and the study of English authors, among whom one of the most important was Thomas Carlyle. Much later, in an 1892 lecture to the Dialectic Society of the University of Glasgow, Caird identified Carlyle as "the greatest literary influence" of his student days. He emphasized Carlyle's role in bringing German literature and philosophy, especially the work of Johann Wolfgang von Goethe and Johann Gottlieb Fichte, to England. Caird noted that Carlyle's reputation gradually waned as the issues he had addressed so vehemently were resolved, and his answers to other problems came to seem simplistic, but his major contribution was "to make us see through the external puppet-show of human life, to the internecine struggle of good and evil which it half reveals and half conceals."

Caird shared the radical political ideas of many members of the Old Mortality, especially Green and Nichol. He was a fervent supporter of the North in the American Civil War and of the Italian patriot

Giuseppe Garibaldi's April 1859 rising against Austria. He distrusted both the French emperor Napoleon III and the British prime minister Henry John Temple, Lord Palmerston, but admired the radical British politician John Bright. His radicalism was also evident in his critical resistance to the requirement that all students being admitted to Oxford University sign the Thirty-nine Articles, a 1571 statement outlining the fundamental doctrines of the Church of England.

Caird graduated in 1863 with firsts in Classical Moderations and litterae humaniores. He then supported himself for nearly a year as a private philosophy tutor in Oxford before being elected a fellow of Merton College on 18 May 1864.

Hegel's influence was clear from Caird's first publication, a review of George Grote's *Plato and the Other Companions of Sokrates* (1865) for *The North British Review*. The piece bears striking similarities to Green's essay "The Philosophy of Aristotle," which appeared in *The North British Review* the following year. Caird concludes with a passage that is typical of his writings:

> as the Bible is not a confession of faith or a treatise on doctrine, but a picture of the religious life, its inward trials and difficulties, and its changing relations with the world, so we may say that Plato teaches us not philosophy, but the philosophic life. To live in the world and influence it, and yet not to be of it, not to be overpowered by delusion, or to mistake for eternal truth the passion and the cry of the hour, is a difficulty which besets the thinker as well as the saint, Plato as well as St. Paul.

Caird resigned his fellowship effective 6 May 1866. On 28 May he was appointed to the professorship of moral philosophy at the University of Glasgow. His introductory lecture, delivered on 6 November, was published as *Ethical Philosophy* (1866). Caird married Caroline Frances Wylie on 8 May 1867; Green was his best man.

During his twenty-seven years at Glasgow, Caird established himself as a leading figure in the philosophical life of the time through his teaching, his writings, and his work for the extension of higher education to women. In 1868 he, along with Nichol and two other professors, began lecturing to women. In 1874 Edward and John Caird cast the sole votes against a motion of the university senate to petition Parliament against a bill admitting women to Scottish universities; Edward Caird went on to write a formal dissent from the motion. In 1877 the Caird brothers helped to create the Glasgow Association for the Higher Education of Women. The battles continued

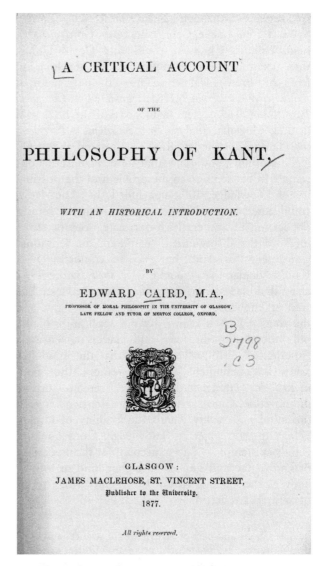

Title page for the book that established Caird as one of the leading British interpreters of the philosophy of Immanuel Kant (Thomas Cooper Library, University of South Carolina)

for most of Caird's time in Glasgow, but women had gained admission to the university by the time he left.

Caird's first book, *A Critical Account of the Philosophy of Kant: With an Historical Introduction,* appeared in 1877. Caird begins by stating the fundamental question of Kant's epistemology (theory of knowledge): how are a priori synthetic judgments possible—that is, how can certain propositions that are fundamental to science, such as "every event has a cause," that are not tautologies (that is, true by definition, such as "bachelors are unmarried males") be known, prior to experience, to be necessarily and universally true? Caird traces the history of epistemology from the Greeks and

Neo-Platonists through René Descartes, Baruch Spinoza, John Locke, George Berkeley, Gottfried Wilhelm Leibniz, Christian Wolff, and David Hume, then examines Kant's philosophical development from the "Pre-Critical period" up to the publication of *Kritik der reinen Vernunft* (1781; translated as *Critique of Pure Reason*, 1855). The main body of the book is a detailed Hegelian analysis of the *Critique of Pure Reason*. Caird acknowledges Kant's genius and philosophical importance but argues that serious contradictions remain in his solution to the problem of the possibility of knowledge. Kant concluded that knowledge could come into existence only through the mind's application of universal a priori categories or structures to the disorganized "manifold" of sensation. Caird sees this claim, however, as conflicting with Kant's "denial that thought is *in itself* synthetic"–a claim that places an irremovable barrier between "the *ideal* of knowledge derived from pure thought, and the *reality* which is known by the application of the pure thought to the form and matter of sensuous experience." In other words, all that the mind can know is "phenomena," or appearances; the "noumena," or "things-in-themselves," remain forever unknowable. Caird argues that this barrier between the mind and reality entails the inability of human beings to gain objective knowledge. Consequently, Kant's epistemology fails to account for the possibility of knowledge and implies "a higher kind of union" between thought and reality. Caird ends with a series of optimistic reflections:

> The labour and pain of experience, of science, and of philosophy, are not wasted in a vain effort after the unattainable; nor are we, as Kant supposes, tempted to pursue a lower good, by the illusive hope of something better. Rather we should say that every step of spiritual progress implies the end, and is, in a sense, the anticipation of the fruition of it. Slow as is the advance of knowledge, the hope by which it is moved is nothing less than certainty, for it is a faith bound up with the very idea of knowledge, and the consciousness of self.

The book established Caird as one of the leading British Kant scholars of the day. In a review in *Mind*, T. M. Lindsay described the work as "the best on Kant's philosophy that I am acquainted with either in our own language or in German, and cannot fail to be the standard upon the subject for a long time to come." Lindsay went so far as to describe Caird and Green as "two of the recognised leaders" of the "small and energetic" English Hegelian school. In his own review of the book in *Academy* (1877) Green eschewed the label "Hegelian" for himself and Caird and said that Caird "has done his work with admirable lucidity and completeness, and as it only could be done by one who has passed through Kant to a position beyond."

Caird defended Kant's conception of the thing-in-itself in two exchanges in *Mind:* an acrimonious one with Arthur J. Balfour in 1879 and a far more respectful one with Henry Sidgwick in 1879–1880. He reviewed Robert Adamson's *On the Philosophy of Kant* (1879) in *Mind* in 1880 and wrote several articles and reviews on Kantian epistemology over the next few years. Most of his philosophical writings after 1879 demonstrate a far greater knowledge of and debt to Kant than his work before 1879. In all of them, however, he reiterates the Hegelian reservations of *A Critical Account of the Philosophy of Kant*.

In the winter of 1879 Caird helped set up a philosophical discussion society called The Witenagemote, after the Anglo-Saxon term for a high council, or, literally, an "assembly of the wise." Its membership included some of those who led British philosophy over the next forty years, including Jones, Muirhead, G. C. MacCallum, J. S. MacKenzie, and Andrew Seth.

In *The Problem of Philosophy at the Present Time: An Introductory Address Delivered to the Philosophical Society of the University of Edinburgh* (1881) Caird says that "The need for philosophy arises out of the broken harmony of a spiritual life, in which the different elements or factors seem to be set in irreconcilable opposition to each other." The intellectual problems of the current world "all, directly or indirectly, turn upon the difficulty of reconciling the three great terms of thought,–the world, self, and God: the difficulty of carrying out to their legitimate consequences what seem to be our most firmly based convictions as to any one of these factors in our intellectual life, without rejecting in whole or in part the claims of the others." Partial answers can never be satisfactory, because human reason cannot rest until it conceives the world as a complete and internally coherent system. What is needed is a rearticulation of the truths of natural science, religion, and philosophy that brings out their interrelationships.

Green died of blood poisoning in March 1882. Caird reviewed his friend's final work, *Prolegomena to Ethics* (1883), in *Mind* in 1883. That same year he contributed the preface to *Essays in Philosophical Criticism,* a collection of nine tracts by some of those who became leading figures in the British idealist movement, including Bosanquet, Ritchie, Jones, and W. R. Sorely, as well as Seth and Richard B. Haldane, who were co-editors of the volume. The collection was dedicated to Green's memory. In his preface Caird notes that Kant and Hegel, along with Green, were inspirations for every contributor to the work.

Also in 1883 Caird published *Hegel* in Blackwood's Philosophical Classics for English Readers, a series of short introductory texts in the history of philosophy. Here he says that the most important fundamental truth that Hegel brought into clear view is the necessary unity of thought and knowledge. Yet, for all of his evident admiration, Caird insists that Hegel's system was not the culmination of philosophy but only an important stage in its development:

> To us, at this distance of time, Hegel, at the highest, can be only the last great philosopher who deserves to be placed on the same level with Plato and Aristotle in ancient, and with Spinoza and Kant in modern times, and who, similar to them, has given an "epoch-making" contribution to the development of the philosophic, or, taking the word in the highest sense, the idealistic, interpretation of the world. In other words, he can only be the last writer who has made a vitally important addition to the proof, that those ideas, which are at the root of poetry and religion, are also principles of science.

Caird contributed the article "Metaphysic" to the ninth edition of the *Encyclopædia Britannica* (1883). The piece is a succinct and powerful defense of Caird's own form of absolute idealism. He argues that the Absolute realizes itself in thought, and that thought is an activity rather than an unchanging state of being. The sympathy Caird exhibits for Hegel's philosophy of nature in this article is particularly striking given the reservations about that part of Hegel's system that Caird had expressed earlier that year in *Hegel*.

In 1885 Caird published *The Social Philosophy and Religion of Comte,* a revision of four articles that had appeared in *The Contemporary Review* in 1879. Caird seeks to establish that the French positivist Auguste Comte was logically precluded from professing his "religion of Humanity" without also professing the "religion of God" that he rejected. Most notable throughout this work is Caird's determination to see merit in a system with which he has profound disagreements.

In 1886 Caird filed a lawsuit against William S. Sime, who had published, in the guise of a study aid, lithographs of notes taken of Caird's lectures by a former Glasgow undergraduate. Caird's complaint was upheld by the House of Lords on 13 June 1887. He pursued the matter because he believed that the academic profession would be harmed by the appearance of such unapproved materials.

Caird begins *The Moral Aspect of the Economical Problem: Presidential Address to the Ethical Society. January*

Caird's wife, Caroline, circa 1912

10, 1887 (1888) by noting that young people are taking up the study of economics in greater numbers than ever before, and that they are particularly fascinated with the ethical and social aspects of "the dismal science." He cautions that poorly informed zeal is dangerous in efforts for social reform, and that thorough empirical research, as well as clear moral principles, are required if beneficial changes are to be made in complex socioeconomic situations. The problem of socialism, he says, is "to level up, to make and keep society organic, and not to let any individual or class fall out of the ranks." He attacks Carlyle for romanticizing the "thraldom" of the past and argues that although individualism may have undermined social unity, social unity is worthless unless based on intelligent obedience to the citizens' own laws. Capitalism needs to be tempered by state action, but there can be no general a priori answer to the question of how this tempering should be achieved. Caird notes "the general principle which should be kept in view in discussing such proposals, namely, that the aid which society gives to individuals cannot be a real aid unless it be such as to call out and stimulate their individual energy." Capitalism might crush the lives of some workers, but the total removal of this danger would be possible only at the cost of crushing all chance for individual self-expression and development. The Poor Law is a necessary safety net, "but we are obliged to surround such relief with disagreeable accidents to make it safe." He notes that "competition is as necessary to human development as association," because society is an organism that lives and grows only in the lives and relationships of its members. Caird concludes with a call for the young to learn from past theories of political economy and then go beyond them. The isolation of one area of human life for study must be corrected by bringing the lessons gained there into contact with the lessons of all other spheres of human knowledge.

Clearly, Caird conceived of his radicalism as having its philosophical foundations in his Hegelianism. In "On Pfleiderer's 'The Development of Theology in Germany since Kant, and Its Progress in Great Britain since 1825'" (1891) he criticizes Otto Pfleiderer for arguing that the fundamental doctrine of Hegelian idealism—"the real is the rational, and the rational is the real"—is inherently conservative. Instead, Caird argues, "if Dr. Pfleiderer's book proves anything, it proves that that doctrine is the most revolutionary of all doctrines, because it is the very principle of all progress which finds the roots of the future in the present."

In 1888 Caird helped to found the Women's Protective and Provident League to improve the working lives of women and children. His active involvement with the league continued only until he left Glasgow in 1893, but during that relatively short time he achieved much of practical value and helped to set the tone of an important national organization.

Twelve years after his first book-length study of Kant, Caird published *The Critical Philosophy of Immanuel Kant* (1889). There are many overlaps between this work and *A Critical Account of the Philosophy of Kant*, including the verbatim reproduction of some text. The two works differ markedly in scope, however. In 1877 Caird examined only Kant's epistemology; in the later book he traces out the interconnections of all of the main branches of Kant's philosophy: epistemology, ethics, aesthetics, critique of teleological judgment (the imputing of purpose to nature), and philosophy of religion. The work comprises more than 1,200 pages, of which epistemology occupies

only about a fifth. Caird argues that the dualism of noumena and phenomena that is at the heart of Kant's epistemology is transcended in the rest of his philosophy. In ethics, for example, "in so far as we live morally, we live as inhabitants of the ideal world we think, and treat it as the only real world." Caird thinks that the thrust of Kant's philosophy as a whole, in spite of his intentions, points to a Hegelian reconciliation of the noumenal and phenomenal worlds. Kant's tendency to abstract from phenomena leads him to an empty formalism rather than to synthetic "concretion," which is "a process in which we recognise, behind and beneath experience, certain elements of which it does not usually take account; though without these elements experience could not apprehend anything, and for want of the consciousness of them it does not comprehend anything as it really is." Despite his claims to the contrary, Kant frequently steps beyond his purely analytic role and attempts to correct and deepen the initial conception of the world through such a synthetic process. In doing so, he is better than his professed analytic aims. Caird contends that Kant's synthetic philosophizing constitutes his main permanently valuable contribution and led to the German idealist philosophies developed by Fichte, Hegel, and Friedrich Wilhelm Joseph von Schelling.

In spite of its depth and erudition, the work attracted some criticism. An anonymous reviewer in *The Athenæum* described Caird's book as "ponderous," derivative, and marked by an "intolerable diffuseness" and attacked almost everything in it, from Caird's arguments to his use of "will" and "shall." In contrast, Seth's review in *Mind* (1890) described the work as "in many ways the culmination of the long English endeavour to assimilate Kant. It is the result of a study of Kant, such as perhaps no Englishman will again undertake, and is in every way a thorough and masterly performance." Perhaps the most significant response came from Alexander Bain, a leading British empiricist who, though largely hostile to Kantianism, acknowledged to Caird in a 2 April 1890 letter that his treatment of Kant was superior to anything that had previously appeared on the subject.

Seth ended his review of *The Critical Philosophy of Kant* with a call for Caird to undertake "the working out of" an independent "philosophical position in the role of a Gifford lecturer." Caird was, in fact, soon appointed to this prestigious position; his lectures were published in an augmented and slightly revised form as *The Evolution of Religion: The Gifford Lectures Delivered before the University of St. Andrews in Sessions 1890–91 and 1891–92* (1893). Using a dialectical method, he traces the growth of religion from its objective stage in ancient Greece through its subjective stage in Buddhism, Stoicism, and Judaism to the most adequate–though still imperfect–reconciliation of these moments in Christianity:

> our highest moral and social ideal–reached, as it has been, as the result of all the thought and labour and pain of humanity in the past–is not visionary or illusive, but may be taken as our best key to the nature of the universe of which we are a part, and to the nature of the Divine Being who is its source and its end. And it derives from this a deeper consciousness of the nearness of God to man, a confirmation of the Christian faith that the kingdom of heaven is in the midst of us, and that the service of humanity is the true and the only service of God.

Absolute idealism is the first system of thought to apprehend that the true spirituality of the world necessitates a rational, rather than an imaginative, faith. Moreover, this "new Christianity" necessarily takes one of its main tasks to be the relief of the moral and material condition of the poor.

J. M. E. McTaggart said in his 1893 notice of the published lectures in *Mind* that "it would be difficult to overestimate the importance of" Caird's analysis, although he criticizes Caird's reading of Hegel as unduly unsympathetic. Alfred W. Benn predicted in his 1 April 1893 review in *The Academy* that the book "will, I think, take rank not only as the best Gifford Lectures that have yet been published, but also as, so far, its accomplished author's most important work, and the most valuable contribution made to speculative theology for many years past." *The Athenaeum* reviewer, however, wrote that it "seems to be enough for his purpose if he can somehow identify the ghost of Christianity with the phantom of Hegelianism" and called Caird's use of the concept of evolution "facile." In *The Philosophical Review* (1894) James Seth was also skeptical about Caird's Hegelianism; nevertheless, he described Caird's lectures as "not only a notable contribution to the subject" but also "as its author's most independent and constructive work." He welcomed the fact that "Professor Caird has at last got away from Kant."

Jowett died on 1 October 1893, and Caird was appointed his successor as master of Balliol in November. His election was opposed by some, and the opposition did not end until some time into his tenure. His main opponent was J. L. Strachan-Davidson, who had been an undergraduate with Caird at Balliol. Caird himself had reservations about moving south to Oxford after twenty-seven years in Glasgow. Nevertheless, he took up the post in the summer term of 1894 and appointed Strachan-Davidson to run the

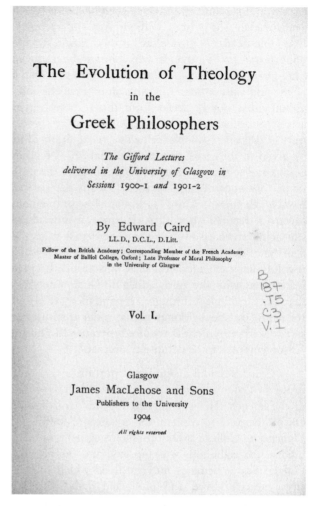

The Evolution of Theology

in the

Greek Philosophers

*The Gifford Lectures
delivered in the University of Glasgow in
Sessions 1900-1 and 1901-2*

By Edward Caird
LL.D., D.C.L., D.Litt.
Fellow of the British Academy; Corresponding Member of the French Academy
Master of Balliol College, Oxford; Late Professor of Moral Philosophy
in the University of Glasgow

Vol. I.

Glasgow
James MacLehose and Sons
Publishers to the University
1904
All rights reserved

Title page for the work in which Caird traces the development of the concept of God from Plato through Aristotle, the Stoics, and the Neo-Platonists to St. Augustine (Thomas Cooper Library, University of South Carolina)

routine business of the college. His lectures were well attended, but he was criticized for concentrating on teaching and pastoral work rather than on promoting the interests of the college within the university. In 1897 Caird was a candidate for the Whyte's Professorship of Moral Philosophy, which had once been held by Green and became vacant on the death of Wallace, another friend of Caird's. Caird failed to secure the professorship.

In 1897 Caird delivered the inaugural address to the Civic Society of Glasgow; it was published that same year as *Individualism and Socialism*. "Logically carried out," he says, individualism "can be nothing less than anarchism," and socialism would be "social despotism." There must be a reconciliation of the two positions. Caird argues for a sphere of "individual energy and resolution" in which each person is left to act as he or she wishes without state interference. Everyone needs "control over his own earnings," the opportunity for "a career in which he can be useful to himself and to society," and the opportunity to own a house and raise a family. At the same time, the individual must not be freed from the responsibilities arising out of such opportunities. "That is the *essential truth of Individualism.*" Nevertheless, recognition must be given to the social and political nature of human beings and to the fact that efficiency requires the public performance of certain tasks. "This is the *essential truth of Socialism.*" Caird sees the slow movement toward a reconciliation of socialism and individualism being powered by "the great idea" that rules the age: "the idea of organic evolution." He condemns revolutionary change because it fails to fill the new institutions with the spirit and individual "energies" that are developed through acquaintance with and reflection on the workings of the older institutions. Gradual development is required, because the future "is too complex to be definitely forecast."

Caird devoted a significant portion of his time to the sort of gradual social reform that he advocated in the speech. He campaigned for the awarding of Oxford degrees to women, the creation of the liberal Manchester College at Oxford, the recognition of labor unions, the eight-hour working day, and the national Universities Settlements movement, in which university graduates lived and interacted daily with the poor. In 1899 he took controversial stands against the Boer War and the awarding of an honorary degree to the African colonialist Cecil Rhodes. Near the end of 1901 he joined Henry Scott Holland in trying to persuade the Church of England to condemn the incarceration of Boer civilians in concentration camps.

On 14 May 1903 Caird read a paper to the British Academy titled "Idealism and the Theory of Knowledge." Published in the *Proceedings* of the academy, it is one of the best succinct defenses of late-nineteenth-century absolute idealism. "We cannot play the game of thought, if one might use such an expression," he says, "without taking our stand upon the idea that the world is a self-consistent and intelligible whole." This idea must be presupposed by all science and philosophy; nevertheless, it is based on "faith," because it is "a principle the complete vindication or realisation of which is for us impossible; for, obviously, nothing short of omniscience could grasp the world as a complete system." It is impossible to say how complete human knowledge is capable of becoming, but its ultimate unity must be presupposed if progress is to be made at all.

Caird returned to the University of Glasgow during the 1900–1901 and 1901–1902 sessions to deliver his second two series of Gifford lectures. They were published in a revised and enlarged form in two volumes as *The Evolution of Theology in the Greek Philosophers* (1904). Caird notes that philosophy first emerged as a distinct intellectual activity in ancient Greece. Although earlier Indian thought was "often subtle and profound," it remained "unmethodical." Aristotle was the first to conceptualize God as the moving principle of the universe; this epochal step made it possible to recognize that all mental activities presuppose "the idea of an all-comprehensive whole." Caird argues that "to believe in God is, in the last resort, simply to realise that there is a principle of unity in that whole, akin to that which gives unity to our own existence as self-conscious beings." He traces the development of theology from the post-Aristotelians through the Stoics and the Neo-Platonists and closes with an examination of the influence of Greek thought on Christianity through St. Augustine.

The book met with widespread, if always qualified, approval. In *Mind* (1905) R. P. Hardie raised questions about certain points of interpretation but concluded that all "students of Greek philosophy will be grateful to Mr. Caird for this brilliant work." In *The Quarterly Review* (1906) F. C. S. Schiller welcomed the book, while criticizing its narrow focus. Reverent praise was paid, in a 1904 notice in *The Athenæum,* and H. N. Gardiner claimed in *The Philosophical Review* (1905) that "since [James Frederick] Ferrier's lectures on Greek philosophy, probably no work has appeared by an English writer, treating of the same general theme," that was "so illuminative and inspiring."

In 1905 Caird suffered a paralytic stroke. His wife tried to restore his health by taking him on an extended tour of Italy, but he never fully recovered. After developing Bright's disease, Caird resigned his mastership on 18 March 1907; his place was taken by Strachan-Davidson.

Caird's final volume, *Lay Sermons and Addresses: Delivered in the Hall of Balliol College, Oxford,* a collection of twelve speeches delivered between 1893 and 1905, was published in 1907. Here he reiterates many of his earlier themes, including the nature of spiritual development and the need for a rational faith in God rather than an uncritical reliance on religious authorities. He also expresses a firm belief in the orthodox doctrine of spiritual immortality.

Caird died at home on 1 November 1908. He is buried in St. Sepulchre's Cemetery, Oxford.

Caird has suffered from the general neglect of British idealism that began at the end of World War

I. Moreover, he did not revel in exposing the errors of other philosophers but sought to highlight what he believed to be of value, and his consequently understated writing style has not attracted much mainstream philosophical interest. Sarah Belinda Paddle's 1986 dissertation, "Edward Caird (1835–1908): Religion, Philosophy and Education," is an examination of the links between Caird's social reformism and his philosophy. Caird looms large in Alan P. F. Sell's important study of British idealist religious thought, *Philosophical Idealism and Christian Belief* (1995). *The Collected Works of Edward Caird,* edited by Colin Tyler, was published in 1999. Volume one includes an introduction by Tyler on Caird's evolutionary conception of the Absolute, a subject also treated in a 2000 essay by William J. Mander.

Biographies:

Henry Jones and John H. Muirhead, *The Life and Philosophy of Edward Caird* (Glasgow: MacLehose, Jackson, 1921);

Sarah Belinda Paddle, "Edward Caird (1835–1908): Religion, Philosophy and Education," dissertation, Queen Mary College, University of London, 1986.

References:

Robert MacKintosh, *Hegel and Hegelianism* (Edinburgh: Clark, 1903);

William J. Mander, ed., *Anglo-American Idealism, 1865–1927* (Westport, Conn. & London: Greenwood Press, 2000)—includes "Caird's Developmental Absolutism," by Mander; "Caird on Kant and the Refutation of Skepticism," by Phillip Ferreira; and "Caird, Watson, and the Reconciliation of Opposites," by Elizabeth Trott;

Rudolf Metz, *A Hundred Years of British Philosophy,* translated by John W. Harvey, Thomas E. Jessop, and Henry Sturt, edited by John H. Muirhead (London: Allen & Unwin, 1938), pp. 254, 288;

Alan P. F. Sell, *Philosophical Idealism and Christian Belief* (Cardiff: University of Wales Press, 1995);

Colin Tyler, "The Evolution of the Epistemic Self: A Critique of the Evolutionary Epistemology of Thomas Hill Green and His Followers," *Bradley Studies,* 4 (Autumn 1998).

Papers:

Major collections of Edward Caird's papers are at the University of Glasgow and at Balliol College, Oxford University.

R. G. Collingwood

(22 February 1889 – 9 January 1943)

David Boucher
Cardiff University

BOOKS: *Religion and Philosophy* (London: Macmillan, 1916);

Ruskin's Philosophy: An Address Delivered at the Ruskin Centenary Conference, Coniston, August 8th, 1919 (Kendal: Wilson, 1922);

Roman Britain (Oxford: Clarendon Press, 1923; revised and enlarged, 1932; revised and enlarged again, 1934);

Ambleside Roman Fort (Ambleside: Printed by George Middleton, St. Oswald Press, 1924);

Speculum Mentis; or, The Map of Knowledge (Oxford: Clarendon Press, 1924);

Outlines of a Philosophy of Art (London: Oxford University Press, 1925);

The Roman Signal-Station on Castle Hill, Scarborough (Scarborough: Printed for the Corporation of Scarborough by E. T. W. Dennis & Sons, 1925);

Roman Inscriptions and Sculptures Belonging to the Society of Antiquaries of Newcastle upon Tyne (Newcastle upon Tyne: Northumberland Press, 1926);

A Guide to the Chesters Museum (Newcastle upon Tyne: Reid, 1926);

A Guide to the Roman Wall (Newcastle upon Tyne: Reid, 1926);

Faith and Reason: A Study of the Relations between Religion and Science (London: Benn, 1928);

Roman Eskdale (Whitehaven: Whitehaven News, 1929);

The Archaeology of Roman Britain (London: Methuen, 1930; New York: Lincoln MacVeagh, Dial, 1930);

The Philosophy of History, Historical Association leaflet, no. 79 (London: Published for the Historical Association by G. Bell & Sons, 1930);

The Book of the Pilgrimage of Hadrian's Wall, July 1st to 4th, 1930 (Kendal: Wilson, 1930);

Philosophical Essays, 2 volumes (Oxford: Clarendon Press, 1933, 1940)—comprises volume 1, *An Essay on Philosophical Method;* and volume 2, *An Essay on Metaphysics;*

R. G. Collingwood *(photograph by Lafayette)*

The Historical Imagination: An Inaugural Lecture Delivered before the University of Oxford on 28 October 1935 (Oxford: Clarendon Press, 1935);

Roman Britain and the English Settlements, by Collingwood and J. N. L. Myres, The Oxford History of England, volume 1 (Oxford: Clarendon Press, 1936; revised, 1937);

The Principles of Art (Oxford: Clarendon Press, 1938; New York: Oxford University Press, 1958);

An Autobiography (Oxford: Clarendon Press, 1939; London & New York: Oxford University Press, 1939);

The First Mate's Log of a Voyage to Greece in the Schooner Yacht Fleur de Lys *in 1939* (London: Oxford University Press, 1939);

The Three Laws of Politics: Read before the London School of Economics at the Mill Lane Lecture Rooms, Cambridge, by A. M. Carr-Saunders, M.A., on 7 May 1941, Hobhouse Memorial Trust Lectures, no. 11 (London: H. Milford, Oxford University Press, 1941);

The New Leviathan; or, Man, Society, Civilization, and Barbarism (Oxford: Clarendon Press, 1942; Westport, Conn.: Greenwood Press, 1984);

The Idea of Nature, edited by T. Malcolm Knox (London: Oxford University Press, 1945);

The Idea of History, edited by Knox (Oxford: Clarendon Press, 1946; New York: Oxford University Press, 1956);

Essays in the Philosophy of Art, edited by Alan Donagan (Bloomington & London: Indiana University Press, 1964);

Essays in the Philosophy of History, edited by William Debbins (Austin: University of Texas Press, 1965; New York & London: McGraw-Hill, 1966);

The Roman Inscriptions of Britain, volume 1: *Inscriptions on Stone,* by Collingwood and R. P. Wright (Oxford: Clarendon Press, 1965);

Faith and Reason: Essays in the Philosophy of Religion, edited by Lionel Rubinoff (Chicago: Quadrangle, 1967);

Essays in Political Philosophy, edited by David Boucher (Oxford: Clarendon Press / New York: Oxford University Press, 1989);

The Roman Inscriptions of Britain, volume 2, 8 fascicules, by Collingwood and Wright, edited by S. S. Frere and R. S. O. Tomlin (Stroud: Published by Alan Sutton for the Administrators of the Haverfield Bequest, 1991–1995);

The Idea of History: With Lectures 1926–1928, edited by Jan van der Dussen (Oxford: Clarendon Press, 1993);

Letters from Iceland and Other Essays, edited by Boucher and Bruce Haddock, Collingwood Studies, volume 3 (Swansea: R. G. Collingwood Society, 1996);

An Essay on Metaphysics: Revised Edition. With The Nature of Metaphysical Study, Function of Metaphysics in Civilization, Notes for an Essay on Logic, edited by Rex Martin (Oxford: Clarendon Press, 1998);

The Principles of History: And Other Writings in Philosophy of History, edited by van der Dussen and William H. Dray (Oxford: Clarendon Press, 1999; New York: Oxford University Press, 1999);

The Philosophy of Enchantment, edited by Boucher, Wendy James, and Philip Smallwood (Oxford: Clarendon Press, forthcoming, 2003).

Editions: *Faith & Reason: Essays in the Philosophy of Religion,* edited by Lionel Rubinoff (Chicago: Quadrangle, 1968);

The Archaeology of Roman Britain, edited by Ian Richmond (London: Methuen, 1969);

The New Leviathan; or, Man, Society, Civilization, and Barbarism, edited by David Boucher (Oxford: Clarendon Press, 1992);

The First Mate's Log of a Voyage to Greece in the Schooner Yacht Fleur de Lys *in 1939,* introduction by Peter Johnson (Bristol: Thoemmes Press, 1994).

OTHER: *The Fothergill Omnibus: For Which Eighteen Eminent Authors Have Written Short Stories upon One and the Same Plot,* introductions by Collingwood, John Fothergill, and Gerald Gould (London: Eyre & Spottiswoode, 1931);

An Economic Survey of Ancient Rome, 6 volumes, edited by Collingwood, Tenney Frank, T. R. S. Broughton, A. Grenier, and others (Baltimore: Johns Hopkins Press, 1933–1940)–includes in volume 3, "Roman Britain," by Collingwood;

J. Collingwood Bruce, *The Handbook to the Roman Wall: A Guide to Tourists Traversing the Barrier of the Lower Isthmus,* edited by Collingwood (Newcastle upon Tyne: A. Reid / London: Longmans, Green, 1933).

TRANSLATIONS: Benedetto Croce, *The Philosophy of Giambattista Vico* (London: Allen & Unwin, 1913; New York: Macmillan, 1913);

Guido de Ruggiero, *Modern Philosophy,* translated by Collingwood and A. Howard Hannay (London: Allen & Unwin, 1921; New York: Macmillan, 1921);

Croce, *Aesthetics as Science and Expression and General Linguistics,* second edition, translated by Douglas Ainslie, translation revised by Collingwood (London: Macmillan, 1922);

Croce, *An Autobiography* (Oxford: Clarendon Press, 1927);

de Ruggiero, *The History of European Liberalism* (London & New York: Oxford University Press, 1927).

R. G. Collingwood was one of the last of the great polymaths; his range of interests was truly remarkable. He is largely remembered for his philosophy of history and his aesthetics, but he also wrote extensively on religion, philosophical method, conceptions of nature, political philosophy, metaphysics, ethics–and fairy tales. As pastimes he composed music, played the piano and the violin, painted, did woodwork and bookbinding, and sailed. Archaeology is often described as another of his hobbies, but this characterization undervalues his

*Collingwood (at right) at an archaeological dig site on
Hadrian's Wall in 1929*

contributions to the field: he was the world's leading authority on Roman inscriptions in Britain and was consulted by museums for advice on their collections. Before he became Waynflete Professor of Metaphysical Philosophy at the University of Oxford, he was a university lecturer there in both philosophy and Roman history. He published hundreds of journal articles on archaeology, as well as several book-length surveys that became immensely popular, including *Roman Britain and the English Settlements* (1936), co-authored with J. N. L. Myres, in the Oxford History of England series. His obituary in *The New York Times* referred to him exclusively as a famous archaeologist of Roman Britain. His reputation as a philosopher was slow to take off, partly because he was a proponent (at least in his early work) of a point of view that was on the wane in Britain—

philosophical idealism—and because the book for which he is best known, *The Idea of History* (1946), was not published until three years after his death. His style of philosophizing was compatible with modern analytic philosophy, however, and adherents of that movement soon found much in Collingwood's work that was original and insightful. The analytic philosophers Alan Donagan, William H. Dray, A. J. M. Milne, and Rex Martin were largely responsible for the first Collingwood revival in the 1960s and 1970s, which was supported by the interest of authors inspired by the Continental tradition in philosophy, including such pioneers as Nathan Rottenstreich, Leon Goldstein, Louis O. Mink, and Lionel Rubinoff. Jan van der Dussen's *History as a Science* (1981) gave a comprehensive indication of what was to be found in the newly deposited manuscripts in the Bodleian Library and precipitated a second wave of interest that brought Collingwood's political philosophy into sharp focus for the first time.

The passion for breadth of learning that is the hallmark of Collingwood's works was inspired by the Victorian-era essayist and critic John Ruskin, who thought that a necessary preliminary to theorizing about a subject was to become completely immersed in it. Robin George Collingwood was born on 22 February 1889 in Gillhead, Cartmel Fell, in the Lake District, to William Gershom Collingwood, an artist, writer, and archaeologist, and Edith Mary Isaacs Collingwood, an artist and pianist. Collingwood's father was Ruskin's secretary; in 1891 he moved his family to within a mile of Ruskin's home at Brantwood, where he wrote *The Life and Work of John Ruskin* (1893). W. G. Collingwood was also a member of William Morris's circle, designed Celtic crosses, and wrote imitations of Norse sagas. He went on an extensive painting tour of Iceland in 1897; many of his watercolors, which constitute some of the few records of the Icelandic landscape in the late nineteenth century, are in the National Museum of Iceland.

Until he was thirteen, Collingwood was educated at home, principally by his father; his mother and his three sisters, Dora, Barbara, and Ursula, also contributed. Two or three hours were set aside each morning for formal lessons, including Greek, Latin, and ancient and modern history. He learned to read and write ancient and modern languages and to sing, play the piano, and draw and paint–all skills that he practiced in his adult life. He and his sisters produced a weekly family magazine, painted their own Christmas cards, and were prodigious writers of letters. During this time Collingwood, on his own initiative, developed his passions for philosophy and natural science. He did, however, share many of the interests of boys his age. In letters of 3 and 10 April 1900 to Beatrice Willink, a family friend, he conveys his enthusiasm for Lord Robert Baden-Powell's Boy Scout manual, especially its instructions for measuring the height of trees and the breadth of rivers. He also includes his own drawings of the hoof-prints of horses walking, cantering, and galloping.

At thirteen Collingwood was sent to a preparatory school at Grange; a year later he enrolled at Rugby School. Public school failed to stimulate his natural inquisitiveness, and he devoted himself to independent study of such subjects as medieval Italian history and early French poetry.

In 1908 Collingwood entered University College of the University of Oxford, where his father had been tutored by the philosopher Bernard Bosanquet. There he was finally able to indulge his insatiable appetite for learning. He became semireclusive, reading all day and most of the night on any subject that attracted his atten-

tion. At this time he developed the insomnia that contributed to his later poor health. In 1910 he took a first in Classical Moderations and in 1912 a first in *Literae Humaniores*. He was elected to a philosophy fellowship at Pembroke College in 1912.

When World War I broke out in 1914, Collingwood was drafted into the intelligence unit of the Admiralty. Fearing that he might die in the war before he had the chance to commit his views to print, Collingwood wrote *Religion and Philosophy* (1916), in which he tries to bring religion and philosophy into a closer relationship. The reader of the manuscript for the publisher, Macmillan, commented that he wondered why Collingwood did not take holy orders.

In 1918 Collingwood returned to his fellowship at Pembroke College, but he vacated it that same year to marry Ethel Winifred Graham. He was soon reelected to the fellowship and became the first Pembroke fellow to obtain permission to live outside the college. After a brief period in North Oxford, the Collingwoods moved to Stapleton's Chantry in Moreton, near Didcott. During school terms Collingwood spent four nights in the college and the weekends at home. Between terms he was a prodigious traveler; his notebooks in the Ashmolean Museum at Oxford show that as soon as a term ended he would travel from one archaeological site to another–sometimes to three or four in a day. Ethel was also a keen archaeologist and sometimes accompanied him. They had two children, William Robert, born in 1919, and Ursula Ruth, born in 1921. In 1924 Collingwood published *Speculum Mentis; or, The Map of Knowledge,* in which he separates religion from philosophy and places both in a hierarchy of "forms of experience." A form of experience for Collingwood is a way of viewing the world based on unquestioned postulates that ultimately prove to be contradictory and thus give rise to a new form of experience. These forms–which include religion, philosophy, art, science, and history–are logically related to one another in a linked hierarchy. Each form has both a theoretical and a practical side. Art, for example, is pure imagination for Collingwood, while its form of action is play. The most comprehensive form is philosophy, which overcomes the limitations of the four special forms.

Between 1924 and 1933 Collingwood assisted his father as joint editor of *Transactions of the Cumberland and Westmoreland Antiquarian and Archaeological Society.* In 1927 he became university lecturer in philosophy and Roman history at Oxford.

In 1933 Collingwood published *An Essay on Philosophical Method.* Here he argues, in opposition to the early views of the analytic philosopher Ludwig Wittgenstein, that theory and practice overlap, and that philosophy has to do more than describe current linguistic usage. Examining current usage is only the preliminary stage in defining a concept. The aim of philosophy is to know better something that is already understood. This view was also that of analytic philosophers such as G. E. Moore and Bertrand Russell, but their method was quite different from Collingwood's. For them, each subject had to be broken down into its structure and components. Collingwood thought that this method was regressive. Instead, he was concerned with the postulates, principles, and presuppositions from which conclusions are drawn. In contrast with the analytic philosophers, Collingwood undertook philosophical study because of its practical value.

In 1934 Collingwood was elected a fellow of the British Academy, and in 1935 he was appointed Waynflete Professor of Metaphysical Philosophy. A gifted teacher, he took singing lessons to improve the projection of his voice in the lecture hall. His lectures became so popular that they were moved from Pembroke to a college with a larger hall to accommodate the audience. Many of his books originated in his lectures, and he clarified his thoughts in tutorials. He preferred to try out his theories on undergraduates rather than present them to his colleagues.

In *The Principles of Art* (1938) Collingwood equates art with the expression of emotion and argues that a successful work of art is one in which the artist shows the audience the expression in itself. He differentiates art from pseudoarts such as magic and amusement, where "magic" encompasses superstitions and folk practices involving elements of enchantment, the primitive survivals of which are still a part of modern life. While magic and amusement have essential roles to play in society, the dominance of either has serious consequences for the future of civilization. Collingwood says that magic has been mistakenly viewed as primitive bad science; as a result, its importance has been undervalued and its influence has been suppressed. Thus, the ritualized and conventionally accepted ways of discharging emotions into practical activities have been undermined. Similarly, the role of amusement has been misunderstood: instead of being seen as an aspect of a healthy society, a way in which emotions are discharged in the amusement itself, it has come to be seen as the dominant purpose of life, the end to which all of one's activities should be directed.

In *The Principles of Art* Collingwood argues that sensations, or "sensa," and the emotions that accompany them are not two separate experiences: a person who is terrified of the dark is not experiencing the sensation of darkness and the emotion of fear but a terrifying darkness. Sensa are immediate and fleeting; if connections are to be made among them, one must be able to retain and recall them. Consciousness converts

sensa into imagination; that is, imagination is what sensa become when one is conscious of them. The intellect then establishes relationships between the converted sensa. Sensa are categorized into those one wishes to acknowledge and those that one does not by means of selective attention. Consciousness also converts emotions into imagination; if it fails to do so, and the emotion is, therefore, not expressed, the intellect will receive distorted emotional expressions and will build thought on them. Collingwood calls this process the "corruption of consciousness."

Collingwood suffered a series of strokes in 1938 and was forced to take a long period off for recuperation. In June he took his nineteen-foot sailing yacht *Zenocrates* down the Thames and around the south coast of England. The boat was wrecked in a storm off Deal; Collingwood was rescued by the Walmer Lifeboat. He spent the early part of 1939 as a paying passenger on a cargo steamer sailing to the East Indies. On this journey he corrected the proofs for *An Autobiography* (1939) and rewrote the last chapter; completed *An Essay on Metaphysics* (1940); and wrote forty thousand words of *The Principles of History: And Other Writings in Philosophy of History* (1999).

In *An Autobiography,* which traces the development of his thought rather than his life, Collingwood works out his doctrine of the importance of questioning. Reporting the conclusions that he had worked out in two unpublished works—"Truth and Contradiction," written in 1917, and "Libellus de Generatione," written in 1920—he argues that "Whether a given proposition is true or false, significant or meaningless, depends on what question it was meant to answer; and any one who wishes to know whether a given proposition is true or false, significant or meaningless, must find out what question it was meant to answer." The meaning of a statement can only be grasped fully in relation to the question it is meant to answer; it follows that no two propositions can be contradictory unless they are answers to the same question. Statements have to be seen as integral aspects of question-and-answer complexes. The logic of question and answer is at the heart of Collingwood's claim that there are no perennial problems in philosophy: questions arise in specific contexts, and those regarding, for example, the ancient Greek city-state are necessarily different from those relating to the seventeenth-century nation-state.

In late 1939 Collingwood joined a group of undergraduates in chartering a boat, the *Fleur-de-Lys,* in the Mediterranean. He gives an account of the journey and his views on ethics, social history, and a variety of other subjects in *The First Mate's Log of a Voyage to Greece in the Schooner Yacht* Fleur de Lys *in 1939* (1940).

An Essay on Metaphysics is an attempt to rescue metaphysics from the criticisms of the logical empiricist A. J. Ayer. Ayer identified statements such as "there is a nonempirical world of values" and "people have immortal souls" as pseudopropositions; since they are neither logical tautologies nor empirically verifiable, they have no meaning and are neither true nor false. For Collingwood, on the contrary, these statements are "absolute presuppositions" that provide the foundation of thought. In Collingwood's view, Ayer had correctly exposed metaphysical statements as lacking the features of propositions; but Ayer had not gone on to determine what sort of statements they were. Since metaphysical propositions are neither true by definition nor empirically verifiable, they fall, for Collingwood, into a third category of statements, to which the question of truth and falsity is inapplicable. Absolute presuppositions are not like propositions, which are answers to questions; and they are not derived from experience. They are "catalytic agents which the mind must bring out of its own resources to the manipulation of what is called 'experience' and the conversion of it into science and civilization." Absolute, or ultimate, presuppositions, not being propositions, are never disproved; when they cease to be useful, they are simply replaced by others.

Collingwood resigned his chair at Oxford in 1941 on grounds of ill health. He returned to his late parents' home, Lanehead in Coniston, not with his wife but with Kathleen Edwardes. In 1942 the Collingwoods were divorced, and Collingwood and Edwardes were married; they had a daughter, Teresa. Also in 1942 Collingwood published *The New Leviathan; or, Man, Society, Civilization, and Barbarism.*

From his first book to his last Collingwood was determined to show that the mind is indistinguishable from its activities. In *Religion and Philosophy* he maintained that the dualism of thought and action is false: "the mind *is* what it *does.*" In *The New Leviathan* he anticipates Gilbert Ryle's better-known discussion in *The Concept of Mind* (1949) by tracing the problem to the seventeenth-century French philosopher René Descartes, who held that the mind inhabits the body in much the same way as a person inhabits a house. Thinking that a person is part material body and part immaterial mind or soul gives rise to the unanswerable question of the relationship in which body and mind stand to each other. According to Collingwood, the person is wholly mind or wholly body depending on whether the mode of understanding employed is that of the natural or that of the human sciences. The relationship between the two modes of understanding, not that between body and mind, constitutes the legitimate, as opposed to the false, philosophical problem.

As its title, which refers to Thomas Hobbes's *Leviathan* (1651), suggests, *The New Leviathan* is primarily a work of political philosophy; the title was originally conceived as the subtitle of a book that was to be called "The Principles of Politics." Collingwood's goal is to provide the social-contract theory with an historical dimension. Freedom, he says, is the essence of mind, cultivated by reason, gradually eliminating caprice from rational choice. Free rational choice, or self-determination, is hindered by force. While force can never be entirely eliminated from the body politic, the ideal of civility assumes its gradual reduction, first among members of the same community, then between communities, and finally between human beings and the rest of nature. A continuous process of conversion from the nonsocial to the social condition occurs within the body politic as the ruling class is constantly replenished by the ruled. Though Collingwood's is an historical philosophy, it is not relativist: reason, defined as the gradual elimination of caprice; freedom, conceived as the capacity for rational choice; and civility, viewed as the gradual reduction of force, constitute universal criteria by which to judge civilizations and the degree to which barbarism—that is, the conscious subversion of these ideals—is present in them. Rational government by majority rule presupposes rationality in the governed, and the principal obligation of a modern democratic state is to provide a sufficient level of education to meet the requirement. Collingwood's recognition that there will always be an element in society that has to be ruled without the presumption of consent—what he calls the "nonsocial community"—an element that coexists with, but is outside of, society, is an important consideration that is generally overlooked in contractarian theories.

The strokes Collingwood had suffered had impressed on him the likelihood of an early death, and he drove himself to exhaustion to try to complete his life's work—thereby accelerating the process. Collingwood died of pneumonia at Lanehead on 9 January 1943. He had almost completed the revisions of *The Idea of Nature,* which was edited by T. Malcolm Knox and published in 1945.

The Idea of Nature, Knox suggests in his introduction, is Collingwood's attempt to apply the principles of *An Essay on Philosophical Method* to science and cosmology. *The Idea of Nature* analyzes the Greek, Renaissance, and modern concepts of nature, showing each to rest on a different analogy. For the Greeks nature was an intelligent organism. The Renaissance viewed nature as a vast complex mechanism with God as its creator, on the model of human beings as creators of machines. The modern conception of nature is based on the analogy of historical process: "Modern cosmology could

THE
IDEA OF HISTORY

BY

R. G. COLLINGWOOD

OXFORD
AT THE CLARENDON PRESS

Title page for Collingwood's best-known work, published three years after his death in 1943, in which he argues that the historian must reenact the past in his or her own mind in order to understand it (Thomas Cooper Library, University of South Carolina)

only have arisen from the widespread familiarity with historical studies, and in particular with historical studies of the kind which placed the conception of process, change, development at the centre of their picture and recognized it as the fundamental category of historical thought." Understanding nature thus requires an understanding of history. The modern idea of nature is historical in that change is conceived as progressive rather than cyclical; nature is no longer viewed as mechanical but as teleological (purposeful); and in both history and the evolutionary view of nature, structure or substance is resolved into function.

At the time of his death Collingwood had completed four chapters of what he considered his life's work, *The Principles of History;* but Knox disregarded Collingwood's instructions and incorporated a chapter of the manuscript for that work into *The Idea of History,* which he published in 1946.

The Idea of History is an exposition of the conditions required for attaining historical knowledge; it is not a speculative philosophy of history that claims to discern a pattern or meaning in past events. History, Collingwood says, is an organized body of knowledge based on rational principles and inferred from evidence. He agrees with the German historian Wilhelm Dilthey that human beings are at home everywhere in this historically understood world and that there is no meaning in it apart from that to be discerned in the activities of the actors in their interrelations with each other.

For Collingwood the past, in being known, is rethought or reenacted by the historian. History is not the mere satisfaction of idle curiosity about the past; history, for Collingwood, is equated with the mind's self-knowledge and the attainment of human freedom. Historical knowledge brings into view the full potential of human nature and better equips those who study it to respond appropriately to the situations they encounter in their own lives. No absolute distinction exists, then, between theory and practice: practice sets the problems out of which theory arises, and theory returns to practice in its conclusions. A false theoretical conception cannot help but have insidious implications for practice. Historical thinking is the key to defeating all types of barbarism and irrationalism, including fascism and Nazism. History prepares people to make the choices and shoulder the responsibilities that freedom entails.

Collingwood's archaeological work first impressed on him the importance of questioning in any form of knowledge: if one does not ask the right questions, then no human artifact can be made to reveal its mysteries. The historian is not simply a receptacle for data; the historian does not merely receive what is given in experience. It is up to the historian to take the initiative by asking the right questions and devising the means by which to make the evidence reveal what the historian wants to know. One has to discover the question that was in a person's mind when he or she created an artifact. Unless one knows the purpose of the object—that is, the reason the person had for producing it—one will be unable to understand what it is. A carved image, for example, may have a wide range of purposes. Only when one discovers that it is the answer to a question relating to religious worship or to voodoo can one understand it as an integral element in a ritual. Such considerations led Collingwood to make his famous, and often misunderstood, claim that all history is the history of thought.

This claim can be seen as part of Collingwood's relentless effort to overcome dualisms, particularly that between the mind and its objects. His principal instrument for doing so is the idea of reenactment. He distinguishes between the inside and outside of an event: the outside of an event is its physical properties, which can be subsumed under general laws. The inside is the thought that informs the manifestation that is seen as the outside of the event, which is unintelligible without it. The inside and outside together constitute human actions, which are the subject matter of history. The various phases in a natural process are separate and distinct: each phase falls outside of and supersedes the preceding ones. The past is part of a natural process; it dies in being replaced by the present. The historical process is quite different: the phases in an historical process are not separate. In becoming something new, mind does not cease to be what it was. Each stage in the development interpenetrates with the others. The past is, therefore, not dead but lives in the present by being rethought in the mind of the historian. The dualism between the mind of the historian and the objects of his or her thinking is overcome by reenacting the thoughts of past actors. Thought can be reenacted not because some sort of telepathic communication exists with minds of the past but because evidence of past thought survives in the present.

Collingwood's theory of "incapsulation" shows how the historian is able to differentiate his or her own thoughts from those that are being reenacted. Without this capacity, an historian thinking Napoleon's thoughts, for example, would be unable to differentiate himself or herself from Napoleon. Collingwood worked out the theory in a 1936 British Academy lecture that constitutes part 5, section 4 of *The Idea of History*. The theory depends on a distinction between thoughts and feelings, with the latter posited as the context in which the former occur. The category of feelings includes emotions and sensations. Rational purposive thoughts to which a criterion of success and failure can be applied are the subject matter of history; history, like aesthetics, is thus a "criteriological" science. Feelings are the subject matter of psychology, and psychology, as Collingwood says in *An Essay on Metaphysics*, is a non-criteriological science.

The distinction is, however, not easy to reconcile with Collingwood's major theories. *An Essay on Philosophical Method* depends on the idea that there are no absolute distinctions. The philosophical concept, he says there, is a combination of differences in degree and kind, as well as a fusion of opposites. It is an overlapping scale of forms in which each lower form embodies the generic essence of the concept as a constituent variable to a lesser extent than the one above it but contains nascent within itself what the higher attempts to be. If action, for example, is taken as the philosophical concept the generic essence of which is freedom of choice, entailing the absence of caprice, its different overlap-

ping forms are utility, right, and duty. The higher form negates the lower by being a more adequate and distinct expression of the lower but affirms it by taking the positive content of the lower up into itself and transforming it. Because the variable generic essence is a constituent of the concept, there can be no point at which it is absent; therefore, the scale of forms does not start at zero and end with its absolute opposite but starts with a unity in which the generic essence is present to the minimum degree. The distinction between feelings and thoughts in *The Idea of History* falls foul of what Collingwood calls in *An Essay on Philosophical Method* the "fallacy of precarious margins." For example, if mind is taken as the generic philosophical concept of which feelings and thoughts are species, one would soon find that an overlap occurs in which some human actions are a mixture of both. To get around the problem, the overlap can be ignored in favor of concentrating on the margin, where the overlap is not yet apparent. Such an approach assumes that the overlap between classes can be relied on not to spread and that the area beyond it is pure and exclusive to each class. The margin is precarious, because to admit the overlap in the first place is to renounce any grounds for expecting it not to spread.

Collingwood has sometimes been accused of an extreme methodological individualism in his understanding of history. Methodological individualism maintains that the actions of any collective or institution can be resolved into the thoughts, purposes, and intentions of the individuals who comprise them. For Collingwood, however, the individual mind is a product of society; society as a whole is reflected in the individuals who comprise it and is not merely the sum of its parts. He also says that it is important to recognize that historical outcomes occur without any one person necessarily intending them; and he talks about knowing the "corporate mind" or the spirit of an age. Although *The Idea of History* does not adequately explain how such collective entities are to be understood, it is clear that he did not wish to exclude them from the practice of history.

The Idea of History was the first full-scale philosophical study in English to attempt to establish the autonomy of historical understanding in opposition to the claims of positivism. No subsequent study has been able to ignore its conclusions, and the book has become a classic in the philosophy of history. The book that Collingwood saw as his life's work, however, *The Principles of History*, was never completed. The manuscript was discovered in 1995 in the archives of Oxford University Press; it was edited by Dray and van der Dussen and published in 1999.

Critics of *The Idea of History* have often thought that Collingwood attributes too high a degree of rationality and purposiveness to historical actors. Human beings are far from completely reasonable, they point out, and to restrict historical inquiry to intentional rational activity is to make it far too intellectualist. *The Principles of History* provides a much clearer picture of what Collingwood meant in restricting the subject matter of history to reflective thought. He does not claim that human beings are perfectly rational; he knows that they are only intermittently so. Nor does he wish to exclude unreasonable actions from historical investigation. It is not that unreasonable people do not have reasons for what they do: they simply have bad ones. Also, *The Principles of History* qualifies the view expressed in *The Idea of History* that past thoughts can be reenacted by the historian, but emotions cannot. In section 7, "The History of Thought," drawing on the theory of mind he put forward in *The Principles of Art*, Collingwood says that language, as the expression of rational thought, does not entirely exclude the emotions. Without elaborating the point in detail, Collingwood makes a distinction between essential and nonessential emotions. The former are necessarily bound up with the thoughts of the person who performs an action, and if one knows those thoughts, one knows the essential emotions that accompanied them. Thus, the claim he made in *The Idea of History*–that all history is the history of thought–is here extended to include the essential emotions.

In *The Idea of History* Collingwood also made the controversial claim that the historian does not rely on any other authority than himself and that his thought is, therefore, "autonomous, self-authorizing, possessed of a criterion to which his so-called authorities must conform and by reference to which they are criticised." At the most basic level this autonomy is expressed in the act of selection: no historian, however incompetent, simply reproduces authorities without engaging in selection. The historian, not the authorities, is responsible for what goes into the work of history.

Critics such as Rex Martin have called Collingwood's contention that the historian is his own criterion a form of radical subjectivism. In *The Principles of History* Collingwood clarifies his position. He argues that the relics that comprise evidence are not important in themselves but because of what they say and their relationship to what they mean. The actions studied by historians are the gestures, or their traces, that express thought, and expressions of thought are languages that can be read by those who are equipped to do so. An historian able to read them has to "reconstruct the gestures in his imagination and so reconstruct as an experience of his own the thought they express." The starting point of any historical investigation is not the evidence itself but what the historian, knowing the language, takes it to mean. The historian says, "I read this evi-

dence to be saying this rather than that," and it is in this respect that the historian is autonomous in relation to the evidence. The evidence, then, is not found but is made in the mind of the historian. By analogy, Collingwood says, it is not food as such that nourishes one; it is the body, which converts the food into energy, that does so. But not just any substance can be used as food. Similarly, if the digestive system is defective, no matter how wholesome the food, nutrition will not result. By the same token, not just any authorities or sources, only pertinent ones, serve as evidence for the well-attuned historical consciousness.

The account that Collingwood gives elsewhere in *The Principles of History* shows more clearly what he was trying to do in the chapter that was published in *The Idea of History*. According to Collingwood, whenever one engages in historical interpretation, one's a priori imagination inevitably comes into play; in other words, one's understanding always entails certain presuppositions without which a person's experience would be inconceivable, such as one's notions of space and time. Through a priori imagination one might be led to presume, for example, that evidence of a person being in Paris one day and Rome three days later precluded the possibility of travel by dematerializing in one place and materializing in another. Collingwood is not recommending that the historian employ his or her a priori imagination, nor is he suggesting that there is a choice to be made in such matters. He is asking: what happens to one each time one interprets a text? How the a priori imagination comes into play is a question of historical method; hence, the historian has to justify his or her reading of the evidence. In other words, historical method imposes on the historian's a priori imagination conditions to which the historical novelist's a priori imagination is not subject. Collingwood's doctrine is not, therefore, radical subjectivism; it is an acknowledgment of personal responsibility in interpretation.

Knox's omission from *The Idea of History* of Collingwood's discussion of the science of human nature disguises the extent to which *The Idea of History* and *An Essay on Metaphysics* are complementary texts. Both works are also closely allied to *The Principles of Art* in that history, metaphysics, and aesthetics are all criteriological sciences. Criteria of success and failure are applicable to all rational activities. Logic, for example, using the criteria of validity and invalidity, explains how a particular argument fails to establish its conclusion. Psychology, on the other hand, as a noncriteriological science, shows how that argument is typical of a certain kind of person and attempts to show why it is so. Criteriology is not incidental to the human sciences; it is a self-critical element that is crucial to them: it "is the way in which a thinker aims at applying certain standards or 'criteria' and thereby finding out whether he is thinking rightly or wrongly," Collingwood says in *The Principles of History*.

R. G. Collingwood's overall standpoint can be characterized as historicist: the modern conceptions of nature, metaphysics, and ethics are more adequate than their predecessors because they have become identified with history. Collingwood was not, however, a relativist. He believed that events could not have been other than they were; but he was always prepared to pronounce judgment as to whether those events could have been better than they were.

Letters:

The Correspondence of R. G. Collingwood, edited by Peter Johnson (Swansea: Collingwood Society, 1998).

Bibliographies:

Donald Taylor, *R. G. Collingwood: A Bibliography* (New York: Garland, 1988);

Christopher Dreisbach, *R. G. Collingwood: A Bibliographical Checklist* (Bowling Green, Ohio: Philosophy Documentation Center, 1993).

References:

David Boucher, *The Social and Political Thought of R. G. Collingwood* (New York: Cambridge University Press, 1989);

Boucher, James Connelly, and Tariq Modood, eds., *Philosophy, History and Civilization* (Cardiff: Wales University Press, 1995);

Alan Donagan, *The Later Philosophy of R. G. Collingwood* (Oxford: Clarendon Press, 1962);

William H. Dray, *History as Re-Enactment* (Oxford: Oxford University Press, 1995);

Michael Hinz, *Self-Creation and History: Collingwood and Nietzsche on Conceptual Change* (Lanham, Md.: University Press of America, 1994);

John P. Hogan, *Collingwood and Theological Hermeneutics* (Lanham, Md.: University Press of America, 1989);

Peter Johnson, *R. G. Collingwood: An Introduction* (Bristol: Thoemmes Press, 1996);

William M. Johnston, *The Formative Years of R. G. Collingwood* (The Hague: Nijhoff, 1967);

Michael Krausz, ed., *Critical Essays on the Philosophy of R. G. Collingwood* (Oxford: Clarendon Press, 1972);

Rex Martin, *Historical Explanation* (Ithaca, N.Y. & London: Cornell University Press, 1977);

Louis O. Mink, *Mind, History, and Dialectic* (Bloomington: Indiana University Press, 1969);

James Patrick, *The Magdalen Metaphysicals: Idealism and Orthodoxy at Oxford, 1901–1945* (Macon, Ga.: Mercer University Press, 1985);

Lionel Rubinoff, *Collingwood and the Reform of Metaphysics: A Study in the Philosophy of the Mind* (Toronto: University of Toronto Press, 1970);

Peter Skagestad, *Making Sense of History* (Oslo: Universitetsforlaget, 1975);

Jan van der Dussen, *History as a Science* (The Hague: Nijhoff, 1981).

Papers:

The principal collection of R. G. Collingwood's papers is in the Bodleian Library of the University of Oxford. Significant holdings also exist in the Pembroke College Library, Magdalen College, and the Ashmolean Museum, all at the University of Oxford; the Archives of Oxford University Press in Oxford; and the British Idealism and Collingwood Centre at Cardiff University.

Michael Dummett

(27 June 1925 –)

Bernhard Weiss
University of Wales, Lampeter

BOOKS: *Frege: Philosophy of Language* (London: Duckworth, 1973; New York: Harper & Row, 1973);

The Justification of Deduction (London: Oxford University Press, 1974);

Elements of Intuitionism, by Dummett and Robert Minio (Oxford: Clarendon Press, 1977);

Truth and Other Enigmas (London: Duckworth, 1978; Cambridge, Mass.: Harvard University Press, 1978);

Immigration: Where the Debate Goes Wrong (London: Action Group on Immigration and Nationality, 1978 [i.e., 1979]);

Catholicism and the World Order: Some Reflections on the 1978 Reith Lectures (London: Catholic Institute for International Relations, 1979);

The Game of Tarot: From Ferrara to Salt Lake City, by Dummett and Sylvia Mann (London: Duckworth, 1980);

Twelve Tarot Games (London: Duckworth, 1980);

Southall, 23 April 1979: The Report of the Unofficial Committee of Enquiry, by Dummett and others (London: National Council for Civil Liberties, 1980);

The Death of Blair Peach: The Supplementary Report of the Unofficial Committee of Enquiry, by Dummett and others (London: National Council for Civil Liberties, 1980);

The Interpretation of Frege's Philosophy (London: Duckworth, 1981; Cambridge, Mass.: Harvard University Press, 1981);

Voting Procedures (Oxford: Clarendon Press, 1984);

What Do I Know When I Know a Language? (Stockholm: Stockholm University Press, 1984);

The Visconti-Sforza Tarot Cards (New York: Braziller, 1986);

Ursprünge der analytischen Philosophie, translated by Joachim Schulte (Frankfurt am Main: Suhrkamp, 1988); English version published as *Origins of Analytical Philosophy* (London: Duckworth, 1993; Cambridge, Mass.: Harvard University Press, 1994);

The Logical Basis of Metaphysics (London: Duckworth, 1991; Cambridge, Mass.: Harvard University Press, 1991);

Frege: Philosophy of Mathematics (London: Duckworth, 1991; Cambridge, Mass.: Harvard University Press, 1991);

Frege and Other Philosophers (Oxford: Clarendon Press, 1991; New York: Oxford University Press, 1991);

Grammar and Style for Examination Candidates and Others (London: Duckworth, 1993);

The Seas of Language (Oxford: Clarendon Press, 1993; New York: Oxford University Press, 1993);

Il mondo e l'angelo: I tarocchi e la loro storia, translated by Mariangela Tempera (Naples: Bibliopolis, 1993);

I tarocchi siciliani, translated by Clelia Mirabella (Palermo: La Zisa, 1995);

A Wicked Pack of Cards: The Origins of the Occult Tarot, by Dummett, Ronald Decker, and Thierry Depaulis (London: Duckworth, 1996; New York: St. Martin's Press, 1996);

Principles of Electoral Reform (Oxford & New York: Oxford University Press, 1997);

On Immigration and Refugees (London: Routledge, 2001);

La natura e il futuro della filosofia, translated by Eva Picardi (Genoa: Il Melangolo, 2001);

The History of Occult Tarot, by Dummett and Decker (London: Duckworth, 2001).

OTHER: *Formal Systems and Recursive Functions: Proceedings of the Eighth Logic Colloquium, Oxford, July 1963,* edited by Dummett and J. N. Crossley (Amsterdam: North-Holland, 1965);

"The Role of Government in Britain's Racial Crisis," by Dummett and Ann Dummett, in *Justice First,* edited by Lewis Donnelly (London: Sheed & Ward, 1969);

Rudolf von Leyden, *Ganjifa: The Playing Cards of India: A General Survey, with a Catalogue of the Victoria and Albert Museum Collection,* contributions by Dummett (London: Victoria and Albert Museum, 1982).

Since the mid 1950s, and certainly since the publication in 1959 of his paper "Truth" (collected in *Truth and Other Enigmas*, 1978), Michael (now Sir Michael) Dummett has exerted a considerable influence on philosophical work in Britain. His influence on American philosophy is less obvious, but he has made his presence felt there, too, partly through his dialogues with and critiques of Nelson Goodman, W. V. O. Quine, Donald Davidson, and Hilary Putnam. Dummett thinks that philosophy, like natural science, aims at discovering truth but that the process of discovery in philosophy is quite different from that in science. The questions in which philosophers are interested are difficult to solve not because the relevant facts are obscure but because it is difficult to bring them within the scope of an explanatory theory. Therefore, Dummett should be distinguished both from those philosophers who think that philosophy should aim at "dissolving" rather than answering philosophical questions and who, thus, separate philosophy from science, and from those who agree that philosophy aims at truth but believe that there is no fundamental distinction between philosophy and science. An important consequence of Dummett's view of philosophy is that he allows philosophy to play a role in validating and justifying ordinary practices such as daily habits of speech or the way language is used in mathematics and science. If those practices are not susceptible to philosophical validation, they stand in need of revision. Dummett is best known for his exposition of the thought of the German logician and philosopher of mathematics Gottlob Frege; his attacks on the principle of bivalence in the philosophy of language and the law of excluded middle in logic; and his antirealism in metaphysics.

Michael Anthony Eardley Dummett was born in London on 27 June 1925 to George Herbert Dummett, a silk merchant, and Iris Eardley-Wilmot Dummett. After attending Winchester College, he served in the Royal Artillery and then in the Intelligence Corps of the British Army from 1943 to 1947, attaining the rank of sergeant; he was stationed in India in 1945 and in Malaya (today Malaysia) in 1946–1947.

Following his military service, Dummett enrolled at Christ Church, a college of the University of Oxford. His main teachers were J. O. Urmson and G. E. M. Anscombe; the latter exerted the greater influence on him. Other major philosophical influences were Frege and Ludwig Wittgenstein, an Austrian-born philosopher who invented two radically different approaches to the analysis of language. Dummett received a B.A. with first-class honors in 1950. In 1951 he married Agnes Margaret Ann Chesney, who has written many works on racism, immigration policy, citizenship, and nationality. They have five children: Christopher, Andrew, Susanna, Tessa, and Paul; another son and daughter died young. Dummett received his M.A. from Oxford in 1954.

Dummett has spent virtually his whole career at Oxford, except for a one-year lectureship at Birmingham University in 1950–1951; a Harkness Fellowship at the University of California at Berkeley in 1955–1956; visiting professorships at the University of Ghana in 1958, Stanford University several times between 1960 and 1966, the University of Minnesota in 1968, Princeton University in 1970, and Rockefeller University in 1973; and a von Humboldt Prize visit to the University of Münster in 1981. He gave the William James Lectures at Harvard University in 1976. He held the Wykeham Chair in Logic at Oxford from 1979 until his retirement in 1992. He was a fellow of the British Academy from 1968 to 1984 and was reelected in 1995. He became an honorary member of the American Academy of Arts and Sciences in 1985. A social activist as well as an academic, in 1967 Dummett helped to found the still-active Joint Council for the Welfare of Immigrants. From 1979 to 1981 he chaired an unofficial committee of inquiry into police violence at Southall in 1979 and the resultant death of antiracism demonstrator Blair Peach. Dummett was knighted in 1999.

The two most prominent strands in Dummett's output are his studies of Frege, to whom four of his eight philosophical books are entirely, and a fifth substantially, devoted; and his work in the philosophy of language and metaphysics. The intertwining of these strands is made clear in the often-made observation that his work in the philosophy of language springs from an attempt to read Wittgensteinian lessons into an essentially Fregean view of the workings of language.

In his first book, *Frege: Philosophy of Language* (1973), Dummett relates that Frege believed that mathematicians had either offered poor accounts or had not bothered to offer any account at all of the most fundamental concept in mathematics: number. As long as this situation was allowed to persist, knowledge of arithmetic was imperiled. Frege wanted to construct a system in which the most fundamental truths about numbers, such as that every number has a successor, could be proved. Every step in the proof would be an application of an explicitly stated rule of inference; in this way, one could be sure that no step involved an illicit and possibly misleading appeal to intuition. Frege called the system he invented a "concept-script." The concept-script categorizes mathematical expressions on the basis of syntax, explains what sort of entities expressions in each category could stand for, and shows how the meaning of a complex expression depends on the meanings of its parts.

Frege realized, however, that this procedure involves the notion that the meaning of a term is the object

FREGE:
Philosophy
of
Language

BY
MICHAEL DUMMETT

Dust jacket for Michael Dummett's first book, published in 1973, in which he argues that the German logician Gottlob Frege, rather than Bertrand Russell, G. E. Moore, or Alfred North Whitehead, was the father of analytic philosophy (Bruccoli Clark Layman Archives)

There is much exegetical controversy about the extent of Frege's interest in language. Some claim that his involvement with the philosophy of language was tangential to his interest in mathematics; others go further and contend that the philosophical views at which he arrived precluded him from having a serious interest in the workings of language as such. Dummett demurs: according to him, Frege constructed a philosophy of language that is still relevant, and many of the concepts Frege used to analyze language are precisely correct. Indeed, Frege's approach to his mathematical concerns provides a method for approaching philosophical issues in general: the goal of philosophy is an analysis of the structure of thought; thought must be sharply distinguished from the psychological process of thinking; and the only way to analyze thought is to analyze language. These three tenets, Dummett claims, constitute the guiding principles of analytic philosophy, of which Frege–rather than Bertrand Russell, G. E. Moore, or Alfred North Whitehead– is, therefore, the father.

Dummett's own approach to philosophy fits the Fregean mold in its overall shape, as well as in many of its details. He argues for the priority of language over thought and for a connection of traditional metaphysical issues with questions about the working of language in many of the papers that are collected in *Truth and Other Enigmas*, *Frege and Other Philosophers* (1991), and *The Seas of Language* (1993). Some of the technical implications of these positions in regard to mathematics are worked out in *Elements of Intuitionism* (1977). *The Logical Basis of Metaphysics* (1991) is a book-length development of his views; it is not, however, a good entry point into Dummett's thought, because much of it is steeped in philosophical logic.

Dummett says in essay 15 in *Frege and Other Philosophers* and in "What Does the Appeal to Use Do for the Theory of Meaning?" and "Language and Communication" in *The Seas of Language* that language is prior to thought in the sense that one cannot make use of the nature of thought in giving an account of linguistic meaning. To believe otherwise is to regard language as a code for thought, and this view, Dummett insists, is seriously confused. First, in most of the interesting cases one cannot give an account of what it is to have a thought, or grasp a concept, without appealing to the subject's ability to use language appropriately. How, for instance, would one ascribe complex expectations to a subject without making such an appeal? Dummett borrows Wittgenstein's observation that one might say that a dog is expecting his master to come home, but one would not say that he is expecting his master to come home *next week*.

The primary reason for rejecting the "code conception" of language, however, is that it rests on the notion of associating a word or expression with a concept; but this

to which it refers. This notion is inadequate, because it fails to take account of the difference in meaning between, for example, the terms "Everest" and "Gaurisanker," both of which refer to the highest mountain on Earth. Although the terms have the same reference, he said, they differ in sense. He identified the sense of a term variously as its cognitive significance (its information content) or as the mode of presentation of its reference (the way the referent is given). The crucial points are that the sense of a term is known by a speaker who understands it and that it determines the term's reference.

Frege's idea that questions about numbers can be approached by asking about numerical terms and arithmetical statements can be generalized into the claim that questions about ontology–that is, about the character of entities in the world–can be restated as questions about language. Dummett takes this move, which he calls "the linguistic turn," to be a distinctive feature of analytic philosophy, and he strongly endorses it.

notion is doubly mysterious. First, if one is to bring a concept to mind, one must be able to form a representation of the concept. But what is the nature of such a representation, and what makes it a representation of that particular concept? Answers to these questions seem entirely lacking, or else they appeal once again to a process of association and thus launch an endless regress. Second, even if a mental bringing together of the word with the concept does occur, an explanation is still needed of how this confers a meaning on the expression–that is, how it determines the use of the expression. If the association can "drift free" of its use, speakers who use an expression in the same way might not share the same understanding of the expression. But this possibility subverts the role of language in communication. Conversely, if agreement in use is the criterion for two speakers having agreed in the process of association, then the latter performs no useful work; one might as well concentrate on explaining meaning in terms of the use to which speakers put expressions.

In the first essay in *The Seas of Language,* "What Is a Theory of Meaning? (I)," Dummett says that the central question in the philosophy of language is the nature of meaning. The best way to attack this question is to consider how one would go about constructing a theory of meaning for a language. This procedure will provide a "sophisticated" answer to the question: it is sophisticated because it illuminates the concept of meaning without presupposing that any interesting way exists of generating direct specifications of meaning (that is, a clause of the form "*x* means that *y*") for every expression of the language; and it allows that many expressions will have quite different roles in language and that the meaning of an expression will be its contribution to the meanings of complex expressions of which it is a constituent. (Dummett attributes this approach primarily to Davidson.)

In the second essay in *The Seas of Language,* "What Is a Theory of Meaning? (II)," Dummett says that Frege provides the clue as to how a theory of meaning should be formulated. At its center, the theory of meaning will comprise a theory of truth and reference; that is, it will specify that to which each of the basic expressions in the language refers and how the references of complex expressions depend on those of their parts. It will also explain how the truth of a sentence is determined by the truth of its component sentences or by the references of its parts. Surrounding this theory of truth and reference will be a theory of sense that systematically explains the sense of expressions in the language on the basis of the specifications of their references. Dummett notes that Frege introduced the concept of knowledge into the theory of meaning through his argument for the notion of sense: one cannot give an adequate account of language by focusing on the referential relationship between language and the world; one needs, in addition, to include the sense that is grasped by the

speaker and that determines the reference of an expression. Frege, however, did not account for the intellectual capacity of grasping sense. Dummett insists that in addition to explaining what speakers know, the theory must also explain what justifies ascribing this knowledge to speakers.

Knowledge of the sense of an expression is the ingredient of a speaker's understanding that is relevant to determining the expression's reference. For instance, the expressions "dog" and "cur" agree in their senses—one would determine whether something is a dog or a cur in exactly the same way; but they differ in their meanings, since the former is neutral while the latter has a negative connotation.

The sense of a sentence must be distinguished from the various linguistic acts that might be performed by uttering that sentence. If one utters the sentence "Dummett is a great philosopher," one might be making a statement, putting forward a conjecture for consideration, making an assumption, or asking a question. The sense of the sentence is available for many linguistic acts, and in each act one must distinguish the sense from the "force"– assertoric, interrogative, imperative, or whatever–that "attends" the sense. Dummett argues in "What Is a Theory of Meaning? (II)" and in chapter 5 of *The Logical Basis of Metaphysics* that a systematic theory of meaning depends on the sense/force distinction.

In "What Is a Theory of Meaning? (I)" Dummett says that an adequate theory of meaning must be "molecular" rather than "holistic" and "full-blooded" rather than "modest." Explaining the first distinction, he says that an account of meaning that deserves to be called a "theory" will be compositional: that is, the meaning of a complex expression will be determined by the meanings of its components and the way they are combined. Theories differ, however, as to what more the speaker needs to know. According to the holistic account, the additional component is invariable across the language as a whole or, at least, across large regions of it; it might just be general linguistic competence. In contrast, in a molecular account the additional component will vary from expression to expression; the understanding of a given expression will presuppose, at most, an understanding of a fragment of language; and the relevant fragment will be determined by the complexity of the expression.

In regard to the second distinction, Dummett says that one way of providing an account of the meaning of linguistic expressions is to assume that the speaker grasps a basic set of concepts and then to explain the meanings of complex expressions on the basis of those concepts. To do so is to offer a modest theory of meaning. A full-blooded theory, on the other hand, explains the meanings of all of the expressions in the language without presupposing any such "conceptual competence." It, therefore, displays

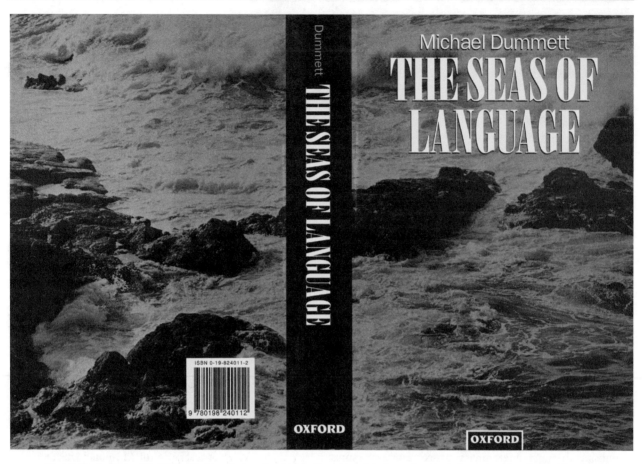

Dust jacket for Dummett's 1993 collection of papers, in which he discusses such topics as the nature of meaning, the priority of language to thought, realism, and the distinction between the sense and the force of a proposition (Bruccoli Clark Layman Archives)

more of the workings of language than a modest theory of meaning, which Dummett considers to be little more than a translation manual. A translation manual specifies the meanings of expressions in a foreign language in terms of those of a "home" language; it can provide no illumination of the concept of meaning, since it takes that concept for granted in regard to the home language. A modest theory of meaning, similarly, portrays the meanings of complex expressions in terms of those of a basic set, and it, too, takes the concept of meaning for granted.

A theory of meaning, then, must give an account of the knowledge possessed by competent speakers of a language. For Dummett, this account must make use only of capacities that a speaker can publicly manifest, that are "visible" from a third-person perspective. If it fails to do so, the character of a speaker's understanding will be "hidden from view"; meaning would then be essentially private. In this case, first, the social role of language would be subverted; and second, one's ability to learn language on the basis of the behavior displayed by competent speakers would be threatened, since a "leap" would be required from the available evidence to the cor-

rect understanding. For these reasons—called the "manifestation" and "acquisition challenges"—Dummett insists on the "publicity of meaning." The publicity of meaning is a main thesis of Wittgenstein's *Philosophical Investigations* (1953); Dummett's "manifestation" and "acquisition" challenges are his way of applying the Wittgensteinian lesson to the construction of a theory of meaning (an enterprise with which Wittgenstein would have had little sympathy). Thus, a theory of meaning must give an account of the knowledge possessed by competent speakers, must specify what constitutes possession of this knowledge, and must do so in a way that makes possession of the knowledge available to public scrutiny.

It might appear that the theory for which Dummett is calling is a behaviorist one. He thinks, however, that he avoids behaviorism because he is searching not for a theory that predicts speakers' behavior but for one that describes their behavior as rational agents. As rational agents, speakers want to understand the intentions, motives, and purposes underlying each other's actions. So the public behavior in terms of which understanding is characterized is described in distinctively rational terms. It thus both adheres to the twin demands of full-bloodedness and publicity and avoids crude behaviorism, as Dummett says in "What Do I Know When I Know a Language?" in *The Seas of Language* and in chapter 4 of *The Logical Basis of Metaphysics*.

In some cases knowledge of an expression's meaning will be explicit; that is, the speaker will be able to formulate an informative explanation of the meaning of the expression. This capacity is publicly observable and is, thus, an adequate account of what the speaker's understanding consists in. But it explains one linguistic capacity in terms of another; so if it were all that could be said, it would be circular. Thus, some aspects of a speaker's understanding must be implicit knowledge, and in such cases it is harder to say what possession of the knowledge consists in and what manifests possession of the knowledge. Dummett's solution is that possession of such knowledge must, at least in large measure, be constituted by possession of a "recognitional capacity": a capacity to recognize, for instance, whether circumstances warrant the assertion of a sentence.

Armed with these resources, Dummett goes on to develop an argument against the traditional conception of meaning. The traditional conception assumes that every statement is either true or false: this is the "principle of bivalence." There are, however, sentences that one understands, but one does not know how to discover whether they are true or false. For example, one understands statements about the past for which decisive evidence is lacking. No one knows, for instance, what Julius Caesar had for breakfast a fortnight before he crossed the Rubicon, nor does anyone know a way of settling the matter; yet, clearly one can understand a multitude of sentences concerning what Caesar might or might not have eaten. Or one can understand the sentence "There is intelligent life in the galaxy," but, though one may be lucky enough to come across decisive evidence for its truth, one would have no way of definitely furnishing oneself with such evidence. Such sentences are "undecidable." The traditional conception construes understanding of a statement as grasping the conditions under which it is true; this is the "truth-conditional account of meaning." One understands the sentences in these examples because one knows what would have to be the case for them to be true. One knows what it would be for there to be intelligent life in the galaxy, and this knowledge is part of one's understanding of the relevant sentence. This account has considerable plausibility, since it is correct to assert a declarative sentence only when it is true. So an ability to use the sentence correctly—an understanding of the sentence—should be captured through a knowledge of the sentence's truth-conditions.

Dummett argues that the traditional conception encounters an overwhelming problem in accounting for speakers' understanding of undecidable sentences. What, according to the traditional account, constitutes knowledge of the truth-conditions of undecidable sentences? Such knowledge cannot be explicit knowledge, since if what is to be explained is undecidable then the explanation will be so, too. Knowledge of the truth-conditions of these kinds of sentences therefore has to be implicit. Speakers will then, however, only be able to use the sentence in response to circumstances that they are capable of recognizing, and nothing in such a use could demonstrate that an undecidable sentence has a determinate truth-value, which, precisely, lies beyond what speakers can be sure to recognize. The upshot of the argument is that one cannot assume that the principle of bivalence holds for undecidable sentences. One should note that the argument is premised on Frege's conception of language, since it takes an issue about the notion of truth to depend on questions about how speakers understand language. In other words, the theory of truth for a language will depend on the character of an adequate theory of sense. Dummett claims that no adequate theory of sense will be based on a theory of truth and reference that adheres to the principle of bivalence. He concludes that the principle of bivalence should be rejected and that one should give an account of meaning not in terms of truth-conditions but in terms of what counts as evidence for or against the statement.

The logical positivists thought that the meaning of a sentence was its verification procedure; sentences that are not verifiable are, therefore, meaningless. Though this claim superficially resembles Dummett's position, Dummett accepts that one can understand undecidable sentences. His point is that since that understanding consists in grasping what would count as evidence for or against such a sentence, one cannot assume in the absence of such evidence that the sentence is, nevertheless, determinately either true or false. That is, whereas the logical positivists were skeptical about the possibility of understanding such sentences, Dummett only doubts the applicability of the principle of bivalence to them.

Dummett's position leads to the abandonment of a basic rule of inference of classical logic, the law of excluded middle, which entitles one to assert, for any sentence p, the necessarily true sentence "p or not-p." For example, applying the law of excluded middle to the sentence "World War II broke out in 1939," entitles one to assert that "World War II broke out in 1939 or World War II did not break out in 1939." Since each sentence is either true or false and is true if its negation is false and false if its negation is true, either p is true or "not-p" is true. The sentence "p or not-p" is true in either case, so it is always true. This rationale, however, appeals to the principle of bivalence; if that principle is rejected, then the law cannot be justified in this way. Since Dummett insists in "The Justification of Deduction" in *Truth and Other Enigmas* and in chapter 8 of *The Logical Basis of Metaphysics* that logical laws should be justifiable, he is doubtful about the acceptability of classical logic. Instead, he advocates the adoption of intuitionistic logic, in which the law of the excluded middle is not assumed to be valid. His *Elements of Intuitionism* is an attempt to reconstruct significant portions of mathematics using intuitionistic rather than classical logic.

Another of Dummett's philosophical concerns is realism, a topic discussed in "Realism" in *Truth and Other Enigmas;* in two essays in *The Seas of Language,* "Realism" and "Realism and Anti-realism"; and in chapter 15 of *The Logical Basis of Metaphysics.* Realism maintains that the world, or some portion of it, is independent of mind and language; rejection of realism is, accordingly, often taken to be the view that the world, or at least a certain portion of the world, is dependent on, or constructed through, thinking or talking. Dummett was drawn to look at debates about realism in the hope of discovering the general features of such debates. If one could discern what the debates were about, he thought, one might have a better understanding of what realism involves; and that understanding might provide more plausible ways of rejecting realism than those that depend on the notion of construction, as well as a way of deciding whether realism with respect to a given subject matter is justified or not.

A first point to note, Dummett says, is that one should resist seeing debates about realism as being about the status of entities. Realism about mathematics or mental states might be seen as views about numbers and other minds, respectively. But realism about the past or future cannot be construed as involving a set of entities. One might, instead, interpret realism as a view about states of affairs or facts; but these items are themselves controversial. Dummett thinks that it is best to see a realist view as a view about how certain statements, such as those concerning the past or mathematical statements, relate to the world—that is, how they are made true or false. Thus, realism is a semantic thesis. The precise characterization of realism along these lines is a complex matter, and Dummett does not think that it can be achieved. Rather, there are various views about the semantics of regions of language, and disputes between these competing views will be disputes relating to realism. One feature, however, is of overriding significance: the notion of mind- and language-independence involved in realism. Dummett claims that the best way to make sense of this notion is to think of the problematic statements as being true independently of one's knowledge. Thus, for the realist, the truth of these statements goes beyond anyone's ability to discover it. He calls this position an "objectivist" notion of truth. Dummett's argument against the principle of bivalence can be reformulated to apply to an objectivist notion of truth. He

has, thus, provided an argument against any realist position that holds to an objectivist notion of truth.

In his essay "Realism" in *The Seas of Language* Dummett notes that philosophers have often contrasted realism with reductionism. Thus, realism in regard to statements ascribing mental states to others would be rejected by claiming that such statements can be reduced to complex statements about how a person would be disposed to behave in various circumstances. In Dummett's example, the statement "Jones is brave" would be taken to mean that if Jones were placed in a position of danger, he would behave courageously. Dummett does not think that such a claim is a clear rejection of realism, because to decide whether "Jones is brave" is true, one would have to decide whether the sentence "If Jones were to be placed in a position of danger, then he would behave courageously" or the sentence "If Jones were to be placed in a position of danger, then he would *not* behave courageously" is true. But one might think that one or the other of these complex sentences was true not because Jones possesses or lacks the trait of bravery but because of his neurophysiological makeup. In this case, Dummett says, reductionism would *support* realism. On the other hand, one might doubt that either of the sentences is determinately true, because what Jones does may be determined by some unspecified factor. In this case, one would relinquish one's realism about ascriptions of bravery and the like. So reductionism is quite distinct from antirealism—one may be both a realist and a reductionist—though it may provide a reason for rejecting realism.

Michael Dummett has also made important contributions to the philosophies of time, causation, logic, and mathematics. Outside of philosophy he has maintained a keen interest in church and theological matters; has been an active and passionate campaigner against racism; and has developed his enthusiasm for the game of Tarot—and his disdain for the use of the cards in occult practices—into an intellectual study that has resulted in seven books.

References:

Karen Green, *Dummett: Philosophy of Language* (Cambridge: Polity Press, 2001);

Darryl Gunson, *Michael Dummett and the Theory of Meaning* (Aldershot: Ashgate, 1998);

Richard Heck, ed., *Language, Thought and Logic: Essays in Honour of Michael Dummett* (Oxford: Oxford University Press, 1997);

Anat Matar, *From Dummett's Philosophical Perspective* (Berlin: De Gruyter, 1997);

Brian McGuiness and Gianluigi Oliveri, eds., *The Philosophy of Michael Dummett* (Dordrecht: Kluwer, 1994);

Barry Taylor, ed., *Michael Dummett: Contributions to Philosophy* (Dordrecht: Nijhoff, 1987).

William Godwin

(3 March 1756 – 7 April 1836)

Susan Spencer
University of Central Oklahoma

See also the Godwin entries in *DLB 39: British Novelists, 1660–1800; DLB 104: British Prose Writers, 1660–1800; DLB 142: Eighteenth-Century British Literary Biographers; DLB 158: British Reform Writers, 1789–1832;* and *DLB 163: British Children's Writers, 1800–1880.*

BOOKS: *The History of the Life of William Pitt, Earl of Chatham,* anonymous (London: G. Kearsley, 1783);

A Defence of the Rockingham Party: In their Late Coalition with the Right Honourable Frederic Lord North, anonymous (London: Printed for J. Stockdale, 1783);

An Account of the Seminary that will be opened on Monday the Fourth Day of August at Epsom in Surrey, for the Instruction of Twelve Pupils in the Greek, Latin, French, and English Languages, anonymous (London: Printed for T. Cadell, 1783);

Damon and Delia: A Tale, anonymous (London: Printed for T. Hookham, 1784);

Imogen: A Pastoral Romance from the Ancient British, 2 volumes, anonymous (London: Printed for W. Lane, 1784; New York: New York Public Library, 1963);

Italian Letters: or, The History of the Count de St. Julian, anonymous, 2 volumes (London: Printed for G. Robinson, 1784; Lincoln: University of Nebraska Press, 1965);

Sketches of History, in Six Sermons (London: Printed for T. Cadell, 1784);

The Herald of Literature: or, A Review of the Most Considerable Publications That Will Be Made in the Course of the Ensuing Winter: With Extracts, anonymous (London: Printed for J. Murray, 1784);

Instructions to a Statesman: Humbly inscribed to the Right Honourable George Earl Temple, anonymous (London: Printed for J. Murray, J. Debrett & J. Sewell, 1784);

The History of the Internal Affairs of the United Provinces, from the Year 1780, to the Commencement of Hostilities in June, 1787, anonymous (London: Printed for G. G. J. & J. Robinson, 1787);

William Godwin; portrait by J. W. Chandler, 1798 (Tate Gallery, London)

The English Peerage; or, A View of the Ancient and Present State of the English Nobility: To Which is Subjoined, a Chronological Account of Such Titles as Have Become Extinct, from the Norman Conquest to the Beginning of the Year MDCCXC, anonymous, 3 volumes (London: Printed by T. Spilsburg for G. G. J. & J. Robinson, 1790);

An Enquiry Concerning Political Justice, and Its Influence on General Virtue and Happiness, 2 volumes (London: G. G. J. & J. Robinson, 1793; revised edition, London: G. G. J. & J. Robinson, 1796; Philadelphia:

Bioren & Madan, 1796; revised again, London: G. G. J. & J. Robinson, 1798);

Things As They Are; or, The Adventures of Caleb Williams (3 volumes, London: B. Crosby, 1794; 2 volumes, Baltimore: H. & P. Rice, 1795; revised edition, 3 volumes, London: G. G. J. & J. Robinson, 1796; revised again, 3 volumes, London: G. G. J. & J. Robinson, 1797); revised as *Caleb Williams* (1 volume, London: H. Colburn & R. Bentley, 1831; 2 volumes, New York: Harper, 1831);

Cursory Strictures on the Charge delivered by Lord Chief Justice Eyre to the Grand Jury, October 2, 1794, anonymous (London: D. I. Eaton, 1794);

A Reply to An Answer to Cursory Strictures, Supposed to Be Wrote by Judge Buller, by the Author of Cursory Strictures, anonymous (London: Printed and sold by D. I. Eaton, 1794);

Considerations on Lord Grenville's and Mr. Pitt's Bills: Concerning Treasonable and Seditious Practices, and Unlawful Assemblies, by a Lover of Order, anonymous (London: Printed by J. Johnson, 1795);

The Enquirer: Reflections on Education, Manners, and Literature: In a Series of Essays (London: Printed for G. G. J. & J. Robinson, 1797; Philadelphia: Printed by J. Birch for R. Campbell, 1797; revised edition, Edinburgh: J. Anderson, 1823; London: W. Simpkin & R. Marshall, 1823);

Memoirs of the Author of a Vindication of the Rights of Woman (London: Printed by G. G. J. & J. Robinson for J. Johnson, 1798; revised edition, London: J. Johnson, 1798); republished as *Memoirs of Mary Wollstonecraft Godwin, Author of "A Vindication of the Rights of Woman"* (Philadelphia: J. Carey, 1799);

St. Leon: A Tale of the Sixteenth Century (4 volumes, London: Printed for G. G. J. & J. Robinson, 1799; 2 volumes, Alexandria, Va.: Printed by J. & J. D. Westcott, 1801; revised edition, 1 volume, London: H. Colburn & R. Bentley, 1831);

Antonio, a Tragedy in Five Acts (London: Printed by Wilks & Taylor for G. G. J. & J. Robinson, 1800; New York: D. Longworth, 1806);

Thoughts: Occasioned by the Perusal of Dr. Parr's Spital Sermon, preached at Christ Church, April 15, 1800. Being a Reply to the Attacks of Dr. Parr, Mr. Mackintosh, the Author of an Essay on Population, and Others (London: Printed by Wilks & Taylor and sold by G. G. J. & J. Robinson, 1801);

Bible Stories: Memorable Acts of the Ancient Patriarchs, Judges, and Kings: Extracted from their Original Historians. For the Use of Children, 2 volumes, as William Scholfield (London: R. Phillips, 1802; Albany, N.Y.: Charles R. & George Webster, 1803); republished as *Sacred Histories; or, Insulated Bible Stories,* 2 volumes (London: R. Phillips, 1806);

Life of Geoffrey Chaucer, the Early English Poet, including Memoirs of his Near Friend and Kinsman, John of Gaunt, Duke of Lancaster: With Sketches of the Manners, Opinions, Arts and Literature of England in the Fourteenth Century, 2 volumes (London: Printed by T. Davison for R. Phillips, 1803);

Fleetwood; or, The New Man of Feeling (3 volumes, London: R. Phillips, 1805; 2 volumes, New York: Printed by I. Riley for S. Gould, 1805; Alexandria, Va.: Cotton & Stewart, 1805; revised edition, 1 volume, London: R. Bentley, 1832);

Fables, Ancient and Modern: Adapted for the Use of Children, as Edward Baldwin (London: Printed for T. Hodgkins, 1805; New Haven, Conn.: Printed by Sidney's Press for Increase Cooke, 1807);

The Looking Glass: A True History of the Early Years of an Artist. Calculated to Awaken the Emulation of Young Persons of Both Sexes, in the Pursuit of Every laudable Attainment: particularly in the Cultivation of the Fine Arts, as Theophilus Marcliffe (London: Printed for T. Hodgkins, 1805);

The Pantheon; or Ancient History of the Gods of Greece and Rome: Intended to facilitate the Understanding of the Classical Authors, and of the Poets in General. For the Use of Schools, and Young Persons of Both Sexes, as Baldwin (London: Printed for T. Hodgkins, 1806; edited by Burton Feldman, 1 volume, New York: Garland, 1984);

The History of England: For the Use of Schools and Young Persons, as Baldwin (London: T. Hodgkins, 1806);

Life of Lady Jane Grey, and of Lord Guildford Dudley, her Husband, as Marcliffe (London: Printed for T. Hodgkins, 1806);

Faulkener: A Tragedy (London: Printed by R. Taylor for R. Phillips, 1807);

Dramas for Children: Imitated from the French of L. F. Jauffret, by the Editor of Tabart's Popular Stories (London: Printed for M. J. Godwin, 1808);

History of Rome: From the Building of the City to the Ruin of the Republic, as Baldwin (London: M. J. Godwin, 1809);

Essay on Sepulchres; or, A Proposal for erecting some Memorial of the Illustrious Dead in All Ages on the Spot where their Remains have been interred (London: W. Miller, 1809; New York: M. & W. Ward, 1809);

Outlines of English History, Chiefly Abstracted from the History of England, For the Use of Children from Four to Eight Years of Age, as Baldwin (London: M. J. Godwin, 1814);

Lives of Edward and John Philips, Nephews and Pupils of Milton: Including Various Particulars of the Literary and Political History of Their Times (London: Longman, Hurst, Rees, Orme & Brown, 1815);

Letters of Verax, to the Editor of the Morning Chronicle, on the Question of a War to be commenced for the Purpose of putting an End to the Possession of Supreme Power in France by Napoleon Bonaparte (London: Printed by R. & A. Taylor, 1815);

Mandeville: A Tale of the Seventeenth Century in England (3 volumes, Edinburgh: A. Constable / London: Longman, Hurst, Rees, Orme & Brown, 1817; 2 volumes, New York: W. B. Gilley/C. Wiley, 1818; Philadelphia: M. Thomas/J. Maxwell, 1818);

Letter of Advice to a Young American, on the Course of Studies It Might Be Most Advantageous for Him to Pursue (London: Printed by R. & A. Taylor for M. J. Godwin, 1818);

Of Population: An Enquiry concerning the Power of Increase in the Numbers of Mankind, being an Answer to Mr. Malthus's Essay on that Subject (London: Longman, Hurst, Rees, Orme & Brown, 1820; New York: A. M. Kelly, 1964);

The History of Greece, as Baldwin (London: M. J. Godwin, 1821);

History of the Commonwealth of England: From Its Commencement to the Restoration of Charles the Second, 4 volumes (London: Printed for H. Colburn, 1824–1828);

Cloudesley: A Novel, 3 volumes, as the author of *Caleb Williams* (London: H. Colburn & R. Bentley, 1830); republished as *Cloudesley: A Tale,* 2 volumes, as the author of *Caleb Williams* (New York: Printed by J. J. Harper and sold by Collins & Hannay, 1830);

Thoughts on Man, His Nature, Productions, and Discoveries: Interspersed with Some Particulars Respecting the Author (London: E. Wilson, 1831; New York: A. M. Kelly, 1969);

Deloraine (3 volumes, London: R. Bentley, 1833; 2 volumes, Philadelphia: Carey, Lea & Blanchard, 1833);

Lives of the Necromancers; or, An Account of the Most Eminent Persons in Successive Ages, who have claimed for themselves, or to whom has been imputed by Others, the Exercise of Magical Powers (London: F. J. Mason, 1834; New York: Harper, 1835);

Essays Never Before Published, edited by C. Kegan Paul (London: H. S. King, 1873);

The Elopement of Percy Bysshe Shelley and Mary Wollstonecraft Godwin, as Narrated by Godwin, edited by Harry Buxton Forman (London: Bibliophile Society, 1911; Boston: Privately printed, 1912);

Tragical Consequences: or, A Disaster at Deal: Being an Unpublished Letter of William Godwin Dated Wednesday, November 18th, 1789, edited by Edmund Blunden (London: Printed for Fytton Armstrong, 1931);

Uncollected Writings: Articles in Periodicals and Six Pamphlets, One with Coleridge's Marginalia, edited by Burton R. Pollin and Jack W. Marken (Gainesville, Fla.: Scholars' Facsimiles and Reprints, 1968)–includes *Lord Chief Justice Eyre to the Grand Jury, October 2, 1794; Thoughts Occasioned by the Perusal of Dr. Parr's Spital Sermon, preached at Christ Church, April 15, 1800;* and *Letters of Verax, to the Editor of the Morning Chronicle.*

Editions and Collections: *Four Early Pamphlets, 1783–1784,* edited by Burton R. Pollin (Gainesville, Fla.: Scholars' Facsimiles and Reprints, 1966)–comprises *A Defence of the Rockingham Party; An Account of the Seminary that will be opened on Monday the Fourth Day of August at Epsom in Surrey, for the Instruction of Twelve Pupils in the Greek, Latin, French, and English Languages; The Herald of Literature;* and *Instructions to a Statesman;*

Enquiry Concerning Political Justice and Its Influence on Modern Morals and Happiness, edited by Isaac Kramnick (London: Penguin, 1976);

The Anarchist Writings of William Godwin, edited by Peter H. Marshall (London: Freedom, 1986);

Collected Novels and Memoirs of William Godwin, 8 volumes, edited by Mark Philp (London: Pickering, 1992).

OTHER: *Memoirs of the Life of Simon Lord Lovat; Written by Himself in the French Language; and Now First Translated from the Original Manuscript,* translated anonymously by Godwin (London: Printed for George Nicol, 1797);

Mary Wollstonecraft Godwin, *Posthumous Works of the Author of a Vindication of the Rights of Woman,* 4 volumes, edited by Godwin (London: Printed for G. G. & J. Johnson, 1798);

William Mylius, *School Dictionary of the English Language: To which is prefixed a New Guide to the English Tongue,* preface by Godwin as Edward Baldwin (London: M. J. Godwin, 1809);

Mary Shelley, *Valperga: A Novel,* revised by Godwin (London: G. & W. B. Whittaker, 1823);

William Godwin Jr., *Transfusion; or, The Orphans of Unwalden,* 3 volumes, preface by Godwin (London: J. Macrone, 1835; New York: Wallis & Newell, 1835).

Regarded by some of his contemporaries as a dangerous radical and by others as a prophetic visionary, the anarchist William Godwin had a profound effect on British liberalism and, through his son-in-law, the poet Percy Bysshe Shelley, on the politically charged literary movement known as Romanticism. In his best-known work, *An Enquiry Concerning Political Justice, and Its Influence on General Virtue and Happiness*

AN

E N Q U I R Y

CONCERNING

POLITICAL JUSTICE,

AND

ITS INFLUENCE

ON

GENERAL VIRTUE AND HAPPINESS.

BY

WILLIAM GODWIN.

IN TWO VOLUMES.

VOL. I.

LONDON:

PRINTED FOR G. G. J. AND J. ROBINSON, PATERNOSTER-ROW.

M.DCC.XCIII.

Title page for Godwin's best-known philosophical work,
in which he argues for the abolition of government
(Bruccoli Clark Layman Archives)

(1793)–usually referred to simply as *Political Justice*–Godwin tried to show that the search for political and ethical principles, or "moral philosophy," was essentially the same process as the search for the laws of nature, or "natural philosophy." Inquiry into the philosophical basis of government could establish, he believed, the scientific principles against which political questions could be judged. With these principles established, a political system could be built that was so rational that laws would be unnecessary, since every individual would acknowledge its precepts and, thus, agree on what constituted proper behavior.

Godwin was born on 3 March 1756 to John and Ann Hull Godwin in Wisbech in the Cambridgeshire Fens. John Godwin, like his father and brother, was a poverty-stricken Dissenting minister and had to move his family twice before settling in 1858 in the village of Guestwick in Norfolk, where William and his five brothers and sisters grew up. The strict discipline and joyless Calvinism that Godwin experienced as a child led to puritanical strains in his political theory.

At eleven Godwin was sent to Norwich to be educated for the ministry in the household of the Reverend Samuel Newton, who whipped him frequently and chastised him on a regular basis for the sin of arrogance, instilling a sense of guilt that remained with Godwin for the rest of his life. Since Dissenters were barred from attending Anglican universities such as Oxford or Cambridge and from holding government jobs, after his father's death in November 1772 Godwin was enrolled in September 1773 at the Hoxton Academy, a school for Dissenters in London, where he remained for five years. Dissenting academies were known for their intellectual rigor and academic excellence, and the tutors at Hoxton were particularly forward-looking: they encouraged debate and critical thinking concerning metaphysical questions and helped Godwin develop the logical thought processes that characterized his later writings.

In 1778 Godwin took religious orders, and at the end of 1779 he accepted a permanent appointment as a minister at Stowmarket, Suffolk. After quarreling with neighboring ministers about his democratic view that the congregation should participate in decision making, he resigned in 1782 and moved to London, where he prepared to open a seminary. The plan was abandoned, but Godwin's prospectus, *An Account of the Seminary that will be opened on Monday the Fourth Day of August at Epsom in Surrey, for the Instruction of Twelve Pupils in the Greek, Latin, French, and English Languages* (1783), is one of the first accounts of his developing educational theory. Influenced by John Locke, Claude-Adrien Helvétius, and, especially, Jean-Jacques Rousseau, Godwin began to believe that rather than being a vessel of original sin, a child is a tabula rasa with an unlimited capacity for goodness if only he or she can be educated properly. This idea developed into the paradox put forth in *An Enquiry Concerning the Principles of Political Justice:* since human beings and institutions are capable of infinite progress toward perfection, perfection can never be attained.

At about this time Godwin became an agnostic. Giving up any idea of a religious career, he began to earn a living as a literary reviewer. He produced several works in a short time, including a parody of contemporary literary reviews, *The Herald of Literature: or, A Review of the Most Considerable Publications That Will Be Made in the Course of the Ensuing Winter: With Extracts* (1784); three sensationalistic novels; and several historical studies and political pamphlets. His occupation as a reviewer made him a welcome guest at parties given by booksellers, particularly the radical Joseph Johnson, whose circle included William Blake. Exposure to Johnson's literary milieu, especially during the turbulent period of the French Revolution, led Godwin to contemplate the nature of what he called "political justice," a concept that covered all human interactions from personal relationships to the formation of governments.

Political Justice appeared in February 1793 and catapulted Godwin to instant fame. Because the work condemned all government systems and presented a blueprint for a British revolution, the members of the Privy Council debated whether to suppress publication of the work and prosecute the author. They decided against taking action, because Prime Minister William Pitt the Younger advised them that "a three guinea book could never do much harm among those who had not three shillings to spare" and that those who could afford it would be likely to balk at its suggestions for the abolition of private property. Comprising two quarto volumes, *Political Justice* was, indeed, expensive. Nevertheless, it became a best-seller, mainly because members of subscription libraries joined together to purchase copies. Many who did not read it at least heard about it.

Godwin argues in *Political Justice* that individual human beings should not be subject to general laws, which, by their nature, will always favor some more than others. Since such a system is not possible in a large state, Godwin suggests that nations and even provinces be replaced by self-ruled parishes in which everyone would have contact with, and presumably a stake in the welfare of, everyone else. Political authority could thus be replaced by public persuasion, and law and government by public opinion. Wealth would be eliminated, and with it the incentive for most crime. Punishment would also be abolished: an individual's actions would be judged on a case-by-case basis, and if there were a general consensus in the community that the offense was not an isolated incident, the community would persuade the offender not to do it again, much as a parent would persuade a recalcitrant child:

> The right of the parent over his offspring lies either in his superior strength, or his superior reason. If in his strength, we have only to apply this right universally in order to drive all morality out of the world. If in his reason, in that reason let him confide. It is a poor argument of my superior reason that I am unable to make justice be apprehended and felt, in the most necessary cases, without the intervention of blows.

Another precept of Godwin's philosophy is his doctrine of necessity or determinism, which, in keeping with his mission to unite the moral and the natural sciences, follows the model of Sir Isaac Newton's physics. Since all things and events are inextricably interconnected, no human action is without consequence; thus, every action is a moral choice. Having observed that all

The feminist Mary Wollstonecraft in 1797, the year she and Godwin were married; portrait by John Opie (National Portrait Gallery, London)

children do not appear to have equal potential, Godwin suggests that the chain of cause and effect begins with "the accidents which pass during the months of percipiency in the womb," a departure from Locke's tabula rasa theory.

Godwin equates necessity with virtue: if a person is taught to recognize virtuous actions, he or she will perform such actions as a matter of course. If, after sincere argument, individuals are unable to agree on what the virtuous action in a given situation is, it is because human reason has further progress to make toward perfection. Open debate is a prerequisite for that progress. There is no room for half-truths in Godwin's utopia: like the seventeenth-century Puritans, he asserts that every person has a duty to speak fearlessly and to censure friends so as to exhort them to correct behavior. There is also little room for domestic affection because it might lead to the neglect of one's duty—another Puritan idea surviving from his early Calvinist beliefs. Among the institutions Godwin attacks, marriage comes under fire as particularly debilitating and absurd: not only does he agree with many of his contemporaries that it is inhumane to tie two people together for life, but "cohabitation is also hostile to that fortitude which should accustom a man, in his actions, as well as in his opinions, to judge for himself, and feel competent to the discharge of his own duties."

In 1794 Godwin sought to influence a larger audience by writing a popular novel. *Things As They Are; or, The Adventures of Caleb Williams* puts the principles of *Political Justice* into the form of a thrilling tale of pursuit and mystery, exposing social evils as it engages the reader's sympathy for its unfortunate hero. Corrupted by England's monolithic and unpitying justice system and an outdated code of pride and chivalry, Squire Falkland murders a vicious man. After Caleb accidentally discovers his guilt, Falkland hounds him across the length and breadth of England, capitalizing on his superior rank to ensure his own safety and destroy Caleb's credibility. Caleb, one of the few characters in the novel who believes in the concept of extenuating circumstances, remarks that Falkland "might yet be a most excellent man, if he did but think so"–an echo of Godwin's argument in *Political Justice* that capital punishment robs the community of any future good an individual might do. At one point Caleb takes up with a highwayman who complains that although he would like to abandon his profession,

> the institutions . . . leave no room for amendment, and seem to have a brutal delight in confounding the demerits of offenders. It signifies not what is the character of the individual at the hour of trial. How changed, how spotless, and how useful, avails him nothing. If they discover at the distance of fourteen or of forty years an action for which the law ordains that his life shall be the forfeit, though the interval should have been spent with the purity of a saint and the devotedness of a patriot, they disdain to enquire into it. . . . Am I not compelled to go on in folly, having once begun?

Godwin appears to have considered *Political Justice* a work in progress. A second edition, with extensive revisions, was published in 1796. In the preface Godwin comments that while "the spirit and great outlines of the work" have not been changed, "many things . . . now appear to the author upon a review, not to have been meditated with a sufficiently profound reflection, and to have been too hastily obtruded upon the reader." As the promise of the French Revolution lapsed into the Reign of Terror, most of England's intellectual community, including Godwin's former supporters William Wordsworth and Samuel Taylor Coleridge, began to embrace a far more conservative point of view than they had at the beginning. The first edition of *Political Justice* had been hurriedly sent to press as the situation in France was heating up: King Louis XVI had been executed on 1 February, and Godwin's book had gone on sale in London on 14 February. The second edition makes its points with less

rigidity, perhaps as a reaction to the shock of recent events. One of the best-known passages in the first edition, for example, posits a predicament in which the palace of the great educator and author Archbishop François de Salignac de la Mothe-Fénelon is on fire. Fénelon and his chambermaid are trapped by the flames, and only one of them can be saved. Godwin concludes that since Fénelon contributes more to the public good, he must be the one to be rescued, regardless of personal loyalties: "Supposing the chambermaid had been my wife, my mother or my benefactor. This would not alter the truth of the proposition. The life of Fénelon would still be more valuable than that of the chambermaid; and justice, pure, unadulterated justice, would still have preferred that which was most valuable." In the second edition the chambermaid has been replaced by Fénelon's valet, eliminating the possibility of outraging the sensibilities of readers by abandoning a woman to her fate and, possibly, reflecting the more conservative, less egalitarian view of gender relations that was coming into fashion.

Isaac Kramnick suggests that certain alterations in the second and the third (1798) editions of *Political Justice* having to do with "greater receptivity to the realm of feeling" owe their existence to a more personal situation than the progress of the French Revolution: Godwin's relationship with Mary Wollstonecraft. The author of the groundbreaking feminist manifesto *A Vindication of the Rights of Woman: With Strictures on Political and Moral Subjects* (1792), Wollstonecraft had recently returned from three years in France when she and Godwin again met in 1795. They had disliked each other when they first met in November 1791, but this time they became friends and, within a year, lovers. Although Wollstonecraft shared Godwin's distaste for marriage as an institution, they decided to marry when she became pregnant; the ceremony took place at St. Pancras Church on 29 March 1797. Godwin adopted Fanny, her illegitimate daughter by Gilbert Imlay. Wollstonecraft died on 10 September 1797, ten days after giving birth to Mary Wollstonecraft Godwin.

The grief-stricken Godwin published *Memoirs of the Author of a Vindication of the Rights of Woman* and *Posthumous Works of the Author of a Vindication of the Rights of Woman,* both in 1798. Godwin's inclusion, in the former work, of the facts of Wollstonecraft's relationship with Imlay and in the latter of her letters to him, written during her sojourn in France, proved to be a mistake. In an increasingly conservative era the knowledge that feminism's most vocal advocate had had an illicit affair and, worse, an illegitimate child, damaged Wollstonecraft's posthumous reputation, the cause she had championed, and, by association, the reputation of of her husband.

By the turn of the nineteenth century Godwin had slipped into infamy and relative obscurity. He augmented his sparse income and simultaneously pursued his interest in the education of youth by publishing pseudonymously a series of children's books—at that time a relatively new genre. In December 1801 he married Mary Jane Clairmont, a pioneer in the children's literature field. Clairmont, a widow, had two children by her previous marriage, and she and Godwin had a son, William, in 1803. In 1805 the Godwins purchased a book and toy shop to market their own productions, as well as a selection of English and French children's books.

In 1812 the nineteen-year-old poet Shelley became a frequent visitor in the Godwin household. Shelley admired *Political Justice* and incorporated many of its principles into his political treatise in verse, *Queen Mab: A Philosophical Poem, with Notes* (1813), a radical work that was banned by the government. Shelley loaned Godwin much-needed funds and flattered him profusely. Godwin was displeased, however, when Shelley took the antimatrimonial injunctions of *Political Justice* to heart and eloped to the Continent with sixteen-year-old Mary in 1814 despite the fact that he was already married. Shelley and Mary returned to England at the end of the year, but Godwin refused to see them. Two years later the couple, accompanied by Godwin's stepdaughter, Jane "Clair" Clairmont, joined George Gordon, Lord Byron, in Switzerland. There Mary wrote the first draft of the novel *Frankenstein; or, The Modern Prometheus* (1818), which she dedicated to Godwin as "the Author of Political Justice, Caleb Williams, Etc.," and Clair became pregnant with Byron's daughter, Allegra. On 9 October 1816 Fanny, Wollstonecraft's daughter by Imlay who had been adopted by Godwin, poisoned herself in Swansea, Wales. Shelley and Mary were married in December 1816, after Shelley's first wife, Harriet, drowned herself. Godwin then reconciled with the couple. Shelley drowned in a boating accident in July 1822 in Italy, where he was attempting to influence the Italian and Greek freedom fighters with Godwinian notions of political justice; Mary returned to England the following year.

On 8 September 1832 William Godwin Jr. died of cholera, leaving behind the manuscript for a novel, *Transfusion; or, The Orphans of Unwalden*. Godwin added a prefatory memoir of his son and published the work in 1835.

Godwin continued to write children's books, novels, and nonfiction, but his best work was behind him, and he is remembered almost exclusively for *An Enquiry Concerning the Principles of Political Justice* and *Things As They Are*. He died on 7 April 1836 after suffering for several days from catarrhal fever and was buried beside

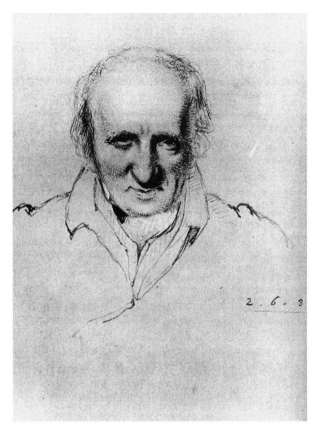

Godwin in 1832; portrait by William Brockendon
(National Portrait Gallery, London)

Wollstonecraft in St. Pancras Churchyard. His second wife died in 1841. In 1851 Godwin and Wollstonecraft were reburied in the churchyard at Bournemouth, near the Shelley home, Boscombe Manor, alongside Mary Shelley, who had died on 1 February of that year.

Letters:
Godwin and Mary: Letters of William Godwin and Mary Wollstonecraft, edited by Ralph M. Wardle (Lawrence: University of Kansas Press, 1966).

Bibliography:
Burton R. Pollin, *Godwin Criticism: A Synoptic Bibliography* (Toronto: University of Toronto Press, 1967).

Biographies:
C. Kegan Paul, *William Godwin: His Friends and Contemporaries,* 2 volumes (London: H. S. King, 1876);
Henry Noel Brailsford, *Shelley, Godwin, and Their Circle,* Home University Library of Modern Knowledge, no. 77 (New York: Holt, 1913; London: Oxford University Press, 1951);
Ford K. Brown, *The Life of William Godwin* (London & Toronto: Dent, 1926; New York: Dutton, 1926);

George Woodcock, *William Godwin: A Biographical and Critical Study* (London: Porcupine, 1946);

Rosalie Glynn Grylls, *William Godwin and His World* (London: Odhams, 1953);

Don Locke, *A Fantasy of Reason: The Life and Thought of William Godwin* (London & Boston: Routledge & Kegan Paul, 1980);

Peter H. Marshall, *William Godwin* (New Haven, Conn. & London: Yale University Press, 1984);

William St. Clair, *The Godwins and the Shelleys: The Biography of a Family* (Baltimore: Johns Hopkins University Press, 1989).

References:

David Fleisher, *William Godwin: A Study in Liberalism* (London: Allen & Unwin, 1951);

Kenneth W. Graham, *The Politics of Narrative: Ideology and Social Change in William Godwin's* Caleb Williams, AMS Studies in the Eighteenth Century, no. 16 (New York: AMS Press, 1990);

Graham, *William Godwin Reviewed: A Reception History, 1783–1834,* AMS Studies in the Nineteenth Century, no. 20 (New York: AMS Press, 2001);

Gary Kelly, *The English Jacobin Novel, 1780–1805* (Oxford: Clarendon Press, 1976);

David H. Monro, *Godwin's Moral Philosophy: An Interpretation of William Godwin* (London: Oxford University Press, 1953);

Mark Philp, *Godwin's Political Justice* (Ithaca, N.Y.: Cornell University Press, 1986);

Burton R. Pollin, *Education and Enlightenment in the Works of William Godwin* (New York: Las Americas, 1962);

Elton Edward Smith and Esther Greenwell Smith, *William Godwin* (New York: Twayne, 1965);

B. J. Tysdahl, *William Godwin as Novelist* (London: Athlone, 1981);

Gerald P. Tyson, *Joseph Johnson: A Liberal Publisher* (Iowa City: University of Iowa Press, 1979).

Papers:

Most of William Godwin's papers are in the Abinger Collection at the Bodleian Library, Oxford University. Other collections are in the British Museum; the Forster Collection of the Victoria and Albert Museum, London; Cambridge University; Harvard University; Yale University; Columbia University; and the Carl H. Pforzheimer Library of the Harry Ransom Humanities Research Center, University of Texas at Austin.

T. H. Green

(7 April 1836 – 26 March 1882)

Colin Tyler
University of Hull

See also the Green entry in *DLB 190: British Reform Writers, 1832–1914.*

BOOKS: *An Estimate of the Value and Influence of Works of Fiction in Modern Times: A Prize Essay, Read in the Theatre, Oxford, July 2nd, 1862* (Oxford: T. & G. Shrimpton, 1862; edited by Fred Newton Scott, Ann Arbor, Mich.: Wahr, 1911);

Liberal Legislation and Freedom of Contract: A Lecture (Oxford: Slatter & Rose, 1881);

The Work To Be Done by the New Oxford High School: A Lecture Addressed to the Wesleyan Literary Society (on December 19th, 1881) (Oxford: Slatter & Rose, 1882; London: Simpkin, Marshall, 1882);

Prolegomena to Ethics, edited by A. C. Bradley, preface by Edward Caird (Oxford: Clarendon Press, 1883);

The Witness of God, and Faith: Two Lay Sermons, edited by Arnold Toynbee (London: Longmans, 1883);

Works of Thomas Hill Green, 3 volumes, edited by R. L. Nettleship (London & New York: Longmans, Green, 1885–1888);

Lectures on the Principles of Political Obligation (London & New York: Longmans, Green, 1895);

Lectures on the Principles of Political Obligation and Other Writings, edited by Paul Harris and John Morrow (Cambridge & New York: Cambridge University Press, 1986);

Collected Works of T. H. Green, edited by Peter P. Nicholson, 5 volumes (Bristol: Thoemmes Press, 1997).

OTHER: David Hume, *The Philosophical Works,* 4 volumes, edited by Green and Thomas Hodge Grose (London: Longmans, Green, Reader & Dyer, 1874–1875).

T. H. Green

T. H. Green was a seminal liberal political theorist. The various aspects of his philosophical system—in particular, his conceptions of society, positive freedom, and the common good—remain profound and rich areas for research. Historically, he played a key role in transforming Anglo-American philosophy in the late nineteenth and early twentieth centuries: he helped to foster the study of Immanuel Kant and Georg Wilhelm Friedrich Hegel in Great Britain and the United States, and his own philosophy exerted a significant influence over such figures as F. H. Bradley, Bernard Bosanquet, Leonard T. Hobhouse, Herbert H. Asquith, Edward Caird, John Dewey, and

Josiah Royce. Few philosophers are as challenging–or as misunderstood–as Green.

Thomas Hill Green was born on 7 April 1836 in Birkin, a village near Pontyfract in the West Riding of Yorkshire, the youngest of four children and the second son of the Reverend Valentine Green and his first wife. After his mother's death in 1837, Green was raised by a nanny. The lack of class division that Green experienced in the village had a decisive effect on his later social and political convictions. He was educated at home from 1840 until he entered Rugby School in August 1850. He arrived there exactly two years before another vicar's son, Henry Sidgwick, who later became Green's friend and utilitarian combatant. Green rarely shone at Rugby, although his lethargy occasionally gave way to an enthusiasm for debating. In 1855 he surprised everyone by winning a prize for his translation from Latin into English of a passage in John Milton's *Areopagitica* (1644).

Green's interest in philosophy and religion was already evident at Rugby. In his edition of the *Works of Thomas Hill Green* (1885–1888) R. L. Nettleship quotes a fellow pupil to whom Green attempted "to impart some 'elementary metaphysical conceptions' in connexion with a bridge on the Newbold road; 'he endeavoured to make me understand that we each of us saw a different bridge.'" Nettleship's notebooks reveal that the fellow pupil was Sidgwick. Their discussions lasted for the rest of Green's life.

Green matriculated at Oxford on 30 May 1855 and entered Balliol College the following October. Benjamin Jowett was appointed as Green's tutor and played a pivotal role in his intellectual development. One thing that Jowett could not do, however, was force Green to work. In 1857 he gained only a second in Classical Moderations. Shocked by this relative failure, Green applied himself for the next two years and achieved a first in *Literae Humaniores*. Six months of cramming brought him a respectable third in law and modern history.

The philosophy curriculum at Oxford in Green's undergraduate days placed great emphasis on the Greeks, especially Aristotle, and on John Stuart Mill's *A System of Logic, Ratiocinative and Inductive: Being a Connected View of the Principles of Evidence, and the Methods of Scientific Investigation* (1843). Green was required to produce weekly essays on various topics, including "The Effect of Commerce on the Mind of a Nation," "Loyalty," "The Duties of the University to the State," "Conservatism," and "Legislative Interference in Moral Matters" (all of which are included in the fifth volume of *Collected Works of T. H. Green* [1997]). Each piece anticipates some aspect of

Green's mature writings: the duty to foster the moral improvement of one's fellows and, as a means to that end, to secure a minimum level of material well-being for each member of society; the need for state action, coupled with a fear of trampling on individual initiative and effort; and the importance of principled pragmatism in political reform.

Aside from his formal studies, Green took part in debates in the Oxford Union and, most significantly, was elected to the Old Mortality Club in May 1858. The club had been created the previous year by Green's friend John Nichol primarily for the discussion of philosophical and religious questions; its favorite public figures were radicals such as Thomas Carlyle and John Bright. Other members included James Bryce, Albert Venn Dicey, and Caird, who joined in 1860. The relationships that Green formed in the Old Mortality Club remained some of the strongest of his life; Caird became a particularly close friend.

Green's religious beliefs became increasingly unorthodox at Oxford, especially after his exposure to the biblical criticism of the Hegelian Tübingen School of David Strauss and F. C. Baur. Green was probably introduced to the writings of Hegel and the Tübingen School by Jowett, who had studied Hegel while traveling in Germany in 1844 and continued to do so after his return to England. He fostered an interest in Hegelianism at Oxford in opposition to the established British empiricist tradition of Mill and John Locke.

Green received his B.A. in 1859. He served as a lecturer on ancient and modern history at Balliol during the absence of W. L. Newman in 1860 and was appointed a college fellow in November of that year. In 1862 he was awarded an M.A. and won the Chancellor's Prize for an essay that was published the same year as *An Estimate of the Value and Influence of Works of Fiction in Modern Times: A Prize Essay, Read in the Theatre, Oxford, July 2nd, 1862*. On his return to England in June 1863 from a trip to Tübingen with a friend from Oxford, John Addington Symonds, Green toyed with the idea of becoming a Dissenting preacher. Later that year he declined the editorship of *The Times of India*. He was appointed librarian of Balliol in 1864, but he wanted to make a more meaningful contribution to society. In 1865 he accepted the post of assistant commissioner to the Schools Inquiry Commission. This experience gave Green an interest and expertise in educational reform. He resigned from the commission in 1866. Later that year he was named senior dean of Balliol and decided to pursue an academic career.

Henry Scott Holland, who was Green's pupil between 1866 and 1870, wrote that before coming under Green's influence

> we had lost all touch with the Ideals of life in Community. . . . Then at last, the walls began to break. . . . He gave us back the language of self-sacrifice, and taught us how we belonged to one another in the one life of high idealism. We took life from him at its spiritual value. And then we were startled and kindled by seeing this great intellectual teacher give himself over to civic duties, and take up personally the obligations of citizenship, and work for poor despised Oxford city. This had an immense practical effect on us.

Throughout these years Green developed his knowledge of Hegelian philosophy. Commentators have often assumed that Green's interest in Hegel remained strong from the time of his first acquaintance with Jowett. In reality, until at least 1855, and maybe as late as 1859, Green had had no discernible knowledge of Hegel. Among his papers is an unfinished essay, begun in the early 1860s, in support of Hegel's claim that "Whatever is real is rational, whatever is rational is real." This essay reveals that Green's knowledge of Hegel was not yet well developed.

Green's study of Hegel first bore real fruit with the appearance in September 1866 of "The Philosophy of Aristotle" in *The North British Review*. The piece shows a significant debt to Hegel in both terminology and methodology. The structure and content of the article closely follow Hegel's discussion of Aristotle's metaphysics in the second volume of his *Vorlesungen über die Philosophie der Geschichte* (1837; translated as *The Philosophy of History*, 1899), the enlarged 1840 German edition of which was available to Green in the Balliol College library. Like Hegel, Green sought to establish that Aristotle's conception of God as "the prime mover" prefigured Hegel's notion of the Absolute and that the latter represented the most permanently valuable element of Christian thought.

Green developed his conception of the Absolute in a somewhat different form in a paper for the Old Mortality Club, "Essay on Christian Dogma." Although its exact date of composition is unclear, its mature style and depth of philosophical insight strongly suggest that it was written in the mid 1860s at the earliest, and its Hegelian orientation indicates that it was unlikely to have been written later than the mid 1870s. In any case, it marks an important point in Green's development. Green argues that the times in which a literal reading of Scripture could satisfy a questioning Christian intellect were passing. The "thoughtful" Christian "is asking the faith which he professes for some account of its origin and authority," and "it is a

Benjamin Jowett, Green's tutor and mentor at Balliol College of the University of Oxford, in 1893 (photograph by H. H. H. Cameron)

pity that the answer should be confused by the habit of identifying christianity with the collection of propositions which constitute the written New Testament." The eternal truth of Christianity is contained in its spirit, not in the merely contingent letter of the Bible. Green calls for theology, as a system of orthodoxy and established creeds, to be replaced by a sustained philosophical examination of Christian life. The proper role of philosophy is to draw out the essence of Christianity by rationally articulating the intuitively presented kernel of religious thought. Modern human beings need to be able to express, both in knowledge and in action, the harmony underlying the world. In this way, the person can express his or her higher essence as a being created in God's image. This harmony is an inherent aspect of humanity's spiritual nature, although its manifestation is hindered by the physical medium through which it must be expressed. It is an inescapable part of the human condition that the individual's spiritual being must be realized slowly and imperfectly via his or her "animal" form.

Few orthodox Christian beliefs remain intact in Green's rereading of evangelical Protestantism. "Jesus of Nazareth was not divine from his birth," according to Green. He became so because the social influences that helped to form his adult character enlivened his immanent spiritual essence, which may have struggled to be realized in practice but was incapable of doing so without a sympathetic and nurturing cultural context. Jesus was special in that he realized to a unique extent the spiritual potential possessed by every human being, according to Green. Nevertheless, all humans have the potential to become "Christ" or "God's anointed one."

The necessary function of social roles, institutions, and social duties in the individual's spiritual self-realization is a central theme of the "Essay on Christian Dogma." Green concludes by arguing that St. Paul "appeals to the vision of Christ, yet he says that the 'seal' of his apostleship is found in the congregation that he founded." For Green, Paul's recognition of "God in the crucified Jesus" on the road to Damascus was only one stage in his spiritual growth. The next and equally important stage was the foundation of his "church." This church was not a collection of unquestioned and formalized services and dogmas such as is found in the later Christian tradition but a family of believers earnestly and conscientiously seeking to serve God as members of a living and inquiring spiritual community.

The requirement of rigorous inquiry is a vital ingredient of Green's moral, social, and religious thought. The same attitude is evident in his essays for the Ellerton theological prizes of 1860 and 1861, neither of which he won. His fellow Balliol undergraduate Lionel Tollemache recounts a revealing, although undated, incident in his 1895 biography of Jowett. Tollemache brought to Green's attention a passage from Jowett's essay "Casuistry and Confession" (1855) that concluded with an affirmation of "the rule of the Apostle, which may be paraphrased, 'Do as other men do in a Christian country.'" Tollemache says that Green "told me that he was aware that Jowett had laid down this principle, but that he himself thought it most immoral." For Green, even customary Christian morality, to be worthy of respect, must be rationally thought through and conscientiously judged by the individual for himself or herself.

Green's advocacy of active Christian citizenship was not a merely intellectual position: he had been actively involved in political discussions within the university since his arrival at Oxford. He took this involvement a stage further in the 1860s by moving into local politics. On 25 March 1867 he allied himself with the Oxford Reform League by speaking in favor of universal suffrage and secret ballots for Parliamentary elec-

tions to an audience mainly composed of workingmen. From that time onward he fulfilled a grueling schedule of public speaking and administrative work in support of various liberal causes, including the creation of a free, coeducational, national educational system; support for the North in the American Civil War; intelligent trade-union action for the improvement of wages and working conditions; the exposure of corrupt electoral practices; and the greater devolution of public powers to local governments. Green was convinced that by far the most important of the latter powers was the power to grant licenses for the sale of alcohol. One of Green's brothers was an alcoholic, and drunkenness afflicted all ages of the Victorian working class, including children. Alcoholism prevented individuals from realizing their potential; buying ale and liquor wasted money that could have been used to set up self-help groups, including cooperative societies; and public houses created a threat of violence in their neighborhoods. Green's preferred method of countering the liquor trade was "the local option," whereby town councils controlled the granting of licenses to sell alcohol and could close down unwelcome shops and public houses. The local option helped to foster community spirit and active Christian citizenship. For Green, political participation by the poor performed an educative role by encouraging them to develop their intellectual and moral capacities.

Political participation was, however, insufficient by itself for human spiritual development. Also needed was a proper intellectual orientation of the individual to the self and to the world. Evolutionary theory and geological discoveries were making it increasingly difficult for thoughtful individuals to believe in orthodox Christian dogma, opening the door to materialism and moral skepticism. Green regarded this movement away from a spiritual conception of life as a threat to human moral development, and the need to safeguard this conception was probably a large part of what attracted Green to Hegel.

In his 1868 essay "Popular Philosophy in Its Relation to Life" Green seeks to establish that the popular empiricist tradition derived from Locke, Hume, Mill, and Herbert Spencer and evident in the new popular "scientific" mind was too shallow to answer the spiritual needs of humanity. Hegel provided precisely what empiricism failed to give the inquiring modern soul: "formulae adequate to the action of reason as exhibited in nature and human society, in art and religion." For Green, Hegelianism was the philosophy of the future.

In 1868 Jowett put Green in charge of Balliol Hall, which provided cheap accommodation for poorer and older Balliol students. In 1869 he became a lecturer in ethics and a tutor at Balliol. In 1928 Asquith, the

Green (standing, center) and other members of the Old Mortality discussion club at Oxford. Seated, second from left,
is the future poet A. C. Swinburne; to the right of Swinburne is the founder of the club, John Nichol.

British prime minister from 1908 to 1916, recalled in his memoirs that in 1870 Green was "undoubtedly the greatest personal force in the real life of Oxford." On 1 July 1871 Green married Charlotte Byron Symonds, the sister of his friend John Addington Symonds.

Green's important critique of empiricism, "Introductions to Hume's 'Treatise of Human Nature,'" the preface to the edition of Hume's writings edited by Green and Thomas Hodge Grose and published from 1874 to 1875, represents a major step in his philosophical development. He argues that the self cannot be a Humean stream of sensations or a Lockean tabula rasa, because the coherent experiences that human beings have are only possible if the self employs a coherent system of a priori categories and relations to organize its sensations. This account is the conceptual foundation of Green's equivalent to Hegel's Absolute, which he later labeled "the spiritual principle" or "the eternal consciousness." He concludes his critique by expressing the hope that "the attention of Englishmen 'under

five-and-twenty' may be diverted from the anachronistic systems hitherto prevalent among us to the study of Kant and Hegel"; if so, "an irksome labour"–his attack on empiricism–"will not have been in vain."

Green was awarded an honorary degree by Glasgow University in April 1875. In 1876 he became classical tutor at Balliol, president of the Oxford Temperance Union, and the first member of the university to be elected to the local council by the people of Oxford, rather than being appointed to a seat by the university authorities. David George Ritchie reports that Green "went straight from the declaration of the poll, when he was elected a town councillor, to lecture on *The Critique of Pure Reason.*"

Among his acquaintances Green was renowned for his sharp tongue and sardonic humor, but in his writings he almost always treated his opponents with respect. Spencer, the proponent of materialism and Social Darwinism, was probably the only person to attract public sarcasm from Green. In the first of two articles on Spencer's epistemology in *The Contemporary Review* in 1877 and 1878 Green accuses Spencer of having the philosophical knowledge of "a raw undergraduate." The tone of both articles betrays a clear contempt for Spencer. Later, Green regretted his vitriol, but he could not bring himself to apologize to Spencer. He expressed his regret instead in an 1881 letter to the editor of *The Contemporary Review,* saying that "I make this acknowledgment merely for my own satisfaction, not under the impression that it can at all concern Mr. Spencer." As Green was more friendly and respectful in two otherwise similar 1885 articles on the materialist George Henry Lewes, it is likely that his antipathy to Spencer was more than strictly philosophical. He seems to have seen Spencer as little more than a dangerously influential charlatan.

After years of seeking a university chair in Scotland and England, Green was appointed to the coveted Whyte's Professorship of Moral Philosophy at Oxford in 1878. One of his most important acts was to instigate a series of lectures at which he could present more advanced research than was possible in regular courses. Some insight into their effect can be gained from Sidgwick's journals. The entry for 22–26 December 1884 reports that a letter from Alfred Marshall, then professor of economics at the University of Cambridge, where Sidgwick also taught, "contrasted my lecture-room, in which a handful of men are taking down what they regard as useful for examination, with that of (T. H.) Green, in which a hundred men–half of them B.A.'s–ignoring examinations, were wont to hang on the lips of the man who was sincerely anxious to teach them the truth about the universe and human life."

One of Green's most influential and philosophically significant practical activities was a lecture, "Liberal Legislation and Freedom of Contract," that he gave to the Leicester Liberal Association in Temperance Hall on 18 January 1881. In this talk Green argues that state intervention in factory conditions, land reform, and the liquor trade can be justified on the ground of securing greater personal liberty. He says that "freedom in all the forms of doing what one will with one's own, is valuable only as a means to an end. That end is what I call freedom in the positive sense: in other words, the liberation of the powers of all men equally for contributions to a common good." This kind of freedom is "a positive power or capacity of doing or enjoying, and that, too, something that we do or enjoy in common with others." Green also accords a necessary place to what he calls "negative" or "subjective" freedom.

In a laudatory 1877 *Academy* review of Edward Caird's *A Critical Account of the Philosophy of Kant* (1877) Green rejects the label "Hegelian" both for Caird and for himself, saying that he remains unclear as to precisely what Hegel was arguing. In his *Academy* "Review of J. Caird, 'Introduction to the Philosophy of Religion'" (1880) Green gently admonishes John Caird, Edward Caird's elder brother, for being "too much overpowered by Hegel." He argues that even though one "cannot drink too deep of Hegel," one "should sit rather looser to the 'dialectical' method than Dr. Caird has done." Even so, Green concludes that Hegel's system demonstrates "the vital truth" that every human mind is a manifestation of "one spiritual self-conscious being, of which all that is real is the activity or expression." Expounding, clarifying, and developing the implications of this message is the main task of what proved to be Green's last and most important philosophical work, *Prolegomena to Ethics* (1883).

Green did not live to complete *Prolegomena to Ethics.* Twenty to thirty pages were still to be written when he fell ill on 15 March 1882. Symptoms of blood poisoning began to appear on 22 March, and he died on 26 March. The cause of the blood poisoning remains uncertain. He was reported to have cut his hand while gardening the week before the symptoms appeared, but the official cause of death was "Ulcerated tonsils 10 days. Pyamia [*sic*] 4 days." More than two thousand people attended his funeral at St. Sepulchre's Cemetery, including many Oxford townspeople. Jowett gave the eulogy.

Green left instructions for the publication of two lay sermons he had delivered at Balliol; they appeared in 1883 as *The Witness of God, and Faith.* He also asked that A. C. Bradley edit the manuscript of *Prolegomena to Ethics* for publication. The work is important as Green's mature philosophical position; it is important historically because it formed the basis of his initial reputation and influence after his death.

The first of the four books of *Prolegomena to Ethics* includes a series of three articles that were originally published in 1881 in *Mind* under the title "Can There Be a Natural Science of Man?" Here, Green reiterates the position he had developed in the "Introductions to Hume's 'Treatise of Human Nature.'" In book 2 Green presents his theory of the will. He argues that the individual's intellect develops through acquaintance with, and rationalization of, existing human knowledge and institutions as they are expressed in the individual's society. Gradually, the agent's consciousness presents ideal or potential objects to itself that may or may not trigger desires for those objects. To the extent that the agent's character has reached its highest self-realization, the will seeks those objects that best accord with its true good as a manifestation of "the spiritual principle" or "eternal consciousness."

In book 3 Green develops his conception of the true good as the common good. He follows Hegel in stressing the importance of social life and social institutions as storehouses of the collective, but still imperfect, wisdom of humanity:

> Social life is to personality what language is to thought. Language presupposes thought as a capacity, but in us the capacity of thought is only actualised in language. So human society presupposes persons in capacity—subjects capable each of conceiving himself and the bettering of his life as an end to himself—but it is only in the intercourse of men, each recognised by each as an end, not merely a means, and thus as having reciprocal claims, that the capacity is actualised and that we really live as persons.

Green argues that the individual develops as a moral agent through recognizing and helping to manifest more fully the spiritual essence shared by all human beings. By helping others to develop, the individual also realizes himself or herself. In doing so, he or she experiences a contentment that is qualitatively different from and superior to a mere fleeting pleasure. It is "an abiding satisfaction of an abiding self"—the contentment of the eternal consciousness. Values are intersubjectively developed, validated, critiqued, and reformulated with largely subconscious reference to the demands of the eternal consciousness as the latter becomes determinate in the particular culture. (Green had expressed the same idea in "The Force of Circumstances," written in 1858 when he was an undergraduate: "The very essence of a true reformer consists in his being the corrector and not the exponent of the common feeling of his day.") This process of social criticism causes the individual to develop over time in both knowledge and ethical status. An essential aspect of this human progress is the widening of the area of the common good as individuals come to conceive of people of other nations and cultures as their fellow citizens. Ultimately, humans are all striving to live in a Kantian "kingdom of ends."

Throughout this discussion Green stresses the personal nature of social organizations and ethics. Just as there can be no nation except in the ideas that real people have about one another, so the "ultimate standard of worth is an ideal of *personal* worth. All other values are relative to value for, of, or in a person." Green distances himself from what he considers the fanciful positions of Giuseppe Mazzini and Auguste Comte, arguing that moral progress occurs only in actual persons, not "in some impersonal Humanity."

In the last chapter of book 3 and all of book 4 Green turns away from abstract analysis to the question of how one goes about performing one's duty in practice. The individual should begin by examining the virtues and expectations of his or her social roles. The next stage is to consider conscientiously whether or not acting in accordance with these virtues and expectations would tend to secure the greatest ethical good of one's society. The moral individual should ask:

> Does this or that law or usage, this or that course of action—directly or indirectly, positively or as preventive of the opposite—contribute to the better being of society, as measured by the more general establishment of conditions favourable to the attainment of the recognized virtues and excellences, by the more general attainment of those excellences in some degree, or by their attainment on the part of some persons in higher degree without detraction from the opportunities of others?

The decision cannot be predicted in advance or in the abstract. Only particular individuals can identify the particular moral dilemmas they face. Only the conscientious individual can judge which course of action is most likely to push his or her imperfect society toward embodying most perfectly a kingdom of ends. Green ends *Prolegomena to Ethics* with a detailed comparison of his own position and that of his friend and rival, Sidgwick.

Nettleship's *Works of Thomas Hill Green* includes "Lectures on the Principles of Political Obligation," which Green gave in 1879–1880. Green argues that political obligation arises out of the formative and sustaining role played by social forms in the development of personal moral agency and the need for the state to provide the conditions in which these social forms can function and develop. There can be no individuality without a sympathetic social context in which the agent can act. Once this social context grows to the size and complexity of a modern nation, the state is necessary to sustain a vibrant and self-developing culture and collective life. At the heart of the culture is a specific conception of the common good.

Green spends a significant amount of space attacking the social-contract theories of Locke, Thomas Hobbes, Benedict Spinoza, and Jean-Jacques Rousseau. According to Green, they all rely on an atomistic conception of the individual that is a mere fiction of the abstracting mind. This fiction caused social-contract theorists to misconceive the true nature of rights, which are not possessed by persons independently of their societies. Instead, "A right is a power of which the exercise by the individual or by some body of men is recognized by a society either as itself directly essential to a common good or as conferred by an authority of which the maintenance is recognized as so essential." There may be morally valid claims that society and the state have failed to recognize, but they do not become rights until they are so recognized. Following the legal philos-

*Charlotte Byron Symonds at the time of her marriage
to Green in 1871*

opher John Austin, Green says that a legitimate state is an organization that exercises complete coercive power within a certain territory in accordance with the common good of the society that it governs.

Throughout his analysis Green reiterates the necessity of uncoerced subjective identification with the common good. Nettleship expresses this thought in one of the section headings he added to the lectures: "Will, not force, is the basis of the state." Citizens must freely identify their own highest good with their community's values if the social customs, rules, and laws that embody these values are to exercise legitimate force over them; and the closer a culture comes to answering the demands of the eternal consciousness, the more completely and adequately the individual will identify with it.

Green anticipates the objection that his argument opens the door to totalitarian manipulation of the agent's self-image in the manner of Rousseau's civil religion in *Du Contrat social* (1762; translated as *An Inquiry*

into the *Nature of the Social Contract; Or, Principles of Political Right,* 1791). First, no culture perfectly satisfies the demands of the eternal consciousness, and no one can legitimately claim knowledge of how to perfect it that is reliable enough to justify totalitarianism. Second, for a political system or common good legitimately to command a citizen's obedience, it must accord with—and be recognized by the citizen through the exercise of his or her own reason as according with—the citizen's highest moral interests; unthinking obedience is slavery. The state should foster the social conditions under which rational agency is possible; it should, in Bosanquet's phrase, act as a "hindrance of hindrances" to the individual's self-realization. Where the state fails to fulfill this purpose, civil disobedience and—in the most extreme circumstances—revolution become not just a right but a duty.

Individuals should be left as "negatively" free as possible to develop their own highest capacities. External factors, however, often constitute obstacles too powerful for an unaided individual to overcome. Consequently, the state is required to ensure that everyone receives at least a basic level of education and that no one is forced by circumstances to accept dangerous or exploitative employment. Nevertheless, state officials should bear in mind that government action often removes the moral motivation, and hence the moral character, of a particular act. A person who would have performed a good act out of a sense of duty may act primarily out of fear if ordered to do so by the government. Also, leaving a problem to be solved by individuals and nongovernmental organizations brings home to the people the seriousness and complexity of that problem.

The basic principle of legitimate state action is the imperative to foster the best conditions for the citizens' moral self-realization. Punishment should aim to make good citizens of the guilty and of those who may be tempted to commit crimes. Family rights, particularly that of divorce, should balance the right of wives and husbands to live rewarding lives with the right of their children to live in morally enriching homes. In regard to the right to private property, Green argues that capitalism allows individuals to exercise their virtuous wills. Nevertheless, he reiterates that the state has a duty to force the modification or ending of harmful and exploitative contracts and practices in the name of fostering individual self-development.

Like that of *Prolegomena to Ethics,* the manuscript of *Lectures on the Principles of Political Obligation* was unfinished at the time of Green's death. Nevertheless, it remains his most important work after *Prolegomena to Ethics,* which forms its intellectual foundation. It was republished eleven times between 1901 and 1950.

Green's reputation has fluctuated wildly since his death. Initially, the British idealist movement that he helped to inspire flourished. Bosanquet, Ritchie, John H. Muirhead, Green's friend Edward Caird, and F. H. Bradley, who had attended Green's lectures in 1867, developed Green's philosophy in the years following his death. Even when, as in the case of Bradley, they came to disagree with Green on certain fundamental issues, their debt to him remained evident. *Essays in Philosophical Criticism,* a collection of pieces by his followers, including Bosanquet and Caird, was published in 1883. Leading philosophical journals such as *Mind* and *The International Journal of Ethics* were dominated by British idealists and their opponents. Green was even fictionalized as Professor Grey in Mrs. Humphry Ward's popular novel *Robert Elsmere* (1888). He was a seminal influence on British "new liberalism," as well as on important American philosophers such as Dewey and Royce. Through Asquith, he helped to set the tone of Edwardian politics. Theologically, his influence was evident in the slow liberalization of Anglicanism.

On the other hand, Sidgwick continued his criticisms following Green's death. Spencer acrimoniously attacked Green's "New Toryism" in *The Man versus the State* (1884). Bertrand Russell and G. E. Moore's critiques of Green, particularly the chapter "Metaphysical Ethics" in Moore's *Principia Ethica* (1903), dealt the first serious blows to Green's philosophical standing. World War I hastened the reaction against Hegelianism and its allegedly mystical and conservative implications. Although L. T. Hobhouse sought to distinguish Green's political philosophy from Bosanquet's, his attack on the latter in *The Metaphysical Theory of the State: A Criticism* (1918) greatly damaged Green's reputation. R. G. Collingwood was the only important sympathetic figure, and his influence was not strong enough to save Green's reputation. Between the two world wars many further attacks that used Green as a straw man occurred; the work of H. A. Pritchard and John Plamenatz are the most significant examples. The extent to which the tide had turned against Green by the middle of the twentieth century is shown by the fact that on the rare occasions when studies of his thought did appear, it was portrayed as dead dogma. In Melvin Ritcher's *The Politics of Conscience: T. H. Green and His Age* (1964), for example, Green is treated as a figure of purely historical interest.

The revival of philosophical interest in Hegelianism in the 1960s began to rehabilitate Green's philosophical reputation. The revival has gained momentum since then, mainly through the work of largely sympathetic critics such as Paul Harris, Peter Hylton, Alan Milne, Maria Dimova-Cookson, John Morrow, Peter P. Nicholson, Avital Simhony, Geoffrey Thomas, Ben

Wempe, and Colin Tyler. John Rawls, author of the widely acclaimed *A Theory of Justice* (1971), has expressed admiration for Green. Peter Gordon and John White's *Philosophers as Educational Reformers: The Influence of Idealism on British Educational Thought and Practice* (1979) is an important work on the educational thought of Green and the other British idealists, while Alan P. F. Sell's *Philosophical Idealism and Christian Belief* (1995) deals with their religious thought. Harris and Morrow brought out *Lectures on the Principles of Political Obligation and Other Writings* in 1986. Nicholson's edition of *Collected Works of T. H. Green* includes important previously unpublished material, such as lecture notes for an 1867 course on the history of moral and political philosophy and selections from Green's lectures and public speeches; he prefaces the volume with an introduction to Green's practical citizenship. T. H. Green is beginning to receive recognition as a major philosopher and liberal political theorist.

Biographies:

R. L. Nettleship, "Memoir," in *Works of Thomas Hill Green,* edited by Nettleship, volume 3 (London: Longmans, Green, 1888): xi–clxi;

Melvin Richter, *The Politics of Conscience: T. H. Green and His Age* (London: Weidenfeld & Nicolson, 1964).

References:

Olive Anderson, "The Feminism of T. H. Green: A Late-Victorian Success Story?" *History of Political Thought,* 12 (1991): 671–693;

Herbert H. Asquith, *Memories and Reflections, 1852–1927,* 2 volumes, edited by Alexander Mackintosh (London: Cassell, 1928);

Spencer Cecil Carpenter, *Church and People 1789–1889: A History of the Church of England from William Wilberforce to "Lux Mundi,"* 3 volumes (London: S.P.C.K., 1959), III: 483–484;

Maria Dimova-Cookson, *T. H. Green's Moral and Political Philosophy: A Phenomenological Perspective* (Basingstoke: Palgrave, 2001);

Sandra M. Den Otter, *British Idealism and Social Explanation: A Study in Late Victorian Thought* (Oxford & New York: Clarendon Press, 1996);

Peter Gordon and John White, *Philosophers as Educational Reformers: The Influence of Idealism on British Educational Thought and Practice* (London & Boston: Routledge & Kegan Paul, 1979);

W. D. Hait, "Motions of the Mind," in *Psychoanalysis, Mind, and Art: Perspectives on Richard Wolheim* (Oxford: Blackwell, 1992), pp. 220–236;

Christopher Harvie, *The Lights of Liberalism: University Liberals and the Challenge of Liberal Democracy 1860–86* (London: John Lane, 1976);

Leonard T. Hobhouse, *The Metaphysical Theory of the State: A Criticism,* Studies in Economic and Political Science, no. 51 (London: Allen & Unwin, 1918; New York: Macmillan, 1918);

Peter Hylton, "The Metaphysics of T. H. Green," *History of Philosophy Quarterly,* 2 (1985): 91–110;

Alan J. M. Milne, *The Social Philosophy of English Idealism* (London: Allen & Unwin, 1962), pp. 124–164;

Peter P. Nicholson, *The Political Philosophy of the British Idealists: Selected Studies* (Cambridge & New York: Cambridge University Press, 1990);

Nicholson, "T. H. Green and State Action: Liquor Legislation," *History of Political Thought,* 6 (1985): 517–550;

David George Ritchie, *The Principles of State Interference: Four Essays on the Political Philosophy of Mr. Herbert Spencer, J. S. Mill, and T. H. Green* (London: Swan Sonneschein, 1891);

Alan P. F. Sell, *Philosophical Idealism and Christian Belief* (Cardiff: University of Wales Press, 1995; New York: St. Martin's Press, 1995);

Andrew Seth and R. B. Haldane, eds., *Essays in Philosophical Criticism* (London: Longmans, Green, 1883);

Arthur Sidgwick and Eleanor M. Sidgwick, *Henry Sidgwick: A Memoir* (London & New York: Macmillan, 1906);

Henry Sidgwick, *Lectures on the Ethics of T. H. Green, Mr. Herbert Spencer, and J. Martineau,* edited by E. E. Constance Jones (London & New York: Macmillan, 1902);

Avital Simhony, "Idealist Organicism: Beyond Holism and Individualism," *History of Political Thought,* 10 (1991): 515–535;

Simhony, "T. H. Green's Theory of the Morally Justified Society," *History of Political Thought,* 10 (1989): 481–498;

Geoffrey Thomas, *The Moral Philosophy of T. H. Green* (Oxford: Clarendon Press, 1987; New York: Oxford University Press, 1987);

Lionel Tollemache, *Benjamin Jowett: Master of Balliol* (London & New York: Arnold, 1895), p. 118;

Colin Tyler, *Thomas Hill Green (1836–1882) and the Philosophical Foundations of Politics: An Internal Critique* (Lampeter, Wales & Lewiston, N.Y.: Edwin Mellen Press, 1997);

Andrew Vincent and Raymond Plant, *Philosophy, Politics, and Citizenship: The Life and Thought of the British Idealists* (Oxford: Blackwell, 1984);

Vincent, ed., *The Philosophy of T. H. Green* (Aldershot: Gower, 1986; Brookfield, Vt.: Gower, 1986);

David Weinstein, "Between Kantianism and Consequentialism in T. H. Green's Moral Philosophy," *Political Studies,* 16 (1993): 618–635;

Ben Wempe, *Beyond Equality: A Study of T. H. Green's Theory of Positive Freedom* (Delft, Netherlands: Eburon, 1986).

Papers:

T. H. Green's papers are in the Bodleian Library of the University of Oxford.

Sir William Hamilton

(3 March 1788 – 6 May 1856)

Anita R. Rose
Converse College

BOOKS: *De melaenae natura et curatione* (Edinburgh, 1819);

Sir William Hamilton and Phrenology: I. Correspondence Published in the Caledonian Mercury between Sir William Hamilton and Dr. Spurzheim, and between Sir William Hamilton and Mr. George Combe (Edinburgh: J. Anderson, 1828);

An Account of Experiment on the Weight and Relative Proportions of the Brain, Cerebellum, and Tuber Annulare, in Men and Animals, under the Various Circumstances of Age, Sex, Country, &c., prefix to Alexander Munro, The Anatomy of the Brain, with Some Observations of Its Functions (Edinburgh: Carfrae, 1831);

Character and Authorship of the Epistolae Obscurorum Virorum (Edinburgh, 1831);

The Works of George Dalgarno: A Critique (Edinburgh, 1835);

To the Right Honourable the Lord Provost, Magistrates, and Town Council, Patrons of the University of Edinburgh . . . 23d April, 1836 (Edinburgh, 1836);

Letter to the Right Honourable the Lord Provost of Edinburgh on the Election of a Professor of Mathematics: Comprising Observations on the Value of Mathematical Science as an Object of Liberal Study (Edinburgh: Ballantyne, 1838);

A Correspondence Relative to Certain Proceedings of the Town Council of Edinburgh Affecting the Philosophical Professors of the University, and in Particular the Professor of Logic and Metaphysics, anonymous (Edinburgh: Ballantyne & Hughes, 1839);

Be Not Schismatics, Be Not Martyrs by Mistake: A Demonstration, that "the Principle of Non-Intrusion," So Far from Being "Fundamental in the Church of Scotland," is Subversive of the Fundamental Principles of That and Every Other Presbyterian Church Establishment. Respectfully Submitted to the Reverend Convocation Ministers (Edinburgh: Maclachlan & Stewart, 1843; enlarged, 1843);

Discussions on Philosophy and Literature, Education and University Reform, Chiefly from the Edinburgh Review; Corrected, Vindicated, Enlarged, in Notes and Appendices

(London & Edinburgh: Longman, Brown, Green & Longmans, 1852; revised and enlarged edition, London: Longman, Brown, Green & Longmans, 1853; New York: Harper, 1853);

Lectures on Metaphysics and Logic, edited by H. L. Mansel and John Veitch (4 volumes, Edinburgh & London: Blackwood, 1859–1860; 2 volumes, Boston: Gould & Lincoln / New York: Sheldon, 1860);

The Worship of Priapus: An Account of the Fête of St. Cosmo and Damiano, Celebrated at Isernia, in a Letter to Sir Joseph Banks (London: Redway, 1883).

Editions and Collections: *Philosophy of Sir William Hamilton, Bart., Professor of Logic and Metaphysics in Edinburgh University,* edited by O. W. Wight (New York: D. Appleton, 1853);

The Metaphysics of Sir William Hamilton, Collected, Arranged, and Abridged, for the Use of Colleges and Private Students for Use in Colleges and Schools, edited by Frances Bowen (Cambridge, Mass.: Sever & Francis, 1861);

Works of William Hamilton, 7 volumes, edited by Savina Tropea (Bristol: Thoemmes Press, 2001).

OTHER: *The Works of Thomas Reid, D.D. Now Fully Collected, with Selections from His Unpublished Letters,* edited by Hamilton (Edinburgh: Maclachan & Stewart, 1846);

The Collected Works of Dugald Stewart, 11 volumes, edited by Hamilton (Edinburgh: Constable, 1854–1860; London: Hamilton, Adams, 1854–1860).

Today Sir William Hamilton, ninth baronet of Preston, is little more than a footnote in philosophy texts and histories. In his own time, however, he was regarded as one of the greatest and most erudite among living philosophers, and after his death his name was often mentioned alongside that of John Stuart Mill in discussions of philosophy and logic. Hamilton received this posthumous attention in part because of Mill's meticulous dissection of his ideas in *An Examination of Sir William Hamilton's Philosophy, and of the Principal Philosophical Questions Discussed in His Writings* (1865). That Mill viewed Hamilton as a major representative of intuitionism and dogmatism testifies to Hamilton's significance in the decades following his death.

Hamilton was the most influential proponent of Scottish common sense philosophy, also called common sense realism, a school of thought founded in the late eighteenth century by Thomas Reid and elaborated by George Campbell, James Oswald, James Beattie, and, most significantly, Dugald Stewart. Reid set out to disprove the skeptical epistemology (theory of knowledge) of his fellow Scot David Hume, who thought that reason was unable to prove the existence of things outside the mind; according to Reid, their existence does not need to be proved: it is directly perceived. Hamilton was, however, also influenced by the epistemology of the German philosopher Immanuel Kant, which held that things cannot be known as they are in themselves; all that can be known are phenomena, or appearances. As S. A.

Graves puts it, Hamilton gave the philosophy of common sense "a Kantian transformation with the axiom of relativity," dividing "things as they are 'absolutely' from things as they appear."

William Stirling Hamilton was born in Glasgow 3 March 1788 to William Hamilton, a surgeon and professor of anatomy and botany at the University of Glasgow, and Elizabeth Stirling Hamilton. Hamilton's father died when Hamilton was two. Hamilton attended the Glasgow grammar school from 1797 to 1800 and took Greek and Latin classes at the University of Glasgow in 1800. He was sent to schools in Chiswick, near London, and then in Bromley, Kent, from 1801 to 1803, then returned to the University of Glasgow from 1803 to 1806. He studied medicine at Edinburgh University in the winter of 1806–1807 before entering Balliol College, Oxford, in 1807 on a Snell Exhibition scholarship. Around this time he dropped his middle name, writing to his mother in 1807 that it was "nonsense having three long names." At Oxford he was acknowledged as a premier Aristotelian and won first honors on his examinations in 1811. His examination reading list became the stuff of legend; his tutor declared that he was prepared "in a much greater number of abstruse and difficult books than is usually the case." He received his B.A. in 1811. Despite gaining firsts in his examinations and being recognized as a first-rate scholar, Hamilton was not offered a fellowship at Oxford. Some sources suggest that this slight stemmed from the unpopularity of Scots in England at that time.

Hamilton had attended Oxford with an eye toward becoming a physician, but after graduation he turned his ambitions to law. He returned to Edinburgh, where he studied mainly antiquarian and civil law and was admitted to the bar in 1813. He received his M.A., in absentia, from Oxford in 1814. One of his first legal projects was to establish himself in 1816 as the rightful heir to the baronetcy of Robert Hamilton of Preston, thus earning the right to add "Sir" to his name.

Hamilton made two brief trips to the Continent, both to Germany on legal business: one in 1817 and the other in 1820. It may have been these visits that sparked his interest in Kant.

Hamilton was not a particularly successful or diligent lawyer. According to John Veitch's flattering *Memoir of Sir William Hamilton, Bart., Professor of Logic and Metaphysics in the University of Edinburgh* (1869), law was a "secondary pursuit" to scholarship and a life of the mind. On the death of Thomas Brown in 1820, Hamilton was nominated to succeed him in the chair in moral philosophy at Edinburgh University but lost out to his friend John Wilson. In 1821 he was appointed professor of civil history at the university for a negligible salary.

Hamilton's mother never remarried, and the two shared a residence until her death in January 1827. On 31 March 1829 Hamilton married Janet Marshall, his first cousin, who had acted as companion to his mother during the ten years before her death. The Hamiltons had a son, William, who became a military officer, and a daughter, Elizabeth.

In 1829 the editor of *The Edinburgh Review* asked Hamilton to contribute a review of Victor Cousin's *Cours de philosophie* (1828). Hamilton's piece, titled "The Philosophy of the Unconditioned," brought Continental speculative philosophy to the attention of British philosophers. Although Hamilton's review was critical, he and Cousin carried on a friendly correspondence for some years.

Hamilton continued to contribute regularly to *The Edinburgh Review* until he was elected to the chair of logic and metaphysics at Edinburgh in 1836; one more article appeared in 1839. The articles—on perception, the writings of Reid, and logic—established his reputation and led to his being offered the post. They locate his epistemological position between the Kantian view that knowledge is limited and the Scottish common sense belief that human beings have direct acquaintance with the eternal world.

Hamilton was, by all accounts, a compelling presence, described by contemporaries as "handsome," "athletic," and "manly." Veitch quotes the writer Thomas De Quincey as saying that he was struck by Hamilton's apparent lack of the "ostentation of learning" and his calm and unaffected "air of dignity and massy self-dependence." Hamilton's public demeanor, however, was stiff and portentous, a mode of presentation that carried over into his written work. His prose style was characterized, even by his friends and supporters, as "painful" and "elaborate," and Veitch admits that he was sometimes a "monster of erudition," intent on citing references and precedents rather than attaining clarity. On the other hand, Hamilton's precise scholarship helped him to translate Continental and ancient philosophy into terms his countrymen could appreciate. Later critics, however, have found inaccuracies in Hamilton's accounts of the thought of other philosophers.

Hamilton admired William Wordsworth's early poetry and thought that he detected a touch of Kantian philosophy in it. His younger brother, Thomas, was Wordsworth's neighbor in the Lake District, and in a letter quoted in Veitch's biography he reports that he asked Wordsworth "about that passage in the 'Excursion' that, according to William, refers to the doctrine of Kant. Wordsworth says he is utterly igno-

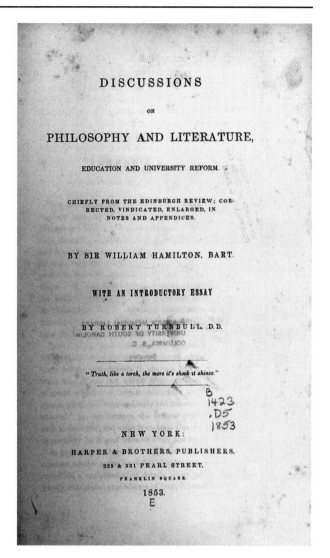

Title page for the U.S. publication of the revised and enlarged edition of Hamilton's collection of articles written between 1829 and 1839 (Thomas Cooper Library, University of South Carolina)

rant of everything connected either with Kant or his philosophy."

Hamilton suffered a paralytic stroke in 1844. With his wife acting as his amanuensis, he published an edition of Reid's writings in 1846; his preface, notes, and "supplementary dissertations" to the edition constitute an important statement of his own philosophy. The *Edinburgh Review* articles were collected in 1852 as *Discussions on Philosophy and Literature, Education and University Reform, Chiefly from the Edinburgh Review: Corrected, Vindicated, Enlarged, in Notes and Appendices* (1852).

In 1853 Hamilton's health was further damaged by a fall. In 1854 he began editing *The Collected*

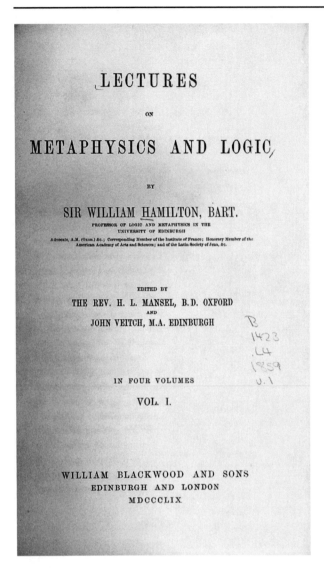

LECTURES

ON

METAPHYSICS AND LOGIC

BY

SIR WILLIAM HAMILTON, BART.
PROFESSOR OF LOGIC AND METAPHYSICS IN THE
UNIVERSITY OF EDINBURGH
Advocate, A.M. (Oxon.) &c.; Corresponding Member of the Institute of France; Honorary Member of the
American Academy of Arts and Sciences; and of the Latin Society of Jena, &c.

EDITED BY

THE REV. H. L. MANSEL, B.D. OXFORD
AND
JOHN VEITCH, M.A. EDINBURGH

IN FOUR VOLUMES

VOL. I.

WILLIAM BLACKWOOD AND SONS
EDINBURGH AND LONDON
MDCCCLIX

*Title page for the posthumous collection of Hamilton's Edinburgh
University lectures (Thomas Cooper Library,
University of South Carolina)*

Works of Dugald Stewart (1854–1860). He died on 6 May 1856 of complications from his fall and was buried in St. John's Chapel in Edinburgh. His 8 May 1856 obituary in *The Times* (London) calls his erudition "unrivaled" and says that his research was "enormous, and amid the general poverty of Scottish scholarship he achieved a reputation as one of the most learned men of his time." Veitch and H. L. Mansel edited and published his Edinburgh University lectures in four volumes as *Lectures on Metaphysics and Logic* (1859–1860).

In these works Hamilton, along with the other members of the Scottish common sense school, holds that perception provides direct knowledge of the existence of external objects, or the "nonego"; it is not the case that one is acquainted only with mental con-

tents, or "ideas," from which the existence of external objects must be inferred. Similarly, the existence of the "ego," or self, is known through self-consciousness; it is not inferred as some sort of unknown "stage" that supports the sensations and feelings that are directly perceived. Hamilton refers to his position as "natural or intuitive realism" or "natural dualism." On the other hand, the knowledge both of objects and of the self is relative, not absolute. What is perceived in regard to external objects are their appearances as modified by the senses, the medium through which they are perceived, and the mind itself. In regard to the self, what is directly perceived are subjective experiences, such as sensations, feelings, and emotions. In both cases, a "law of thought" compels one to think of something absolute as the source of the relative phenomena that are perceived.

Furthermore, the mind always thinks of objects in relation to other objects; it classifies them or subsumes them under a concept—in Hamilton's terms, thought "conditions" its objects. Thus, every whole is conceived of as composed of parts and as being itself a part of a greater whole; knowledge is, then, only of "the relative manifestations of an existence, which in itself it is our highest wisdom to recognize as beyond the reach of philosophy." The human mind can never arrive at the totally unconditioned, or the absolute, but it must acknowledge that the absolute exists. Hamilton points out that it is impossible for the mind to conceive of either space or time as infinite or as finite; yet, in themselves they must be one or the other, since the two possibilities are mutually exclusive. The human mind, in its weakness, operates in the realm of the "Conditioned," which "is the mean between two extremes—two unconditionates, exclusive of each other, neither of which can be conceived as possible, but of which . . . one must be admitted as necessary." Like Kant, Hamilton contends that even though God, freedom, and immortality cannot be directly known or demonstrated to exist, one is entitled to believe in their existence.

In logic, Hamilton's major innovation was his doctrine of the quantification of the predicates of categorical propositions. In traditional logic, the four kinds of categorical statements were "All *S* are *P*," "No *S* are *P*," "Some *S* are *P*," and "Some *S* are not *P*." In each case the subject term is quantified as universal ("all," "no") or particular ("some"), but the predicate term is left unquantified. Hamilton says that the predicate is always thought of as quantified, and that the quantification should be made explicit. For example, "All humans are all rational beings" would mean that all and only humans are rational, while "All humans are some mammals" would mean that all humans are mammals but that other creatures are also mammals. According to Hamilton, this innovation would allow all propositions to be treated as equations of subject and predicate, which, in turn, would make it possible to develop a "logical calculus" or "scheme of logical notation" that would permit arguments to be analyzed "with even a mechanical simplicity." Hamilton did not go on to develop such a calculus, and the systems of symbolic logic that were soon elaborated did not make use of his predicate-quantification idea.

In *An Examination of Sir William Hamilton's Philosophy and of The Principal Philosophical Questions Discussed in His Writings* (1865), Mill shows that Hamilton's attempt to combine common sense philosophy with Kantianism is untenable and leads, as he says in his *Autobiography* (1873), to an "almost incredible number of inconsistencies which shewed themselves on comparing different passages with one another." A major contradiction is that between Hamilton's doctrine of the relativity of knowledge and his realism: he should have said that only the knowledge not contributed by the object itself is relative. Mill opposes what he called Hamilton's philosophy of "Intuition" with his own empiricist philosophy of "Experience and Association." He denies that the mind immediately perceives the existence of an external reality, as Hamilton and the other common sense realists claim; according to Mill, repeated experiences lead to a belief in external reality, or matter, as "a permanent possibility of sensation." Hamilton claimed that the existence of free will was a direct deliverance of "consciousness"; Mill counters that "If our so-called consciousness of what we are able to do is not borne out by experience, it is a delusion. It has no title to credence but as an interpretation of experience, and if it is a false interpretation, it must give way." Mill is convinced that in "clinging" to the doctrine of free will, Hamilton "was thoroughly his own dupe, and that his speculations have weakened the philosophical foundation of religion fully as much as they have confirmed it."

One of Mill's primary objections to Hamilton's philosophy is the way that it was developed by Mansel after Hamilton's death. In *The Limits of Religious Thought Examined in Eight Lectures: Preached before the University of Oxford, in the Year M.DCCC.LVIII, on the Foundation of the Late Rev. John Bampton, M.A., Canon of Salisbury* (1858), Mansel argues that although, as Hamilton showed, positive knowledge can be had only of the finite and the conditioned, one can have "negative knowledge" of the Unconditioned by attributing conditioned qualities to it and then removing their normal limits. For example,

goodness, knowledge, and power are only known in their limited or conditioned human manifestations; but they can be attributed to God in an unconditioned and infinite sense. But these attributes as applied to God must be understood analogically and not literally. God's goodness, for example, differs from human goodness in kind, not just in degree: "The infliction of physical suffering, the permission of moral evil, the adversity of the good, the prosperity of the wicked, these are facts which no doubt are reconcilable, we know not how, with the Infinite Goodness of God, but which certainly are not to be explained on the supposition that its sole and sufficient type is to be found in the finite goodness of man." Mill devotes the seventh chapter of *An Examination of Sir William Hamilton's Philosophy* to Mansel's views. He says that this kind of circular reasoning requires people to worship a being who is unrecognizable in terms of anything considered virtuous by humans: "I will call no being good, who is not what I mean when I apply that epithet to my fellow-creatures; and if such a being can sentence me to hell for not so calling him, to hell I will go."

Mill's critique provoked a firestorm of rebuttal and defense of Hamilton's ideas. Within a few years of the publication of *An Examination of Sir William Hamilton's Philosophy* Mansel, Veitch, James McCosh, and W. G. Ward responded to Mill's criticism of Hamilton and brought the debates pitting intuitionism against empiricism to the fore of philosophical debate. The third edition (1867) of *An Examination of Sir William Hamilton's Philosophy* included Mill's rejoinders.

Common sense philosophy in general, and Hamilton's works in particular, were widely read in American universities in the years after his death. O. W. Wight edited a compilation of Hamilton's works in 1853 for use as a textbook; the work went into its sixth edition in 1860. In 1861 Frances Bowen of Harvard University edited *The Metaphysics of Sir William Hamilton, Collected, Arranged, and Abridged, for the Use of Colleges and Private Students for Use in Colleges and Schools.* McCosh, a fellow Scotsman and member of the common sense school, brought Hamilton's philosophy to Princeton University, of which he was president from 1868 to 1888. Nevertheless, Hamilton has been dismissed as a minor figure in Great Britain and the United States since the early part of the twentieth century.

Biography:
John Veitch, *Memoir of Sir William Hamilton, Bart., Professor of Logic and Metaphysics in the University of Edinburgh* (Edinburgh & London: Blackwood, 1869).

References:

M. P. W. Bolton, *Examination of the Principles of the Scoto-Oxonian Philosophy,* revised edition (London: Chapman & Hall, 1861);

S. A. Graves, *The Scottish Philosophy of Common Sense* (Oxford: Oxford University Press, 1960);

H. L. Mansel, *The Limits of Religious Thought Examined in Eight Lectures: Preached before the University of Oxford, in the Year M.DCCC.LVIII, on the Foundation of the Late Rev. John Bampton, M.A., Canon of Salisbury* (Oxford: Printed by J. Wright for J. Murray, 1858);

Mansel, *The Philosophy of the Conditioned: Comprising Some Remarks on Sir W. Hamilton's Philosophy, and on Mr. J. S. Mill's Examination of That Philosophy* (London & New York: Strahan, 1866);

Terrence Martin, *The Instructed Vision: Scottish Common Sense Philosophy and the Origins of American Fiction* (Bloomington: Indiana University Press, 1961);

James McCosh, *Philosophical Papers* (London: Macmillan, 1868; New York: R. Carter, 1869);

McCosh, *The Scottish Philosophy: Biographical, Expository, Critical, from Hutcheson to Hamilton* (London: Macmillan, 1875);

John Stuart Mill, *Autobiography* (London: Longmans, Green, Reader & Dyer, 1873);

Mill, *An Examination of Sir William Hamilton's Philosophy, and of the Principal Philosophical Questions Discussed in His Writings* (London: Longman, Green, Longman, Roberts & Green, 1865; revised edition, London: Longmans, Green, Reader & Dyer, 1867); republished as volume 9 of *Collected Works of John Stuart Mill,* edited by J. M. Robson (Toronto: University of Toronto Press, 1979; London: Routledge & Kegan Paul, 1979);

Daniel Robinson, *The Story of Scottish Philosophy: A Compendium of Selections from the Writings of Nine Pre-Eminent Scottish Philosophers, with Bibliographical Essays* (New York: Exposition, 1961);

James Hutchinson Stirling, *Sir William Hamilton: Being the Philosophy of Perception. An Analysis* (London: Longmans, Green, 1865);

John Veitch, *Hamilton,* Philosophical Classics for English Readers, no. 6 (Edinburgh & London: Blackwood, 1882).

R. M. Hare

(21 March 1919 – 29 January 2002)

Peter Dalton
Florida State University

BOOKS: *Oxford's Traffic: A Practical Remedy* (Buckingham: Privately printed, 1948);

The Language of Morals (Oxford: Clarendon Press, 1952; revised edition, Oxford: Oxford University Press, 1961);

Freedom and Reason (Oxford: Clarendon Press, 1963);

Practical Inferences (London: Macmillan, 1971);

Essays on Philosophical Method (London: Macmillan, 1971);

Essays on the Moral Concepts (London: Macmillan, 1972);

Applications of Moral Philosophy (London: Macmillan, 1972);

Moral Thinking: Its Levels, Method and Point (Oxford: Clarendon Press, 1981);

Plato (Oxford: Oxford University Press, 1982);

Essays in Ethical Theory (Oxford: Clarendon Press, 1989);

Essays on Political Morality (Oxford: Clarendon Press, 1989);

Essays on Religion and Education (Oxford: Clarendon Press, 1992);

Essays on Bioethics (Oxford: Clarendon Press, 1993);

Sorting Out Ethics (Oxford: Clarendon Press, 1997);

Objective Prescriptions and Other Essays (Oxford: Clarendon Press, 1999; New York: Oxford University Press, 1999).

OTHER: "Religion and Morals," in *Faith and Logic: Oxford Essays in Philosophical Theology,* edited by Basil Mitchell (London: Allen & Unwin, 1957), pp. 176–193;

"Conventional Morality," "Decision," "Deliberation," "Ethics," "Intention," and "Right and Wrong," in *A Dictionary of Christian Ethics,* edited by John McQuarrie (London: SCM, 1967), pp. 74, 85, 86, 114–116, 170–171, 299;

"Drugs and the Role of the Doctor," in *Personality and Science: An Interdisciplinary Discussion,* edited by I. T. Ramsey and Ruth Porter (Edinburgh: Churchill Livingstone, 1971), pp. 85–92;

"Non-Descriptivist Ethics" and "Utilitarianism," in *Encyclopedia of Bioethics,* edited by Warren Reich

R. M. Hare (photograph by Ellin Hare)

(New York: Free Press, 1979), pp. 447–450, 424–428;

"Moral Conflicts," in *The Tanner Lectures on Human Values,* edited by Sterling M. McMurrin (Salt Lake City: University of Utah Press, 1980; Cambridge: Cambridge University Press, 1980), pp. 169–193;

"Do Agents Have to Be Moralists?" in *Gewirth's Ethical Rationalism: Critical Essays with a Reply by Alan Gewirth,* edited by Edward Regis Jr. (Chicago: University of Chicago Press, 1984), pp. 52–58;

"The Ethics of Experimentation on Human Children," in *Logic, Methodology and Philosophy of Science: Proceedings of the Seventh International Congress of Logic, Methodology, and Philosophy of Science, Salzburg, 1983,* edited by Ruth Barcan Marcus, Georg J. W. Dorn, and Paul Weingartner VII, Studies in Logic and the Foundation of Mathematics, volume 114 (Amsterdam & Oxford: North Holland, 1986);

"Conventional Morality," "Decision," "Deliberation," "Ethics," "Intention," "Right and Wrong," "Universalizability," and "Utilitarianism," in *A New Dictionary of Christian Ethics,* edited by McQuarrie and James F. Childress (London: SCM, 1986); republished as *The Westminster Dictionary of Christian Ethics* (Philadelphia: Westminster Press, 1986), pp. 127, 147–148, 149–150, 206–207, 306–307, 555–556, 636–638, 640–643;

Hare and Critics: Essays on Moral Thinking, edited by Douglas Seanor and Nicholas Fotion, contributions by Hare (Oxford: Clarendon Press, 1988), pp. 199–293;

"Universal Prescriptivism," in *A Companion to Ethics,* edited by Peter Singer (Oxford: Blackwell, 1991), pp. 451–462;

"Moral Terms," "Prescriptivism," "Slavery," "Universalizability," and "Weakness of Will," in *Encyclopedia of Ethics,* edited by Lawrence C. Becker and Charlotte B. Becker, Garland Reference Library of the Humanities, volume 925 (New York: Garland, 1992), pp. 868–871, 1007–1010, 1159–1160, 1258–1261, 1304–1307;

"Utilitarianism and Deontological Principles," in *Principles of Health Care Ethics,* edited by Raanan Gillon (Chichester & New York: Wiley, 1993);

"Objective Prescriptions," in *Ethics,* edited by A. Phillips Griffiths, Royal Institute of Philosophy Supplement, no. 35 (Cambridge & New York: Cambridge University Press, 1993), pp. 1–17;

"Brandt's Methods of Ethics," in *Rationality, Rules and Utility: New Essays on the Moral Philosophy of Richard Brandt,* edited by Brad Hooker (Boulder, Colo. & Oxford: Westview Press, 1993), pp. 67–80;

"The Structure of Ethics and Morals," in *Ethics,* edited by Singer (Oxford: Oxford University Press, 1994), pp. 319–331;

"Hare: A Philosophical Self-Portrait," in *A Dictionary of Philosophy,* edited by Thomas Mautner (Cambridge, Mass. & Oxford: Blackwell, 1996), pp. 177–178;

"Towards Objectivity in Morals," in *Contemporary British and American Philosophy and Philosophers,* edited by Ouyang Kang and S. Fuller (Beijing: People's Press, 1998).

SELECTED PERIODICAL PUBLICATIONS–UNCOLLECTED: "The Objectivity of Values," *Common Factor,* 1 (1964);

"Geach on Murder and Sodomy," *Philosophy,* 52 (1977): 467–472;

"An Ambiguity in Warnock," *Bioethics,* 1 (1987): 175–178;

"The Poverty of Ideas," *Guardian* (London), 11 October 1988; republished in *Political Studies Association* (June 1990);

"Brandt on Fairness to Happiness," *Social Theory and Practice,* 15 (1989): 59–65.

R. M. Hare was the leading British moral philosopher of the last half of the twentieth century. His overarching aim, which he relentlessly pursued, was to demonstrate how rational argumentation about morality is possible. He achieved this aim by using the logic of language to formulate a theory of moral reasoning. With the support of facts about human preferences, he used this theory to construct, in turn, a normative theory basing personal obligation on an impartial concern for the interests of all people. A prolific author and an adviser to university, church, local, and national organizations, he applied these theories to provide guidance on a host of practical issues. While developing and defending his theories over a fifty-year span, he maintained a remarkable consistency—a challenging task, given that he was attempting to harmonize elements that many philosophers consider irreconcilable: a morally neutral logic capable of yielding substantive moral conclusions; statements with both prescriptive (action-guiding) and descriptive (objectively truthful) meanings; and principles that are Kantian (nonconsequentialist) and utilitarian (consequentialist). The result is a body of work that speaks to nearly every issue in contemporary moral philosophy.

Richard Mervyn Hare was born in Backwell, near Bristol, on 21 March 1919 to Charles Francis Aubone Hare, a paint manufacturer, and Louise Kathleen Simonds Hare. He attended Rugby School, then enrolled at Balliol College of Oxford University. He left college after the outbreak of World War II in 1939 to join the British army; serving with the Indian Mountain Artillery, he was taken prisoner after the fall of Singapore in 1942 and spent eight months as a slave laborer building the Burma Railway—an ordeal in which many of his fellow prisoners died. Freed in 1945, he returned to Balliol. He received his B.A. and M.A.

degrees in 1947 and was named a fellow and tutor at Balliol. His duties involved some lecturing and seminar work but for the most part called on him to serve as tutor to about twenty students each term. Like many faculty members, he also took on some administrative responsibilities (for example, for a while he was in charge of maintenance of the college buildings). In December 1947 he married Catherine Verney; they have a son, John Edmund, and three daughters: Bridget Rachel, Amy Louise, and Ellin Catherine.

From the beginning Hare's philosophical work focused on morality. He has said that he took up the study of philosophy because he thought that it could provide answers to the kinds of moral questions that had confronted him during the war, such as whether a citizen is obligated to serve in the military or whether it is ever right to kill or injure other human beings. The dominant ethical theorists of the time denied that answers to such questions could be rationally defended, and some questioned whether moral statements could be true or even meaningful. H. A. Prichard and W. D. Ross promulgated intuitionism, the view that moral beliefs are self-evident convictions held by all or, at least, all thoughtful, educated people. A. J. Ayer and other logical positivists held that moral statements are cognitively meaningless because they cannot be verified as scientific and logical statements can. The leading proponent of emotivism, the American philosopher C. L. Stevenson, disagreed with the positivists that moral statements are meaningless but held that they are expressions of attitudes, feelings, and desires that function to influence conduct. Finally, ordinary-language philosophy, originated by J. L. Austin and Ludwig Wittgenstein, surveyed the uses to which moral statements could be put but viewed the uses themselves as deriving, like spelling and grammar, from custom and tradition and, therefore, as not rationally defensible.

In opposition to all these views, Hare set out to show how language embodies a method of rationally supporting moral beliefs. He defended his approach in a dissertation that won the T. H. Green Moral Philosophy Prize in 1950. In 1951, in addition to his tutoring duties, he was named a university lecturer in philosophy. The publication of *The Language of Morals* in 1952 established Hare as a major thinker in the field of ethics.

Though *The Language of Morals* is a "logical study of the language of morals," Hare does not focus exclusively on English but deals with any language that embodies certain concepts. No language has to incorporate these concepts; a few languages may not have them; and any language that does include them can alter or eliminate them. Nonetheless, these concepts are, according to Hare, the basic constituents of moral

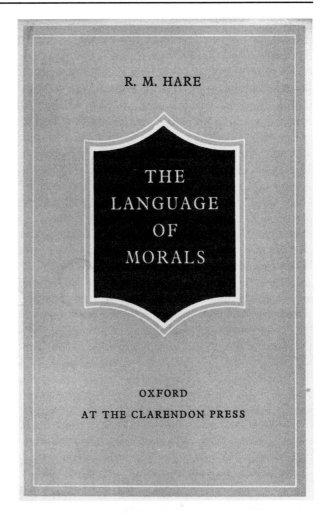

*Dust jacket for the 1952 work that established
Hare as a major thinker in the field of ethics
(Bruccoli Clark Layman Archives)*

thinking. Foremost among them is the prescription, which is any linguistic act that guides conduct: examples include advising, approving, grading, commanding, and criticizing. Almost any word or statement can be prescriptive, but most languages include special structural forms, such as the imperative sentence, and special words for this purpose. Some prescriptive words, such as "ought," "right," and "good," are highly general; Hare calls them "primary." They function largely to evaluate and have little descriptive content. Other prescriptive words, such as "industrious," "modest," and "mean-spirited," are more specific; Hare calls them "secondary." These words are also evaluative, but they include a substantial descriptive component. Hare says that a prescription reveals a decision, choice, or preference on the part of the speaker: if a person sincerely utters a prescription, he or she will act—or, at least, will be strongly disposed to act—in accordance with the prescription.

Though prescriptions always have a descriptive component, they are not descriptions. They do not tell one what is the case; they tell one to make something the case. They do not represent something in the world; they guide one to do something in the world. Because prescriptions are not descriptions, some philosophers have concluded that they cannot be true or false and, hence, cannot figure in inferences. If this argument is correct, and if Hare is right in thinking that all evaluative language is prescriptive, then there can be no reasoning about values, including morality. But Hare insists that there can be prescriptive inferences, because prescriptive words and statements include meanings that allow for entailments and inconsistencies: "You ought to do it" entails "There is a reason to do it," and "It is not wrong" contradicts "You ought not to do it." A study of language use reveals many prescriptive inferences. Common ones begin with a rule-like prescription that Hare calls a "principle"–"One ought to help strangers," for example–then cite certain facts about a situation and conclude with a specific prescription, such as "You ought to show this man the way to the bus station." All prescriptive inferences conform to a stricture laid down by the eighteenth-century Scottish philosopher David Hume: an "ought" judgment cannot be inferred from "is" judgments alone. Hence, these inferences must not begin only with facts and conclude with a prescription; they must begin with at least one prescription–preferably, a principle.

Principles are not self-evident; their merits are debated, and one is free to adopt or reject them. Thus, moral reasoning, while logical, does not begin or end with certainties. Most principles are learned in childhood; as children become adults they may alter or give up the principles their elders or society taught them and choose principles of their own. One chooses principles primarily by considering the likely consequences of acting on them and considering one's own preferences for some consequences over others. This consideration should be undertaken thoughtfully, in cognizance of all relevant facts, and without the influence of anything, such as emotion or bias, that impedes sound reasoning. Ultimately, however, a person must choose his or her principles; thinking alone will not provide them.

Hare illustrates his notion of a prescription by analyzing the word *good*. He points out that something is not merely good; it is good because of what is. For example, a strawberry is good because it is ripe, red, and sweet. While *good* is prescriptive, its use is always linked to some descriptive properties. One is guided in its usage by a standard that tells one what descriptive properties merit an application of the prescriptive term. Since this standard is rule-like, it is a principle. With the backing of this standard, descriptive properties provide the reason for a prescription and, hence, for the action it guides a person to take: for example, "I'll eat this strawberry because it is a good one, and it is good because it is ripe, red, and sweet."

The descriptive properties designated by standards reveal a key feature of prescriptive language: it is "covertly universal." That is, a person who prescribes in one case is logically committed to prescribing in the same way in any identical case, because he or she has prescribed for a reason that refers to certain descriptive properties that can be found in many other cases. For the person to prescribe differently in other cases, there would have to be a reason for the difference; but reasons refer only to descriptive properties, which by hypothesis are the same in all the cases. The only way around this difficulty, other than prescribing irrationally–for example, on a whim or out of emotion–is to change one's standards of prescription. And one can do so: one can decide, for example, that a good strawberry is firm and tart rather than ripe, red, and sweet.

Despite this dependence of prescriptions on what can be described, Hare rejects all "descriptivist" theories of evaluative concepts. Such theories either identify an evaluative property with a descriptive one, as in the claim by the founder of utilitarianism, Jeremy Bentham, that goodness is simply pleasure, or assert that a descriptive property entails an evaluative one, as in theories that assert that anything God commands is good. Such theories are logically incoherent, Hare says; since one is free to prescribe and to choose standards for prescribing, nothing that one describes can make one prescribe anything in particular. More important, since what one describes is the reason for one's prescription, the two are only contingently related: if a strawberry is good because it is sweet, saying that it is good cannot be just another way of saying that it is sweet; *good* and *sweet* would be redundant if goodness and sweetness were identical. Nor can a strawberry's being sweet entail its being good, since one can deny, without being guilty of inconsistency, that a sweet strawberry is good. *Good* is used for commending, which it could not be if it were merely descriptive. The same holds for all other evaluative terms: since they have a prescriptive component, they cannot be merely descriptive.

Hare argues that since moral words and judgments are evaluative, they have the logical features of prescriptions. Moral language is distinctive because it is about human conduct, and all users of language are human. Moral language is also of social importance, since one person's moral conduct has effects on others.

While many moral philosophers discussed Hare's first book and his other early published work, foremost among his critics were three of his female colleagues at Oxford. G. E. M. Anscombe challenged all leading contemporary philosophers to explain whether their theories could substantiate absolute obligations, such as "Do not punish the innocent." Hare's theory seemed vulnerable, since his principles can be chosen or rejected. Philippa Foot claimed that some moral terms, such as *courteous,* include necessarily related prescriptive and descriptive components. She also argued, using examples such as praising someone for clasping his hands three times, that some principles cannot be chosen, while others must be. Iris Murdoch objected that since most evaluative concepts depict something–a polite daughter-in-law, for example–some prescriptive terms are inherently descriptive. She also worried that Hare was similar to the existentialists in claiming that people are utterly free to choose, with no basis whatsoever, the principles by which they will live.

Hare remained a tutor until 1966; from 1951 to 1966 he was also a university lecturer in philosophy, and from 1963 to 1966 he was Wilde Lecturer on Natural and Comparative Religion. In *Freedom and Reason* (1963), begun while he was a visiting professor at Princeton in 1957, Hare develops his ethical theory to show that the freedom to choose principles is consistent with the rationality of moral reasoning. Moral judgments, he says, are evaluative and, hence, prescriptive; but they are also descriptive, since what they describe is the reason for the prescription. Standards for these reasons are set out in moral principles. These principles commit one to "universalizability"–the same concept that he called "covert universality" in *The Language of Morals:* if what one describes is the reason for a prescription in one case, such as "Never hit an infant for crying," then to avoid inconsistency one must prescribe in the same way in any identical situation. Moral principles have two other key logical features. They are universal, in that they apply to all moral agents in the same kind of situation. And they have a degree of generality, since they always refer to properties–*infant* is less general than *human* or *child* but more general than *English infant*– with a limited range.

The core of *Freedom and Reason* is Hare's account of the reasoning one uses to choose moral principles. The reasoning is hypothetical in form: one considers a situation in which one is faced with a decision and initially chooses a prescription for that situation–"Insult her because she has angered me," for example. If a moral principle is to support this choice, that principle will endorse the same prescription in any identical situation. One then reflects on all the kinds of situations in which someone might act on this principle, all the positions in which one might find oneself in these situations, and the likely consequences for the people in those positions if the principle is followed. This reflection requires factual knowledge about actual cases as

Dust jacket for the 1989 collection in which Hare critiques the American philosopher John Rawls's highly regarded theory of justice (Bruccoli Clark Layman Archives)

well as imagination to conjure up possible cases. The key test is whether one can prescribe the proposed principle in all cases, regardless of who one might be and or how one might be affected. If there is even a single case in which one cannot make the prescription, then it must be rejected, since universalizability allows no exceptions. If the prescription can be made in all cases, then it can be accepted tentatively. This hypothetical method of reasoning permits the derivation of the moral principles common to most societies, because people generally have similar preferences based on their inclinations, desires, feelings, and attitudes; these preferences lead to similar prescriptions, which are the tests of principles.

Hare illustrates his account by using the example of racism. The racist dislikes people because of their appearance or origin. The racist might think that this preference is morally allowable; the racist might even think that he or she is morally obliged to exclude, harass, injure, or kill people who differ from him or her in appearance or origin. But Hare argues that moral reasoning cannot justify racism: while the racist may prescribe intolerant or harmful treatment of people who differ from himself or herself, the racist cannot universalize these prescriptions. If the racist considers all situations in which one might act on these prescriptions, he or she will find some in which he or she is the victim of racist actions. Since the racist would hate to be treated in this way in those situations, he or she cannot endorse a prescription sanctioning racist treatment in those situations. As a matter of logic, then, the racist must reject the principle he or she tried to universalize. In short, since racism cannot be endorsed in all situations, it cannot be moral.

Hare concedes, however, that two kinds of people would not be swayed by this reasoning. The "amoralist" is indifferent to or dismissive of morality and refuses to use universal moral prescriptions. The amoralist cannot be refuted with moral reasoning or judgments, since he or she does not employ them. About all one can do is to point out some of the prudential disadvantages of living as an amoralist. The fanatic poses a different problem. The fanatic is willing to universalize prescriptions, but one kind of prescription—that expressing the fanatic's racial, artistic, or political "ideal"—is paramount. What Hare calls the "pure" fanatic is impervious to hypothetical moral reasoning: such a person's ideal is so important that he or she will continue to prescribe it even in situations where it conflicts with other prescriptions, including strongly held ones. An extreme example would be a Nazi who believed so strongly in the superiority of the Aryan race that he would condemn himself to death if he discovered that he was of Jewish descent. Most fanatics, however, are "impure": their fanaticism stems from ignorance, error, emotion, or flawed thinking. If they thought more rationally, they would not be fanatics—an impure Nazi fanatic could be made to realize that Jews were not responsible for Germany's decline in the 1920s, for example. Pure fanatics are rational and informed but have an ideal that takes utter precedence over all of their other preferences. The only consolation, Hare says, is that there are few such fanatics.

All those other than these two odd characters, Hare says, will find that the logic of their moral language compels them to use his hypothetical method of moral reasoning. This logic leads them to think as the "Golden Rule" recommends: they should only endorse actions that they could accept no matter who they might be. Logic thus requires an impartial consideration of the interests of all. When interests conflict, as is common in moral dilemmas, it is a matter of logic that the stronger interest must be chosen, because the stronger interest, as shown by a stronger inclination, is simply the one that the person will prescribe in the face of competing prescriptions—for example, one's desire not to be a victim of racism is stronger than any desire one might have to act as a racist. Hare concedes that this account is not complete: some notion of maximizing interests to deal with competing prescriptions within a group of people may be necessary. The development of such a notion would call for a substantive utilitarian theory, which, he says, he cannot offer in detail in *Freedom and Reason.*

Hare was elected to membership in the British Academy in 1964. In 1966 he was named White's Professor of Moral Philosophy at Oxford and a fellow of Corpus Christi College. He was a visiting professor at the Australian National University in 1966 and at the University of Michigan in 1968. He collected many of his journal articles in *Practical Inferences* (1971), *Essays on Philosophical Method* (1971), *Essays on the Moral Concepts* (1972), and *Applications of Moral Philosophy* (1972). He was elected president of Britain's oldest philosophical organization, the Aristotelian Society, in 1972.

Since the late 1960s moral philosophy in Britain and especially in the United States had taken an "applied turn." Motivated in part by the civil rights, antiwar, and feminist movements and in part by disappointment that philosophers using the reigning analytic and linguistic methods had written little about how people should live, many younger philosophers began to write about current practical issues. Articles on abortion, affirmative action, and civil disobedience began to appear in traditional philosophical journals, and journals devoted to such topics, such as *Philosophy and Public Affairs,* were founded. The high point in this change of direction in moral philosophy was the publication in 1971 of *A Theory of Justice* by the Harvard University philosopher John Rawls. The book sold more than 150,000 copies, was read by many outside the world of academic philosophy, and was the subject of several books and hundreds of articles. In this elaborately structured and densely argued work Rawls uses a variation on the traditional "social contract" theory to defend the liberties and social welfare programs found in Western democracies. Rawls gives the work an unusual twist by using a group of highly rational, self-interested, but amnesiac "Everypersons" to devise the contract. Ensconced behind a "veil of ignorance," these people have no knowledge of who they will be when the society is up and running—they do not know what their race, their sex, their talents, or their particular interests will be, but they do know general principles of economics and sociology. Under these conditions, each person will vote to set up the rules of the society so as to make sure that no matter how things turn out, he or she will not be too badly off (in decision theory, this strategy is called the "maximin rule": the person wants to be sure of maximizing the minimum outcome for himself or herself). For example, the parties will not vote to set up a society that includes slavery, because none of them can guarantee that he or she will wind up as a master rather than as a slave. Rawls concludes that the people would decide to set up a society in which each had the maximum amount of liberty consistent with a comparable liberty for the rest, and inequalities in power and wealth would be allowed only if they improved the lot of the worst-off group in the society.

Hare was among the minority of philosophers who were unenthusiastic about *A Theory of Justice*. In a two-part critical study that appeared in *The Philosophical Quarterly* in 1973 (it was republished in his *Essays in Ethical Theory* in 1989) Hare argues that the methodology of the work is irredeemably flawed. Rawls begins with the moral and political beliefs held by thoughtful people in Western democracies. He refers to these beliefs as "intuitions," by which he means that they are strongly held but are not arranged in a hierarchy allowing one to take precedence over another. Rawls's aim is to devise a theory, consisting of a set of higher-level principles and a method of argumentation that would justify these intuitions and put them in some kind of order. Perhaps a few of these intuitions will have to be given up or altered, but Rawls aims to preserve all of them if possible. Hare finds this method circular: since Rawls has admittedly devised his principles and method of argumentation to arrive at those very intuitions and no others, he seems to have rigged his theory to get the results he wants. Rawls does tinker with some intuitions, as well as with some elements in the theory, calling the result "reflective equilibrium." What he should have done, Hare argues, was to provide a morally and politically neutral justification of those intuitions.

Hare was a visiting professor at the University of Delaware in 1974. He was named an honorary foreign member of the American Academy of Arts and Sciences in 1975 and received a Tanner Award in 1979.

Hare grew increasingly concerned about reliance on intuition in philosophical works on morality and politics and the apparent ignorance or unconcern of the authors of the need for a rigorous method of argumentation. If philosophy is to do anything, he insisted, it is to show people how to be rational when forming their opinions and making decisions; but philosophers were not fulfilling that responsibility. He addresses these issues in *Moral Thinking: Its Levels, Method and Point* (1981), drafted in 1980 while he was a fellow at the Center for Advanced Studies in the Behavioral Sciences at Stanford University. Philosophers who rely on intui-

Cover for the 1996 paperback edition of the 1993 collection of articles in which Hare applies his ethical theory to practical moral issues that arise from advances in the biological sciences

tions think that they do not need a defense, or, at least, provide none for them. Instead, such philosophers announce their intuitions, assume that their readers share the intuitions, and then demonstrate, often by rigorous arguments, what follows from these intuitions. This approach, Hare points out, proves nothing to people who do not share the assumed intuitions; it has no response to those who will not accept an intuition unless some defense of it is given, or to those who worry that some intuition of theirs is vulnerable to an attack and want to know how to respond; it cannot deal with situations in which intuitions conflict, as when a person thinks a fetus has a right to life but also thinks that a woman has a right to control her own body; nor can it deal with situations in which it is not clear which intuition applies, or in which no intuition seems to apply.

The main purpose of *Moral Thinking* is to provide a method of rational argumentation to resolve these problems about intuitions and, more generally, to help solve practical problems. To accomplish this task, Hare says, three levels of moral thought must be distinguished. The highest is the metaethical, at which the meanings and logic of moral language are analyzed. The metaethical is the level at which Hare operates as a philosopher. His focus in this book, however, is on the other two levels. The "intuitive" is the level of day-to-day life, where a person must make decisions and act. Intuitions are simple, firmly held moral beliefs, such as "Honor thy father and mother" or "A businessman always fulfills his contracts." They must be simple if they are to be easily learned and readily followed. They must also be backed by strong desires, attitudes, or other motives so that one will be disposed to act on them, especially in situations where one might be tempted to reject or evade them. People who are generally regarded as highly moral have firm intuitions on which they reliably act, and a society works best if its members can be counted on to follow their intuitions in nearly all cases.

This account, however, leaves unresolved the problems with intuitions that Hare has cited. All the intuitive level offers is the old intuitions. Nor will new intuitions alone resolve the quandary; some criteria must be established for the acceptance of the new intuitions. The solution, Hare says, is to move to another level of moral thought: the "critical." At this level one chooses the principles that will not only guide one in picking the intuitions by which to live but will also resolve the problems posed by intuitions.

What is needed at this level is a method for choosing principles. Hare uses the method he developed in his first two books and adds some new features. Principles should be considered hypothetically, but they may be of unlimited specificity. A complex principle forbidding the killing of humans but allowing several exceptions would be an example. In assessing principles, one is to rely on logic and facts and on "nothing else." The key logical concept is universalizability. As Hare showed previously, the descriptive properties in a principle are universalizable. They can occur in a vast number of situations, so if one commits to a principle in one situation one must, on pain of inconsistency, commit to it in all situations featuring the same descriptive properties. A principle is not only descriptive but also prescriptive, and if a prescription is to be moral it, too, must be universalizable. Universalizability means that one must be willing to commit to a principle in any situation in which it applies. One could occupy various positions in these situations—for example, pregnant woman, fetus, doctor, or parent of the

woman—and one must be willing to commit to a principle no matter which position one might occupy. The universalizability of principles is the Kantian element in Hare's method. The factual elements include carefully inquiring into what the consequences would be if everyone acted on the principle, using experience to gauge the consequences in actual situations and imagination to project the consequences in possible situations. Only likely situations and consequences should be considered, Hare warns. The point of a principle is to help choose the intuitions one will need in real life, not in some fantasy world. This qualification allows one to ignore some bizarre cases that have taxed the wits of philosophers: for example, if one were at the wheel of a runaway trolley heading for a fork in the track, and taking one fork would result in running over one person and taking the other would result in running over five people, which way should one steer? The most important factual feature in these situations is the preferences people have in them, since preferences determine which principles can be prescribed. To find these preferences, one must consider what it would be like to be in any position in a situation—for example, how would one feel if one were pregnant, had no husband and little money, and did not think that one could raise a child? This procedure may require the use of the imagination, and it must eventuate in one's actually having a preference—for example, deciding that one would not want to remain pregnant in such circumstances. Not any preference will do, however: only rational preferences should be used, that is, those that one would have if one were logical and well informed about the relevant facts. Only then will this hypothetical method of reasoning be rational. If it is, then in cases when there are only two competing principles, the critical thinker will choose the one supported by the stronger prescription, which derives from the stronger preference—for example, rejecting torture done for enjoyment. This procedure parallels cases where a moral dispute involves two people. Where more than two people are involved, the critical thinker must consider their positions one by one, and, under the guidance of the prescriptions and preferences found in each, pick a principle that everyone, or almost everyone, can endorse. Hare thinks an individual can do this by himself or herself, but not all of his critics have agreed; some asked, for example, whether a man could know what it is like to be a woman.

In later writings focusing on how to pick a principle for more than two people, which is what one would be doing when choosing moral principles for an entire society, as Rawls's parties in the veil of ignorance did, Hare introduces a further crucial step that does not involve only facts and logic. It is a traditional utilitarian step, calling on one to maximize the preference satisfaction of all those who are affected by conformity to a principle. Hare describes it in rather general terms, and his wording varies: in *Essays in Ethical Theory* (1989) he claims that one should "maximize the satisfaction [of the 'equal interests of all the affected parties'] in total"; or, one should strive for a principle that "maximizes the preference satisfactions, in sum, of all affected by [one's] action considered impartially"; or, he claims in *Essays in Political Morality* that one should seek "moral principles whose general adoption will do the best for all those affected considered impartially"; or, one should aim for principles with "the highest acceptance utility; that is, whose acceptance in society . . . is most likely to do the best, all in all, to satisfy the preferences of those affected"; or, he claims in *Sorting Out Ethics* (1997) that one should "will only such maxims [which become one's universal laws] as do the best, all in all, impartially, for all those affected by [one's] action [on them]." Critics have pointed out that more-specific accounts of maximization might involve Hare in some of the problems that have marred other utilitarian theories, such as condoning unfair treatment of some individuals or groups as long as the overall welfare is served; Hare never offered a detailed theoretical response to this criticism.

In 1983 Hare resigned from Oxford and took a position as Graduate Research Professor of Philosophy at the University of Florida in Gainesville. For the next decade he spent the late fall, winter, and early spring at the University of Florida and the rest of the year at his home in Ewelme, a village outside Oxford. In the 1980s and 1990s his work focused more and more on practical problems. It consists largely of articles, some originating as conference papers and nearly all appearing in books and journals of an "applied" nature. Their range is broad, covering topics in politics, bioethics, education, and religion. The articles indicate that he thinks that his method of moral reasoning can deal with practical issues without becoming entangled in traditional maximization problems. Nearly all begin with a summation of his method or of some facet of it; next he carefully clarifies what is at stake in the issue; and only then does he argue for a specific solution to the problem. What a philosopher can add to a moral controversy, Hare continually points out, has to rest on the cardinal philosophical virtues of clarity and rationality. Otherwise, the philosopher has no distinctive role in a practical debate and no hope of making a difference in day-to-day life. Hare assembled these "applied" articles in *Essays on Political Morality, Essays on Religion and Education* (1992), and *Essays on Bioethics* (1993).

In his courses at Oxford and the University of Florida and as a visiting professor at Florida State University in Tallahassee, Hare developed a "taxonomy"

Dust jacket for the 1999 collection that includes some of Hare's early essays (Bruccoli Clark Layman Archives)

of the main ethical theories of the twentieth century that reveals their distinctive features, their strengths, and their weaknesses. He presented a condensed version of the material as the Axel Hagerstrom Lectures at Uppsala University in 1991. He hoped to work the text into a full-length book, but several strokes in the mid to late 1990s left him, as he put it in the preface to *Sorting Out Ethics,* "incapable, not only of typing with more than one hand, but of thinking book-length thoughts." He explained that "Formerly, when writing a book, I used to hold the whole of it in my head from start to finish. This is the only way to avoid repetitions and even contradictions. But I can no longer do it." He published the text of the Hagerstrom lectures as *Sorting Out Ethics* in 1997.

Describing the book in its preface as a "taxonomy of ethical theories [for] all those who are lost in the moral maze, including many of my philosophical colleagues," Hare divides ethical theories into two logically exclusive groups; each of the subdivisions within each of these main groups likewise consists of two logically exclusive groups. The main division is between descriptivist and nondescriptivist theories. Descriptivist theories regard moral beliefs as stating something that purports to be true; on this view, the meaning of a moral belief is determined solely by its truth conditions–that is, by what makes it true. On this view, "Lying is wrong" is similar in its logic to "Cats have tails." Nondescriptivist theories hold that a moral belief does something other–or, at least, more–than purport to tell the truth. Nondescriptivists disagree about what this further factor is: emotivists say that it is expressing a desire, feeling, or attitude; Hare says that it is prescribing. Whatever it is, it seems to have something to do with a moral belief functioning as a guide to conduct. That is why, on a nondescriptivist view, "Lying is wrong" is similar in its logic to "Don't step on a cat's tail." The descriptivist/nondescriptivist division of ethical theories is a logically exclusive one, since any theory must either affirm or deny that the meaning of a moral belief is determined solely by its truth conditions.

Descriptivist theories are either objective or subjective: they claim either that a moral belief is true of something existing independently of minds or that its truth is somehow dependent on minds. Objective descriptivist theories, in turn, fall into two groups, depending on whether they claim that what exists independently is of a moral or a nonmoral nature. Intuitionistic theories are an example of an objective descriptivist theory that the independent element is inherently moral: intuitionists think that one can just perceive, perhaps with the aid of a special "moral sense," such things as evil, rightness, and justice. Naturalistic theories are an example of the other kind of objective descriptivist theory, which says that moral beliefs refer to something independent but nonmoral. Naturalistic theories view moral beliefs as representing something in nature that is not described by moral terms: for example, goodness is pleasure, and evil is pain; right and wrong are determined solely by what is conducive to evolutionary survival; or what is just is whatever helps a society to function.

Most moral theories in the history of philosophy have been of the objective descriptivist variety, and they all suffer from a fatal flaw, Hare argues: they collapse into relativism because they have to concede that people disagree about morality. Disagreement cannot result solely from incompetence, misunderstanding, ignorance, or poor reasoning; there is just too much sincere, thoughtful disagreement for that to be the case. Objectivists must claim that such disagreement is the product either of different moral concepts and, hence,

of different meanings being expressed in moral beliefs, or of different realities and, hence, different truths being represented by those beliefs. But this position is relativism: it means that there is no one set of objective moral beliefs but several, each relative to a different concept or reality. Examples of such relativistic views are the views that some humans (for example, Europeans and savages) just think differently, or that some moralities pertain only to some people (for example, slavery was not wrong in classical Greece). This position is ruinous for objective theories, since they purport to provide the one and only truth about morality.

The other descriptivist alternative is subjective: it claims that the truth of moral beliefs is dependent on minds. Egoism is an example: it asserts that what is moral is whatever is in a person's perceived self-interest. Other examples are the views that what is moral is a matter of what people approve, or desire, or sympathize with, or take as their purpose. All of these subjective descriptivist theories, like the objective ones, succumb to relativism. They, too, must acknowledge moral disagreement, and the only way to explain it is to attribute it to the different workings of human minds.

Since the only two possible versions of descriptivism fail, a correct ethical theory must be nondescriptivist. These theories are divided into two groups according to whether they are nonrational or rational. Emotivism is an example of nonrational nondescriptivism. It claims that moral beliefs merely express some feeling, desire, or attitude ("Murder is wrong," for example, expresses only the speaker's disapproval of murder). While the expression and what is being expressed have psychological causes, and while they can function as causes of behavior, they are not the conclusions of any reasoning process. Ethics then becomes a branch of psychology. Hare finds that the fundamental problem with emotivism and all other forms of nonrational nondecriptivisms is that they deny that reasoning about moral matters is possible. Yet, an examination of the logic of moral language reveals that this kind of reasoning is possible, and in daily life people do offer reasons for their moral views. The correct version of nondescriptivism, Hare concludes, must be a rational one.

In the final chapter, "Rationalism," Hare outlines his prescriptive version of nondescriptivism by summing up the points he made in his previous writings. He concedes that there might be other, perhaps even superior, forms of rational nondescriptivism; if so, they must meet the six conditions he sets out for any sound ethical theory: its account of the meaning and logic of moral language must be neutral, so that it can be used by people taking different sides in a moral argument; it must be practical, in that the moral conclusions one reaches by it must make some difference in how one acts; it must show how people can disagree about moral matters; it must allow for logical relations between moral statements, which makes moral reasoning possible; it must provide a way to resolve moral disagreements by argument; and it must allow "moral discourse and moral thought in general to fulfill the purpose that they have in society," which is to allow people who disagree to "reach agreement by rational discussion."

While working on the text that became *Sorting Out Ethics*, Hare made occasional forays against the main contemporary competitors to his approach in ethical theory. Some, such as virtue theory and naturalism, were revivals of older theories. Realism, which used the sophisticated tools of epistemology and the philosophy of science to argue for the existence of moral entities, such as justice, was new. Hare was critical of all of them.

In 1994 Hare began living in retirement with his wife in Ewelme; he did no writing after the last of his strokes. Some of his earlier pieces, including his major critical essays and some articles defending his form of rational prescriptivism, appeared in 1999 in the collection *Objective Prescriptions and Other Essays*. Hare died at his home on 29 January 2002. His final original book, *Sorting Out Ethics*, has left philosophers of the future with a road map for theorizing. If its arguments are correct, it reveals all the dead ends and shows that only a nonde-scriptivist, rational course remains open. Hare would hope that philosophers will take the open road.

Interview:

"Applied Philosophy and Moral Theory: R. M. Hare Talks to *Philosophy Today*," *Philosophy Today,* 38 (1994).

Bibiliography:

R. M. Hare and Ulla Wessels, "References and Bibliography," in *Sorting Out Ethics,* by Hare (Oxford: Clarendon Press, 1997), pp. 167–182.

References:

G. E. M. Anscombe, "Modern Moral Philosophy," *Philosophy,* 33 (1958): 1–19;

Philippa Foot, *Virtues and Vices and Other Essays in Moral Philosophy* (Oxford: Blackwell, 1978);

Iris Murdoch, *Existentialists and Mystics: Writings on Philosophy and Literature,* edited by Peter J. Conradi (New York & London: Allen Lane/Penguin, 1998), pp. 62–64, 66, 69, 83, 85–91, 177, 206, 308, 327, 343.

Papers:

R. M. Hare left his letters, drafts, unpublished works, and other papers to his son and literary executor, John Hare.

J. M. E. McTaggart

(3 September 1866 – 18 January 1925)

W. J. Mander
Harris Manchester College, Oxford

BOOKS: *Studies in the Hegelian Dialectic* (Cambridge: Cambridge University Press, 1896);

Studies in the Hegelian Cosmology (Cambridge: Cambridge University Press, 1901; New York: Russell & Russell, 1964);

Some Dogmas of Religion (London: Arnold, 1906); selections republished as *Human Immortality and Pre-Existence* (London: Arnold, 1915; New York: Longmans, Green, 1915);

A Commentary on Hegel's Logic (Cambridge: Cambridge University Press, 1910; New York: Russell & Russell, 1964);

"Dare to Be Wise": An Address, Delivered before the Heretics Society in Cambridge on 8th December, 1909 (London: Watts, 1910);

The Nature of Existence, 2 volumes, volume 2 edited by C. D. Broad (Cambridge: Cambridge University Press, 1921, 1927; Grosse Pointe, Mich.: Scholarly Press, 1968);

Philosophical Studies, edited by S. V. Keeling (London: Arnold, 1934; New York: Longmans, Green, 1934).

Editions: *Some Dogmas of Religion* (New York: Greenwood Press, 1968);

Philosophical Studies, edited by S. V. Keeling, introduction by Gerald Rochelle (Bristol: Thoemmes Press, 1996);

Some Dogmas of Religion, introduction by C. D. Broad, foreword by Rochelle (Bristol: Thoemmes Press, 1997).

OTHER: "Ontological Idealism," in *Contemporary British Philosophy: Personal Statements,* first series, edited by John H. Muirhead (London: Allen & Unwin / New York: Macmillan, 1924), pp. 249–269.

J. M. E. McTaggart

Known today mainly as the author of a paradox designed to prove the unreality of time—which, even if it has not convinced many, nonetheless served as the starting point for the great majority of philosophical discussions about time in the twentieth century—J. M. E.

McTaggart was a philosopher whose contributions to scholarship on Georg Wilhelm Friedrich Hegel and to metaphysics established him as a leading thinker of the first quarter of the twentieth century. Although McTaggart is usually identified as a member of the school of British idealism, a movement that also included Bernard Bosanquet, F. H. Bradley, Edward Caird, and T. H. Green, he was an original thinker and in many respects quite unlike the other members of this school. He was, for example, a personal idealist, in that he believed that reality is best understood as a community of finite spirits; but unlike most other personal idealists, such as

Andrew Seth Pringle-Pattison or Hastings Rashdall, he was unsympathetic to religion. By the time of the posthumous publication of the final volume of his principal work, *The Nature of Existence* (1921, 1927), metaphysics in general and idealism in particular were largely out of intellectual favor.

John McTaggart Ellis was born 3 September 1866 at Norfolk Square, London, the eldest surviving son of Francis Ellis, a judge, and Caroline Ellis. The family adopted the surname McTaggart as a condition for obtaining a legacy from a wealthy relative, the Scottish baronet Sir John McTaggart, giving Jack (as he was always called), who had already been named after a great-uncle, the memorable appellation John McTaggart Ellis McTaggart–a name he always delighted in using in its full form. He was educated at Clifton College, an institution to which he remained immensely loyal: in later years he became a governor of the institution, and his will stipulated that the remainder of his estate should go to the college after the death of his wife. In 1885 he entered Trinity College of the University of Cambridge. There he studied under the philosophers Henry Sidgwick and James Ward and became a member of the Apostles, a debating society that had great influence on the British intellectual scene. He gained a first-class degree in 1888, and in 1891, on the strength of a specially composed dissertation, he was awarded a fellowship at Trinity College. In 1897 he became a college lecturer, a post that he held until his retirement. In 1891–1892 and 1898–1899 he visited his mother in New Zealand, to which she had immigrated. There he met and, in 1899, married Mary Elizabeth Bird. The couple had no children.

McTaggart's philosophical opinions were formed early and never substantially changed. The dissertation on the basis of which he was awarded his fellowship at Trinity College was on Hegel's dialectic, and it set the topic that consumed his philosophical attentions during the next twenty or so years. He became a celebrated Hegel scholar, and his many critical articles were collected in three important books: *Studies in the Hegelian Dialectic* (1896), the first four chapters of which are based on his dissertation; *Studies in the Hegelian Cosmology* (1901); and *A Commentary on Hegel's Logic* (1910). The British idealists were all inspired by Hegel, but their allegiance to his ideas tended to be rather loose. McTaggart is notable among the idealists for the close and detailed attention he paid to Hegel's actual writings.

For McTaggart, the heart of Hegel's philosophy was his logic, particularly the dialectical method. He understands Hegel's logic as essentially a more rigorous version of that of Immanuel Kant: each higher category of thought is a necessary presupposition of a lower cate-

gory to which the thinker is committed, starting with the lowest and most inescapable category of all–Being. For McTaggart, the contradictions and transitions of the Hegelian dialectical process take place only in the human mind, not in reality: imperfections and contradictions are not intrinsic to objects themselves but result from one's manner of apprehending them. The fundamental aspect of the dialectic, he thinks, is not the tendency of each finite category to negate itself but, rather, its drive for self-completion; as the process approaches its consummation, negation becomes less important and the transitions become more direct. McTaggart notes that Hegel has often been accused of attempting the seemingly impossible feat of deducing existence from mere thought, but he denies that this task is what the dialectic is designed to do. He rejects any view of the dialectic as a movement of pure thought, insisting that it cannot be understood without reference to the matter of experience.

McTaggart's work on Hegel was much respected in his day, and it can be argued that the "Hegel" against whom such philosophers as Bertrand Russell reacted was in large part McTaggart's interpretation. Today, however, McTaggart is regarded as a poor and idiosyncratic commentator, and his work is little read by Hegel scholars. This decline in his reputation is, perhaps, the result of changing fashions in Hegel scholarship: McTaggart's is an unashamedly metaphysical interpretation of Hegel, while the interpretations that have found popularity in recent years are nonmetaphysical. The modern assessment of McTaggart also stems in part from a failure to note that much of McTaggart's work is critical of Hegel. He aims not only at exposition but also at pointing out errors and showing what he thinks Hegel should have done instead.

For example, he objects that Hegel was wrong to see philosophy as the highest expression of the Absolute. Philosophy may be the highest level of human knowledge, but it is not the highest level of reality. Instead of being regarded as the synthesis of art and religion, as in Hegel's system, philosophy and religion should together form the antithesis to art, leaving room for a new synthesis. Furthermore, he says, the finite differentiations of the Absolute should be taken as individual spirits, while the whole to which they belong should not be viewed as some kind of superperson or overarching Spirit. The Absolute should be understood as a community of interrelated selves. McTaggart is also suspicious of Hegel's detailed applications of his system and of the uniqueness of the dialectical path: there might be many different yet equally valid approaches to the Absolute.

For all his dissent, however, McTaggart thinks that Hegel's general conclusions were sound. At the

*McTaggart in 1886, when he was a student at
Trinity College of the University of Cambridge*

end of his *Commentary on Hegel's Logic* he says, "I would wish, therefore, in concluding the exposition of Hegel's philosophy which has been the chief object of my life for twenty one years, to express my conviction that Hegel has penetrated further into the true nature of reality than any philosopher before or after him."

Another reason McTaggart's critical work on Hegel has been neglected may be that most commentators have concentrated on his original philosophy, which they have generally regarded as independent of his earlier scholarly studies. But most of McTaggart's mature positions were reached through his critique of Hegel; to understand them, a clear view of their origin is essential.

The central characteristic of McTaggart's constructive work, which occupied him during the second half of his career, is its unabashedly metaphysical character. McTaggart defines metaphysics as the systematic study of the ultimate nature of reality. The justification for this study lies in the profound difference it can make

to human life. Dissenting from the logical positivist view that things that make no empirical difference can make no other kind of difference, McTaggart holds that much human happiness or misery hangs on the answers to such metaphysical questions as whether God exists, whether human beings are free, whether they are immortal, and whether the world is, on balance, good or evil. He considers metaphysical dogma an essential component of religion, which he defines as an emotion resting on a conviction of a harmony between oneself and the universe. The strength of McTaggart's belief in the practical value of metaphysics led him throughout his Cambridge career to give philosophy classes to nonphilosophers and to republish portions of his *Some Dogmas of Religion* (1906) in a cheap format as *Human Immortality and Pre-Existence* in 1915 to comfort those bereaved by World War I.

The production of comforting metaphysical rabbits from complex and obscure logical hats ought to arouse suspicion of wishful thinking in all except the most credulous; but while few have spoken so openly as McTaggart of the consolation that metaphysics can afford, few have warned so clearly of the dangers of emotional bias or strived so hard to avoid it in their own work. Metaphysics, in his view, demands great clarity and precision–and his work is notable for these qualities–but also great courage: for, he argues, if one is to think about these matters at all, one must accept the beliefs for which one has evidence and reject those for which one has none, however much the first may repel or the second may allure one.

One conclusion to which McTaggart's metaphysical reasoning led him was atheism, a view on which he settled in his early youth and openly and vigorously defended. He was one of the first British philosophers to be so openly an atheist. He rules out an omnipotent creative God on the ground that omnipotence is intrinsically absurd: such a God would not even be bound by the laws of logic. But even if the omnipotence requirement were relaxed so that God would not be able to violate logical laws, the notion of a creator God must be rejected because of the existence of evil. A nonomnipotent and noncreator God who is nothing more than an extremely powerful spirit might exist, he allows, although it would be of little religious value and is not something in whose existence there is any good reason to believe.

In all of his discussions of the topic McTaggart maintains the traditional concept of God as a personal being. He rejects the path taken by many of his idealist colleagues of calling the Absolute "God." To do so, he thinks, offends against ordinary usage and renders the question of whether God exists a trivial one. Also, he argues, human beings are parts of the Absolute and are persons, but no person can include another as one of its parts. Thus, identifying the Absolute with God contradicts the notion that God is a person. In this respect, at least, the atheist McTaggart stands with other personal idealists, who were all theists.

In 1923 McTaggart resigned his lectureship with the intention of devoting time to the completion of his magnum opus, *The Nature of Existence,* but died of the effects of a circulatory disease on 18 January 1925. At his death he had completed only two and a half of his customary five drafts of the second volume of the final statement of his philosophical system. Nevertheless, the bulk of the work was done, and there is no reason to think that the book would have been much different had he lived to finish revising it.

In *The Nature of Existence* McTaggart says that everyone must accept two general principles. The Principle of Sufficient Description holds that a unique and wholly general description of the nature of every object must exist. This principle follows from the fact that every individual being must have a unique nature in virtue of which it exists as a separate being. The Principle of Infinite Divisibility holds that every substance is divisible into substances that are themselves further divisible, and so on, in an endless process. Together, the two principles require an infinity of sufficient descriptions, one for each of the infinite number of distinct substances. The most obvious way to attempt to arrive at such descriptions would be to proceed in an ascending fashion, using sufficient descriptions of the parts to construct descriptions of the wholes to which they belong; but if substance is infinitely divisible, this procedure could never get started. The only alternative is to try to derive the required descriptions in a descending fashion, using descriptions of wholes to construct descriptions of their parts.

McTaggart concludes that substance must be structured in a way that will permit such a downward derivation of the sufficient descriptions of the infinitely many parts. He devises an abstract schematism, which he calls a Determining Correspondence System, in which parts are so related to wholes as to give each part a sufficient description by referring only to the whole from which it came.

To fill in this sketch, McTaggart presents as a possibility a world that consists solely of atemporal and immaterial selves who do nothing but perceive each other and themselves. If A and B are two such individuals, A will consist of A's perception of B–or, in McTaggart's symbolism, A!B–and A's perception of itself, or A!A. At the next level A's perception of B will consist in A's perception of B's perception of A (A!B!A) and A's perception of B's perception of itself (A!B!B), while A's perception of itself will consist of its perception of its perception of B (A!A!B) and its perception of its perception of itself (A!A!A). This system meets McTaggart's requirement, since, starting with sufficient descriptions of A and B, one can derive sufficient descriptions of each of their infinite parts.

Such a system, McTaggart claims, is the only possible one, for nothing else–especially not matter or sense-data–is able to satisfy the demands set out for an infinitely divisible yet generally describable reality. (Sense-data were postulated by many philosophers in the early twentieth century as the immediate objects of sensory experience, reducible neither to mind nor to matter.)

At first sight McTaggart's argument appears weak, for it would seem easy enough to use spatial qualities to meet the demands of infinite divisibility:

HUMAN IMMORTALITY AND PRE-EXISTENCE

BY

JOHN M'TAGGART ELLIS M'TAGGART,
LITT.D. (CAMBRIDGE), LL.D. (ST. ANDREWS)
FELLOW AND LECTURER OF TRINITY COLLEGE IN CAMBRIDGE
FELLOW OF THE BRITISH ACADEMY

SECOND IMPRESSION

LONDON
EDWARD ARNOLD
1916

Title page for the second printing of McTaggart's abridgment of his Some Dogmas of Religion *(1906), published to comfort those who had lost loved ones in World War I (Thomas Cooper Library, University of South Carolina)*

one could identify the parts of a repeatedly bisected line as, say, the longest part, the shortest part of the longest part, the shortest part of the shortest part of the longest part, and so on. But McTaggart argues, in a manner reminiscent of Gottfried Wilhelm Leibniz, a German rationalist philosopher of the late seventeenth and early eighteenth centuries, that all spatial properties require a nonspatial basis, and that, for all that it may appear to be otherwise, ultimate reality consists in nothing but a timeless realm of mutually perceiving immaterial selves.

The timelessness of the selves in McTaggart's system stems from his celebrated argument for the unreality of time. He begins by noting that the ways in which one speaks about time fall into two quite different kinds. Because a set of events may be placed in a given order using either of these ways of speaking,

McTaggart calls them the A series and the B series (philosophers today call them the tensed and the tenseless modes of expression, respectively). The A series orders events as past, present, and future, while the B series orders them as before, after, and simultaneous. The principal difference between the series is that A-series statements change their truth-values according to the time at which they are uttered (for example, though it was once false, it is now true that the lives of McTaggart and his wife are both past), while B-series statements are timelessly true or false (for example, it was, is, and always will be true that McTaggart died before his wife).

The reality of the A series is crucial to the reality of time, because there could be no change without the A series, and without change there could be no time. The B series alone cannot account for change, because change is more than just the possession of different properties at different times. Though no doubt essential, this characteristic alone does not capture the true passage or dynamism of change; for that, one needs the flow of time that is expressed by the A series. But while every event must have a past, present, and future, these characteristics are incompatible. The A series is, then, self-contradictory and, therefore, impossible.

McTaggart anticipates the obvious objection that no event is past, present, and future at the same time; it might be, for instance, that it was future, is present, and will be past. But to say that, McTaggart argues, is just to say that its futurity is past, its presence present, and its pastness future, and thereby to replace one problem with three: since nothing is always past, always present, or always future, each of these predications must be joined by the other two, which reintroduces the original problem. For this reason, then, the A series is unreal; and since it is necessary to the existence of time, then time, too, must be unreal.

If McTaggart's conclusions are correct, the real nature of the universe differs vastly from the nature it appears to possess: though it appears to contain matter and sense-data, it contains nothing but spirits, or selves, each of which perceives itself, other selves, and their parts; though these selves appear to be made up not merely of perceptions but also of judgments, assumptions, sensations, volitions, and emotions, they are in reality composed of nothing but perceptions; and though the universe seems to exist in time, there is no time. The everyday view of the world, then, contains a great deal of error, and McTaggart's next move is to account for it. He argues that error must be a species of perception, for perception is all that exists. It is, in fact, misperception. The most pervasive misperception, and the one from which all others follow, is that of seeing things as in time. But this misperception cannot be a pure fiction, pulled out of thin air: to misperceive is to take one thing for another, not to invent. Therefore, although time is unreal, a real series must exist that serves as a basis for the perception of things as temporal. This real series, which is misperceived as a temporal series, he calls the C series.

But how could the C series come into being? Insofar as McTaggart's Determining Correspondence System consists in a community of spirits, each made up of perceptions of each other's parts, it seems to leave no room for error. Once the requirements of Determining Correspondence have been met, however, there is nothing to preclude the possibility that objects might also be divided in other ways and no reason why the parts formed in these ways need be regarded as accurate perceptions. McTaggart, therefore, suggests that a subject's perceptual errors be thought of as a series of "Fragmentary Parts" strung out along a dimension of division other than that of the Determining Correspondence System. With the most illusory at one end and the least illusory at the other, these parts can be arranged into a "Misperception Series." McTaggart says that the series should be thought of as an "Inclusion Series," where, as in an intensive magnitude such as light or weight, increments may be added but not individually identified. If such a series is to view itself, it must misrepresent its members as exclusive of one another, that is, as appearing to have no content in common; but since this is just how temporally distinct perceptions manifest themselves, to regard it in this way is to view it as a temporal series. In this manner the Inclusion Series becomes the C series for the temporal misperception of oneself. The heart of error, in other words, is that in self-perception one inevitably misconstrues oneself as temporal. When one perceives oneself as in time, one perceives the world as in time, and from this misperception all the other errors follow.

McTaggart's account of misperception enables him to believe in immortality. Like atheism, this belief was immensely important to McTaggart and one that he held from an early age. It was closely related to his view of love and friendship: all people feel that their loves are special and mourn their passing, and many hope for a future life in which their loves will be restored. For McTaggart, friendships are not accidental but are built into the very fabric of the universe: they are the relationships between finite selves.

McTaggart holds that no good argument for immortality can fail to bring in preexistence, as well;

as he wryly comments in *Some Dogmas of Religion,* "If the universe got on without me a hundred years ago, what reason could be given for denying that it might get on without me a hundred years hence?" The most obvious reason for taking an asymmetrical attitude here would be memory, for, notwithstanding the occasional mystical claim to the contrary, it is certain that most people do not remember any past lives; but McTaggart argues that the lack of direct experiential evidence should be no bar to a belief in preexistence if there are strong enough indirect arguments of another kind. Alternatively, it might be objected that memory is essential to personal continuity; but McTaggart responds that while personal identity is the identity of a conscious being, it does not have to be an identity of which the possessor is conscious.

McTaggart realizes that it might be objected that his claim that time is but an appearance of an underlying timeless reality does not provide the self with genuine preexistence or immortality but with eternity, which is altogether different. He admits that in the strictest sense, people are not immortal; but he argues that, nonetheless, on his theory it can be shown that they appear to be immortal, just as they appear to exist in time, and that this fact captures all that anyone needs or desires. He suggests that the time series and the Misperception Series of his system be correlated. In that case, one would, as time progressed, get ever closer to a final state of wholly adequate perception in which the illusion of time itself would be overcome and the eternity of the world perceived. To creatures bound within the illusion of time, eternity appears to be in the future; yet, it would be a future that, once arrived at, could never go on to appear present or past, since to reach it would be precisely to see through and transcend the misperception that is time. On this view, it would appear as though eternity, or timelessness, were the final or culminating moment of time. Thus, for McTaggart, the claim that eternity awaits one in the future, though not wholly true, is as true as many other temporal claims—as true, for example, as the claim that one has lived through the past twenty-four hours.

Such an apparent immortality, McTaggart finds, would be a state of great goodness. It would be a state of unmixed good except for a residue of sympathetic pain for the evil and suffering endured in the prefinal stages. Moreover, although humanity is approaching the good, it may not do so steadily and without backsliding, which implies that there is, in all probability, much evil still ahead.

McTaggart's belief that the final stages of the universe are the ones that are of the greatest personal

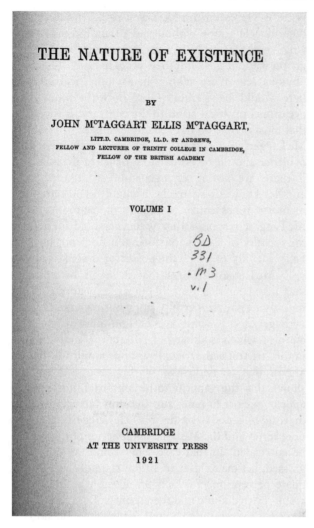

THE NATURE OF EXISTENCE

BY

JOHN M^cTAGGART ELLIS M^cTAGGART,

LITT.D. CAMBRIDGE, LL.D. ST ANDREWS,
FELLOW AND LECTURER OF TRINITY COLLEGE IN CAMBRIDGE,
FELLOW OF THE BRITISH ACADEMY

VOLUME I

BD
331
.M3
v.1

CAMBRIDGE
AT THE UNIVERSITY PRESS
1921

Title page for the first volume of McTaggart's principal work, in which he argues that time is unreal (Thomas Cooper Library, University of South Carolina)

same characteristics and to continue loving a person even if he or she changes in respect of the characteristic the lover most admires. McTaggart's emphasis on love highlights a paradox in his philosophy: by holding that reality consists of a community of individual spirits united in personal love and transcending time, McTaggart, of all the British idealists, came the closest to presenting a traditional Christian metaphysics; yet, he, of all the British idealists, was the most committed atheist, one who missed no opportunity to attack traditional religious conceptions.

McTaggart's contributions to ethics, as presented in *The Nature of Existence,* were not of great note. Like much moral philosophy at that period, his thinking was strongly influenced by G. E. Moore's *Principia Ethica* (1903), and it adds little to that work. He does, however, make some important observations about the individuality of value, holding that nothing is ultimately good or bad except conscious beings and their conscious states. In this respect McTaggart takes his stand against the Hegelians, who urged the value of wholes—both metaphysical, such as the universe, and social, such as the state. On the alleged intrinsic value of the latter he was quite outspoken, arguing in the posthumously published collection *Philosophical Studies* (1934) that

> whatever activity it is desirable for the State to have, it will only be desirable as a means, and that the activity, and the State itself, can have no value but as a means. And a religion which fastens itself on a means has not risen above fetish-worship. Compared with worship of the State, zoolatry is rational and dignified. A bull or a crocodile may not have great intrinsic value, but it has some, for it is a conscious being. The state has none. It would be as reasonable to worship a sewage pipe, which also possesses considerable value as a means.

J. M. E. McTaggart never had the sort of influence that some of the other British idealists did—indeed, he seems not to have had a single disciple—but this lack of influence should not be taken as a reflection on the value of his ideas. Unlike some of the other idealists, who were content to follow each other, he was fiercely original; and while his thought has not attracted as much attention from scholars as has that of some of his contemporaries, this relative neglect owes more to its intimidating complexity and to the age, hostile to all metaphysics, in which it finally appeared, than to its own merit or lack thereof.

Biographies:

G. Lowes Dickenson, S. V. Keeling, and Basil Williams, *J. McT. E. McTaggart* (Cambridge: Cambridge University Press, 1931);

value is intimately linked to what he considered the most important of his doctrines: that the mutual perceptions linking the community of finite spirits that make up ultimate reality are relationships of love, that all spirits are bound together in an interlocking system of loving perception. Love, for McTaggart, is a fundamental relationship in the universe that holds outside the appearances of space, time, and matter. He makes a sharp distinction between its object and its cause, arguing that love of an individual, while it may be caused by certain characteristics in that individual, is not necessarily maintained because of them: a great passion may be inspired by a minor cause. Indeed, he suggests that genuine love for individuals does not persist because of any characteristics those individuals possess, since it is possible to love one person but not to love another person who has all the

Gerald Rochelle, *The Life and Philosophy of J. McT. E. McTaggart, 1866–1925,* Studies in the History of Philosophy, volume 22 (Lewiston, N.Y.: Edwin Mellen Press, 1991).

References:

Timo Airaksinen, *The Ontological Criteria of Reality: A Study of Bradley and McTaggart* (Turku, Finland: Turun Yliopisto, 1975);

Leslie Armour, "Love, Reason, and Reality: Argument and Emotion in McTaggart's System," in *Anglo-American Idealism, 1865–1927,* edited by W. J. Mander, Contributions in Philosophy, no. 74 (Westport, Conn.: Greenwood Press, 2000), pp. 163–181;

Armour, "Russell, McTaggart, and I," *Idealistic Studies,* 9 (1979): 66–76;

James Bradley, "Hegel in Britain: A Brief History of British Commentary and Attitudes," *Heythrop Journal: A Quarterly Review of Philosophy and Theology,* 20 (1979): 1–24, 163–182;

C. D. Broad, *An Examination of McTaggart's Philosophy,* 2 volumes (Cambridge: Cambridge University Press, 1933, 1938);

Broad, "John McTaggart Ellis McTaggart, 1866–1925," *Proceedings of the British Academy,* 13 (1927): 307–334;

Michael Dummett, "A Defence of McTaggart's Proof of the Unreality of Time," *Philosophical Review,* 59 (1960): 497–504;

Richard M. Gale, "McTaggart's Analysis of Time," *American Philosophical Quarterly,* 3 (1966): 145–152;

Peter T. Geach, "McTaggart," *Philosophy,* 70 (1995): 567–579;

Geach, *Truth, Love and Immortality: An Introduction to McTaggart's Philosophy* (London: Hutchinson, 1979);

John Knox, "McTaggart's Theory of the Self," *Idealistic Studies,* 11 (1981): 151–166;

E. J. Lowe, "The Indexical Fallacy in McTaggart's Proof of the Unreality of Time," *Mind,* 96 (1987): pp. 62–70;

W. J. Mander, "McTaggart on Time and Error," *Modern Schoolman,* 75 (1998): 157–169;

Mander, "McTaggart's Argument for Idealism," *Journal of Speculative Philosophy,* 11 (1997): 53–72;

Mander, "On McTaggart on Love," *History of Philosophy Quarterly,* 13 (1996): 133–147;

N. M. L. Nathan, "McTaggart's Immaterialism," *Philosophical Quarterly,* 41 (1991): 442–456;

Hilda D. Oakeley, "McTaggart's Theory of Immortality," *Hibbert Journal,* 45 (1946–1947): 350–353;

Oakeley, "The Philosophy of Time and the Timeless in McTaggart's *Nature of Existence,*" *Proceedings of the Aristotelian Society for the Systematic Study of Philosophy,* 47 (1947): 105–128;

Oakeley, "Time and the Self in McTaggart's System," *Mind,* 39 (1930): 175–193;

Robert L. Patterson, "McTaggart's Contribution to the Philosophy of Religion," *Philosophy,* 23 (1931): 323–335;

Patterson, "On Broad's Refutation of McTaggart's Arguments for the Unreality of Time," *Philosophical Review,* 50 (1941): 602–609;

Nicholas Rescher, "McTaggart's Logical Determinism," *Idealistic Studies,* 12 (1982): 231–241;

Gerald Rochelle, *Behind Time: The Incoherence of Time and McTaggart's Atemporal Replacement* (Aldershot: Ashgate, 1998);

J. D. B. Walker, "Some Amendments to McTaggart's Theory of Selves," *Idealistic Studies,* 12 (1982): 242–250;

Gregory Williams, "McTaggart's Logical Determinism—A Reply to Professor Rescher," *Idealistic Studies,* 17 (1987): 219–229;

John Wisdom, "McTaggart's Determining Correspondence of Substances: A Refutation," *Mind,* 37 (1928): 414–438.

Papers:

J. M. E. McTaggart's papers are in the Wren Library, Trinity College, University of Cambridge.

James Mill

(6 April 1773 – 23 June 1836)

Ann-Barbara Graff
University of Toronto

See also the Mill entries in *DLB 107: British Romantic Prose Writers, 1789–1832, First Series* and *DLB 158: British Reform Writers, 1789–1832.*

BOOKS: *An Essay on the Impolicy of a Bounty on the Exportation of Grain: And on the Principles Which Ought to Regulate the Commerce of Grain* (London: Printed for C. & R. Baldwin, 1804; New York: Augustus M. Kelley, 1966);

Commerce Defended. An Answer to the Arguments by Which Mr. Spence, Mr. Cobbett, and Others, Have Attempted to Prove That Commerce Is Not a Source of National Wealth (London: Printed for C. & R. Baldwin, 1808; New York: Augustus M. Kelley, 1965);

Schools for All, in Preference to Schools for Churchmen Only; or, The State of the Controversy between the Advocates for the Lancasterian System of Universal Education, and Those Who Have Set Up an Exclusive and Partial System under the Name of the Church and Dr. Bell, anonymous (London: Longman, Hurst, Rees, Orme & Brown, 1812);

The History of British India, 3 volumes (London: Printed for Baldwin, Cradock & Joy, 1817);

Elements of Political Economy (London: Printed for Baldwin, Cradock & Joy, 1821; revised, 1824; revised again, 1826; New York: Augustus M. Kelley, 1965);

Essays on I. Government, II. Jurisprudence, III. Liberty of the Press, IV. Prisons and Prison Discipline, V. Colonies, VI. Law of Nations, VII. Education: Reprinted from "The Supplement to the Encyclopædia Britannica" (London: J. Innes, 1828);

Analysis of the Phenomena of the Human Mind, 2 volumes (London: Printed for Baldwin & Cradock, 1829);

A Fragment on Mackintosh: Being Strictures on Some Passages in the Dissertation by Sir James Mackintosh Prefixed to the Encyclopædia Britannica (London: Printed for Baldwin & Cradock, 1835).

Editions and Collections: *Essays on Government, Jurisprudence, Liberty of the Press, and Law of Nations* (Lon-

James Mill (portrait by an unknown artist; from Alexander Bain, James Mill: A Biography, *1882)*

don: J. Innes, 1828; New York: Augustus M. Kelley, 1967);

Analysis of the Phenomena of the Human Mind, 2 volumes, edited by John Stuart Mill, with notes by Alexander Bain, Andrew Findlater, and George Grote (London: Longmans, Green, Reader & Dyer, 1869; New York: Augustus M. Kelley, 1967);

James & John Stuart Mill on Education, edited by F. A. Cavenagh (Cambridge: Cambridge University Press, 1931; New York: Harper, 1969);

An Essay on Government, edited by Ernest Barker (Cambridge: Cambridge University Press, 1937);

An Essay on Government, edited by Currin V. Shields (New York: Liberal Arts Press, 1955; Indianapolis: Bobbs-Merrill, 1955);

Selected Economic Writings, edited by Donald Winch (Edinburgh & London: Published by Oliver & Boyd for the Scottish Economic Society, 1966; Chicago: University of Chicago Press, 1966);

James Mill on Education, edited by W. H. Burston (London: Cambridge University Press, 1969);

Utilitarian Logic and Politics: James Mill's "Essay on Government," Macaulay's Critique and the Ensuing Debate, edited by Jack Lively and John Rees (Oxford: Clarendon Press, 1978; New York: Oxford University Press, 1984);

Political Writings, edited by Terence Ball (Cambridge: Cambridge University Press, 1992);

The Collected Works of James Mill, 7 volumes (London: Routledge/Thoemmes Press, 1992).

OTHER: Charles de Villers, *An Essay on the Spirit and Influence of the Reformation of Luther: The Work Which Obtained the Prize on the Question Proposed in 1802 by the National Institute of France; with a Sketch of the History of the Church from Its Founder to the Reformation, Intended as an Appendix to the Work,* edited and translated by Mill (London: Printed for C. & R. Baldwin, 1805);

"Beggars" (1816), "Benefit Societies" (1816), "Banks for Saving" (1816), "Caste" (1817), "Economists" (1819), "Education" (1819), "Government" (1820), "Colonies" (1820), "Jurisprudence" (1821), "Liberty of the Press" (1821), "Prisons and Prison Discipline" (1823), and "Law of Nations" (1823), in *The Encyclopædia Britannica: Supplement to the Fourth, Fifth, and Sixth Editions. With Preliminary Dissertations on the History of the Sciences,* edited by Macveigh Napier, 6 volumes (Edinburgh: Printed for A. Constable / London: Hurst, Robinson, 1815–1824);

"Regulations of the Political Economy Club," in *Political Economy Club of London: Minutes of Proceedings, 1899–1920, Roll of Members and Questions Discussed, 1821–1920. With Documents Bearing on the History of the Club* (London: Macmillan, 1921), pp. 2–5.

SELECTED PERIODICAL PUBLICATIONS– UNCOLLECTED: "State of the Nation," *Westminster Review,* 6 (12 October 1826): 249–278;

"The Ballot," *Westminster Review,* 13 (25 July 1830): 1–39.

James Mill has suffered the unfortunate distinction of being overshadowed by both his philosophical mentor—the founder of utilitarianism, Jeremy Bentham—and his own son, the philosopher John Stuart Mill. James Mill, however, distinguished himself as an historian, educational theorist, economist, political philosopher, psychologist, civil servant, and as perhaps the single most important popularizer of utilitarianism, extending Bentham's limited agenda of political and legal reform into a comprehensive, self-sufficient ethical system. Mill influenced Bentham to appreciate the role of economic factors in social life and political institutions and also turned him away from advocating rule by an enlightened aristocracy in favor of increasing democratic participation in government.

James Mill was born on 6 April 1773 in Northwater Bridge, Forfarshire, Scotland, to James Mill, a shoemaker, and Isabel Fenton Mill, a farmer's daughter with a forceful personality and social pretensions. Isabel Mill is thought to have changed the family name from the Scottish "Milne" to the English-sounding "Mill" before James's birth, and she was resolved to raise her son as a gentleman. Mill was sent to the parish school, then to Montrose Academy, where he conceived the desire to become a clergyman. He tutored Wilhelmina Stuart, the daughter of his neighbors Sir John and Lady Jane Stuart; Lady Jane Stuart had started a fund for the education of poor young men intended for the ministry, and her support enabled Mill to enroll at Edinburgh University in 1790. There he studied Greek, especially the works of Plato; Latin; and moral philosophy under Dugald Stewart. He began his studies in divinity in 1794 and was licensed to preach on 4 October 1798. After delivering some sermons locally without success—they were regarded as learned but obscure—Mill supported himself as an itinerant preacher and tutor.

In 1802 Mill moved to London, where he found employment as a journalist with the *Anti-Jacobin Review.* While working there he began collaborating with the clergyman Henry Hunter in rewriting *Nature Delineated* (1740), the English translation of Noël Antoine Pluche's *Le spectacle de la nature* (1732). Hunter died in 1802, before the work was completed; but the firm of C. and R. Baldwin, the prospective publisher, offered Mill the editorship of a new periodical, the weekly *Literary Journal,* which started publication at the beginning of 1803. Supplementing his income by writing a pamphlet attacking the taxation of grain exports (1804) and translating Charles de Villers's *Essai sur l'esprit et l'influence de la Reformation de Luther* (1804) as *An Essay on the Spirit and Influence of the Reformation of Luther* (1805), Mill was secure enough financially to marry Harriet Burrow on 5 June 1805; they took up residence in a house in Pentonville that they rented from Burrow's mother. Mill's editorship of the *Literary Journal* continued for a year after it became a monthly in 1806; from 1805 until 1808 he also edited the *St. James Chronicle.* In 1806 he began a history of India that he estimated would take three years to complete. Also in 1806–

The utilitarian philosopher Jeremy Bentham, Mill's friend and mentor (engraving by J. Posselwhite of a portrait by J. Watts)

though he is described as being neither a loving husband nor a loving father—he and his wife had the first of their nine children: John Stuart Mill, named for the husband of his father's patron. The others were Wilhelmina, Clara, Harriet, James Bentham, Jane, Henry, Mary, and George Grote. Mill took great interest in his children's education and spent a portion of each day giving them personal instruction. He is depicted in this role in the early chapters of John Stuart Mill's *Autobiography* (1873), and his stringent system of education is satirized in Charles Dickens's novel *Hard Times* (1854).

The loss of both of his editorships forced Mill to depend for his income on contributions, often published anonymously, to periodicals such as the *British Review,* the *Monthly Review,* and, especially, the *Eclectic Review.* In 1808 the Scottish Whig politician Henry Brougham helped Mill obtain employment with the prestigious *Edinburgh Review,* of which Brougham was one of the founders, and Mill contributed three long articles a year on a variety of subjects for the journal until 1813.

Mill met Bentham in 1808, and they almost immediately formed an alliance. Bentham was the leading exponent of what later came to be called utilitarianism, a philosophy that defined right actions as those that maxi-

mized the happiness and minimized the suffering of the greatest number of the sentient beings (including animals) affected by the actions. At that time utilitarianism was concerned with promoting legal, penal, and electoral reforms, religious toleration, and freedom of speech and of the press. Mill revised Bentham's writings and took an active part in his circle, known as the Philosophical Radicals, which included the labor leader Francis Place, the Swiss jurist Etienne Dumont, the historian George Grote, the legal philosopher John Austin, and the economist David Ricardo. Their relationship was so productive that Bentham wanted Mill constantly at hand, and the Mills spent the summers of 1809 and several other years with Bentham in Surrey. In 1810 they moved into a house on Bentham's property that had previously belonged to John Milton and William Hazlitt; the unhealthy condition of the ancient building forced them to leave after a few months, however, and they moved to Newington Green. From 1814 to 1830 the Mills rented a house from Bentham at 1 Queen Square that was next door to his own home; they also spent lengthy periods with Bentham in Somerset between 1814 and 1818.

By this time an agnostic, Mill wrote for William Allen's Quaker periodical *Philanthropist* from 1811 to 1817 on subjects such as law reform, the antislavery movement, and, especially, the controversy between the educational reformers Andrew Bell and Joseph Lancaster. In 1809 Mill had joined the Royal Lancasterian Association, which supported the founding of nondenominational primary schools on the monitorial system, which was claimed to be a cheap and efficient way of providing a good education. Mill believed that the monitorial system would work because it balanced competing self-interests and provided an incentive to the monitors, who were held personally responsible for the failings of their pupils. The Church of England disagreed with the pedagogy and curriculum of the Royal Lancasterian Association, and a debate raged in the press, with the *Quarterly Review* supporting the church and the *Philanthropist* and *Edinburgh Review* supporting Lancaster. In 1813 Allen, Place, and Mill tried to establish a Lancasterian school to educate children in west London, but because of a lack of funds and a schism within the Royal Lancasterian Association—which by then had been renamed the British and Foreign Schools Society—the school did not materialize. Undeterred, Mill moved on to promote a nondenominational secondary school. His pamphlet *Schools for All, in Preference to Schools for Churchmen Only; or, The State of the Controversy between the Advocates for the Lancasterian System of Universal Education, and Those Who Have Set Up an Exclusive and Partial System under the Name of the Church and Dr. Bell* (1812) appeared as part of this campaign, as did Bentham's *Chrestomathia: Being a Collection of Papers, Explanatory of the Design of an Institution, Proposed to Be Set on Foot, under the Name of the*

Chrestomathic Day School, or Chrestomathic School, for the Extension of the New System of Instruction to the Higher Branches of Learning, for the Use of the Middling and Higher Ranks of Life (1817), edited by Mill. Attempts to build this school were also foiled. He also called for the establishment of rehabilitation programs in humanely designed prisons, free trade, freedom of speech, freedom of the press, and extension of the franchise to ensure the active participation and continual education of all classes in society.

Although Mill wrote about politics, psychology, economics, and history, the theme that unifies all of his work is education. For Mill, education meant not just schooling but the formation of character and conduct by association and habituation; for him it was the answer to most social ills. He argued that education was the best way to ensure good citizens, whereas miseducation led inevitably to the formation of a criminal class. He also called for the establishment of rehabilitation programs in humanely designed prisons, free trade, freedom of speech and of the press, and extension of the franchise to ensure the active participation and continual education of society.

Mill's reputation was established with the publication of *The History of British India* (1817), a "philosophical history" in the tradition of Edward Gibbon's *The History of the Decline and Fall of the Roman Empire* (1776–1788) that took ten years to complete, rather than the three Mill had anticipated. The book provided a defense of British imperialism in India, mild criticism of the shortcomings of the East India Company, and a critique of the weaknesses of English trading policy, all on utilitarian principles. In his preface he defends his authority to write about the subcontinent without ever having visited the region and with no knowledge of Indian languages by characterizing these lacks as an advantage, arguing that he is unlikely to have formulated any "partial impressions" colored by personal association. Mill was distancing himself from orientalist scholars such as William Jones, who traveled extensively in Asia; studied Sanskrit, Persian, and Hindi; and became submerged in the culture of the subcontinent before commenting, usually admiringly, on the culture of ancient India. Mill, on the contrary, argues in the chapter "Of the Hindus" that India had never had a high degree of civilization by European standards. His examination of the caste system, government, laws, arts and sciences, religion, and manners of Indian society leads Mill to conclude that it is comparable to the society of the English feudal period. He concludes: "Exactly in proportion as Utility is the object of every pursuit may we regard a nation as civilized. Exactly in proportion as its ingenuity is wasted on contemptible and mischievous objects, though it may be, in itself, an ingenuity of no ordinary kind, the nation may safely be denominated barbarous." Despotic rule is justified until a society is capable of self-government; on this basis, as well

as for economic reasons, Mill defends the British East India Company's role in India. Though utilitarians were in principle opposed to colonial governments, which they regarded as inefficient, corrupt, and inclined to perpetuate the interests of the ruling class, and were also opposed to monopolistic trading practices, India is deemed exceptional. Mill never implies that racial inferiority accounts for the abject level of civilization reached by India; he suggests that its lowliness is a function of poor education. Furthermore, Mill argues that Indians should be instructed in their own languages—unlike Thomas Babington Macaulay, who, in his "Minute on Indian Education" (1835), defines the aim of British educational policy in India as the creation of "a class of persons, Indian in blood and colour, but English in taste and intellect"—and says that this aim is achievable only through the use of English as a medium of instruction.

The significance of *The History of British India* cannot be overestimated; according to Javed Majeed's *Ungoverned Imaginings: James Mill's* The History of British India *and Orientalism* (1992), "*The History of British India* shaped a theoretical basis for the liberal program to emancipate India from its own culture." The work established Mill as an expert on India and quickly became the official textbook of the East India Company's college at Haileybury. The book, as well as the support of influential friends, led to Mill's appointment on 12 May 1819 as assistant to the examiner of Indian correspondence for the East India Company.

In 1814 Mill had been invited by the editor, Macveigh Napier, to contribute to the six-volume *Supplement to the Fourth, Fifth, and Sixth Editions* of the *Encyclopædia Britannica*. Between 1816 and 1823 he wrote twelve articles expounding utilitarian principles. For modern critics the most significant of these pieces are "Education" (1819) and "Government" (1820), on the latter of which his modern reputation largely rests. In "Education" Mill says that the aim of education is "to render the individual, as much as possible an instrument of happiness, first to himself, and next to other beings." Happiness, he continues, depends on intelligence, temperance, justice, and generosity; it is not identical with pleasure. Education equips individuals to conduct themselves to provide the greatest happiness for the greatest number; citizens must be taught to avoid short-range pleasures in favor of the collective good. Conformity, self-denial, and censure ensure a happy and healthy polity. In his *Autobiography* John Stuart Mill criticizes the practical application of his father's educational theories, which led in his own case to the nervous breakdown he describes in the chapter "A Crisis in My Mental History."

At the time of its publication James Mill's essay "Government" was regarded as radical, dangerous, and extreme in its advocacy of democracy. In the essay,

COMMERCE DEFENDED.

AN

ANSWER TO THE ARGUMENTS

BY WHICH

Mr. SPENCE, Mr. COBBETT,

AND OTHERS,

HAVE ATTEMPTED TO PROVE THAT

Commerce

IS NOT A

SOURCE OF NATIONAL WEALTH.

BY JAMES MILL, Esq.

Author of an Essay on the Impolicy of a Bounty on the Exportation
of Corn.

London:

PRINTED FOR C. AND R. BALDWIN, NEW BRIDGE-STREET.

1808.

Price Four Shillings.

*Title page for Mill's second book, in which he argues in
favor of business against thinkers who wanted to
return Britain to an agrarian economy
(Library of Congress)*

which was written during a period of political unrest and instability in Europe, Mill attempts to elaborate a science of good government. The central issue he addresses is how government can be prevented from using its power to victimize rather than benefit the greatest number; that is, given the utilitarian tenet that individuals are motivated by self-interest, how the interests of governors can be attuned with those of the governed. Mill's answer is representative government, which, he argues, provides the best alternative to the unwieldy and expensive "participatory" democracy advanced by the Swiss-born French philosopher Jean-Jacques Rousseau, and the "virtual representation" advocated by Whigs, especially Macaulay and Edmund Burke, in which an unelected aristocracy is trusted to safeguard the interests of the majority. Representative government, with its frequent elections and short terms in office, ensures an "identity of interests" between electorate and representative.

Arguing for the extension of the franchise to male householders over the age of forty, Mill says: "One thing is pretty clear, that all those individuals whose interests are indisputably included in those of other individuals, may be struck off without inconvenience. In this light may be viewed all children, up to a certain age, whose interests are involved in those of their parents. In this light, also, women may be regarded, the interest of almost all of whom is involved either in that of their fathers or in that of their husbands." William Thompson responded in his *Appeal of One Half of the Human Race, Women, Against the Pretensions of the Other Half, Men, to Retain Them in Political and Thence in Civil and Domestic Slavery: In Reply to a Paragraph of Mr. Mill's Celebrated "Article on Government"* (1825) that women ought not to be excluded from Mill's proposed reforms.

Macaulay also attacked Mill in an article in the March 1829 issue of the *Edinburgh Review*. He challenged the "law" that individuals always act according to self-interest and criticized Mill for depicting democracy as morally neutral. Mill does not argue that individuals have a natural right to the vote or an innate need to participate in the political process; he depicts the vote simply as a way of checking selfish interests. Democracy, in other words, is a negative limit, and Mill recommends no more of it than will deter the rulers from acting to promote their "sinister interests."

The Political Economy Club, founded in 1820, arose from meetings held at Ricardo's house on the subject of free trade. Henry Bickersteth, John and Charles Austin, William Ellis, Walter Coulson, and John Stuart Mill were regular attendees at club meetings. James Mill drafted the rules of the club, and his *Elements of Political Economy* (1821), along with Ricardo's *On the Principles of Political Economy, and Taxation* (1817), which Mill had encouraged Ricardo to publish, became definitive texts in the new discipline of economics. In 1821 Mill was promoted to second assistant to the examiner of Indian correspondence and in 1823 to assistant examiner.

The Westminster Review, begun in 1824 with Bentham's backing, replaced the *Morning Chronicle* as the recognized organ of utilitarianism. Bentham invited Mill to edit the journal, but his position with the East India Company prevented him from accepting the offer. With the exception of his defense of the extension of the franchise in 1830, Mill stopped writing for the *Westminster Review* after a dispute with the editors in 1826.

In 1829 Mill published *Analysis of the Phenomena of the Human Mind,* on which he had worked during vacations from his East India Company job since 1822. All human beings seek pleasure and try to avoid pain, Mill says, but custom, habituation, and environment determine what they will experience as pleasurable. Fusing the empirical tradition of John Locke, according to which knowledge is produced by sense experience and the introspective experience of feelings, with David Hartley's association theory, which holds that when sensations have repeatedly been experienced simultaneously or in succession, the idea of one will call up the idea of the others, Mill presents a model of the human mind as rational and that supports his view of the role and importance of education.

In 1830 Mill was made head examiner of Indian correspondence for the East India Company. That same year he moved from Queen Square to Church Street in Kensington. In 1831 and 1832 he testified before committees of the House of Commons regarding the renewal of the East India Company's charter in 1833, and he wrote the final dispatches in which the company argued its case for renewal. His views on India did not change over the course of his career; it seems that his official experiences confirmed for him that the natives of India were unfit for self-government and that even free trade would not produce an improvement without despotic controls. His final book was *A Fragment on Mackintosh: Being Strictures on Some Passages in the Dissertation by Sir James Mackintosh Prefixed to the* Encyclopædia Britannica, written in 1830 but not published until 1835, in which he attacks Mackintosh for attempting to combine utilitarianism with a "moral sense" theory. Mill suffered during his last years from lung disease, and he died on 23 June 1836 after an attack of bronchitis. He was buried in Kensington Church.

James Mill addressed epistemological and methodological concerns that are still relevant today. His work provides an historical and philosophical context for modern debates about the nature of authority, the role of government, and the rationality of the human mind. Mill's ascetic, rational utilitarian philosophy was a precondition for both democratic reform and modern moral relativism.

Bibliography:

Robert A. Fenn, "Concise List of the Works of James Mill," in his *James Mill's Political Thought* (New York: Garland, 1987), pp. 156–186.

Biographies:

Alexander Bain, *James Mill: A Biography* (London: Longmans, Green, 1882);

Bruce Mazlish, *James and John Stuart Mill: Father and Son in the Nineteenth Century* (New York: Basic Books, 1975).

References:

Terence Ball, "Utilitarianism, Feminism, and the Franchise: James Mill and His Critics," *History of Political Thought,* 1 (Spring 1980): 91–115;

W. H. Burston, *James Mill on Philosophy and Education* (London: Athlone Press, 1973);

Stefan Collini, Donald Winch, and John Burrow, *That Noble Science of Politics: A Study in Nineteenth-Century Intellectual History* (Cambridge & New York: Cambridge University Press, 1983);

Robert A. Fenn, *James Mill's Political Thought* (New York: Garland, 1987);

Duncan Forbes, "James Mill and India," *Cambridge Journal,* 5 (1951/1952): 19–33;

Knud Haakonsen, "James Mill and Scottish Moral Philosophy," *Political Studies,* 33 (1985) 628–636;

Elie Halévy, *The Growth of Philosophic Radicalism* (London: Faber & Faber, 1949);

Joseph Hamburger, *James Mill and the Art of Revolution* (New Haven: Yale University Press, 1963);

Thomas Babington Macaulay, "Mill's *Essay on Government:* Utilitarian Logic and Politics," *Edinburgh Review,* 49 (March 1829): 159–189;

Javed Majeed, *Ungoverned Imaginings: James Mill's* The History of British India a*nd Orientalism* (Oxford: Clarendon Press, 1992; New York: Oxford University Press, 1992);

Bruce Mazlish, *The Revolutionary Ascetic: Evolution of a Political Type* (New York: Basic Books, 1976);

Alan Ryan, "Two Concepts of Politics and Democracy: James and John Stuart Mill," in *Machiavelli and the Nature of Political Thought,* edited by Martin Fleisher (London & New York: Atheneum, 1972), pp. 72–113;

Leslie Stephens, *The English Utilitarians* (London: Duckworth, 1900);

Eric Stokes, *The English Utilitarians and India* (Oxford: Clarendon Press, 1959);

William Thomas, *The Philosophical Radicals* (Oxford: Clarendon Press, 1979);

William Thompson, *Appeal of One Half of the Human Race, Women, Against the Pretensions of the Other Half, Men, to Retain Them in Political and Thence in Civil and Domestic Slavery: In Reply to a Paragraph of Mr. Mill's Celebrated "Article on Government"* (London: Printed for Longman, Hurst, Rees, Orme, Brown & Green, 1825; republished, with introduction by Richard Pankhurst, London: Virago, 1983).

Papers:

The London Library has volumes one through four of James Mill's commonplace books; the London School of Economics has volume five. Other relevant collections include the Place, Napier, and Bentham Papers at the British Museum and the Bentham and Brougham Collections at University College London.

John Stuart Mill

(20 May 1806 – 7 May 1873)

Lou J. Matz
University of the Pacific

See also the Mill entries in *DLB 55: Victorian Prose Writers Before 1867* and *DLB 190: British Reform Writers, 1832–1914*.

BOOKS: *A System of Logic, Ratiocinative and Inductive, Being a Connected View of the Principles of Evidence and the Methods of Scientific Investigation* (2 volumes, London: Parker, 1843; 1 volume, New York: Harper, 1846);

Essays on Some Unsettled Questions of Political Economy (London: Parker, 1844; New York: Kelley, 1974);

The Principles of Political Economy with Some of Their Applications to Social Philosophy (London: Parker, 1848; Boston: Little, Brown, 1848);

On Liberty (London: Parker, 1859; Boston: Ticknor & Fields, 1863);

Thoughts on Parliamentary Reform (London: Parker, 1859; revised and enlarged, 1859);

Dissertations and Discussions: Political, Philosophical, and Historical; Reprinted Chiefly from the Edinburgh and Westminster Reviews (4 volumes; volumes 1 and 2, London: Parker, 1859; volume 3, London: Longmans, Green, Reader & Dyer, 1867; volume 4, London: Parker, 1875; 5 volumes; volumes 1–4, Boston: Spencer, 1864–1867; volume 5, New York: Holt, 1875);

Considerations on Representative Government (London: Parker & Bourn, 1861; New York: Harper, 1862);

Utilitarianism (London: Parker & Bourn, 1863; Boston: Small, 1887);

Auguste Comte and Positivism (London: Trübner, 1865; Philadelphia: Lippincott, 1866);

An Examination of Sir William Hamilton's Philosophy, and of the Principal Philosophical Questions Discussed in His Writings (1 volume, London: Longmans, Green, Longmans, Roberts & Green, 1865; 2 volumes, Boston: Spencer, 1865);

Speech of John Stuart Mill, M.P., on the Admission of Women to the Electoral Franchise (London: Trübner, 1867);

John Stuart Mill

Personal Representation: Speech of John Stuart Mill . . . Delivered in the House of Commons, May 29, 1867, with an Appendix, Containing Notices of Reports, Discussions, and Publications on the System in France, Geneva, Germany, Belgium, Denmark, Sweden, the Australian Colonies, and the United States (London: Printed by Henderson, Rait & Fenton, 1867);

Inaugural Address Delivered to the University of St. Andrews, Feb. 1st, 1867 (London: Longmans, Green, Reader & Dyer, 1867; Boston: Littell & Gay, 1867);

England and Ireland (London: Longmans, Green, Reader & Dyer, 1868);

The Subjection of Women (London: Longmans, Green, Reader & Dyer, 1869; Philadelphia: Lippincott, 1869; New York: Appleton, 1869);

Autobiography (London: Longmans, Green, Reader & Dyer, 1873; New York: Holt, 1873);

Nature, The Utility of Religion, and Theism, edited by Helen Taylor (London: Longmans, Green, Reader & Dyer, 1874); republished as *Three Essays on Religion* (New York: Holt, 1874);

Early Essays by John Stuart Mill, edited by J. W. M. Gibbs (London: Bell, 1897);

The Spirit of the Age, edited by Frederick A. von Hayek (Chicago: University of Chicago Press, 1942);

Mill on Bentham and Coleridge, edited by F. R. Leavis (London: Chatto & Windus, 1950; New York: Stewart, 1950);

Prefaces to Liberty: Selected Writings of John Stuart Mill, edited by Bernard Wishy (Boston: Beacon, 1959; Lanham, Md. & London: University Press of America, 1983);

John Mill's Boyhood Visit to France: Being a Journal and Notebook Written by John Stuart Mill in France, 1820–21, edited by Anna Jean Mill (Toronto: University of Toronto Press, 1960);

The Early Draft of John Stuart Mill's Autobiography, edited by Jack Stillinger (Urbana: University of Illinois Press, 1961);

Mill's Essays on Literature and Society, edited by J. B. Schneewind (New York: Collier, 1965; London: Collier-Macmillan, 1965);

Literary Essays, edited by Edward Alexander (Indianapolis: Bobbs-Merrill, 1967);

The Nigger Question, by Thomas Carlyle, and *The Negro Question,* by Mill, edited by Eugene R. August (New York: Appleton-Century-Crofts, 1971);

Essays on Poetry, edited by F. Parvin Sharpless (Columbia: University of South Carolina Press, 1976);

John Stuart Mill on Ireland, with an essay by Richard Ned Lebow (Philadelphia: Institute for the Study of Human Issues, 1979).

Collection: *The Collected Works of John Stuart Mill,* 31 volumes, edited by John M. Robson and others (Toronto & London: Toronto University Press, 1963–1990).

OTHER: Jeremy Bentham, *The Rationale of Judicial Evidence, Specially Applied to English Practice,* 5 volumes, edited by Mill (London: Hunt & Clarke, 1827);

Public Agency or Trading Companies: Memorials on Sanitary Reform, and on the Economical and Administrative Principles of Water-Supply for the Metropolis, Including Correspondence between John Stuart Mill and the Metropolitan Sanitary Association (London: Gadsby, 1851);

Henry Romilly, *Public Responsibility and Vote by Ballot,* includes letter by Mill (London, 1867);

James Mill, *Analysis of the Phenomenon of the Human Mind, with Notes Illustrative and Critical by Alexander Bain, Andrew Findlater, and George Grote,* 2 volumes, edited by John Stuart Mill (London: Longmans, Green, Reader & Dyer, 1869);

Programme of the Land Tenure Reform Association, explanatory statement by Mill (London: Longmans, Green, Reader & Dyer, 1871);

Henry Aime Ouvry, *Stein and His Reforms in Prussia, with Reference to the Land Question in England: And an Appendix Containing the Views of R. Cobden, and J. S. Mill's Advice to Land Reformers* (London: Kerby & Endean, 1873);

Four Dialogues of Plato, Including the "Apology of Socrates," translated and annotated by Mill (London: Watts, 1946).

John Stuart Mill was the most influential philosopher in the English-speaking world in the nineteenth century. He wrote extensively on logic and scientific methodology, economics, moral theory, political philosophy, feminism, metaphysics, religion, poetry, history, and botany, as well as on virtually all of the pressing social and political issues of his time; his *Collected Works* (1963–1990) comprise thirty-one volumes. In the opinion of his contemporary, the eminent philosopher Herbert Spencer, Mill was "the one conspicuous figure in the higher regions of thought." In his writings and his speeches as a member of Parliament, Mill espoused liberal views that shaped the opinions of intellectuals and members of the working class alike. Even in his most abstract and technical philosophical works, such as his writings on logic and scientific method, his goal was the moral improvement of humanity. For Mill, philosophical speculation was not distinct from practical affairs: as a member of Parliament, for example, Mill gained infamy as the first person to propose women's suffrage in a legislative assembly. He left an autobiography—rare among philosophers—that is the principal source of information on his life and intellectual development.

Mill was born in Pentonville, outside London, on 20 May 1806, the first of the four sons and five daughters of James Mill, who was then editor of the *Literary Journal* and the *St. James Chronicle,* and Harriet Burrow Mill. James Mill was the son of a Scottish shoemaker; through the patronage of the wife of a local aristocrat, Sir John Stuart, after whom he named his son, he had studied divinity at Edinburgh University and become licensed as a Presbyterian preacher; but soon afterward he had become an agnostic and never took up the profession. In 1808 his editorships came to an end, and he turned to freelance journalism. That same year he met

Miniature of Harriet Hardy Taylor, who married Mill in 1851; artist unknown (British Library of Political and Economic Science)

the utilitarian Jeremy Bentham, the leader of a group of utilitarian political and legal reformers known as the Philosophical Radicals; he soon became one of Bentham's principal disciples. The Mills eventually took up residence near Bentham and spent summers at his country mansion in Devonshire. After the publication of his three-volume work *The History of British India* (1817), James Mill was appointed an examiner of Indian correspondence in the East India Company. His article "Education" (1819) in the supplement to the fourth, fifth, and sixth editions of the *Encyclopaedia Britannica* and his *Analysis of the Phenomena of the Human Mind* (1829) articulated the theories that shaped his son's early education. John Stuart Mill's mother was a beautiful, good-natured, but uneducated woman, ten years younger than her husband. Their intellectual disparity led James Mill to treat her with contempt.

John Stuart Mill's early education, which he famously describes in his *Autobiography* (1873), gained him a reputation for intellectual greatness by his teenage years but elicited horror in his contemporaries. His education was an experiment conducted by his father—the essayist and historian Thomas Carlyle characterized John Stuart Mill as "the son of a demonstration"—and its aim was to create a formidable future leader of the cause of Philosophical Radicalism. James Mill accepted the prevailing empiricist philosophy that the mind at birth is a tabula rasa and that associations of

ideas are built up as a result of experience. While the mind always absorbs impressions, he believed, their force is much greater before many experiences have been accumulated. As a result, the earlier education was begun, the more lasting its effects would be; and whoever controlled this education could permanently shape the person's intellect and character. Thus, at age three Mill began learning ancient Greek and arithmetic. Before he was eight he read many works of history, and he recited for his father what he had learned during their frequent walks in Newington Green. His father explained to him fundamental ideas about civilization, government, and morality and required him to restate them in his own words, thereby avoiding the then-standard method of rote learning. As Mill says in his *Autobiography*, his education was not a passive repetition and cramming of facts but an active one that promoted critical scrutiny and independence of thought; James Mill pushed his son to find things out for himself, intervening only when the boy was incapable of going farther on his own. Mill rarely read children's books, and he had no toys other than occasional gifts from relatives. He also had no friends his own age, because his father feared the corrupting and vulgar influences of other boys. Mill's friends were his father's—Bentham, the economist David Ricardo, and Francis Place, a master tailor and self-taught leader of the working class. At eight Mill began learning Latin and prepared lessons for his siblings. By age twelve he had read many of the Greek and Latin classics, including the works of Homer, Thucydides, Aeschylus, Sophocles, Euripides, Aristophanes, Plato, Aristotle, Virgil, Horace, Livy, Ovid, Lucretius, and Cicero in the original languages. He also learned elementary geometry and algebra; but he had difficulty with differential calculus and more-advanced mathematics, since his father was not competent to help him in those subjects. Because of the low assessment of its value by the Benthamites, Mill read little poetry—"Prejudice apart, the game of push-pin is of equal value with the arts and sciences of music and poetry. If the game of push-pin furnish more pleasure, it is more valuable than either," Bentham says in *Théorie des peines et des récompenses* (Theory of Punishments and Rewards, 1811), first published in a French translation by Etienne Dumont and retranslated as *The Rationale of Reward* (1825). Mill delighted, however, in writing histories and reading treatises on chemistry.

At twelve Mill began to learn logic; in his *Autobiography* he attributes his ability to think clearly to his early study of the subject. Logic also impressed on him the importance of using precise language and avoiding vague or ambiguous terms. The next year he began studying classical economics with Adam Smith's *An*

Inquiry into the Nature and Causes of the Wealth of Nations (1776) and Ricardo's *On the Principles of Political Economy and Taxation* (1817).

Recounting the moral influences of his upbringing in the *Autobiography,* Mill notes that he was raised without any religious belief; thus, unlike many of his contemporaries, he never experienced a loss of faith. Mill's father had rejected his own former religious convictions on the grounds that the amount of evil and suffering in the world was inconsistent either with God's alleged omnipotence or with his goodness; that a deity who would create a hell knowing that the majority of the human race would be consigned to it for eternity was unworthy of worship; and that the Christian religion sets up false virtues, such as devotion to religious creeds and ceremonies, that are contrary to morality since they do not promote the good of humanity as a whole but lead to divisions between believers and nonbelievers. James Mill embraced, and held out to his son as examples of moral excellence, the ethical virtues embodied by Socrates and the Stoics: justice, temperance, a life of exertion, and regard for the public good. Many of his father's moral and religious ideas can be found in John Stuart Mill's writings.

From May 1820 to July 1821 Mill lived in France with the family of Bentham's brother, Sir Samuel Bentham, traveling around the country and attending lectures on chemistry, zoology, and metaphysics at the Faculté des Sciences in Montpellier. He came to prefer the French temperament to that of the English, which he believed to be lacking in feeling; he decided that the feelings, not just the intellect, were important and could be educated.

During the winter of 1821–1822 Mill studied Roman law with John Austin, the Benthamite legal theorist, and read Jeremy Bentham's *Traités de législation civile et pénale* (Treatise on Civil and Penal Legislation, 1802), which had originally been edited and published in a French translation by Dumont (a retranslation into English appeared in 1830 as *Principles of Legislation*). Mill claims in the *Autobiography* that the work inspired a turning point in his mental history. Bentham's application of the principle of utility—the principle that morally right actions are those that promote the greatest happiness of the greatest number—to legislation and institutions "gave unity to my conceptions of things. I now had opinions: a creed, a doctrine, a philosophy; in one of the best senses of the word, a religion; the inculcation and diffusion of which could be made the principal outward purpose of a life."

Mill first appeared in print at the end of 1822 with letters to the newspaper *The Traveller.* In early 1823 he organized the Utilitarian Society, which met fortnightly at Bentham's house to discuss ethics and

politics until it was disbanded in 1826. During 1823 he contributed to *The Morning Chronicle* many pieces critical of the political and legal institutions of the day, including a series of letters defending freedom of speech in regard to religion, written in response to recent persecutions of people who had published opinions hostile to Christianity or who had refused to take an oath in court. In May 1823 Mill was hired as a clerk under his father in the examiner's office of the East India Company. His principal role was to supervise the political department's dealings with independent states. He remarks in the *Autobiography* that this practical experience was invaluable to him as a reformer.

In 1824 Bentham founded *The Westminster Review* as the organ of the Philosophical Radicals, who sought to supersede the Whigs as the progressive voice of the middle class. There appeared to be an opportunity to form a third party alongside the liberal Whigs and conservative Tories. Mill was an ardent proponent of Radical views, such as advocacy of representative government, freedom of the press, and full employment at high wages for workers. If not for his position with the East India Company, Mill probably would have become editor of *The Westminster Review.*

Mill and the other Philosophical Radicals accepted the economist Thomas Robert Malthus's view, expressed in *An Essay on the Principle of Population, as it affects the Future Improvement of Society, with Remarks on the Speculations of Mr. Godwin, M. Condorcet, and Other Writers* (1798), that the geometrical increase in the population would inevitably outstrip the mere arithmetical increase in the production of food, leading to famine. Malthus pointed out, however, that famine and war were not the only possible checks on population growth: moral restraints, such as deferring marriage—an idea contrary to the teaching of the Church of England—were also available. Place wrote a pamphlet that extended Malthus's ideas by recommending the use of birth control. On his way to work at India House one day in 1824 Mill discovered a newborn baby that had been strangled and abandoned. Horrified, Mill began handing out copies of Place's pamphlet in slum tenements. He and others helping him were arrested and charged with distributing obscene literature. Mill and his companions were sentenced to fourteen days imprisonment, but their term was reduced to only three or four days after their friends convinced the authorities that their intention was to prevent infanticide, not to promote vice or obscenity.

In 1825 Mill participated in the founding of the Society of Students of Mental Philosophy, which met twice a week until 1828 at the home of George Grote, the historian of Greece, to discuss economics, logic, and analytic psychology. Also in 1825 Mill and his friends

Miniature of John Taylor, Harriet Taylor's first husband; artist unknown (British Library of Political and Economic Science)

educational program had emphasized his intellectual cultivation and the abstract pursuit of the general good at the expense of feelings and emotions. His education, he says, had provided him with "a well equipped ship and a rudder, but no sail; without any real desire for the ends which I had been so carefully fitted out to work for; no delight in virtue or the general good." He asked himself:

> Suppose that all your objects in life were realized; that all the changes in institutions and opinions which you are looking forward to, could be completely effected at this very instant: would this be a great joy and happiness to you? An irrepressible self-consciousness distinctly answered, "No!" At this my heart sank within me: the whole foundation on which my life was constructed fell down. All my happiness was to have been found in the continual pursuit of this end. The end had ceased to charm, and how could there ever again be any charm in the means? I seemed to have nothing left to live for.

Afraid to confide in his father and lacking intimate friends to share his distress, Mill felt isolated. Fearing that he had lost his capacity to feel, he tried to revive it by turning to Romantic poetry, especially that of William Wordsworth, and to novels and music. In the process he came to the painful realization that Bentham's views on the place of the feelings in human nature and on the value of poetry and the imagination were disastrously mistaken. Cultivating the feelings through the imagination, Mill decided, was essential for individual well-being.

Mill visited followers of the socialist Claude-Henri de Rouvron, Comte de Saint-Simon, in Paris during the July Revolution of 1830. After his return to England he wrote articles on events in France for *The Examiner,* including weekly summaries of French politics.

In the summer of 1830 Mill met Harriet Taylor, the wife of a London merchant, John Taylor. The encounter proved to be one of the most significant events of Mill's life. Harriet Taylor had been married in her late teens and had two children. Domestic life bored her, however, and her intellectual vivaciousness immediately attracted Mill. They developed an intimate but chaste friendship, despite the attempts of her husband and Mill's family and friends to end it. They came to an agreement with John Taylor: Mill and Harriet could continue their relationship and could even vacation together, but they must avoid being seen in each other's company in public.

Mill's first significant publication, *The Spirit of the Age,* was serialized in *The Examiner* from January through May 1831, during the first reform movement that reconstituted Parliament and extended the vote to

debated the Owenites of the Cooperative Society on the merits of communism. These debates resulted that same year in the founding, under Mill's leadership, of the London Debating Society, which included several members of Parliament and members of the Cambridge Union and the Oxford United Debating Society. Many of the participants, among them Thomas Babington Macaulay, Albany Fonblanque, and Samuel Wilberforce, went on to become notable political or literary figures. Mill enlisted many prominent members of the society to write articles and reviews of literary and historical works for *The Westminster Review;* Mill himself contributed pieces on issues such as libel law, the corn laws, and the laws against gambling.

In the fall of 1826 Mill experienced the beginning of a mental crisis that continued for many months, though no one else was apparently aware of it. The nature of Mill's melancholy has been the subject of debate. Some scholars contend that he was simply mentally exhausted from the arduous work of preparing Bentham's *The Rationale of Judicial Evidence, Specially Applied to English Practice* (1827) for publication. Mill's own assessment in the *Autobiography* is that his father's

the industrial middle class by lowering property qualifications. In "The Spirit of the Age" he appropriates the Saint-Simonian distinction between "natural" and "transitional" periods to interpret the historical meaning of the reform movement. During natural periods a social consensus exists in regard to the locus of political, religious, moral, and intellectual authority in society and how this authority is to be maintained; in transitional periods the consensus is lost. Mill says that his own time is a transitional age. While he recognizes the need for authority—in this respect he rejects the individualistic tendencies of the Radicals—he argues that the traditional institutions admired by conservatives, such as the Church of England and the House of Lords, are deficient by the conservatives' own standards. He predicts that the next natural period will be based on social science. Mill's essay did not attract much attention, but it was noticed by Carlyle. When Carlyle came to London in 1831, a friendship between the two began.

In 1834 Mill published in *The Monthly Repository* abstracts of several of Plato's dialogues, including the *Apology, Protagoras, Gorgias,* and *Euthyphro;* they were his best-known writings to that time. He also wrote articles on the Poor Law reform of 1834 for *The Morning Chronicle* and *The Examiner* in which he supported the principle of "least eligibility," that is, giving only an amount of relief that would not make poverty more attractive than work. The most important event of the year for Mill was becoming the actual, though not the official, editor of Sir William Molesworth's newly created *London Review,* which replaced *The Westminster Review* as the periodical organ of the Philosophical Radicals.

After the death of his father in June 1836, Mill says in his *Autobiography,* he felt liberated from the "restraints and reticences" that had hindered the full expression of his political ideas. Opening the pages of *The London Review*—renamed *The London and Westminster Review* after its amalgamation with *The Westminster Review* in April 1836—to writers who shared his views on progress, Mill used his position to distance Philosophical Radicalism from the narrow constraints of Benthamism and to promote the development of a Radical political party, or, failing that, to put pressure on the moderate Whigs, whose leader declared in 1837 that no further reform of Parliament was necessary. Mill purchased *The London and Westminster Review* from Molesworth in 1837. The Radical Party never materialized, and Mill left the staff of the journal in 1840 but continued to contribute occasional articles to it.

Mill had reviewed the first volume of Alexis de Tocqueville's *De la Démocratie en Amerique* (Democracy in America, 1835) in *The London Review* in October 1835; he reviewed the second volume, which appeared five years later, in the October 1840 issue of *The Edinburgh Review.* The work changed the direction of his political thinking and led to the ideas he later expressed in *On Liberty* (1859) and *Considerations on Representative Government* (1861). Tocqueville describes the strengths and deficiencies of democracy and suggests correctives for the latter. Mill found Tocqueville's analysis of centralization especially compelling. Tocqueville warns that it is necessary for the people to be involved in local government to prevent what he calls "soft despotism." Citizen involvement could also foster the social feelings and practical intelligence of the people, qualities that are essential not only for sound government but also for personal well-being. Mill's 1840 review focused on Tocqueville's analysis of the "tyranny of the majority," a concept that became the central theme of *On Liberty.*

After Bentham's death in 1832 Mill had written an anonymous critical review of his *Introduction to the Principles of Morals and Legislation* (1789); the review appeared as an appendix to Edward Bulwer-Lytton's *England and the English* (1833). In 1838 Mill made his views public in his essay "Bentham" in *The London and Westminster Review.* Two years later, in the same review, he published "Coleridge," the complement to his essay on Bentham. For Mill, Bentham and the Romantic poet Samuel Taylor Coleridge represent, respectively, the essential truths of liberal and conservative thought. Bentham compels one to inquire into the validity of existing customs and institutions, and Coleridge, in the spirit of the conservative political philosopher Edmund Burke, prompts one to search for their meaning. In "Bentham" Mill praises Bentham's criticisms of existing laws and institutions and his unrelenting demand that they be reformed to promote human happiness. Most of all, Mill lauds Bentham's "method of detail," which exhausts every question and illustrates how a scientific philosophy can be applied to ethical problems. While Bentham was himself no practical reformer, Mill notes, his ideas inspired those who were. Mill, however, criticizes the "half-truths" in Bentham's psychological, moral, and political doctrines. Bentham's hedonistic view that human welfare is identical with pleasure and the absence of suffering is correct, Mill says, but Bentham's generalizations about human nature were projections from his own limited psychology. He was wrong, for example, to dismiss the value of natural feelings and of the imaginative and aesthetic dimensions of experience. Bentham "was a boy to the last. Self-consciousness . . . never was awakened in him." He also neglected the importance of internal moral motives, such as self-respect, and focused too exclusively on the outward consequences of conduct. As a result, Bentham's account of the "springs of action" is incomplete. In political philosophy Bentham invests the numerical majority with absolute authority, neglecting the necessity for a cultivated intellectual elite to inform

*Mill with his stepdaughter, Helen Taylor, who served as his companion
and secretary after Harriet Taylor Mill's death in 1858*

the public will. Many of the Radicals believed that Mill's criticisms were too severe, and in later years Mill expressed misgivings about them.

By the end of the 1830s Mill had limited his friends to a small circle, of which the principal members were Harriet Taylor, George Grote, and his future biographer Alexander Bain. Mill had grown tired of hearing the gossip about his relationship with Harriet; moreover, several of his friends had died. Also, Mill was occupied with his East India Company job and his writing projects, especially the preparation of the monumental *A System of Logic, Ratiocinative and Inductive, Being a Connected View of the Principles of Evidence and the Methods of Scientific Investigation* (1843).

A treatise on logic and scientific method had been on Mill's mind since he reviewed Richard Whateley's *Elements of Logic, Comprising the Substance of the Article in the* Encyclopaedia Metropolitana, *with Additions* (1826) in *The Westminster Review* in 1828. Mill had begun *A System of Logic* in 1832 but had been unable to resolve problems connected with inductive reasoning. He resumed writing in 1837, stimulated by his reading of the work of Auguste Comte and William Whewell's *History of the Inductive Sciences: From the Earliest to the Present Times* (1837). Mill's aim in *A System of Logic* is to demonstrate

that all knowledge derives from sense experience and the association of ideas. He is thus carrying on the tradition of the great British empiricists John Locke and David Hume; but he identifies his position as the "School of Experience," dismissing empiricism as "bad generalization" and "unscientific surmise."

Mill argues that profound practical consequences will result from the victory of one side or the other in the contest between the rival epistemologies of "Experience" and "Intuition." Proponents of the latter position, such as the "moral sense" schools and the German idealists, hold that truth is attainable by direct intellectual insight, independently of sense experience. Mill contends that the intuitive theory supports false moral, political, and religious doctrines and inhibits social reform because it consecrates its purported truths without justifying them by reason. The intuitive view claims that moral and religious propositions, like those in logic and mathematics and some in the natural sciences, can be known a priori. Mill attacks the view by demonstrating that logical, mathematical, and scientific knowledge stems from sense experience alone.

One of Mill's most important claims in *A System of Logic* is that deductive reasoning is actually a form of inductive inference. He supports this contention by analyzing the epitome of deductive arguments, the syllogism. In a valid syllogism such as "All human beings are mortal [major premise], John Stuart Mill is a human being [minor premise], therefore, John Stuart Mill is mortal [conclusion]" the conclusion is not actually inferred from the major premise, since it is already included in it; as a result, deductive reasoning does not amplify knowledge. Accordingly, Mill terms it "apparent" inference. The evidence for the conclusion derives from the experience of past particular cases; the major premise is a generalization based on these past cases and the assumption that the future will resemble the past—in other words, it is an example of inductive reasoning. Syllogistic inference is, therefore, ultimately not deductive but inductive, and inductive reasoning is the only basis for knowledge.

Mill notes that Hume had argued that the assumption that the future will resemble the past, or the assumption of the uniformity of nature, cannot be used to justify induction since it is itself a product of induction; thus, it commits the fallacy of circular reasoning. Mill responds that it is a mistake to demand deductive certainty from an inductive process.

The centerpiece of *A System of Logic* is Mill's discussion of the four methods of inductive reasoning: agreement, difference, residues, and concomitant variations. The purpose of the methods is to support hypotheses about causal connections by eliminating alternative hypotheses.

After presenting a catalogue of fallacies, Mill contends in the final part of *A System of Logic* that social phenomena can be explained by causal laws and that, therefore, the four inductive methods can be applied to psychology, sociology, and morality. He sketches a science of "ethology" that could serve as a scientific basis for progressive social reforms by discovering how social circumstances modify character. Recognizing that a conflict exists between his deterministic account of human behavior and his commitment to fostering individual freedom and moral responsibility, Mill adopts a "compatibilist" position on the free will-versus-determinism issue: a person's desires can be intervening causes of action, so that behavior is not completely determined by the character that has resulted from socialization.

A System of Logic was an immediate success not only in traditionally empiricist Britain but even on the Continent, where the a priori approach of German idealism predominated. It went into eight editions during Mill's lifetime. His contemporaries considered it his most significant work, and Mill himself believed in later life that it and *On Liberty* were destined to survive longer than any of his other writings. It was used for decades as a textbook in most English universities and some foreign ones. The work is still considered a seminal contribution to logic, but critics today contend that Mill's four inductive methods, which he considered methods of discovery, are not accurate descriptions of how scientific discovery takes place; they are actually methods of justification or proof. Mill had virtually no personal experience with scientific experimentation; he relied on Bain to furnish examples to illustrate his methods.

In 1844 Mill published *Essays on Some Unsettled Questions of Political Economy*. A more systematic work on economics, *The Principles of Political Economy with Some of Their Applications to Social Philosophy,* appeared in 1848, during the political revolutions in Europe and the acceleration of industrialization in England. Mill's views were formed by the works of the great classical economists Smith, Ricardo, and Malthus. From Ricardo, Mill learned that basic economic theory is a priori and deductive, much like geometry, and is derived from the axiom that human beings desire to amass the greatest amount of wealth with the least amount of labor. Smith, however, showed Mill that such "pure" economic theory is incomplete because it does not take account of actual social conditions. Mill believed that his own contribution to economics lay in updating Smith's analysis by applying the best social science of his own day to economic phenomena.

Mill distinguishes between production, which is subject to invariable economic laws, and distribution, which is a human convention and can be altered. The question for Mill, as a utilitarian, is what institutional

arrangements will not only assure a means of subsistence for all but also promote "that diversity of tastes and talents, and variety of intellectual points of view, which not only form a great part of the interest of human life, but by bringing intellects into stimulating collision, and by presenting to each innumerable notions that he would not have conceived himself, are the mainspring of mental and moral progression." The capitalist ideal that wealth should be based on the fruits of one's labor and on self-denial is contradicted by the facts, since the labor and sacrifice of workers are not fairly compensated; indeed, remuneration dwindles as work becomes more disagreeable. Opponents of socialism charge that it would reduce incentives to work and would foster a collective mentality, but these are claims that must be tested empirically. Ideally, Mill supports the organization of labor into producer cooperatives in which each worker is both manager and employee, but, contrary to most socialists, he advocates competition among the cooperatives. From a practical standpoint, it is more realistic to reform the system of the private ownership of the means of production than to abolish it. Mill, therefore, supports unionization so that workers' bargaining power can be made equal to that of the factory owners. Like other classical economists, Mill predicts that capitalistic economies will eventually become stagnant; but he points out the moral and environmental superiority of such a "stationary state" over rapid growth. Whatever system of economic organization a society chooses, universal education and voluntary restriction of the birthrate are imperative. In regard to the role of government in the economy, laissez-faire should be the rule, with exceptions based on expediency. Government should not only protect individuals against force and fraud but also provide goods that would be inadequately produced by market forces, such as utilities, poor relief, and education. Mill's most radical proposal is an inheritance tax that would insure that heirs received only a reasonable amount of wealth. The tax would mitigate the unjust distribution of wealth, and it is consistent with the basic capitalist principle that no one has a right to the fruits of the skill and labor of others—in this case, of one's own parent. Overall, Mill's advocacy of limited government stems less from considerations of economic efficiency than from his belief in the importance of promoting the development of the citizens' capacity for self-rule.

The Principles of Political Economy appeared in thirty-two editions over the next fifty years, but its importance was diminished by the rise of new economic theories. The historical significance of Mill's work lies in its combination of application of analytic theory to social issues; in that respect it is a direct ancestor of Alfred Marshall's *Principles of Economics* (1890).

Illustration from the Illustrated London News, *22 July 1865, showing Mill in Covent Garden receiving the nomination for the Westminster seat in the House of Commons*

John Taylor died in July 1849, but Harriet Taylor, Mill's partner in thought, feeling, and writing, did not become his wife until April 1851. At the time of their marriage Mill renounced in writing all legal rights that husbands acquired over their wives.

In 1854 Mill was diagnosed with consumption, the disease that had killed his father and two of his brothers. His health was largely restored by an eight-month trip to Italy, Sicily, and Greece. In 1856 he was promoted to chief examiner of correspondence by the East India Company, the same position his father had held. He retired at the end of 1858, when the company was transferred to the Crown.

After his retirement Mill and his wife traveled to France, intending to spend the winter in Montpellier, but Harriet Taylor Mill died of pulmonary congestion in Avignon. It was the greatest tragedy of Mill's life; for a time, he says in the *Autobiography,* he was doubtful whether he was "fit for anything public or private," but he soon resolved to complete the writing projects that he and Harriet had planned. For the rest of his life Mill and his stepdaughter, Helen Taylor, lived for most of each year near Avignon, where Harriet was buried.

Mill's first publication after his wife's death was *On Liberty* in 1859. Most of the manuscript had been drafted in 1857–1858, and Mill and Harriet had scrutinized it repeatedly line by line, prompting Mill to claim in the *Autobiography* that "none of my writings have been either so carefully composed, or so sedulously corrected as this." In Harriet Taylor Mill's memory, Mill never altered the work for any of the four editions that appeared in his lifetime.

The fundamental theme of *On Liberty* is the value of freedom for individual and social well-being and the extent to which political and social power can legitimately limit it. Mill's reviews of *Democracy in America,* his correspondence with social reformers such as Comte, and his experience of the moralism of the Victorian Era convinced him that a defense of individual liberty was necessary against the most oppressive power in democracies, the "tyranny of the majority." The majority can oppress either by law or by social pressure, and Mill contends that the latter is the greater threat since it is far more difficult to escape: the opinions of one's peers can become internalized and enslave the individual's own thoughts and desires. Individuals must be protected against the tendency of society to impose its collective opinion—which is usually based on emotion rather than on reason—on those who disagree. *On Liberty* was written to educate legislators and citizens about the basic principle that should guide the making of law, as well as the exercise of social approbation and disapprobation. This principle—which is not applicable to children or to backward societies—is

> that the sole end for which mankind are warranted, individually or collectively, in interfering with the liberty of action of any of their number, is self-protection. That the only purpose for which power can be rightfully exercised over any member of a civilized community, against his will, is to prevent harm to others. His own good, either physical or moral, is not a sufficient warrant. He cannot rightfully be compelled to do or forbear because it will be better for him to do so, because it will make him happier, because, in the opinions of others, to do so would be wise, or even right. These are good reasons for remonstrating with him, or reasoning with him, or persuading him, or entreating him, but not for compelling him, or visiting him with any evil in case he do otherwise. To justify that, the conduct from which it is desired to deter him, must be calculated to produce evil to some one else. The only part of the conduct of any one, for which he is amenable to society, is that which concerns others. In the part which merely concerns himself, his independence is, of right, absolute. Over himself, over his own body and mind, the individual is sovereign.

Applying this principle, Mill advocates the complete freedom to express one's opinions, except when such expression would lead directly to harm to others (as in the case of a person delivering a speech declaring that corn dealers starve the poor to an angry mob assembled before the house of a corn dealer). Mill poses a hypothetical scenario in which all members of a society but one hold the same opinion. There are only two possibilities. One is that the majority opinion is mistaken and that the dissenting view is wholly or partially true. If so, society would benefit by replacing error with truth. Hence, it must leave open the means to discover the truth: free discussion. Mill says, "The beliefs which we have most warrant for, have no safeguard to rest on, but a standing invitation to the whole world to prove them unfounded." The other possibility is that the majority opinion is true. Society still stands to benefit from tolerating a dissenting opinion that is false, because it compels the majority to reevaluate the grounds for its opinion; this process gives a vitality to beliefs that makes them "living" convictions rather than "dead" dogmas.

Mill's defense of liberty of conduct rests in part on the same arguments as his defense of freedom of thought and expression: society should permit a variety of "experiments in living" that inflict no harm on anyone but those who pursue them. If some of these experimental lifestyles prove to be superior to those of the majority, they will be imitated, and the overall happiness of society will increase. If they prove to be unhappy, as the majority of them no doubt will, society still benefits, since it gains a clearer understanding of the grounds for its traditional customs. Mill's central argument, however, appeals to the moral value of liberty. He holds that what is distinctive about a human life, and what makes it meaningful, is self-cultivation. Humans are not meant to be socially directed automata but to use their intellects to choose a way of life that brings out their highest potentials. True individuality is thus at one with self-development. According to Mill, "It really is of importance, not only what men do, but also what manner of men they are that do it." In another memorable passage he declares that "Human nature is not a machine to be built after a model, and set to do exactly the work prescribed for it, but a tree, which requires to grow and develop itself on all sides, according to the tendency of the inward forces which make it a living thing." The influence of Romantic poets such as Wordsworth and Coleridge on Mill's conception of individuality is clearly resonant in such passages.

Mill states that legal and social coercion are legitimate only when individuals violate, or are likely to violate, their distinct and assignable obligations to others, which Mill terms "rights." Rights are social rules that have paramount utility because they protect the interests that are most essential to human security and well-being. Actions that are merely offensive or discomfiting to others must be distinguished from those that are truly harmful. For example, although eating pork in a predominately Muslim society, or singing and dancing in a predominately Puritan one, or having more than one wife in a Christian society might be offensive to the majorities in the respective societies, such actions do not sacrifice any of the essential interests of a society. On the other hand, if someone is unable, through intemperance or extravagance, to pay his debts or support his family, he is justly punished—not for the intemperance or extravagance but for his breach of his duty to others.

Conduct that harms others, therefore, may rightfully be punished; but paternalistic legislation to punish conduct that is only harmful to the actor is illegitimate. Mill adduces several arguments for this position: society, not the individual, is to blame if it cannot educate its citizens to be prudent; controlling such "self-regarding" conduct will only prompt rebellion; the best means to educate people to be prudent is to tolerate, rather than prohibit, self-destructive behavior, since others will then be able to witness the painful consequences it produces; and, finally, an individual is more likely to know what is good for him or her than is society, which is not acquainted with the circumstances of particular individuals. Mill denies that his theory of liberty implies indifference to the character and conduct of others, arguing that society has other means besides the law to encourage prudence and high-mindedness: education and social encouragement. Strictly speaking, there are no moral duties to the self; there are self-regarding faults, such as a lack of moderation or neglect of talents, but these qualities only display a lack of personal dignity or self-respect and are not immoral. On the other hand, qualities of character such as cruelty, envy, greed, and insincerity are genuine moral vices, since they are likely to harm others. Society rightly expresses moral disapprobation of such qualities.

Applying his principle to various specific issues, Mill points out that the sale of poisons should not be prohibited, even though they can be used to harm others, because they also have legitimate uses; on the other hand, manufacturers can rightfully be forced to label products to warn consumers of their dangerous character. Parents can be forced to work to support their children. Gambling should be permitted in private homes, but casinos may be prohibited. The imposition of additional taxes on activities such as smoking or drinking on the grounds that they are vices is not legitimate. An individual should not be allowed to sell himself or herself into slavery. Strict divorce laws are unjust. In some respects, Mill points out, his principle would allow less liberty than prevailing opinions countenance: the state can make education compulsory, and those who cannot financially support a family can be forbidden to marry.

Mill anticipated a hostile reaction to *On Liberty,* and indeed, virtually all of its doctrines were subjected to criticism. His distinction between self-regarding and other-regarding conduct was attacked as unrealistic, and it was pointed out that the utilitarianism on which his principle was based could justify far more legal and social control of individual behavior than he admitted. Critics also found his assessment of the suppression of individuality in contemporary England greatly exaggerated and called his critique of Christian morality unfair. The eminent utilitarian jurist James Fitzjames Stephen was incited to publish a book-length attack on *On Liberty* in the year of Mill's death.

In *Considerations on Representative Government* (1861) Mill says that the purpose of government is to advance individual and social progress; representative government is best suited to this end, since it promotes the development of the citizens' intellectual, moral, and practical talents. Mill rejects the view expressed in his father's influential article "Government" (1820) in the supplement to the *Encyclopaedia Britannica* that the primary function of government is to protect the interests and rights of the people and that popular participation

is unnecessary to secure that end. For John Stuart Mill, only empowered citizens can make sure that their rights are protected and that their interests are represented in Parliament by people who share and can passionately defend them. Moreover, political participation has an educational function in directing citizens to look beyond their narrow self-interest to the public good.

Mill's proposals on the suffrage, which he had expressed previously in his *Thoughts on Parliamentary Reform* (1859), are the most radical aspect of *Considerations on Representative Government*. At this time many men, including manual laborers, and all women were excluded from the suffrage. Mill says that anyone who pays taxes and passes a modest literacy test should be allowed to vote: those who do not pay taxes should not decide how others' money should be spent, and people must be literate enough to participate in the political process. He also advocates a proportional-representation scheme in which voters would rank candidates in order of preference and quotas would be set to determine the minimum number of votes needed to elect a candidate; surplus votes for the top candidate would be transferred to the second-choice candidate, and the process would continue until the requisite number of candidates were elected. The purpose of proportional representation is to represent the voters' preferences more accurately. Mill also proposes a system of plural voting, in which better-educated voters—particularly the professional classes—would be able to cast multiple ballots. The purpose of plural voting is to give greater weight to more informed voters: all are to have a voice, but not equally. Mill recognizes the difficulty in determining who are the "better educated," and he proposes that an educational system be created to administer tests to citizens. (England did not establish a formal system of public education until the 1870s.) Mill rejects the secret ballot: since voting is a social act, how a person has voted should be open to public debate. An open ballot would lessen the likelihood that voters make their choices for purely selfish reasons.

Parliament should not draft laws; an expert commission should do so, and Parliament should be limited to accepting or rejecting the proposals. The administration of the government should be left to a professional civil service. Mill endorses the Northcote-Trevelyan Report of 1854, which advocated the recruitment of officials through competitive examinations irrespective of social class. An educated bureaucracy would act as a check on popular enthusiasms, while public debate and electoral participation would prevent the bureaucracy from becoming inefficient and corrupt.

Drawing on his experience with the East India Company, Mill concludes *Considerations on Representative Government* with a discussion of dependent states.

England's rule over its colonies is justified, since it expands and protects trade, preserves the peace, relieves population pressures at home, and provides a model of enlightened governance for the natives. Mill supports colonial autonomy when it is practicable, but autonomy is not an option for India because of its diverse cultures and low literacy rate. The East India Company was the best trustee of India's development toward self-rule; its authority should not have been transferred to the Crown. Mill believed that politicians were unfit to decide matters affecting the welfare of India, and he refused invitations to serve on the New Council of India.

In 1861 Mill published *Utilitarianism* in three installments in *Fraser's Magazine;* it was republished in book form in 1863. *Utilitarianism* was the first systematic statement of the utilitarian ethics; Mill wrote it to correct widespread misunderstandings of the doctrine. Like Bentham, Mill is an unwavering critic of a priori, intuitionist, and natural-rights ethical theories. The supreme moral standard is the "greatest happiness principle," according to which the morality of actions and institutions is determined by how much they promote the "happiness," defined as pleasure or, at least, the absence of pain, of all those affected by the action or institution. It is based on what, for Mill, is the undeniable empirical fact that the goal of all sentient beings is to experience pleasure and avoid suffering. To those who object that utilitarianism is vulgar and promotes a carpe diem attitude, Mill responds with a distinction between higher pleasures, which involve the intellect, and lower pleasures that can also be enjoyed by animals, such as eating and sex. Bentham believed that pleasure should be measured solely in quantitative terms—intensity, duration, fecundity (whether the pleasurable action led to more pleasure later), purity (whether the pleasurable action involved or led to painful experiences, such as a hangover), propinquity or remoteness (how closely the pleasure followed on the performance of the action), certainty (how certain it was that the action would produce the desired pleasure), and extent (how many sentient beings would experience pleasure as a result of the act). Mill, however, says that competent judges who have experienced both forms of pleasure would prefer a life devoted primarily to the higher ones: they would prefer to be Socrates dissatisfied rather than a fool satisfied, or a human being dissatisfied rather than a pig satisfied. To those who claim that people seek ends in life besides happiness, such as virtue, Mill responds that virtuous conduct is precisely that which minimizes suffering and increases happiness. Self-sacrifice is justified only if it advances others' happiness; it is pointless to pursue it as an end in itself. To those who complain that utilitarian-

ism is a godless doctrine, Mill replies that the Judeo-Christian God commands actions that promote happiness and forbids those that increase suffering. To those who charge that the utilitarian standard is impracticable, since there is not enough time to calculate the consequences for happiness of every decision one makes, Mill responds that one usually only needs to follow the "secondary principles" of customary morality: experience teaches that theft, lying, and murder cause suffering, while acts of kindness relieve misery and increase happiness. Appeal to the primary principle of utility is needed only when a conflict arises between secondary principles.

Conscience is the ultimate sanction of the principle of utility, according to Mill. While the specific dictates of the conscience are not innate but acquired, feelings of preference for the pleasures of others and of aversion to their pains may be innate. This feeling is not originally moral, however, since without training it extends only to members of one's immediate circle and not to all human beings. Social feelings are a fact of human nature, and when they are sufficiently cultivated, they are the source of individual happiness. Mill's answer to the moral skeptic's question why the individual should be moral is that those who have a developed conscience would not be willing to live without it if it were taken away. He says that if the feeling of regard for others' happiness were "to be taught as a religion, and the whole force of education, of institutions, and of opinion, directed, as it once was in the case of religion, to make every person grow up from infancy surrounded on all sides both by the profession and by the practice of it, I think that no one, who can realize this conception, will feel any misgiving about the sufficiency of the ultimate sanction for the Happiness morality."

Mill agrees with Bentham that the principle of utility is so basic that it is not subject to proof; nevertheless, he offers an "indirect" proof of the principle. Just as the fact that an object is seen shows that it is visible, so the fact that happiness is desired by all shows that it is desirable; the general happiness is desirable as the aggregate of the happiness of all individuals. Furthermore, happiness is the ultimate goal of all human actions. The twentieth-century philosopher G. E. Moore criticized Mill's argument for committing the "naturalistic fallacy": that is, it erroneously deduces "moral" from "nonmoral" goods by confusing what is normatively desirable—that is, what ought to be desired—with what is, in fact, desired. Critics today argue that the principal flaws in Mill's argument are the purely hedonistic psychology on which it is based and, even granted that assumption, its illicit move from the

Illustrated initial caricaturing Mill as "The Father of Political Economy" in the 21 March 1868 issue of the humor magazine Punch

desire of the individual for his or her own happiness to a purported desire for the general happiness.

Mill concludes *Utilitarianism* by explaining the relationship of justice to utility. A survey of conceptions of justice throughout history leads him to isolate two essential elements of the idea of justice: a right that ought to exist and the threat of punishment for its violation. There are no "natural" rights that are justified independently of happiness. Rights are the social rules that are most essential for well-being, such as protection of one's person and property. Such rules preserve security, which is the most vital of human interests: humans depend on security "for the whole value of all and every good, beyond the passing moment; since nothing but the gratification of the instant could be of any worth to us, if we could be deprived of everything the next instant by whoever was momentarily stronger than ourselves." The sentiment of justice arises from two originally nonmoral feelings: the impulse to self-defense and the feeling of sympathy. The natural desire to retaliate against an injury to oneself is extended to others when the individual realizes that a threat to them is also a threat to himself or herself. Through the feeling of sympathy the impulse to retaliate is widened to include injuries done to all human beings.

In 1865 Mill published *An Examination of Sir William Hamilton's Philosophy, and of the Principal Philosophical Questions Discussed in His Writings*. Hamilton was one of the most eminent philosophers in England at the time, and Mill, as an empiricist, thought it was his duty to critique Hamilton's rival intuitionist epistemology. Most of the work is devoted to exposing Hamilton's misunderstanding of empiricists such as Thomas Reid and David Hartley; in the course of the discussion Mill presents his own views on traditional metaphysical problems such as the existence of the external world, the nature of personal identity, and the relationship between determinism and free will. In the empiricist spirit of David Hume, Mill gives a phenomenalist explanation for the belief in an external world. The regularity of human experience leads people to form the hypothesis that certain conditions will produce certain sensations. Material objects are thus "permanent possibilities of sensation." Mill admits, however, that his explanation accounts only for the belief in an external reality and does not prove that objects exist independently of the human mind. On the question of personal identity, Mill rejects the common view that the mind is an immaterial substance and accepts Hume's psychological observation that there is no separate self apart from the succession of mental states. Nonetheless, Mill believes that the concept of a unitary self is necessary to explain memories and expectations, since there must be an abiding self that is remembered or that expects a future experience. Ultimately, Mill confesses that the nature of personal identity is a "final inexplicability." Mill returns to the issue of freedom and necessity from his earlier discussion in book 6 of *A System of Logic* by restating his determinist view and showing how it is perfectly consistent with moral responsibility and punishment.

Mill's application of empiricism to the question of God's moral attributes created a public controversy. For Mill, moral terms must have the same meaning when used in reference to God as they do when they are applied to human beings; otherwise, they are meaningless. Those who insist that God's justice is beyond human comprehension are simply confused about how the meaning of terms is established. Mill states, "I will call no being good, who is not what I mean when I apply that epithet to my fellow-creatures; and if such a being can sentence me to hell for not so calling him, to hell I will go." Despite being the major statement of Mill's views on metaphysical questions, *An Examination of Sir William Hamilton's Philosophy* is seldom read today—

largely because of Hamilton's obscurity, which Mill's exhaustive critique helped to secure.

Also in 1865 Mill published *Auguste Comte and Positivism* as two essays in *The Westminster Review;* the work came out in book form the same year. Comte invented the term *positivism* to characterize the empirical and scientific method of acquiring knowledge, in contrast to the "volitional" or "ontological" methods of theology. His claim that the scientific method could yield general laws of social phenomena earned Comte the title "the father of sociology." Mill was first exposed to Comte's ideas during his association with the Saint-Simonians in 1829–1830; his reading of Comte's *Cours de philosophie positive* (Course of Positive Philosophy, 1830–1842) enriched Mill's ideas in *A System of Logic* and motivated him to establish a correspondence with Comte that continued for three years before irreconcilable differences of opinion ended it. Mill views positivism as the true approach to knowledge but rejects Comte's idiosyncratic interpretation of it–for example, his reduction of psychology to phrenology. Most of all, Mill finds fault with Comte's *Système de politique positive* (System of Positive Polity, 1851–1854), which opposes representative government, advocates a strong centralized authority, and rejects freedom of thought in certain realms. In his *Autobiography* Mill judges Comte's theory as "the completest system of spiritual and temporal despotism, which ever yet emanated from a human brain, unless possibly that of Ignatius Loyola." He says that Comte's greatest contribution to social philosophy is the notion of a "Religion of Humanity," which coincides with the utilitarian ethical perspective and puts an end to the long-standing prejudice that morality requires belief in a supernatural religion. Mill, however, finds Comte's proposed priesthood of philosophers, sacraments, and rituals too rigid an imitation of Roman Catholicism. Mill later created his own version of the "Religion of Humanity" in "The Utility of Religion" (1874).

In 1865 Mill was asked to become the Liberal Party candidate for the Westminster seat in the House of Commons. In a letter to a friend he wrote, "I am, indeed, reduced to wondering whether I shall ever be able to resume those quiet studies which are so prodigiously better for the mind itself than the tiresome labour of chipping off little bits of one's thoughts of a size to be swallowed by a set of diminutive practical politicians incapable of digesting them." The prospect of placing his ideas before a wider audience was appealing, though, and he agreed to run on the conditions that he not be expected to deal with local concerns, that he would be loyal only to the views expressed in his writings and not to the Liberal Party itself, that he would not spend his own money on the campaign (he considered it unjust to buy one's way into office and

thought that the best people were deterred from running for lack of wealth), and would not answer any questions about his religious convictions. Mill spoke to his potential constituents only twice during the campaign. On one of these occasions he was addressing a group of working people, who were not allowed to vote, when a placard was presented bearing a quotation from his *Thoughts on Parliamentary Reform:* "the lower classes, though mostly habitual liars, are ashamed of lying." Asked whether he had written these words, Mill unhesitatingly said that he had. The crowd responded approvingly, having expected the usual equivocation from a politician. The leader of the group said that the working class wanted friends, not flatterers.

Mill won the election, and he was a conscientious member of Parliament who patiently listened to all sides in every debate. He frequently spoke in favor of unpopular causes, such as radical land-tenure reform in Ireland–though he did not go so far as to support Irish independence–and protested against English abuses of power in Ireland and Jamaica. Unlike many members of Parliament, Mill, who had attacked Carlyle's pro-slavery views in *Fraser's Magazine* in 1850, supported the North in the American Civil War. He advocated policies that he had advanced in his writings, including Thomas Hare's proportional-representation plan during the debate over Benjamin Disraeli's Reform Bill, and he proposed the creation of a London city council (such a body was not established until 1888). In his own judgment his most lasting contribution as a member of the House of Commons was his proposal that any reference to the sex of householders entitled to vote be left out of the 1867 Reform Bill. The idea was considered so preposterous that he was subjected to ridicule and caricature in political cartoons, and even prominent women such as the novelists George Eliot (Mary Ann Evans) and Elizabeth Cleghorn Gaskell, the poet Elizabeth Barrett Browning, and Queen Victoria herself did not support extending the suffrage to women. Mill's amendment failed, but it called attention to the cause of gender equality and helped to lead to the founding of the National Union of Women's Suffrage Societies in 1897.

Mill lost his reelection bid in 1869; his support of reformist working-class candidates against incumbents and his financial assistance to an openly atheistic candidate doomed his chances. That year he published *The Subjection of Women,* his last major work to appear during his lifetime. He had essentially completed the book by 1861, but his anticipation of a hostile reaction had led him to delay its publication. Three editions appeared in 1869, including two in the United States. It was immediately translated into seven languages and prompted more correspondence than any of his previous works.

Portrait of Mill by G. F. Watts, 1873
(National Portrait Gallery, London)

Mill's aim in *The Subjection of Women* is to defend the principle of absolute equality between the sexes and to show that the legal subordination of women is not only unjust but also one of the main hindrances to human improvement. He says in the *Autobiography* that this view was one of his earliest political convictions but was nothing more than an abstract principle until the commencement of his friendship with Harriet Taylor, which gave him a vivid understanding of the injustice of inequality. Indeed, Mill attributed what was most striking and profound in *The Subjection of Women* to his wife and the many conversations they had had on the topic. Much of the argument echoes themes from Harriet Taylor Mill's essay "The Enfranchisement of Women" (1851).

Mill's strategy in the book is to compare the legal condition of the married state–which was called "coverture," since a woman was under the "cover" of her husband–to slavery. When a woman married, she lost all rights to her property and the proceeds of her labor; she had no legal right to determine the kind of education her children received; she even had no right to custody of her children if her husband died. Until 1857 a woman could only obtain a divorce through an expensive act of Parliament–only four women ever

acquired a divorce under this provision–and a double standard of proof existed: the husband needed only to prove that his wife had committed adultery, whereas the woman had to prove that her husband had not only been unfaithful but had also committed some other "abominable act" such as bigamy, incest, or extreme cruelty. Mill points out that the legal status of married women is thus worse than that of ancient slaves, for Greek slaves were sometimes released from their bondage, and Roman slaves were able to own property (their so-called *peculium*).

Mill acknowledges that he has to contend against convictions that are rooted in feelings rather than based on rational arguments or experiments that proved the present system to be the most beneficial one. Nonetheless, he addresses the two prevailing public arguments for inequality. First, it was claimed that inequality is natural, inasmuch as men and women have different natures that justify different social roles: men are more aggressive, competitive, and adept at abstract thinking, making them fit for the economic and political functions in society, whereas women are more nurturing and emotional and less capable of abstract reasoning and so are suited to be wives and the caretakers of children. Mill replies that if *natural* means whatever is customary, calling female subjection "natural" cannot justify it because custom teaches what has been, not what ought to be; other practices that were formerly regarded as natural, such as slavery, have been abolished because they were finally seen to be unjust. The second argument is that inequality is voluntarily accepted by women. Mill retorts that this claim is empirically false, since some women do reject the present system; there would be more resistance if women were not socialized to be submissive and did fear the repercussions of speaking out.

Mill's fundamental objection to the arguments supporting inequality is an epistemological one: no one can make reliable statements about the nature of women, since their development has taken place under unequal conditions that obscure their natural desires and capacities. The ideal of a woman's character is to be submissive and self-abnegating and to live in the emotions–qualities that are desirable because they are attractive to men. Since women have not been free to develop themselves independently of the control of men, no one can plausibly assess women's nature. Women, Mill says, "have always hitherto been kept, as far as regards spontaneous development, in so unnatural a state, that their nature cannot but have been greatly distorted and disguised; and no one can safely pronounce that if women's nature were left to choose its direction as freely as men's, and if no artificial bent were attempted to be given to it except that required by the condition of human society, and given to both sexes alike, there would be any material difference, or perhaps any difference at all, in the character and capacities which would unfold themselves." A science of ethology would be necessary to make legitimate inferences about the sexes, and Mill laments the small amount of progress that has been made, including his own attempts in book 4 of *A System of Logic,* toward the establishment of this science. Nevertheless, he cites several examples of women who have shown themselves as capable as men in politics, science, and literature. He admits that this evidence is "humble," since it proves only what women have done under conditions of oppression; the implication is that they would rival the accomplishments of men if given equal opportunities.

Mill goes on to argue that the basic tenet of the modern age–that merit and personal preference, not birth, are the basis for opportunity–is not consistently applied to women. This tenet has been extended to other formerly excluded groups, such as the working class and blacks; why are women the solitary breach of this modern principle?

Mill recognizes, however, that it is not enough to show that inequality has no legitimate defense. He must further show the advantages of equality, such as doubling the talents that could be of service to humanity in the various professions, the moral improvement of men, the civilizing effects of women's opinions–particularly their aversion to war and their support of philanthropy–on society, and the improvement of marriage, since genuine love and friendship are possible only between equals.

Contemporary critics denounced Mill's arguments on a variety of grounds. The jurist Stephen, as well as women such as the editor and essayist Anne Mozley and the novelist and reform writer Margaret Oliphant, argued that natural differences between the sexes did justify different social functions. Moreover, they said, most women accepted their position and neither wanted suffrage nor found the marriage laws burdensome; thus, Mill was attempting to impose an abstract conception of well-being on women independently of their preferences. Another criticism was that Mill was silent about the issue of divorce, which would become a practical problem for women if men could decide to annul their marriages on a whim; the existing marriage laws actually protected women rather than harming them. Modern critics point out that Mill accepted the traditional division of labor between the sexes as optimal and that he regarded certain differences between men and women, such as a woman's supposedly greater susceptibility to a nervous temperament, as inherent.

A political issue involving sexual equality moved Mill to one of his last public acts. In 1871, despite having no direct acquaintance with the issue, he was asked to testify before a royal commission investigating whether the Contagious Diseases Acts, which mandated compulsory medical inspection of prostitutes to control venereal disease among troops in garrison towns, should be repealed. Although he did not support the acts, since they implied state endorsement of immoral conduct, he argued that if they were to continue, men, too, should be compelled to submit to examinations. Mill's position was not well received.

After his term in Parliament, Mill was internationally renowned. People in England and abroad solicited his advice on social and political questions, his support for their causes, and even his assistance regarding personal hardships. His correspondence became so enormous that his stepdaughter, Helen Taylor, managed most of it. In his final years Mill was occupied with writing articles for the *Fortnightly Review,* including one on the empiricist philosopher George Berkeley's life and writings; preparing the eighth edition of *A System of Logic;* revising his essay "Theism"; working on a treatise on socialism; and indulging his passion as an amateur botanist. He contributed a considerable amount of money to causes such as the Society for the Prevention of Cruelty to Animals, the Working Men's Library in Ireland, and the Women's Suffrage Society.

On 7 May 1873, Mill died suddenly in Avignon. Shortly before his death he had said to Helen Taylor, "You know that I have done my work." He was buried next to his wife in Avignon. He willed half of his estate to charity.

The story of Mill's arrest in 1824 had been hushed up at the time, but it was resurrected in a scathing obituary in *The Times* (London). The revelation led William Gladstone, the leader of the Liberal Party in the House of Commons, to resign from a committee set up to commemorate Mill with a statue in Temple Gardens.

Several works appeared posthumously. The first was Mill's *Autobiography,* published in the year of his death. An early draft of the work had been written in the winter of 1853–1854, when Mill feared that he might soon die of consumption. He had revised it in 1861 and added the last chapter in the winter of 1869–1870. Mill's self-avowed purposes in the *Autobiography* are to describe his "unusual and remarkable" education so as to demonstrate that children are capable of learning more in their earliest years than is commonly supposed, to show how a willingness to accept new ideas and discard old ones is beneficial "in an age of transition of opinions," and to acknowledge those–especially his wife–who had furthered his intellectual and moral development. The bulk of the book records his educa-

AUTOBIOGRAPHY

BY

JOHN STUART MILL

LONDON
LONGMANS, GREEN, READER, AND DYER
MDCCCLXXIII

*Title page for Mill's account of his life, focusing on his education
and the development of his ideas, published shortly after
his death (Library of Congress)*

tion and intellectual development until age thirty-six. In the early draft Mill disclosed that his mother was not a warmhearted person and that he "grew up in the absence of love and the presence of fear," but she is not mentioned at all in the final version. Some scholars have speculated that Mill omitted her from the story of his life because he resented the fact that her weakness left him prey to the rigorous intellectual upbringing imposed by his father, which led to his mental breakdown; others contend that Mill believed that she had insulted his wife.

In 1874 Helen Taylor published three of Mill's essays in the volume *Nature, The Utility of Religion, and Theism.* The first two essays had been written during the 1850s, at the same time as *On Liberty;* "Theism" was written in the late 1860s and is Mill's last considerable work. Speculation that Mill purposely withheld publication of his views on religion until after his death is implausible, since they had already been publicly expressed in works such as *Utilitarianism, On Liberty,* and

Auguste Comte and Positivism. It is more likely, as Taylor supposes in her introduction to the volume, that because Mill wanted his speculations on religion to be as precise and comprehensive as possible, he had continually revised the essays.

In "Nature" Mill demonstrates that the ideas of natural justice, natural law, and natural right, which originated with the Stoics and were developed by the Roman jurists, St. Thomas Aquinas, and modern theorists such as Thomas Hobbes and John Locke, are untenable. No appeal to "nature" or "the natural" can be a standard to determine right and wrong. The two most popular definitions of *nature* are, first, "all the powers existing in either the outer or the inner world and everything which takes place by means of those powers" and, second, everything that happens "without the voluntary and intentional agency, of man." Neither definition implies that what is natural is good and what is unnatural is bad. According to the first definition, everything that happens is natural; in that case murder, for example, is natural and, hence, good. By the second definition, anything that results from human intelligence is opposed to the natural and, therefore, to the good; in that case such actions as building houses or inventing medicines are bad. Both definitions thus lead to absurd conclusions. Mill points out that the very idea of a natural moral law conflates two different senses of law. Real natural laws, such as the law of gravity, describe uniformities, and no one can act against them. Moral laws do not describe uniformities, since human conduct is not uniform; such laws are really imperatives prescribing how people ought to act. For Mill, moral virtue is not a matter of following nature but of controlling it: virtues such as courage and altruism result from taming natural feelings of fear and selfishness. Mill challenges the notion that the ways of a benevolent God are manifested in nature: "however offensive the proposition may appear to many religious persons, they should be willing to look in the face of the undeniable fact, that the order of nature, in so far as unmodified by man, is such as no being, whose attributes are justice and benevolence, would have made, with the intention that his rational creatures should follow it as an example."

In "The Utility of Religion" Mill considers whether belief in traditional supernatural religions, such as Christianity, might be useful for individual happiness and as an incentive for moral behavior, even if it is intellectually unsustainable because of the success of scientific explanations of natural and social phenomena. He concludes that traditional religious belief is not only unnecessary but is actually a threat to human well-being and ought to be supplanted by a secular religion of humanity. Religious belief results from the combined effects of authority, early education, and public opinion; if the utilitarian ethic were inculcated in the same way, it would be as strongly held as traditional religious belief. Mill admits that Christianity has had good effects, and he praises the beauty of Jesus' moral ideals; but he objects to giving these ideals a supernatural origin, since such an origin protects them from rational criticism. If "the essence of religion is the strong and earnest direction of the emotions and desires toward an ideal object, recognized as of the highest excellence and as rightfully paramount over all selfish objects of desire," a religion of humanity could fulfill all the functions of traditional religion. The "ideal object" of a religion of humanity would be the promotion of the happiness of all sentient beings and the perfection of human talents, goals that are worthy of the deepest feelings of commitment. In times of crisis, individuals could find consolation and inspiration in the examples of noble and venerated persons, past and present. A religion of humanity is preferable to traditional religion on moral and intellectual grounds. Morally, it is more altruistic, since it does not treat moral conduct as a means to obtaining a reward for oneself in the afterlife; furthermore, it does not involve the veneration of a being that, if it existed, would be responsible for the unjustified suffering in this world and that also is depicted as having created a hell for sinners and unbelievers in the next life with the foreknowledge that many would be consigned to eternity there. Intellectually, the religion of humanity encourages the active exercise of the mind; Christianity, on the contrary, punishes free thought and compels people to believe in fantastic notions such as miracles and revelations. Mill acknowledges that a religion of humanity does not promise a life after death, but he questions whether an eternal prolongation of one's existence is even desirable.

In "Theism" Mill critiques the principal arguments for the existence of God. The "first cause" argument holds that a God must be posited as the starting point for the series of causes and effects observed in nature. Like Hume, Mill points out that more likely than intelligence as an explanation of the origin of the universe are forces such as chemical action and gravity, which are responsible for mechanical motion on a far larger scale than any intelligence with which humans are familiar. Also, the first-cause argument creates another "infinite regress" problem in place of the one it was intended to solve: if God is posited as the cause of the universe, something else must be posited as the cause of God, and something else as the cause of that cause, and so on. Mill's final judgment on the argument is that while science cannot disprove it, science provides no evidence for it, either.

Some of Mill's friends were surprised to discover that his assessment of the argument from "marks of design in nature" to the postulation of a divine architect was more favorable. The argument is strongest, he says, with regard to a biological phenomenon such as

the eye, the parts of which are arranged in such a complex fashion that a slight alteration would destroy its functionality. The likelihood that the eye originated from a random concurrence of independent causes seems lower than that it resulted from a plan in the mind of a designer. Mill concludes that the argument is an inductive one and is warranted by the principles of inductive logic. He points out, though, that the then-recent theory of the "survival of the fittest" proposed by the naturalist Charles Darwin offers an alternative explanation that does not presuppose conscious intention. Mill finds the Darwinian theory improbable, however, although he remains open to future developments in it that might make it more credible. Regarding the likely attributes of a deity, Mill points out that God, if he exists, is not omnipotent, since he required means—matter and force—to achieve his ends. God's imperfection is also revealed by the defects in nature. On the issue of immortality, Mill says that the scientific demonstration that the brain is necessary for mental operations does not absolutely prove that the mind cannot survive the death of the body. He concludes that indulgence in the hope of an afterlife might be salutary, as long as it does not pervert intelligence and morality in this life.

Some commentators allege that Mill's goal in his writings on religion was to destroy belief in Christianity and convert his readers to a secular religion. But he told Bain in a letter of 6 August 1859, "certainly I am not anxious to bring over any but really superior intellects & characters to the whole of my own opinions—in the case of all others I would much rather, as things now are, try to improve their religion than to destroy it."

In 1879 Mill's unfinished "Chapters on Socialism" appeared in the *Fortnightly Review.* Expanding the analysis of socialism he had given in *The Principles of Political Economy,* he opposes the fostering of class hatred and the violent revolutionary seizure of power but supports small-scale experiments such as the introduction of cooperatives. He is also against nationalization of the means of production and distribution because of the increase in the power of the state that it would entail. The principal value of socialist theory, he says, lies in exposing the injustices of capitalism and proposing radical reforms that could make people receptive to more moderate social change.

Mill remains a central figure in the history of philosophy. The twentieth-century philosopher Bertrand Russell judged in a 1955 lecture that Mill's importance is less in the originality of his thought than in his intellectual virtues. Some scholars contend that Mill's standing is owed to his skill in reformulating dominant trends of his age, such as empiricism and Romanticism, and creating a compelling view of self and society that affected the attitudes of his era. It is fitting that Mill's moral, social, and political views are the most significant and influential aspects of his philosophy today, for he considered himself above all a public moralist. Along with Aristotle's *Nicomachean Ethics* and Kant's *Grundlegung zur Metaphysik der Sitten* (1785; translated as *Groundwork of the Metaphysic of Morals,* 1948), Mill's *Utilitarianism* is considered an essential reading in ethics. *On Liberty* is standard fare in social and political philosophy at universities as a reminder of the inherent dangers of democratic culture; it is widely excerpted in textbooks on constitutional law and frequently cited by English and American judges in their opinions. Mill's liberalism was invoked during the public debate in Great Britain to decriminalize homosexuality in the wake of the 1957 Wolfenden Report of the Committee on Homosexual Offences and Prostitution. Finally, *The Subjection of Women* is revered as a foundational text in early feminist thought. John Stuart Mill's life and secular liberal view of society continue to inspire both admirers and critics.

Letters:

John Stuart Mill and Harriet Taylor: Their Correspondence and Subsequent Marriage, edited by F. A. Hayek (London: Routledge & Kegan Paul, 1951).

Bibliographies:

Mill News Letter, 1–23 (1965–1988); combined with *Bentham Newsletter* as *Utilitas: A Journal of Utilitarian Studies,* 1– (1989–);

Michael Laine, *Bibliography of Works on John Stuart Mill* (Toronto & Buffalo, N.Y.: University of Toronto Press, 1982).

Biographies:

Alexander Bain, *John Stuart Mill: A Criticism with Personal Recollections* (London: Longmans, Green, 1882; New York: Holt, 1882);

W. L. Courtney, *Life of John Stuart Mill* (London: Scott, 1889);

Michael St. John Packe, *The Life of John Stuart Mill* (New York: Macmillan, 1954);

Ian Cumming, *A Manufactured Man: The Education of John Stuart Mill,* Educational series II, no. 55 (Auckland, New Zealand: University of Auckland, 1960);

Bruce Mazlish, *James and John Stuart Mill: Father and Son in the Nineteenth Century* (New York: Basic Books, 1975).

References:

R. P. Anschutz, *The Philosophy of J. S. Mill* (Oxford: Clarendon Press, 1953);

Eugene August, *John Stuart Mill: A Mind at Large* (New York: Scribners, 1975);

Fred R. Berger, *Happiness, Justice, and Freedom: The Moral and Political Philosophy of John Stuart Mill* (Berkeley: University of California Press, 1984);

Isaiah Berlin, "John Stuart Mill and the Ends of Life," in his *Four Essays on Liberty* (London: Oxford University Press, 1969), pp. 173–206;

Karl Britton, *John Stuart Mill* (New York: Dover, 1969);

Elie Halévy, *The Growth of Philosophic Radicalism,* translated by Mary Morris (London: Faber & Faber, 1952);

Gertrude Himmelfarb, *On Liberty and Liberalism: The Case of John Stuart Mill* (New York: Knopf, 1974);

Iris Wessel Mueller, *John Stuart Mill and French Thought* (Urbana: University of Illinois Press, 1956);

J. C. Rees, *Mill and His Early Critics* (Leicester: University College, 1956);

John M. Robson, *The Improvement of Mankind: The Social and Political Thought of John Stuart Mill* (London: Routledge & Kegan Paul, 1968);

Bertrand Russell, *John Stuart Mill* (London: Oxford University Press, 1955);

Alan Ryan, *J. S. Mill* (London & Boston: Routledge & Kegan Paul, 1974);

Ryan, *The Philosophy of John Stuart Mill* (London: Macmillan, 1970);

J. B. Schneewind, ed., *Mill: A Collection of Critical Essays* (London: Macmillan, 1969);

James Fitzjames Stephen, *Liberty, Equality, Fraternity* (London: Smith, Elder, 1873);

Leslie Stephen, *The English Utilitarians,* volume 3: *J. S. Mill* (London: Duckworth, 1900);

William Thomas, *Mill* (Oxford & New York: Oxford University Press, 1985).

Papers:

John Stuart Mill's letters and manuscripts are in the Mill-Taylor Collection of the British Library of Political and Economic Science at the London School of Economics, the National Library of Scotland in Edinburgh, and the Osborn Collection in the Beinecke Rare Book and Manuscript Library at Yale University.

G. E. Moore

(4 November 1873 – 24 October 1958)

Darlei Dall'Agnol
Federal University of Santa Catarina, Brazil

BOOKS: *Principia Ethica* (Cambridge: Cambridge University Press, 1903; revised and enlarged, edited by Thomas Baldwin, Cambridge & New York: Cambridge University Press, 1993);

Ethics (London: Williams & Norgate, 1912; New York: Holt, 1912);

Philosophical Studies (London: Kegan Paul, Trench, Trübner / New York: Harcourt, Brace, 1922);

Some Main Problems of Philosophy (London: Allen & Unwin / New York: Macmillan, 1953);

Philosophical Papers (London: Allen & Unwin / New York: Macmillan, 1959);

Commonplace Book, 1919–1953, edited by Casimir Lewy (London: Allen & Unwin / New York: Macmillan, 1962);

Lectures on Philosophy, edited by Lewy (London: Allen & Unwin / New York: Humanities Press, 1966);

G. E. Moore: The Early Essays, edited by Tom Regan (Philadelphia: Temple University Press, 1986);

The Elements of Ethics, edited by Regan (Philadelphia: Temple University Press, 1991);

Lectures on Metaphysics, 1934–1935: From the Notes of Alice Ambrose and Margaret Macdonald, edited by Alice Ambrose, American University Studies, Series V: Philosophy, volume 130 (New York: Peter Lang, 1992);

Selected Writings, edited by Baldwin (London & New York: Routledge, 1993).

OTHER: "Cause and Effect," and "Change," in volume 1, and "Nativism," "Quality," "Real," "Reason," "Relation," "Relativity of Knowledge," "Substance," "Spirit," "Teleology," and "Truth," in volume 2, of *Dictionary of Philosophy and Psychology: Including Many of the Principal Conceptions of Ethics, Logic, Aesthetics, Philosophy of Religion, Mental Pathology, Anthropology, Biology, Neurology, Physiology, Economics, Political and Social Philosophy, Philology, Physical Science, and Education; and Giving a Terminology in English, French, German and Italian, Written by*

Many Hands, 3 volumes, edited by James Mark Baldwin (London: Macmillan, 1901–1902);

Frank P. Ramsey, *The Foundations of Mathematics and Other Logical Essays*, edited by R. B. Braithwaite, preface by Moore (London: Kegan Paul, Trench, Trübner / New York: Harcourt, Brace, 1931);

"An Autobiography" and "A Reply to My Critics," in *The Philosophy of G. E. Moore*, edited by Paul Arthur Schilpp, The Library of Living Philosophers, volume 4 (Evanston, Ill. & Chicago: Northwestern University Press, 1942), pp. 3–39, 535–667;

Ludwig Wittgenstein, *Notebooks, 1914–1916,* edited by G. E. M. Anscombe and Georg Henrik von Wright, translated by Anscombe, includes notes on logic dictated to Moore (Oxford: Blackwell, 1961).

SELECTED PERIODICAL PUBLICATIONS–
UNCOLLECTED: Review of Franz Brentano's *The Origin of the Knowledge of Right and Wrong, International Journal of Ethics,* 14 (October 1903): 115–123;

Review of George Santayana's *The Life of Reason, International Journal of Ethics,* 17 (January 1907): 248–253.

G. E. Moore is known for his attack on idealism and defense of common-sense realism and for being, together with Bertrand Russell and Ludwig Wittgenstein, one of the founders of analytic philosophy. His main stimulus for investigating philosophical problems was what other philosophers had written, rather than the problems of science or the world itself; for this reason he is known as the "philosopher's philosopher." He took pains to analyze what philosophers meant when they enunciated metaphysical theses such as the claim that time is unreal–a position that he himself held in his younger years–and to refute such propositions. In *Principia Ethica* (1903) he argues for the autonomy of ethical concepts. The book had a strong influence in literary circles, especially on members of the Bloomsbury Group, such as the writer Virginia Woolf and the economist John Maynard Keynes. Writing to a friend in 1940, Woolf asked, "did you ever read the book that made us all so wise and good: *Principia Ethica?*" Moore's later works include the articles "A Defence of Common Sense" (1925) and "The Proof of an External World" (1939), in which he argues against idealism and skepticism and for the common-sense view of reality.

George Edward Moore was born in Upper Norwood, Surrey, a suburb of London, on 4 November 1873, the third of the three sons and fifth of the eight children of Daniel Moore, a physician, and Henrietta Sturge Moore. At eight he was enrolled at Dulwich College, a boarding and day school near his home, where his aptitude for Greek and Latin resulted in his specializing in classics, rather than natural science or mathematics. Under the influence of his headmaster he read Plato and developed a great admiration for Socrates. At twelve he was converted to evangelical Christianity and became a member of the Children's Special Service Mission, an organization similar to the

Salvation Army; but two years later his oldest brother, the poet Thomas Sturge Moore, persuaded him to become an agnostic, a position Moore retained for the rest of his life.

Moore entered Trinity College of the University of Cambridge in 1892 to continue his classical studies. During his first year he met Russell, who was a year and a half older than he. Russell invited Moore to join him and the idealist philosopher J. M. E. McTaggart, a Hegelian idealist, in Russell's rooms for tea. During the conversation McTaggart discussed his well-known view that time is unreal. Moore recalled in his autobiographical statement in the Library of Living Philosophers volume *The Philosophy of G. E. Moore* (1942) that the claim struck him as a "perfectly monstrous proposition" and that he argued against it, pointing out that he had had breakfast before coming to Russell's room and could not have done so if time did not exist. Noting Moore's skill at philosophical argument, Russell urged him to change his specialization from classics to philosophy; Moore did so in his third year at Cambridge.

Moore took a first in part 1 of the classical tripos in 1894, and in 1896 he took a first in part 2 of the moral sciences tripos. His first published paper, "In what Sense, If Any, Do Past and Future Time Exist?" appeared in the journal *Mind* in April 1897; it has been collected in *G. E. Moore: The Early Essays* (1986). Here Moore, influenced by the idealist F. H. Bradley, himself argues for the unreality of time: "I would say that neither Past, Present, nor Future exists, if by existence we are to mean the ascription of full Reality and not merely existence as Appearance."

In 1898 Moore was awarded a six-year fellowship at Trinity College on the basis of a dissertation on Immanuel Kant's ethical theory. In the article "Freedom," published in *Mind* in April 1898 and republished in *G. E. Moore: The Early Essays,* Moore argues in favor of Kant's doctrine that human beings' actions are, as part of the phenomenal world, completely causally determined, but that humans are, as atemporal "things-in-themselves," free in a transcendental sense. He also criticizes Kant, however, for inconsistently restricting freedom to human–or "rational"–beings, contending that Kant is confusing the transcendental and psychological senses of freedom. He says in the introduction to the paper that he has chosen to deal with Kant "at such length mainly because I think that reference to the views of the philosopher, with whom you are most in agreement, is often the clearest way of explaining your own view to an esoteric audience; but partly, also, because I think he has been much misunderstood." He also says:

Moore's parents, Daniel and Henrietta Sturge Moore

That time itself cannot be conceived to be fundamentally real is always admitted by Kant himself, and indeed he has attempted a proof of it. How far that proof is satisfactory, and whether, if unsatisfactory, any other proof is forthcoming, is too large a question to be discussed here. I can only state that the arguments by which Mr. Bradley has endeavoured to prove the unreality of Time appear to me perfectly conclusive.

In "The Nature of Judgment," published in *Mind* in April 1899 and collected in *G. E. Moore: The Early Essays,* Moore undertakes to make Bradley's idealism more consistent than Bradley had: he argues that concepts are not mental phenomena but universals that exist independently of the mind; and,

further, that "all that exists is . . . composed of concepts related to each other in specific manners." He admits that he is "fully aware how paradoxical this theory must appear, and even how contemptible. But it seems to me to follow from premisses generally admitted, and to have been avoided [by Bradley] only by lack of logical consistency." He goes on to try to show that this position would be Kant's if Kant, too, were perfectly consistent.

Toward the end of 1898 Moore and Russell rebelled against idealism, with Moore leading the way and Russell following. As Russell puts it in "My Mental Development," his autobiographical statement in *The Philosophy of Bertrand Russell* (1944),

Bradley had argued that everything that common sense believes in is mere appearance; we reverted to the opposite extreme, and thought that *everything* is real that common sense, uninfluenced by philosophy or theology, supposes real. With a sense of escaping from prison, we allowed ourselves to think that grass is green, that the sun and the stars would exist if no one was aware of them, and also that there is a pluralistic timeless world of Platonic ideas. The world which had been thin and logical, suddenly became rich and varied and solid.

Russell says in the preface to *The Principles of Mathematics* (1903) that he accepted from Moore the nonexistential nature of propositions, except for those that explicitly assert existence, and their independence of any knowing mind, as well as a conception of the universe as composed of an infinite number of mutually independent entities. The latter view was in direct opposition to the monistic metaphysics of absolute idealism.

In the fall of 1898 Moore gave his first lectures, speaking on Kant's ethics at the Passmore Edwards Settlement in London under the auspices of the London School of Ethics and Social Philosophy. The lectures form the main outline of his *Principia Ethica,* although Moore spent six years rewriting the material delivered in London, and some parts of the book, such as the last chapter, are entirely new. The original lectures were published in 1991 as *The Elements of Ethics.* Moore also wrote entries such as "Cause and Effect" and "Teleology" for James Mark Baldwin's *Dictionary of Philosophy and Psychology* (1901–1902). He was also the subeditor for English books for the *International Journal of Ethics.*

Moore established his reputation as an original philosopher in 1903 with two works. In "The Refutation of Idealism" in *Mind* (republished in his *Philosophical Studies,* 1922) he attacks the fundamental contention of idealism: that everything that can be proved to be real is mental or spiritual. He argues that the act of judging and the contents of a judgment must be separated; the existence of the color blue, for example, must be conceived as quite distinct from the sensation of blue, because a person can understand that the color exists without having the sensation.

The other major work of 1903 was *Principia Ethica,* one of the most influential works in twentieth-century moral philosophy. Defining ethics as "the general enquiry into what is good," Moore proceeds to show that *good* is a nonnatural property that is indefinable and unanalyzable. According to Moore, if "horse" is defined as "a hoofed quadruped of the genus Equus," the definition establishes that a "certain object, which we all of us know, is composed in a certain manner": it has four legs, a head, a heart,

and so forth. *Good,* by contrast, is indefinable, since it is a simple property and so not composed of any more-basic parts. To prove that *good* is indefinable, Moore constructs the "open question argument": "whatever definition be offered, it may be always asked, with significance, of the complex so defined, whether it is itself good." Suppose someone defines *good* as "pleasant" or "desired" or "approved":

> But whoever will attentively consider with himself what is actually before his mind when he asks the question "Is pleasure (or whatever it may be) after all good?" can easily satisfy himself that he is not merely wondering whether pleasure is pleasant. And if he will try this experiment with each suggested definition in succession, he may become expert enough to recognise that in every case he has before his mind a unique object, with regard to the connection of which with any other object, a distinct question may be asked. Everyone does in fact understand the question "Is this good?" When he thinks of it, his state of mind is different from what it would be, were he asked "Is this pleasant, desired, or approved?"

The validity of Moore's open-question argument is still debated. Stephen Darwall, Allan Gibbard, and Peter Railton contend that it is effective against an ethical theory such as naturalism, because it shows that ethical concepts cannot be explained by scientific ones. They think that the open-question argument can do its job case by case, showing that any naturalist definition of good is false. On the other hand, philosophers such as Dennis Rohatyn consider Moore's conception of definition flawed; they maintain that there are various kinds of definitions, and that the open question argument is not relevant to most of them. Consequently, they say, *good* is not indefinable.

Moore also argues in *Principia Ethica* that to reduce ethical concepts to natural ones is to commit "the naturalistic fallacy." Natural objects are studied by the empirical sciences; but ethical judgments cannot be established by observation and induction. Thus, ethics cannot be replaced by psychology, biology, sociology, or any other science. Ethics does not deal with natural phenomena such as instincts; on the contrary, "sometimes what we feel to be our duty is to abstain from some action to which a strong *natural* impulse tempts us." And ethical judgments do not describe properties of objects; they prescribe actions that ought to be performed or avoided. While statements in science presuppose causality, ethical statements are based on the assumption that human beings have free will, that choice and deliberation are possible. Moore's main target is the application of biological concepts, particularly the theory of evolution, to ethics by Social Darwinists such as Herbert Spencer.

After rejecting the naturalistic approach to ethics, Moore engages—mainly in the last chapter, "The Ideal"—in the constructive task of identifying the possible bearers of intrinsic value. A thing may have only instrumental value: a pen, for example, is useful for writing. Other things, such as pleasure, are valued for their own sake, not because they are useful for some further purpose; such things have intrinsic value.

Moore uses two complementary strategies to identity that which has worth in itself: the method of isolation and the principle of organic unities. In the method of isolation one imagines a thing "existing absolutely by itself" in the universe and asks whether its existence would still be considered good. According to the principle of organic unities, "*the value of a whole must not be assumed to be the same as the sum of the values of its parts.*"

Moore says that unmixed goods, which are composed only of good parts (for example, a pleasant mind contemplating a beautiful work of art), are more valuable than mixed ones, which have good and bad parts (for instance, a virtue such as courage, which requires the existence of danger, or knowledge, which includes awareness of evil). "By far the most valuable things, which we know or can imagine, are certain states of consciousness, which may be roughly described as the pleasures of human intercourse and the enjoyment of beautiful objects. . . . personal affections and aesthetic enjoyments include *all* the greatest, and *by far* the greatest, goods we can imagine." Moore is not saying that states of mind are the only things that are good in themselves; as an organic unity, an unmixed good involves states of mind, but they are not the only ingredient: "the value which a thing possesses *on the whole* may be said to be equivalent to the sum of the value which it possesses *as a whole, together with* the intrinsic value which may belong to any of its parts." The best possible values are composed of at least three elements: a state of mind; pleasure; and what is contemplated (such as a work of art). Each of them has worth independently and can be part of different goods, including mixed ones.

According to Moore, friendship is the most valuable good. It involves the recognition of good qualities among "admirable persons" or exists toward a "good person," and it involves "reciprocal affection": "we may admit that the appreciation of a person's attitude towards other persons, or, to take one instance, the love of love, is far the most valuable good we know, and far more than the mere love of beauty, yet we can only admit this if the first be understood to *include* the latter, in various degrees of directness."

Moore's older brother, the poet Thomas Sturge Moore

This chapter particularly impressed the Bloomsbury Group, since it praises the values of love, friendship, and beauty. Moore came to be seen as what Tom Regan calls "Bloomsbury's Prophet" because he defended aesthetic values as one of the best things in the world. The Bloomsbury Group's understanding of Moore's work is exemplified by Keynes:

> Nothing mattered except states of mind, our own and other people's of course, but chiefly our own. These states of mind were not associated with action or achievement or with consequence. They consisted in timeless, passionate states of contemplation and communion, largely unattached to "before" and "after."

Moore, however, denies that states of mind, by themselves, can have intrinsic value. Russell points out in "My Mental Development" that "Moore gave due weight to morals and by his doctrine of organic unities avoided the view that the good consists of a series of isolated passionate moments, but those who considered themselves his disciples ignored this aspect of his teaching and degraded his ethics into advocacy of a stuffy girl's-school sentimentalizing." *Principia Ethica* does not claim that moral duties are subservient to art.

The ethical philosopher Sir David Ross said of the principle of organic unities, "its truth in the abstract seems unquestionable"; but Ross did not think that it could be applied to all kinds of values. There seem to be examples of the principle "in the regions of aesthetic and of economic value"; but they are irrelevant to ethics, since they are instances of instrumental rather then intrinsic value. For example, Ross says, "a pair of boots is worth more than twice as much as a single boot." Ross did believe that some moral values may be instantiations of the principle: "Few people would hesitate to say that a state of affairs in which *A* is good and happy and *B* bad and unhappy is better then one in which *A* is good and unhappy and *B* bad and happy, even if *A* is equally good in both cases, *B* equally bad in both cases, *A* precisely as happy in the first case as *B* is in the second, and *B* precisely as unhappy in the first case as *A* is in the second."

After his fellowship expired in 1904, Moore moved to Edinburgh. His lack of employment was not a concern, since he had received an inheritance. In Edinburgh he read Sir Walter Scott's novels and William James's *Pragmatism* (1907) and wrote some articles related to the latter. In 1910–1911 he gave a series of lectures at Morley College in London; they were first published in 1953 as *Some Main Problems of Philosophy*. In his early idealist works Moore had upheld the coherence theory of truth, according to which a statement is true if concepts are correctly related within it. He changes this view in the lectures, holding that a statement is true if it corresponds to a fact:

> To say of this belief that it is true would be to say of it that the fact to which it refers *is*–that there is such a fact in the Universe as the fact to which it refers; while to say of it that it is false is to say of it that *the fact to which it refers* simply is not–that there is no such fact in the Universe.

Moore returned to Cambridge in 1911 as a university lecturer in moral science. His second book, *Ethics* (1912), presents substantially the same views as *Principia Ethica* but is much clearer and uses stronger arguments than the earlier work. According to his autobiographical statement in the Library of Living Philosophers volume, Moore preferred *Ethics* to *Principia Ethica;* nevertheless, he was, and is, known mainly as "the author of *Principia Ethica.*"

In both books Moore defends what is now called "ideal consequentialism." In evaluating an action, he says in *Principia Ethica,* one should consider:

(a) If the action itself has greater intrinsic value than any alternative, whereas both its consequences and those of the alternatives are absolutely devoid either of intrinsic merit or intrinsic demerit; or

(b) if, though its consequences are intrinsically bad, the balance of intrinsic value is greater than would be produced by any alternative; or

(c) if its consequences being intrinsically good, the degree of value belonging to them and it conjointly is greater than that of any alternative series.

In 1912 Moore met Ludwig Wittgenstein; according to his autobiographical statement, Moore "soon came to feel that he was much cleverer at philosophy than I was, and not only cleverer, but also much more profound, and with a much better insight into the sort of inquiry which was really important and best worth pursuing, and into the best method of pursuing such inquiries."

In 1913 Moore received a D.Litt. from Cambridge. The following year he went to Norway to meet Wittgenstein, who dictated to him some notes on logic. The notes were later published in Wittgenstein's *Notebooks, 1914–1916* (1961).

In 1916 Moore married Dorothy Ely; they had two sons, Nicholas and Timothy. In 1918 Moore received an honorary LL.D. from St. Andrews University and was elected a fellow of the British Academy. In 1921 he became editor of *Mind* on the retirement of G. F. Stout. Also in 1921 he wrote a preface for a proposed second edition of *Principia Ethica;* the preface was not published until it appeared in Thomas Baldwin's 1993 edition of the work. In the preface Moore attempts to clarify his concept of intrinsic value:

> (1) *G* [good] *is a property which depends only on the intrinsic nature of the thing which possesses it.* . . .
> (2) *Though G thus depends only on the intrinsic properties of things which possess it, and is, in that sense, an intrinsic kind of value, it is yet not itself an intrinsic property.*

Moore has to deny that good is an intrinsic property; otherwise, he will be committed to naturalism. A slightly different approach to intrinsic value appears in "The Nature of Moral Philosophy," published for the first time in Moore's *Philosophical Studies.* Here Moore presents an Aristotelian analysis of intrinsic value. According to Moore, Aristotle says

> first, that nothing can be good, in the sense he means, unless it is something which is worth having for its own sake, and not merely for the sake of something else; it must be good in itself; it must not, like wealth (to use one example which he gives) be worth having merely for the sake of what you can do with it; it must be a thing which is worth having even if nothing further comes of it. . . . secondly, . . . it must, he says, be some-

thing that is "self-sufficient": something which, even if you had nothing else would make your life worth having.

In 1925 Moore succeeded James Ward as professor of philosophy at Cambridge and became a fellow of Trinity. That same year he published "A Defence of Common Sense" in the second series of *Contemporary British Philosophy: Personal statements,* edited by J. H. Muirhead. The article, which is collected in Moore's posthumous *Philosophical Papers* (1959), is an example of his use of the analytic method while he was at the height of his powers.

Moore takes "common sense" to mean good judgment in everyday life: the ability to distinguish true from false and right from wrong. "A Defence of Common Sense" begins with a long list of propositions that belong to the ordinary way of looking at things; these statements seem to be truisms that are not even worth expressing, such as "there exists at present a living body, which is my body; this body was born at a certain time in the past, and has existed continuously ever since, though not without undergoing changes; at every moment since this body was born, there have also existed many other things, having shape and size in three dimensions; among the things which have existed there have been other living human bodies; the earth had existed for many years before my body," and so forth. Moore then states what he regards as another truism: that everyone knows, with regard to himself or herself, that these statements are true. Although these propositions of common sense are meaningful, Moore says, one cannot be sure about the correct analysis of them:

> Such an expression as "The earth has existed for many years past" is the very type of an unambiguous expression, the meaning of which we all understand. Anyone who takes a contrary view must, I suppose, be confusing the question whether we understand its meaning (which we all certainly do) with the entirely different question whether we *know what it means,* in the sense that we are able to *give a correct analysis* of its meaning.

The task of the philosopher is to give meaning to the language in which these beliefs are cast.

Moore acknowledges that many philosophers disagree with his realist position. Philosophers from various traditions have questioned whether there are material things that exist in spatial relations to one another, the reality of space and time, and even whether the self exists. Moore's defense of common sense consists in a reiteration of the truth of such propositions: he simply says that he knows them to be true.

Moore after he became university lecturer in moral science at the University of Cambridge in 1911

He does not present an argument to rebut skeptical doubts about the reality of material things, space, time, and the self.

In 1939 Moore published "Proof of an External World" in the *Proceedings of the British Academy;* it was republished in his *Philosophical Papers.* In this article he tries to show that the common-sense view is true:

> I can prove now, for instance, that two human hands exist. How? By holding up my two hands, and saying, as I make a certain gesture with the right hand, "Here is one hand," and adding, as I make a certain gesture with the left, "and here is another." And if, by doing this, I have proved *ipso facto* the existence of external things, you will all see that I can also do it now in numbers of other ways: there is no need to multiply examples.

Moore seems to think that this proof is a demonstration—that is, a valid deductive argument from true premises to a necessary conclusion, as in a mathematical proof or a logical inference. As such, only a few philosophers have accepted it as valid; the argument is generally regarded as incapable of refuting either idealism or skepticism. Some, however, have claimed that Moore is not actually presenting a formal demonstration, even though Moore himself says immediately afterward that his argument meets the conditions of a rigorous proof: the premises are different from the conclusion; the premises are known, not merely believed, to be true; and the conclusion follows from the premises. But Moore recognizes that there are many sorts of proof, and he does not rule out the possibility that he is here offering a "nonformal" proof. Some commentators contend that his proof of the common-sense view of the existence of the external world can be better understood as an exhibition that proves its point not by inference but by showing evidence in a particular context. Moore gives an example of such an exhibition:

> Suppose, for instance, it were a question whether there were as many as three misprints on a certain page in a certain book. A says there are, B is inclined to doubt it. How could A prove that he is right? Surely he *could* prove it by taking the book, turning to the page, and pointing to three separate places on it, saying "There's one misprint here, another here, and another here."

What Moore is describing is clearly not a formal demonstration; but, as he says, "we all of us do constantly take proofs of this sort as absolutely conclusive proofs of certain conclusions." An exhibition is sufficient to provide conviction under the circumstances.

Moore retired from his professorship in 1939. His former students R. B. Braithwaite, Gilbert Ryle, and Norman Malcolm provide vivid portraits of him as a teacher. In an essay collected in Alice Ambrose and Morris Lazerowitz's *G. E. Moore: Essays in Retrospect* (1970), Braithwaite recalls that "in 1922–1923, when I attended both courses of Moore's lectures, we hunted for the correct analysis of propositions about the self on Monday, Wednesday and Friday mornings and the correct analysis of propositions of the form 'This is a pencil' on Tuesday, Thursday, and Saturday morning throughout the year." According to Ryle's 1971 biography of Moore,

> He gave us courage not by making concessions, but by making no concessions to our youth or to our shyness. He treated us as corrigible and therefore as responsible thinkers. He would explode at our mistakes and muddles with just that genial ferocity with which he would explode at the mistakes and muddles of philosophical high-ups, and with just the genial ferocity with which he would explode at mistakes and muddles of his own.

And Malcolm, in another essay from Ambrose and Lazerowitz's collection, says that Moore's qualities included "complete modesty and simplicity, saving him from the dangers of jargon and pomposity; thorough absorption in philosophy, which he found endlessly exciting; strong mental powers; and a pure integrity that accounted for his solidity and his passion for clarity." Malcolm adds: "I believe that what gave Moore stature as a philosopher was his *integrity,* an attribute of character rather than of intellect."

From 1940 to 1944 Moore visited the United States. He gave lectures and held visiting professorships at several universities, including Princeton, Columbia, and the University of California. Two of the lectures he presented during his American sojourn, "Certainty" and "Four Forms of Scepticism," were first published in *Philsophical Papers*. In 1951 he was appointed to the Order of Merit. He died on 24 October 1958.

G. E. Moore was not fertile in ideas, as Russell was; he was not a profound thinker, like Wittgenstein. But no other philosopher had a greater ability to analyze problems, detect ambiguities, expose fallacies, and formulate and work out alternative possibilities. Moore's literary style is simple, lucid, and direct. His *Principia Ethica* is still regarded as the classic work in analytic philosophy, and "A Defence of Common Sense" and "Proof of an External World" are still at the center of epistemological discussions. The qualities of his character are also a model for philosophers and students around the world.

Letters:

Ludwig Wittgenstein, *Letters to Russell, Keynes, and Moore,* edited by G. H. von Wright and B. F. McGuinness (Ithaca, N.Y.: Cornell University Press, 1974).

Interview:

Constantine Cavarnos, *A Dialogue on G. E. Moore's Ethical Philosophy, Together with an Account of Three Talks with G. E. Moore on Diverse Philosophical Questions* (Belmont, Mass.: Institute for Byzantine and Modern Greek Studies, 1979).

Biographies:

Paul Levy, *G. E. Moore and the Cambridge Apostles* (London: Weidenfeld & Nicolson, 1970);

Gilbert Ryle, "G. E. Moore," in his *Collected Papers* (London: Hutchinson, 1971), pp. 268-271.

References:

Alice Ambrose and Morris Lazerowitz, eds., *G. E. Moore: Essays in Retrospect* (London: Allen & Unwin / New York: Humanities Press, 1970);

A. J. Ayer, *Russell and Moore: The Analytical Heritage* (London: Macmillan, 1971);

Thomas Baldwin, *G. E. Moore* (London & New York: Routledge, 1990);

Peter Butchvarow, *Skepticism in Ethics* (Bloomington & Indianapolis: Indiana University Press, 1989);

Darlei Dall'Agnol, "Intrinsic Value: Analysing Moore's Ethics," dissertation, University of Bristol, 2000;

Stephen Darwall, Allan Gibbard, and Peter Railton, eds., *Moral Discourse and Practice: Some Philosophical Approaches* (New York & Oxford: Oxford University Press, 1997);

John Hill, *The Ethics of G. E. Moore: A New Interpretation* (Amsterdam: Van Gorcum, 1976);

John Maynard Keynes, "My Early Beliefs," in his *Essays in Biography* (London: Macmillan, 1993), pp. 433–450;

E. D. Klemke, *The Epistemology of G. E. Moore* (Evanston, Ill.: Northwestern University Press, 1969);

Klemke, ed., *Studies in the Philosophy of G. E. Moore* (Chicago: Quadrangle, 1969);

David O'Connor, *The Metaphysics of G. E. Moore* (Dordrecht, Netherlands & London: Reidel, 1982);

Tom Regan, *Bloomsbury's Prophet: G. E. Moore and the Development of His Moral Philosophy* (Philadelphia: Temple University Press, 1986);

Dennis Rohatyn, *The Reluctant Naturalist: A Study of G. E. Moore's* Principia Ethica (Lanham, Md., New York & London: University Press of America, 1987);

Sir David Ross, *The Right and the Good* (Indianapolis: Hackett, 1988);

Bertrand Russell, "My Mental Development," in *The Philosophy of Bertrand Russell,* edited by Paul Arthur Schilpp, The Library of Living Philosophers, volume 5 (Evanston, Ill. & Chicago: Northwestern University Press, 1944), pp. 3–22;

Russell, *The Principles of Mathematics* (Cambridge: Cambridge University Press, 1903);

Schilpp, ed., *The Philosophy of G. E. Moore,* The Library of Living Philosophers, volume 4 (Evanston, Ill. & Chicago: Northwestern University Press, 1942);

William Shaw, *Moore on Right and Wrong: The Normative Ethics of G. E. Moore* (Dordrecht, Netherlands: Kluwer, 1995);

Robert Peter Sylvester, *The Moral Philosophy of G. E. Moore* (Philadelphia: Temple University Press, 1990);

Allan White, *G. E. Moore: A Critical Exposition* (Oxford: Blackwell, 1958).

Papers:

G. E. Moore's personal papers and unpublished manuscripts are in the Cambridge University Library.

R. L. Nettleship

(17 December 1846 – 25 August 1892)

Phillip Ferreira
Kutztown University of Pennsylvania

BOOKS: *Philosophical Lectures and Remains of Richard Lewis Nettleship,* 2 volumes, edited by A. C. Bradley and G. R. Benson (London & New York: Macmillan, 1897); volume 1 republished as *Philosophical Remains of Richard Lewis Nettleship* (London & New York: Macmillan, 1901); volume 2 republished as *Lectures on the* Republic *of Plato* (London & New York: Macmillan, 1901);

Memoir of Thomas Hill Green, Late Fellow of Balliol College, Oxford, and Whyte's Professor of Moral Philosophy in the University of Oxford, preface by Charlotte Byron Green (London, New York & Bombay: Longmans, Green, 1906);

The Theory of Education in the Republic *of Plato* (Chicago: University of Chicago Press, 1906); republished as *The Theory of Education in Plato's* Republic (Oxford: Clarendon Press, 1935).

OTHER: Hermann Lotze, "Book I: Of Logic (Pure Thought)," translated by Nettleship, in Lotze, *Logic: In Three Books, of Thought, of Investigation, and of Knowledge,* translated by Nettleship, F. H. Peters, Bernard Bosanquet, F. C. Conybeare, and R. G. Tatton, edited by Bosanquet (Oxford: Clarendon Press, 1884), pp. 1–148;

Works of Thomas Hill Green, 3 volumes, edited by Nettleship (London: Longmans, Green, 1885–1888);

"'Viaggio del pellegrino' di G. Bunyan, pt. ii" and "'Il Paradiso perduto' di Milton," in *Studi di Letteratura Straniere,* edited by Bonaventura Zambini (Florence: Successor Le Monnier, 1893).

SELECTED PERIODICAL PUBLICATION–
UNCOLLECTED: "An Italian Study of Bunyan's *Pilgrim's Progress,*" *Macmillan's Magazine* (November 1878).

Remembered today primarily for his commentaries on Plato, R. L. Nettleship had an influence that extended well beyond the study of Greek philosophy.

Although he published no major works expressing his own views during his lifetime, he made major contributions to the field of philosophy through his editing of *Works of Thomas Hill Green* (1885–1888) and the book-length memoir–republished separately in 1906–that introduces the collection. And, though they have been largely ignored by later writers, Nettleship's lectures on logic remain one of the most concise and accessible accounts of the theory of knowledge that came to dominate late-nineteenth-century British philosophy.

Richard Lewis Nettleship was born on 17 December 1846 in Kettering, Northamptonshire, to John Henry Nettleship, a solicitor, and Isabella Ann Hogg Nettleship. Reports conflict as to the size of the Nettleship family, but the best evidence indicates that Richard was the youngest of five brothers. The eldest, Henry, became a professor of Latin at Oxford; John had a successful career as a painter; Edward was an ophthalmologist; and James, of whom the least is known, attended Christ's College, Cambridge.

After first attending a school in Wing, Buckinghamshire, Nettleship–as his brother James had three years earlier–became a boarder at Uppingham School a few months before his twelfth birthday. There he won many academic prizes, participated in athletic activities, and was a member of the school choir. He also took on at various times the duties of school librarian and edited the *Uppingham School Magazine.*

Nettleship entered Balliol College of the University of Oxford on a scholarship in 1865. His tutor was the unorthodox classicist Benjamin Jowett. He was deeply influenced by the idealist philosopher T. H. Green, who became a tutor at Balliol in late 1866 and was later appointed Whyte's Professor of Moral Philosophy. His acquaintances included A. C. Bradley, who became a noted Shakespeare scholar, and Bernard Bosanquet, later an important idealist philosopher. But his closest friend was H. S. Holland, who was eventually named canon of St. Paul's.

After winning the Hertford Scholarship in 1866, the Ireland Scholarship in 1867, and the Gaisford Greek Verse Prize in 1868, and taking the expected first in Classical Moderations, Nettleship shocked his teachers and fellow students by failing to obtain a first in litterae humaniores ("Greats") when he wrote his final examination in 1869. Some speculated that this failure was the result of the teaching of the controversial Green; his friend and biographer Bradley attributes it "to the incapacity of certain examiners." Nettleship believed that it had other causes, not the least of which was his commitment to the Balliol rowing team. Even so, Nettleship always said that he regretted neither rowing nor the teaching of Green. He was advised to seek a fellowship at another college, but he wanted to remain at Balliol. He applied for a fellowship there later in the year and was elected to it.

Though he briefly considered becoming a lawyer or a schoolmaster, Nettleship most wanted to write about art and its relation to the history of ideas. He originally planned to reside in Oxford as a fellow only

for a year or two; but the success of his lectures on Plato's *Republic,* along with pressure from Green and Jowett, led him to abandon the idea of writing about art and to throw himself into his academic duties. He was at first regarded primarily as a classical scholar, and he taught Latin and Greek composition; philosophy, however, held the greatest attraction for him. When Green assumed the Whyte's Professorship in 1878, Nettleship became the principal teacher of the subject at Balliol. He also held at various times the post of junior or senior dean of the college. He maintained his interest in rowing and coached the Balliol team for many years. During his frequent travels abroad he engaged in strenuous hiking and, when the opportunity presented itself, mountain climbing.

As a tutor, Nettleship most frequently lectured on the *Republic* and on logic. He also sometimes taught Aristotles's *Nicomachean Ethics* and the history of moral philosophy. Most of his notes on the latter topics have been lost, and little is known of the contents of these lectures. His views on Plato, however, are well documented. In 1880 the work for which he is best remembered, "The Theory of Education in the *Republic* of Plato," was published in *Hellenica: A Collection of Essays on Greek Poetry, Philosophy, History, and Religion* (1880), edited by Evelyn Abbott. This commentary was his only publication on Greek philosophy during his lifetime. In 1897, five years after Nettleship's death, his lectures on the *Republic* were published as the second volume of *Philosophical Lectures and Remains of Richard Lewis Nettleship,* edited by Bradley and G. R. Benson. According to Benson, the editor of the second volume, the published version of the lectures is a redaction of Nettleship's own notes, Benson's student notes from 1885, and the 1887–1888 notes of other students.

Nettleship sees Plato as a thinker who, despite the distance at which his ideas stand from ordinary views, still has profound lessons to teach. His lectures show little concern for historical influences and none for scholarly feuds. He is interested only in penetrating to the heart of Plato's difficult philosophy, and his characterization of Plato's thought stands in marked contrast to the standard interpretation. Nettleship's Plato does not propound a fantastic "two-world" dualism of "Forms" and "physical existence" but emphasizes the continuity and interdependence of reality and of human beings' experience of it. According to Nettleship, Plato sees the failure of sense experience to provide reliable knowledge as arising not from the radical separation of sensation from the Forms but from its fragmentary and limited apprehension of them. In Nettleship's account of Plato's "divided line," the ascent from opinion to knowledge involves grasping from a fuller and more encompassing perspective that which was previously seen in only a limited and

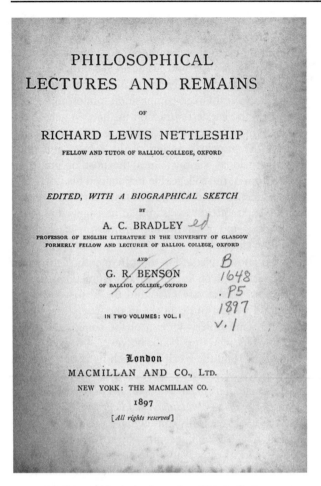

PHILOSOPHICAL
LECTURES AND REMAINS

OF

RICHARD LEWIS NETTLESHIP

FELLOW AND TUTOR OF BALLIOL COLLEGE, OXFORD

EDITED, WITH A BIOGRAPHICAL SKETCH

BY

A. C. BRADLEY

PROFESSOR OF ENGLISH LITERATURE IN THE UNIVERSITY OF GLASGOW
FORMERLY FELLOW AND LECTURER OF BALLIOL COLLEGE, OXFORD

AND

G. R. BENSON
OF BALLIOL COLLEGE, OXFORD

IN TWO VOLUMES: VOL. I

London
MACMILLAN AND CO., LTD.
NEW YORK: THE MACMILLAN CO.
1897
[All rights reserved]

*Title page for the posthumously published collection
of Nettleship's works (Thomas Cooper Library,
University of South Carolina)*

truncated fashion. Because of his emphasis on the unity of Plato's metaphysical vision, some critics have seen Nettleship's commentaries as excessively colored by the thought of the seventeenth-century Dutch rationalist philosopher Baruch Spinoza and the neo-Hegelianism that dominated Oxford philosophy in the late nineteenth century. Nettleship, however, always makes it clear just how far Plato's text allows his reading.

Nettleship's lectures on logic were published in the first volume of *Philosophical Lectures and Remains of Richard Lewis Nettleship*. While the content of the Oxford examinations forced Nettleship to discuss the views of Aristotle and Francis Bacon, in his lectures on logic he makes only occasional historical references. The lectures are a synthesis and restatement of what were at the time new—even revolutionary—views. During the composition of the lectures Nettleship translated the first book of Hermann Lotze's *Logik: Drei Bücher vom Denken, vom Untersuchen und vom Erkennen* (1843), which was published, under Bosanquet's editorship, in 1884 as *Logic: In Three Books, of Thought, of Investigation, and of Knowledge*. Nettle-

ship was also in regular contact with Green and was familiar with the latter's "Logic of the Formal Logicians." He had studied F. H. Bradley's *The Principles of Logic* (1883), one of the most widely read works of the day, and Bosanquet's *Knowledge and Reality: A Criticism of Mr. F. H. Bradley's "Principles of Logic"* (1885). Nettleship also submitted to the Oxford University Press a lengthy reader's report on the manuscript for Bosanquet's *Logic, or the Morphology of Knowledge* (1888).

The dominant theme of Nettleship's logic is the systematic nature of knowledge. The judgment, the basic unit of thought, begins with a limited apprehension of its object and attempts to incorporate itself progressively into higher and higher forms. All legitimate inferential advance is realized through the explicit recognition of the relations that these acts of systematic apprehension include. Thus, the reader finds in Nettleship's "Lectures on Logic" such idealist themes as the relativity of universal and particular, otherwise known as the doctrine of the "concrete universal"; the coextensiveness of intension and extension, that is, the idea that the number of objects to which a term refers increases with the term's internal complexity; and the rejection of the wholly categorical judgment on the ground that since they are less than perfectly systematic, all judgments are incapable of denoting fact whole and complete.

For the modern reader, Nettleship's discussion is striking for its focus on language. Most noteworthy about the holistic conception of knowledge developed in his lectures is his insistence that linguistically embodied thought, not "intuition," allows the fullest apprehension of reality. The contents of thinking experience, though they include only a fragmentary apprehension of their object, are continuous with it and are much more than mere "duplicates" or "representations." That is, in thinking experience one may progressively, though never completely, identify with or even become one's object.

In 1873 Nettleship won the Arnold Prize for his essay "The Normans in Italy and Sicily." The examiners urged Nettleship to develop the essay into a fuller study, which they guaranteed to have published. For the next six years Nettleship devoted most of his vacations to traveling in Italy and Sicily; in 1875 he took a year off from his tutor's duties so that he could more fully devote himself to research in Italian history. By 1879 he had accumulated massive notes and had written a good part of the projected book.

Over the next few years, however, two events combined to bring the project to a halt. The first was E. A. Freeman's announcement that he was planning a history of Italy and Sicily and that Nettleship should confine himself to a discussion of the Normans. Nettleship acquiesced, apparently without protest.

(Freeman's four-volume *History of Sicily from the Earliest Times* was published between 1891 and 1894.) Nettleship planned to continue with his more limited history after a brief return to philosophical writing; but when Green died in March 1882, he took on the task of preparing his friend and mentor's voluminous notes for publication. In addition, he wanted to write a memoir of the individual whose life had so greatly influenced his own. For the better part of the next four years most of Nettleship's working hours aside from his tutor's duties were devoted to these tasks. The memoir, at more than 160 pages, goes far beyond biography: it is possibly the most focused—if not the lengthiest—account of Green's philosophy ever published. Though Nettleship sometimes expresses dissatisfaction with Green's manner of expression, overall he provides a restatement and defense of Green's moral and metaphysical vision. While it is not on the same scale as Green's *Prolegomena to Ethics* (1883), on which it is largely a commentary, or F. H. Bradley's *Ethical Studies* (1876), Nettleship's account remains one of the more important discussions of moral philosophy produced during the period.

Another demanding literary project that Nettleship undertook during these years was a work on Platonism that was commissioned by the Society for the Promotion of Christian Knowledge. The book, intended as a companion to William Wallace's *Epicureanism* (1880) and W. W. Capes's *Stoicism* (1880) in the Chief Ancient Philosophies series, was originally conceived as a relatively limited discussion of 250 pages or less. Nettleship's work on the first part soon became so involved, however, that the editors decided to change the title from "Platonism" to "Plato." Though he had written hundreds of pages by the time of his death, Nettleship regarded only one chapter as ready for publication. Aware of his views, his literary executors included only that chapter, "Plato's Conception of Goodness and the Good," in *Philosophical Lectures and Remains of Richard Lewis Nettleship*.

Though he continued tutoring at Balliol, in 1882 Nettleship gave up his college rooms and moved with his mother into a house on Banbury Road next door to Green's widow, Charlotte Symonds Green. Around this time a "passionate attachment," as A. C. Bradley calls it in his biographical sketch, became a source of great frustration for Nettleship. Little is known of this relationship other than that Nettleship's feelings were not fully reciprocated. Nettleship consoled himself with frequent attendance at concerts and art galleries and by traveling, including several mountain-climbing trips to Switzerland.

By this time he had achieved a considerable reputation as a mountaineer, and he climbed in Grindelwald in 1890 and in Saas-Fee the following year. In August 1892 he tried to climb the Dôme du Gôuter of Mont Blanc with two Swiss guides, Alfred Comte and Gaspard Simond. Halfway up, the party encountered a violent storm. After spending the night in an ice cave they decided to try to descend, even though the storm was still raging. Before they had traveled far, Nettleship, thought by his companions to be the strongest of the group, collapsed. On 25 August, with Comte and Simond holding his hands, he died of exposure. The following Monday, with his brother Henry's family in attendance, he was buried in the English Church in Chamonix-Mont-Blanc, France. The inscription on his tombstone, suggested by his mother, reads: "He maketh the storm a calm."

In his obituary in *The Times* (London) Nettleship is described as "the least Donnish of the Dons"—not only in reference to his generosity to students but also to emphasize his commitment to perfection in scholarly work. This commitment, the writer suggests, explains why Nettleship left many projects unfinished.

It is, of course, impossible to know what contributions R. L. Nettleship would have made to philosophy had his life been even of average length. Bosanquet says in a letter that everyone who knew Nettleship expected something of the highest order. While the *Philosophical Lectures and Remains of Richard Lewis Nettleship* and his other published works provide only a hint of what could have been, Nettleship's importance as a teacher should not be underestimated. A memorial in the Balliol Chapel sanctuary perhaps best summarizes his effect on his students: "He loved great things, and thought little of himself: desiring neither fame nor influence, he won the devotion of men and was a power in their lives; and, seeking no disciples, he taught to many the greatness of the world and of man's mind."

Biographies:

"In Memoriam Richard Lewis Nettleship," *Uppingham School Magazine,* 30 (1892);

P. D., "A Reminiscence of R. L. Nettleship," *Uppingham School Magazine,* 30 (1892);

G. R. B. [G. R. Benson?], "R. L. Nettleship," *Uppingham School Magazine,* 31 (1893);

A. C. Bradley, "Biographical Sketch," in *Philosophical Lectures and Remains of Richard Lewis Nettleship,* volume 1, edited by Bradley and G. R. Benson (London & New York: Macmillan, 1897);

Bryan Matthews, "R. L. Nettleship," in his *Eminent Uppinghamians* (Cranbrook: Neville & Harding, 1987).

Papers:

R. L. Nettleship's papers are held by Balliol College and include letters catalogued in the Benjamin Jowett papers, reminiscences in the T. H. Green archives, and lecture notes on Christianity and moral philosophy transcribed by J. A. Spender and dated 1884.

Derek Parfit

(11 December 1942 –   )

Kathy Behrendt
University of Oxford

BOOKS: *Reasons and Persons* (Oxford: Clarendon Press, 1984; revised, 1987);
Equality or Priority? The Lindley Lecture, 1991 (Lawrence: University of Kansas, 1995).

OTHER: *Eton Microcosm,* edited by Parfit and Anthony Cheetham (London: Sidgwick & Jackson, 1964);
"Later Selves and Moral Principles," in *Philosophy and Personal Relations: An Anglo-French Study,* edited by Alan Montefiore (London: Routledge & Kegan Paul, 1973), pp. 137–169;
"Personal Identity," in *Personal Identity,* edited by John Perry (Berkeley: University of California Press, 1975), pp. 199–223;
"Overpopulation and the Quality of Life," in *Applied Ethics,* edited by Peter Singer (Oxford: Oxford University Press, 1986), pp. 145–164;
"Against the Social Discount Rate," by Parfit and Tyler Cowen, in *Justice between Age Groups and Generations,* edited by Peter Laslett and James S. Fishkin (New Haven & London: Yale University Press, 1992), pp. 144–161;
"The Unimportance of Identity," in *Identity: Essays Based on Herbert Spencer Lectures Given in the University of Oxford,* edited by Henry Harris (Oxford: Clarendon Press, 1995), pp. 13–45.

SELECTED PERIODICAL PUBLICATIONS–
UNCOLLECTED: "Prudence, Morality, and the Prisoner's Dilemma: Annual Philosophical Lecture, Henriette Hertz Trust, 1978," *Proceedings of the British Academy,* 65 (1979): 540–564;
"Future Generations: Further Problems," *Philosophy and Public Affairs,* 11 (1982): 113–172;
"Personal Identity and Rationality," *Synthese,* 53 (1982): 227–241;
"Rationality and Time," *Proceedings of the Aristotelian Society,* new series 84 (1984): 47–82;
"Reasons and Motivation," by Parfit and John Broome, *Proceedings of the Aristotelian Society,* supplementary volume, 71 (1997): 99–146;

Derek Parfit (photograph by S. L. Hurley; from the dust jacket for Reasons and Persons*)*

"Why Anything? Why This?" parts 1 and 2, *London Review of Books* (27 January 1998): 24–27; (5 February 1998): 22–25;
"Experiences, Subjects, and Conceptual Schemes," *Philosophical Topics,* 26 (1999): 217–270.

Derek Parfit's career is unusual in that it largely revolves around a single work: *Reasons and Persons* (1984). Most of his previous writings rehearse the central themes of that work, and much of his subsequent output responds to the critical reactions the book has elicited. Yet, any suggestion of narrowness is dispelled by the scope, ambition, and impact of *Reasons and Persons,* in which Parfit establishes complex interrelationships among the important themes of rationality, morality, and personal identity. His arguments have significantly revised or set the agenda for debate in each of these areas of philosophical thought.

Derek Antony Parfit was born in western China on 11 December 1942 to Dr. Norman Parfit and Dr. Jessie Parfit, née Browne, both of whom taught medicine at the University of Chengtu. The family returned to Great Britain in 1945. Parfit attended the Dragon School in Oxford from 1950 to 1956 and Eton School from 1956 to 1961. At Eton he gained a reputation for his verbal wit and writing talent. He went to Oxford in 1961 to read modern history at Balliol College. After a year he considered switching to the philosophy, politics, and economics program; but, discouraged by the mathematical demands of economics, he remained in modern history. He received his B.A. in that subject with first-class honors in 1964; he has no formal academic training in philosophy.

While spending the following two years on a non-degree Harkness Fellowship at Columbia and Harvard Universities in the United States, Parfit began seriously to explore his interest in philosophy. In 1967 he received a prestigious Prize Fellowship at All Souls, a research-based college at Oxford. This fellowship, granted to young academics for a total of seven years' tenure at the college, leaves the holder free to pursue academic research for part or all of his or her stay. Parfit became a junior research fellow at All Souls in 1974 and a senior research fellow in 1984. The lack of teaching duties at All Souls was indispensable to the production of *Reasons and Persons,* as it afforded him time to work out his ideas in a series of papers that he published over the span of more than a decade. During this time he held visiting professorships at several American universities, including Princeton, Harvard, and New York University.

In his 1971 *Philosophical Review* article "Personal Identity" Parfit says that persons are complex entities and that the relations that make up their identities are, in part, a matter of degree. He thus opposes the seventeenth-century French rationalist philosopher René Descartes's view that humans are essentially simple and indivisible beings whose identities are an all-or-nothing matter. His opposition has its roots in the treatment of persons by the seventeenth- and eighteenth-century British empiricist philosophers John Locke and David Hume as complex beings composed of various and changing psychological elements. Parfit, however, goes beyond his historical predecessors by contending that continued identity, in itself, does not matter, as long as certain psychological connections are retained between the present and future subject. His arguments against the importance of personal identity were immediately recognized as provocative and significant; "Personal Identity" was rapidly incorporated into the canon of views on the issue.

Parfit draws out the ethical implications of his view of personal identity in "Later Selves and Moral Principles" (1973) with respect to the utilitarian rejection of distributive principles of justice. His view of persons as complex conglomerates of physical and mental elements allows him to focus less on individual persons and more on particular experiences as the loci of moral importance. Hence, as in utilitarianism, the aim is for the greatest sum, rather than the most even distribution, of benefits. In "Personal Identity and Rationality" (1982) he argues against what he calls the "Classical Prudence" view that one ought rationally to be equally concerned about all parts of one's future. Granting his account of persons, it is rational for one's degree of concern to be in proportion to the degree of psychological connectedness between oneself now and at the future time in question. Parfit hastens to add that while it is not irrational on his view to care less about one's further future, it still may be immoral to do so. He leaves open the question of whether the grounds for paternalistic state intervention are strengthened or weakened by viewing such cases as immoral rather than irrational. Again drawing on his concept of persons as complex entities, he argues in "Rationality and Time" (1984) against the widely held view that acting in one's self-interest is the ideal model of rational behavior, especially given that the Self-interest Theory does not account for the discrepancy between one's attitude toward one's past versus one's attitude toward one's present or future suffering. Not all of Parfit's work of this period deals, at least explicitly, with personal identity; "Prudence, Morality, and the Prisoner's Dilemma" (1979) concerns the view that the rational choice is always the self-benefiting or "prudent" one, and that it is irrational to do anything that one believes would be worse for oneself. Parfit explores several examples, including ethical ones—cutting into a line of people, overfishing depleted seas, promoting the welfare of one's friends and family over that of others—in which if each person involved were to exercise prudence, all would be worse off. He raises but does not answer the question of whether prudence itself, in the case of morality, dictates that one reject prudence in favor of altruism.

Much of the material from Parfit's early papers is incorporated into *Reasons and Persons.* The book is expressly intended as a revisionist text: that is, Parfit's aim is to alter, rather than merely describe, the way the issues of rationality, morality, and personal identity are approached. In the first of the four parts of the book he discusses three theories that he calls "the Self-interest Theory," "Consequentialism," and "Common-Sense Morality." He focuses the most attention on the Self-interest Theory, because he contends that it has been the predominant theory of rationality for more than two millennia. The Self-interest Theory holds that everyone has the most reason to do whatever is in his or her own best interest, and that it would be irrational to do something that he or she believes would make himself or herself worse off. Parfit, however, agrees with the nineteenth-century utilitarian Henry Sidgwick that it cannot be assumed that what one has the most reason to do will be the same as what it is right to do. From an ethical point of view, it is, thus, important that the Self-interest Theory undergo careful scrutiny. Parfit examines the most common charge brought against that theory: that it is self-defeating. He allows that the Self-interest Theory is "indirectly self-defeating": many people would actually be worse off if they never did what they believed would make them worse off. Parfit gives the example of a man stranded in the desert, whose best means of persuading a passerby to save him is the promise of a reward. If he is rescued, however, he knows that it will no longer be in his self-interest to bestow the reward; hence, he has no intention of fulfilling his promise when he encounters the passerby. But this state of mind renders him incapable of telling a convincing lie, and so he cannot persuade the passerby to save him. The moral is that sometimes the most rational course is to make oneself disposed to act in a way that, according to the self-interest theory, is irrational.

Parfit obtains similar results in his examination of Consequentialism, according to which one ought always to perform that action that one believes will result in the best outcome for all concerned. He argues that "if we were all pure do-gooders, the outcome would be worse than it would be if we had certain other sets of motives." One would, for instance, have to refrain from acting on desires concerning certain people or projects in order not to show favoritism toward particular individuals. This refraining would reduce the sum of happiness overall, contrary to the aims of Consequentialism; the result is, again, an indirectly self-defeating theory.

Despite these conclusions, Parfit contends that neither the Self-interest Theory nor Consequentialism is *directly* self-defeating. The Self-interest Theory does not tell one never to do what one believes will be worse for oneself; one should, on the terms of the Self-interest Theory, change one's disposition to do that

which is irrational on the terms of the theory in order to meet the aims of the theory. Consequentialism, likewise, dictates that one should choose a set of motives that helps one to achieve the aims of Consequentialism, even if those motives are not directly attuned to those aims. Thus, both the Self-interest Theory and Consequentialism are, according to Parfit, only indirectly and, therefore, "undamagingly" self-defeating. He goes on to subject the Self-interest Theory to a series of prisoner's-dilemma-type cases that reveal it to be directly self-defeating when applied collectively. In a basic version of the prisoner's dilemma two people are separately interrogated about a crime they have jointly committed. If one confesses and the other does not, the one who confesses will go free, and the one who does not will be sentenced to twelve years in prison; if both confess, both will receive ten years; and if neither confesses, both will receive two years. Thus, the prisoners collectively do better if they both stay silent, but in so doing each pursues an option that goes against his or her rational self-interest—that is, against the aim of procuring the most self-interested result of being freed immediately by confessing. Nevertheless, Parfit concludes that the Self-interest Theory succeeds on its own terms, because it is a theory of individual, not collective, rationality.

Parfit then turns to Common-Sense Morality, which endorses favoring friends, loved ones, or other groups to which one has special obligations—what Parfit calls "M-related people." Exposing Common-Sense Morality to analogues of the prisoner's dilemma reveals it, too, to be collectively directly self-defeating; and, since its aims are collective, it risks failing on its own terms. Parfit suggests, however, that Common-Sense Morality can be revised to avoid this outcome. The revision consists of treating moral aims as common or universal, as opposed to each individual favoring his or her own M-related people. The result would be that "though *each* is doing what is worse for his M-related people," all of them would "*together* be doing what is better for all these people," and thus all of them would better achieve the original aim of helping their own M-related people. One of Parfit's goals is to establish a more impersonal approach to morality: "if we were all rational altruists, this would be better for everyone."

Having overcome the most common objection to the Self-interest Theory—that it is self-defeating—Parfit notes in part 2 of *Reasons and Persons* that "many bad theories do not condemn themselves." He then develops a different line of attack against the Self-interest Theory, arguing that it is incompletely relative in that it demands personal bias but maintains temporal neutrality: that is, it does not take into consideration whether the rational self-interest in question is directed primarily toward one's past, present, or future. But it is difficult to justify maintaining neutrality in one regard but not in the other: if reasons can be relative to agents, Parfit asks, then why not to times? The fundamental problem with the Self-interest Theory, however, is that it treats bias in a person's own favor as supremely rational and as outweighing all other considerations, regardless of circumstances or of one's actual desires. Parfit favors what he calls the "Critical Present-aim Theory," according to which some desires are intrinsically irrational and others are rationally required. One has the most reason to fulfill those present desires that are not irrational. The desire to do what is in the interest of others, when doing so is morally admirable or a moral duty, is not irrational. Thus, the Critical Present-aim Theory is compatible with the view of Common-Sense Morality outlined in part 1, and Parfit recommends that moral theorists adopt it because it "can give to moral reasons all of the weight which they believe that these reasons ought to have." While the Critical Present-aim Theory does not deny that self-interest or temporal neutrality are rational—Parfit insists that temporal neutrality is generally desirable—it does not say that they will be always supremely rational; thus, it avoids the pitfall of incomplete relativity that undermines the Self-interest Theory. The Critical Present-aim Theory allows, for instance, that the interests of others, or desires for artistic or intellectual achievement, or a desire not to act wrongly could also stand as rational requirements. Because the Critical Present-aim Theory rejects the supreme rationality of self-interest, it is more impersonal than the Self-interest Theory; and because it allows for the agent to act according to his or her present values or desires, it is not a wholly impartial theory of the sort advocated by utilitarians.

In part 3 of *Reasons and Persons* Parfit offers his account of personal identity. He observes that it is generally believed that one's identity must be determinate: that is, that for any given person, there must be a definite yes-or-no answer to the question of whether that same person exists at different times. Such beliefs are misguided, Parfit argues. In a thought experiment, he asks the reader to envision a spectrum of cases, in each of which a different percentage of a person's body and psychological states is replaced with someone else's. At the low end of the spectrum the changes are inconsequential, and the original person remains after the procedure; at the farthest end nothing of the original individual remains. Those committed to the determinacy of identity must hold that at some point in the spectrum a sharp borderline exists in which the balance of identity is tipped so that the original person meets his or her demise and the new one begins. The difficulty is that the differences between any two adjacent cases in

Dust jacket, featuring Parfit's photograph of Venice, for his 1984 book, dealing with the interrelationships of rationality, morality, and personal identity (Collection of Kathy Behrendt)

the spectrum are relatively minor, so that to single out one case as that in which the person's identity is altered seems arbitrary and makes identity hinge on a trivial physical and/or psychological change.

Parfit contends that only if persons were like Cartesian "egos"—simple, indivisible entities that could exist separate from brain, body, and experiences—could a nonarbitrary, determinate answer be given to the question of whether or not the original person remains in each case in the spectrum. The notion of the Cartesian ego has its own difficulties, however, and is rejected by most believers in determinate identity. But in the absence of recourse to such a notion, Parfit concludes, it must be admitted that in the middle range of cases in the spectrum, identity is indeterminate.

Parfit argues that nothing is involved in the existence of a person other than his or her brain, the rest of his or her body, and related and interrelated mental and physical events. At the same time, he claims that persons are distinct from these elements in the same way that a nation is distinct, though not separate, from the land, the people, and the activities that constitute it; one can continue to refer to the same nation, even though all of those elements have changed. This view that persons are distinct but not separate from that of which they are constituted is the core of Parfit's "Reductionist" position on persons. A significant advantage of Reductionism is that it allows the facts in which a person's identity and existence consists to be fully described without referring to that person or to any person at all. Indeed, Parfit adds, the whole of reality can be so redescribed. Such impersonal redescriptions will be complete, because persons do not exist separately from the elements that constitute them.

This argument leads to one of the more revisionist aspects of Parfit's account: his claim that personal identity should not matter, rationally or morally, to one's concern about one's future. What does matter is that there be a strong degree of psychological connectedness and continuity between one's present self and some future self—that one's memories, goals, beliefs, and so forth carry on. But all of those things could continue even if one ceased to exist or if one's continued existence became an indeterminate matter. Such a situation may not, in fact, ever occur, but it is a logical possibility. Parfit points out in another thought experiment that one can imagine dividing, amoeba-like, into two or more persons, both or all of whom inherit one's psychology. While one might intuitively be appalled at such a prospect, one ought not to be, according to Parfit. For although one cannot reasonably be said to survive such a division, all that is of primary importance to one would survive.

Parfit next examines the implications of his Reductionist view of persons for rationality and morality. On the Reductionist account, one's concern for the future should decrease in proportion to any decrease in psychological connectedness between one's present and future selves. This decrease in concern should not be confused with discounting the distant future simply because it is distant—a position that Parfit explicitly rejects. But though imprudence with respect to the future may not be irrational, it can still be morally objectionable. One can view one's future self in a way similar to that in which future generations ought to be viewed: they "have no vote, so their interests need to be specially protected." Because Reductionism allows one's future self to be seen as on a par with other persons, it is in accord with the impersonal aspect of utilitarianism: the quantity or quality of individual suffering is not a determiner of action. Rather, one should do the most one can to relieve whatever suffering is going on now, regardless of any resulting unevenness of distribution of benefits among various persons. By allowing

that the identity of persons may be indeterminate, Reductionism also has a bearing on practical ethical issues. Parfit suggests that abortion and euthanasia may be subject to varying degrees of moral acceptability depending on the degree of existence of the person in question, and that punishment can be tempered as the psychological connections between the one who committed an act and his or her later self weaken. Parfit also says that acceptance of his Reductionist view can reduce one's fear of death and worry about the future, while increasing one's concern for others.

In part 4 of *Reasons and Persons* Parfit considers the effects of present public policies on future generations. He calls attention to the obvious fact that if a person had not been conceived when he or she was, he or she would never have existed. Therefore, a change in public policy that has a great impact on the general standard of living so that, in time, no one is alive who would have lived had that change not taken place creates what Parfit calls the "Non-Identity Problem": public policies, no matter how bad, may actually make no one worse off, because the people who come into existence under such policies would not have done so had those policies not been in place; therefore, if their lives are, on the whole, worth living, they cannot be said to have been harmed by the bad policies. The question, then, is: how can public policies be regulated if they cannot be said to harm anyone?

According to Parfit, a theory of beneficence is needed to solve the Non-Identity Problem. Such a theory would compare the value of various prospective populations on the supposition that, other things being equal, it is wrong knowingly to make a choice that results in a worse outcome. Any such theory, however, encounters two significant obstacles. First, it seems inevitably to lead to what Parfit calls "the Repugnant Conclusion": for any population of reasonably content people that can be envisioned, a much larger population of considerably less content—though still not badly off—people is preferable, because if it is large enough, its collective quantity of happiness will outweigh that of the smaller but individually more-content population.

The second difficulty faced by a beneficence theory is what Parfit calls "the Mere Addition Paradox." In another thought experiment, he asks the reader to consider a series of imaginary populations. A is a large population whose members all have a good quality of life. B is twice as large as A, and its members' quality of life is only four-fifths as high as that of the members of A. Intuitively, then, it seems that B is worse than A. A third population, A+, consists of one group as large as and with as high a quality of life as A but also has members whose lives, while still good, are about half the quality of those in A. Merely adding these extra people does not make the outcome worse: it lowers no one's quality of life, because these extra people live so far from the other A+ people that neither group is even aware of the other's existence. Parfit argues that A+ is not worse than A: to say otherwise would be to claim that the extra people should not have existed simply because, unknown to them, a better-off group exists. He then brings in a fourth population, Divided B, which is the same as B except that it is divided into two roughly equal groups located far from, and unaware of, each other. The paradox is that Divided B is better than A+: the average quality of life is better, and there is less inequality between members of the overall population; and clearly, Divided B is as good as B; therefore, if Divided B is better than A+, then B is also better than A+; but it has already been shown that A+ is not worse than A; therefore, contrary to one's initial intuition, B is not worse than A. In summary: one is inclined to believe that B is worse than A, while B is better than A+, and A+ is not worse than A. To assert all of these propositions at the same time is to embrace a contradiction.

The Repugnant Conclusion and the Mere Addition Paradox confront any policy that affects future generations. Parfit has no solutions to offer to these problems. He leaves the reader with the challenge of finding a theory of beneficence that will solve the problems and is optimistic that others will succeed where he has failed.

Reasons and Persons was immediately recognized as an important work and lauded for integrating such a wide range of philosophical concerns. Critics have, however, raised objections to specific aspects of the book. Parfit's ethical views, for example, have met with variations on the standard criticisms of utilitarianism—for instance, that he subordinates distributive justice to general well-being. Others, however, contend that Parfit's Reductionist metaphysics can supply the utilitarian approach with needed support by justifying a focus on experiences rather than the individuals who are the subjects of them: if the separateness of persons is weakened in Parfit's account, the utilitarian approach gains credence over its rivals that are based on the rights of individuals.

Other critics maintain that any acceptable ethics must treat persons holistically, taking into consideration all the contingent features that shape their individual identities and characters, rather than viewing them as loci of consequences or vehicles of rational action. The Reductionist account, it is argued, does not allow for full-fledged, unified moral agents, as distinct from mere conglomerates of parts and events. Parfit's defenders retort that Parfit's metaphysics can, in fact, account for moral agency insofar as agency itself can be reduced to

constitutive elements, such as beliefs, desires, and intentions. These criticisms may be seen in the broader context of the debate over the role of metaphysics in ethics. Parfit is a firm believer in placing metaphysics at the foundation of one's overall philosophy, but some critics worry that this approach can lead to the acceptance of abhorrent or otherwise undesirable ethical conclusions. For example, in "Self-Interest and Interest in Selves," her contribution to a 1986 issue of *Ethics* devoted to Parfit, Susan Wolf suggests that Parfit's view of persons, by admitting of degrees of psychological connectedness that weaken over time, demands that one care much more for one's present children than for the adults that they will become. This idea undermines the prime motive for disciplining, or even educating, the child now: "why would the parent reduce the happiness of the child she loves so much for the sake of an adult she loves so little?" Wolf concludes that one's metaphysical view of persons ultimately does not and should not inform one's interest in individual persons or one's actions that arise from this interest. In contrast, Parfit upholds his conviction that actions are inextricably linked to metaphysical beliefs and that most morally wrong actions come from false metaphysical beliefs. Hence, even if some results are undesirable, the benefits of divesting oneself of those beliefs will outweigh the losses. If Parfit is taken to be claiming that metaphysics alone can decide among moral views, many philosophers would oppose him. Robert Stern suggests, however, that it is more plausible to read Parfit as holding the less controversial position that metaphysical considerations can overrule others but that morality has other bases as well.

Parfit's views on rationality and time have attracted considerable interest. Some have been moved by Parfit's treatment of this issue to argue that people need not sustain a bias toward the future but may be equally—or at least strongly—concerned about their own past suffering. Others oppose Parfit's leaning toward temporal neutrality, arguing that it is reasonable to base preferences solely on considerations of time. There is also some dispute as to whether any serious inconsistency is involved in being biased toward the self but neutral about time. Some philosophers have taken Parfit's discussion as a basis for exploring the question of why people find the idea of their posthumous nonexistence sad or terrifying but have no strong feelings about their prenatal nonexistence.

The impact of *Reasons and Persons* has been greatest in regard to personal-identity theory. While Parfit's views are seldom fully embraced, they are rarely ignored. His Humean "bundle theory" of persons as complex beings has met with little opposition from his contemporaries, and many—though by no means all—

agree with what Parfit sees as a corollary to this view: that personal identity admits of indeterminacy. The alternative to the complex view, Cartesianism, which treats persons as essentially simple, indivisible, and of determinate identity, is largely out of favor. Those few who still hold a Cartesian view tend not to feel obliged to defend themselves against the details of Parfit's position, since it is the starting points of the respective views that are in conflict.

Among those who agree with Parfit's depiction of persons as complex entities, there is a growing tendency to question his essentially psychological criterion of personal identity. While straightforward physical identity views have always struggled to win adherents, the related but more subtle "animalist" position has been gaining adherents. According to this view, people should consider themselves members of the natural kind "human being." Their identity will, thus, be bound up with the distinctive criteria of identity for an animal of that kind. One goal of this attempt to narrow the focus from personal to animal identity is to thereby circumvent what Paul Snowdon condemns as "the chaotic mess, and the evident arbitrariness, exhibited by the debate about criteria of personal identity." This move is in keeping with a more general reaction to the proliferation of diverse opinions on personal identity that Parfit's book has generated: a feeling that "person" may be too broad and unwieldy a category on which to base any meaningful pronouncements concerning identity.

Other critics take issue with Parfit's claim that although persons exist, a complete account of their identity and existence need not mention them. One line of criticism accepts the idea that persons consist of mental and physical elements but denies that these elements can be adequately described in impersonal terms. Quassim Cassam argues that one cannot "specify the truth condition of an I-thought" without ascribing it to the person whose thought it is. Therefore, mention of persons cannot be eliminated without undermining certain common and crucial elements of referential thought and speech. This criticism is related to the neo-Kantian view that to experience the world as consisting of mind-independent, objectively existing things, one must view oneself as the same person or subject of experience over time.

Conversely, others contend that the complex nature of persons undermines Parfit's entitlement to claim that persons exist at all: if Parfit's Reductionism is taken to its logical conclusion, they say, the result is an "eliminativist" view, according to which there are no persons but only subatomic mental and/or physical elements. A different and essentially sympathetic group of commentators links Parfit's emphasis on the impersonal

in ethics and metaphysics to Buddhist views on the self and moral action.

A debate has arisen within personal-identity theory concerning the value of Parfit's thought experiments. While the "method of cases," as Mark Johnston calls it, has a long history in philosophy, both the extent of Parfit's appeal to it and the fact that the thought experiments are often a crucial part of his arguments, rather than serving merely to illustrate them, are unusual features. Kathleen V. Wilkes views thought experiments as "a highly misleading philosophical tool," at least when applied to personal-identity theory, because the counterfactual and often science-fictional nature of such experiments renders one's intuitions about them dubious. Many philosophers, nevertheless, agree that the method is a legitimate means by which to analyze and, perhaps, to reform one's metaphysical commitments.

Many have taken Parfit up on his challenge at the end of part 4 of *Reasons and Persons* to find a theory of beneficence that will avoid the Repugnant Conclusion and solve the Mere Addition Paradox. Some have tried to "defuse" the paradox by attacking Parfit's claim that population A+ is not worse off than population A, arguing that the addition of lower-quality items to a set of high-quality ones can result in a worse all-around situation. David Boonin-Vail has pointed out, however, that while this argument may be valid in regard to works of art or athletic achievements, it is not clear that it is applicable to the situation described by Parfit. The arguments and examples of part 4 are especially relevant to debates about environmental protection and the use of natural resources.

Much of Parfit's work since *Reasons and Persons* has been occupied with responding to the criticisms of the book. He has remained committed to most of the views presented there, but certain changes in and additions to his position are noteworthy. In response to the charge that when Reductionism is pushed to its logical conclusion, all that end up mattering are subatomic particles, he argues in his article "The Unimportance of Identity" (1995) that Reductionism cannot be taken all the way down to the subatomic level, because it would fail to capture certain important facts about persons and personal identity. This article is Parfit's first explicit move to distance his Reductionist view of personal identity from Reductionism as a position in the mind/body debate, a topic about which he remains neutral. Another notable change occurs in a 1997 article, "Reasons and Motivation," co-authored with John Broome, in which Parfit announces his abandonment of the Critical Present-aim Theory on the grounds that, though some reasons depend on one's having certain desires, it is never the desires themselves that provide reasons.

In "Experiences, Subjects, and Conceptual Schemes" (1999) Parfit tempers his claim that reality can be fully described in impersonal terms, largely because he concedes the justice of the criticism that the content of I-thoughts depends in part on what those thoughts are about—a person, or subject of experience—and that, therefore, one ought to say that persons exist. "This . . . is not, however, an objection to Reductionism about persons," he hastens to add; for, while it may not be possible to drop all reference to subjects of experience from one's thought and speech, such subjects are nothing more than brains, bodies, and interrelated mental and physical events. Therefore, one can analyze the facts in which a person's identity consists without presupposing identity. The core Reductionist claim that one's identity over time consists in physical and/or psychological continuity can, then, be sustained, according to Parfit. To reinforce this point he puts forward a new thought experiment: one can imagine beings who know roughly as much as humans do and experience the world as humans do and yet have no concept of a person or subject of experience. This experiment confirms his oppostion to the neo-Kantian view that self-consciousness is required to experience the world as humans do. "Experiences, Subjects, and Conceptual Schemes" is the first to be published of what was intended to be a series of short responses to criticisms in the collection *Reading Parfit* (1997), edited by Jonathan Dancy. The responses became so lengthy that the book was published without them.

Since the mid 1990s Parfit has done much thinking and writing about matters beyond those covered in *Reasons and Persons* and the critical responses to it. In the article "Why Anything? Why This?" (1998) he delves into the question of why the universe exists. While he does not answer the question, he shows that the inquiry is a sensible and worthwhile one, and that more progress can be made on it than many assume. As of mid 2002 he was writing a book to defend the nonreductionist account of reasons that he propounds briefly at the end of "Experiences, Subjects, and Conceptual Schemes."

Parfit, who has never been married, is still senior research fellow at All Souls College; he is also a fellow of the British Academy and of the American Academy of Arts and Sciences. Aside from his own publications, he has influenced the thinking of many of his contemporaries by commenting on their manuscripts. Apart from philosophy, he is known for his interest in architectural photography, particularly of Venice, Italy, and St. Petersburg, Russia, and he hopes to produce books of photographs of each city. One of his Venetian photographs is reproduced on the dust jacket of *Reasons and Persons*.

Derek Parfit's work is of interest to metaphysicians, ethicists, political and legal theorists, economists, decision theorists, and those who are concerned with public policy. His views are controversial and provocative, and he is a familiar presence in debates. It is not unusual for theorists to define themselves in relation to Parfit's views, and the labels "Parfitian" and "anti-Parfitian" are common currency in several fields. Many of the thought experiments and examples that he has employed in his works have become standard topics of philosophical discussion. Fully realizing his ambition to be a revisionist philosopher, he has altered the contemporary philosophical landscape.

References:

David Boonin-Vail, "Don't Stop Thinking about Tomorrow: Two Paradoxes about Duties to Future Generations," *Philosophy and Public Affairs*, 25 (1996): 267–307;

Quassim Cassam, "Reductionism and First-Person Thinking," in *Reduction, Explanation, and Realism*, edited by David Charles and Kathleen Lennon (Oxford: Clarendon Press, 1992), pp. 361–380;

Jonathan Dancy, ed., *Reading Parfit* (Oxford: Blackwell, 1997);

Ethics, special Parfit issue, 96 (1986);

Mark Johnston, "Human Beings," *Journal of Philosophy*, 84 (1987): 59–83;

Paul Snowdon, "Persons, Animals, and Ourselves," in *The Person and the Human Mind: Issues in Ancient and Modern Philosophy,* edited by Christopher Gill (Oxford: Clarendon Press, 1990), pp. 83–107;

Robert Stern, "The Relation between Moral Theory and Metaphysics," *Proceedings of the Aristotelian Society,* 92 (1992): 143–159;

Kathleen V. Wilkes, *Real People: Personal Identity without Thought Experiments* (Oxford: Clarendon Press, 1988).

Karl Popper
(28 July 1902 – 17 September 1994)

Nicholas Maxwell
University of London

BOOKS: *Logik der Forschung: Zur Erkenntnistheorie der modernen Naturwissenschaft* (Vienna: Springer, 1935); translated by Popper as *The Logic of Scientific Discovery* (London: Hutchinson, 1959; New York: Basic Books, 1959); retranslated by Popper and J. and L. Freed as *The Logic of Scientific Discovery* (New York: Harper & Row, 1965); German version enlarged (Tübingen: Mohr, 1966); translation revised (London: Hutchinson, 1968); German version enlarged (Tübingen: Mohr, 1969; revised, 1971); translation revised (London: Hutchinson, 1972; revised again, 1980); German version enlarged (Tübingen: Mohr, 1982; revised, 1989; revised and enlarged, 1994);

The Open Society and Its Enemies, 2 volumes (London: Routledge, 1945; revised edition, Princeton: Princeton University Press, 1950; London: Routledge & Kegan Paul, 1952; revised again, London: Routledge & Kegan Paul, 1962; Princeton: Princeton University Press, 1962; revised again, Princeton: Princeton University Press, 1966)—comprises volume 1, *The Spell of Plato,* and volume 2, *The High Tide of Prophecy: Hegel, Marx, and the Aftermath;*

The Poverty of Historicism (London: Routledge & Kegan Paul, 1957; Boston: Beacon, 1957; revised edition, London: Routledge & Kegan Paul, 1960; New York: Basic Books, 1960; revised edition, London & New York: Routledge, 1961; New York: Harper & Row, 1964);

Conjectures and Refutations: The Growth of Scientific Knowledge (New York: Basic Books, 1962; London: Routledge & Kegan Paul, 1963; revised, 1969; revised again, 1989);

Of Clouds and Clocks: An Approach to the Problem of Rationality and the Freedom of Man, The Arthur Holly Compton Memorial Lecture, 1965 (St. Louis: Washington University, 1966);

Revolution oder Reform? Herbert Marcuse und Karl Popper: Eine Konfrontation, edited by Franz Stark (Munich: Kösel, 1971); translated by Michael Aylward and

Karl Popper

A. T. Ferguson, edited by Ferguson as *Revolution or Reform? A Confrontation: Herbert Marcuse and Karl Popper* (Chicago: New University Press, 1976);

Objective Knowledge: An Evolutionary Approach (Oxford & New York: Clarendon Press, 1972; revised, 1979);

Unended Quest: An Intellectual Autobiography (La Salle, Ill.: Open Court, 1976; London: Fontana/Collins, 1976);

The Self and Its Brain: An Argument for Interactionism, by Popper and John C. Eccles (London & New York: Springer International, 1977; revised, 1985);

Die beiden Grundprobleme der Erkenntnistheorie: Aufgrund von Ms. aus der Jahren 1930–1933, edited by Troels Eggers Hanson (Tübingen: Mohr, 1979);

The Postscript to The Logic of Scientific Discovery, 3 volumes, edited by W. W. Bartley III (Totowa, N.J.: Rowman & Littlefield, 1982; London: Hutchinson, 1983)—comprises volume 1, *Realism and the Aim of Science;* volume 2, *The Open Universe: An Argument for Indeterminism;* and volume 3, *Quantum Theory and the Schism in Physics;*

Auf der Suche nach einer besseren Welt: Vorträge und Aufsätze aus dreissig Jahren (Munich: Piper, 1984); translated by Laura J. Bennett as *In Search of a Better World: Lectures and Essays from Thirty Years,* includes additional material by Melitta Mew (London & New York: Routledge, 1992);

A World of Propensities (Bristol: Thoemmes, 1990);

Gegen den Zynismus in der Interpretation der Geschichte (Regensburg: Pustet, 1992)—includes "Karl Popper: Ein Jünger von Sokrates," by Hubert Kiesewetter;

Alles Leben ist Problemlösen: Über Erkenntnis, Geschichte und Politik (Munich: Piper, 1994); translated by Patrick Camiller as *All Life Is Problem Solving* (London & New York: Routledge, 1999);

Knowledge and the Body-Mind Problem: In Defence of Interaction, edited by M. A. Notturno (London & New York: Routledge, 1994);

The Myth of the Framework: In Defence of Science and Rationality, edited by Notturno (London & New York: Routledge, 1994);

The Lesson of This Century: With Two Talks on Freedom and the Democratic State, translated by Camiller (London & New York: Routledge, 1997);

The World of Parmenides: Essays on the Presocratic Enlightenment, edited by Arne F. Petersen and Jørgen Mejer (London & New York: Routledge, 1998).

Collection: *A Pocket Popper,* edited by David Miller (Oxford: Fontana, 1983); republished as *Popper Selections* (Princeton: Princeton University Press, 1984).

OTHER: "The Propensity Interpretation of the Calculus of Probability, and the Quantum Theory," in *Observation and Interpretation: A Symposium of Philosophers and Physicists: Proceedings of the Ninth Symposium of the Colston Research Society Held in the University of Bristol, April 1957,* edited by S. Körner and M. H. L. Pryce, Colston Papers, volume 9 (London: Butterworth Scientific, 1957), pp. 65–79, 88–89;

"A Theorem on Truth-Content," in *Mind, Matter and Method: Essays in Philosophy and Science in Honor of Herbert Feigl,* edited by Paul Feyerabend and

Grover Maxwell (Minneapolis: University of Minnesota Press, 1966), pp. 343–353;

"Normal Science and Its Dangers," in *Criticism and the Growth of Knowledge: Proceedings of the International Colloquium in the Philosophy of Science, London, 1965,* volume 4, edited by Imre Lakatos and Alan Musgrave (London & New York: Cambridge University Press, 1970), pp. 51–58;

"Autobiography of Karl Popper" and "Replies to My Critics," in *The Philosophy of Karl Popper,* 2 volumes, edited by Paul Arthur Schilpp, The Library of Living Philosophers, volume 14 (La Salle, Ill.: Open Court, 1974), I: 1–181; II: 962–1197.

SELECTED PERIODICAL PUBLICATIONS—UNCOLLECTED: "What Can Logic Do for Philosophy?" *Proceedings of the Aristotelian Society,* 22, supplement (1948): 141–154;

"A Note on Natural Laws and So-Called Contrary-to-Fact Conditionals," *Mind,* 58 (1949): 62–66;

"Indeterminism in Quantum Physics and in Classical Physics," *British Journal for the Philosophy of Science,* 1 (1950): 117–133, 173–195;

"The Principle of Individuation," *Proceedings of the Aristotelian Society,* 27, supplement (1953): 97–120;

"The Arrow of Time," *Nature,* 177 (1956): 538;

"Probability Magic or Knowledge out of Ignorance," *Dialectica,* 11 (1957): 354–372;

"Irreversibility; or Entropy since 1905," *British Journal for the Philosophy of Science,* 8 (1957): 151–155;

"The Propensity Interpretation of Probability," *British Journal for the Philosophy of Science,* 10 (1959): 25–42;

"Philosophy and Physics," *Proceedings of the XIIth International Congress of Philosophy* (1961): 367–374;

"A Note on Verisimilitude," *British Journal for the Philosophy of Science,* 27 (1976): 147–159;

"Natural Selection and the Emergence of Mind," *Dialectica,* 32 (1978): 339–355.

Karl Popper is regarded by many commentators as the greatest philosopher of the twentieth century. His most significant work is found in his first four published books—*Logik der Forschung: Zur Erkenntnistheorie der modernen Naturwissenschaft* (Logic of Discovery: Toward an Epistemology of Modern Natural Science, 1935; translated as *The Logic of Scientific Discovery,* 1959), *The Open Society and Its Enemies* (1945), *The Poverty of Historicism* (1957), and *Conjectures and Refutations: The Growth of Scientific Knowledge* (1962)—which attack fundamental problems with ferocious integrity, clarity, simplicity, and originality. They have wide and fruitful implications for science, philosophy, the social sciences, education, art,

Moritz Schlick, one of Popper's dissertation examiners
at the University of Vienna and the founder of the
Vienna Circle, a group whose logical positivist
views influenced Popper's thought

political philosophy, and practical politics. A volume of The Library of Living Philosophers series (1974) is devoted to Popper's work; like all volumes in the series, it includes the subject's intellectual autobiography. Popper's was published separately, with revisions, as *Unended Quest: An Intellectual Autobiography* (1976).

Karl Raimund Popper was born in Vienna on 28 July 1902. His parents were of Jewish origin but had converted to Protestantism before their children were born. His father, Simon Carl Siegmund Popper, was a successful lawyer whose real interests lay in scholarship and literature. Popper's mother, Jenny Schiff Popper, came from a musical family and was a talented pianist.

During Popper's early childhood the family was prosperous. They lived in a large apartment in an eighteenth-century house in the center of Vienna, where Popper's father conducted his legal practice. His father had an enormous library, which included many works of philosophy; books were everywhere, Popper says in his autobiography, except in the dining room, where a concert grand piano stood.

In *Unended Quest* Popper recounts an early brush with philosophy. His father had suggested that he read some volumes of the Swedish dramatist and novelist August Strindberg's autobiography. Popper tried to point out to his father that Strindberg gave too much importance to words and their meanings and was surprised to discover that his father did not agree. He later regarded this incident as the first skirmish in his lifelong battle against the influential view that philosophy must concern itself with analysis of meaning.

Bored with his classes, Popper left secondary school at sixteen and enrolled at the University of Vienna as a nonmatriculated student. Any student could take any lecture course, and Popper sampled lectures in history, literature, psychology, and philosophy before concentrating on physics and mathematics. In these fields he had excellent, if remote and autocratic, teachers: Hans Thirring, Wilhelm Wirtinger, Philipp Furtwängler, and Hans Hahn.

Popper's father lost much of his savings in the inflation brought on by World War I. For a time Popper was employed as a laborer but found the work too hard; he then tried his hand at cabinetmaking but was distracted by the intellectual problems with which he was wrestling. In 1919 he was a volunteer in the clinic of the psychologist Alfred Adler; he was also a social worker dealing with neglected children.

In the winter of 1919–1920 Popper moved out of his parents' home and into an abandoned military hospital that had been converted into a primitive students' home and joined socialist groups seeking political change. For a time he thought of himself as a communist, but an event that he later described as one of the most important in his life caused him to become critical of Marxism and led years later to the writing of *The Open Society and Its Enemies:* the communists organized a demonstration to free some of their comrades who were being held in a police station in Vienna; the police opened fire, and some of the demonstrators were killed. Popper was deeply shocked and felt some personal responsibility for the tragedy because he had endorsed a doctrine–Marxism–that required that such incidents occur so that the struggle to overcome capitalism might be intensified. Nevertheless, Popper continued to think of himself as a socialist and to associate with socialist groups. In his autobiography he celebrates these working people for their dedication and their eagerness to become educated. The economic and political outlook was bleak, but Popper and his friends were exhilarated by the challenges that lay before them.

Around this time the Pedagogic Institute was established in Vienna to train teachers in new methods of education. Popper was enrolled at the institute from 1925 to 1928; in 1927 he presented a thesis that qualified him to teach physics and mathematics in secondary schools. During these same years, influenced by the lectures of Karl Bühler and the writings of Otto Selz, he devoted himself to the study of the psychology of thinking.

Shortly before he was to submit his Ph.D. dissertation at the University of Vienna in 1928, Popper's interest shifted from the psychology to the methodology of thought and problem solving–in particular, to the methodology of science. This change came about partly as a result of long discussions with two friends, the philosophers Julius Kraft and Heinrich Gomperz. He hastily rewrote the dissertation. His examiners were Bühler and Moritz Schlick; Popper thought that he had failed, but he passed with distinction. On 11 April 1930 he married a former fellow student at the institute, Josefine Anna (Hennie) Henninger.

While employed full time as a teacher, Popper continued to work on epistemological and methodological problems in science; he wrote down his thoughts as an aid to research, rather than with the idea that they might eventually be published. During this time he became acquainted with several people associated with the logical-positivist group known as the Vienna Circle. The Vienna Circle was essentially an informal seminar convened by Schlick; its members included Hahn, Rudolf Carnap, Otto Neurath, Herbert Feigl, Kurt Gödel, Friedrich Waismann, Victor Kraft, Karl Menger, Philipp Frank, Richard von Mises, Hans Reichenbach, and Carl Hempel. The logician Ludwig Wittgenstein, who was much admired by Schlick, was an intellectual godfather of the group, together with the physicist Ernst Mach and the British philosopher Bertrand Russell. Visitors from abroad included A. J. Ayer and Frank Ramsey from England, Ernst Nagel and W. V. Quine from the United States, Arne Naess from Norway, and Alfred Tarski from Poland. Popper was never invited to join the Vienna Circle, possibly because Schlick was aware of Popper's low opinion of Wittgenstein. Nevertheless, Popper attended and gave papers at several fringe seminars. His work was strongly influenced by, but also critical of, the ideas of the Vienna Circle.

Two issues were of central concern to Popper. The first was how to distinguish science from pseudoscience. Popper was impressed by a particular difference between the economic theory of Karl Marx and the psychoanalytic theories of Adler and Sigmund Freud, on the one hand, and Albert Einstein's general theory of relativity, on the other hand. The former theories seemed able to explain phenomena, whatever happened; no evidence, it seemed, could count against them. Einstein's theory, by contrast, issued in a definite prediction: light traveling near the sun would pursue a curved path because of the sun's gravitational field. If this curving did not occur, Einstein's theory would be refuted. Around 1921, according to his autobiography, Popper decided that what distinguished pseudoscientific theories from genuine ones was that the former were irrefutable, while the latter were open to empirical refutation.

The other problem that preoccupied Popper was that of the methodology of scientific discovery: how does science acquire new knowledge? Suddenly, he says in his autobiography, he realized that the solution to the first problem was also the solution to the second: there is no such thing as the verification of theories in science; there is only refutation. Scientists put forward theories as empirically falsifiable conjectures or guesses; the theories are then subjected to sustained attempts at empirical refutation. Science advances through a process of trial and error, of conjecture and refutation. (Popper's biographer Malachi H. Hacohen challenges key elements of Popper's account of his intellectual development, claiming that Popper accepted an inductivist conception of science–that is, the idea that theories gain increasing support through experiment and observation–throughout the 1920s and did not develop his falsifiability criterion until 1932).

Encouraged by Feigl, Popper wrote the first volume of what was intended to be a two-volume work, "Die beiden Grundprobleme der Erkenntnistheorie" (The Two Fundamental Problems of the Theory of Knowledge). The first volume was accepted for publication by Schlick and Frank, the editors of a series of publications written mostly by members of the Vienna Circle, but the publisher, Axel Springer, insisted that the book be shortened. In the meantime Popper had completed the second volume. He offered a new work consisting of extracts from both volumes, but Springer still judged it to be too long. Popper's uncle, Walter Schiff, cut the manuscript by about half, and this work was published in late 1934 (with a title-page date of 1935) as *Logik der Forschung*. Thus emerged onto the public stage one of the most important books on scientific method to be published in the twentieth century. It was published in Popper's English translation, with many additional appendices and footnotes, as *The Logic of Scientific Discovery* in 1959; the original *Die beiden Grundprobleme der Erkenntnistheorie* was finally published in one 476-page volume in 1979.

Logik der Forschung begins by laying out what Popper considers the two fundamental problems about the nature of scientific inquiry. The first is "the problem of induction": how can scientific theories be verified by evidence, in view of the eighteenth-century Scottish empiricist philosopher David Hume's argument that verification is based on the assumption that the future will resemble the past, an assumption that is itself unverifiable? The second problem is "the prob-

Popper with his wife, Hennie, in New Zealand, where Popper taught from 1937 to 1946
(photograph reproduced with the permission of Melitta Mew)

lem of demarcation": how is science to be demarcated from nonscience—that is, from pseudoscience and metaphysics? Popper's solution to the second problem is that to be scientific a theory must be empirically falsifiable; and this solution solves the first problem, as well: scientific laws and theories cannot be verified by evidence at all; they can only be falsified. However much evidence may be amassed in support of a theory, the probability of the theory being true remains zero. But despite this negative conclusion, science can still make progress. Progress comes about as a result of theories being proposed as conjectures in response to problems; these conjectures are then subjected to a ruthless barrage of attempted empirical refutations. The purpose of observation and experimentation is not to prove or verify but to disprove or refute. Refutation creates the problem of discovering a new conjecture, a new theory, that meets with all the success of its predecessor, predicts the phenomena that refuted its predecessor, and predicts new phenomena, as well. When such a theory is formulated, the task then becomes to try to refute this new theory. Thus science advances from one falsifiable conjecture to another, each successfully predicting more than its predecessor, but none ever having a probability greater than zero. Scientific theories are irredeemably conjectural in character; but science makes progress precisely because, in science, it is possible to discover that theories are false and need to be replaced by better ones.

Popper has been criticized for not appreciating that even empirical refutations are not decisive: it is always a conjecture that a theory has been falsified, since it is always a conjecture that a given observation or experiment has yielded a falsifying result. But Popper gives at least two replies to such criticisms in *Logik der Forschung*. First, there is a logical asymmetry between verification and falsification. Any theory has infinitely many empirical consequences in infinitely many times and places; only a finite number of these consequences can ever be verified, and, thus, one will forever remain infinitely far from verifying the theory. But only one false empirical consequence of a theory need be discovered to show decisively that the theory is false. Second, a theory is only falsifiable with respect to the adoption of a methodology. If a theory is empirically falsified, it is always possible to rescue it by adopting what Popper calls "conventionalist stratagems" such as explaining away the experimental result in some manner or modifying the theory in an ad hoc fashion so that it no longer clashes with the empirical result. Popper proposes that scientists adopt methodological rules designed to expose theories to the maximum risk of empirical refutation. Conventionalist stratagems, in particular, are to be banned. Faced with a refutation, a theory may be modified so as to overcome the refutation only if the modification increases the empirical content, and thereby the openness to falsification, of the theory. Scientists should always strive to put forward theories that say as much as possible about the empirical world, that expose themselves to the greatest risk of refutation, that have the highest possible degree of falsifiability. The supreme methodological principle of science, according to Popper, "says that the other rules of scientific procedure must be designed in such a way that they do not protect any statement in science against falsification."

Though theories cannot be verified, they can be "corroborated." Corroboration is a measure of how well a theory has stood up to attempts to refute it. A highly falsifiable theory that has survived an onslaught of severe testing has proved its worth; it deserves to be taken more seriously than an untested theory or an unfalsifiable speculation. Science, then, progresses by means of wild imagining and bold guesswork controlled by ferocious attempted empirical refutation.

Logik der Forschung was influenced by the ideas of the Vienna Circle but is highly critical of some of the group's main tenets. For example, logical positivists such as the members of the Vienna Circle claimed that only propositions that are capable in principle of being verified are meaningful, hoping that all meaningful factual propositions would be scientific. Popper points out that this verifiability criterion actually condemns scientific theories as meaningless, since they can never be verified. The positivists wanted to rule out metaphysical statements as meaningless; but for Popper, metaphysical claims, though neither verifiable nor falsifiable, may be meaningful and may even have a fruitful role to play in the development of science. Metaphysical theses such as atomism may suggest—and, as a result of acquir-

ing precision, may be transformed into–falsifiable scientific theories.

In *Logik der Forschung* Popper also deals with two problems concerning probability: how are probabilistic statements or theories to be interpreted, and how can probabilistic theories be falsifiable, given that they are in principle "impervious to falsification"? In response to the first problem he defends a version of von Mises's objective frequency interpretation of probability. The basic idea of the frequency interpretation is that in a vast number of random events (such as repeated tosses of a die), with each event having a fixed number of different possible outcomes (such as the die showing one to six), the probability of one of these outcomes (such as the die showing three) is the fraction of events that have this outcome of the total number of events. In response to the second problem, Popper insists that probabilistic statements become falsifiable as a result of a methodological decision to treat them as such.

In *Logik der Forschung* Popper also criticizes Niels Bohrs and Werner Heisenberg's orthodox interpretation of quantum theory, which gives equal weight to the two "complementary" pictures of subatomic entities as particles and waves; Popper interprets the theory as an objective, realistic, statistical one about particles. Popper also criticizes Heisenberg's interpretation of his own uncertainty principle: Heisenberg interprets the principle as placing restrictions on simultaneous measurement of the position and momentum of a particle. Popper argues that the principle should be interpreted as restricting what can be predicted, not what can be measured.

Logik der Forschung was widely reviewed and discussed and led to Popper's being invited to give lectures in England, Denmark, and elsewhere; he later claimed that his criticisms of logical positivism in the book led to the downfall of that doctrine. Three great merits of *Logik der Forschung* are its originality, its clarity, and its tight structure: everything revolves around the key idea of falsifiability. But this virtue also lays the book open to criticism. Nicholas Maxwell argues in his *From Knowledge to Wisdom: A Revolution in the Aims and Methods of Science* (1984) and *The Comprehensibility of the Universe: A New Conception of Science* (1998) that the book fails to solve its basic problems because of its treatment of simplicity. Popper claims that the more falsifiable a theory is, the greater its degree of simplicity. But Maxwell says that this proposal fails. He points out that the falsifiability of a reasonably simple scientific theory, T, can be increased by adding on an independently testable hypothesis, h_1, to form the new theory $T + h_1$. The new theory will be more falsifiable than T but much less simple. And one can add on as many independently testable hypotheses as one pleases to form new theories, $T + h_1 + h_2 + h_3$ and so on, each of which is highly empirically falsifiable but drastically lacking in simplicity. Thus, simplicity cannot be equated with falsifiability. Maxwell makes what he considers an even more devastating point: Popper's methodological rules favor $T + h_1 + h_2 + h_3$ over T, especially if h_1, h_2, and h_3 have been severely tested and corroborated (that is, not falsified). But in scientific practice $T + h_1 + h_2 + h_3$ would never even be considered, however highly corroborated it might be if it were considered, because of its extreme lack of simplicity or unity, its grossly ad hoc character. Thus, according to Maxwell, there is a fundamental flaw in the central doctrine of *Logik der Forschung*.

In 1936 Popper was offered a lectureship at the University of Canterbury in New Zealand. Rising anti-Semitism ensured that he had no hope of an academic career in Austria, and the increasing influence of fascism meant that the future there looked grim in general. Popper accepted the offer, and he and his wife left Vienna for New Zealand early in 1937.

For some years Popper had privately believed that because of the influence of Marxism, the policies of socialists in Germany and Austria played into the hands of the fascists and Adolf Hitler. But he had feared that any public criticism would weaken the forces opposing Hitler. When Nazi Germany occupied Austria in March 1938, Popper decided that all grounds for restraint had disappeared and began writing *The Poverty of Historicism*. But as the sections on essentialism and on totalitarian tendencies in Plato grew, driven by the desperation of the times, Popper found that he had a new work on his hands. It became what is, perhaps, his best-known and most influential book: *The Open Society and Its Enemies*. Without referring anywhere to Hitler or to Soviet dictator Joseph Stalin, the book is an urgent and passionate investigation of totalitarianism, whether of the right or the left. It seeks to understand the appeal of totalitarianism and how it has come to be a threat to civilization. Popper regarded the writing of the book as his contribution to the war effort.

In *The Open Society and Its Enemies* Popper argues that a fundamental problem confronting humanity is that of moving from a closed, tribal way of life to an "open society." The closed society has just one view of the world, one set of values, and one basic way of life. It is dominated by dogma, taboo, and magic and devoid of doubt and uncertainty. The open society, by contrast, tolerates diversity of views, values, and ways of life, which makes learning through criticism possible. The open society is the civilized society, in which individual freedom and responsibility, justice, democracy,

humane values, reason, and science can flourish. The transition from the closed to the open society is "one of the deepest revolutions through which mankind has passed." But it imposes a great psychological burden, "the strain of civilization," on the individuals involved. The organic, dogmatic, and doubt-free security of the tribe is replaced by uncertainty, insecurity, the necessity of taking personal responsibility for one's life in a state of ignorance, and the lack of intimacy of an "abstract society" in which the individual constantly rubs shoulders with strangers. Many cannot bear the burden and they long for the security and certainty of the closed society. Some of the greatest thinkers of Western civilization have given in to this temptation, Popper says, and have urged a return to the closed society under the guise of Utopia. Such thinkers include the ancient Greek philosophers Plato and Aristotle, the nineteenth-century German idealist philosopher Georg Wilhelm Friedrich Hegel, and the Communist theoretician Marx. The lure of totalitarianism, Popper says, is built deep into Western history and traditions. The two greatest enemies of the open society, according to Popper, are Plato, treated in volume one of *The Open Society and Its Enemies*, and Marx, treated in volume two. Both uphold versions of historicism, the doctrine that history unfolds according to a fixed pattern or rigid set of laws of evolution.

The revolutionary transition from closed to open society first occurred, according to Popper, with the "Great Generation" of ancient Athens in the fifth century B.C. Those who are associated with the birth and affirmation of the open society include Pericles, Herodotus, Protagoras, Democritus, Alcidamas, Lycophron, Antisthenes, and, above all, Socrates. The main source of information for later centuries concerning Socrates' passionate skepticism, searching criticism of current beliefs and ideals, and conviction that one must acknowledge one's own ignorance before one can acquire knowledge and wisdom is the dialogues of his disciple Plato. But Popper argues that Socrates was ultimately betrayed by Plato: the greatest advocate of the open society became, in Plato's *Republic*, the spokesman for a return to a closed society. Deeply disturbed by the beginnings of the open society in democratic Athens, Plato came to fear all social change as embodying decay and corruption. Synthesizing elements from Parmenides, the Pythagoreans, and Socrates, Plato turned these fears into an entire cosmology and social theory, the famous Doctrine of Forms: every kind of material object has its perfect model, its ideal representation, in an immaterial Form in a Platonic Heaven; the Forms initiated the material universe by imprinting themselves on space, thus producing nearly perfect material copies of themselves. But as time passed, the copies of copies became more and more corrupt, further and further removed from their ideal progenitors. The same corruption occurred in the social and moral sphere as the material. The primary task of the rulers of society is, therefore, to arrest all social change and try to keep society resembling, as closely as possible, the ideal Forms of order, justice, and the Good. Most people know only imperfect material things, but a few philosophers, as a result of studying mathematics—which enables one to acquire knowledge of abstract, perfect objects and not just their imperfect material copies—are able to arrive at an intellectual apprehension of the Forms and, eventually, of the supreme Form, that of the Good (represented by the sun in Plato's myth of the cave in *The Republic*). These enlightened philosophers alone know the form society should take and how it can be protected from the corrupting effects of change. Philosophers, then, must rule, aided by "guardians"—a class of soldiers or police who ensure that the rest of the population obeys the commands of the philosopher-kings. Plato's republic, as Popper depicts it, is a nightmarish, totalitarian closed society, rigidly ordered, with individual liberty, freedom of expression and discussion, art, democracy, and justice ruthlessly suppressed. But Plato presents his scheme with great subtlety and a kind of twisted logic, so that he is ostensibly arguing for a just, wise, and harmonious society of legal and moral perfection. Popper even suggests that Plato wrote *The Republic* as a kind of manifesto to promote himself as a philosopher-king.

Since Plato believed that historical change inevitably involves decay and degeneration, and that all that enlightened philosopher-kings can do is to slow down the changes, he was what Popper calls a pessimistic historicist. Marx, on the other hand, was an optimistic historicist: for him, historical development will result in socialism and freedom. Popper traces a direct lineage from Plato to Marx via Aristotle and Hegel. Prompted by his interest in biology, Aristotle modified Plato's doctrine of the Forms so that it could give an account of organic growth and development. Aristotle, so to speak, inserts a Platonic Form into each individual object; the Form becomes the essence of the object, an inherent potentiality that the object, through movement, change, or growth, strives to realize. Thus, the oak tree is inherent in the acorn as a potentiality. Germination and growth are to be understood as the acorn striving to actualize its potentiality by becoming an oak tree.

In short, Aristotle modifies Plato's doctrine of the Forms so that the Form ceases to be the perfect copy of an object from which the object can only decay and becomes, instead, an inherent potentiality that the object strives to realize. This modification potentially transforms Plato's pessimistic historicism of inevitable

Popper in 1946, the year he began working at the London School of Economics (photograph reproduced with the permission of Melitta Mew)

decline into an optimistic historicism of social growth, development, and progress. But Hegel was the first fully to exploit Aristotelianism in this way.

Popper depicts Hegel as a complete intellectual fraud. He endorses Arthur Schopenhauer's verdict: "Hegel, installed from above, by the powers that be, as the certified Great Philosopher, was a flat-headed, insipid, nauseating, illiterate charlatan, who reached the pinnacle of audacity in scribbling together and dishing up the craziest mystifying nonsense." Hegel's great idea was to depict history as the process of Spirit, the Aristotelian essence and potentiality of the State and the Nation, striving to realize itself through war and world domination. Taking over and corrupting the antinomies (paradoxes) of Immanuel Kant's *Kritik der reinen Vernunft* (1781; translated as *Critique of Pure Reason*, 1855), Hegel depicted history as a kind of pseudorational or logical dialectical process, thesis giving way to antithesis, and the two then combining in a higher synthesis. What matters is not individual liberty or democracy but the triumph of the strongest State on the stage of history, its inner essence interpreted and directed by the Great Leader by means of dictatorial power.

Despite—or because of—his intellectual fraudulence, Popper argues, Hegel exercised a powerful influence over the development of subsequent nationalist, historicist, and totalitarian thought of both the extreme right and the extreme left. Both Hitler and Stalin stumble onto the world stage out of Hegel, Popper implies, although neither man is mentioned by name in *The Open Society and Its Enemies*.

For Popper, Marx is in a quite different category from Hegel. Popper pays tribute to Marx's humanitarianism, intellectual honesty, hatred of moralizing verbiage and hypocrisy, grasp of the facts, sincere quest for the truth, contributions to historical studies and social science, and burning desire to help the oppressed. Nevertheless, according to Popper, Marx is one of the most dangerous enemies of the open society, his thought disastrously corrupted by its Hegelian inheritance.

In a well-known passage in the first volume of his *Das Kapital* (1867; translated as *Capital*, 1887) Marx declares that Hegel "stands dialectics on its head; one must turn it the right way up again." In another passage he announces that "It is not the consciousness of man that determines his existence—rather, it is his social existence that determines his consciousness." For the idealist Hegel, history is the dialectical development of ideas; for Marx, history is determined by the dialectical development of material processes—in particular, those associated with the means of production. Distinct historical phases—prefeudal, feudal, capitalist, and postrevolutionary socialist—owe their existence to distinct phases in the means of production and the social arrangements these phases generate. Each phase leads, as a result of inevitable dialectical processes, to its own destruction and the creation of the next phase. Thus, capitalism concentrates wealth and ownership of the means of production into fewer and fewer hands until the workers unite, overthrow the capitalists, and establish socialism. The historical processes of dialectical materialism work themselves out through class struggle, with classes and the conflicts between them determined by the means of production. The laws that determine the evolution of the economic base decide the path of history; ideas and political and legal institutions form an ideological superstructure that reflects and preserves the economic base and the interests of the dominant class but is powerless to influence the path of history. Marx condemned as "Utopian" those socialists who sought to bring about the revolution by means of political policies and planning; the proper "scientific" approach to achieving socialism is to discover the dialectical laws that govern the evolution of the eco-

nomic base of society and then to help this evolution along, insofar as such is possible, thus speeding up the coming of the final and inevitable socialist revolution. Popper argues that several elements of Marxist thought are of value, if not taken too far: the idea that the social cannot be reduced to the psychological; the thesis that much of history has been influenced by class struggle; the idea that economic circumstances play an important role in influencing the development of other aspects of social and cultural life, even of something as apparently remote from economic conditions as mathematics; and, above all, the recognition and depiction of the appalling conditions of life of the poor in the unrestrained capitalism of Marx's time and the recognition of the hypocrisy of much of the morality, law, and politics of that time. After describing Marx's account of the working conditions of children as young as six, Popper writes: "Such were the conditions of the working class even in 1863, when Marx was writing *Capital;* his burning protest against these crimes, which were then tolerated, and sometimes even defended, not only by professional economists but also by churchmen, will secure him forever a place among the liberators of mankind."

But these good points are, for Popper, more than counterbalanced by the defects in Marx's thought, most of which stem from the historicism he inherited from Hegel. The central tenet of Marxism—that the laws of dialectical materialism determine the evolution of the means of production, and that this evolution, in turn, determines the evolution of everything else, from class struggle to culture, religion, law, and politics—is, Popper says, manifestly false. For one thing, the interaction between economic conditions and ideas goes in both directions: eliminate scientific and technological ideas, and the economy would collapse. Furthermore, nonscientific ideas can themselves influence the course of history: Marxism itself is an example. Historical predictions made by Marx on the basis of his economic historicism have been falsified by subsequent historical events. The Russian Revolution is, for example, entirely at odds with Marx's theory, as is the way in which the unrestricted capitalism of Marx's time has become both more economically successful and more just and humane as a result of political intervention. Marx's economic historicism is not just false: it is pseudoscientific. Only for exceptionally simple systems, such as the solar system, is long-term prediction, based on scientific theory, possible. In the case of social systems, which are incredibly complex and open to the influence of a multitude of unpredictable factors, the idea that science should be able to deliver long-term predictions is hopelessly unwarranted. Marx's historicism leads him to turn good points into bad ones by exaggeration. His claim that "The history of all hitherto existing society is a history of class struggle" is a good point if "all" is not taken too seriously, but as it stands it is an oversimplification and exaggeration; it ignores, for example, power struggles within the ruling class. Again, Popper says, Marx was right to see the legal and political institutions of his time as biased in favor of the interests of the ruling classes, but he was wrong to condemn all legal and political institutions as inevitably having this function, as his economic historicism compelled him to do.

For Popper, the most damaging feature of Marx's historicism has to do with the limitations that it places on the power of politics—on the capacity of people to solve social problems. Marx is famous for his eleventh thesis on the philosopher Ludwig Feuerbach: "The philosophers have only interpreted the world in various ways; the point however is to change it." But Marx's economic historicism leads to a severely restricted view about what political intervention can achieve. In *Capital* he declares: "When a society has discovered the natural law that determines its own movement . . . even then, it can neither overleap the natural phases of its evolution, nor shuffle them out of the world by a stroke of the pen. But this much it can do; it can shorten and lessen its birth-pangs." The very factors that improved the unrestrained capitalism of Marx's time beyond anything he would have recognized—political intervention and trade unions—are thus discounted by Marx's economic determinism as necessarily impotent. Political planning and policy making for socialism are condemned by Marx as inherently inefficacious. One disastrous consequence was that when Marxists gained power in Russia, they found that their literature gave them no guidelines as to how to proceed. Another disastrous consequence was that Marxism, blind to the potency of political power, failed to anticipate the dangers inherent in handing over power to political leaders after the revolution—dangers that, after the Russian Revolution, became all too manifest.

The full force of Popper's criticism is devoted, however, to the central argument of *Capital,* which seeks to establish the inevitable downfall of capitalism and the triumph of socialism. Popper presents Marx's argument as having three steps, only the first of which is elaborated in *Capital.* The first step is the claim that an inevitable increase in the productivity of work will lead to the accumulation of more and more wealth by the ruling class and to a corresponding increase in the poverty and misery of the working class. The second step is the claim that all classes will disappear except for a small, wealthy ruling class and a large, impoverished working class and that this situation will inevitably lead to a revolution. The third step is the claim that the revolution will result in the victory of the working class, which will lead to the withering away of the state and

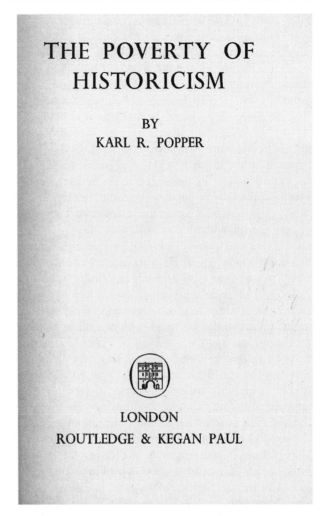

THE POVERTY OF
HISTORICISM

BY
KARL R. POPPER

LONDON
ROUTLEDGE & KEGAN PAUL

Title page for the book, published in 1957, in which Popper criticizes the doctrine that human history unfolds according to a fixed pattern or rigid laws of evolution (Thomas Cooper Library, University of South Carolina)

the creation of socialism. Popper demonstrates that none of these steps is inevitable by showing that alternative developments are possible and, in many cases, actually happened, after Marx wrote *Capital.* Even if there is a tendency under capitalism for the means of production and wealth to be concentrated in fewer and fewer hands, the state can intervene to counteract this tendency by such means as taxation and death duties. The increasing poverty of workers can be counteracted by the formation of trade unions and by collective bargaining backed up by strikes. The brutal, unrestricted capitalism of Marx's time has been transformed by just such interventionist methods. Again, even if the ruling class did become increasingly wealthy and the working class increasingly poor, all other classes would not necessarily disappear, since landowners, rural workers, and a new middle class may well exist under Marx's assumptions. Even if violence broke out, it would not necessarily constitute the social revolution as envisaged by Marx. Finally, even if the workers united and overthrew the ruling class, a classless society and socialism would not necessarily result. It is all too easy to suppose that the new political leaders would seize and hold onto power, justifying their actions by exploiting and twisting the revolutionary ideology and invoking the threat of counterrevolutionary forces. And many other possible outcomes can be envisaged. It is, in fact, Popper says, implausible to suppose that the victory of the working class would mean the creation of a classless society and the withering away of the state.

Marx condemned planning for socialism, and, in a sense, Popper agrees. He distinguishes two kinds of social planning or government intervention, which he calls "Utopian social engineering" and "piecemeal social engineering." Utopian social engineering seeks to attain an ideal social order by bringing about holistic changes in society; this approach is, Popper argues, doomed to failure. Piecemeal social engineering, by contrast, searches out and fights against "the greatest and most urgent evils of society"; Popper advocates this approach. Piecemeal social engineering can take the form of state intervention or of the creation of legal and institutional curbs on freedom of action. The latter is to be preferred, Popper argues, as the former carries with it the danger of increasing the power of the state.

Central to *The Open Society and Its Enemies* is the idea that reason is a vital component of the open society; by "reason" Popper means "critical rationalism," which is arrived at by generalizing his falsificationist conception of scientific method. For Popper, both scientific method and rationality need to be understood in social terms. He criticizes Karl Mannheim's sociology of knowledge for overlooking the "social aspect of scientific method." He also criticizes moral historicism, oracular philosophy, the revolt against reason, and the idea that history might have a meaning. Both volumes include extensive footnotes discussing a great variety of issues tangentially related to the main argument, such as the development of ancient Greek mathematics, the problem of putting an end to war, and the proper aims of a liberal education.

Popper's fiercely polemical book provoked much controversy. His critical onslaughts against Plato, Aristotle, Hegel, and Marx were angrily repudiated or simply ignored by many scholars who specialized in the thought of those men.

Popper expounds on and criticizes historicism in more general terms in *The Poverty of Historicism,* first published as three articles in the journal *Economica* in 1944 and 1945 (thus, somewhat before *The Open Society and Its Enemies*) and in book form in 1957. Popper divides historicist views and arguments into two classes: the "anti-naturalist doctrines," which hold that the methods of the social and natural scientists are quite different, and the "pro-naturalist doctrines," which hold they are the same or similar. According to the anti-naturalists, social phenomena exhibit novelty, complexity, and a holistic aspect that are lacking in physical phenomena. These differences ensure that historicist social science, in trying to predict the evolution of society in rough outline, must employ methods that differ from those of natural science. Pro-naturalists, on the other hand, make much of the success of long-term predictions in astronomy: just as states of the solar system can be predicted far into the future by natural science, historicist social science ought to be able to predict states of society. Such predictions will, however, employ social laws of succession that specify how one characteristic phase of social development gives way to a subsequent phase.

Popper effectively criticizes the anti-naturalist version of historicism, pointing out that novelty, complexity, and holistic features arise just as much in physical contexts as in social ones; there is no reason here for physical and social sciences to have different methods. His criticism of the pro-naturalist standpoint is, however, the more important aspect of the book. Historicist "laws" of succession, he points out, are trends, and "*trends are not laws.*" A law provides a causal explanation of an event when the law, plus the initial conditions, imply that the event will occur. Whenever a succession of causally connected events occurs in one's environment, such as the wind shaking a tree and causing an apple to fall to the ground, laws—usually several quite different laws—plus the specification of a sequence of initial conditions are required to predict the sequence of events. Trends can, then, be explained by laws, but it is always laws *plus relevant initial conditions* that provide explanations. The crucial point, according to Popper, is that, given some trend, in particular a social trend, the initial conditions that must persist if the trend is to continue are likely to be multitudinous, and most of them will be easy to overlook. This situation ensures that trends, such as the growth of a population, that have persisted for centuries may suddenly cease if some condition necessary for the persistence of the trend ceases to exist. "The poverty of historicism," Popper declares, "is a poverty of imagination"—an inability to imagine that conditions necessary for the persistence of a trend might themselves suddenly change. This point is highly relevant to Popper's idea of piecemeal social engineering, for the piecemeal engineer may seek to change the conditions required for the persistence of some undesirable trend.

In 1946 Popper became a reader in logic and scientific method at the London School of Economics (LSE); he was promoted to professor of those subjects in 1949. Initially the only philosopher at the LSE, he was joined by J. O. Wisdom in 1948, Joseph Agassi in 1957 (Agassi left in 1960), John Watkins in 1958, W. W. Bartley III and Imre Lakatos in 1960, and Alan Musgrave in 1964. In 1956–1957 Popper was a fellow at the Center for Advanced Study in the Behavioral Sciences in Stanford, California.

Throughout the 1950s and 1960s ordinary-language philosophy and conceptual analysis prevailed in British philosophy departments, which were dominated by the influence of Wittgenstein: the task of philosophy was to dismantle pseudoproblems that arose as a result of the misuse of ordinary language. At the LSE, by contrast, Popper's approach prevailed. The philosophy department there conceived of itself as an island of reason and seriousness surrounded by an ocean of trivialization and scholasticism.

The LSE philosophy department was famous—or notorious—for its weekly seminar, at which visiting speakers rarely succeeded in concluding the announcement of the titles of their talks before being interrupted by Popper, who would proceed to attack them almost sentence by sentence. The seminars were always dramatic and sometimes farcical, but they revealed Popper's passionate determination to get at the truth even if conventions of politeness had to be sacrificed.

Popper received an honorary LL.D. from the University of Chicago in 1962. That same year he published *Conjectures and Refutations,* a collection of essays restating, extending, and applying his views on scientific method, philosophy, and rationality. It is, perhaps, the single best introduction to his thought. In the introduction to the volume he notes the widespread tendency to believe that truth is readily available; when it turns out not to be so easy to obtain, epistemological optimists become pessimists and either deny that knowledge is possible at all or resort to conspiracy theories to account for the inaccessibility of the truth. The seventeenth-century French philosopher René Descartes and the seventeenth-century British philosopher Francis Bacon are famous for their anti-authoritarian stance in epistemological matters; and yet, Popper points out, authoritarianism is implicit in their views. For Descartes and the rationalists who followed him, reason is the authoritative source of knowledge; for Bacon and the empiricists who followed him, the senses are the authoritative source. Popper argues against the idea that conjectural knowledge has any authoritative source.

In "The Nature of Philosophical Problems and Their Roots in Science" Popper contends that philo-sophical problems have their roots in science and mathematics, and he argues against the Wittgensteinian view that they are pseudoproblems that arise when ordinary language is misused. In "Three Views Concerning Human Knowledge" he discusses essentialism, which holds that science can grasp the ultimate essence of things; instrumentalism, which claims that scientific theories are merely tools for the prediction of observable phenomena; and realism, according to which science puts forward falsifiable conjectures about aspects of reality that often go beyond what is observable. Popper criticizes the first two views and defends the third.

In "Back to the Presocratics" Popper depicts the philosophers Thales, Anaximander, Anaximenes, Heraclitus, and Parmenides as proposing successive theories about the origins and ultimate constituents of the universe and the problem of how to understand change and critically assessing the theories of their predecessors. The pre-Socratics, he argues, almost unintentionally created critical rationality, the tradition of proposing bold conjectures that are then subjected to criticism—a tradition that led eventually to modern science. In "On the Status of Science and Metaphysics" he takes up the problem of how philosophical or metaphysical doctrines can be rationally assessed, given that they cannot be empirically falsified as scientific theories can. His solution is that philosophical doctrines can be assessed in terms of their success in dealing with the problems that they are intended to solve.

In "Truth, Rationality, and the Growth of Scientific Knowledge" Popper restates and develops somewhat his falsificationist conception of scientific method, putting forward a new methodological principle that, when added to those of *Logik der Forschung,* excludes theories such as $T + h_1 + h_2 + h_3$ from scientific consideration. According to Popper, a new theory, to be acceptable, "should proceed from some *simple, new, and powerful, unifying idea* about some connection or relation (such as gravitational attraction) between hitherto unconnected things (such as planets and apples) or facts (such as inertial and gravitational mass) or new 'theoretical entities' (such as field and particles)." $T + h_1 + h_2 + h_3$ does not "proceed from some *simple, new, and powerful, unifying idea*" and is to be rejected on that account, even if it is more highly corroborated than T. But critics have pointed out that the adoption of this "requirement of simplicity," as Popper calls it, as a basic methodological principle of science has the effect of permanently excluding from science all ad hoc theories (such as $T + h_1 + h_2 + h_3$) that fail to satisfy the principle, however empirically successful such theories might be if they were considered. The principle, then, amounts to assuming the substantial metaphysical thesis that the

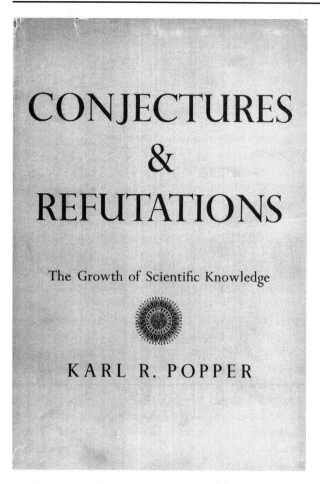

*Dust jacket for Popper's 1962 collection of essays and lectures
on such subjects as philosophy of science, knowledge,
Immanuel Kant, ancient Greek philosophy, the
mind/body problem, and political philosophy
(Bruccoli Clark Layman Archives)*

universe is non-ad hoc, in the sense that no theory that fails to satisfy Popper's principle of simplicity is true. But such acceptance, Maxwell says, clashes with Popper's criterion of demarcation, which holds that no unfalsifiable metaphysical thesis is to be accepted as a part of scientific knowledge. Maxwell says that Popper's criterion of demarcation must be rejected and the metaphysical thesis of "non-ad hocness" must be explicitly acknowledged as part of scientific knowledge, because the thesis, in the form in which it is implicitly adopted at any given stage in the development of science, may well be false, and scientific progress may require that it be modified. The thesis needs to be made explicit, in other words, for good Popperian reasons: so that it can be critically assessed and, perhaps, improved, Maxwell concludes.

Popper also formulates and tries to solve what has come to be known as "the problem of verisimilitude": what can be meant by "scientific progress" if sci-

ence merely advances from one false theory to another? Popper's solution is that given two theories, T_1 and T_2, even though both are false, T_2 may, nevertheless, be closer to the truth than T_1. Suppose, he says, that T_2 implies everything true that T_1 implies and more besides but does not imply anything false that T_1 does not imply. Granted that assumption, there is a perfectly good sense in which T_2 can be said to be "closer to the truth" than T_1 and, thus, an advance over T_1. P. Tichý and David Miller, however, have argued that this proposed solution to the problem does not work. If T_2 has more true implications than T_1 does, then T_2 necessarily has some false implications that T_1 does not. Popper's requirements for T_2 to be "closer to the truth" than T_1, when both are false, cannot be satisfied, according to Tichy and Miller.

One of the themes that runs through *Conjectures and Refutations* and much of Popper's subsequent work is that the proper task of philosophy is to attack, in an imaginative and critical way, real and fundamental problems that have their roots outside philosophy in science, politics, art, and life. This Popperian conception of philosophy stands in sharp contrast both to what some consider the obscurities of much Continental philosophy and to what others regard as the aridity of philosophy in the British analytic tradition, which is restricted to the analysis of meaning in ordinary language. Popper fought against both of these rival conceptions of philosophy and sought to put into practice his own critical-rationalist, problem-solving conception of philosophy. His first four books are exemplary in this respect and have exercised an enormous but often unacknowledged influence on subsequent philosophy. The basic impulse behind these works might almost be summed up in a stray remark Popper makes in *The Open Society and Its Enemies:* "We have to learn the lesson that intellectual honesty is fundamental for everything we cherish."

Popper's work has exercised a substantial influence far beyond philosophy in such fields as the physical, biological, and social sciences; education; politics; and even art history. The basic thesis of *The Logic of Scientific Discovery* has been accepted by many scientists, including Peter Medawar, Herman Bondi, and John C. Eccles. And the book has influenced scientific practice, for inductivism has been influential not just in the philosophy of science but in science itself. Popper's argument that there is no such thing as inductivism has persuaded many that scientific research and teaching should no longer try to conform to inductivist edicts. In this respect, Popper's work stands in marked opposition to a vast body of literature in the philosophy of science that has sought to justify induction. *The Open Society and Its Enemies* not only includes what many consider the definitive refutation of Marxism but is also a classic exposition and defense of liberalism. For a book of political philosophy it has been widely read, highly influential, and admired and hated in almost equal measure. With the advent of the Cold War it was taken up by the political right as an ideological cudgel with which to belabor the left and combat communism. In the West many on the left refused to read the book under the impression that it amounted to no more than right-wing propaganda. Behind the Iron Curtain, however, it was circulated in samizdat form and was influential along with such anticommunist works as George Orwell's *Animal Farm* (1945).

A central backbone of argument runs through Popper's first four books. The falsificationist view of scientific method elaborated in *The Logic of Scientific Discovery* is generalized to form Popper's conception of critical rationality, a general methodology for solving problems or making progress. As Popper says in that work, "inter-subjective *testing* is merely a very important aspect of the more general idea of inter-subjective *criticism,* or in other words, of the idea of mutual rational control by critical discussion." But to make sense of the idea of severe testing in science, one needs to see the experimenter as having at least the germ of an idea for a rival theory; otherwise, testing might degenerate into performing essentially the same experiment again and again. All experiments are, thus, crucial experiments, attempts to decide between competing theories. Theoretical pluralism, in other words, is necessary for science to be genuinely empirical. More generally, to criticize an idea, one needs to have a rival idea in mind; rationality requires a plurality of ideas, values, and ways of life. Thus, for Popper, the rational society is the open society. In contrast, for pre-Popperian conceptions of reason, with their emphasis on proof rather than criticism, the idea that the rational society is the open society is almost a contradiction in terms. There is, thus, a close link between *The Logic of Scientific Discovery,* on the one hand, and *The Open Society and Its Enemies, The Poverty of Historicism,* and *Conjectures and Refutations,* on the other hand. And the argument does not just go from *The Logic of Scientific Discovery* to *The Open Society and Its Enemies;* it goes in the other direction, as well. For in *The Open Society and Its Enemies* Popper argues that rationality, including scientific rationality, needs to be conceived in social and institutional terms. This argument is also echoed in *The Poverty of Historicism* in connection with the conditions required for scientific progress to be possible. The doctrines of *The Logic of Scientific Discovery* are illuminated and enriched by the three later books.

Popper was knighted in 1965. That same year he received the Prize of the City of Vienna for contributions to the moral and mental sciences. In 1966 he was awarded an honorary LL.D. by the University of Denver, and he was a visiting fellow at the Salk Institute for Biological Studies in La Jolla, California, in 1966–1967. He retired from the LSE in 1969.

Much of the work Popper published after *Conjectures and Refutations* restates, extends, and finds further applications for the ideas elaborated in the first four books. Where his subsequent work does go in new directions, these are not always well chosen. Battles against subjectivity, antirealism, and physical determinism lure Popper into defending opposing views that are sometimes exaggerated almost to the point of absurdity. A subtle shift of perspective can also be discerned as one moves from Popper's earlier to his later work. In the early books he speaks up on behalf of humanity, on behalf of any concerned person of goodwill and against those traditional "great thinkers" and "experts" who threaten to beguile people and lead them to disaster. In his later work he speaks up on behalf of great science and great scientists and against fraudulent academics, mostly philosophers and social scientists.

In 1970 appeared *Criticism and the Growth of Knowledge,* edited by Lakatos and Musgrave. The fourth volume of the proceedings of a conference on philosophy of science held in London in 1968, it is devoted to a comparison of the views of Popper and Thomas Kuhn; among the contributors are Popper, Kuhn, Lakatos, Watkins, Stephen Toulmin, and Paul Feyerabend. In his contribution Popper praises Kuhn for discovering "normal science": science that takes some "paradigm" for granted and devotes itself to puzzle solving. Popper points out that he had made the same discovery more than thirty years earlier, as recorded in the preface to *Logik der Forschung.* But, Popper says, the normal scientist "has been badly taught. He has been taught in a dogmatic spirit: he is the victim of indoctrination." Normal science is "a danger to science and, indeed, to our civilization."

Popper received an honorary Lit.D. from the University of Warwick in 1971. In 1972 he published a second collection of his essays as *Objective Knowledge: An Evolutionary Approach.* In one of the essays, "Two Faces of Common Sense," he notes that common sense tends to combine two incompatible theses: common sense realism, the view that things around one, such as stones, trees, and other physical entities, really exist, and the notion that knowledge floods into the mind via the senses like water being poured into a bucket—a view that Popper dubs "the bucket theory of the mind." Philosophers, he says, have generally held onto the bucket theory and rejected realism, but they should have done just the opposite: the bucket theory assumes that knowledge is acquired passively as it pours in through the senses, when actually it is acquired by active trial and error.

Much of the rest of the book is devoted to developing and defending Popper's three-world view: the physical world is world 1, the psychological or mental world is world 2, and the world of objective theories, propositions, arguments, and problems is world 3. World 3, he says, interacts with world 1 via world 2. This interaction is demonstrated, Popper says, by the fact that scientific theories from world 3 lead to new technologies, which are world 1 phenomena. Popper puts world 3 into a biological and evolutionary context: like the webs, nests, and dams created by spiders, birds, and beavers, world 3 is created by human beings; and, like those other products, once it has been created it acquires an objective existence independent of its makers.

In 1973 Popper was awarded an honorary doctorate by the University of Canterbury and the Sonning Prize by the University of Copenhagen. In 1976 he became a fellow of the Royal Society and received the Grand Decoration of Honour in Gold from the Austrian government, the American Political Science Association Lippincott Award for *The Open Society and Its Enemies,* and honorary degrees from the University of Salford and the City University of London.

In *The Self and Its Brain: An Argument for Interactionism* (1977), co-authored with the neurologist Eccles, Popper develops a sustained argument in support of mind-body interactionism and his three-worlds view and criticizes materialism, physicalism, and the claim that the physical world is a causally closed system. In a chapter on the history of the mind/body problem, Popper argues for the questionable thesis that the problem was recognized before the arrival of anything like the modern scientific view of the world.

What is one to make of the three-worlds view? In his *The Human World in the Physical Universe: Consciousness, Free Will, and Evolution* (2001) Maxwell argues that Popper is surely right to hold that the contents of theories need to be distinguished from their linguistic forms and from the causal effects these linguistic forms can have on appropriately educated brains. He says that Popper is also right to stress that in order to make sense of human action, one must attend to the contents of theories. But Maxwell contends that it is quite another matter to argue, as Popper does, that world 3 entities, such as the contents of theories, exist as full-blooded, almost Platonic entities, poltergeistic intellectual objects capable of influencing material phenomena via their influence on conscious minds. Maxwell alleges that Popper has overlooked or ignored the possibility that the material world may be causally closed but not explanatorily closed. That is, he overlooks the possibility that physical phenomena such as these associated with human actions and technology can be explained in two distinct but perhaps interdependent ways: in terms of physical causes, on the one hand, and "personalistically," in terms of the intentions, plans, and ideas of people, on the other hand. Personalistic explanation, on this view, is compatible with, but not reducible to, physical explanation. This view gives the contents of theories a vital role in the personalistic explanation of human actions and the development of technology, without undermining the possibility of a purely physical, causal explanation of these phenomena. Popper insists that his world 3 entities differ from Platonic Forms in that they consist of theories, including false ones, and problems, rather than reified concepts or essences, and in that there is no suggestion that world 3 objects can, like the Forms, be known with certainty. But Maxwell argues that even if Popper's world 3 entities do not have implausible Platonic epistemological features, they do have implausible Platonic metaphysical features in that they have causal effects on the material world via their influence on conscious minds. That the elderly Popper should espouse such a Platonic doctrine, Maxwell notes, almost seems like Plato's revenge for the youthful Popper's onslaught against him.

It is true that in the essay "Epistemology without a Knowing Subject" in *Objective Knowledge,* Popper, despite the title of the essay, does not altogether neglect the personal dimension of the search for knowledge, but he does argue that subjective knowledge is irrelevant to science: only objective, impersonal, "world 3" knowledge is important. But Maxwell points out that this position ignores the fact that objective knowledge stored in books and libraries is of value only insofar as it is understood and used by people. Albert Einstein remarked in his *Ideas and Opinions* (1954) that "Knowledge exists in two forms—lifeless, stored in books, and alive in the consciousness of men. The second form of existence is after all the essential one; the first, indispensable as it may be, occupies only an inferior position." Maxwell comments that Einstein's priorities seem saner than the elderly Popper's, and altogether saner, more humane, and down to earth than the elderly Popper's "spooky" world 3 objects is the viewpoint of the youthful Popper of *The Open Society and Its Enemies,* which sees science and reason in personal, social, and institutional terms, with no appeal to ghostly, quasi-Platonic Forms.

In 1978 Popper received the Karl Renner Prize, as well as honorary doctorates from the University of Guelph, the University of Vienna, and the University of Manheim. The following year he was awarded an

Dust jacket for the 1977 book, co-authored with the neurologist Eccles, in which Popper argues for mind-body interactionism
(Bruccoli Clark Layman Archives)

honorary doctorate by the University of Salzburg and received the American Museum of Natural History Gold Medal for distinguished service to science. In 1980 he received honorary doctorates from the University of Cambridge and the University of Frankfurt am Main and the Ehrenzeichen für Wissenschaft und Kunst from Austria and was made a member of the Order of Merit of the Federal Republic of Germany. He was made a member of the Order of the Companions of Honour of the United Kingdom in 1982.

In 1982 appeared *The Postscript to The Logic of Scientific Discovery,* a three-volume work in which he extends and elaborates some of the doctrines and arguments of *The Logic of Scientific Discovery.* Much of the material was actually written between 1951 and 1956 and had reached proof stage by 1957, but the work was abandoned because Popper suffered from detached retinas and had to have operations on both eyes. After some additions and rewriting, the work finally appeared under the editorship of his former LSE colleague Bartley. Volume one, *Realism and the Aim of Science,* restates and elaborates Popper's views and arguments concerning induction, falsification, corroboration, demarcation, realism, metaphysics, and probability. At one point he contrasts how a scientific paper might be writ-

ten in the style of inductivism and in the critical, problem-solving approach of falsificationism and critical rationalism.

In volume two, *The Open Universe: An Argument for Indeterminism,* Popper distinguishes between "scientific" determinism, which asserts that future states of physical systems can be predicted by means of theories and initial conditions that are specified with sufficient precision, and "metaphysical" determinism, which claims merely that "all events in this world are fixed, or unalterable, or predetermined." Popper gives an argument that, he claims, refutes scientific determinism: even in a universe in which all events occurred in accordance with a deterministic physical theory, T, a predictor placed in an isolated system could not predict all future states of the system with unlimited precision, because it could not acquire up-to-date information about its own state; it could not acquire such information because the attempt to do so would continually alter its state. Popper admits, however, that his argument does not refute a second version of scientific determinism that asserts that past states of physical systems can be predicted by employing prior initial conditions and physical theory. And critics have claimed that Popper ignores a third version of scientific determinism that asserts that the universe is such that a discoverable, true, deterministic "theory of everything" T exists. This version of determinism deserves to be called "scientific," the critics point out, because T is scientifically discoverable; furthermore, once discovered, T will be falsifiable and, hence, scientific by Popper's own standards. Critics also point out that it is curious that Popper, who is elsewhere opposed to instrumentalism and in favor of realism, should discuss at length a version of scientific determinism that is thoroughly instrumentalist in that it makes assertions about predictability but ignores a version of scientific determinism that is much more in keeping with scientific realism in that it makes an assertion about the nature of the universe. This oversight, they claim, seriously weakens Popper's argument for indeterminism.

Popper goes on to argue against metaphysical determinism. He says that nothing in the world of experience warrants it; that determinism of this kind includes a massive amount of redundancy, in that all of the future is contained in any past instantaneous state of the universe; and that it is not easy to see how the view can do justice to the flow of time as it is experienced. Popper all but acknowledges, however, that these arguments are not very convincing. Critics have said that Popper is making the mistake of conflating determinism with the thesis that the universe is four-dimensional, with time as the fourth dimension, so that there are no such things as the objective "now" or the objective "flow of events." In fact, these critics say, such a "block universe" view neither implies nor is implied by determinism.

Volume three, *Quantum Theory and the Schism in Physics,* is concerned with quantum theory and probability, interconnected issues that preoccupied Popper throughout his working life. His positions on these issues, first stated in *Logik der Forschung,* are restated and further developed, taking into account relevant developments such as John Bell's proof that local-hidden-variable versions of quantum theory cannot reproduce all the predictions of orthodox quantum theory and experiments such as those of Alain Aspect that seem to have refuted these local-hidden-variable theories. The main changes in Popper's views are his "propensity" interpretation of probability and his application of it to quantum theory. A propensity is a probability of a *"whole repeatable experimental arrangement."* The probabilistic statements of quantum theory can be interpreted as attributing propensities, not to individual electrons or photons, but to electrons or photons in the context of some specific, repeatable measurement.

The introduction to *Quantum Theory and the Schism in Physics* is an expanded version of a paper that Popper delivered at the International Symposium on the Foundation of Physics in Oberwolfach, Germany, in 1966; it was published in *Quantum Theory and Reality* (1967), edited by Mario Bunge. Responding to this paper, Feyerabend criticized Popper's views on quantum theory in 1968 in "On a Recent Critique of Complementarity." According to Feyerabend, Popper attacks Bohr but ends up defending a position that is quite close to Bohr's. Because propensities are defined in terms of experimental arrangements, Popper's propensity interpretation of quantum theory, like Bohr's, brings in measurement in an essential way. Popper's reply in *Quantum Theory and the Schism in Physics* is that propensities relate to "physical situations" that may, but need not be, experimental arrangements. Some have found this reply to be unsatisfactory; but here, as elsewhere in his work, Popper's ideas, even when they may be wrong or inadequate, are rich in fruitful suggestions and implications for further development.

After *Postscript to the Logic of Scientific Discovery* Popper published several collections of essays restating and elaborating themes of his earlier works: *Auf der Suche nach einer besseren Welt: Vorträge und Aufsätze aus dreissig Jahren* (1984; translated as *In Search of a Better World: Lectures and Essays from Thirty Years,* 1992), *A World of Propensities* (1990), and *The Myth of the Framework: In Defence of Science and Rationality* (1994). Hennie Popper died of cancer in 1985. In his last years Popper continued to be showered with honors, including the Prix Alexis de Tocqueville in 1984, the International Prize of the Catalonian Institute of Mediterranean Studies in 1989, honorary Ph.D. degrees from the University of Eichstatt and the University of Madrid in 1991, and the Kyoto Prize of the Inamori Foundation and an honorary Ph.D. from the University of Athens in 1992. Academic societies in which he was a member, honorary member, or fellow included the International Academy for Philosophy of Science; the Academic Internationale d'Histoire des Sciences; the British delegation to the Academie Européenne des Sciences, des Arts, et des Lettres; the Institut de France; the Academie Royale Belgique; the American Academy of Arts and Sciences; the British Society for the History of Science; the Aristotelian Society; the British Society for the Philosophy of Science; the Association for Symbolic Logic; the Royal Institute of Philosophy; the Royal Society of New Zealand; and the Harvard University chapter of Phi Beta Kappa. Many conferences were dedicated to discussions of his philosophy.

Karl Popper died in Croydon on 17 September 1994 of pneumonia, cancer, and kidney failure, a week after undergoing an operation. Posthumous collections of his work include *Knowledge and the Body-Mind Problem: In Defence of Interaction* (1994), *Alles Leben ist Problemlösen: Über Erkenntnis, Geschichte und Politik* (1994; translated as

All Life Is Problem Solving, 1999), *The Lesson of This Century: With Two Talks on Freedom and the Democratic State* (1997), and *The World of Parmenides: Essays on the Presocratic Enlightenment* (1998). During his working life of some seventy-five years Popper produced an immense body of work: the bibliography of his publications comprises more than 1,200 entries, including reprints and translations.

Bibliography:

T. E. Hansen, "Bibliography of the Writings of Karl Popper," in *The Philosophy of Karl Popper*, edited by Paul Arthur Schilpp (La Salle, Ill.: Open Court, 1974), pp. 1201–1287.

Biographies:

J. Watkins, "Karl Popper: A Memoir," *American Scholar*, 66 (1977): 205–219;

Watkins, "Karl Raimund Popper 1902–1994," *Proceedings of the British Academy*, 94 (1997): 645–684;

David Miller, "Sir Karl Raimund Popper, C. H., F. B. A.," *Biographical Memoirs of Fellows of the Royal Society*, 43 (1997): 367–409;

Malachi H. Hacohen, *Karl Popper: The Formative Years, 1902–1945. Politics and Philosophy in Interwar Vienna* (New York & Cambridge: Cambridge University Press, 2000).

References:

Theodor W. Adorno and others, *The Positivist Dispute in German Sociology*, translated by Glyn Adey and David Frisby (London: Heinemann, 1976);

Joseph Agassi, *A Philosopher's Apprentice: In Karl Popper's Workshop*, series in the Philosophy of Karl R. Popper and Critical Rationalism, volume 5 (Amsterdam, Netherlands & Atlanta: Rodopi, 1993);

Hans Albert, *Between Social Science, Religion and Politics: Essays in Critical Rationalism*, Series in the Philosophy of Karl R. Popper and Critical Rationalism / Schriftenreihe zur Philosophie Karl R. Poppers und des kritischen Rationalismus, volume 13 (Amsterdam: Rodopi, 1999);

Dariusz Aleksandrowicz and Hans Günther Russ, eds., *Realismus, Disziplin, Interdisziplinarität*, Series in the Philosophy of Karl R. Popper and Critical Rationalism / Schriftenreihe zur Philosophie Karl R. Poppers und des kritischen Rationalismus, volume 14 (Amsterdam: Rodopi, 2001);

Renford Bambrough, ed., *Plato, Popper and Politics: Some Contributions to a Modern Controversy* (Cambridge: Heffer, 1967; New York: Barnes & Noble, 1967);

William Berkson and John Wettersten, *Learning from Error: Karl Popper's Psychology of Learning* (La Salle, Ill.: Open Court, 1984);

Mario Bunge, ed., *The Critical Approach to Science and Philosophy* (New York: Free Press of Glencoe, 1964; London: Collier-Macmillan, 1964);

Gregory Curie and Alan Musgrave, eds., *Popper and the Human Sciences* (The Hague & Boston: Nijhoff, 1985);

David Edmonds and John Eidinow, *Wittgenstein's Poker: The Story of a Ten-Minute Argument between Two Great Philosophers* (London: Faber & Faber, 2001; New York: Ecco, 2001);

Paul Feyerabend, "On a Recent Critique of Complementarity," *Philosophy of Science*, 35 (1968): 309–331; 36 (1969): 82–105;

Volker Gadenne, ed., *Kritischer Rationalismus und Pragmatismus*, Series in the Philosophy of Karl R. Popper and Critical Rationalism / Schriftenreihe zur Philosophie Karl R. Poppers und des kritischen Rationalismus, volume 10 (Amsterdam & Atlanta: Rodopi, 1998);

Bernward Gesang, *Wahrheitskriterien im kritischen Rationalismus: Ein Versuch zur Synthese analytischer, evolutionärer und kritisch-rationaler Ansätze*, Series in the Philosophy of Karl R. Popper and Critical Rationalism / Schriftenreihe zur Philosophie Karl R. Poppers und des kritischen Rationalismus, volume 7 (Amsterdam: Rodopi, 1995);

Norbert Hinterberger, *Der Kritische Rationalismus und seine antirealistischen Gegner*, series in the Philosophy of Karl R. Popper and Critical Rationalism / Schriftenreihe zur Philosophie Karl R. Poppers und des kritischen Rationalismus, volume 9 (Amsterdam: Rodopi, 1996);

Max Jammer, *The Philosophy of Quantum Mechanics: The Interpretations of Quantum Mechanics in Historical Perspective* (New York: Wiley, 1974), pp. 174–176;

Ian Jarvie and Sandra Pralong, eds., *Popper's Open Society after Fifty Years: The Continuing Relevance of Karl Popper* (London & New York: Routledge, 1999);

Imre Lakatos and Alan Musgrave, eds., *Criticism and the Growth of Knowledge: Proceedings of the International Colloquium in the Philosophy of Science, London, 1965*, volume 4 (London & New York: Cambridge University Press, 1970);

Paul Levinson, ed., *In Pursuit of Truth: Essays on the Philosophy of Karl Popper on the Occasion of His 80th Birthday* (Atlantic Highlands, N.J.: Humanities Press, 1982; Sussex: Harvester, 1982);

Bryan Magee, *Popper* (London: Fontana, 1973);

Nicholas Maxwell, *The Comprehensibility of the Universe: A New Conception of Science* (Oxford: Clarendon Press, 1998; New York: Oxford University Press, 1998);

Maxwell, "A Critique of Popper's Views of Scientific Method," *Philosophy of Science*, 39 (1972): 131–152;

Maxwell, *From Knowledge to Wisdom: A Revolution in the Aims and Methods of Science* (Oxford & New York: Blackwell, 1984);

Maxwell, *The Human World in the Physical Universe: Consciousness, Free Will, and Evolution* (Lanham, Md.: Rowman & Littlefield, 2001);

Maxwell, "Instead of Particles and Fields," *Foundations of Physics,* 12 (1982): 607–631;

Maxwell, "Particle Creation as the Quantum Condition for Probabilistic Events to Occur," *Physics Letters: A,* 187 (1994): 351–355;

Maxwell, "Quantum Propensiton Theory," *British Journal for the Philosophy of Science,* 39 (1988): 1–50;

David Miller, *Critical Rationalism: A Restatement and Defence* (Chicago: Open Court, 1994);

Miller, "Popper's Qualitative Theory of Verisimilitude," *British Journal for the Philosophy of Science,* 25 (1974): 166–177;

P. W. Musgrave, *Essays on Realism and Rationalism,* Series in the Philosophy of Karl R. Popper and Critical Rationalism / Schriftenreihe zur Philosophie Karl R. Poppers und des kritischen Rationalismus, volume 12 (Amsterdam: Rodopi, 1999);

Anthony O'Hear, ed., *Karl Popper: Philosophy and Problems* (Cambridge & New York: Cambridge University Press, 1995);

Sheldon Saul Richmond, *Aesthetic Criteria: Gombrich and the Philosophies of Science of Popper and Polanyi,* Series in the Philosophy of Karl R. Popper and Critical Rationalism / Schriftenreihe zur Philosophie Karl R. Poppers und des kritischen Rationalismus, volume 1 (Amsterdam: Rodopi, 1994);

Paul Arthur Schilpp, ed., *The Philosophy of Karl Popper,* 2 volumes, The Library of Living Philosophers, volume 14 (La Salle, Ill.: Open Court, 1974);

Jeremy Shearmur, *The Political Thought of Karl Popper* (London & New York: Routledge, 1996);

Colin Simkin, *Popper's Views on Natural and Social Science* (Leiden, Netherlands & New York: Brill, 1993);

P. Tichý, "On Popper's Definition of Verisimilitude," *British Journal for the Philosophy of Science,* 25 (1974): 155–160;

Gerhard Zecha, ed., *Critical Rationalism and Educational Discourse,* Series in the Philosophy of Karl R. Popper and Critical Rationalism / Schriftenreihe zur Philosophie Karl R. Poppers und des kritischen Rationalismus, volume 11 (Amsterdam: Rodopi, 1999).

Papers:

The Hoover Institute at Stanford University is the main repository for Karl Popper's papers, including manuscripts for his works from 1927 to 1980, correspondence from 1932 to 1987, teaching materials from 1937 to 1970, conference proceedings, letters of reference, and additional biographical material. The register can be accessed on the Internet via the Karl Popper Web: <www.eeng.dcu.ie/~tkpw/>. Microfilmed copies of the Hoover originals are held by the London School of Economics and Political Science; the Karl Popper Institute in Vienna; the Karl-Popper-Sammlung at the University of Klagenfurt, Austria; and the Popper Project at Central European University in Budapest.

Frank P. Ramsey

(22 February 1903 – 19 January 1930)

Pascal Engel
University of Paris–Sorbonne

BOOKS: *The Foundations of Mathematics and Other Logical Essays,* edited by Richard B. Braithwaite, International Library of Psychology, Philosophy, and Scientific Method, volume 5 (London: Kegan Paul, Trench, Trübner / New York: Harcourt, Brace, 1931); revised and enlarged as *Foundations: Essays in Philosophy, Logic, Mathematics, and Economics,* edited by D. H. Mellor (London: Routledge & Kegan Paul, 1978; Atlantic Highlands, N.J.: Humanities Press, 1978); revised as *Philosophical Papers,* edited by Mellor (Cambridge & New York: Cambridge University Press, 1990);

On Truth: Original Manuscript Materials (1927–1929) from the Ramsey Collection at the University of Pittsburgh, edited by Nicholas Rescher and Ulrich Majer (Dordrecht, Netherlands & Boston: Kluwer Academic, 1990);

Notes on Philosophy, Probability and Mathematics, edited by Maria Carla Galavotti (Naples: Bibliopolis, 1991).

In spite of his short life and consequently abbreviated career, Frank P. Ramsey is a major figure in twentieth-century British philosophy. His work ranges from logic to economics, probability and decision theory, epistemology, and metaphysics. He is considered, with Bertrand Russell, G. E. Moore, and Ludwig Wittgenstein, one of the main representatives of Cambridge philosophy during the first part of the century, and his work has inspired many contemporary philosophers in the analytic tradition.

Frank Plumpton Ramsey was born in Cambridge on 22 February 1903 to Arthur Stanley Ramsey, a mathematician and president of Magdalene College of the University of Cambridge, and Agnes Mary Ramsey, née Wilson. Ramsey's brother, Michael, went on to become archbishop of Canterbury. Ramsey was educated at Winchester, one of England's leading public schools, and at Trinity College, Cambridge. At Cambridge he became acquainted in 1921 with the economist John Maynard Keynes, who became his mentor and introduced him

Frank P. Ramsey

to the famous discussion group the Cambridge Apostles, of which he became a member, and to the philosophers Moore, Russell, and Alfred North Whitehead, all of whom quickly recognized his genius. Self-taught in German, Ramsey read Wittgenstein's *Logisch-Philosophische Abhandlung* (1921) under the direction of his teacher C. K. Ogden and assisted Ogden in translating the work under the title suggested by Moore:

Tractatus Logico-Philosophicus (1922). He received a bachelor's degree in mathematics with first-class honors in 1923. At twenty-one he became a fellow of King's College; two years later he was named lecturer in mathematics. His interests included all of the topics that were then at the center of Cambridge intellectual life: mathematics, logic, economics, and social and political theory. He mastered the substance of Whitehead and Russell's *Principia Mathematica* (1910–1913), as well as most of the work done in mathematical economics in Cambridge.

In 1923 Ramsey met Wittgenstein for the first time in the Austrian village of Puchberg, where the latter was teaching at an elementary school. Their conversations resulted in modifications to the second edition of the *Tractatus Logico-Philosophicus,* published in 1923, and in an extended correspondence on related philosophical and logical matters. The two men met again in Vienna in 1924.

In September 1925 Ramsey married Lettice Baker; they had two daughters, Jane and Sarah. He met Wittgenstein once more, in 1929; the prospect of discussing philosophy with Ramsey was one of the reasons Wittgenstein had come back to Cambridge, although, according to Wittgenstein's diaries, their personal relationship was sometimes strained. Many of Wittgenstein's doctrines of the 1930s and later can be traced to Ramsey's influence.

Ramsey was a tall, well-built man; he weighed, according to his own report, about seventeen stone (238 pounds). He died at Guy's Hospital in London on 19 January 1930 of jaundice contracted after an operation. Keynes declared in an obituary that

> The loss of Ramsey is . . . to his friends, for whom his personal qualities joined most harmoniously with his intellectual powers, one which it will take long to forget. His bulky Johnsonian frame, his spontaneous gurgling laugh, the simplicity of his feelings and reactions, half-alarming sometimes and occasionally almost cruel in their directness and literalness, his honesty of mind and heart, his modesty, and the amazing, easy sufficiency of the intellectual machine which ground away between his wide temples and broad smiling face, have been taken from us at the height of their excellence and before their harvest of work and life could be gathered.

In 1931 Ramsey's friend and former pupil Richard B. Braithwaite published *The Foundations of Mathematics and Other Logical Essays,* a collection of papers that became classics in analytic philosophy, logic, and economics: "A Critical Notice of Wittgenstein's *Tractatus*" (1923), "The Foundations of Mathematics" (1925), "Universals" (1925), "Mathematical Logic" (1926), "Truth and Probability" (1927), "A

Contribution to the Theory of Taxation" (1927), "A Mathematical Theory of Saving" (1928), "Facts and Propositions" (1927), "On a Problem of Formal Logic" (1928), "Reasonable Degree of Belief" (1928), "Statistics" (1928), "Chance" (1928), "Theories" (1929), "General Propositions and Causality" (1929), "Probability and Partial Belief" (1929), "Knowledge" (1929), "Causal Qualities" (1929), and "Philosophy" (1929). Some of these papers are short notes, the full import of which was not perceived at once; the significance of others, such as the title essay, was recognized immediately. "Truth and Probability," which lays the foundations of the subjective approach to probability theory and decision theory, and the papers on economics began to be appreciated only in the 1950s, when these disciplines were systematized by mathematicians and economists such as Leonard J. Savage, John Von Neumann, and Oscar Morgenstern. One reason the importance of these works was not recognized at once was their originality; another is Ramsey's style of writing, which is often elliptical and understated. In 1978 the collection, with additions, was republished by D. H. Mellor under the title *Foundations: Essays in Philosophy, Logic, Mathematics, and Economics.* In 1990 Nicholas Rescher and Ulrich Majer published Ramsey's unfinished manuscript *On Truth,* and in 1991 Maria Carla Galavotti published a collection of manuscripts from the Ramsey Collection at the Hillman Library of the University of Pittsburgh as *Notes on Philosophy, Probability and Mathematics.*

Although he was well read in classical philosophy, Ramsey conceived of philosophy as a technical discipline closely allied to logic. He shared Russell's ideal of a scientific philosophy and Wittgenstein's and Moore's conception of philosophy as the clarification of ideas. In "A Critical Notice of Wittgenstein's *Tractatus*" he calls Russell's analysis of descriptions of nonexistent objects, such as the present king of France, "a paradigm of philosophy," and he attempted to give such analyses of several important philosophical concepts.

Ramsey was, however, also critical of Russell's and Wittgenstein's work. In a piece used as the epilogue to *The Foundations of Mathematics and Other Logical Essays,* Ramsey responds to Russell's conception of philosophy as parasitic on scientific knowledge of nature:

> Where I seem to differ from some of my friends is in attaching little importance to physical size. I don't feel in the least humble before the vastness of the heavens. The stars may be large, but they cannot think or love; and these are qualities which impress me far more than size does. I take no credit for weighing nearly seventeen stone. My picture of the world is drawn in perspective,

and not like a model to scale. The foreground is occupied by human beings and the stars are all as small as threepenny bits. I don't really believe in astronomy, except as a complicated description of part of the course of human and possibly animal sensation. I apply my perspective not merely to space but also to time. In time the world will cool and everything will die; but that is a long time off still, and its present value at compound discount is almost nothing.

Of Wittgenstein he says in "Philosophy": "The chief proposition of philosophy is that philosophy is nonsense. And again we must take seriously that it is nonsense, and not pretend, as Wittgenstein does, that it is serious nonsense." He did not approve of Wittgenstein's mystical tone, saying with some irony of Wittgenstein's famous dictum, "What we cannot speak about we must pass over in silence": "what we can't say we can't say, and we can't whistle it either."

Ramsey devoted his first efforts to understanding and criticizing Whitehead and Russell's *Principia Mathematica,* which sets out to reduce mathematics to logic. "The Foundations of Mathematics" is an attempt to revise Russell's "theory of logical types" as a solution to paradoxes such as the paradox of the class of classes that are not members of themselves and the "liar paradox." The paradox of the class of classes that are not members of themselves, which has come to be known as Russell's Paradox, begins with what seems to be the obvious fact that some classes, such as the class of all classes, are members of themselves, while other classes, such as the class of all philosophers, are not members of themselves. What, then, of the class of all classes that are not members of themselves? If this class is a member of itself, then it cannot be a member of itself; but if it is not a member of itself, then it *is* a member of itself. Thus, it seems, at one and the same time, both to be and not to be a member of itself, which violates the principle of contradiction. The classical form of the liar paradox is "Epimenides the Cretan says, 'All Cretans are liars,'" meaning that everything any Cretan says is a lie. Thus, his own statement, if true, is a lie and, therefore, false; but if it is false, it supports his contention and is, therefore, true. The paradox can be put more simply as "This sentence is false": if the sentence is true, it is false; but if it is false, it is true. Thus, it seems to be both true and false at the same time—again violating the principle of contradiction. Russell held that to avoid the first kind of paradox one had to arrange entities into hierarchies of types: individuals, classes of individuals, classes of classes, classes of classes of classes, and so forth. Thus, a class can only be a member of a class of a higher type; since no class can be a member of

Ramsey on Red Pike in the Lake District in 1925
(photograph by Lettice Ramsey)

itself, the paradox disappears. To solve the liar paradox and other semantic paradoxes Russell proposed the "ramified" theory of types, according to which statements are arranged in a hierarchy so that a statement can refer only to statements of a lower type; thus, self-referential statements such as "This statement is false" become meaningless.

Ramsey's chief contribution consists in making a distinction, which is today widely accepted, between paradoxes of the "logical" kind, such as the paradox of class membership, and paradoxes of the "semantical" kind, such as the liar paradox. The first do not require Russell's ramified hierarchy; the second are treated by postulating a hierarchy of symbols instead of a hierarchy of objects. The latter solution anticipates, in part, one that the Polish logician Alfred Tarski later proposed to the liar paradox, which involves a hierarchy of languages and metalanguages.

In "Mathematical Logic" Ramsey defends Whitehead and Russell's reduction of mathematics to logic against David Hilbert's formalism, according to which mathematics concerns the manipulation of possibly meaningless symbols according to a set of prescribed rules, and L. E. J. Brouwer's intuitionism, which holds that mathematics is a mental construction and that mathematical objects have no existence independent of thought. In "On a Problem of Formal Logic," first published in 1928, Ramsey demonstrates a theorem, known today as "Ramsey's theorem," which has been shown to be equivalent in one of its versions to Kurt Gödel's famous incompleteness theorem, which did not appear until three years later. According to these theorems, it is impossible for a formal system, such as arithmetic, to be both fully consistent and totally complete. This paper gave rise to a whole branch of combinatorial analysis—which is itself a branch of logic—called "Ramsey theory." In a paper first published in 1989, "Principles of Finitist Mathematics," Ramsey abandons his logicist standpoint and comes close to an intuitionist position in the philosophy of mathematics.

Of all of Ramsey's contributions, those that are today considered the most outstanding belong to the theory of probability and decision theory. His long essay "Truth and Probability" is particularly regarded as a classic. It sets forth the "subjective" or "personalist" conception of probability that was anticipated in the writings of the British mathematician Thomas Bayes in the eighteenth century and developed independently by the Italian mathematician Bruno de Finetti in the 1930s. According to this conception, the probability of a proposition is equivalent to a subject's degree of belief in the proposition. Belief, in turn, is defined in terms of actions that an agent would be disposed to take in some possible set of circumstances—not his or her actual actions. Ramsey treats actions as bets: that is, a bet is proposed to an agent to see what the lowest stakes are that the agent will accept. These need not be literal bets: as Ramsey says, "in all our life we are in a sense betting," as when one gambles that the train one intends to catch will be on time. Ramsey uses what he calls "a general psychological theory, today universally rejected, but approximately true," according to which "we act in the way which we consider as most likely to realize the objects of our desires." The choices made by an agent, then, are the products of two psychological factors: the values that the agent places on the results of the various actions that are available to be performed in the circumstances, and the probability that the agent attributes to these results occurring if the actions are performed. If one knows the agent's degrees of belief in, or "subjective probabilities" for, various outcomes, it is easy to calculate his or her "subjective utilities," or preferences,

from the actions that the agent chooses to perform; conversely, if one knows the agent's preferences, it is easy to infer his or her degrees of belief from his or her actions. The problem is to discover the agent's preferences and beliefs when one only has information about his or her actions. Ramsey's procedure consists in postulating propositions that are "ethically neutral"—a proposition or statement is ethically neutral if two possible worlds that differ only with regard to the truth of that proposition are of equal value. Such ethically neutral propositions are believed at a degree of one half if and only if the agent is indifferent with respect to two bets: winning A if the proposition is true and winning B otherwise, on the one hand, and winning B if the proposition is true and winning A otherwise, on the other hand. For instance, if the agent is indifferent between, on the one hand, getting $100 if it rains tomorrow and getting nothing if it does not rain, and, on the other hand, getting nothing if it rains and getting $100 if it does not rain, then he or she considers it equally probable that it will rain as that it will not rain. From this point Ramsey is able to calculate a scale of intermediate degrees of belief and to derive the "fundamental laws of partial belief" that are the basic axioms of the calculus of probabilities; these axioms will necessarily be true of all coherent systems of beliefs. This claim is today known as the "Dutch book argument" in favor of the Bayesian conception of decision theory: a clever bookmaker could make and win a series of bets against a person holding an incoherent system of beliefs. Rationality is thus identified as the coherence of an agent's subjective probabilities and preferences. Nevertheless, Ramsey, unlike modern Bayesian theorists, does not take his decision theory to prescribe "acting in the way we think most likely to realize the objects of our desires"; he takes it to be merely an approximation to the truth about the way people do behave. During the second half of the twentieth century, Ramsey's methods of measuring belief and preference were rediscovered by the statistician Savage and applied in mathematical psychology by philosophers such as Patrick Suppes and Donald Davidson to give rise to a huge literature on decision making, expected utility, and scientific inference. Ramsey's conception of probability, however, is not totally subjectivist: he thinks that connections exist between subjective degrees of belief and objective frequencies of events.

Ramsey's analysis of belief leads him to a new conception of the nature of logic: deductive or formal logic, he says, is a "logic of coherence"; but it is not the whole of logic: there is also a logic of discovery, which he calls "the logic of truth" or "human logic."

006-02-02 (6)

The General Nature of Philosophy   April 1928

1. Philosophy consists of logical analysis and clarification but not all of this is regarded as philosophy, since the clarification of ideas of a particular science is often regarded as part of that science. Only when it is of sufficient general importance is it called philosophy.

2. There are fundamental difficulties about the nature of analysis (or philosophy) of which we may take first the question whether it relates to things or to words. Thus is a typical result of analysis such as "Justice is the will of the stronger" to be regarded as giving us information about justice or the word "justice".

3. It seems impossible to take it as being about justice, because then it becomes a pure tautology; for it is evidently intended as definition not as a description. It does not assert as a fact that the stronger always will what is just, but that that is what justice is, that 'this is just' and 'this is the will of the stronger' are the same proposition. Consequently all that we have discovered by our pains is that the will of the stronger is the will of the stronger. Philosophy is not so trivial as this.

An additional reason for saying that analysis is not
4. analysis of things is that we can perfectly well ask for an analysis of "the lion beat the unicorn" in which case there is nothing no fact to analyse. Obviously, however, if we wished to we could escape this objection

One of the notes that Ramsey left behind at his death (Ramsey Collection, Hillman Library of the University of Pittsburgh)

The best-justified beliefs are those that have the best chances of success and are correlated with the highest relative frequencies of events. These general beliefs are laws and become mental habits. Thus, Ramsey accepts the "pragmatist" principle that the beliefs that are the most likely to be true are those that have the best chances of success. This position is not, however, the crude pragmatist doctrine that identifies truth with usefulness; it is the distinctive view that the meaning of a belief is determined by its "utility conditions," or, those conditions under which a proposition or thought is useful or leads to the success of the actions of the one who thinks it, given that person's desires. Ramsey says in "Truth and Probability" that "any set of actions for whose utility p is a necessary and sufficient condition might be called a belief that p, and so would be true if p, i.e. if they are useful." Ramsey's pragmatism was inspired by that of the American philosopher Charles Sanders Peirce, whose doctrines he was among the first in Cambridge to appreciate. Like Peirce, Ramsey believed that in the long run, or at the ideal limit of scientific inquiry, the truth will be reached.

In another paper that is considered a classic, "Facts and Propositions," Ramsey formulates what has come to be called a "redundantist" theory of truth. According to this view, the concept of truth amounts to nothing more than the simple equivalence of "It is true that p" and "p" (p stands for any proposition); "true" is a redundant or superfluous predicate that does not express any "deep" property of thoughts or propositions, such as correspondence to facts or coherence with one's other beliefs. Ramsey shows that statements of the form "What you said is true" can be reformulated as "For all p, if you asserted that p, then p." This view, which was held later by some logical positivist philosophers and by Wittgenstein, is supposed to eliminate "metaphysical" anxieties about the nature or essence of truth; today it is debated within the philosophy of language under the name "deflationary conception of truth." But given that Ramsey identified the truth conditions of beliefs with their utility conditions, and that he defends an ideal-limit conception of truth, it is clear that he did not propose to get rid of the concept of truth altogether. Instead, he reconceived the problem of the truth of propositions as the problem of the nature of belief.

In the brief note "Knowledge" Ramsey says that one knows that p if one has a reliable method for knowing that p. This statement is the first formulation of what is now called the "reliabilist" or "causal" theory of knowledge. Reliable beliefs are those that lead, in the long run, to the success of the human species and that, therefore, become habits of mind. Some writers have drawn from this idea a biological-evolutionary conception of belief and meaning known as "teleosemantics."

In "General Propositions and Causality" Ramsey says that empirical beliefs about particular facts, such as "this is a lump of sugar," are "maps by which we steer" that "help us to move in the neighbouring space." General beliefs and laws, such as "sugar dissolves in water," are neither true nor false and have no cognitive content: instead, they express rules that one follows to form particular maps. (Wittgenstein held a similar view in the 1930s: a hypothesis is a law for the formation of propositions, he said, but it is not in itself a genuine proposition that describes a state of affairs.) Like the eighteenth-century Scottish empiricist David Hume, who held that causal beliefs are projections of the mind onto the world, Ramsey takes general beliefs and scientific laws to be projections of one's degrees of confidence in singular facts. This notion leads him to analyze universally quantified propositions—that is, statements of the form "For all x, Fx" (which is read "For all x, x is F," or, more simply, "All x are F," as in "All dogs are mammals")—as expressing "an inference that we are at any time prepared to make, given our singular beliefs of the form "'a is F'" (for example, "Lassie is a mammal"). In a 1928 essay, "Universals of Law and of Fact," republished in *Philosophical Papers,* Ramsey holds that a scientific law differs from an accidental regularity because the former would remain a law to someone who was omniscient. The "ultimate laws of nature" are the consequences of the general propositions that one would take as axioms if one knew everything and organized all of that knowledge in the simplest manner within a deductive system. He later renounced this view in "General Propositions and Causality, "because we are not omniscient," but it has played an important role in modern conceptions of the laws of nature. The idea is that scientific laws must track facts; these facts are often conditional, taking the form "If circumstances C obtain, facts of kind F would follow." To accept such a conditional statement, Ramsey says, one tries adding its antecedent (the "If . . ." clause) to one's existing stock of beliefs; if a contradiction follows from this addition, one adjusts one's system of beliefs in the most economical way that will make it coherent with the addition. This position is known today in the field of "epistemic logic" (the logic of belief revision) as "the Ramsey test" for conditional beliefs.

In "Theories" Ramsey defends the view that theoretical statements in science, such as those about protons or genes, do not denote real entities and are neither true nor false. Instead, they serve as instruments for the prediction of observable events and can be eliminated from the language of science through a procedure of rewriting that has come to be called "Ramsey's method for theoretical terms" and that results in what are known as "Ramsey sentences." The method has been widely discussed in the context of positivistic philosophy of science and the debate between "realism" (the view that theoretical entities such as electrons are real) and "instrumentalism" (the view that theories are just convenient means for predicting observations). Some modern philosophers of mind, such as the American David Lewis, have held that Ramsey's method could also be applied to "folk psychology" and to common-sense descriptions of mental phenomena so as to reduce beliefs, desires, hopes, fears, and so forth to physical states of the brain. Others have recommended applying the procedure to the entities posited by economic theory, such as "values," "utilities," and "expectations." Ramsey himself, however, never attempted a reduction of beliefs to behavior or to physical states.

The traditional problem of the nature of abstract entities and universals occupied Cambridge philosophers such as Russell and Wittgenstein. In "Universals" Ramsey rejects the ontological distinction between universals (or properties) and particulars, holding that there is no difference between the statement "Socrates is wise" and the statement "Wisdom is a characteristic of Socrates"; hence, there is no essential distinction between the subject of a proposition and its predicate and, therefore, no distinction between the kinds of entities—particulars and universals—that they purport to denote. This thesis questions one of the main concepts of logic as it has existed since the work of Russell and Gottlob Frege: that there is an asymmetry between the subject and predicate of a proposition. Ramsey says that a logician can take "any type of objects whatever as the subject of his reasoning, and call them individuals, meaning by that simply that he has chosen this type to reason about." Ramsey's argument anticipates the view of philosophers such as Rudolf Carnap and Nelson Goodman that ontology is arbitrary and relative to language. But it is not an argument for the elimination of universals; on the contrary, Ramsey's pragmatism is compatible with the existence of universals.

Ramsey's work in economic theory was also rediscovered long after his death. His discussions of the views of Cambridge economists, such as Keynes and Arthur Pigou, led him to important contributions in mathematical economics. His two major papers in the field, "A Contribution to the Theory of Taxation" and "A Mathematical Theory of Saving" were published in *The Economic Journal* in 1927 and 1928, respectively, but they were not appreciated until around 1960. The problem with which he deals in his paper on taxation is how to adjust sales-tax rates to increase government revenue by a certain amount, while minimizing the negative effects on consumer well-being. Ramsey's answer is that the rates should be set so that they reduce the production of each taxed commodity in the same proportion; to minimize the loss of income for the consumer, taxes must be augmented in such a way that the pattern of consumption is maintained. Ramsey presupposes that one can ignore the fact that individual consumers have different sets of values, or "utility functions" (the problem of "interpersonal utility comparisons"), and he proposes that the general utility function can be expressed in a quadratic equation. In economics Ramsey's theory led to the notion of "Ramsey prices," a notion that was elaborated by Pigou, Marcel Boiteux, and Paul Samuelson in the 1970s and that is used today in the theory of the firm. It also has implications for the theory of general equilibrium, as well as for market theory through the theorem of "the weak invisible hand."

Ramsey's paper on savings answers a question he was asked by Keynes: what proportion of its income should a nation save? Ramsey's solution is that the savings rate multiplied by the money's marginal utility (the increase in well-being produced by the addition of the next unit of money) should equal the quantity by which the total sum of utility differs from the maximal possible rate. This result holds only if the population and the citizens' preferences are stable (this restriction is known as the "Keynes-Ramsey" rule). The main contribution of this paper consists in proposing a method of analysis, "the intertemporal maximization of well-being," by using the techniques of "dynamical optimization"—in this case, the calculus of variations. The method is called "Ramsey's model." Ramsey's paper on savings is generally considered one of the most important contributions to mathematical economy, since it sets the foundations of the theories of accumulation and optimal growth, as well as the general theory of saving and interest rates. Ramsey did not live to draw out the implications of his economic theories for social and political philosophy, but it is clear from some notes that he left for papers on socialism, happiness, and equality that he had such concerns.

If one considers the breadth and significance of Frank P. Ramsey's contributions, and the number of scientific and philosophical principles that bear his name, one can only be astonished by the imprint he left on the history of ideas in such a short career. His pioneering work in so many fields not only led to many independent developments but also constituted a theoretical system that is regarded today as one of the greatest achievements of twentieth-century philosophy.

Letters:

Ludwig Wittgenstein, *Letters to C. K. Ogden with Comments on the English Translation of the* Tractatus Logico-Philosophicus; *with an Appendix of Letters by Frank Plumpton Ramsey,* edited by Georg Henrik von Wright (Oxford: Blackwell, 1973; Boston: Routledge & Kegan Paul, 1973).

Biographies:

Richard B. Braithwaite, "Frank Plumpton Ramsey," *Journal of the London Mathematical Society,* 6 (1931): 75–78;

John Maynard Keynes, "Frank Plumpton Ramsey," in his *Essays in Biography* (London: Macmillan, 1933), pp. 293–300;

F. Harary, "A Tribute to Frank P. Ramsey, 1903–1930," *Journal of Graph Theory,* 7 (1983): 1–7;

Jérôme Dokic and Pascal Engel, *Ramsey, vérité et succès* (Paris: Presses Universitaires de France, 2001).

References:

Richard Jeffrey, *The Logic of Decision,* second edition (Chicago: University of Chicago Press, 1983), pp. 40–58, 153–154, 157–159;

David Lewis, "Psychophysical and Theoretical Identifications," in his *Philosophical Papers,* volume 1 (Oxford & New York: Oxford University Press, 1983);

D. H. Mellor, ed., *Prospects for Pragmatism: Essays in Memory of F. P. Ramsey* (Cambridge: Cambridge University Press, 1980);

Nils-Eric Sahlin, *The Philosophy of F. P. Ramsey* (Cambridge & New York: Cambridge University Press, 1990);

Leonard J. Savage, *The Foundations of Statistics,* revised edition (New York: Dover, 1972), pp. 7, 60, 96–97;

Raffaella Simili, ed., *L'epistemologia di Cambridge: 1850–1950* (Bologna: Il Mulino, 1987), pp. 329–355.

Papers:

Frank P. Ramsey's papers are in the Archives of Scientific Philosophy in the Twentieth Century at the University of Pittsburgh.

Bertrand Russell

(18 May 1872 – 2 February 1970)

Elizabeth R. Eames
Southern Illinois University at Carbondale

See also the Russell entry in *DLB 100: Modern British Essayists, Second Series.*

BOOKS: *German Social Democracy: Six Lectures,* Studies in Economics and Political Science, volume 7, by Russell and Alys Russell (London & New York: Longmans, Green, 1896; New York: Simon & Schuster, 1965);

An Essay on the Foundations of Geometry (Cambridge: Cambridge University Press, 1897; New York: Dover, 1956);

A Critical Exposition of the Philosophy of Leibniz: With an Appendix of Leading Passages (Cambridge: Cambridge University Press, 1900); republished as *The Philosophy of Leibniz* (New York: Macmillan, 1937);

The Principles of Mathematics (Cambridge: Cambridge University Press, 1903; revised edition, London: Allen & Unwin, 1937; New York: Norton, 1938);

Philosophical Essays (London & New York: Longmans, Green, 1910; revised edition, London: Allen & Unwin, 1966; New York: Simon & Schuster, 1966);

Principia Mathematica, 3 volumes, by Russell and Alfred North Whitehead (Cambridge: Cambridge University Press, 1910–1913; revised edition, Cambridge & New York: Cambridge University Press, 1927);

The Problems of Philosophy (London: Williams & Norgate, 1912; New York: Holt, 1912);

Our Knowledge of the External World as a Field for Scientific Method in Philosophy (London: Allen & Unwin, 1914; revised, 1926; Chicago & London: Open Court, 1914);

Scientific Method in Philosophy: The Herbert Spencer Lecture, 1914 (Oxford: Clarendon Press, 1914);

War: The Offspring of Fear (London: Union of Democratic Control, 1914);

Justice in War-Time (Chicago & London: Open Court, 1916; London: Allen & Unwin, 1916);

Bertrand Russell (photograph © BBC)

Principles of Social Reconstruction (London: Allen & Unwin, 1916); republished as *Why Men Fight: A Method of Abolishing the International Duel* (New York: Century, 1916);

Political Ideals (New York: Century, 1917; London: Allen & Unwin, 1963);

Mysticism and Logic, And Other Essays (London & New York: Longmans, Green, 1917); republished as *A Free Man's Worship, and Other Essays* (London: Unwin, 1976);

Roads to Freedom: Socialism, Anarchism, and Syndicalism, Library of Philosophy (London: Allen & Unwin,

203

1918); republished as *Proposed Roads to Freedom: Socialism, Anarchism, and Syndicalism* (New York: Holt, 1919);

Introduction to Mathematical Philosophy (London: Allen & Unwin, 1919; New York: Macmillan, 1919);

The Practice and Theory of Bolshevism (London: Allen & Unwin, 1920); republished as *Bolshevism: Practice and Theory* (New York: Harcourt, Brace & Howe, 1920);

The Analysis of Mind (London: Allen & Unwin, 1921; New York: Macmillan, 1921);

Free Thought and Official Propaganda, Conway Memorial Lecture, no. 13 (New York: Huebsch, 1922; London: Watts, 1922);

The Problem of China (London: Allen & Unwin, 1922; New York: Century, 1922);

The Prospects of Industrial Civilization, by Russell and Dora Russell (New York & London: Century, 1923; London: Allen & Unwin, 1923);

The ABC of Atoms (New York: Dutton, 1923; London: Kegan Paul, Trench, Trübner, 1923; revised, 1925);

Icarus; or, The Future of Science (New York: Dutton, 1924; London: Kegan Paul, Trench, Trübner, 1924);

The ABC of Relativity (New York & London: Harper, 1925; London: Kegan Paul, Trench, Trübner, 1925; revised edition, edited by Felix Pirani, London: Allen & Unwin, 1958);

What I Believe (New York: Dutton, 1925; London: Kegan Paul, Trench, Trübner, 1925);

On Education, Especially in Early Childhood (London: Allen & Unwin, 1926); republished as *Education and the Good Life* (New York: Liveright, 1926);

Why I Am Not a Christian (London: Watts, 1927; Girard, Kans.: Haldeman-Julius, 1929); enlarged as *Why I am Not a Christian and Other Essays on Religion and Related Subjects,* edited by Paul Edwards (London: Allen & Unwin, 1957; New York: Simon & Schuster, 1957);

The Analysis of Matter (London: Kegan Paul, Trench, Trübner, 1927; New York: Harcourt, Brace, 1927);

An Outline of Philosophy (London: Allen & Unwin, 1927); republished as *Philosophy* (New York: Norton, 1927);

Selected Papers of Bertrand Russell (New York: Modern Library, 1927);

Sceptical Essays (London: Allen & Unwin, 1928; New York: Norton, 1928);

Marriage and Morals (London: Allen & Unwin, 1929; New York: Liveright, 1929);

Has Religion Made Useful Contributions to Civilization? An Examination and a Criticism (London: Watts, 1930; Girard, Kans.: Haldeman-Julius, n.d.);

The Conquest of Happiness (London: Allen & Unwin, 1930; New York: Liveright, 1930);

The Scientific Outlook (London: Allen & Unwin, 1931; New York: Norton, 1931);

Education and the Social Order (London: Allen & Unwin, 1932); republished as *Education and the Modern World* (New York: Norton, 1932);

Freedom and Organization 1814–1914 (London: Allen & Unwin, 1934); republished as *Freedom versus Organization 1814–1914* (New York: Norton, 1934);

In Praise of Idleness and Other Essays (London: Allen & Unwin, 1935; New York: Norton, 1935);

Religion and Science (London: Butterworth, 1935; New York: Holt, 1935);

Which Way to Peace? (London: Joseph, 1936);

Power: A New Social Analysis (London: Allen & Unwin, 1938; New York: Norton, 1938);

An Inquiry into Meaning and Truth (London: Allen & Unwin, 1940; New York: Norton, 1940);

Let the People Think: A Selection of Essays, Thinker's Library, no. 84 (London: Watts, 1941);

How to Become a Philosopher: The Art of Rational Conjecture (Girard, Kans.: Haldeman-Julius, 1942);

How to Become a Logician: The Art of Drawing Inferences (Girard, Kans.: Haldeman-Julius, 1942);

How to Become a Mathematician: The Art of Reckoning (Girard, Kans.: Haldeman-Julius, 1942);

An Outline of Intellectual Rubbish: A Hilarious Catalogue of Organized and Individual Stupidity (Girard, Kans.: Haldeman-Julius, 1943);

The Value of Free Thought: How to Become a Truth-Seeker and Break the Chains of Mental Slavery (Girard, Kans.: Haldeman-Julius, 1944);

A History of Western Philosophy: And Its Connection with Political and Social Circumstances from the Earliest Times to the Present Day (New York: Simon & Schuster, 1945; London: Allen & Unwin, 1946);

Ideas That Have Helped Mankind (Girard, Kans.: Haldeman-Julius, 1946);

Ideas That Have Harmed Mankind (Girard, Kans.: Haldeman-Julius, 1946);

Physics and Experience (Cambridge: Cambridge University Press, 1946; New York: Macmillan, 1946);

Philosophy and Politics (London: Cambridge University Press, 1947);

Human Knowledge: Its Scope and Limits (London: Allen & Unwin, 1948; New York: Simon & Schuster, 1948);

Authority and the Individual: The Reith Lectures for 1948–9 (London: Allen & Unwin, 1949; New York: Simon & Schuster, 1949);

Unpopular Essays (London: Allen & Unwin, 1950; New York: Simon & Schuster, 1950);

New Hopes for a Changing World (London: Allen & Unwin, 1951; New York: Simon & Schuster, 1951);

How Near Is War? (London: Ridgway, 1952);

Dictionary of Mind, Matter, and Morals, edited by Lester E. Denonn (New York: Philosophical Library, 1952);

What Is Freedom? (London: Batchworth, 1952);

The Impact of Science on Society (London: Allen & Unwin, 1953 [i.e., 1952]; New York: Simon & Schuster, 1953 [i.e., 1952]);

What Is Democracy? (London: Batchworth, 1953);

The Good Citizens Alphabet (London: Gaberbocchus, 1953; New York: Philosophical Library, 1958);

Satan in the Suburbs, and Other Stories (New York: Simon & Schuster, 1953; London: Bodley Head, 1953);

History as an Art, Hermon Ould Memorial Lecture, no. 2 (Aldington: Hand and Flower Press, 1954);

Nightmares of Eminent Persons, and Other Stories (London: Bodley Head, 1954; New York: Simon & Schuster, 1954);

Human Society in Ethics and Politics (London: Allen & Unwin, 1954; New York: Simon & Schuster, 1955);

Logic and Knowledge: Essays 1901–1950, edited by Robert Charles Marsh (London: Allen & Unwin, 1956; New York: Macmillan, 1956);

Portraits from Memory, and Other Essays (London: Allen & Unwin, 1956; New York: Simon & Schuster, 1956);

Understanding History, and Other Essays (New York: Philosophical Library, 1957);

The Will to Doubt (New York: Philosophical Library, 1958);

Bertrand Russell's Best: Silhouettes in Satire, edited by Robert Egner (New York: New American Library, 1958);

Common Sense and Nuclear Warfare (London: Allen & Unwin, 1959; New York: Simon & Schuster, 1959);

My Philosophical Development (London: Allen & Unwin, 1959; New York: Simon & Schuster, 1959);

Wisdom of the West: A Historical Survey of Western Philosophy in Its Social and Political Setting, edited by Paul Foulkes (London: Macdonald, 1959; Garden City, N.Y.: Doubleday, 1959);

Bertrand Russell Speaks His Mind (Cleveland & New York: World, 1960; London: Barker, 1960);

Fact and Fiction (London: Allen & Unwin, 1961; New York: Simon & Schuster, 1962);

Has Man a Future? (London: Allen & Unwin, 1961; New York: Simon & Schuster, 1962);

History of the World in Epitome: For Use in Martian Infant Schools (London: Gaberbocchus, 1962);

Unarmed Victory (London: Allen & Unwin, 1963; New York: Simon & Schuster, 1963);

War and Atrocity in Vietnam (London: Bertrand Russell Peace Foundation, 1965);

Appeal to the American Conscience (London: Bertrand Russell Peace Foundation, 1966);

War Crimes in Vietnam (London: Allen & Unwin, 1967; New York: Monthly Review, 1967);

The Autobiography of Bertrand Russell, 3 volumes (volumes 1 and 2, London: Allen & Unwin, 1967, 1968; Boston: Little, Brown, 1967, 1968; volume 3, London: Allen & Unwin, 1969; New York: Simon & Schuster, 1969);

The Art of Philosophizing, and Other Essays (New York: Philosophical Library, 1968);

Russell's Logical Atomism, edited by D. F. Pears (London: Fontana, 1972);

The Life of Bertrand Russell in Pictures and His Own Words, edited by Christopher Farley and David Hodgson (Nottingham: Bertrand Russell Peace Foundation, 1972);

My Own Philosophy (Hamilton, Ont.: McMaster University Library Press, 1972);

Essays in Analysis, edited by Douglas Lackey (London: Allen & Unwin, 1973; New York: Braziller, 1973);

The Collected Papers of Bertrand Russell, McMaster University Edition, edited by Kenneth Blackwell and others, 14 volumes to date (volumes 1, 7, 8, and 12, London & New York: Allen & Unwin, 1983–1986; volumes 2, 9, and 13, London & Boston: Unwin Hyman, 1988–1990; volumes 3, 4, 6, 10, 11, 14, and 15, London & New York: Routledge, 1992–2000).

Collections: *Authority and the Individual* (Boston: Beacon, 1960);

The Basic Writings of Bertrand Russell, edited by Robert E. Egner and Lester E. Denonn (London: Allen & Unwin, 1961; New York: Simon & Schuster, 1961);

Atheism: Collected Essays, 1943–1949 (New York: Arno, 1972);

The Collected Stories of Bertrand Russell, edited by Barry Feinberg (London: Allen & Unwin, 1972; New York: Simon & Schuster, 1973);

Mortals and Others: Bertrand Russell's American Essays 1931–1935, 2 volumes, edited by Harry Ruja (volume 1, London: Allen & Unwin, 1975; revised, 1991; volume 2, London: Routledge, 1998).

OTHER: John B. Watson, *Behavior: An Introduction to Comparative Psychology,* introduction by Russell (New York: Holt, 1914);

Ludwig Wittgenstein, *Tractatus Logico-Philosophicus,* translated by C. K. Ogden and Frank Ramsey, intro-

*Russell's parents, John and Katharine Louisa Stanley Russell,
Viscount and Lady Amberley, in October 1871*

duction by Russell (London: Kegan Paul, Trench,
Trübner, 1922);

John Russell Amberley and Katharine Russell Amberley, *The Amberley Papers: The Letters and Diaries of
Lord and Lady Amberley,* 2 volumes, edited by Russell and Patricia Russell (London: Leonard and
Virginia Woolf at Hogarth Press, 1937); republished as *The Amberley Papers: The Letters and Diaries
of Bertrand Russell's Parents,* 2 volumes (New York:
Norton, 1937);

"My Mental Development" and "Reply to Criticisms,"
in *The Philosophy of Bertrand Russell,* edited by Paul
Arthur Schilpp, The Library of Living Philosophers, volume 5 (Evanston & Chicago: Northwestern University, 1944), pp. 3–22, 681–741.

Bertrand Russell was well known during his lifetime as a controversial public figure; in retrospect, he
has been evaluated primarily as a philosopher and
social critic. As a public figure he opposed World War I,
supported World War II, headed a campaign for
nuclear disarmament (although immediately after
World War II he had advocated the nuclear bombing of
the Soviet Union to prevent the spread of Stalinist communism), opposed the Vietnam War, served jail sentences, and was involved in lawsuits, love affairs, and
marriages that supplied fodder for gossip for at least
sixty years of his life. As a philosopher, Russell is seen
as both a pioneer and a transitional figure between the
nineteenth- and twentieth-century trends in Anglo-
American thought. He was a pioneer in the development of mathematical logic, an abstract discipline that

he applied to theory of knowledge and metaphysics and
that influenced a generation and more of philosophers.
As a transitional figure he moved from the systematic
idealism of late-nineteenth-century philosophers such as
F. H. Bradley to a position he called "analytic realism."
Russell criticized the tendency of nineteenth-century
philosophers to erect comprehensive systems to ratio-
nalize their own religious and ethical values, urging
instead a piecemeal, tentative, and technical approach
to philosophy. As a leader in "scientific" philosophizing
Russell was open to change and revision and was often
charged with developing a new philosophy every few
years. By the end of his career some philosophers were
criticizing him for his formal mode of philosophizing,
while others were accusing him of belonging on the
older side of a twentieth-century watershed in philosophical thought in still seeking a metaphysical synthesis and epistemological justification. Late in life, in *My
Philosophical Development* (1959), Russell remarked, "It is
not an altogether pleasant experience to find oneself
regarded as antiquated after having been, for a time, in
the fashion." It is true that, although Russell used analytic modes of argument, his philosophic aim remained
traditional in that he sought a comprehensive view of
the nature of reality through science and attempted an
epistemological analysis that would give the knowledge
people think they have of reality the strongest possible
base, however flawed it might remain.

Throughout his life Russell engaged in lively
debates and dialogues with his contemporaries, influencing and being influenced by them. He was constantly attentive to current social and political problems
and devoted much time, thought, and published work
to such issues as women's suffrage, education, laws governing marriage and sexual relations, international relations, labor conditions, censorship, the treatment of
prisoners, foreign affairs, war crimes, and military policies. His analyses of political and social issues and theories give his work a wide range and popular influence
not often achieved by technical philosophers. He published more than ninety books and pamphlets during
his lifetime, and the editing of *The Collected Papers of Bertrand Russell* (1983–) has revealed that he wrote many
articles, reviews, and comments that were not recognized as his work and one philosophical book that was
never published.

Bertrand Arthur William Russell was born at the
estate of Ravenscroft in Trelleck, Monmouthshire,
Wales, on 18 May 1872, the third and last child of John
and Katharine Louisa Stanley Russell, Viscount and
Lady Amberley. The Russells and the Stanleys had
been active in politics for generations; Russell's father, a
political radical and an atheist, had served a term in
Parliament in 1867–1868 and had written a book on

religious belief. His mother and sister died of diphtheria when Russell was two; his father died a year later. The father left Bertrand and his older brother, John Francis Stanley Russell, known as Frank, under the guardianship of two freethinkers; but Russell's paternal grandparents had the will set aside, and Russell and his brother received a Christian upbringing in their home, Pembroke Lodge, in Surrey. The grandfather, Lord John Russell, a former prime minister, died in 1878, and the boys were raised by their grandmother, Lady Frances Anna Maria Elliot Russell. She was a strong, puritanical figure whose favorite Bible verse, "Thou shalt not follow a multitude to do evil," influenced Russell profoundly. A radical in her own way, she espoused equality for women and became a Unitarian in her eighties. Frank, seven years older than Bertrand, was sent to school, but "Bertie" was tutored at home and became a shy, lonely, and thoughtful child. He had the advantage of encountering the many famous people of the period who came to his grandparents' home and of reading widely in his grandfather's library; but, except for a short period when his tutor was a freethinker, he had no one with whom to share his thoughts. In his early teens he kept a diary—written in Greek letters for the sake of secrecy—in which he recorded his doubts about the existence of God, freedom of the will, and immortality.

At eighteen Russell entered Trinity College of the University of Cambridge, where he found other young men with whom he could talk freely. With a kind of intoxication he shared his feelings and thoughts, displayed his wit, and formed lifelong friendships and important intellectual collaborations. Among the ten close friends of his undergraduate days that he lists in his intellectual autobiography, "My Mental Development," in *The Philosophy of Bertrand Russell* (1944) are two philosophers, the Hegelian J. M. E. McTaggart, who was six years his senior, and G. E. Moore, who was a year younger but, like McTaggart, extremely influential in Russell's philosophical development. Alfred North Whitehead, a fellow at Trinity, was much impressed by Russell's entrance papers on mathematics and mentioned the promising new student to others in that small, elite society. But as Whitehead was eleven years his senior, the two did not become friends and collaborators until some years later. Russell and his friends met every weekend for late-night discussions at which they read papers and argued on wide-ranging topics, and for long Sunday walks.

When he was seventeen, Russell had met a family of American Quakers, the Pearsall Smiths, who lived near his uncle. They were wealthy, religious, ready to discuss any idea, and welcoming to the young Russell. Among the children were Logan Pearsall Smith, who

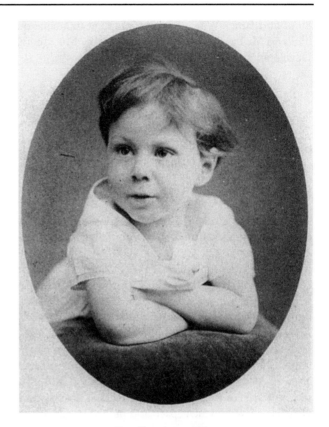

Russell at about age three

became a writer, and Alys Pearsall Smith, who was several years older than Russell and had just graduated from Bryn Mawr College. Despite opposition from his family, Russell and Alys became engaged when Russell reached his majority and came into his inheritance from his parents' estate, which yielded a modest income sufficient to support a family. After completing the moral sciences tripos in 1894, Russell planned to become a candidate for a fellowship, study economics, and marry Alys. In the hope of ending the engagement, his grandmother persuaded him to take a three-month appointment as an attaché at the British embassy in Paris. Throughout their friendship, engagement, and separation during the Paris assignment Russell and Alys corresponded daily, and Russell's letters reveal much about his reading, his conversations, and the development of his philosophical ideas. Russell returned from Paris and married Alys in December 1894. The couple traveled extensively in Europe and collaborated on a book, *German Social Democracy,* published in 1896.

At the end of his third year at the university Russell turned with relief from mathematics to philosophy. The prevailing mode of philosophizing in Britain at the time was idealism, and the chief debates were carried on between upholders of Kantian and Hegelian versions of that philosophy. Russell was instructed by G. F.

Stout and James Ward, but the dominant influence on him was McTaggart's neo-Hegelianism. In "My Mental Development" he recalls

> the precise moment, one day in 1894, as I was walking along Trinity Lane, when I saw in a flash (or thought I saw) that the ontological argument is valid. I had gone out to buy a tin of tobacco; on my way back, I suddenly threw it up in the air, and exclaimed as I caught it: "Great Scott, the ontological argument is sound." I read Bradley at this time with avidity, and admired him more than any other recent philosopher.

A major issue in Russell's philosophical reflections was whether spatial and temporal relations were absolute and objective or relative and subjective. He wanted his philosophical position on the issue to be consistent with the mathematical treatment of such relations, and he experimented with various idealist solutions to the problem. His fellowship dissertation, *An Essay on the Foundations of Geometry,* published in 1897, presents a Kantian view of space and time as structures imposed on experience by the mind; Moore castigated it as unduly psychological and subjective, and in a series of articles he wrote in 1901 Russell developed a Hegelian view in which space and time were aspects of the Absolute.

Although elements of neo-Hegelianism lingered in his thought for some time, during the last years of the nineteenth century Russell, under Moore's influence, moved away from idealism. Russell remembers this time in "My Mental Development":

> Bradley argued that everything common sense believes in is mere appearance; we reverted to the opposite extreme, and thought that *everything* is real that common sense, uninfluenced by philosophy or theology, supposes real. With a sense of escaping from prison, we allowed ourselves to think that grass is green, that the sun and the stars would exist if no one was aware of them, and also that there is a pluralistic timeless world of Platonic ideas. The world, which had been thin and logical, suddenly became rich and varied and solid.

In 1900 Russell taught a course on the philosophy of the late-seventeenth- to early-eighteenth-century German rationalist philosopher Gottfried Wilhelm Leibniz and published his third book, *A Critical Exposition of the Philosophy of Leibniz,* in which he worked out a criticism of the idealist view of relations. The most important event of that year, however, was his attendance at a philosophical congress in Paris, where he met the Italian mathematician Giuseppe Peano and heard papers by Peano and Peano's pupils. Russell was impressed by the elegance and simplicity of the mathematical symbolism Peano had developed and by

Peano's idea that a system of mathematics could be built up by deduction from a minimum of definitions and axioms. He mastered Peano's works and applied Peano's symbolism and deductive method to a wide range of topics, including the logic of relations. The fruit of this labor was *The Principles of Mathematics* (1903).

In *The Principles of Mathematics* Russell, while accepting Peano's symbolism and method of deduction, disputes the Italian's distinction between a class and its members. The distinction allowed Peano to discuss the null class (a class with no members), infinite classes, and finite classes of which the members are not identifiable. But Russell, holding that terms and propositions are real, has to identify the class with its members: for example, the class of human beings is the sum of John, Mary, and so forth. This position leads to difficulties with the null class, the infinite class, and the class with unidentifiable members (such as the class of persons in the statement "I met a person"). The most serious problem is a paradox that arises in regard to classes that are not members of themselves. Some classes are members of themselves, such as the class of classes; others are not members of themselves, such as the class of teaspoons. What about the class of classes that are not members of themselves? It must both be and not be a member of itself, which is absurd. Russell concludes that the paradox results from classes including themselves among their members and that some restriction on class membership is required; but he thinks that this solution has an ad hoc air. Russell was tortured by this problem for several years, and he tried out various solutions to it and to other problems that had emerged in the book.

Russell had told Whitehead about Peano's new symbolism and method; Whitehead was contemplating a second volume to complete his *A Treatise on Universal Algebra, with Applications* (1898), and Russell was planning a continuation of *The Principles of Mathematics,* but the two decided instead to collaborate on a book that would take the place of both proposed second volumes. Russell was to be responsible for the basic definitions, axioms, and postulates and the logic of relations, Whitehead for the section on geometry; each man would write the first version of his part of the book, the other would criticize and edit it, and then the original writer would rewrite it. The work went on for ten years and produced a landmark in mathematical logic and philosophy: *Principia Mathematica,* published in three volumes in 1910, 1912, and 1913, respectively.

Russell published many articles between *The Principles of Mathematics* and the first volume of *Principia Mathematica.* Some treated the logical issues he was working out in what he and Whitehead called "the big book"; one of the most notable essays is "On Denoting," published in the journal *Mind* in 1905 and repub-

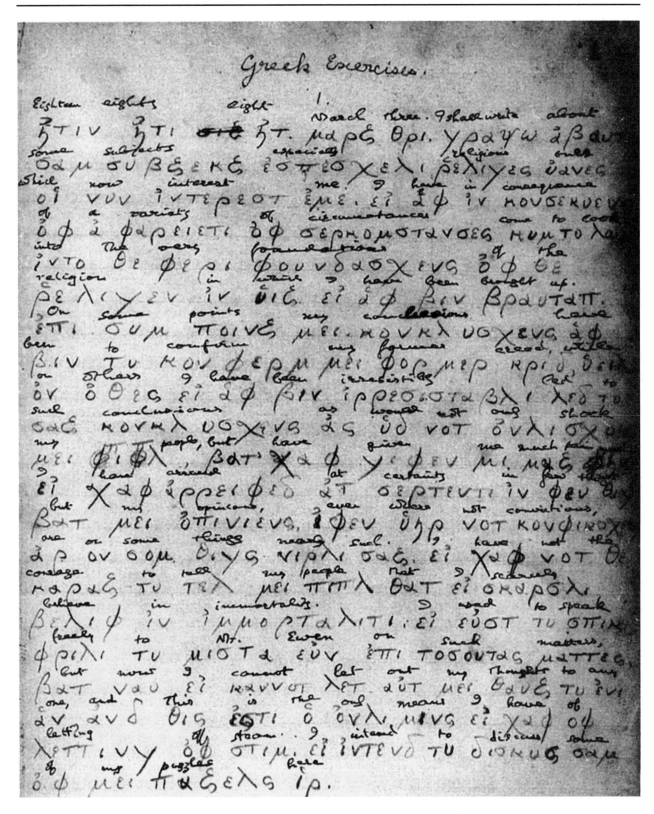

First page of Russell's private journal, written in English in Greek characters to conceal his unorthodox views.
Dated 3 March 1888, the entry begins: "I shall write about some subjects which now interest me"
(Bertrand Russell Archives, McMaster University).

Russell as an undergraduate at Trinity College of the University of Cambridge in 1891

lished in Russell's *Logic and Knowledge: Essays 1901–1950* (1956). The topic of this piece has proved to be of permanent significance and continues to be debated among philosophers today. The problem is the denotation of expressions in which an entity is referred to not by name but indirectly as "the such and such," "a such and such," or "some such and such," as in "the author of Waverly" or "the man who is knocking at the door." The solution to the problem should also deal with expressions that refer to nonexistent entities such as "the winged horse" or "the square circle." Russell is concerned with how such a proposition as "the king of France is bald" can be said to be false, not because the king of France is hairy but because there is no king of France. How can a proposition be meaningful if it does not denote (that is, point to) any specific thing or even to anything at all? Russell reviews what he believes the Austrian philosopher and psychologist Alexius Meinong and the German mathematician and logician Gottlob Frege offer as solutions to the problem (much of the recent debate centers on the extent to which these reviews are accurate and fair). He then puts forward his

own view, which became known as the "theory of descriptions": the problematic expressions are "incomplete symbols," and one can translate propositions in which they appear into a series of propositions about which it is possible to say what they refer to and whether they are true or false. "Sir Walter Scott is the author of *Waverley*" becomes "there is one and only one person who wrote *Waverley,* and that person is Scott"; "The present king of France is bald" becomes "there is one and only one person who is the king of France, and that person is bald." In the second case, it can now be seen that the falsity of the proposition derives from the falsity of the first conjunct–"there is one and only one person who is the king of France"–and not the presence or absence of hair. Stated in more-technical terms, the theory of descriptions, under the title "the method of construction," was intended to be the basic method of the definition of points and instants in a projected fourth volume of *Principia Mathematica* to be written by Whitehead. In nontechnical terms it later figured as a basic premise of Russell's theory of "knowledge by acquaintance and knowledge by description" and as the method of the "construction of the external world."

In "Transatlantic 'Truth,'" published in *The Albany Review* in 1908, and "Pragmatism," published in *The Edinburgh Review* in 1909, Russell criticizes the pragmatist definition of truth as "what works"; in contrast, Russell maintains a form of realism of which the outlines–as the philosopher F. C. S. Schiller complained to him in a letter of 23 March 1909–are not clear. Both essays were republished in Russell's *Philosophical Essays* (1910). In an important series of articles titled "Meinong's Theory of Complexes and Assumptions," published in *Mind* in 1904 and collected posthumously in Russell's *Essays in Analysis* (1973), Russell says that true and false propositions differ as do red and white roses, although he admits to problems about the reference of false propositions. "The Nature of Truth," published in *Mind* in 1906, became part of a series on truth in *Philosophical Essays*. Russell criticizes the idealist "monistic theory of truth," as found in Bradley's philosophy, for holding that no particular truth can be completely true because it must cohere with the entire rest of the world of thought, and for allowing that any coherent body of thought is true as any other; Russell maintains, on the contrary, that specific inquiries can yield specific truths apart from their connections with the rest of reality. Russell also criticizes Bradley for allowing relations to absorb their terms; Russell holds that terms and relations are separate realities. In *Philosophical Essays* Russell defends a relational theory of truth: a belief is true if the relation between the components of the belief correspond to the relation between the components of the reality to

Russell and his first wife, Alys Pearsall Smith, in 1894, the year they were married

which the belief refers. Hence, if Othello believes that Desdemona loves Cassio, his belief is true if she does and false if she does not. But the reality of the referents is not undermined: Othello, Desdemona, Cassio, the belief, and love all exist, but the relation does not hold as the belief asserts it to hold.

One of Russell's best-known essays, "A Free Man's Worship," a poetic renunciation of traditional religious belief, appeared in *The Independent Review* in 1903; "The Study of Mathematics," an exalted statement of commitment to a realm of eternal mathematical truth, was published in *The New Quarterly* in 1907. Both were republished in *Philosophical Essays*. Russell later found the style of the first of these two essays overly rhetorical and the sentiments of the second inappropriate to his changing view of the nature of mathematics.

Another topic addressed in a 1908 article, "Mathematical Logic as Based on the Theory of Types"–published in *The American Journal of Mathematics* and later collected in *Logic and Knowledge*–was worked out in detail in *Principia Mathematica*. The theory of types is Russell's solution to the paradox of classes that are not members of themselves. The tenta-

tive suggestion of *The Principles of Mathematics* is now strengthened into the prohibition of a proposition including itself in its reference. The result is a hierarchy of classes in which first-order propositions refer only to what are not propositions, while second-order propositions refer only to first-order propositions, and so on. The theory of types also requires that no statement of an order higher than the first could make a statement about all the properties of a class. Yet, to ground parts of mathematics it must be possible to make such statements. Thus, the "axiom of reducibility" is required: it asserts that statements can be made about all the properties of a class, such as the class a, "providing we remember that it is really a number of statements and not a single statement that could be regarded as assigning another property to a, over and above all properties." Russell and Whitehead found this axiom necessary, but neither of them thought that it was justified on other than pragmatic grounds.

During this period of intense professional activity Russell's personal life was far from tranquil. On the surface all seemed well: the Russells cooperated in Bertrand's candidacy for Parliament in 1907, although both understood it as an educational effort with no danger of election; they exchanged visits with Whitehead and his wife, Evelyn, while the two men worked on *Principia Mathematica;* and they followed their usual routine of charitable works, social engagements, and letter writing. But their marriage was in trouble. Russell says in *The Autobiography of Bertrand Russell* (1967–1969) that one day in 1902, while riding his bicycle, he discovered to his surprise that he no longer loved Alys. When he imparted this information to her, an emotional storm of threatened suicide and real suffering resulted. Russell, for his part, had longed for sexual fulfillment but had found it impossible to achieve with Alys. This emotional turmoil, combined with the continuing frustrations of the logical problems he faced in working on *Principia Mathematica,* caused him much pain. He says in the autobiography:

> The strain of unhappiness combined with very severe intellectual work, in the years from 1902 till 1910, was very great. At the time I often wondered whether I should ever come out at the other end of the tunnel in which I seemed to be. I used to stand on the footbridge at Kennington, near Oxford, watching the trains go by, and determining that tomorrow I would place myself under one of them.

As the volumes of "the big book" went through stages of proof and publication, Russell was continuing to write reviews, articles on current topics such as the women's suffrage movement, and technical mathematical and philosophical papers. In March 1911 he was scheduled to present three papers in Paris. Spending the night before his departure at the home of Philip and Lady Ottoline Morrell, he fell passionately in love with Ottoline. He was determined that they should get divorced and marry each other; but she did not want to give up her family, and he had to be content with being her lover. Amid much grief and distress, Alys agreed to a separation on the condition that Russell's relationship with Morrell be kept secret. During its five years the relationship resulted in a dazzling correspondence on Russell's part that shows the intensity of his desire to share every aspect of his life with Morrell, as well as his jealousy, despair, and, finally, his turning to others when Morrell was involved with other lovers. The correspondence also reveals an important watershed in the development of Russell's philosophy, and, some critics say, the collapse of his dream of a systematic and logically rigorous solution to the philosophical problems that engaged him during this period.

In 1911 Russell wrote a short book for the Home University Library that he called his "shilling shocker." Published in 1912, *The Problems of Philosophy* offers an overview of Russell's point of view at the time, a sketch

of what he planned as his next big work after *Principia Mathematica,* and discussions of a large number of unsolved problems. It is regarded as a classic and has been the means of introducing many students to philosophy. Russell's primary concern in the work is what can be known. After a skeptical review of instances of purported knowledge, he concludes that two kinds of knowledge are not open to doubt: what is immediately and directly perceived and what are intuited as the basic propositions of logic and mathematics. Such directly given, uninferred knowledge he calls "knowledge by acquaintance." From it a body of reliable knowledge can be built up by logical inference; this kind of knowledge is "knowledge by description." The distinction between knowledge by acquaintance and knowledge by description was an important topic in Russell's work for many years, and it constituted the link between his general epistemological concerns and his logical techniques. In *The Problems of Philosophy,* which was intended for a popular audience, the distinction is sketched out in a nontechnical fashion.

Another subject discussed in *The Problems of Philosophy* is the problem of induction. Russell says that it is impossible to prove that the way things have behaved in the past, however great their regularity, will be the way they behave in the future. At best, the uniformity of nature is a principle that has not been disproved and is useful; thus, one is justified in using it to make probable inferences. A similarly skeptical treatment of induction, "On the Notion of Cause," was presented to the Aristotelian Society in 1912 and published in Russell's *Mysticism and Logic, and Other Essays* (1917). Here Russell argues that all that can be said about causal laws is that certain regularities exist that scientists can express in mathematical formulas; the idea of a cause "forcing" or "necessitating" an effect is a metaphysical one with no basis in experience. For this reason, the concept of cause has no relevance to the issue of determinism versus free will. The problem of induction continued to be a concern of Russell's and was a major topic that occupied him during his final years of philosophical work.

In 1911 a young engineer named Ludwig Wittgenstein came from Austria to study mathematical logic with Russell. He joined Russell's course on the *Principia Mathematica* and found it "like music," as Russell reported to Morrell in a letter of 19 March 1912. Russell worried about Wittgenstein's stability but found his companionship stimulating and his ideas brilliant, if not always clear; he appreciated Wittgenstein's criticisms of the *Principia Mathematica* and began to see the Austrian as his successor, one who could bring new vigor and insights to the subject. The tenor of their interaction became less that of teacher and student than of colleagues. Russell told Morrell that Wittgenstein did not like the "shilling shocker" and thought that nothing could be said about the value of philosophy: if one is interested, one studies it, and that is that.

By 7 May 1913 the term was over at Cambridge; Wittgenstein had left; and Morrell was in Switzerland for an extended visit. Russell turned to his next major work, which was to be either one long or two shorter volumes on the theory of knowledge. According to Russell's letters to Morrell, it was to begin with an analysis of what is given in experience, including a treatment of logical ideas and relations, then move on to judgments, propositions, truth and falsity, and probability; a third section would consist in a logical construction of matter, points in space, moments in time, and cause. He showed the manuscript to Wittgenstein on at least two occasions; Wittgenstein criticized it severely, and on 20 June, Russell, having produced three hundred pages, abandoned the work because he could find no answers to Wittgenstein's objections. Of the original manuscript, only chapters 7 to 11 of part 1 and chapters 1 to 7 of part 2 are extant. It has been established that the first six chapters of part 1 were published, probably with revisions, as articles in the *Monist* in 1914 and 1915. The reconstructed manuscript was published in 1984 as *Theory of Knowledge: The 1913 Manuscript,* volume seven of *The Collected Papers of Bertrand Russell.*

Russell did not tell Morrell what Wittgenstein's criticisms were—in fact, he told her that he was not sure what Wittgenstein meant—but it seems likely that Wittgenstein criticized Russell's theory of relations, theory of judgment, and treatment of propositions. Russell replaced his relational theory of 1910 with a more complex five-term relation, but Wittgenstein apparently objected that the new theory left the relation between Othello and what he believes on the same level as the relation of love between Desdemona and Cassio. Russell's attempt to build atomic propositions from the materials of experience and logical form, to build molecular propositions from the atomic propositions, and to construct scientific objects from molecular propositions with the apparatus of mathematical logic could not proceed if the theory of judgment and the theory of relations on which it depended would not hold. Wittgenstein's criticisms brought Russell's project to a halt and, Russell wrote to Morrell on 20 June, made "a large part of the book I meant to write impossible for years to come probably." With the exception of the six *Monist* articles, none of it was published during Russell's lifetime, although remnants of the project appear in various forms in Russell's later work.

Although Russell's chief concerns in philosophy during this period were logic and theory of knowledge, he was interested in ethics and religion as well. Two of his essays on ethics reveal the influence of Moore: a

Russell in 1918

favorable review of Moore's *Principia Ethica* (1903), published in *The Independent Review* (March 1904), and a statement of ethical realism modeled on Moore's ethics, published in the *Hibbert Journal* in 1908 as "Determinism and Morals" and republished in *Philosophical Essays* as "The Elements of Ethics." Russell abandoned the view that the good is real after reading George Santayana's comment in the chapter "Hypostatic Ethics" of Santayana's *Winds of Doctrine: Studies in Contemporary Opinion* (1913) that it was equivalent to saying that whiskey stood dead drunk in the bottle. Although Russell had long since abandoned traditional religious beliefs, he had retained the attitude of awe toward the majesty of nature and the Spinozistic acceptance of its impersonality and unresponsiveness to human desires that is expressed in "A Free Man's Worship." He and Morrell tried to combine her religious commitment with his views in a book on the theme of escape from the prison of the senses and the self. They gave the manuscript for "Prisons" to Evelyn Whitehead; her response was highly critical, and they gave up on the project. All that remains of it is Russell's article "The Essence of Religion" in the *Hibbert Journal* in 1912 (republished in 1986 in volume twelve of *The Collected Papers of Bertrand*

Russell); he told Morrell in a letter dated 9 February 1912 that he had used part of the penultimate chapter of "Prisons" for the article. They also worked together on "The Perplexities of John Forstice," a philosophical novel in dialogue form. Readers of the manuscript recommended major revisions, and that project, too, was abandoned; the novel was finally published in the twelfth volume of *The Collected Papers of Bertrand Russell* with a note, which Russell specified should accompany it if it ever were published, to the effect that it represented his views during only a short period of time.

Invited to give the Lowell Lectures in Boston in the spring of 1913, Russell offered to speak on good and evil in the universe; but the grant that established the lectures stipulated that they were not to involve religion, and Russell had to choose another topic. At the same time he had to prepare lectures for Harvard University, where he would be teaching seminars on logic and on the theory of knowledge. In the fall of 1913, on his return from a vacation following the collapse of his book on the theory of knowledge, he began work on these projects. The Lowell Lectures were published in 1914 as *Our Knowledge of the External World as a Field for Scientific Method in Philosophy* (generally known simply as *Our Knowledge of the External World*); they cover much the same ground as Russell's articles "Knowledge by Acquaintance and Knowledge by Description" in the *Proceedings of the Aristotelian Society* for 1910–1911, "The Ultimate Constituents of Matter" in *The Monist* (July 1915), and "The Relation of Sense-Data to Physics" in *Scientia* (1914), and his *Scientific Method in Philosophy: The Herbert Spencer Lecture, 1914* (1914). All were republished in *Mysticism and Logic, and Other Essays*.

Russell calls *Our Knowledge of the External World* a sketch of what could be accomplished by distinguishing those philosophical problems that can be addressed scientifically from those that cannot. The former sort of problems would be solved by the method of construction, which was invented by Whitehead and was to be used to offer definitions of geometrical terms in the forthcoming fourth volume of *Principia Mathematica*. Russell begins by presenting his familiar skepticism concerning what one learns from perception and how many common-sense beliefs have no firm foundation beyond habit and assumption. One thinks that one sees a penny, but all one really "sees" is a colored shape. The penny is a set of inferences from what one sees or from what others report that they see. The method of construction, however, holds out the hope that a penny may be logically inferred—that is, constructed—from the materials of sensation. For instance, one can look at the penny from a series of different perspectives—from above, on edge, tilted, and so forth—arrange these perspectives into a series of images, or sense-data, and then consider the penny to *be* this series of sense-data. That is, one can take the materials presented through direct acquaintance, which cannot be doubted, submit them to logical arrangement and logical construction, and arrive at the common-sense objects of experience. The points, instants, and elements of matter in physics can be constructed in a similar way, Russell argues. One thus moves from knowledge by acquaintance to knowledge by description. The book concludes with a discussion of the difficulties of the concept of cause and suggests that the philosophical problem of determinism versus free will is based on a metaphysical inflation of what knowledge by acquaintance shows cause and effect to be: sequences of perceived events following each other in temporal sequence. This concept of cause, which is similar to that elaborated by the eighteenth-century empiricist David Hume, still permits one to speak of causal laws but merely as mathematical representations of the observed sequences. As Russell states the basic epistemological premise of his view: "Every proposition which we can understand must be composed wholly of constituents with which we are acquainted." He goes on to say that

> a complete application of the method which substitutes constructions for inferences would exhibit matter wholly in terms of sense-data, and even, we may add, of the sense-data of a single person, since the sense-data of others cannot be known without some elements of inference. This, however, must remain for the present an ideal, to be approached as nearly as possible, but to be reached, if at all, only after a long preliminary labour of which as yet we can only see the very beginning.

The book became a model for the Vienna Circle and other logical positivists of what might be accomplished by a scientific philosophy, and Russell's criticism of traditional metaphysical issues such as free will versus determinism inspired the positivist attack on metaphysics. Rudolf Carnap used the ideas of *Our Knowledge of the External World* and the methodology of the *Principia Mathematica* in his *Der Logische Aufbau der Welt* (1928; translated as *The Logical Structure of the World,* 1967). Other philosophers were less impressed; in "The Existence of the World as a Logical Problem" (1915) the American pragmatist John Dewey found Russell's construction to depend not on pure experiential givens but on elementary sense-data produced by sophisticated analyses and used to address an artificial problem. More seriously for Russell, Whitehead was displeased by Russell's preempting of the method he was proposing to use in a different context, and with different assumptions about experience, in the fourth volume of the *Principia Mathematica*. For this reason,

r

He said that as late as July 1917 the Bolsheviks were not only persecuted, but even assaulted by the Moscow mob. He said that very few understand the theory of the govt, but that many support it out of instinct. I got the impression that he despises the populace & is an intellectual aristocrat.

May 19. Morning, visit to Marchand, former correspondent of Figaro, now Bolshevik, though not materialist; agreeable, not important. Afternoon, walk round Kremlin — extraordinarily beautiful churches. Evening, interview with Lenin, one hour. His room is very bare — a big desk, some maps on the walls, 2 book-cases, one easy chair, for visitors. Throughout the time I was there, a sculptor was working on a bust of him. Conversation in English, very fairly good. He is friendly & apparently simple — entering without a trace of hauteur, a great contrast to Trotsky. Nothing in his manner or bearing suggests the man who has power. He looks at his visitor very close, & screws up one eye. He laughs a great deal; at first, his laugh seems merely friendly & jolly, but gradually one finds it grim. He is dictatorial, calm, incapable of fear, devoid of self-seeking, an embodied theory. The materialist conception of history is his life-blood. He resembles a professor in his desire to have the theory understood & his fury with those who misunderstand or disagree; also in his love of expounding. I put three questions to him. (1) I asked whether & how far he recognized the peculiarity of English conditions. The answer was unsatisfactory to me. He admits that there is little chance of revolution now, & that the working man is not yet disgusted with Parliamentary government. He hopes this result may be brought about by a Labour Ministry, particularly if Henderson is premier. But when I suggested that whatever is possible in England may occur without bloodshed, he waved aside the suggestion as fantastic. I got little impression of knowledge or psychological imagination. (2) I asked him whether he thought it possible to establish communism firmly & fully in a country containing such a large majority of peasants. He admitted it was difficult. He laughed over the exchange the peasant is compelled to make, of food for paper — the worthlessness of Russian paper struck him as comic. But he said things would right themselves when there are goods to offer to the peasant. For this he looks partly to electrification in industry, which he says is a technical necessity in Russia [& will take 10 years]; but chiefly he looks to the raising of the blockade. He described the division between rich & poor peasants, & the

Page from Russell's diary for 1920, recounting his interview with Soviet leader Vladimir Lenin (Bertrand Russell Archives, McMaster University)

*Russell's second wife, Dora Black,
whom he married in 1921*

dence of Wittgenstein's rejection of the *Principia Mathematica* approach appears in notes of the seminar taken by T. S. Eliot, a student of Russell's at the time. During the period from 1913 to 1919 references to Wittgenstein in Russell's writings give him general credit for important and yet unpublished ideas, but little change is noticeable in Russell's own views.

After completing his seminars at Harvard, Russell lectured at several other American universities and then returned to Britain in June 1914. The threat of war was becoming ever more ominous, and Russell tried to rally opposition to Britain's participation in the looming conflict. When war did break out in August, he threw himself into efforts to protect interned alien residents, supported conscientious objectors, and argued against the continuation of the war. These activities consumed most of his time and energy for the next three years. Aside from works that had been written prior to the war, Russell's publications from August 1914 to November 1918 were all related to the conflict; ranging from letters to the editors of newspapers to books such as *Principles of Social Reconstruction* (1916) and *Justice in War-Time* (1916), they constitute more than one hundred entries in his bibliography. These efforts alienated him from many friends, cost him his fellowship at Trinity, and resulted in fines; finally, in 1918 an article referring to American soldiers as strikebreakers landed him in prison, charged with "having in a printed publication made certain statements likely to prejudice His Majesty's relations with the United States of America." He was sentenced to six months, which he occupied in reading works in psychology and composing *Introduction to Mathematical Philosophy* (1919) and a response to Dewey's critique of *Our Knowledge of the External World*. The latter piece appeared as "Professor Dewey's *Essays in Experimental Logic*" in *The Journal of Philosophy, Psychology and Scientific Methods* in 1919 and is republished in volume eight of *The Collected Papers of Bertrand Russell* (1986).

In a series of lectures titled "The Philosophy of Logical Atomism," given in London in 1918–1919, he summarized his earlier views and amended them in the light of what he thought he had learned from Wittgenstein, from whom he had not heard since Wittgenstein joined the Austrian army at the beginning of the war. The lectures were published in the October 1918 issue of *The Monist* and the three following issues in 1919 and republished in *Logic and Knowledge*.

The lectures on logical atomism show Russell at a time when he was most under the influence of Wittgenstein. They demonstrate Russell's response to Wittgenstein's criticisms in letters to Russell and in the transcribed notes from 1913. In the lectures Russell

when the publisher, Open Court, refused to allow Russell to use any material from the book after World War I, and he turned to Whitehead, requesting the notes of their discussions that Whitehead was using, Whitehead, too, refused. Volume four of *Principia Mathematica* was never published; instead, Whitehead wrote *An Enquiry Concerning the Principles of Natural Knowledge* (1919).

While Russell was preparing for the Boston lectures in the fall of 1913, Wittgenstein had arrived in Cambridge with some new ideas about logic. Russell had trouble following them, and Wittgenstein said that he was unable to write them down. Russell had a stenographer make a record of Wittgenstein's discussion of the ideas. Wittgenstein then went to Norway to work in seclusion. Russell sent Wittgenstein a copy of the notes and kept one for himself; Wittgenstein's copy became the basis for his posthumously published *Notebooks, 1914–1916* (1961). Russell, still trying to understand Wittgenstein's comments, took his copy of the notes to Harvard, apparently intending somehow to incorporate them into his logic seminar; but little evi-

credits Wittgenstein with the recognition that the two verbs—the one that refers to the "judging" or "believing" of a proposition, and the one within the proposition that refers to what is judged or asserted—are on different levels that must be sharply distinguished. He agrees with Wittgenstein that the proposition itself must be taken as the unit of analysis, without bringing in its assertion, denial, or doubt. He analyzes the atomic proposition, which consists of names—symbols that directly refer to entities outside the proposition—and distinguishes names for components of the proposition from the proposition itself, which is not a name (Wittgenstein had criticized Russell for holding that an atomic proposition is a name). An atomic proposition consists of names for terms and relations, and it refers to a fact composed of the referents of those names; it has no parts that are themselves propositions. The external relation of the proposition to the fact determines its truth or falsity: if it points toward the fact, the proposition is true; if it points away from the fact, it is false. This view of truth and falsity, taken from Wittgenstein, avoids the problem, which had been present in Russell's 1913 manuscript, of comparing the internal relation of the proposition with the internal relation of the fact to which it refers. Molecular propositions consist of two or more atomic propositions connected by logical connectives such as those specified in *Principia Mathematica*. Russell also deals with the theory of descriptions, the theory of types, and classes. The lectures became highly popular because they advanced the seductive possibility of using a precise language and thereby making philosophy scientific.

Another work of this period, "On Propositions: What They Are and How They Mean," published in supplementary volume two of *The Proceedings of the Aristotelian Society* in 1919 and republished in *Logic and Knowledge* and in volume eight of *The Collected Papers of Bertrand Russell*, begins with an analysis of facts into terms and relations and gives an account of atomic propositions similar to that in the lectures, then shifts to a discussion of John B. Watson's theory of behaviorism. (Russell had written an introduction to Watson's 1914 book, *Behavior: An Introduction to Comparative Psychology*). Russell proposes to use psychology to develop a theory of meaning along behavioristic lines. In his prison reading he had been impressed with William James's psychological theories, and he goes on to connect Watson's treatment of meaning in terms of images and movements of the larynx with James's metaphysics of neutral monism, which contends that reality is neither material nor mental but consists of some more-basic stuff that can appear as either mind or matter. If the laws of psychology and the laws of physics could be

Title page for Russell's 1940 work, written during his six-year sojourn in the United States, in which he seeks a secure foundation for knowledge in basic sentences that express pure experience (Bertrand Russell Archives, McMaster University)

derived from a flow of particulars such as images and bodily responses to stimuli, Russell says, neutral monism would be an attractive position. He leaves the issue open and the theory of meaning not fully developed. Along with the lectures on logical atomism, this article shows the direction in which Russell's thought was moving and forms a link to his next major work, *The Analysis of Mind* (1921).

Another work of this period, *Introduction to Mathematical Philosophy*, written in prison and published in 1919, is a nontechnical overview of mathematical philosophy in which none of the issues of the lectures on logical atomism are broached and the only reference to Wittgenstein is a passing mention that he had pointed out to Russell that logic and mathematics consist of tautologies. In his 1944 autobiographical sketch Russell reveals the impact this view had on him:

My intellectual journeys have been, in some respects, disappointing. When I was young I hoped to find religious satisfaction in philosophy; even after I had abandoned Hegel, the eternal Platonic world gave me something non-human to admire. I thought of mathematics with reverence, and suffered when Wittgenstein led me to regard it as nothing but tautologies.

Russell and Wittgenstein met in Holland in December 1919, after Wittgenstein was released from an Italian prisoner-of-war camp, and went over a manuscript Wittgenstein had written during the war. The work had been rejected by publishers; Wittgenstein and Russell decided that it would have a better reception if it were accompanied by an introduction by Russell. But when Russell sent the introduction to Wittgenstein in May 1920, the latter rejected it, claiming that Russell had misunderstood him. He left the work in Russell's hands. It was published in a German journal, *Annalen der Philosophie,* in 1921 as "Logisch-philosophische Abhandlung"; a bilingual edition, with the English translation by C. K. Ogden and Frank Ramsey prepared with Wittgenstein's assistance, was published in 1922 as *Tractatus Logico-Philosophicus.* Russell's introduction remained in this version. The publication marked the end of the friendship and collaboration between Russell and Wittgenstein. For the early logical positivists, the *Principia Mathematica* and the *Tractatus Logico-Philosophicus* together were manifestos of a new scientific philosophy, and, even after they were disowned by their alleged fathers, the members of the Vienna Circle considered themselves heirs of Russell and Wittgenstein.

After his affair with Morrell ended in 1916, Russell had begun a stormy four-year relationship with Lady Constance Malleson, who acted under the stage name Colette O'Niel. In 1919 he had become interested in a bright, radical, and unconventional young student, Dora Winifred Black. They traveled to Russia in 1920 to see the results of the revolution; during the trip Russell interviewed the Bolshevik leader Vladimir Lenin. Russell despised the Communist system, while Black admired it; Russell published his critique in *The Practice and Theory of Bolshevism* (1920). Russell and Black spent the academic year 1920–1921 in China, where Russell taught at the National University of Peking and Black lectured on women's rights. Russell became ill with pneumonia in China, and Dora nursed him; with his returning health they discovered to their delight that she was pregnant. Their son, John Conrad Russell, was born seven weeks after Russell and Black married in September 1921, following his divorce from Alys.

In 1921 Russell published *The Analysis of Mind,* a work of logical construction in which he tries to show how a picture of the workings of the mind and an explanation of the development of belief and knowledge can be built up from the materials provided by perception, given the psychological mechanisms of sensation, memory, and imagination. He begins by adopting the neutral monism he had rejected in "On Propositions: What They Are and How They Mean." Although he identifies this position with James's, he rejects what he calls James's "lingering idealism" in the idea of "pure experience"; but he accepts the notion that the laws of physics and the laws of psychology can both be shown to be constructed from "particulars" that are neither matter nor mind. He no longer sees such "particulars" as directly given in experience, without inference or the possibility of error. Each perception includes elements of memory, habit, and expectation, and the given particulars have to be disentangled from this accompanying "encrustation" through a causal analysis of the origin of the various elements of the perception. For example, if one sees a star, the perception may include a causal line of light transmitted from the distant sun through intervening space to the atmosphere of the darkened earth to the retina and to the sensation of light that is a response to that stimulus. But one may also imagine or dream about a star, and these "perceptions" have causal origins as well. When particulars are thus disentangled and ordered in temporal patterns, one has the basis for psychological constructions of minds, emotions, and beliefs. Were the particulars to be ordered spatially instead of temporally, one would have the construction of physical entities. The laws of psychology belong to the first ordering, the laws of physics to the second. In the case of the psychological analysis, repeated perceptual experienced images are the referents for the meanings that one connects into beliefs, formulates in propositions, and tests for truth and falsity through future perceptual experiences. It seems that Russell is attempting in this book to reforge, by way of psychology, the link that had been destroyed in 1913 by Wittgenstein's criticism, between given experiences, formerly called "acquaintance," and propositions.

The construction in *The Analysis of Mind* is a draft or sketch; it is not worked out and expressed in the logical symbols and mathematical form in which such constructions should, according to Russell, ultimately be done. The "neutral monism" in this book actually has little in common with James's; also, Russell's theory of truth remains a realistic one, and his criticism of pragmatism on that issue is as severe as ever.

Russell published *The Problem of China* in 1922; the following year there appeared *The Prospects of Industrial Civilization,* co-authored with Dora, and *The ABC of Atoms.* The Russells' daughter, Katharine Jane, was born in December 1923. In 1924 Russell published *Icarus; or, The Future of Science.*

Russell with his third wife, Patricia Spence, and their son, Conrad, in Cambridge, circa 1947

Russell used the method of construction again in *The Analysis of Matter* (1927). In this work, which he called "a long dull book on matter," his many years of work with the construction of scientific concepts was finally completed. As with the construction of psychological and epistemological concepts in *The Analysis of Mind*, this construction is not worked out in full mathematical logical form. The book is, however, a technical one in which Russell, starting with the particulars—here called "events"—of which one is aware as elements of perception or that are extrapolated from the perceived elements, constructs points in space, moments in time, causal centers, and causal lines, such that the needs of physics for these concepts and the complicated structure of matter can be supplied. He deals with competing views of relativity and competing constructions of space-and-time series by Whitehead and Sir Arthur Eddington; the theory of relativity naturally makes the process of construction more difficult than it had seemed in the essays of the 1910 period.

Also in 1927 Russell published a second edition of *Principia Mathematica*. In the introduction he tried to work out a Wittgensteinian view of the topics, such as identity, atomicity, and extensionality, on which Witt-

genstein had most severely criticized the first edition of the book. But this reworking neither satisfied Wittgenstein nor represented a conversion on the part of Russell, who appeared to regard the intention of the work as unaffected by the changes he proposed as possible alternatives. The correspondence between Wittgenstein and Ramsey, who was consulted by Russell about the new edition, reveals the degree to which Wittgenstein saw the changes as inadequate. Other publications of 1927, such as the famous *Why I Am Not a Christian* and *An Outline of Philosophy*, dealt with nontechnical philosophical topics.

As the Russell children reached school age, their parents became concerned about their education. Russell published several works on the subject, including *On Education, Especially in Early Childhood* (1926). In 1927 the Russells opened their own school, Beacon Hill, on Russell's brother Frank's estate, based on the principles of not inculcating fear or unwholesome prudery in the students. Managing the school and lecturing and writing to raise funds to support it took up a great deal of their time, and their own children, who had to be treated the same as the other pupils while the school was in session, felt neglected by their parents. On

Frank's death in 1931, Russell succeeded to the title of third Earl of Russell, Viscount Amberley. The Beacon Hill School closed in 1932.

Bertrand and Dora Russell thought that marriage should permit the partners the freedom to engage in sexual relationships with others, while maintaining their friendship and their commitment to their children; this view is expressed in Russell's *Marriage and Morals* (1929). But when Dora returned from a lecture tour in the United States with a lover, subsequently bore his child, and became pregnant by him again, Russell rebelled. He did not want another man's children to bear his name; Dora believed he had deserted their principles. A bitter divorce in 1935 included a struggle over the children's custody, schooling, and support. In January 1936 Russell married his children's former governess, Patricia Helen Spence, known as "Peter," by whom he had a third child, Conrad Sebastian Robert–named, like his half brother, in honor of the writer Joseph Conrad–in 1937.

This period was sad, difficult, and trying financially because of the Great Depression, the drying up of Russell's income from a series of popular articles he had written for the Hearst newspapers, and the financial burden of supporting several households, including that of his brother's widow. It was, then, with a sense of relief that Russell and his new family set sail in September 1938 for the United States, where Russell had arranged for a one-year lectureship at the University of Chicago.

In contrast to his pacifism during World War I, Russell supported the fighting of World War II, which began in 1939, to stop the aggression of Adolf Hitler's Germany. He was anguished at being away from England during the conflict, but he was glad to have his children safe in the United States. The American sojourn, too, had its difficulties–Peter was unhappy in Los Angeles, where Russell was professor of philosophy at the University of California in 1939–1940; a contract for Russell to teach at City College of New York was blocked by court action because of his unconventional views on marriage; and Russell was fired from a lectureship on the history of culture at the Barnes Institute in Merion, Pennsylvania, in 1941–1942, and had to sue for his fee.

Russell's most significant philosophical work of the American period was *An Inquiry into Meaning and Truth* (1940). As before, he seeks the most reliable foundation for knowledge: the epistemological premises that are most free from doubt and from which inferences can be built up with the least risk of error. Russell attempts to find atomic sentences that express as closely as possible the nub of experience that is left when the effects of habit, memory, and expectation are analyzed away. He refers to this process as the "asymptotic approach to the pure datum." He finds the sentences closest to the datum

to be those that indicate and express "egocentric particulars" such as "here," "now," "this," and "I." A sentence such as "hot here now," for example, includes a minimum of inference; in contrast, a sentence such as "the sun is hot" leaves a gap between what is expressed and what is indicated and, thus, an opening for error. Although his own approach is more concerned with language and meaning than it formerly was, he faults logical positivists such as Carnap for keeping their analysis too bounded within language. His old complaint against Schiller, James, and Dewey is here directed against Hans Reichenbach as well: such philosophers fail to distinguish between how propositions are *known* to be true and what it means for propositions to *be* true. Russell agrees that they are known to be true by verification, but he insists that what makes them true is that they are in accord with the facts, even if those facts are inaccessible and verification is, therefore, impossible.

In 1945 Russell's *A History of Western Philosophy: And Its Connection with Political and Social Circumstances from the Earliest Times to the Present Day* was published, providing much-needed income. That same year the Russells returned to England, where Russell had been offered a fellowship at his old college, Trinity. *A History of Western Philosophy* proved to be one of Russell's most popular books; although criticized as flippant and opinionated, it is clear and readable and provides historical, social, and political contexts for the philosophical ideas discussed.

In *Human Knowledge: Its Scope and Limits* (1948) Russell turns his attention to the problem that had troubled him since 1910: induction–or, as he terms it, nondemonstrative inference. The first four parts of the book treat topics on which he had already written extensively and include little that is new. "The World of Science" brings together what is known in the various sciences; Russell had always believed that philosophy should start with the most reliable human knowledge, that of science, and should end its analysis by justifying what science says. He also believed that the contribution of philosophy was to adumbrate new hypotheses for science to explore. The second part deals with language in a way similar to *An Inquiry into Meaning and Truth*. The third part, concerning perception and science, is largely an updating of *The Analysis of Mind*. The fourth part, "Scientific Concepts," reviews and adds to the material covered in *The Analysis of Matter*. The fifth and sixth parts add new material. The fifth, "Probability," reviews the chief theories of probability in relation to mathematical probability and the problem of induction. This discussion leads to the concluding part of the work, "The Postulates of Scientific Inference," in which Russell, finding the "uniformity of nature" inadequate, develops what he considers the minimum postulates necessary to support the kind of inductive inferences needed to justify the conclusions of science:

Russell receiving the 1950 Nobel Prize in literature from King Gustav VI Adolph of Sweden

quasi permanence, separable causal lines, spatiotemporal continuity in causal lines, the common causal origin of similar structures ranged about a center, and analogy–in other words, assumptions about structure, substance, cause, and continuity. These postulates cannot be proved; but if they are necessary, no experience refutes them, and they are generally believed: they have all the justification of which the case admits.

Russell and his third wife separated in 1949. That year he was awarded the British Order of Merit and published *Authority and the Individual: The Reith Lectures for 1948–9*. In 1950 he received the Nobel Prize in literature; the following year he published *New Hopes for a Changing World*. In 1952 he and Peter were divorced, and he married an old friend, Edith Finch.

Human Knowledge: Its Scope and Limits was part of a synthesis that Russell found to be too large for one volume. The other volume, *Human Society in Ethics and Politics*, was published in 1954. The two books can be seen as the fulfillment of a plan that, Russell says in "My Mental Development," he had entertained while walking in the snow in the Tiergarten in Berlin in 1897:

to write a series of books in the philosophy of the sciences, growing gradually more concrete as I passed from mathematics to biology; I thought I would also write a series of books on social and political questions, growing gradually more abstract. At last I would achieve a Hegelian synthesis in an encyclopaedic work dealing equally with theory and practice. The scheme was inspired by Hegel, and yet something of it survived the change in my philosophy. The moment had had a certain importance: I can still, in memory, feel the squelching of melting snow beneath my feet, and smell the damp earth that promised the end of winter.

Human Knowledge: Its Scope and Limits and *Human Society in Ethics and Politics* can be regarded as Russell's final works in philosophy. He wrote many more works, some of them philosophical, but they were either retrospective analyses of his earlier views and development or polemical pieces. By the 1950s the kind of philosophy that Russell exemplified was widely attacked, particularly by the ordinary-language analysts. Russell's defenses of his philosophy against J. O. Urmson, G. F. Warnock, and P. F. Strawson, along with his critical review of Gilbert Ryle's *The Concept of Mind* (1949), appear in *My Philosophical Development,* published in 1959. The book is a useful overview of the development of Russell's thought, and the criticisms of ordinary language philosophy as an "idle tea-table amusement" show how far that thought was from the current mode of British philosophizing. In the chapter "The Impact of Wittgenstein" Russell is critical of some of the doctrines of the *Tractatus* that had originally impressed him.

After the brief period of "respectability" during which he received the Order of Merit and the Nobel Prize, Russell returned to notoriety in the mid 1950s as head of the Campaign for Nuclear Disarmament and, later, of the Committee of 100, organizations devoted to mass civil disobedience in the cause of halting the nuclear arms buildup. In a wonderful publicity boost for the cause, Russell and his wife were arrested and briefly imprisoned; pictures of the frail-looking eighty-eight-year-old Russell being hauled off to jail evoked widespread sympathy for them and disapproval of government actions. During the 1950s and 1960s he produced a steady flow of speeches, articles, and books in the cause of peace, of which *Common Sense and Nuclear Warfare* (1959) and *Has Man a Future?* (1961) are probably the best known. He attempted to intervene in international conflicts such as the border dispute between India and China and the 1962 Cuban Missile Crisis between the United States and the Soviet Union; he recounts these events in *Unarmed Victory* (1963). He also used his prestige on behalf of political prisoners. In 1963 he resigned from the Committee of 100 and founded the Bertrand Russell Peace Foundation; he was actively involved in the foundation and set up an endowment so that its work would continue after his death. Russell was outspoken in his opposition to American actions in the Vietnam War, and in 1966 he and the leftist French philosopher Jean-Paul Sartre set up a self-styled International War Crimes Tribunal to "try" American officials for alleged atrocities in the war.

Russell's personal life during his final decades was generally happy, although differences of policy and direction within the organizations with which he worked left wounds. There was also the strange case of Russell's secretary and "assistant," Ralph Schoenman, who exercised a Svengali-like hold over Russell from 1960 until his rejection by Russell in 1966. Edith, however, gave him the contentment and support he needed. She helped him with his autobiography and other writing and with his correspondence, visitors, and engagements, and worked for peace and went to jail with him. Russell's older son fell ill, and Russell and his wife found themselves caring for their grandchildren. Their home in Penrhyndeudraeth, Merionethshire, Wales, where they had lived since 1955, was a pleasant place for children's holidays and for entertaining family and friends, and a ref-

uge from the publicity that surrounded them because of their participation in the peace movement.

Russell retained an interest in philosophy; he entertained and corresponded with many philosophers and found the friendship of some, such as A. J. Ayer, delightful. He told his wife when they were working on his autobiography that recalling the old issues between himself and Meinong and between himself and Wittgenstein led him to think that he could return to the debate and finally give definitive answers. But his concern for peace was more pressing.

Russell's death on 2 February 1970 left people around the world feeling bereft of the clear voice of reason to which they had come to look amid the Cold War, the arms race, and incidents such as the Cuban Missile Crisis that had seemed to place humanity on the brink of a nuclear holocaust. Even the critics who had discounted his warnings and accusations as the ravings of a senile old man had to admit that Russell spoke eloquently and without fear or favor; the gadfly was sorely missed.

The evaluation of Russell by philosophers has been highly divergent. While Russell was alive and active, he could and did inflame opponents such as the idealists and pragmatists with what they considered—and sometimes were—unfair criticisms of their ideas. Logical positivists and empiricists who considered him their mentor were shaken by his rejection of some of their ideas. Still other contemporaries were frankly contemptuous of Russell's work. British ordinary-language analysts objected to the model of a simplified and precise logical language that began with *Principia Mathematica;* to them, the intuitions and nuances of everyday speech are philosophically informative and not to be ignored. Russell, in turn, regarded such concerns as trivial.

Another criticism, shared by ordinary-language and analytic philosophers and those with other points of view, is of Russell's "foundationalism," his attempt to trace beliefs back to some unquestioned and reliable starting point. Throughout his writings Russell strove to find elements of knowledge that could be taken as given and that could serve as the basis for inferences to common-sense and scientific beliefs. Early in his career he found these elements in logical truths and in acquaintance—that is, direct reference from words to objects. Russell admits in the chapter "The Retreat from Pythagoras" in *My Philosophical Development* that he was unable to achieve his goal. With respect to mathematical truth, he quotes from his 1907 essay "The Study of Mathematics," where he had said that "Mathematics, rightly viewed, possesses not only truth, but supreme beauty," then goes on: "All this, though I still remember the pleasure of believing it, has come to seem to me largely nonsense. . . . I have come to believe, though very reluctantly, that it consists of tautologies." With respect to the world as known

*Russell addressing Edinburgh members of the Campaign for Nuclear Disarmament
in Trafalgar Square, London, on 24 September 1960*

through the senses, Russell had to retreat from knowledge by acquaintance to a view that what is presented by perception must submit to extensive analysis before the nugget of reliable knowledge can be elicited from it. Russell acknowledged the difficulties in establishing what can be known; in the chapter from *My Philosophical Development* titled "Non-Demonstrative Inference," however, he explains that

> Universal scepticism cannot be refuted, but also cannot be accepted. I have come to accept the facts of sense and the broad truth of science as things which the philosopher should take as data, since, though their truth is not quite certain, it has a higher degree of probability than anything likely to be achieved in philosophical speculation.

In other places Russell takes the task of philosophy to be the building of bridges between science and common sense, and these bridges require not only the data of science but also those of perception, as well as the disciplined inferences derived from logic and mathematics. This concept of the scope of philosophy has something in common with his early dream in the Tier-

garten, as Russell points out in the postscript to his autobiography:

> My work is near its end, and the time has come when I can survey it as a whole. How far have I succeeded, and how far have I failed? From an early age I thought myself as dedicated to great and arduous tasks. Nearly three-quarters of a century ago, walking alone in the Tiergarten through melting snow under the coldly glittering March sun, I determined to write two series of books: one abstract, growing gradually more concrete; the other concrete, growing gradually more abstract. They were to be crowned with a synthesis, combining pure theory with a practical social philosophy. Except for the final synthesis, which still eludes me, I have written these books. They have been acclaimed and praised, and the thoughts of many men and women have been affected by them. To this extent I have succeeded.

Russell goes on to recount his failures: the outer failures of a world torn with strife and its loss of ideals; the inner failure of giving up his dream of finding a world of pure truth through mathematics. But, he says, "beneath all this load of failure I am still conscious of

Russell with his fourth wife, Edith Finch Russell, and his assistant, Ralph Schoenman, in the 1960s
(photograph © McMaster University)

something that I feel to be victory. I may have conceived theoretical truth wrongly, but I was not wrong in thinking that there is such a thing, and that it deserves our allegiance."

Contemporary philosophers by and large reject this vision of a truth that is "there" and deserves to be pursued and the conviction that the philosopher and the scientist are colleagues in this pursuit. Richard Rorty, for example, sees philosophy not as a search for truth but as "edification." Even some philosophers who consider themselves, like Russell, in the empiricist tradition, reject his foundationalism.

On the other hand, Russell's philosophical fame is secure in the realm that most disappointed him: mathematical logic. His and Whitehead's *Principia Mathematica* remains a milestone in that area of philosophy and a model for many in what remains of the logical positivist or logical empiricist tradition, although this technical subject seems less and less part of the general area of academic philosophy and more and more a subject matter of its own.

Russell himself was unsure of the extent to which his writings on individual ethics, social problems, and political theory should be considered philosophy.

Answering his critics in *The Philosophy of Bertrand Russell*, he says, "I come now to what is, for me, an essentially different department of philosophy—I mean the part that depends upon ethical considerations. I should like to exclude all value judgments from philosophy, except that this would be too violent a breach with usage." In the preface to *Human Society in Ethics and Politics* he says, "I had originally intended to include this discussion of ethics in my book 'Human Knowledge,' but I decided not to do so because I was uncertain as to the sense in which ethics can be regarded as 'knowledge.'" Russell certainly regarded his writings in this area an important part of his lifework, whether or not they should be considered philosophical in a technical sense.

However philosophers of the future view such questions as whether philosophy should commit itself to the pursuit of truth, whether science and philosophy can or should collaborate in that pursuit, whether philosophy is properly concerned with the experiential basis of knowledge, and whether value areas such as ethics ought to be included within philosophy, Bertrand Russell's work has left certain influences that seem likely to endure. The clarity of his writing, the cogency of his arguments, and his insistence on analy-

Memorial placque to Russell in Trinity College Chapel, Cambridge
(photograph by Edward Leigh)

sis as a method have had long-lasting effects on his successors, whether or not they explicitly espouse his methodology. If one compares the current level of philosophical argumentation with that of much of the nineteenth century, it seems clear that a debt is owed to Russell. The model of the philosopher as a person of wisdom and a citizen of the world, exemplified by Russell in his life and his work, has also struck many of his heirs as an ideal to be admired and emulated.

Letters:
The Selected Letters of Bertrand Russell, 2 volumes, edited by Nicholas Griffin and Alison Roberts Miculan (volume 1, Boston: Houghton Mifflin, 1992; volume 2, London & New York: Routledge, 2001).

Bibliographies:
Martin Werner, *Bertrand Russell: A Bibliography of His Writing 1895-1976* (Munich, New York, London & Paris: Saur / Hamden, Conn.: Linnet, 1981);
Kenneth Blackwell, Harry Ruja, and others, *A Bibliography of Bertrand Russell* (London & New York: Routledge, 1994).

Biographies:
H. W. Leggett, *Bertrand Russell, O.M.* (London: Lincolns-Prager, 1949; New York: Philosophical Library, 1950);
Alan Wood, *Bertrand Russell: The Passionate Sceptic* (London: Allen & Unwin, 1957);
Rupert Crawshay-Williams, *Russell Remembered* (London: Oxford University Press, 1970);

Dora Russell, *The Tamarisk Tree: My Quest for Liberty and Love* (New York: Putnam, 1975);
Katharine Tait, *My Father, Bertrand Russell* (New York: Harcourt Brace Jovanovich, 1975);
Ronald W. Clark, *The Life of Bertrand Russell* (New York: Knopf, 1976);
Maurice Cranston, "Bertrand Russell: Towards a Complete Portrait," *Encounter,* 46 (1976): 65–79;
Clark, *Bertrand Russell and His World* (London: Thames & Hudson, 1981);
Caroline Moorehead, *Bertrand Russell: A Life* (London: Sinclair-Stevenson, 1992);
Alan Ryan, *Bertrand Russell: A Political Life* (New York: Oxford University Press, 1993).

References:
Lillian Woodworth Aiken, *Bertrand Russell's Philosophy of Morals* (New York: Humanities Press, 1963);
A. J. Ayer, *Russell and Moore: The Analytic Heritage* (Cambridge, Mass.: Harvard University Press, 1971);
Kenneth Blackwell, *The Spinozistic Ethics of Bertrand Russell* (London & Boston: Allen & Unwin, 1985);
Wayne C. Booth, *Modern Dogma and the Rhetoric of Assent* (Chicago & London: University of Chicago Press, 1974);
Tom Burke, *Dewey's New Logic: A Reply to Russell* (Chicago: University of Chicago Press, 1994);
John Dewey and H. M. Kallen, eds., *The Bertrand Russell Case* (New York: Viking, 1941);
Alan Dorward, *Bertrand Russell: A Short Guide to His Philosophy* (London & New York: Published for the British Council by Longmans, Green, 1951);

Elizabeth R. Eames, *Bertrand Russell's Dialogue with His Contemporaries* (Carbondale & Edwardsville: Southern Illinois University Press, 1989);

Eames, *Bertrand Russell's Theory of Knowledge* (London: Allen & Unwin, 1969; New York: Braziller, 1969);

C. A. Fritz, *Bertrand Russell's Construction of the External World* (New York: Humanities Press, 1952);

A. C. Grayling, *Russell* (Oxford & New York: Oxford University Press, 1996);

Nicholas Griffin, *Russell's Idealist Apprenticeship* (Oxford: Clarendon Press / New York: Oxford University Press, 1991);

Paul J. Hager, *Continuity and Change in the Development of Russell's Philosophy* (Dordrecht, Netherlands & Boston: Kluwer Academic Publishers, 1994);

Claire Ortiz Hall, *Rethinking Identity and Metaphysics: On the Foundations of Analytic Philosophy* (New Haven: Yale University Press, 1997);

Peter Hylton, *Russell, Idealism, and the Emergence of Analytic Philosophy* (Oxford: Clarendon Press / New York: Oxford University Press, 1990);

Philip Ironside, *The Social and Political Thought of Bertrand Russell: The Development of an Aristocratic Liberalism* (Cambridge & New York: Cambridge University Press, 1996);

A. D. Irvine, ed., *Bertrand Russell: Critical Assessments,* 4 volumes (London & New York: Routledge, 1998);

Irvine and G. A. Wedeking, eds., *Russell and Analytic Philosophy* (Buffalo, N.Y. & Toronto: University of Toronto Press, 1993);

Ronald Jager, *The Development of Bertrand Russell's Philosophy* (London: Allen & Unwin, 1972; New York: Humanities Press, 1972);

C. W. Kilmister, *Russell* (New York: St. Martin's Press, 1984);

Gregory Landini, *Russell's Hidden Substitutional Theory* (New York: Oxford University Press, 1998);

Margaret Moran, "Bertrand Russell's Early Approaches to Literature," *University of Toronto Quarterly,* 54 (1984): 56–78;

George Nakhnikian, ed., *Bertrand Russell's Philosophy* (London: Duckworth, 1974);

Ramendra Nath, *The Ethical Philosophy of Bertrand Russell* (New York: Vantage, 1993);

L. Nathan Oaklander, *Temporal Relations and Temporal Becoming: A Defense of a Russellian Theory of Time* (Lanham, Md.: University Press of America, 1984);

J. Obi Oguejiofor, *Has Bertrand Russell Solved the Problem of Perception? A Critical Exposition of Bertrand Russell's Analysis of Sense Perception and Its Relation with the External World* (Frankfurt am Main & New York: Peter Lang, 1994);

Wayne A. Patterson, *Bertrand Russell's Philosophy of Logical Atomism* (New York: Peter Lang, 1993);

D. F. Pears, *Bertrand Russell and the British Tradition in Philosophy* (London: Collins, 1967; New York: Random House, 1967);

A. P. Rao, *Understanding* Principia *and* Tractatus: *Russell and Wittgenstein Revisited* (San Francisco: International Scholars Publications, 1997);

George Roberts, ed., *Bertrand Russell Memorial Volume* (London: Allen & Unwin / New York: Humanities Press, 1979);

Alan Ryan, *Bertrand Russell's Politics: 1688 or 1968?* (Austin: College of Liberal Arts, Harry Ransom Humanities Research Center, University of Texas at Austin, 1991);

R. M. Sainsbury, *Russell* (London & Boston: Routledge & Kegan Paul, 1979);

George Santayana, *Winds of Doctrine: Studies in Contemporary Opinion* (New York: Scribners, 1913);

C. Wade Savage and C. Anthony Anderson, eds., *Rereading Russell* (Minneapolis: University of Minnesota Press, 1989);

Paul Arthur Schilpp, ed., *The Philosophy of Bertrand Russell,* The Library of Living Philosophers, volume 5 (Evanston, Ill. & Chicago: Northwestern University Press, 1944);

Ralph Schoenman, ed., *Bertrand Russell: Philosopher of the Century. Essays in His Honour* (London: Allen & Unwin, 1967; Boston: Little, Brown, 1967);

William W. Tait, ed., *Early Analytic Philosophy: Frege, Russell, Wittgenstein. Essays in Honor of Leonard Linsky* (Chicago: Open Court, 1997);

J. E. Thomas and Kenneth Blackwell, eds., *Russell in Review: The Bertrand Russell Century Celebrations* (Toronto: Stevens, Hakkert, 1976);

Eric Wefald, *Truth and Knowledge: On Some Themes in Tractarian and Russellian Philosophy of Language* (Lanham, Md.: University Press of America, 1996).

Papers:

The Bertrand Russell Archives are at McMaster University in Hamilton, Ontario. T. S. Eliot's notes on Russell's spring 1914 logic seminar at Harvard University are held at the Houghton Library, Harvard University.

Gilbert Ryle

(19 August 1900 – 6 October 1976)

Konstantin Kolenda
Rice University

BOOKS: *Locke on the Human Understanding* (London: Oxford University Press, 1933);

Philosophical Arguments: An Inaugural Lecture Delivered before the University of Oxford, 30 October 1945 (Oxford: Clarendon Press, 1945);

The Concept of Mind (London & New York: Hutchinson's University Library, 1949);

Dilemmas: The Tarner Lectures, 1953 (Cambridge: Cambridge University Press, 1954; Cambridge & New York: Cambridge University Press, 1960);

A Rational Animal: Delivered on 26 April 1962 at the London School of Economics and Political Science, Auguste Comte Memorial Trust Lecture, no. 5 (London: Athlone, 1962);

Plato's Progress (Cambridge: Cambridge University Press, 1966);

Studies in the Philosophy of Thought and Action: British Academy Lectures, by Ryle and others, edited by P. F. Strawson (London & New York: Oxford University Press, 1968);

The Thinking of Thoughts, University Lectures, no. 18 (Saskatoon, Saskatchewan: University of Saskatchewan, 1968);

Collected Papers, 2 volumes (London: Hutchinson, 1971; New York: Barnes & Noble, 1971);

On Thinking, edited by Konstantin Kolenda, introduction by G. J. Warnock (Oxford: Blackwell, 1979; Totowa, N.J.: Rowman & Littlefield, 1979);

Aspects of Mind, edited by René Meyer (Oxford & Cambridge, Mass.: Blackwell, 1993).

OTHER: *Proceedings of the Seventh International Congress of Philosophy, Held at Oxford, England, September 1–6, 1930,* edited by Ryle (London: Oxford University Press, 1931);

"Systematically Misleading Expressions," in *Essays on Logic and Language,* edited by Antony Flew (Oxford: Blackwell, 1951; New York: Philosophical Library, 1951), pp. 11–36;

Gilbert Ryle in the mid 1920s

"The *Timaeus Locrus*" and "*Plato's Progress:* Counter-Queries," in *The Progress of* Plato's Progress, edited by Richard Freis (Berkeley, Cal.: Agon, 1970);

Contemporary Aspects of Philosophy, edited by Ryle (Stocksfield, U. K. & Boston: Oriel, 1976 [i.e., 1977]).

Gilbert Ryle was one of the most influential British philosophers of the twentieth century. Along with Ludwig Wittgenstein and J. L. Austin, he called attention to the centrality of language in the formation of concepts. For that reason he is celebrated as one of the founders of what has been labeled "language analysis" or "ordinary language philosophy." Such labels, however, fail to take into account the broad historical background against which Ryle conducted his investigations. That background included classical Greek philosophy, as manifested in his original interpretation of Plato, and the work of German phenomenologists, whose views sometimes provided a foil for his approach. Philosophers all over the world have been affected by his eloquently and vigorously stated views, which provided extensive additions to available philosophical tools. A prediction by a reviewer of his seminal work, *The Concept of Mind* (1949), has certainly come true: "Professor Ryle writes with Aristotelian pregnancy, and almost every paragraph contains observations which require, and will certainly be given, thousands of words of discussion."

Besides influencing the philosophical scene through his original writings, Ryle contributed to the spread of ideas generated in England to other parts of the world through his editorship of *Mind* from 1948 to 1971. He made that journal into a forum for professional exchange across the Atlantic, including among the contributors many young and not yet well-known philosophers and causing an occasional grumble that he favored American over British authors. But this disregard of national boundaries is more readily explained by his conviction that philosophical endeavor is inherently international in character. Symbolic of that attitude is the fact that at both ends of his career Ryle edited collections representing collaborative ventures: in 1930 he served as editor of the proceedings of an international conference held in Oxford, and in 1975, the year before his death, he was the chairman of the Oxford International Symposium and the editor of its proceedings.

Ryle was born in Brighton on 19 August 1900 to Reginald John and Catherine Scott Ryle. His philosophical interests received early stimulation from his father, a physician who was also an amateur astronomer and philosopher. Ryle became, as he himself reported, "an omnivorous reader" in his father's large and variegated library. He was educated at Brighton College and at Queens College of the University of Oxford. His formal studies at Oxford were supplemented by participation in the meetings of an informal dining club, the "Wee Teas," of which he was one of six members. He graduated with first-class honors and became a lecturer in philosophy at Christ Church College at Oxford in 1924. The following year he became a tutor at the same college.

After becoming an Oxford don, Ryle acquainted himself with German philosophy and the German language through travel and dictionary-aided reading. From this period stems his interest in the ideas of Edmund Husserl and other phenomenologists, which led to a short-lived course of lectures titled "Logical Objectivism: Bolzano, Brentano, Husserl and Meinong"–a course that was referred to at Oxford as "Ryle's three Austrian railway stations and one Chinese game of chance." In subsequent years logical positivism and the work of Wittgenstein led Ryle to regard philosophy as conceptual analysis. In 1945 he returned to Oxford from military service in World War II, during which he rose to the rank of major in the Welsh Guards, and was appointed Waynflete Professor of Metaphysical Philosophy at Magdalen College.

The Concept of Mind was published four years later. It is a concerted and many-pronged assault on the idea that the mind has its own sphere of operation parallel to but independent of what is going on in the body or in the world. Dubbing that idea "the myth of the ghost in the machine," Ryle attributes its popularity to the influence of the seventeenth-century French rationalist philosopher René Descartes. Some commentators have pointed out, however, that the notion of the mind as an independent entity has older and more-diffuse origins, including Plato and religious doctrines that emphasize the immateriality of the human soul or spirit.

According to the Cartesian metaphysics, every human being is a combination of a body and a mind; what goes on in the mind is wholly distinct from what happens to and is done by the body, and when the body dies, the mind may continue to exist and function. The behavior of the body is publicly observable, while the working of the mind is completely private: each subject is directly and immediately conscious of the content of his or her mental life, but this content is accessible only to that subject and remains a closed book for others. The human body is subject to mechanical laws, as are other bodies in space; since minds are not in space, their operations are not subject to mechanical laws. Each person's life thus proceeds on two separate tracks–the bodily and the mental, the public and the private. The relationship between the two realms is sometimes described in spatial terms: the mental life is "internal," the bodily life "external." But Ryle observes that if one presses the metaphor, one will see that its explanatory power is illusory, since, according to Cartesianism, minds are not in space at all.

This mind-body dualism leads to the perennial philosophical problem of how the two can interact. How can something intrinsically private become public? What transactions occur between the private and public episodes in the history of an individual? It seems that the language referring to such transactions would contain unavoidable self-contradictions as it tried to describe something nonspatial breaking out into space, and something immaterial causally affecting matter and vice versa.

That the connection between a person's body and mind is inexplicable and mysterious, Ryle says, is but one absurd consequence of the insistence on the intrinsic privacy of the mental. Another consequence is the inevitable isolation of minds from one another, for the only "evidence" for the existence of minds other than one's own comes from their bodily manifestations. But how does one know that these are manifestations of minds? One observes another person's body and its various ways of behaving, but, being shut up in one's private consciousness, one cannot get at the mind of someone else. "Absolute solitude is on this showing the ineluctable destiny of the soul. Only our bodies can meet."

Ryle makes some conjectures as to the motives behind the emergence of the "ghost in the machine": Descartes was impressed by the success of the new physics and its mechanical laws and attracted by the explanatory powers of materialistic doctrines, but, unlike his British contemporary Thomas Hobbes, he could not bring himself to adopt them as applicable to all phenomena, including mental ones; therefore, he discussed the mind in "paramechanical" terms: if matter obeys mechanical causal laws, then the mind must obey nonmechanical causal laws. Ryle observes that the Cartesian description of mental phenomena is always expressed in negative terms: "They are not in space, they are not motions, they are not modifications of matter, they are not accessible to public observation. Minds are not bits of clockwork, they are just bits of not-clockwork." Ryle concedes that the paramechanical model may be an advance over the previous "parapolitical" model of the mind as a series of hierarchical faculties, a model in which ruling, obeying, collaborating, and rebelling were the accepted idioms.

The paramechanical model is clearly at work in the Cartesian concept of will, which represents volitions as inner mental thrusts that link the mind with its "expressions" in the public world. These episodes are said to exhibit transactions between minds and bodies, although the theory forbids such transactions. The theory and its application are thus in conflict. Moreover, Ryle points out, if every bodily action, to be called voluntary, must issue from a mental volition, then every volition, if it is to claim voluntary status, must issue from another voluntary volition, and so on, ad infinitum. The causal model, then, cannot explain how action comes about. It strikes Ryle as significant that the language of volitions is never used by ordinary people: for instance, no one ever says that someone performs a few difficult and many easy volitions in a day.

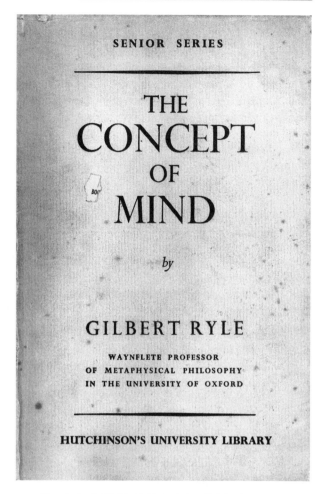

Dust jacket for Ryle's 1949 work, in which he characterizes the theory that the mind and body are separate entities as "the myth of the ghost in the machine" (Bruccoli Clark Layman Archives)

Another area into which the dogma of the ghost in the machine has brought conceptual confusion is the theory of perception. Here philosophers introduced another dubious term, *sensation,* thus creating the discipline of "paraoptics"—a pseudoscience of mental life of which the British empiricists John Locke and David Hume were especially fond. The key mistake, says Ryle, was the assimilation of sensation to observation. According to the theory, sensing is a kind of seeing, and since every act of seeing has an object, every sensation must have an object. Thus, Locke concluded that people do not really experience objects but, rather, their "primary and secondary qualities." Hume believed that the foundation of knowledge is "impressions," verdicts of the senses of which one is directly aware in perception.

Ryle's criticism of the doctrine of sensations begins with a confession of uneasiness even in discussing it, for to talk about sensations is to accept the philosophers' theory that such entities exist and that there are mental acts of "observing" them. But the philosophers' talk about sensations clearly deviates from that of ordinary people, who do not say that looking, for example, at a yellow flower gives them a sensation of yellow; ordinary perceptual reports refer not to sensations but to objects. Sensations are typically described by employing the vocabulary of common objects and cannot be described otherwise. As Ryle puts it, one never talks about sensations "neat," in isolation from the common context in which colors, sounds, shapes, and tastes are experienced. Sensation words draw their significance from the objects in the presence of which the sensations may be had, such as fleas, needles, and stoves. Moreover, the description of sensations often includes the way they strike the person who is experiencing them: as pleasant, painful, disturbing, exciting, or annoying.

Furthermore, if sensations were things that could be observed, then it should be possible to make the observations more or less successfully. People make mistakes in observation, but having a sensation is not something about which one can either make or avoid a mistake; sensations can be neither correct nor incorrect. Furthermore, one does not witness them: there can be witnesses to a fire, but no witness to a qualm. It is also incorrect to say that sensations are something that one feels. When grit gets in one's eye, one may rightly report a strange or unpleasant sensation in the eye, and when the grit is removed, it makes sense for someone to ask, "How does your eye feel now?" But when one switches one's gaze from one object to another, it would make no sense for someone to inquire: "Did the feeling in your eye change when you switched your gaze from the table to the chair?"

The sense-datum theory, which claims that people do not see objects but only sense-data out of which the mind "logically constructs" objects, also assimilates the concept of sensation to the concept of observation. It borrows verbs applicable to the latter, such as *observe, scan,* or *savor,* and transplants them into the shadowy realism of inner episodes called *sensations,* so that words such as *intuit, cognize,* and *sense* supposedly refer to special cognitive relationships in which the mind stands to its sense-data. But the whole notion of sensations is sheer mystification, Ryle says: "Sensations, then, are not perceivings, observings, or findings; they are not detectings, scannings, or inspectings; they are not apprehendings, intuitings, or knowings. To have a sensation is not to be in cognitive relation to a sensible object. There are no such objects nor is there any such relation."

Another area in which the dogma of the ghost in the machine does epistemological damage is the analysis of imagination. Imaginings, like sensations, are supposed to be ghostly seeings. Although imaginings do occur, it is false to say that they are "seen" by an "inner eye." Hume's account of "ideas" as less-forceful and less-vivid copies of impressions is a typical example of such a mistake: "An imagined shriek is neither louder nor fainter than a heard murmur. It neither drowns it nor is it drowned by it." The characterizations that are typically applied to sights seen and sounds heard cannot be applied to sights "seen" or sounds "heard" in the imagination. *Within* the imagination one can distinguish between vivid and hazy pictures, but Humean impressions cannot properly be described as vivid: one may imagine vividly, but one does not see vividly. Hume's notion of ideas as weaker copies of their stronger originals is based on a misleading analogy: "One actor may be more convincing than another actor; but a person who is not acting is neither convincing nor unconvincing, and cannot therefore be described as more convincing than an actor." The temptation to construe imaginings as a kind of seeing is strong for those who have accepted the sense-datum theory of perception: if one can "see" sense-data, then one can contemplate one's imaginings. But if it is wrong to say that one can witness oneself sensing—that is, seeing, hearing, smelling, tasting, and feeling—then it is also wrong to say that one can observe one's imagined seeing, hearing, and so on.

In the first chapter of *The Concept of Mind* Ryle insists that he is not denying that mental processes occur. He thinks, however, that the account of them in terms of the Cartesian myth is misleading: it does not square with what is known to be true of minds and mental processes or with what is already embedded in linguistic distinctions that everyone makes in daily life. He does not claim that ordinary people's distinctions cannot be wrong, only that the working distinctions and discriminations of which people ordinarily avail themselves in making sense of their experiences should not be ignored.

One type of mistake to which philosophers are especially prone, according to Ryle, is to assimilate a mode of speaking in one area of experience to another area where the mode is not applicable. Ryle calls this error a "category mistake" and gives many illustrations of it. A person watching a division of soldiers marching by would make a category mistake if he wondered why he does not see the division but only battalions, batteries, and squadrons; he would think that a division must be something in addition to the elements that make it up. The same would be true of a person touring a campus who saw the classroom and administration buildings, laboratories, dormitories, quadrangles, students, professors, and so on and then asked, "But where is the university?" Similarly, a sports team's esprit de corps is not exhibited alongside the particular performances; a player cannot display it as something separate from his actual playing of the game. The U. S. Constitution is not an item parallel to the executive, legislative, and judiciary branches of the government; none of them is related to the Constitution in the ways in which it is related to the other branches of government. It would be a category mistake to regard the Constitution as one of the institutions that it delineates.

Ryle's warning against the category mistake is a warning against improper linguistic assimilations. This sort of assimilation is what happened when the theory of mind was couched in paramechanical and paraoptical terminology. The consequence was a displacement of one's attention from concretely available facts of experience to a ghostly realm of inner mental processes. The way to correct this mistake is to return one's attention to situations in which the presence of mental operations and characteristics is acknowledged in one's actual use of language.

In the chapter "Knowing How and Knowing That" Ryle reminds the reader that the notion of human intelligence is much broader than the overly intellectualized account given by philosophers. In an important sense, "knowing how" is logically prior to the more sophisticated "knowing that." It is also a more appropriate context in which to explore the nature of mind. To know how to do something is to display a certain capacity and competence; it is a disposition, an exercise of a skill. When one says that a person knows how to do something, one is not referring to any processes or acts or episodes going on within his or her mind, brain, or head. A disposition is not an act or a series of acts; to think of it in that way is to make a category mistake. A student gives the right answer on an arithmetic test because she knows arithmetic and therefore can give correct answers in this area. Her knowledge is a dispositional property: "To possess a dispositional property is not to be in a particular state, or to undergo a particular change; it is to be bound or liable to be in a particular state, or undergo a particular change, when a particular condition is realized."

Thinking of mental phenomena in dispositional terms avoids the pitfalls of the dualistic Cartesian picture. Being intelligent does not consist of two operations: thinking about what one is doing and doing it. When a clown trips on purpose, his action is both physical and mental; there are not two separate processes going on. Intelligent performance satisfies the criteria of competence that the agent knows how and when to apply. The agent does not have to be able to state these

DILEMMAS

"I want to discuss issues which are more than riddles, issues which interest us because they worry us; not mere intellectual exercises, but live intellectual troubles."

GILBERT RYLE

CAMBRIDGE UNIVERSITY PRESS

Dust jacket for the published version (1954) of Ryle's 1953 Tarner lectures, in which he further develops some of the ideas of The Concept of Mind *(Bruccoli Clark Layman Archives)*

criteria; a person may know, for example, how to tie a knot without being able to give a verbal account of how it is done.

Skills and competencies are acquired by learning, but learning should not be equated with mere drill: to do so would be to make another category mistake. Human learning is, typically, training, which involves more than mechanical habituation: "It is of the essence of intelligent practices that one performance is modified by its predecessors. The agent is still learning. . . . Drill dispenses with intelligence, training develops it." Furthermore, intelligent dispositions are not one-track responses. A polite person, for example, is one who has been trained to respond politely in infinitely heterogeneous situations.

Ryle points out that linguistic devices exist to capture the meaning of dispositional descriptions. When one says that glass is brittle, one is making a law-like statement: one is saying that under certain conditions glass is likely to shatter. The statement can be rephrased as a hypothetical one: if such and such conditions obtain, then glass will shatter. Everyone understands the meaning of such statements and uses them daily. Only an epistemologist's prejudice would confine the use of sentences to the job of reporting facts that actually obtain at the time of utterance. One receives information when one is told that a substance is soluble or that a person knows Latin. The former means that if a substance is placed in a liquid, it will dissolve; the latter means that if a person is shown an original text by Cicero, he or she will understand it. Words such as *would* and *could* convey information and should not be relegated to an epistemological limbo. Using them, one can formulate statements that function as "inference licences" and allow one to predict events that will occur in the future.

Ryle observes that many statements, especially those used to describe mental characteristics, fall into the border area between categorical and hypothetical: he calls them "semi-hypothetical" or "mongrel-categorical." Such a statement functions in some respects as a statement of brute fact and in others as an inference license; it is both narrative and predictive. As an example he gives the colloquial accusation "You *would* miss the train." The statement refers both to the particular error for which a reproach is made (the categorical aspect) and also to the propensity that makes the error predictable (the hypothetical aspect). The hypothetical aspect allows one to conclude that other similar actions could be predicted of that person. The recognition of mongrel-categorical statements also helps to account for such celebrated perceptual puzzles as the elliptical appearance of a round plate when it is tilted toward or away from one or the bent look of a stick in the water. "The plate has an elliptical look" is a mongrel-categorical statement, whereby one applies a rule about untilted elliptical plates to the actual appearance of the plate.

Thus, the topic of mind is "not the topic of untestable categorical propositions, but the topic of testable hypothetical and semi-hypothetical propositions." It is an inquiry into capacities, skills, habits, propensities, liabilities, and bents. One discovers that other minds exist by understanding what people say and do; but this discovery is not an inference about some operations going on "behind the scenes." When one person follows another's speech, appreciates his or her joke, or understands his or her chess move, they are in the presence of each other's minds. Of course, they can misunderstand each other, but misunderstanding makes sense only against a background of possible understanding.

The topic of mind, Ryle says, is concerned with the "characterization of such stretches of human behavior as exhibit qualities of intellect and character." Here typically dispositional words such as *know, believe, aspire, clever,* and *humorous* have determinable meanings. Similarly, dispositional accounts are in order when one refers to inclinations and motives. Explanations by motive are inquiries into the agent's character, or at least into his or her temporary bents or propensities. This procedure is used by novelists and biographers, who describe what people do and undergo rather than what goes on in their minds. In this respect the novelists' and biographers' method is to be preferred to the epistemologists'. Ryle gives an account of what one ordinarily understands by "conceit," a mental characteristic par excellence: "To be conceited is to tend to boast of one's excellences, to pity or ridicule the deficiencies of others, to day dream about imaginary triumphs, to reminisce about actual triumphs, to weary quickly of conversations which reflect unfavorably upon oneself, to lavish one's company upon distinguished persons and to economize in association with the undistinguished."

Ryle describes the intellect as a sophisticated kind of mental competence. Intellectual work is an activity of a specific sort, with its own criteria of achievement and excellence, but it is wrong to think of it as being the cause of all intelligent activities. Mastery of arguments is a skill in which one can be instructed, but people learn to argue logically and coherently without ever taking a course in logic. Words such as *judgment, deduction, inference,* and *abstraction* refer not to processes but to verdicts. They are referees' words, not biographers' words.

In *Dilemmas: The Tarner Lectures, 1953* (1954) and in various articles in the second volume of his *Collected Papers* (1971) Ryle develops some of the themes of *The Concept of Mind* in greater detail, particularly the category mistake. He considers a variety of intellectual troubles that result when "theorists of one kind may unwittingly commit themselves to propositions belonging to quite another province of thinking." But he became dissatisfied with some of his earlier formulations of what it means to have a mind. He continually returned to the topic, and many of his articles on it were published posthumously in *On Thinking* (1979). The verb *thinking,* he says, often functions in a way that can be characterized as "adverbial." When one learns, for instance, that the soldier obeyed the sergeant's order to eat breakfast, or that he performed the order reluctantly, one learns something about the soldier's mind without having to ascribe to him some invisible "pushes" or "pulls." Autonomous verbs of doing may have multiple layers of "adverbialness" attached to them. The soldier may eat his breakfast obediently but also obey the order to do so reluctantly, and, on top of that, may be pretending not to be reluctant. He is not doing four things—eating breakfast, obeying, being reluctant, and pretending—but only one. This ability to act on such pyramiding levels of sophistication is a familiar characteristic of the human mind.

Ryle disputes the claim that thought must be carried on in language or any other kind of symbols and says that this "vehicle-cargo" model should be discarded. A person who is making up a speech does not think in words, phrases, and sentences that finally constitute his speech; rather, he searches for the words, phrases, and sentences that will suit his purpose. Nor does he necessarily engage in "internal soliloquies": "Some thinking does, but most thinking does not require the saying or sub-saying of anything." Soliloquies differ according to the purposes with which they are performed, and each purpose has its own criteria of success: "Meditating composingly and meditating self-practisingly are different things; their successes and failures are different, and can be interdependent."

Returning to the imagination, Ryle distinguishes among various ways in which the relation between imagination and thought may be conceived. He observes that there is an exercise of imagination that is not a rival or supplanter of thinking but "adverbially" qualifies thinking. It is, thus, a mistake to contrast thought and imagination. The exercise of the imagination is undesirable in some intellectual tasks, such as producing correct answers in arithmetic, and an historian must not allow his or her imagination to distort or ignore the facts. But for some tasks, hard factual thinking and imaginative thinking go hand in hand. The inventions of a Thomas Edison or the theoretical discoveries of a Michael Faraday are a result of a successful blend of the two mental powers.

Ryle calls attention to a connection between the concepts of thinking and self-teaching: "Thinking is trying to better one's own instructions, it is to try out promissory tracks which will exist, if they ever do exist, only after one has stumbled exploringly over ground where they are not." In Plato's dialogue *Meno,* Socrates gets a slave boy who is ignorant of geometry to formulate the Pythagorean Theorem by asking him a series of leading questions. If Socrates forgot how to prove a particular theorem, Ryle suggests, he could rediscover the proof by asking himself similar leading questions. His thinking would then take the form of self-teaching. "Explorers always do have to start off chartless; yet, as we know, some of them, sometimes with luck, flair, patience, and an already trained eye for the country, end up with a bit of what had been no-man's-land now properly charted."

The appearance of elusiveness in some mental phenomena can be remedied when one considers verbs characterizing "negative actions." Verbs such as *refraining, postponing, overlooking, letting,* and *pausing* refer to the agent's intentional nonperformance of some specifiable actions. Although in some cases there seem to be reasons for regarding such verbs as verbs of doing, the preponderance of reasons is against regarding them in that way. Ryle finds the notion "of a higher order" helpful here. Negative "actions" provide the "supra-factor" (such as postponing) ascribable to "infra-doings" (such as writing a letter). While not actions proper, negative "actions" are intentional sustained actualities that are truly or falsely predicable of agents. They may be used to identify "lines of action" that agents at any given time may be correctly said to pursue. The acknowledgment of the presence of negative "actions" in behavior enlarges the concept of the "mental" without forcing one into a Cartesian position.

Ryle had a strong interest in ancient Greek philosophy and published several critical essays in that field. In 1966 he surprised the philosophical world with his book *Plato's Progress,* which advances a provocative thesis about Plato's intellectual development that he arrived at by combing through the writings of Plato, Aristotle, and their contemporaries. The thesis is that an abrupt change occurred in Plato's method of philosophizing. In the early dialogues the character Socrates practices the "elenctic argument," which consists of asking a series of questions that drives the proponent of a thesis to admit its falsity and abandon it. But about twenty years after Socrates' execution in 399 B.C., on charges of undermining belief in the state religion and corrupting the youth of Athens, Plato himself was tried and punished for writing offensive speeches about some politicians and for corrupting the youth by teaching the dialectical method. As a result of that crisis, Plato, according to Ryle, was forbidden to teach dialectic to young men in his school, the Academy, and had to adopt a different method of philosophizing. Argumentation became "internal"; the soul of the thinker was to "converse with itself," to weigh alternatives in an inner dialogue.

As evidence for his conclusion Ryle cites the absence of any reference to dialectic in Aristotle's writings about Plato's Academy. Aristotle came to the Academy a few years after Plato's "crisis," by which time dialectic was no longer part of its curriculum; instead, Aristotle's training was in mathematics and theoretical astronomy. Furthermore, Ryle points out, all jollity disappears from Plato's "post-crisis" dialogues, and the Socrates character flattens out into a professor or a preacher. Book 7 of *The Republic* startlingly vetoes the participation in dialectical disputation by young men on the grounds that "they themselves and the whole business of philosophy are discredited with other men." Ryle suggests that *The Apology,* which depicts Socrates' trial, should be read as a conflated defense of charges brought almost twenty years apart against both Socrates and Plato. Ryle also produces a new chronology of the composition of the Platonic dialogues, disputing the timetable worked out by previous scholars. Although the findings of Ryle's book were met with much skepticism, the reader is bound to be impressed by his mastery of the scholarly material and by his use of it to produce an original philosophical detective story.

Ryle retired from his professorship at Oxford in 1968. He received honorary doctor of letters degrees from the University of Birmingham and the University of Warwick in 1969, from the University of Sussex in 1971, and from the University of Hull in 1972.

The last paper Gilbert Ryle published before his death on 6 October 1976 was "Improvisation," which appeared in *Mind* in January 1976 and is collected in *On Thinking.* In *The Concept of Mind* he contrasted drill and training and said that the latter requires alertness to the nonroutine elements in one's experience. In this paper, that alertness is declared to be logically necessary: "To a partly novel situation the response is necessarily partly novel, else it is not a response." Ryle claims that innovative thinking is not absent even from inference: no intermediate steps exist between some premises and some conclusions, and in some situations a person trained in inference can find the solution from data and premises that were always available—not because some intermediate steps have turned up, thus changing the problem, but simply because the person has changed and can now "see" with "new eyes," so to speak, what he or she previously failed to see. The penultimate paragraph of the paper includes a sentence that can be regarded as a summary of Ryle's conclusions: "So thinking, I now declare quite generally is, at the least, the engaging of partly trained wits in a partly fresh situation."

References:

Richard Freis, ed., *The Progress of* Plato's Progress (Berkeley, Cal.: Agon, 1970);

Konstantin Kolenda, ed., "A Symposium on Gilbert Ryle," *Rice University Studies,* 58 (Summer 1972);

William Lyons, *Gilbert Ryle: An Introduction to His Philosophy* (Brighton: Harvester Press / Atlantic Highlands, N.J.: Humanities Press, 1980);

Archana Roy, *A Short Commentary on* The Concept of Mind (Calcutta: Naya Prokash, 1973);

Oscar P. Wood and George Pitcher, eds., *Ryle: A Collection of Critical Essays* (New York: Doubleday, 1970).

Henry Sidgwick
(31 May 1838 – 28 August 1900)

David Crossley
University of Saskatchewan

BOOKS: *The Ethics of Conformity and Subscription* (London: Williams & Norgate, 1870);

The Methods of Ethics (London: Macmillan, 1874; revised, 1877; London & New York: Macmillan, 1890);

A Supplement to the First Edition of The Methods of Ethics: *Containing All the Important Additions and Alterations in the Second Edition* (London: Macmillan, 1877);

Three Lectures on Subjects Connected with the Practice of Education: Delivered in the University of Cambridge in the Easter Term, 1882, by Sidgwick and others (Cambridge: Cambridge University Press, 1883);

The Principles of Political Economy (London: Macmillan, 1883; London & New York: Macmillan, 1887);

The Scope and Method of Economic Science: An Address Delivered to the Economic Science and Statistics Section of the British Association at Aberdeen, 10 September, 1885 (London: Macmillan, 1885; New York: Kraus, 1968);

Outlines of the History of Ethics for English Readers (London & New York: Macmillan, 1886);

The Elements of Politics (London & New York: Macmillan, 1891; revised, 1897);

Practical Ethics: A Collection of Addresses and Essays (London: Sonnenschein, 1898; New York: Macmillan, 1898);

Philosophy, Its Scope and Relations: An Introductory Course of Lectures, edited by James Ward (London & New York: Macmillan, 1902);

Lectures on the Ethics of T. H. Green, Mr. Herbert Spencer, and J. Martineau, edited by E. E. Constance Jones (London & New York: Macmillan, 1902);

The Development of European Polity, edited by Eleanor Sidgwick (London & New York: Macmillan, 1903);

Miscellaneous Essays and Addresses, edited by Eleanor Sidgwick and Arthur Sidgwick (London & New York: Macmillan, 1904);

Lectures on the Philosophy of Kant and Other Philosophical Essays, edited by Ward (London & New York: Macmillan, 1905);

Presidential Addresses to the Society for Psychical Research, 1882–1911, by Sidgwick and others (Glasgow: Society for Psychical Research, 1912);

The Works of Henry Sidgwick, 15 volumes (Bristol: Thoemmes Press, 1996).

Edition: *The Methods of Ethics,* foreword by John Rawls (Indianapolis & Cambridge: Hackett, 1981).

235

OTHER: *Moral Sciences Tripos,* edited by Sidgwick, Student's Guide to the University of Cambridge, part 8 (Cambridge: Deighton, Bell, 1881);

P. F. Aschrott, *The English Poor Law System, Past and Present,* translated by Herbert Preston-Thomas, preface by Sidgwick (London: Knight, 1888).

Although mainly remembered as the author of what many critics consider the most important book on ethics written in nineteenth-century Britain, *The Methods of Ethics* (1874), Henry Sidgwick was a man of broad interests and wide-ranging knowledge. He studied classical languages and literature, and his lectures, addresses, and reviews dealt with history, economics, politics, and poetry, in addition to philosophy. His enthusiasm for spiritualism reflected his hope that scientific evidence of paranormal events would support religious belief. He also took practical steps to improve educational opportunities for women.

Sidgwick was born in Skipton, Yorkshire, on 31 May 1838, the third son and fourth of the six children of the Reverend William Sidgwick, the head of the local grammar school, and Mary Crofts Sidgwick. One of his brothers died when Sidgwick was two, and his father died the following year. After some wanderings, during which one of Sidgwick's sisters died, Mary Sidgwick settled near Bristol in 1844.

In early childhood Sidgwick developed a stammer that remained with him for the rest of his life. At twelve he went to boarding school in Blackheath, and in 1852 he entered Rugby School. There he made many lifelong friends, including T. H. Green, who went on to become a philosopher at the University of Oxford. Edward White Benson, an older second cousin of Sidgwick's, took up the position of assistant master of Rugby the year Sidgwick entered and remained an influence and frequent correspondent. Benson married Sidgwick's sister Mary in 1859 and became archbishop of Canterbury in 1882.

In 1855 Sidgwick entered Trinity College of the University of Cambridge, having won two prestigious scholarships. In his second year he began suffering attacks of indigestion; this condition, and the insomnia it caused, plagued him for the rest of his life. He also had hay fever and difficulties with his mucous membranes, both of which affected his breathing. These health problems often made research and writing impossible and were probably the cause of the occasional bouts of depression of which he complained. In spite of these problems he performed the rare achievement of passing the tripos in both classics and mathematics and still found time to read novels and poetry. He was especially fond of poetry and had a fine memory for it; he was partial to the works of Alfred Tennyson and Arthur Hugh Clough.

During his undergraduate days Sidgwick joined the spiritualist Ghost Society and the discussion group the Apostles. At meetings of the Apostles no topic was barred; questions of religion, politics, and ethics were often debated. The influence of his experiences in the group can be seen in Sidgwick's writings, in his constant attempts to understand and weigh the merits of each side of every issue impartially and objectively, and in his readiness to acknowledge weaknesses in his own position. In an 1897 letter he told Benson's son that his guiding ideal was "a complete revision of human relations, political, moral and economic, in light of science directed by comprehensive and impartial sympathy; and an unsparing reform of whatever, in the judgment of science, was pronounced to be not conducive to the general happiness."

In the period between his graduation in June 1859 and taking up his fellowship at Trinity in October, however, Sidgwick was uncertain what occupation would best permit him to pursue this goal. He thought for a time about becoming a minister, but, though he considered himself a theist, he had serious doubts about many of the doctrines of Christianity.

During this period his future projects began to take shape. His concern for the status of women is reflected in a note he sent in late 1862 to the members of a correspondence discussion group, in which he deplored the deficient "mental training" afforded women and said that they ought to be granted "certain rights which they could fairly claim." Some of the themes of *The Methods of Ethics* can already be seen in a series of letters he wrote to his friend H. G. Dakyns in 1862. In March he remarked that he thought he could see a way of reconciling "the moral sense and utilitarian theories." On 7 April he wrote Dakyns that "[Alexander] Bain is the only thoroughly honest Utilitarian philosopher . . . and he allows self-sacrifice . . . to constitute a 'glorious paradox,' whereas [Auguste] Comte and all practical Utilitarians exalt the same sentiments into the supreme Rule of life. These are the views I am trying to reconcile." On 1 December he told Dakyns: "I want intuitions for Morality; at least one (of Love) is required to supplement the utilitarian morality and I do not see why, if we are to have one, we may not have others." Although he was beginning to focus his attention on ethics, he was also reading theological works, and he began to learn Aramaic and Hebrew in the hope that some of his religious doubts might be resolved by comparative studies of the sacred texts of the world's great religions in their original languages. He was also reading books on economics, and in a letter to a friend,

O. Browning, on 27 September 1865 he mentioned that he was "designing a treatise on Politics."

Moral science had become a degree course at Cambridge, and Sidgwick began to lecture on the subject in 1867. In 1869, no longer able to endorse the official doctrines of the Church of England, which was a condition for holding his fellowship, he resigned from the position. On 13 June he wrote Benson that although he would not leave the Church of England, he could not "accept the dogmatic obligation of the Apostles' Creed." Resigning the fellowship could have ended his career at Cambridge, but Trinity College appointed him lecturer in moral sciences.

Sidgwick presented a course of lectures for women at Cambridge; more than seventy attended the first offering in 1870. An appeal for money to provide scholarships brought a contribution from the utilitarian philosopher John Stuart Mill. Sidgwick rented a house where women students from outside Cambridge could live, and he engaged Anne Jemima Clough to run it. But as female demand for education increased, larger premises were needed, and Newnham Hall was built in 1875.

Parliament abolished religious tests for obtaining and holding fellowships in the Test Act of 1871, and Sidgwick was reappointed to the fellowship at Trinity. In 1872 F. D. Maurice died, leaving vacant the professorship of moral philosophy. Sidgwick applied for the position but was not selected. He was clearly disappointed, despite the humorous assurances he gave his mother in a 30 April letter that he did not care about having been passed over, since professorships are "Mere dust, mere dross, in comparison with Knowledge and Virtue (This is Philosophy)"; he would get little increase in income–"This is Common-Sense"; and success would have brought many woes, such as having to dine with "several more stupid people," having "more comparatively ineligible men" ask him for letters of recommendation, and having to tell "several white lies" to "dull writers" who would send him their manuscripts.

The Methods of Ethics appeared in 1874. That the title refers to "methods" rather than to a "theory" of ethics reflects the nature of the task Sidgwick has undertaken. He does not begin by announcing an ethical theory and then spend the rest of the book defending it. He is concerned, instead, with the process of arriving at a theory, which requires one to think things through carefully and completely and with as much clarity and precision as possible. Sidgwick is struck by the fact that certain actions are considered obligatory, even though they conflict with other obligations and their rationale is uncertain–for example, expressing belief in the Thirty-Nine Articles as a condition of holding a college fellowship. This sort of situation raises two questions for Sidgwick:

Sidgwick's mother, Mary Crofts Sidgwick, circa 1870

to what extent can one's own sense of what is right be substituted for the demands of custom or authority, and how is one to resolve conflicts about how to act?

By the middle of the nineteenth century there were four main rival ethical theories. Egoism, which had been presented most forcefully by Thomas Hobbes in the seventeenth century, claimed that one's sole obligation is to promote one's own good. Intuitionism held that self-evident moral axioms could be discovered by a "moral sense" or moral faculty. Intuitionism was the view against which Mill had proposed his empirically grounded ethical theory, utilitarianism, according to which morally right actions are those that promote the greatest happiness of the greatest number. By the time Sidgwick published his book, utilitarianism was the dominant ethical theory in Britain. Finally, various forms of theological ethics claimed either that moral obligations were dependent on the commands of God or that human beings were supposed to attempt to achieve the moral perfection exemplified in the life of Christ; the latter sort of theory was being developed by Green. Turning from the theories of the philosophers to the moral deliberations of ordinary people, Sidgwick finds them sometimes appealing to their own happiness and at other times considering the effects of actions on the general welfare, while considering some actions, such as keeping promises, as simply right in and of themselves. The history of ethics and the deliverances of common sense, then, offer several competing methods for determining moral obligations. The issue for Sidgwick is whether these approaches can be reconciled.

Sidgwick's first task is to clarify the central concepts of ethical discourse: right, good, obligation, and so forth. He points out that ethical terms can appear in judgments that are either hypothetical or categorical. An example of the former is "If you wish to be healthier you should give up smoking." Giving up smoking is obligatory only if one desires to be healthier. By contrast, a categorical judgment asserts that something is good not as a means to other things but for its own sake. Sidgwick contends that moral terms are "logically primitive," meaning that they are "too elementary to admit of any formal definition." Moral judgments are also logically primitive, because they cannot be inferred from nonnormative premises. An empirical science such as psychology can show how people do act but not why they ought to act in certain ways. For this reason, Jeremy Bentham's attempt to base a utilitarian ethics on psychological hedonism—the psychological claim that people are necessarily motivated to seek pleasure and avoid pain—failed. These fundamental ethical concepts are connected to reason: to say that something is right or good is to say that one has some reason to do or pursue it.

Sidgwick says that judgments of what it is right to do seem to be binding in a way that judgments about what is good are not. If one judges a certain kind of conduct to be right, one is claiming that there is "an authoritative prescription to do it; but when one has judged conduct to be good, it is not yet clear that one ought to prefer this kind of good to all other good things: some standard for estimating the relative value of different 'goods' has still to be sought." *Good,* that is, is a comparative term, whereas *right* is not. Questions of what is right are focused on people's conduct as agents acting in the world, while questions of the good answer to the sentient aspect of human life, for in the final analysis people judge things to be good if they contribute to the production or maintenance of "desirable states of consciousness."

That the right and the good make rational demands on human beings introduces objectivity into moral reasoning, for whatever is claimed to be reasonable can be discussed and debated; and an action that it is reasonable for one person to perform should, other things being equal, be reasonable for others. The methods employed in ethics are "rational proce-

dures for determining right conduct" that appeal to a principle that is taken as ultimate. For example, utilitarianism advances universal happiness as the ultimate principle and determines which actions ought to be performed by calculating the happiness that is expected to result from those actions.

Sidgwick divides the methods of ethics into teleological and nonteleological. Teleological theories justify actions by appeal to a moral good to be promoted and differ among themselves by virtue of the ultimate moral end they advocate. Common sense identifies two types of moral goal: perfection and happiness. The latter is divided into egoistic versions, according to which the ultimate end is one's own happiness, and universalistic versions, such as utilitarianism, which hold that the end is the happiness of all persons or all sentient creatures. "Happiness" is understood as achieving pleasure and avoiding pain, so these methods are forms of hedonism—though Sidgwick prefers to describe the end as "desirable states of consciousness" rather than "pleasure." By contrast, nonteleological theories hold that certain actions are obligatory simply because they are morally right and not because they promote some further end, such as increasing happiness. Respecting the rights of individuals would be a nonteleological moral demand, because the obligation flows from the right itself, not from any result achieved by respecting the right.

Sidgwick concludes that there are three distinct methods of ethics: intuitionism, egoistic hedonism, and universal hedonism or utilitarianism. He considers perfectionist or self-realization views, which would seem to be teleological, to be intuitionist, because they extol virtue as desirable for its own sake, not because it promotes some further end. He omits them from consideration, because they must be based on a theory of the nature of the true self that one is to develop; in that respect, they illegitimately attempt to ground their basic ethical principle on nonethical premises.

Sidgwick is concerned not only to examine each method but also to see whether one of the three could systematize all moral reasoning; therefore, two questions dominate his discussion: can intuitionism and utilitarianism be reconciled? And can the two teleological methods, egoism and utilitarianism, be reconciled? The answer to the first question depends on whether the intuitionist is claiming that actions can be intuitively seen to be morally obligatory on a case-by-case basis or that actions must be judged by moral principles that themselves are intuitively certain. When difficult cases arise, people's intuitions about what is morally demanded, or about the moral principle to be applied, often conflict, whereupon they tend to turn to considerations of the benefits attained by accepting one of the conflicting opinions—that is, they fall back on the utilitarian method. And there is a third role for intuitions: since no teleological theory can prove its ultimate principle by appeal to any further principle, it needs an intuition to secure it.

Yet a further place for intuitive principles is evident if one considers practical reasoning more generally. No matter what conception of the good one holds, or what actions one thinks are morally obligatory, all would agree that reason demands that similar cases be treated similarly. If doing X is morally obligatory for one person under certain conditions, then it must be obligatory for anyone else who is similarly situated. Also, if a person's moral obligation is to maximize the good, then it should make no difference whose is the good in question, or whether it can be achieved sooner or later. These considerations, Sidgwick says, reveal three self-evident axioms of practical reasoning to which people generally subscribe.

First, the axiom of justice states that "whatever action any of us judges to be right for himself, he implicitly judges to be right for all similar persons in similar circumstances." He restates the axiom in negative terms: it cannot be right to treat two people differently "merely on the ground that they are two different individuals, without there being any difference . . . which can be stated as a reasonable ground of difference of treatment." Sidgwick sees a general commitment to this axiom reflected in the belief that the law must be administered impartially.

Second, the axiom of prudence states that one "ought to have an impartial concern for all parts of one's conscious life." Sidgwick gives this axiom, too, a negative formulation: "the mere difference of priority and posteriority in time is not a reasonable ground for having more regard to the consciousness of one moment than to that of another." Even if the rational egoist accepts no other axioms, he or she should endorse this one.

The third axiom is that of benevolence. This axiom is not strictly self-evident; but it is self-evident that "the good of any one individual is of no more importance from the point of view of the universe than the good of any other" and that rational creatures are obliged "to aim at good generally . . . not merely at a particular part of it." From these insights one can deduce the axiom of benevolence, which holds "that each of us is morally bound to regard the good of any other individual as much as his own, except in so far as he judges it to be less, when impartially viewed, or less knowable or attainable by him." Clearly, Sidgwick says, this axiom is one to which the utilitarian would subscribe.

Sidgwick's intuited self-evident axioms allow for the possibility of what he calls "Utilitarianism on an Intuitional basis." The egoist, however, remains a prob-

Sidgwick as an undergraduate at Trinity College of the University of Cambridge in the mid-to-late 1850s

lem. Following the eighteenth-century Anglican bishop and ethical philosopher Joseph Butler, Sidgwick insists that pursuit of one's own good is reasonable—in fact, most people would think that anyone who did not look out for his or her own well-being was odd, if not irrational. How, then, can the utilitarian convince the egoist to regard the happiness of others as being as important as his or her own? Although utilitarians are committed to equal concern for all persons, in that they say that the interests of each must be taken into account, the requirement of maximizing happiness opens up the possibility that any particular person's interests will not be promoted. The axiom of benevolence does not prohibit this result, for saying that one cannot treat A differently from B unless one has a good reason for doing so implies that one can treat A differently if one does have such a reason. The egoist, then, can conclude that whenever treating A differently from B will maximize overall "utility" (that is, happiness), the utilitarian will have a good reason for treating them differently. For example, that A will be made healthy and, therefore, much happier is a reason to direct resources toward A rather than to recreational facilities desired by B, who will gain only a small increment in happiness from such facilities. The principle of utility functions as a principle of trade-offs, indicating when it is morally acceptable to sacrifice one person's interests to another's and thereby offering the rational egoist no assurance that his or her interests will not be sacrificed to the general welfare of society. The crucial point for the egoist is "that the distinction between any one individual and any other is real and fundamental, and that consequently 'I' am concerned with the quality of my existence as an individual in a sense, fundamentally important, in which I am not concerned with the quality of existence of other individuals." Thus, a motivational gap exists between interest in one's own good and interest in the good of others that cannot be closed by any rational argument. Feelings of sympathy will often fill this gap, but Sidgwick finds no reason to expect all people to have these sympathies. If, as some religions maintain, people will be compensated for their sacrifices by being rewarded in the afterlife, this problem would be overcome. But that doctrine is far from proven, and besides, to rely on theological arguments at this stage would be to confess that ethical theory cannot itself discover a way to reconcile the two hedonistic methods. Unfortunately, Sidgwick admits, this is exactly what ethical science cannot do, and so the attempt to systematize the methods of ethics ends in failure.

Sidgwick's book elicited many responses. Because the discussion is so dense, with every point followed by qualifications, counterexamples, and restatements, readers had difficulty being sure exactly what position he was advocating. Since Sidgwick described himself as a utilitarian, some took *The Methods of Ethics* as simply a defense of utilitarianism; but because Sidgwick argues that intuition is required to secure utilitarianism's ultimate moral principle, others thought that the book supported intuitionism. A case was even made that Sidgwick had shown egoism to be the basic theory: since the utilitarian's universal happiness is the aggregate of the happiness of individuals, the egoist's conception of his or her own good must underwrite the notion of the good of all. The truth, however, is that Sidgwick attempts to examine all of the methods objectively and fairly, and his reluctant acceptance of their irreconcilability shows that *The Methods of Ethics* is not a polemic in support of any one of them.

The Oxford idealists Green and F. H. Bradley mainly attacked the hedonism of *The Methods of Ethics;* Sidgwick's substitution of "desired states of consciousness" for "pleasure" did nothing to persuade them that hedonism was not central to the book. They raised the traditional objections to hedonism: from the fact that achieving a goal brings satisfaction, hedonists erroneously conclude that pleasure is itself the goal of all actions; pleasures cannot be measured and compared, so hedonistic methods are unworkable; and the focus on pleasure emphasizes the sentient aspect of human beings at the expense of their spiritual nature. Mill had tried to avoid the last criticism by introducing the notion of qualitatively different types of pleasures; but Sidgwick refused to follow Mill on this point, arguing that the distinction between "higher" and "lower" pleasures would either reduce to estimates of the quantity of pleasure produced by various activities or would require a separate criterion that would challenge the principle of utility for supremacy. One objection brought by the idealists was derived from the German idealist philosopher Georg Wilhelm Friedrich Hegel: since pleasures are a perishing series, not a stable state, the demand to obtain the most pleasure is the impossible demand to sum an infinite series. Talking about the greatest possible quantity of pleasure is as meaningless, they claimed, as talking about the greatest possible quantity of time. Sidgwick responded to these criticisms in articles, but the issue became moot as utilitarians moved away from the hedonistic version of their principle.

Modern commentators generally agree that Sidgwick's discussions of the intuitionist's treatment of virtues and duties—justice, benevolence, truth telling, keeping promises and agreements, and so forth—and of difficult topics such as the measurement of happiness are thorough and illuminating and that his analyses of central ethical concepts and his efforts to make obscure points clear and precise are exemplary. In his foreword to the 1981 edition of *The Methods of Ethics* the American ethical and political philosopher John Rawls says that Sidgwick's book shows more awareness of the difficulties classical utilitarianism faces and works through the theory more carefully than do other accounts. He calls Sidgwick the first modern ethical thinker, for *The Methods of Ethics* "is the first truly academic work in moral philosophy which undertakes to provide a systematic comparative study of moral conceptions."

In 1875 Sidgwick was appointed lecturer in moral and political philosophy. That same year, at a séance at the home of Arthur Balfour, a friend and fellow enthusiast for spiritualism who later became prime minister of Britain, he met Balfour's sister, Eleanor Mildred (Nora). They became engaged in December and were married on 4 April 1876. Nora Sidgwick worked with her husband on projects related to women's education and in 1892 became principal of Newnham College.

Around the time of his marriage Sidgwick's interest in spiritualism was at its peak. He was reading about medieval miracles, which he saw as linked to spiritualist phenomena in that both promised support for religious beliefs. He frequently attended séances, and he met many of the prominent mediums of the day, including Eva Anna Fay and one of the Fox sisters. Public interest in psychic phenomena was increasing, spurred in part by experiments conducted by W. F. Barrett that purported to show the reality of "thought transference," or telepathy; some believed that thought transference substantiated the claims of prophets and others to "hear" God speaking to them. Sidgwick was in constant contact with like-minded intellectuals who were studying the paranormal, such as the writer Edmund Gurney, the psychologist Frederic W. H. Myers, the physicist and chemist Sir William Crookes, and the naturalist Alfred Russel Wallace; this association led to the foundation of the Society for Psychical Research. In his inaugural address in July 1882 as its first president, Sidgwick notes that the new society's studies are to include thought reading, clairvoyance, ghosts, the appearance of the dead at séances, the powers of spirits to perform tasks such as moving objects, and mesmerism (hypnotism). The aim of the society is to ascertain the facts by applying scientific methods, making no prior assumptions about the truthfulness of witnesses. Sidgwick admits that they will be facing an uphill battle, given the skepticism of most scientists and the failures of previous attempts to authenticate spiritualist phenomena. Yet, he thinks that the prejudice against spiritualism will fall away as scientists attest to their beliefs, which, he notes, has already happened with mesmerism.

Sidgwick's investigations uncovered many fraudulent mediums, and he knew that there were conceptual problems with spiritualism, such as how ghosts could be material enough to be seen or move objects but immaterial enough to pass through walls. But such concerns never dampened his enthusiasm for long. His hope that spiritualism might be true and that it could provide the evidence he sought for religious beliefs was too strong. He may also have been misled by the apparent success of investigations done in supposedly controlled scientific experiments. In one such experiment Crookes had the medium Fay hold the handles of his galvanometer during a séance in which objects on the table were moved. Crookes concluded that spirits had moved the objects, because the galvanometer showed that the current was never broken—supposedly proving that Fay had not been able to handle the objects herself. But Fay later revealed the trick: she had put one handle behind her knee, thereby keeping both handles in contact with her body and the electrical current flowing, while at the same time freeing one hand to move the objects.

Sidgwick's *The Principles of Political Economy* appeared in 1883, the year he was appointed professor of moral philosophy at Cambridge. He begins the book by noting disagreement among economists as to whether their discipline should be restricted to the theoretical study of the production, exchange, and distribution of wealth or should also include practical advice to

Eleanor Mildred Balfour circa 1870, six years before she and Sidgwick were married (photograph by John William Strutt)

individuals and governments. Sidgwick opts for the second alternative. On the theoretical side he is interested in the central terms and categories used in economics, such as capital, rent, wealth, and so forth, and in the laws of production and exchange formulated by economists. His aim is to clarify the language where it is obscure and to systematize and reconcile doctrines when they are at odds. This approach echoes the one he used in ethics, and his treatment of the problems involved in measuring wealth and value parallels his discussions of the measurement of pleasure and pain in *The Methods of Ethics*. Sidgwick is aware of the problem of the subjectivity of values—the fact that people may not value or desire the same things—and of the problem of providing a comparative evaluation of things in altered circumstances or when their enjoyment lies in the future as opposed to being available now.

On the practical side, Sidgwick notes that since governments have goals that require material resources and ready funds, officials will be interested in what economics can teach about the production of wealth and its efficient use. Nevertheless, there are two points on which politicians and economists part company. First, politicians are likely to be more concerned about the distribution of wealth than economists are. Second, government policies aimed at increasing or making better use of wealth run against a central tenet of economics: the laissez-faire doctrine, which holds that production and efficiency are highest when left to the self-interest of individuals competing in a free market; that is, wealth will be greatest when government interferes least. The laissez-faire doctrine is based on the "system of natural liberty," a presumption in favor of individuals being free to pursue their plans and projects without interference except for constraints required to prevent harm to, and loss of freedom for, others.

Sidgwick subscribes to this libertarian view, with some qualifications. For example, he says, the provision of social goods, such as protecting land from floods or water from becoming polluted, cannot be left to individuals. Sidgwick illustrates the point by presenting a version of the "tragedy of the commons": all of the farmers in a given area need the common land for grazing their cattle, and so they should take care of it; but self-interest will lead each to allow his cattle to overgraze, and the commons will be destroyed. Voluntary self-restraint will not work, for some will take advantage of the self-restraint of others. Thus, government regulation of industries such as fishing is necessary if material resources important to the community are to be protected.

Sidgwick then moves to a discussion of the dangers of government regulation. It will increase the government's powers unduly and will encourage overspending by politicians to please their constituents and thereby win reelection. A more important consideration is that the more the government does for people, the less they will do for themselves, leading to "the repression of energy and self-help." This theme comes up again and again in the last two hundred pages of the book, especially in relation to relief for the poor. Christians and legislators had long been uncertain how to reconcile the moral duty of benevolence to the poor with the fear that charity would, by removing incentive to work, discourage the recipient's self-reliance and industry—qualities that were considered prime virtues during the Victorian era. This dilemma plagued the many volunteer charity organizations to which people such as Sidgwick belonged.

Sidgwick distinguishes government interventions aimed at reducing harm to others, such as laws requiring the labeling of drugs, from paternalistic ones, such as safety regulations to protect workers from their own carelessness, and from "socialistic" programs designed to provide communal goods, such as roads. He points out that the private sector might not be able to provide common goods such as a nationwide telegraph or electric-power system if the capital required is too large, or the profits from the investment will be realized far in the future, or if right-of-way for the telegraph or electric lines cannot be obtained without the power to compel sale of the land. He pays considerable attention to land ownership, a major concern of Victorian political theorists, arguing that private interests cannot guarantee protection of a communal resource such as land, since, for instance, timber merchants want the trees and do not care about the land on which they grow. He discusses free trade, which had been hotly debated since the eighteenth century. The case for free trade, he says, hinges on the claim of the natural-liberty theory that individuals acting from self-interest will create a situation most conducive to the production of wealth and well-being in the community.

In regard to demands for a more equitable distribution of wealth, Sidgwick holds that economic theory does not have a clear and workable criterion of equity. A fair return is usually defined in terms of the prices of goods and services established in a freely competitive market; but this definition is suspect, since truly free markets exist only in economic theory. Justice demands that workers share in the wealth of the society in proportion to their desert. But if doing so means measuring the value of labor by the effort of the worker, it will be difficult to calculate; and it is morally suspect in that it depends on the worker's natural abilities, which are a matter of luck. Desert should be measured according to the worker's actual production of goods and services, since doing so will stimulate production. A different perspective is presented by communism, which says that justice demands distributing wealth according to need rather than desert; an example of policy based on this perspective is the Poor Laws. In addition to the problems of reducing self-reliance and discouraging the exercise of voluntary charity, a central concern is how to distinguish those who truly need help from those who are simply too lazy to work. The traditional way of weeding out the latter by making the conditions of receiving relief so obnoxious that no one would choose it over honest labor—for example, sending people to the workhouse—unfairly penalizes those who do need help through no fault of their own. From the standpoint of economic theory the problem is that the poor and the ill draw from the nation's wealth but contribute nothing to it; Sidgwick admits that unemployment relief and medical aid to the poor cannot be supported on purely economic grounds.

Socialistic policies require funds, a fact that raises the question of establishing a fair tax system. Sidgwick suggests that taxes be levied in proportion to services received and be used to redistribute incomes so as to exact equal sacrifices. Taxation should not render individuals unable to subsist, which means that necessities should not be taxed. He sees, however, no clear way to distinguish necessities from items of superfluous consumption. If this line could be drawn, proportional taxes on superfluous consumption would best equalize sacrifices. Savings should not be taxed, since they will enable people to avoid becoming burdens on society.

Sidgwick worries that economic theory's emphasis on allowing free rein to private interests often runs counter to one's moral feelings. He offers examples and settles the conflicts by appealing to utilitarian considerations. For instance, although morality values openness and sincerity, the economic loss the community would incur justifies a geologist's keeping secret the presence of minerals on a piece of land until he can buy it. Another worry is that economists' emphasis on self-interest has reduced people's natural sympathy for the less fortunate. While he acknowledges that this effect has occurred, Sidgwick argues that the suffering of the disadvantaged may be necessary for the greater good of the community. People need to learn the importance of saving or buying insurance against the possibility of illness and unemployment. Sidgwick adds one of the economic remedies so often urged on the poor: have fewer children.

In 1886 Sidgwick revised and enlarged the article on ethics he had contributed to the ninth edition of the *Encyclopædia Britannica* (1975–1889) and published it as *Outlines of the History of Ethics for English Readers*. He traces the origins of Christian morality, which, he claims, developed on two fronts. Under the influence of Roman law and Jewish theocracy it took a judicial form in which the chief task was to apply the divine code of morality. Obedience to the law was motivated in the Jewish tradition by the obligations resulting from the special covenant with God and by the fear of punishment and the promise of reward in the afterlife. To these sanctions the Roman Catholic Church added removal from membership in the religious community–excommunication–and acts of penitence for serious offenses, gradually building up an elaborate system of ecclesiastical jurisprudence. This emphasis on rules of external conduct was counterbalanced by a concern with "inwardness," with "rightness of heart and spirit." In this respect Christianity followed Stoicism, which stressed right intentions and the suppression of vicious desires. But whereas the Stoics emphasized knowledge, agreeing with Socrates that a person who knows the good will necessarily choose it, Christian moralists emphasized faith and love. Some believed that the divine law is arbitrary in that God was not forced to set out the laws he did, and that, therefore, reason is useless in discovering the provisions of the law, while others

Sidgwick in 1876, the year after he was appointed lecturer in moral and political philosophy at Cambridge

stressed the inability of fallible human beings to know the truth; in either case, it is necessary to accept the divine code on faith, supplemented by loyalty to Christ and trust in his example. The chief motive is love of God and of fellow beings with whom one shares a common "humanity ennobled by the incarnation." Love is the root of moral virtues such as beneficence. Emphasis on the "inward" spiritual values leads to disapproval of the things of the material world, such as wealth.

Opposition to the Catholic Church's development of the external side of moral and religious experience was one root of the Reformation, which, along with its emphasis on faith and the inward life, maintained "the right of private judgement against the dictation of ecclesiastical authority [and] the individual responsibility of every human soul before God in opposition to the papal control over purgatorial punishments." With the Reformation the legalistic treatment of moral obligation began to fade, opening the way for an ethical method that relied "solely on the common reason and common moral experiences of mankind." Into the void left by the retreat of divine codes grounded on authority or revelation came the notion of the natural law, a set of rules that could be seen to be obligatory by the light of reason.

The natural law doctrine of writers such as Hugo Grotius left unanswered the question of why one should obey the law. Hobbes's answer to the question marks the beginning of ethical philosophy in England. While Hobbes grounded a hedonistic ethical theory on psychological egoism, he saw that the successful pursuit of one's own happiness depends on the existence of a powerful "sovereign," or government, that can settle conflicts and keep the peace. Thus, matters of practical morality are decided by the "positive" laws of states, and the push toward universal principles exerted by Hobbes's psychological theory was eliminated by the relativity of legal codes. This relativism was what most exercised Hobbes's opponents, with intuitionists such as Ralph Cudworth and his fellow Cambridge Platonists arguing that reason can distinguish absolute rules of right conduct. Lack of agreement on what these self-evident moral principles are, however, reduced confidence in intuitionist ethics, as did Anthony Ashley Cooper, third Earl of Shaftesbury's substitution of emotional impulses to do one's duty for the role usually assigned to reason. Shaftesbury's writings, Sidgwick says, were important for English ethics because they turned the debate away from abstract principles of reason to psychological studies of the mind's impulses and sentiments. Much of the subsequent debate revolved around what these impulses and sentiments are. Butler thought that there were two: self-love and "conscience," the latter of which discerns certain dictates, such as the duty to be benevolent, as intuitively certain. To this debate David Hume and Adam Smith added the notion of sympathy as a basic feature of the moral sentiments and the source of one's concern for others. The mechanism at work here was the association of ideas, by which "other-regarding" actions are generated by association from feelings of self-love. Sidgwick sees in David Hartley the beginning of the attempt to go deeper than empirical psychological laws by grounding such laws on physiological facts. These attempts to "dissolve ethics into psychology" or physiology survived in the writings of Mill. After the theory of evolution was introduced, attempts were made to ground moral rules in the laws of biology or sociology. As readers of *The Methods of Ethics* know, Sidgwick is suspicious of these sorts of reductionist moves, since he does not think that moral obligations or normative principles can be derived from empirical facts about what people do. Sidgwick notes a countervailing view, which has come to England from Germany, that human beings are not merely material creatures but also rational, self-conscious spiritual ones. This view reintroduces the Christian perspective that the perfected inward spiritual life, rather than external acts, is of primary moral concern. Sidgwick identifies Green as one who defended this view.

Outlines of the History of Ethics for English Readers is still considered one of the best such works ever written. The analysis of medieval Christian morality is unparalleled, and the treatment of modern ethical thought from Hobbes to the late Victorian era provides a lucid and illuminating account of the central disputes of the period.

In 1891 Sidgwick published *The Elements of Politics*. The book carries on from where *The Principles of Political Economy* leaves off and employs a similar strategy. In *The Principles of Political Economy* Sidgwick asked whether government interference with natural liberty is ever justified on economic grounds; *The Elements of Politics* begins with a similar presumption of the value of liberty and asks when and where government interference might be justified by political arguments. Sidgwick says that the ultimate principle of political organization and policy should be that of utility. Having accepted "the utilitarian doctrine that the ultimate criterion for the goodness of law, and of the actions of government generally, is their tendency to increase the general happiness," the "difficult question" is "how far, if at all, the interests of one community are to be postponed by its government to the interests of other sections of humanity."

Sidgwick introduces two related technical notions. The "Individualistic Principle" holds that individuals should be free from interference from others and should only be obliged to render positive services to others that they have voluntarily contracted to perform. The set of rights and obligations required by a strict application of the Individualistic Principle constitutes the "Individualistic Minimum." The rights generated by the Individualistic Principle include protection from physical harms such as assault and battery and from nonphysical harms such as attacks on one's reputation; protection of property, so that the "natural reward of labour is full enjoyment of the utility resulting from it," because without legal protection of the products of one's labor there will be little incentive to work; and enforcement of contracts. These negative rights—that is, rights to noninterference by others—provided by the Individualistic Minimum will not be adequate to provide a suitable life for children and others who cannot fend for themselves. The welfare of children is the responsibility of their parents; therefore, insuring that children get the proper care and education justifies restricting legally recognized marriages to unions between the persons of opposite sexes and making divorce hard to obtain, even though such measures interfere with individual liberty.

Sidgwick notes that recent British governments have shown a trend in the direction of greater restrictions on individual liberty and greater regulation of industry. An example is the Employers' Liability Act, passed by the Liberal government in 1880, which required employers to compensate workers injured on the job. Opposition to this trend comes, first, from the advocates of laissez-faire; in response, Sidgwick repeats the arguments of *The Principles of Political Economy* for government action to provide public goods and protect communal resources. Since "socialistic" policies have costs that are largely defrayed by taxation of property, opposition also comes from property owners, who claim that this practice violates the Individualistic Principle by taking from them something to which they have an entitlement. Sidgwick replies that "the institution of private property as actually existing goes beyond what the individualistic theory justifies." He appeals to the seventeenth-century philosopher John Locke's "proviso" that an appropriation of previously unowned property is legitimate only if it does not reduce the opportunities of others to have and enjoy property–as Locke put it, "that enough and as good be left over for others." To the extent that existing property arrangements violate this moral condition, governments are justified in taxing property and using the proceeds to help the less advantaged through education or poor relief. Moreover, inheritance taxes on land are appropriate, because the heir need not have done anything to deserve the inheritance and so does not have a moral entitlement to it. Sidgwick's conclusion is that an individualistic system based on utilitarianism will sanction a certain level of government "socialism" when it can be shown to be for the common good.

Late in the book Sidgwick introduces the issues of nationalism and the right of peoples to secede from the states that govern them. A state, he says, is a community held together by its adherence to a form of government and a set of established legal rights and duties. As a corporate entity, the state has rights and obligations in regard to other states and has sovereign authority over its own territory. A nation, on the other hand, is a community united by "belief in a common origin, possession of a common language and literature, pride in common historic traditions, community of social customs, community of religion." The bond of the nation is similar to a kinship bond and is crucial for a stable society because it supplies a motivation and sense of unity that cannot be engendered merely by obeying the same legal rules or government dictates. The nation-state–a state comprising a single nationality–would be the ideal arrangement, but Sidgwick recognizes that modern states are usually multinational. While he fears the upheavals such disruptions might cause, Sidgwick endorses the right of a national group to secede and form its own state.

In international relations Sidgwick construes the obligations of states to one another as similar to those of

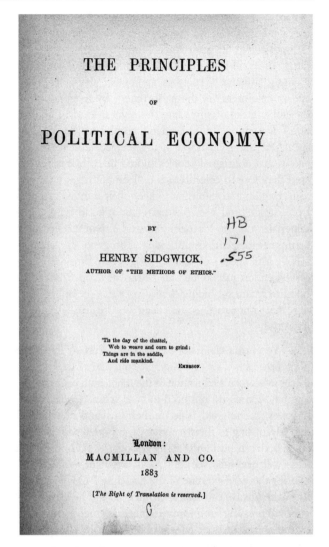

Title page for Sidgwick's major work on economics, in which he argues for a modified laissez-faire system (Thomas Cooper Library, University of South Carolina)

individuals within a state. States have duties of noninterference with other states and a moral obligation to respect treaties and commercial contracts into which they have freely entered. And just as the rational individual accepts certain prudential maxims not expressed in legal requirements, so states should recognize that more generous treatment than is legally required by treaties will often be in their interest. Moreover, states can express disapproval of what other states do, and such sanctions supplement legal requirements just as social sanctions within a community supplement and support its positive laws. But since states are not governed by any authoritative body or legal code that can be used to settle conflicts, war is always possible.

At times in this book Sidgwick displays the less palatable attitudes of his age. For example, he says that excluding some people from the franchise "on the ground of race alone may be expedient if the general intellectual or moral inferiority of the race excluded is sufficiently clear." He speaks without embarrassment of "inferior" or "uncivilized" races, of the gifts of culture and wealth brought to them by "advanced" societies, and of the "justifiable pride" felt by colonizers "in the performance by their nation of the noble tasks of spreading the highest kind of civilization." Forgetting the indigenous peoples of America, he speaks of the great tracts of unoccupied land there. He allows that aboriginal peoples should be compensated for land they lose to colonizers, but "I cannot regard savages as having an absolute right to keep their hunting-grounds from agricultural use." In part this attitude reflects the imperialism of the Victorian era, and in part it reflects the common nineteenth-century idea of progress. In *On Liberty* (1859) Mill speaks of nations progressing through stages of civilization just as human beings develop from childhood to maturity; Sidgwick also uses this metaphor, urging that immature states need to be treated paternalistically.

Women's claim to the franchise falls to the same prejudices; it is a bit of a shock to find one of the moving forces in women's education of the nineteenth century saying that women do not need to vote because the interests of wives "are tolerably safe" in their husband's hands and that "according to the necessary or customary division of labor between husbands and wives, the experience of the latter will, generally speaking, be of less value as a preparation for the wise exercise of the franchise." Sidgwick was, however, always cautious and practical, and he sometimes opposed pressing for improvements in women's university education not because he was opposed to the changes but because he thought the time was not right for them: given the general attitudes of the time, the proposal would probably fail and harm the cause. Moreover, he was always alert to the ways in which society might become unstable, and he might have thought that until women and working-class men had the benefit of better education it would be disruptive to give them the vote.

Sidgwick published no other books in his lifetime, apart from a collection of his addresses and public lectures in 1898. He died of cancer on 28 August 1900. His literary executors brought out several posthumous collections of his lectures, addresses, and essays, including *The Development of European Polity* (1903). This book is based on university lectures Sidgwick gave during the last fifteen years of his life that he never felt were ready for publication. In contrast to the analytical exposition of political principles offered in *The Elements of Politics,* it is an historical and evolutionary study of the development of forms of government.

The four major books Henry Sidgwick published during his lifetime, together with his work for women's education, reveal a man for whom ethical, religious, and political questions were of the utmost importance. *The Elements of Politics* and *Outlines of the History of Ethics for English Readers* are still valued highly, but Sidgwick's place in the history of philosophy is secured by *The Methods of Ethics,* which brilliantly sets out and assesses the principal ethical theories of the nineteenth century and ushers in the era of modern ethics through its clarity and precision and its emphasis on the need for thorough analyses of moral concepts and judgments—characteristics that one can see in the writings of early-twentieth-century ethical theorists such as G. E. Moore.

Biography:

Arthur Sidgwick and Eleanor Sidgwick, *Henry Sidgwick: A Memoir* (London & New York: Macmillan, 1906).

References:

F. H. Bradley, *Mr. Sidgwick's Hedonism: An Examination of the Main Argument of "The Methods of Ethics"* (London: King, 1877);

C. D. Broad, *Five Types of Ethical Theory* (London: Kegan Paul, 1930), pp. 143–256;

T. H. Green, *Prolegomena to Ethics,* fifth edition, edited by A. C. Bradley (Oxford: Clarendon Press, 1906), pp. 447–470;

William Clyde Havard, *Henry Sidgwick and Later Utilitarian Political Philosophy* (Gainesville: University of Florida Press, 1959);

Frank Herbert Hayward, *The Ethical Philosophy of Sidgwick: Nine Essays, Critical and Expository* (London: Sonnenschein, 1901);

David Gwilym James, *Henry Sidgwick: Science and Faith in Victorian England; with a Memoir of the Author by Gwyn Jones* (New York & London: Oxford University Press, 1970);

James Martineau, *Types of Ethical Theory,* third edition, 2 volumes (Oxford: Clarendon Press, 1901), II: 40–58, 277–299;

Hastings Rashdall, *The Theory of Good and Evil: A Treatise on Moral Philosophy,* 2 volumes (Oxford: Clarendon Press, 1907), I: 44–101, 147–151;

Jerome B. Schneewind, *Sidgwick's Ethics and Victorian Moral Philosophy* (Oxford: Clarendon Press, 1977);

Bart Schultz, ed., *Essays on Henry Sidgwick* (Cambridge & New York: Cambridge University Press, 1992).

Papers:

Henry Sidgwick's papers are in the Wren Library at Trinity College of the University of Cambridge. Many of his letters are in the British Museum; Balliol College of the University of Oxford; the Bodleian Library, Oxford; and the Houghton Library at Harvard University.

J. J. C. Smart

(16 September 1920 –   )

Keith Campbell
University of Sydney

BOOKS: *An Outline of a System of Utilitarian Ethics* (Carlton, Australia: Melbourne University Press on behalf of the University of Adelaide, 1961);

Philosophy and Scientific Realism (London: Routledge & Kegan Paul, 1963; New York: Humanities, 1963);

Between Science and Philosophy: An Introduction to the Philosophy of Science (New York: Random House, 1968);

Utilitarianism: For and Against, by Smart and Bernard Williams (London: Cambridge University Press, 1973);

Ethics and Science (Hobart: University of Tasmania, 1981);

Ethics, Persuasion, and Truth (London & Boston: Routledge & Kegan Paul, 1984);

Essays, Metaphysical and Moral: Selected Philosophical Papers (Oxford: Blackwell, 1987);

Our Place in the Universe: A Metaphysical Discussion (Oxford & New York: Blackwell, 1989);

Atheism and Theism, by Smart and J. J. Haldane (Oxford & Cambridge, Mass.: Blackwell, 1996).

OTHER: "The Existence of God," in *New Essays in Philosophical Theology,* edited by Anthony Flew and Alexander MacIntyre (London: SCM, 1955), pp. 28–46;

Problems of Space and Time: Readings, edited by Smart (New York: Macmillan, 1964; London: Collier-Macmillan, 1964);

"Religion and Science," "Space," "Time," and "Utilitarianism," in *The Encyclopedia of Philosophy,* 8 volumes, edited by Paul Edwards (New York: Macmillan, 1967), VII: 158–163, 506–511; VIII: 126–134, 206–212;

"Quine on Space-time," in *The Philosophy of W. V. Quine,* edited by Lewis E. Hahn and Paul Arthur Schilpp, The Library of Living Philosophers, volume 18 (La Salle, Ill.: Open Court, 1986), pp. 495–515;

"Utilitarianism and Its Applications," in *New Directions in Ethics: The Challenge of Applied Ethics,* edited by

J. J. C. Smart

Joseph P. De Marco and Richard M. Fox (London: Routledge & Kegan Paul, 1986), pp. 24–41;

"Verificationism," in *Cause, Mind, and Reality: Essays Honoring C. B. Martin,* edited by John Heil (Dordrecht, Netherlands: Kluwer, 1989), pp. 261–270;

"The Drift to Idealism," in *Science, Mind, and Psychology; Essays in Honor of Grover Maxwell,* edited by Mary Lou Maxwell and C. Wade Savage (Lanham, Md.: University Press of America, 1989), pp. 17–34;

"Explanation–Opening Address," in *Explanation and Its Limits,* edited by Dudley Knowles (Cambridge: Cambridge University Press, 1990), pp. 1–19;

"Wittgenstein, Following a Rule and Scientific Psychology," in *The Scientific Enterprise,* edited by E. Ullman- Margalit (Dordrecht, Netherlands: Kluwer, 1992), pp. 123–137;

"Laws of Nature as a Species of Regularity," in *Ontology, Causality, and Mind; Essays in Honour of D. M. Armstrong,* edited by John Bacon, Keith Campbell, and Lloyd Reinhardt (Cambridge: Cambridge University Press, 1993), pp. 152–169;

"Why Philosophers Disagree," in *Reconstructing Philosophy: New Essays on Metaphilosophy,* edited by Jocelyn Couture and Kai Nielsen, *Canadian Journal of Philosophy,* supplementary volume 19 (Calgary: University of Calgary Press, 1993), pp. 67–82;

"Mind and Brain," in *The Mind-Body Problem: A Guide to the Current Debate,* edited by Richard Warner and Tadeusz Szubka (Oxford: Blackwell, 1994), pp. 19–23;

"Correspondence, Coherence, and Realism," in *The Philosophy of Donald Davidson,* edited by Hahn, The Library of Living Philosophers, volume 27 (Chicago: Open Court, 1999), pp. 109–122;

"Laws and Cosmology," in *Causation and Laws of Nature,* edited by Howard Sankey (Dordrecht, Netherlands: Kluwer, 1999), pp. 211–222;

"The Identity Theory of Mind," *Stanford Electronic Encyclopedia of Philosophy* <http://plato.stanford.edu/entries/mind-identity/>, 2000.

SELECTED PERIODICAL PUBLICATIONS–
UNCOLLECTED: "The River of Time," *Mind,* 58 (1949): 483–494;

"Excogitation and Induction," *Australasian Journal of Philosophy,* 28 (1950): 191–199;

"Heinrich Hertz and the Concept of Force," *Australasian Journal of Philosophy,* 29 (1951): 36–45;

"The Moving 'Now,'" *Australasian Journal of Philosophy,* 31 (1953): 184–187;

"Spatializing Time," *Mind,* 64 (1955): 239–241;

"The Reality of Theoretical Entities," *Australasian Journal of Philosophy,* 34 (1956): 1–12;

"Sensations and Brain Processes: A Rejoinder," *Australasian Journal of Philosophy,* 38 (1960): 252–254;

"Further Remarks on Sensations and Brain Processes," *Philosophical Review,* 70 (1961): 406–407;

"Colours," *Philosophy,* 36 (1961): 128–142;

"Is Time Travel Possible?" *Journal of Philosophy,* 60 (1963): 237–241;

"Quine's Philosophy of Science," *Synthese,* 19 (1968–1969): 3–13;

"Metaphysical Realism," *Analysis,* 42 (1982): 1–3;

"Philosophical Problems of Cosmology," *Revue Internationale de Philosophie,* 41 (1987): 112–126;

"Value, Truth, and Action," *Ethics,* 100 (1990): 628–640;

"Utilitarianism and Punishment," *Israel Law Review,* 25 (1991): 360–375;

"A Form of Metaphysical Realism," *Philosophical Quarterly,* 45 (1995): 301–315;

"'Looks Red' and Dangerous Talk," *Philosophy,* 70 (1995): 545–554;

"Moral Values," *Revue Internationale de Philosophie,* 51 (1997): 479–494;

"Neural Circuits and Block Diagrams," *Behavioral and Brain Sciences,* 22, no. 5 (1999): 84–89.

J. J. C. Smart was one of the most important British philosophers of the second half of the twentieth century, though during that period he worked almost entirely in Australia. He has been a leading figure in the development in philosophy in the English-speaking world of a naturalistic and science-oriented approach to metaphysics and epistemology to replace the emphasis on language and conceptual analysis that dominated at the middle of the century.

John Jamieson Carswell Smart–Jack, as he is known to friends and acquaintances–was born into a Scottish academic family on 16 September 1920. His father, William Marshall Smart, was John Couch Adams Astronomer at the University of Cambridge and wrote many mathematical and popular works on astronomy, including *Text-Book of Spherical Astronomy* (1931) and *Stellar Dynamics* (1938). His mother, Isabel Macquarie Carswell Smart, the daughter of an eminent psychiatrist, published verse, principally for children. In 1937 Smart's father became the Regius Professor of Astronomy at the University of Glasgow. Smart entered the university the following year. Service in World War II as a junior officer in the Royal Corps of Signals, principally in India and Burma, interrupted his education from 1940 to 1945. Returning to Glasgow, he received an M.A. with honors in philosophy, mathematics, and natural philosophy in 1946 and proceeded to the University of Oxford, where he read for the newly established B.Phil. degree and came under the influence of Gilbert Ryle, one of the dominant figures in the linguistic analysis movement in philosophy. After a short period as a junior research fellow at Corpus Christi College, Smart accepted, at twenty-nine, the Hughes Professorship of Philosophy at the University of Adelaide.

Smart's thought took on its characteristic motifs after his move to Australia. He came to view philosophy as best pursued through reflection on the methods and successes of the sciences, and he determined to keep his views attuned to the most plausible and economical of current scientific views. Among the consequences of this orientation were the abandonment of the Christian religion in which he had been raised and a conviction that a thoroughly naturalistic outlook held the key to understanding the human condition. This change carried with it a commitment to dealing directly and straightforwardly with the classic problems in metaphysics and epistemology, problems that the Oxford analysts tended to regard as pseudoproblems generated by a misunderstanding of concepts and of the functioning of the language in which those concepts are expressed. In this respect, Smart became a more traditional philosopher after leaving Oxford.

Smart married Janet Paine in 1956; they had a daughter in 1957 and a son in 1959. Janet Smart died of cancer in 1967. The following year Smart married a friend from his Scottish days, Elizabeth Margaret Warner; the daughter of a former Episcopalian bishop of Edinburgh, she had moved to Melbourne in 1955 and become a social worker.

Smart became a reader at La Trobe University in Melbourne in 1972. In 1976 he was appointed to one of the premier positions in Australian philosophy: a professorship in the Research School of Social Sciences of the Australian National University. He has continued to be active in philosophy since his retirement in 1985.

Showing the influence of both the eighteenth-century Scottish philosopher David Hume and the twentieth-century American logician W. V. Quine, Smart's philosophy has been consistently empiricist, taking human experience as the wellspring and touchstone of reliable knowledge. In logic he has defended extensionalism, the doctrine that statements about matters of actual fact provide one's primary connection to the real world, while claims about iron necessities or mere possibilities are human artifacts. In metaphysics he has championed nominalism, the view that all realities are particular and that red objects and horses do not really share any common universal element, such as Redness or Horseness, respectively. In the philosophy of science he has upheld the Humean view that the laws of nature are no more than important regularities in the unfolding of the cosmos. Unlike the many empiricists who regard imperceptible entities as human constructs, however, he has always been staunchly realist in his account of theoretical entities, claiming that electrons are straightforwardly real components of the world on the same footing as shoes and ships and sealing wax.

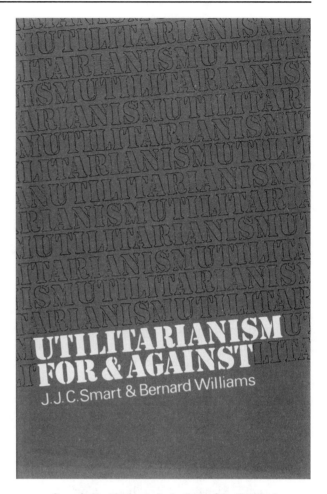

Cover for the 1986 paperback edition of the 1973 book in which Smart defends the utilitarian position in ethics against Williams's critique (Bruccoli Clark Layman Archives)

Smart has been similarly consistent in his ethics: he has defended a rather pure form of act utilitarianism, not flinching from some of its more controversial implications. According to this view, the value of an action lies in the effect it has on all sentient beings affected by the action; this value is to be measured by the net balance of happiness over misery that results, treating every being affected by the action equally. (The other main version of utilitarianism, rule utilitarianism, evaluates individual actions according to whether they conform to a rule that, if generally followed, would tend to maximize happiness and minimize suffering.)

Most of Smart's mature work has revolved around the development of three themes: in cosmology, four-dimensional physical realism; in the philosophy of mind, materialism; and in ethics, utilitarianism. Smart argues that the four-dimensional conception of space-time introduced by Hermann Minkowski for the interpretation of Albert Einstein's Theory of Relativity is superior to all others. This conception implies the equal reality of past, present, and future and rejects as unreal the flow of time that seems to underpin the subjective experience of time passing. In a series of papers beginning with "The River of Time" (1949) and continuing through *Our Place in the Universe: A Metaphysical Discussion* (1989) Smart argues for the space-time conception of reality in two main ways. One way involves the positing of a logical dilemma: if time flows, it must flow at some rate or other; but a flow rate is an interval traversed with respect to time. Therefore, some "super-time" must exist within which time itself can move. But if super-time just exists without flowing and, hence, does not need to be embedded in a super-super-time, why should the same not be the case for time itself? Positing the higher level is unnecessary and uneconomical. If, on the other hand, super-time is on a par with time, it would need a super-super-time in which to flow, resulting in an infinite regress.

The second line of reasoning that leads to acceptance of the four-dimensional space-time theory of the universe connects with Smart's commitment to a philosophy that best interprets scientific advances. Minkowski's account, he says, provides an elegant and perspicuous geometrical explanation of the apparent anomalies of Special and General Relativity, in particular of the apparent contractions of the lengths of rigid bodies along the direction of their relative motion and the mutual mismatches of time periods as measured by systems in relative motion.

Smart's second major theme, materialism, is the claim that there are no spiritual or nonphysical realities; human minds, in particular, are not spiritual or nonphysical. The mind—the organ with which one thinks—is the brain. States of mind, thoughts, feelings, sensations, and dispositions are states or processes or functions of the brain and its associated nervous system. This "central state materialism," as it came to be known, emerged in its contemporary form from two landmark papers written at the University of Adelaide in the 1950s: U. T. Place, regarded by Smart as the true originator of the view, published "Is Consciousness a Brain Process?" in the *British Journal of Psychology* in 1956. Smart's "Sensations and Brain Processes," which appeared in *The Philosophical Review* in 1959 and is collected in his *Essays, Metaphysical and Moral: Selected Philosophical Papers* (1987), gave rise to a literary sensation. The novelty of the view arose mainly from Smart's success in pointing out how insufficient were the then-prevalent reasons for holding that the mental and the physical belonged to

essentially incompatible categories. Smart expanded and defended the claims of this seminal paper in subsequent discussions both of the general issue and of its implications for the "secondary," or subjective, qualities, particularly color.

From *An Outline of a System of Utilitarian Ethics* (1961) through *Ethics, Persuasion, and Truth* (1984) and beyond, Smart has presented a utilitarian theory of moral judgment and action: what matters most is not people's intentions or characters, much less any fixed set of moral rules, but the actual consequences of their behavior. The consequences to consider concern the happiness of all sentient beings as judged from a naturalistic, secular point of view. Whether one's conduct leads one toward God or toward self-mastery is to be taken into account only insofar as such conduct affects human happiness. To adhere blindly to a social or traditional rule of conduct, even in cases where doing so would result in misery, is what Smart calls "rule worship."

Smart recognizes the notorious difficulties that questions of justice generate for any rigorously utilitarian theory: in *Ethics, Persuasion, and Truth* he quotes William James on the enormity of accepting the idyllic happiness of many at the cost of the continuing torture of one lost soul. Smart has not yet been able to formulate a definitive resolution of this conflict between the claims of happiness and justice.

Philosophy and Scientific Realism (1963) marked the first appearance of a line of thought that became a continuing theme in Smart's work through *Our Place in the Universe* and subsequent pieces on the interpretation of the natural sciences: the claims of what is now known as the Argument to the Best Explanation, which holds that one is rationally entitled to accept the best explanation for any given phenomenon as true, until a better one is found; if a better one is found, the path of right reason is to accept the new account and, with it, the reality of the new entities to which it appeals. The issue is whether one can have convincing reasons to accept, as literally real constituents of the universe, entities such as electrons and quarks that must remain forever beyond direct observational validation. This issue has been a particularly salient one for empiricist philosophers such as Smart, since they hold that experience is the sole guide to reality. Smart's position is that the complex, interlocking set of experimental results that have been obtained and validated about electrons, for instance, would constitute an incredible set of coincidences for which there could be no intelligible accounting, unless the electron theory were the literal truth concerning what is going on at levels that transcend direct observation. Therefore, that electrons truly exist and are not merely some overarching conceptual convenience is the only plausible and, hence, the "best explanation" available of the relevant behavior of matter.

In *Ethics, Persuasion, and Truth* Smart presents a sophisticated subjectivist theory in metaethics. Metaethics is the study of the meaning of moral concepts and the logical status of moral judgments, as opposed to normative ethics, which aims to establish the basis and truth of such judgments; utilitarianism is a theory in normative ethics. As an empiricist who regards perceptual experience as the sole basic guide to the nature of the world, Smart rejects the idea that moral judgments state some special kind of "moral facts" about reality. The question, then, is what such judgments must be. They are clearly of great importance—they guide action, they recommend action, and they arise from people's deepest preferences concerning life and society. Smart develops an elaborate semantics to show how moral language works as it does.

Essays, Metaphysical and Moral is a collection of Smart's journal articles and contributions to books. The five sections into which the volume is divided—"Methodology in Philosophy and Science," "Space, Time and Space-time," "Metaphysics and Philosophy of Science," "Philosophy of Mind," and "Ethics"—provide a picture of how Smart looks at his own life's work.

Our Place in the Universe grew out of the Gavin David Young Lectures that Smart delivered at the University of Adelaide in 1987. It recapitulates and draws together many of the central themes of his writings in a coherent naturalistic vision of spatiotemporal physical reality and of the living, conscious systems to be found on earth, a vision that is suffused with a kind of naturalistic piety or philosophic awe. In this view, physics is the fundamental science; the biological and psychological sciences will progress not by finding independent fundamental laws pertaining to living things but, rather, on an analogy with technology, by finding the particular physical circumstances that give rise to life and behavior.

J. J. C. Smart has continued to write on all the major themes of his philosophy. In all of his work he argues for firmly held views with the calm, well-informed courtesy and candor that have made him one of the best loved, as well as most respected, of contemporary philosophers.

Reference:

Philip Pettit, Richard Sylvan, and Jean Norman, eds., *Metaphysics and Morality: Essays in Honour of J. J. C. Smart* (Oxford & New York: Blackwell, 1987).

Herbert Spencer

(23 April 1820 – 8 December 1903)

Fred Wilson
University of Toronto

See also the Spencer entry in *DLB 57: Victorian Prose Writers After 1867.*

BOOKS: *The Proper Sphere of Government: A Reprint of a Series of Letters Originally Published in "The Nonconformist"* (London: Brittain, 1843);

Social Statics; or, The Conditions Essential to Human Happiness Specified, and the First of Them Developed (London: Chapman, 1851; revised and abridged edition, New York: Appleton, 1886);

The Principles of Psychology (London: Longman, Brown, Green & Longmans, 1855; revised and enlarged, 2 volumes, London: Williams & Norgate, 1870, 1872; New York: Appleton, 1871, 1873);

Railway Morals and Railway Policy, Traveller's Library, no. 89 (London: Longman, Brown, Green & Longmans, 1855);

Essays: Scientific, Political, and Speculative, 3 volumes (volume 1, London: Longman, Brown, Green, Longmans & Roberts, 1858; volumes 2-3, London: Williams & Norgate, 1863, 1874; New York: Appleton, 1864, 1874); excerpts from volumes 1 and 2 republished as *Illustrations of Universal Progress: A Series of Discussions* (New York: Appleton, 1864); revised and enlarged as *Essays: Scientific, Political, and Speculative,* 3 volumes (London: Williams & Norgate, 1891; New York: Appleton, 1891);

First Principles (6 parts, parts 1-4, London: G. Mainwaring; parts 5-6, London: Williams & Norgate, 1860-1862; 1 volume, London: Williams & Norgate, 1862); republished as *First Principles of a New System of Philosophy* (New York: Appleton, 1864);

Education: Intellectual, Moral, and Physical (London: Williams & Norgate, 1861; New York: Appleton, 1861);

The Classification of the Sciences: To Which Are Added Reasons for Dissenting from the Philosophy of M. Comte (London: Williams & Norgate, 1864);

The Principles of Biology, 2 volumes (London: Williams & Norgate, 1864, 1867; New York: Appleton, 1864,

Herbert Spencer when 73

1867; revised and enlarged, 2 volumes, London: Williams & Norgate, 1898, 1899; New York: Appleton, 1898, 1900);

The Study of Sociology (London: King, 1873; New York: Appleton, 1874);

The Principles of Sociology, parts 1-3, 3 volumes (New York: Appleton, 1874-1875; London: Williams & Norgate, 1876; enlarged, London: Williams & Norgate, 1885; New York: Appleton, 1886; enlarged again, London: Williams & Norgate, 1893);

Ceremonial Institutions: Being Part IV of The Principles of Sociology (the First Portion of Vol. II) (London: Williams & Norgate, 1879; New York: Appleton, 1880);

The Data of Ethics: The Principles of Ethics, Part 1 (London: Williams & Norgate, 1879; New York: Appleton, 1879; enlarged, London: Williams & Norgate, 1881);

Political Institutions: Being Part V of The Principles of Sociology (The Concluding Portion of Vol. II) (London: Williams & Norgate, 1882; New York: Appleton, 1882);

The Man versus the State: Containing "The New Toryism," "The Coming Slavery," "The Sins of Legislators," and "The Great Political Superstition" (London & Edinburgh: Williams & Norgate, 1884; New York: Appleton, 1884);

Ecclesiastical Institutions: Being Part VI of The Principles of Sociology (London: Williams & Norgate, 1885; New York: Appleton, 1886);

The Factors of Organic Evolution (London: Williams & Norgate, 1887; New York: Appleton, 1887);

Justice: Being Part IV of The Principles of Ethics (London: Williams & Norgate, 1891; New York: Appleton, 1891);

The Principles of Ethics, parts 2 and 3 (London: Williams & Norgate, 1892; New York: Appleton, 1892);

The Principles of Ethics, parts 5 and 6 (London: Williams & Norgate, 1893; New York: Appleton, 1893);

The Inadequacy of "Natural Selection" (London: Williams & Norgate, 1893; New York: Appleton, 1893);

The Principles of Sociology, volume 3 (London: Williams & Norgate, 1896; New York: Appleton, 1896);

Various Fragments (London: Williams & Norgate, 1897; New York: Appleton, 1898; enlarged, 1900);

Facts and Comments (London: Williams & Norgate, 1902; New York: Appleton, 1902);

An Autobiography, 2 volumes (London: Williams & Norgate, 1904; New York: Appleton, 1904).

Collection: *Structure, Function and Evolution,* edited by Stanislaw Andreski (London: Joseph, 1971).

OTHER: *Descriptive Sociology; or Groups of Sociological Facts,* 8 volumes, classified and arranged by Spencer, compiled and abstracted by David Duncan, Richard Schepping, and James Collier (London: Williams & Norgate, 1873–1881; New York: Appleton, 1873–1881)—comprises *English* (London: Williams & Norgate, 1873); *Ancient Mexicans, Central Americans, Chibchas, and Ancient Peruvians* (London: Williams & Norgate, 1874); *Lowest Races: Negrito Races, Malayo-Polynesian Races* (London: Williams & Norgate, 1874); *African Races* (London: Williams & Norgate, 1875); *Asiatic Races* (London: Williams & Norgate, 1876); *American Races* (London: Williams & Norgate, 1878);

Hebrews and Phoenicians (London: Williams & Norgate, 1880); and *French* (London: Williams & Norgate, 1881);

F. Howard Collins, *An Epitome of the Synthetic Philosophy,* preface by Spencer (London: Williams & Norgate, 1889);

Thomas Mackay, ed., *A Plea for Liberty: An Argument against Socialism and Socialistic Legislation,* introduction by Spencer (London: Murray, 1891).

Herbert Spencer is chiefly remembered as an evolutionary philosopher, as one of the founders of sociology, and as a defender of a libertarian version of classical liberalism. He described the evolutionary process and applied it to psychology and biology prior to the publication of Charles Darwin's *On the Origin of Species by Means of Natural Selection, or, The Preservation of Favoured Races in the Struggle for Life* in 1859. Even after the publication of that work Spencer never abandoned the Lamarckian notion that the primary thrust behind evolutionary development is the inheritance of characteristics acquired during the life of the organism through use and disuse. The recognition by biologists that such inheritance is not part of biological evolution has proved to be a fatal flaw in his biological work. In psychology, however, Spencer's ideas proved revolutionary. Moving beyond the associationism of Joseph Priestley and James Mill, he insisted that psychology has to be rooted in physiology, and his work paved the way for the later transformation of psychology into an experimental science by Wilhelm Wundt and William James. In sociology Spencer drew an analogy between society and biological organisms, arguing that both are complex entities with parts functioning interdependently to maintain the whole. He applied the principle of evolution to both but emphasized that, whereas in biology the whole is greater than its parts, in sociology the whole is nothing more than its parts—the individual persons who make up society. A sort of utilitarian in ethics, Spencer defended a radical antistatist individualism in political philosophy and laissez-faire policies in economics.

Spencer's reputation fell considerably with the increasing use of legislation to protect individuals from the worst effects of industrialization. Interest in his views has revived, however, with renewed sympathy for market-based solutions to social problems and with the revival of attempts to provide evolutionary explanations of human psychological traits and social development. But whatever the modern opinion of Spencer may be, his impact in the latter part of the nineteenth century, at least in the English-speaking world, was enormous. Jack London's autobiographical title character in his novel *Martin Eden* (1910) expresses a common impression of the time when he

Spencer circa 1858

says, "here was Spencer, organising all knowledge for him, reducing everything to unity, elaborating ultimate realities, and presenting to his startled gaze a universe so concrete of realisation that it was like the model of a ship such as sailors make and put into glass bottles. There was no caprice, no chance. All was law. It was in obedience to law that the bird flew, and it was in obedience to the same law that fermenting slime had writhed and squirmed and put out legs and wings and become a bird."

Spencer was born in Derby on 23 April 1820, the first and only surviving child of George Spencer and Harriet Holmes Spencer. After a brief attempt at being a schoolmaster, his father took private pupils in geometry, algebra, astronomy, physics, and other mathematical subjects. Spencer attended a day school, where he showed no talent in the required Latin and Greek but advanced beyond what was expected of boys his age in physics and natural history. His father encouraged these interests.

In addition to his formal education, Spencer's mature views were influenced by the atmosphere of the locality in which he grew up. In the eighteenth century

Richard Arkwright, who had invented the first mechanical cotton-spinning machine and introduced the factory system of manufacturing, had joined with a local family, the Strutts, to make Derby a center of the calico industry. But the town was denied representation in Parliament commensurate with its population and economic importance. The middle and working classes joined in political agitation to break the hold of the aristocracy on the political process and to eliminate the tariffs and other trade barriers that kept the price of wheat high by restricting imports in favor of the grain grown on the estates of the aristocrats.

Derby was also a center of religious dissent. Since the restoration of the monarchy in 1660, those who dissented from the established Church of England had been excluded from politics and from the universities of Oxford and Cambridge. The old dissenters, or Nonconformists—the Baptists, Congregationalists, and Presbyterians—were individualists in theology and democrats in church governance. They had been joined since the middle of the eighteenth century by John Wesley's Methodists, who emphasized individual responsibility; all four of Spencer's grandparents were early followers of Wesley. These religious groups joined with others of the middle and working classes to push for parliamentary and electoral reform, but they also developed, through voluntary associations, their own flourishing network of chapels, schools, and cooperative agencies; their academies were in many respects intellectually in advance of the nearly moribund English universities. The dissenters believed that the role of state in education, marriage, and other institutions, exercised through the established church, should be eliminated.

Erasmus Darwin, Charles's grandfather and a successful and wealthy physician, had lived in and around Derby. Erasmus Darwin was a noted naturalist and published speculative evolutionary theories that challenged the orthodox view that each species was specially created by God. In religion he was a deist. His politics were equally radical: he and other members of the Derby Philosophical Society, which he founded, were in favor of the French Revolution and welcomed the founding of the Republic. The society sent a letter of support to the scientist and philosopher Priestley when a Tory mob burned his laboratory, library, and home in Birmingham in reaction to his radical views. Spencer's father was an honorary secretary of the society, and he gave his son access to its scientific library.

At thirteen Spencer was sent to live with his uncle Thomas Spencer, who was curate in Hinton Charterhouse near Bath. Thomas Spencer had established a school and library for his parishioners and was a leader in various social movements, including temperance. Herbert did not enjoy his uncle's rather strict regime and soon ran away, traveling the 115 miles to Derby in three days, with little food and no sleep. But he was sent back to his uncle's home, and his education continued there until he was sixteen.

His formal studies ended, Spencer returned to Derby. In 1840 he became an assistant schoolmaster but resigned after barely three months and took a position as a civil engineer on the Birmingham and Gloucester Railway, which was then under construction. When the line was completed three years later, he turned down an offer of a more permanent post and returned to Derby. There he occupied himself with scientific studies, including natural history and phrenology, and mechanical inventions, some of which were evidently quite ingenious, though of little commercial value.

In 1842 Spencer joined his uncle in working for the Complete Suffrage Union. He also launched his literary career with a series of letters to Edward Miall's *The Nonconformist,* the leading organ of the militant and radical dissenters, in which he calls for strict limitations on the functions of the state. Spencer had the letters reprinted the following year in a pamphlet, *The Proper Sphere of Government.* In 1844 he became subeditor of *The Pilot,* a Birmingham newspaper that was the organ of the Complete Suffrage movement. He was active in organizations opposing the corn laws and slavery and promoting the separation of church and state. His developing antireligious views brought him into conflict with some of the backers of *The Pilot,* and he returned to railway construction as a civil engineer for two years. In 1848 he was appointed subeditor of *The Economist,* a position that provided a good salary and a free room.

While working at *The Economist,* Spencer developed lifelong friendships with the publisher James Chapman, the philosopher G. H. Lewes, the then unknown biologist Thomas Henry Huxley, and the physicist John Tyndall. Through Lewes, Spencer met the essayist and historian Thomas Carlyle and Mary Ann Evans, who later became a novelist under the pseudonym George Eliot. No real friendship developed with Carlyle, but Spencer became close to Evans. He even contemplated marrying her, but, as he relates in his *Autobiography* (1904), he was deterred by her lack of physical beauty.

At this time Spencer began publishing essays in various reviews. After reading several handbooks on rhetoric, he expressed his own views in an essay, "The Philosophy of Style," that he published in *The Westminster Review* in 1852. The theory he proposes is based on psychological views he was then developing: complex ideas are gradually built up by the joining of simpler ideas; therefore, all qualifiers, auxiliaries, embellishments, and subordinate clauses should precede the main subject and verb of a sentence. By carrying the

qualifiers forward, the reader arrives at the main topic directly and with the least trouble and the most force. The theory ignores any role that the emotions might play in the use of language, and it does not attend to the complexities of grammatical structure. But the resulting style is well suited to presenting Spencer's ideas. Throughout his writings he aims to appeal to reason and feels little need for emotive rhetoric; his works are clear and well organized, if somewhat monotonous. His earlier writings adhere fairly closely to the requirements laid down in "The Philosophy of Style"; later, when he dictated his works rather than writing them out, he experimented with variations in style.

At the beginning of 1851 Spencer published his first major book, *Social Statics; or, The Conditions Essential to Human Happiness Specified, and the First of Them Developed.* The work is a deeper and more philosophical defense of the libertarian views he outlined in his letters to *The Nonconformist.* He advocates freedom of speech, religion, and commerce; the right to property; legal equality for women; and the right to refuse to pay taxes, provided that one is willing to forgo the protection provided by the state. He condemns government-supported education, poor laws, and sanitary regulations. The only roles he allows to the state are the provision of police services domestically and the maintenance of an army and navy for protection of the citizens against foreign aggression. These positions are based on the principle that Spencer regards as the sole basis of social and moral obligation: "every man has freedom to do all that he wills, provided he infringes not the equal freedom of any other man." But unlike some more-recent upholders of this principle who justify it by an appeal to "moral intuition," Spencer provides a utilitarian argument for it. Since everyone naturally seeks happiness or pleasure and tries to avoid pain or suffering, the goal of action ought to be the happiness of all; to accomplish this goal each person must have the right to pursue the maximum satisfaction of his or her desires, to the extent that their satisfaction does not interfere with the satisfaction of the desires of others.

Spencer admits that people will often unintentionally reduce rather than increase their happiness or satisfaction. Others, foreseeing this result and wanting to help, might interfere with the person's freedom in an attempt to prevent such consequences. Such ostensibly benevolent interference to constrain one's actions against one's immediate wishes would be coercive, Spencer says. Even though the coercion would be in one's longer-term best interest, it is better to let a person learn, through the natural consequences of his or her actions, which types of action will, in fact, achieve the best results. Thus, Spencer argues against all forms of external control and, in particular, against all forms of

*Spencer's friend, the physicist John Tyndall, who solicited
subscribers to finance the publication of Spencer's
System of Synthetic Philosophy*

government interference except the police functions that aim to prevent harm to others.

Spencer notes that people take pleasure in a variety of things, including the welfare of other people. The deity has placed as instincts in the constitution of human beings the needs for food and shelter but also a sense of altruism or benevolence. This sense extends particularly to one's children and other members of one's family. Spencer argues that this motive will move parents to provide adequate education for their children without the need for support from the government. It is also the appropriate substitute for poor relief. Taxation for poor relief takes property from those to whom it rightfully belongs and gives it to those who have not earned it. Benevolence, in contrast, allows the better off to give voluntarily, while encouraging individual responsibility among the poor rather than increasing their feeling that they have a right to goods taken from others.

Subsequently, Spencer further developed his thinking about the ideas he elaborated in *Social Statics,* but in their basics they remained the same throughout his career. His views were adopted by some of the "rob-

ber barons" in the rapidly industrializing United States, but Spencer was critical of their acquisitiveness to the exclusion of all other motives. He did speak well of the philanthropy of the steel magnate Andrew Carnegie, however. His ideas on personal freedom and freedom of speech were later commended by the anticapitalist anarchist Emma Goldman.

The evolutionary hypothesis had been in the air at Derby, and it was confirmed for Spencer by his observation of fossils in the cuttings made for railroads while he was a civil engineer and by his reading in 1840 of Charles Lyell's *Principles of Geology* (1830–1833). The German physiologist K. E. von Baer's studies of the development of the fetus from homogeneity to heterogeneity, which Spencer came across in 1851, however, inspired him to apply the idea of evolution, or development, to biological species, including the human race; to individual psychology; to society; and even to the universe. In "The Development Hypothesis" (1852), published in the weekly review *The Leader,* Spencer rejects the notion that individual species are the result of special creations, arguing that more-complex organisms have evolved from less-complex ones. To Baer's formula of the transition from homogeneity to heterogeneity Spencer adds that evolution also involves an increase in definiteness and integration. In another essay, "A Theory of Population Deduced from the General Law of Animal Fertility," published in the April 1852 issue of *The Westminster Review,* Spencer argues against the economist Thomas Malthus's claim in his *An Essay on the Principle of Population as It Affects the Future Improvement of Society, with Remarks on the Speculations of Mr. Godwin, M. Condorcet, and Other Writers* (1798) that population growth will inevitably outstrip the food supply and lead to famine. Spencer contends, on the contrary, that increase in population is to be welcomed as providing a drive for progress. The phrase "survival of the fittest" first appears in this essay. In his *Natural Theology: or, Evidences of the Existence and Attributes of the Deity, Collected from the Appearances of Nature* (1802) William Paley had referred to the fitness of organisms for their environments; Spencer adds the idea that organisms *become* fit for their environments. The pressure of population growth leads organisms to develop characteristics that enable them to survive. Like the eighteenth-century biologist Jean-Baptiste de Lamarck and Erasmus Darwin, Spencer says that these characteristics, acquired during the organism's lifetime, can be inherited by its offspring. The term *evolution* itself, which Spencer made popular, first appears in his 1854 essay "On Manners and Fashion."

In 1843 Spencer had made a study of phrenology, which, when first conceived, had had a somewhat scientific basis in the "faculty psychology" of Scottish philosophers such as Thomas Reid: instead of placing these faculties in an immaterial soul, phrenology located them in various parts of the brain. Spencer's involvement with phrenology extended to having his head measured and his capacities evaluated, but he soon became skeptical as to its scientific merits. It did, however, leave him convinced that psychology must be founded on physiology. In *The Principles of Psychology* (1855) he adopts the associationist theory of Lewes, James Mill, and John Stuart Mill. His innovation, which set psychology on a new course that took it beyond mere introspection, is to locate associationist learning theory within the context of the most recent developments in physiology.

Evolutionary concepts are central to *The Principles of Psychology*. When a form emerges in mental life, a corresponding form emerges in the brain; conversely, when environmental factors bring about changes in the brain, corresponding changes occur in the individual's mental life. Emotions and desires are as important as the passively received "impressions" and "ideas" of the associationist psychology: in striving to adapt to a changing environment the organism will develop forms that make it more fit and will pass them on to succeeding generations. Spencer uses the notion of inherited characteristics to illuminate the perception of spatial relations. René Descartes and Immanuel Kant had argued that the capacity to perceive depth is innate, while empiricists such as George Berkeley and David Hume had claimed that innate ideas do not exist and that the perception of depth must, therefore, be learned through a process in which the kinesthetic sensations that arise from one's limbs as one moves nearer to or farther from an object become associated with one's visual and tactile feelings to form the idea of three-dimensional space. Spencer argues that the ideas are innate in the individual but also learned: the learning occurred long ago in the history of the species and was inherited by present individuals. The laws of logic, the principle of induction, and the rules of arithmetic also acquire their a priori certainty from having been learned by one's ancestors and passed down as innate ideas to later individuals.

Spencer applies the same thesis to motivational instincts. In *Social Statics* he had taken benevolence and the capacity for altruistic action to be built into individuals by the deity; in *The Principles of Psychology* these drives are given an evolutionary explanation. Individuals are more likely to survive if they engage in cooperative behavior; the biological usefulness of such behavior causes it to be inherited by succeeding generations. The evolutionary principle thus enables Spencer to thoroughly naturalize his moral theory and develop a purely secular utilitarianism.

While he was working on *The Principles of Psychology,* Spencer developed peculiar sensations in his head and severe insomnia. He spent a year and a half traveling and much time in the country fishing but never fully recovered his health. In need of an income, he returned to London in 1856 and once again began to write articles for the reviews. In "Progress: Its Law and Cause," published in *The Westminster Review* in 1857, he tries to show that evolution is a cosmic phenomenon. The solar system, organic species, the maturation of individual organisms, the psychological development of human beings, and social and cultural change all consist of a movement from an incoherent homogeneity to a complex and interdependent heterogeneity. Paley had seen all aspects of organization in the universe as evidence of the intentional design of a benevolent deity, and Spencer had adopted this position in *Social Statics*. But he now saw the fitness of the universe for organisms and the fitness of organisms to their environment as unplanned effects of evolutionary development. Charles Darwin made much the same point two years later in *The Origin of Species,* but where Darwin's theory is a scientific hypothesis about the adaptation of organisms to their environment, Spencer's is a philosophical speculation about the universe as a whole. Another difference between Spencer and Charles Darwin is that the latter provides an account of the mechanism by which biological evolution occurs: natural selection. Spontaneous random changes–mutations–occur in certain individuals of a species at conception. Most such mutations are detrimental, and the individual is less likely than "normal" individuals of its species to survive long enough to leave offspring. Sometimes, however, a mutation will confer an advantage on the individual in the struggle for survival; such will especially be the case if the environment has changed in some respect. In this situation the individual will be more likely to survive and leave offspring, who will inherit the advantageous change; and they, too, will be more likely to survive and pass the change along to their own offspring. After many generations, the change will become the new norm for the species. After many more generations, the accumulation of such changes may result in a new species of organism. Spencer never did grant natural selection a major role in the origin of species and continued to defend the inheritance of acquired characteristics. But in spite of these differences with Darwin, Spencer warmly welcomed the latter's work and repeatedly defended it against attacks.

In 1857 Spencer was reviewing his articles for republication in the first volume of his *Essays: Scientific, Political, and Speculative* (1858–1874) when the presence of an underlying theme struck him. He immediately conceived a plan to produce a multivolume account of his system, which he dubbed "the Synthetic Philosophy." Unable to find a job that would provide a sufficient income and also allow him time to write, he decided instead to publish the work by subscription. In 1858 he issued a prospectus in which he announced that he would work out the principles of evolution metaphysically and then trace them through psychology, biology, sociology, and ethics. With the backing of such eminent thinkers as John Stuart Mill, he secured more than six hundred subscribers in Britain and the United States. His illness interfered with his work, however, and money from subscribers did not come in as regularly as he had hoped. A legacy from his uncle William Spencer made it possible for him to continue, and the first installment of his system came out in six parts between 1860 and 1862 as *First Principles*.

Spencer distinguishes between reality as it is in itself, on the one hand, and the phenomenal world, or reality as it appears, on the other hand. The first and shortest part of the *First Principles* deals with reality as it is in itself. Spencer takes up and pushes further the view elaborated by Sir William Hamilton and Henry Mansel that the sense impressions of which one is aware in ordinary experience have a cause that is unknowable and even beyond the capacity of humans to conceive. Hamilton and Mansel give a theistic interpretation of this unknowable cause, but Spencer draws out the agnostic implications of their position: if the ultimate is beyond human conception, then nothing can be said about it: it is simply "the Unknowable." All that can be known about the Unknowable is that it is the cause of the appearances of which one is aware in ordinary experience. Even then, since *cause* is a relative term, human beings can only know how it relates to them, not what it is in itself.

Because the Unknowable can at least be known as the cause of the world as it appears, it can be characterized as "Force." It is the force that provides the metaphysical basis for the causal changes that are observed in the phenomenal realm. Other basic categories are like that of cause in pointing to the unknowable mystery. Space and time, for example, are not real in the way that ordinary objects are real, for, if they were, they would possess observable attributes; since they do not possess such attributes, they are not objective. But neither are they subjective, for if they were, they would not exist—but they manifestly do exist. "Time" is an abstract concept summarizing all sequences of phenomena, while "space" summarizes all coexisting ones. But scientists must use these concepts carefully, recognizing the limited cognitive grasp that they have of them. Space, time, force, matter, motion, and infinity can never be completely understood. They all point to the Unknowable.

This account of the Unknowable as cause of the phenomenal world is hard to square with Spencer's account of concept formation in *The Principles of Psychology*. There he draws the standard empiricist distinction between impressions, or sensations, and ideas, which are faint copies of impressions to which words are attached as signs of similarities among them and among the impressions from which they are derived. But if ideas refer only to sensible impressions and ideas, then it would seem that the concept of cause must apply, as Kant pointed out, only within the phenomenal realm; the Unknowable cannot even be conceived as the cause of the world of experience. And if this cause beyond all knowable causes cannot even be thought of, how can one know that it exists?

Spencer does attempt to provide a psychological basis for belief in the Unknowable. In experience, he says, one is aware in two ways of the Unknowable as a force. On the one hand, there is the force of resistance that one feels when one attempts to penetrate objects. On the other hand, there is not only the force of exertion that one experiences when pushing against objects but also the felt continuity of this force as moving forward in time. The self is experienced, as Hume put it, as a bundle of perceptions; but this bundle is also experienced as involving a continuity that is more than its phenomenal aspects: "the aggregate of feelings and ideas constituting the mental *I,* have not in themselves the principle of cohesion holding them together as a whole; but the *I* which continuously survives as the subject of these changing states, is that portion of the Unknowable Power which is statically conditioned in special nervous structures pervaded by a dynamically conditioned portion of the Unknowable Power called energy." To this extent, what is beyond human ideas is encountered within human beings themselves.

Science begins with everyday knowledge of the world and is, in fact, only a more sophisticated and more precise form of that ordinary knowledge. The task of science is to discover regularities among the phenomena of experience. The investigation of specific aspects of the phenomenal world is assigned to specific disciplines. Physicists study matter and have discovered the conservation of energy, the indestructibility of matter, and gravitation; biologists study living things and have discovered the law of evolution; and other scientists have discovered other laws. These laws have a necessity that is not to be found in mere generalizations from observed regularities: they are imposed by the Unknowable on the world as it is experienced.

Spencer takes this sense of a force that is beyond all thought to be the core—at least, the rational core—of religion. Religion is instinctual in human beings: it is the sense of a mystery in the universe that is beyond comprehension. But to this core sense primitive human beings attached many ideas that apply only to the relative world of ordinary experience. The result has been that science and religion have each encroached on the other's appropriate domain. Spencer's account of the Unknowable is meant, on the one hand, to free religion from scientific concepts that apply only to the phenomenal world, and, on the other hand, to free science from the attempts of religion to dictate its doctrines. At the same time, he aims to show that science itself points to the underlying mystery. Both science and religion must acknowledge as the "most certain of all facts that the Power which the Universe manifests to us is utterly inscrutable." Spencer's attempt to reconcile religion and science by making the Unknowable the domain of the former and the phenomenal world the domain of the latter did not please either side.

While the task of the special sciences is to formulate general truths about phenomena of specific kinds, Spencer says, the task of philosophy, as part of this scientific enterprise, is to formulate truths at the most general level–truths that hold for all kinds of phenomena. The fundamental principle of science is the Law of the Persistence of Force, which encompasses the indestructibility of matter and the continuity of motion. This law implies that matter is continuously being redistributed; the redistribution is evolution, which Spencer defines as "an integration of matter and a concomitant dissipation of motion; during which the matter passes from a relatively indefinite, incoherent homogeneity to a relatively definite, coherent heterogeneity and during which the contained motion undergoes a parallel transformation." In 1858 he had published an essay, "The Nebular Hypothesis," in which he adopted the theory of Pierre-Simon, Marquis de Laplace about the origin of the solar system from a gaseous nebula. He adapts this theory to his evolutionary scheme and makes it central to *First Principles*: the world in all its complexity evolved from a homogeneous cloud of gas. The process of evolution tends toward a state of equilibrium, which means that each individual's mental forces will develop until they are in equilibrium with the mental forces of all others in industrial society, where there will be a perfect balance of supply and demand. Thus, Spencer claims to be able to infer from the Law of the Persistence of Force that the process will culminate in a "cosmical equilibrium which brings Evolution under all its forms to a close . . . only in the establishment of the greatest perfection and the most complete happiness." Thus, for Spencer the evolutionary process is directed toward the state of moral perfection in which the utilitarian ideal will be realized. Whereas in *Social Statics* the instantiation of the utilitarian ideal depended on a vaguely conceived God, it now turns on the intrinsic nature of the evolutionary process.

The novelist George Eliot (Mary Ann Evans), to whom Spencer considered proposing marriage but was deterred by her appearance; sketch by Samuel Laurence, actually drawn circa 1860 rather than 1857 (Girton College Library, University of Cambridge)

Spencer's methodology in *First Principles* is hardly that of experimental science; he uses the facts he cites to illustrate his principles rather than to test them. His metaphysics of the Unknowable found little favor in its own time and finds even less today; but his view of science as capable of providing a full and unified account of the world as experienced by the senses served for many Victorians as a substitute for religion.

While working on *First Principles* Spencer put together four articles that had appeared in *The Westminster Review*, *The North British Review*, and *The British Quarterly Review* into a slim volume titled *Education: Intellectual, Moral, and Physical* (1861). The book is strongly critical of the standard educational practices in Victorian Britain. Applying his biological account of human psychology to education, Spencer argues for giving science rather than the classics the central place in the curriculum. Since science yields causal knowledge, it enables people to discover means by which they can adapt to their environment and avoid, or at least mitigate, natural disasters. The study of science should include psychology and the social sciences. But art should also be studied, since the aesthetic pleasure it gives needs no justification beyond itself. Spencer is strongly opposed to rote learning enforced by punishment, which places an undue emphasis on authority. Instead, children should be placed in situations in which experiments occur naturally to them and lead to the discovery of causal laws. Finally, intellectual learning should be accompanied by physical education for the development of the whole person. The work became a widely used text for educators; it has been translated into all the major languages of the world, including Chinese and Arabic, and many minor ones, including Mohawk.

In 1864 Spencer published the first volume of the second part of his Synthetic Philosophy, *The Principles of Biology*. Volume two appeared in 1867, but not without difficulty. Spencer's financial position had deteriorated: the number of subscribers had declined, and those who remained did not always make good on their pledges. John Stuart Mill, Huxley, and Tyndall were among those who tried to obtain further subscribers, but a legacy Spencer received on the death of his father and some $7,000 invested in securities by his American enthusiasts to provide him with an income enabled him to continue the series.

In *The Principles of Biology* Spencer defines life as "the continuous adjustment of internal relations to external relations" and argues that the degree of life is proportional to the degree of correspondence between these two sets of relations. Under changing environmental conditions, organisms that are homogeneous and without structure gradually become complex and differentiated. In primitive single-celled organisms all functions are carried out by the whole body; more advanced organisms exhibit a "physiological division of labour" in which different functions are carried out by different organs. Simple organisms have few parts and, therefore, little coordination among them; highly developed organisms have many distinct parts performing specialized functions, but the parts are coordinated in their operation so as to form an integrated whole. The parts develop to perform activities that the organism needs to survive in its environment; these structures are inherited by succeeding generations and are further modified as evolution proceeds. The eye had long been the standard example for those who, like Paley in *Natural Theology*, argued that the existence of complex organs serving specialized functions could only be explained as the products of an intelligent designer. Spencer offers an alternative and wholly naturalistic account. Light striking a particularly sensitive cell caused it to operate in a way that enabled the organism better to explore and survive in its environment. As the organism's descendants continued the struggle to survive, the organ developed further. These successive changes accumulated over the generations to produce the complex organ that can now be found in higher ani-

mals. Spencer theorizes that the units of heredity are carried by small particles that he calls "physiological units"; later he calls them "constitutional units." He was approaching the modern concept of genes, but his Lamarckism required him to claim that information passes to these units from the environment and causes appropriate changes in them. Spencer's insistence that such transfer of information must occur produced an extended controversy with August Weismann, who presented detailed empirical evidence to the contrary. In the end Weismann prevailed, and *The Principles of Biology* is now largely outdated. It was well received in its day, however, commanding sufficient respect to be used as a textbook at Oxford. The work had the virtue of presenting an account of evolution in easily understood terms, thereby enabling many people to see for the first time that it was possible for science to provide a naturalistic explanation of the origin of species and of the human species, in particular. It thus did much to undermine the traditional natural theology that posited intelligent design and the special creation of the various species. The reception of *The Principles of Biology* matched that of *First Principles* and *The Principles of Psychology*. All were widely read and commanded the attention of the age. William James used both the psychology and the biology works as textbooks in his courses at Harvard University.

In 1864 Spencer was elected a member of the X-Club, to which Huxley, Tyndall, and other leading scientists belonged. In 1866 he, Huxley, Charles Darwin, John Stuart Mill, and John Bright were among the members of the Jamaica Committee, which was formed to agitate for the prosecution of Governor Edward Eyre for atrocities he committed in putting down a revolt by blacks on the island; their campaign was unsuccessful. In 1868 he was elected to the Athenaeum Club. But his health continued to deteriorate, preventing not only most social activities but also almost anything beyond the work of completing the Synthetic Philosophy. The remainder of his life is little more than a record of that effort. In 1871 he declined the lord rectorship of the University of St. Andrews, an honorary post. He also declined a request that he stand for appointment to the professorship in metaphysics and logic at University College London.

After completing *The Principles of Biology*, Spencer revised *The Principles of Psychology* to make it the fifth part of his System of Synthetic Philosophy; the first volume came out in 1870 and the second in 1872. For these works he had relied on his own knowledge, or, in the case of biology, on the help of his friend Huxley. But as early as 1867 he had realized that the sociology on which he proposed to embark would require a mass of information about various societies that was sufficiently large to allow valid generalizations to be drawn. That year he had hired the first of three assistants whose task was to extract cultural data from travelers' accounts, ethnographic works, and historical sources. The data were arranged and classified according to a scheme developed by Spencer and published in eight thick folio volumes as *Descriptive Sociology; or Groups of Sociological Facts* (1873–1881). Spencer could not afford to continue the work, and it was suspended. But he provided in his will for its completion, and many more volumes were published after his death. The work is now almost wholly unknown, but it remains an impressive achievement. It provided Spencer with the material he needed to establish that society, too, fell under the principle of evolution.

While engaged on this project, Spencer published, at the urging of his American friends, *The Study of Sociology* (1873) to demonstrate that a naturalistic scientific study of society is possible. "There can be no complete acceptance of Sociology as a science," Spencer writes, "so long as the belief in a social order not conforming to natural law, survives." He discusses the forms of bias that are liable to warp the judgment of the sociologist; he also makes clear the difference between history and sociology and establishes the proper relationship between the two disciplines. He does not conceal his contempt for most historical writing: it is concerned with kings rather than with the forms of national life and the natural history of society. *The Study of Sociology* rescued sociology from the amateurs and cranks and turned it over to the professionals. William Graham Sumner used it as a textbook at Yale in the first sociology course ever established at an American university. The book was also immensely successful commercially, in part because of the preliminary publication of its chapters in *The Contemporary Review* in Britain and in *Popular Science Monthly* in the United States. The work did much to stimulate interest in Spencer's other writings.

Three volumes, constituting parts 1 to 3 of volume one of *The Principles of Sociology,* appeared in 1874–1875. Subsequent volumes came out irregularly, because of Spencer's precarious health, and under various titles: part 4, the first part of volume two, as *Ceremonial Institutions* (1879); part 5, the second part of volume two, as *Political Institutions* (1882); part 6, the third part of volume two, as *Ecclesiastical Institutions* (1885); and volume three as, once again, *The Principles of Sociology* (1896).

Spencer argues that the phenomena studied by sociology have their roots in biology. Evolution seeks the survival of organisms, including the human organism. Pleasure is the reward that attaches to behavior that contributes to survival and reproduction. As Spencer said in *The Principles of Psychology,* feelings of sociability, sympathy, and benevolence have developed in human beings because cooperation better suits people for survival and reproduction, and these feelings ensure the continuance

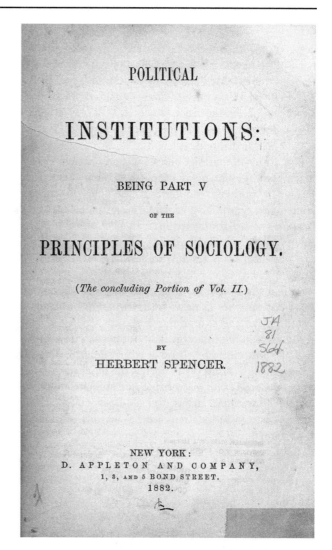

POLITICAL

INSTITUTIONS:

BEING PART V

OF THE

PRINCIPLES OF SOCIOLOGY.

(*The concluding Portion of Vol. II.*)

BY

HERBERT SPENCER.

NEW YORK:
D. APPLETON AND COMPANY,
1, 3, AND 5 BOND STREET.
1882.

Title page for the U.S. edition of a volume of Spencer's work on the evolution of societies (Thomas Cooper Library, University of South Carolina)

of that behavior. The development of the social feelings has led to the emergence of a new kind of entity: society. Sociology is the discipline that studies this entity.

The law of evolution holds for societies as it does for organisms. For this reason Spencer argues that there are close analogies between a society and a biological organism: societies, like biological organisms, develop from infancy through maturity to death. But he also recognizes and emphasizes important dissimilarities between societies and organisms: in a biological organism, consciousness is located in a particular organ, the brain; in a society, consciousness is spread among all the individual members of the society. Also, the various structures in a biological organism function to serve the whole; in society the structures serve the parts. That is, a society exists solely to ensure the well-being of its members.

In the evolutionary development of societies, Spencer says, one finds increasing specialization and differentiation of functions—that is, a movement from homogeneity to heterogeneity. He offers many illustrations, such as the development of elaborate military organizations in both Incan and Spartan societies. Much of *The Principles of Sociology* is devoted to such detailed examples.

Spencer discusses at length primitive social organization, forms of marriage and family, and early concepts of property. Unlike many people at the time, he did not believe in "primitive communism"; he notes that among contemporary primitive peoples tools, ornaments, weapons, and so on are owned individually, which suggests that the same was likely true in prehistoric eras.

Spencer proposes a hypothesis about the origin of religion that came to be known as the "ghost theory." He says that the notion of a soul that inhabits the human body and survives its death is the earliest form of supernatural belief and is a primitive version of what is now recognized as the indestructibility of matter. The primitive person forms the belief that when someone dies, his or her being is conserved and has the ability to return. This notion of a soul that inhabits and animates a body is extended to animals, plants, and inanimate objects. Eventually it is transformed into a belief in gods of multiple forms and powers.

The notion of the inheritance of acquired biological characteristics makes an appearance in Spencer's social theory. He argues that the capacity for the sustained labor that civilized life requires is rooted in a physiological structure that provides the requisite energy; this structure has been inherited from earlier generations of human beings, who acquired it during their lifetimes. There are occasional suggestions that cultural differences are based on innate psychological ones: for example, Spencer contrasts the independence of the ancient Greeks to the submissiveness of Orientals. For the most part, however, he attributes cultural differences to the interplay of cultural and environmental factors. He does not believe that racial differences imply psychological differences. Nor does he impute to primitive peoples a "prelogical" mentality: there is no essential difference in the rational capacities and intelligence of primitive and of civilized persons, he says.

Society, Spencer contends, moves through stages. It is not a linear development, however, as the French sociologist Auguste Comte had suggested, but a process of responding to problems posed by cultural or environmental conditions. Spencer argues that persons in early societies are moved by selfish or egoistic motives rather than by altruism. But some needs can be met only through cooperative behavior, and social forms arise to fulfill these needs. Since cooperation does not come naturally in early societies, it can be secured only by coercion, leading to what Spencer calls "militant" societies with military-type command structures. But in societies so organized, the cooperative behavior that is at first coercively enforced comes to be enjoyed for its own sake; it gradually becomes instinctual, and this instinct is inherited by succeeding generations. Cooperation based on coercion is then replaced by cooperation based on sympathy, benevolence, and altruism, and an "industrial" stage of social organization replaces the militant stage.

Spencer holds that every society must eventually die owing to some external or internal problem that it cannot solve. But he maintains that the Western civilization of the late nineteenth century is entering the highest phase of the industrial stage. Freedom of speech and religion are guaranteed or coming to be guaranteed in all Western countries. Merit, hard work, and enterprise are replacing social status as the means of advancement in society. Representative government is increasing. Sympathy and cooperation in progressive enterprises are becoming universal. Nations are less prone to settle differences through war. With the proper education of citizens, society can approach the moral ideal and continue in that state for a long time.

The Principles of Sociology was followed by *The Principles of Ethics,* which Spencer considered be the culmination of the Synthetic Philosophy. The first part of the *Principles of Ethics* was published as *The Data of Ethics* in 1879; the fourth part appeared as *Justice* in 1891; parts 2, 3, 5, and 6 were published in two volumes as *The Principles of Ethics* in 1892 and 1893. The moral and political theories of the *Principles of Ethics* are similar to those of *Social Statics,* although Spencer now depicts altruistic instincts not as having been implanted innately in human beings by a benevolent deity but as having arisen through an evolutionary process that is described in considerable detail. *Justice* presents Spencer's final and most thorough treatment of the duties of the state; but the main thrust here, as in the earlier work, is that the legitimate role of the government is limited to maintaining order and enforcing contracts at home and repelling aggression from abroad.

Spencer had also argued for these ideas in a series of four essays that appeared in the *Contemporary Review* in 1884 and were published together in the same year as *The Man versus the State: Containing "The New Toryism," "The Coming Slavery," "The Sins of Legislators," and "The Great Political Superstition."* Spencer intended the work as a warning against what seemed to him to be new encroachments on liberty by the government through such programs as state-funded education, sanitation schemes, and the regulation of labor. He found his ideas welcomed by defenders of the status quo, who had formerly most strongly opposed his views.

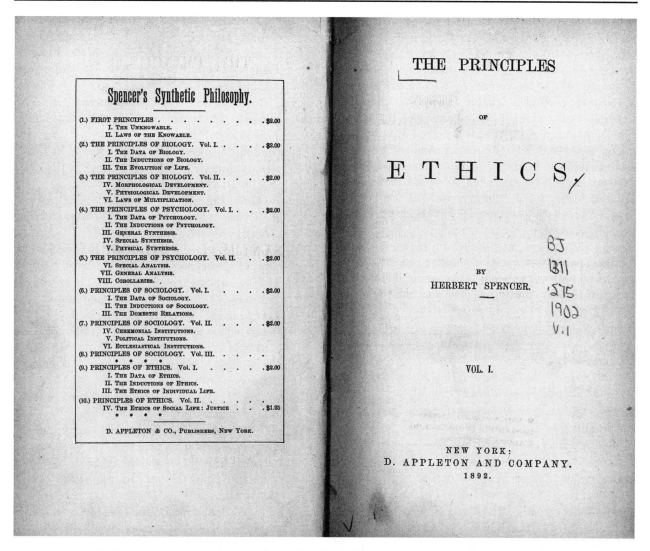

THE PRINCIPLES

OF

ETHICS

BY
HERBERT SPENCER.

BJ
1311
.S75
1902
V.1

VOL. I.

NEW YORK:
D. APPLETON AND COMPANY.
1892.

*Publisher's advertisement and title page for the U.S. edition of a volume of the work in which Spencer describes
the evolution of morality (Thomas Cooper Library, University of South Carolina)*

In 1882 Spencer had visited the United States, where he resisted all attempts to honor him except for a well-attended dinner in New York at which he was lionized as the leading prophet of capitalism. Although his health continued to deteriorate, he continued to work as best he could after completing the exposition of his System of Synthetic Philosophy. In 1882 he had been one of the founders of the Anti-Aggression League; the views that led him to undertake that work moved him to publish in 1902 a collection of essays, *Facts and Comments,* which attracted considerable attention for the vehemence with which Spencer attacked the British policy of aggression in the Boer War. The increasing militarism that seemed to be taking over the society that he had once viewed as culturally and morally progressive, together with the increasing number of tasks being taken on by government, made Spencer's last years a period of embit-

terment. He devoted most of his time to correcting what he considered misrepresentations of his views and answering challenges to their originality. In these efforts justice was usually on his side, but the vehemence of his arguments shows that he was moved by more than devotion to truth. One of the friends of his old age was Beatrice Potter Webb, who as a young woman had learned from Spencer how to do social research. But she was one of many who had become convinced that the utilitarian ends that he proposed could better be achieved by more, rather than less, intervention by the government. She and her husband, Sidney Webb, whom she had married in 1892, were among the early members of the socialist Fabian Society, founded in 1883. The world had moved beyond Spencer, and he no doubt felt abandoned by it. He had moved from London to Brighton in 1898, and he died there on 8 December 1903.

By the time of his death Spencer had been offered no fewer than thirty-two academic honors but had refused almost all of them. History, however, has not been kind to his memory. His metaphysics of the Unknowable and his version of evolutionary theory have largely been forgotten. But Spencer has enduring importance as one who promoted the notion that scientific knowledge and the scientific method are essential to philosophy and to social progress. And while his libertarian views of the role of government seemed out of date as the Victorian Era ended, many have concluded since then that social reformers such as the Webbs expected too much from the state. His criticisms of state planning have been echoed by economists such as the Nobel Prize winners Friedrich A. von Hayek and Milton Friedman. His warnings against the growth of government power can be seen as forecasting the various forms of totalitarianism that dominated the twentieth century, and his objections to imperialistic expansionism are now widely accepted.

Biographies:

David Duncan, *The Life and Letters of Herbert Spencer*, 2 volumes (London: Methuen, 1908);

Hugh S. Elliot, *Herbert Spencer* (London: Constable, 1917; New York: Holt, 1917).

References:

Ernest Barker, *Political Thought in England from Spencer to the Present* (New York: Holt, 1915), pp. 84–132;

Border Parker Bowne, *The Philosophy of Herbert Spencer* (New York: Hunt & Eaton, 1874);

Robert L. Carneiro, "Herbert Spencer as an Anthropologist," *Journal of Libertarian Studies*, 5 (Spring 1981): 153–210;

Frederick B. Churchill, "The Weismann-Spencer Controversy over the Inheritance of Acquired Characters," in *Human Implications of Scientific Advance*, edited by E. G. Forbes (Edinburgh: Edinburgh University Press, 1975), pp. 451–468;

George Bion Denton, "Early Psychological Theories of Herbert Spencer," *American Journal of Psychology*, 32 (January 1921): 5–15;

Denton, "Herbert Spencer and the Rhetoricians," *PMLA*, 34 (1919): 89–111;

Denton, "Origin and Development of Herbert Spencer's Principle of Economy," in *The Fred Newton Scott Anniversary Papers, Contributed by Former Students and Colleagues of Professor Scott and Presented to Him in Celebration of His Thirty-eighth Year of Distinguished Service in the University of Michigan, 1888–1926* (Chicago: University of Chicago Press, 1929), pp. 55–92;

Hugh S. Elliot, *Herbert Spencer* (New York: Constable, 1917);

Mark Francis, "Herbert Spencer and the Myth of Laissez-Faire," *Journal of the History of Ideas*, 39 (April–June 1978): 317–328;

H. G. Good, "The Sources of Spencer's *Education*," *Journal of Educational Research*, 13 (May 1926): 325–335;

Kate Gordon, "Spencer's Theory of Ethics in Its Evolutionary Aspect," *Philosophical Review*, 11 (November 1902): 592–606;

John N. Gray, "Spencer on the Ethics of Liberty and the Limits of State Interference," *History of Political Thought*, 3 (Winter 1982): 465–481;

Tim S. Gray, *Herbert Spencer's Political Philosophy: Individualism and Organicism* (Aldershot: Avebury, 1996);

John C. Greene, "Biology and Social Theory in the Nineteenth Century: Auguste Comte and Herbert Spencer," in *Critical Problems in the History of Science*, edited by Marshall Clagett (Madison: University of Wisconsin Press, 1959), pp. 419–446;

Malcolm Guthrie, *On Mr. Spencer's Formula of Evolution* (London: Trübner, 1879);

Guthrie, *On Mr. Spencer's Unification of Knowledge* (London: Trübner, 1882);

Richard P. Hiskes, "The Nature of Society and the Organic Community: Spencer," in his *Community without Coercion: Getting along in the Minimal State* (Newark: University of Delaware Press, 1982), pp. 57–83;

Hiskes, "Spencer and the Liberal Idea of Community," *Review of Politics*, 45 (October 1983): 595–609;

Geoffrey M. Hodgson, *Economics and Evolution: Bringing Life Back into Economics* (Cambridge: Polity Press, 1993);

Richard Hofstadter, *Social Darwinism in American Thought*, revised edition (Boston: Beacon, 1955), pp. 31–50;

James Iverach, "Herbert Spencer," *Critical Review of Theological and Philosophical Literature*, 14 (January 1904): 99–112; (May 1904): 195–209;

William James, "Herbert Spencer," *Atlantic Monthly*, 94 (July 1904): 99–108;

James, "Remarks on Spencer's Definition of Mind as Correspondence," *Journal of Speculative Philosophy*, 12 (January 1878): 1–22;

J. Vernon Jenson, "The X Club: Fraternity of Victorian Scientists," *British Journal for the History of Science*, 5 (June 1970): 63–72;

James G. Kennedy, *Herbert Spencer* (Boston: Twayne, 1978);

Roy M. MacLeod, "The X-Club: A Social Network of Science in Late-Victorian England," *Notes and*

Records of the Royal Society of London, 24 (1970): 305–322;

Ronald E. Martin, *American Literature and the Universe of Force* (Durham, N.C.: Duke University Press, 1981), pp. 6–95;

P. B. Medawar, "Herbert Spencer and the Law of General Evolution," in his *The Art of the Soluble* (London: Methuen, 1967), pp. 39–58;

William L. Miller, "Herbert Spencer's Theory of Welfare and Public Policy," *History of Political Economy,* 4 (Spring 1972): 207–231;

Ellen Frankel Paul, "Herbert Spencer: The Historicist as a Failed Prophet," *Journal of the History of Ideas,* 44 (October–December 1983): 619–638;

Jeffrey Paul, "The Socialism of Herbert Spencer," *History of Political Thought,* 3 (Winter 1982): 499–514;

J. D. Y. Peel, *Herbert Spencer: The Evolution of a Sociologist* (London: Heinemann, 1971);

Robert G. Perrin, "Herbert Spencer's Four Theories of Social Evolution," *American Journal of Sociology,* 81 (May 1976): 1339–1359;

David C. Rapoport, "Military and Civil Societies," *Political Studies,* 12 (June 1964): 178–201;

Josiah Royce, *Herbert Spencer* (New York: Fox, Duffield, 1904);

Royce, *Herbert Spencer: An Estimate and Review; Together with a Chapter of Personal Reminiscences by James Collier* (New York: Fox, Duffield, 1904);

Jay Rumney, *Herbert Spencer's Sociology: A Study in the History of Social Theory* (London: Williams & Norgate, 1934);

Harold Issadore Sharlin, "Herbert Spencer and Scientism," *Annals of Science,* 33 (September 1976): 456–465;

Henry Sidgwick, *Lectures on the Ethics of T. H. Green, Herbert Spencer and James Martineau* (London: Macmillan, 1906);

C. U. M. Smith, "Evolution and the Problem of Mind: Part 1, Herbert Spencer," *Journal of the History of Biology,* 15 (Spring 1982): 55–88;

Smith, "Herbert Spencer's Epigenetic Epistemology," *Studies in History and Philosophy of Science,* 14 (March 1983): 1–22;

George H. Smith, "Herbert Spencer's Theory of Causation," *Journal of Libertarian Studies,* 5 (Spring 1981): 113–152;

Hillel Steiner, "Land, Liberty and the Early Herbert Spencer," *History of Political Thought,* 3 (Winter 1982): 515–533;

Arthur J. Taylor, "The Originality of Herbert Spencer," *University of Texas Studies in English,* 34 (1956): 101–106;

M. W. Taylor, *Men versus the State: Herbert Spencer and Late Victorian Individualism* (Oxford: Oxford University Press, 1992);

Taylor, ed., *Herbert Spencer and the Limits of the State: The Late Nineteenth-Century Debate between Individualism and Collectivism* (Bristol, U.K. & Dulles, Va.: Thoemmes Press, 1996);

J. Arthur Thomson, *Herbert Spencer* (London: Dent, 1906);

Edward B. Tylor, "Mr. Spencer's *Principles of Sociology,*" *Mind,* 2 (April 1877): 141–156, 415–423;

Norman T. Walker, "The Sources of Herbert Spencer's Educational Ideas," *Journal of Educational Research,* 22 (November 1930): 299–308;

John B. Watson, *Comte, Mill and Spencer: An Outline of Philosophy* (Glasgow: MacLehose, 1895);

Watson, *Hedonistic Theories from Aristippus to Spencer* (London: Macmillan, 1895);

August Weismann, "On Heredity," in his *Essays upon Heredity and Kindred Biological Problems,* 2 volumes, edited by Edward B. Poulton, Selmar Schönland, and Arthur E. Shipley, translated by Schönland and Shipley (Oxford: Clarendon Press, 1889), pp. 67–106;

John White, "Andrew Carnegie and Herbert Spencer: A Special Relationship," *Journal of American Studies,* 13 (April 1979): 57–71;

David Wiltshire, *The Social and Political Thought of Herbert Spencer* (New York: Oxford University Press, 1978);

Chauncey Wright, "The Philosophy of Herbert Spencer," *North American Review,* 100 (April 1865): 423–475.

Papers:

The British Library has the manuscripts for Herbert Spencer's *Social Statics; The Principles of Psychology; First Principles; Essays: Scientific, Political, and Speculative; The Principles of Biology; The Study of Sociology; The Principles of Sociology;* and *The Data of Ethics.* Spencer materials are also at the University of London Library, the London School of Economics Library, the British Library of Political and Economic Science, and the Lyon Playfair Library of the Imperial College of Science and Technology.

Timothy L. S. Sprigge

(14 January 1932 –   )

Leemon B. McHenry

Loyola Marymount University and California State University, Northridge

BOOKS: *Facts, Words and Beliefs* (London: Routledge & Kegan Paul, 1970; New York: Humanities Press, 1970);

Santayana: An Examination of His Philosophy (London & Boston: Routledge & Kegan Paul, 1974; revised and enlarged edition, London: Routledge, 1995);

The Vindication of Absolute Idealism (Edinburgh: Edinburgh University Press, 1983);

Theories of Existence (Harmondsworth & New York: Penguin, 1984);

The Rational Foundations of Ethics (London & New York: Routledge & Kegan Paul, 1988);

The Significance of Spinoza's Determinism (Leiden: Brill, 1989);

James and Bradley: American Truth and British Reality (Chicago: Open Court, 1993);

Spinoza and Santayana: Religion without the Supernatural (Delft: Eburon, 1993).

OTHER: *The Correspondence of Jeremy Bentham,* volumes 1 and 2, edited by Sprigge (London: Athlone, 1968);

"Consciousness," in *The Ontological Turn: Essays in the Philosophy of Gustav Bergmann,* edited by Moltke S. Gram and E. D. Klemke (Iowa City: Iowa University Press, 1974), pp. 114–147;

"Punishment and Moral Responsibility," in *Punishment and Human Rights,* edited by Milton Goldinger (Cambridge, Mass.: Schenkman, 1974);

"The Animal Welfare Movement and the Foundation of Ethics," in *Animal Rights: A Symposium,* edited by David Paterson and Richard Ryder (Fontwell: Centaur, 1978), pp. 87–95;

"Bradley and Russell on Relations," in *Bertrand Russell Memorial Volume,* edited by George W. Roberts (London: Allen & Unwin, 1979), pp. 150–170;

"The Distinctiveness of American Philosophy," in *Two Centuries of Philosophy in America,* edited by Peter Caws (Oxford: Blackwell, 1980), pp. 199–214;

"James, Tarski and Pragmatism," in *Pragmatism and Purpose: Essays Presented to Thomas Goudge,* edited

Timothy L. S. Sprigge

by L. W. Sumner, John G. Slater, and Fred Wilson (Toronto & Buffalo, N.Y.: University of Toronto Press, 1981), pp. 105–120;

"The Self and Its World in Bradley and Husserl," in *The Philosophy of F. H. Bradley,* edited by Anthony Manser and Guy Stock (Oxford: Clarendon Press, 1984), pp. 285–302;

"George Santayana," in *American Philosophy,* edited by Marcus Singer, Royal Institute of Philosophy Lecture Series, no. 19 (Cambridge: Cambridge University Press, 1986), pp. 115–133;

"Utilitarianism," in *An Encyclopedia of Philosophy,* edited by G. H. R. Parkinson (London: Routledge, 1988), pp. 590–612;

"Schopenhauer and Bergson on Laughter," in *Comparative Criticism: An Annual Journal,* volume 10, edited by Elinor S. Shaffer (Cambridge: Cambridge University Press, 1988), pp. 39–65;

"The Ethics of Animal Use in Biomedicine," in *The Importance of Animal Experimentation for Safety and Biomedical Research,* edited by S. Garratini and D. W. van Bekkum (Dordrecht, Netherlands: Kluwer, 1990), pp. 17–28;

"Hartshorne on the Past," in *The Philosophy of Charles Hartshorne,* edited by Lewis E. Hahn, The Library of Living Philosophers, volume 20 (La Salle, Ill.: Open Court, 1991), pp. 397–414;

"Whitehead und Santayana," in *Die Gifford Lectures und ihre Deutung: Materialen zu Whitehead's "Prozess und Realitat,"* edited by Michael Hampe and Helmut Maassen (Frankfurt am Main: Suhrkamp, 1991), pp. 1121–1141;

"Ayer on Other Minds," in *The Philosophy of A. J. Ayer,* edited by Hahn, The Library of Living Philosophers, volume 21 (La Salle, Ill.: Open Court, 1992), pp. 577–595;

"Fundamentalism and International Law," in *International Law and Armed Conflict: United Kingdom Association for Social and Legal Philosophy Sixteenth Annual Conference at Leicester, 5–7 April, 1990,* edited by A. G. D. Bradney (Stuttgart: Steiner, 1992), pp. 103–108;

"Refined and Crass Supernaturalism," in *Philosophy, Religion and the Spiritual Life,* edited by Michael McGhee, Royal Institute of Philosophy Supplement, no. 32 (Cambridge: Cambridge University Press, 1992), pp. 105–125;

"Animal Experimentation in Biomedical Research: A Critique," in *Principles of Health Care Ethics,* edited by Raanon Gillon (Chichester & New York: Wiley, 1994), pp. 1053–1066;

"Bradley," in *The Nineteenth Century,* edited by C. L. Ten, Routledge History of Philosophy, volume 7 (London: Routledge, 1994), pp. 437–458;

"Idealism, Humanism and the Environment," in *Current Issues in Idealism,* edited by Paul Coates and Daniel D. Hutto (Bristol: Thoemmes, 1996), pp. 267–302;

"James, Aboutness and His British Critics," in *The Cambridge Companion to William James,* edited by Ruth Anna Putnam (Cambridge: Cambridge University Press, 1997), pp. 125–114;

"Respect for the Non-Human," in *The Philosophy of the Environment,* edited by T. D. J. Chappell (Edinburgh: Edinburgh University Press, 1997), pp. 117–134;

"Bradley's Doctrine of the Absolute," in *Appearance versus Reality: New Essays on Bradley's Metaphysics,* edited by Stock (Oxford: Clarendon Press, 1998), pp. 193–217;

"Is the Esse of Intrinsic Value Percipi? Pleasure, Pain and Value," in *Philosophy: The Good, the True and the Beautiful,* edited by Anthony O'Hear, Royal Institute of Philosophy Supplement, no. 47 (Cambridge: Cambridge University Press, 2000), pp. 119–140.

SELECTED PERIODICAL PUBLICATIONS–
UNCOLLECTED: "Internal and External Properties," *Mind,* 71 (1962): 197–212;

"Definition of a Moral Judgement," *Philosophy,* 39 (1964): 301–322;

"The Common Sense View of Physical Objects," *Inquiry,* 9 (1965): 339–373;

"The Privacy of Experience," *Mind,* 78 (1969): 512–521;

"Santayana and Verificationism," *Inquiry,* 12 (1969): 265–286;

"Final Causes," *Proceedings of the Aristotelian Society,* 45, supplementary volume (1971): 149–170;

"Ideal Immortality," *Southern Journal of Philosophy,* 10 (1972): 219–235;

"Spinoza's Identity Theory," *Inquiry,* 20 (1977): 419–445;

"Metaphysical Enquiry," *Theoria to Theory,* 12 (1978): 135–149;

"Metaphysics, Physicalism and Animal Rights," *Inquiry,* 22 (1979): 101–143;

"The Importance of Subjectivity: An Inaugural Lecture," *Inquiry,* 25 (1982): 143–163;

"Vivisection, Morals, Medicine: Commentary from an Anti-Vivisectionist Philosopher," *Journal of Medical Ethics,* 9 (1983): 98–101;

"Non-Human Rights: An Idealist Perspective," *Inquiry,* 27 (1984): 439–462;

"Utilitarianism and Idealism: A Rapprochement," *Philosophy,* 60 (1985): 447–463;

"Philosophy and Common Sense," *Revue Internationale de Philosophie,* 40 (1986): 195–206;

"Are There Intrinsic Values in Nature?" *Journal for Applied Philosophy,* 4 (1987): 21–28;

"Ethical Considerations on Animal Experimentation," *Alternatives to Laboratory Animals,* 14 (1987): 307–311;

"Intrinsic Connectedness," *Proceedings of the Aristotelian Society,* new series 88 (1987/1988): 129–145;

"Personal and Impersonal Identity," *Mind,* 97 (1988): 29–49;

"Utilitarianism and Respect for Human Life," *Utilitas,* 1 (1989): 1–21;

"On the Significance of Spinoza's Determinism," *Mededelingen vanwege het Spinozahuis,* 58 (1989): 1–16;

"A. J. Ayer: An Appreciation of His Philosophy," *Utilitas,* 2 (1990): 1–11;

"The Satanic Novel: A Philosophical Dialogue on Blasphemy and Censorship," *Inquiry,* 33 (1990): 377–400;

"Some Recent Positions in Environmental Philosophy Examined," *Inquiry,* 34 (1991): 107–128;

"The Greatest Happiness Principle," *Utilitas,* 3 (1991): 37–51;

"The Unreality of Time," *Proceedings of the Aristotelian Society,* 92 (1992): 1–19;

"Consciousness," *Synthese,* 98 (1994): 73–93;

"Is Spinozism a Religion?" *Studia Spinozana,* 11 (1995): 137–162;

"Pantheism," *Monist,* 80 (1997): 191–217;

"The God of the Philosophers," *Studies in World Christianity,* 4 (1998): 149–172;

"Has Speculative Metaphysics a Future?" *Monist,* 81 (1998): 513–533;

"Is Consciousness Mysterious?" *Anthropology and Philosophy,* 3 (1999): 5–19.

Timothy L. S. Sprigge is a speculative metaphysician who spent most of his career swimming against the current of the dominant linguistic and analytic trends in British philosophy. Working within an intellectual milieu largely hostile to his views, he attempted to provide color to what seemed to him a sterile and narrow orthodoxy. He said in *The Vindication of Absolute Idealism* (1983) that instead of viewing philosophy as a self-contained intellectual game, he attempts to arrive at answers to the "deep ontological questions about the concrete nature of reality." His highly original metaphysics is a bold affirmation of absolute idealism and of panpsychism, the doctrine that the universe is sentient or conscious. His tightly worked-out system combines ideas of the philosophers who have had the greatest impact on his thought: Baruch Spinoza, William James, F. H. Bradley, George Santayana, Josiah Royce, Alfred North Whitehead, and Arthur Schopenhauer. Sprigge also developed a moral philosophy that accords well with his metaphysics but can also stand alone: it is a version of utilitarianism that recognizes the intrinsic value of sentient beings, including nonhuman animals and the environment.

In addition to his metaphysical and moral systems, Sprigge is known for his scholarship in what is sometimes called the "golden age" of American philosophy, centered at Harvard University at the beginning of the twentieth century; in an unpublished 23 September 1981 letter the American philosopher and theologian Charles Hartshorne labeled him the leading expert in Britain on American thought. He found in James, Royce, and Santayana a deeper understanding of the nature of consciousness, time, and existence, and he appreciated the pluralism that their thought inspired in the United States. Sprigge is especially close to James in his emphasis on building up a philosophy from lived experience. The point, he thinks, is to develop a philosophy that is not merely academic but also relevant to one's life. In this respect, Sprigge has always had one foot in and the other out of "professional philosophy." He prefers the diversity of life in cities such as London and Edinburgh to the cloistered atmosphere of Oxford and Cambridge.

Timothy Lauro Squire Sprigge was born in London on 14 January 1932 to Cecil Jackson Squire Sprigge, a journalist, and Katriona Gordon Brown Sprigge. His parents divorced around the time of his birth; he was brought up by his mother and did not get to know his father until he was sixteen. In various places Sprigge records the impact his older brother, intellectual historian Robert, had on his intellectual development, especially for introducing him to various philosophical issues. Sprigge also has a sister, Rosemary Rogan. The seeds of his mature metaphysics were planted while he was serving in the army in 1951–1952. Walking in the countryside near Graz, Austria, he looked up at some clouds and decided that they must be the appearance of some form of consciousness.

In 1952 Sprigge enrolled at Gonville and Caius College of the University of Cambridge. He received his B.A. in English in 1955. The tripos for the degree emphasized the philosophical aspects of literature, making it easy for Sprigge to switch to "moral sciences"—the Cambridge term for philosophy—for the Ph.D. He began his thesis, "The Limits of Morals Defined," under the supervision of R. T. H. Redpath. In 1958 Sprigge left Cambridge for University College London. He received a position at University College as a researcher on Jeremy Bentham's manuscripts in 1959 and as a temporary lecturer in 1961. He finished the work for the Cambridge Ph.D. in 1961 in absentia, working under the analytic philosopher A. J. Ayer at University College. Despite his vast differences with one of the leading British antimetaphysicians, Sprigge admired Ayer's philosophy and learned a great deal from him personally.

The utilitarian philosopher Bentham has been associated with University College London, England's first secular institution of higher education, since he participated in its founding in the late 1820s. In addition to his own body, which is preserved as an "auto-icon" in the lobby of the college's main building,

Bentham left an enormous amount of his manuscript materials on law, economics, politics, and philosophy. Sprigge's appointment involved editing some of these manuscripts for publication in Bentham's collected works; the eventual result was the first two volumes of *The Correspondence of Jeremy Bentham,* published in 1968. Bentham's unqualified hedonism appealed to Sprigge, and a fair amount of Bentham's approach to ethics shows up later in Sprigge's view of intrinsic value.

On 4 April 1960 Sprigge married his first cousin, Giglia Gordon, who had been a nurse at Addenbrooke's Hospital in Cambridge while he was an undergraduate at the university. They have three children: twins Georgina Nessie and Lucy Cecilia, and Samuel Felix. In the preface to *The Vindication of Absolute Idealism* Sprigge says that Giglia is mainly responsible for his contact "with what is known as the real world" as opposed to the abstract speculative constructs of philosophy.

Sprigge lectured in philosophy at University College from 1961 to 1963. In 1963 he was appointed lecturer in philosophy in the School of English and American Studies at the University of Sussex. He was a visiting associate professor at the University of Cincinnati for the academic year 1968–1969 and became a reader in philosophy at the University of Sussex in 1970. In his first book, *Facts, Words and Beliefs* (1970), he investigates the question of what goes on in consciousness when one thinks. Sprigge concludes that consciousness consists of a series of symbols that act as substitutes for perceptual encounters with that of which one is thinking. He approached the question on the basis of a somewhat Russellian point of view on ontological matters, but his style of thinking soon came to owe more to Santayana. He says in "Consciousness" (1974) that "The serious study of Santayana's works transformed my own philosophical outlook and enabled me to escape from a variety of absurdities into which I had been led by premises I did not think to question." His second book, *Santayana: An Examination of His Philosophy* (1974), explores the ontological basis of consciousness from a naturalistic and realistic perspective. Two articles from this period are especially noteworthy as revealing Sprigge's departure from the then-dominant trends in English philosophy: "The Privacy of Experience" (1969) and "Consciousness" both point to his later philosophy of panpsychism based on an examination of the stream of experience known to the subject most intimately and privately.

Philosophical thought in Britain during the latter half of the twentieth century was dominated by the tough-minded, rigorous approach initiated earlier in the century by logical positivism and linguistic analysis. Metaphysics was regarded either as literal nonsense—that is, the use of terms that had no empirically verifiable

Sprigge as a young man

meaning—or as resulting from an inability to understand the way ordinary people use language. The ideas of metaphysicians of the past were held up for ridicule; Bradley and the other absolute idealists were considered some of the worst offenders. Those few philosophers who were interested in metaphysics had to spend their energy in trying to demonstrate its possibility and value rather than in actually practicing it: "meta-metaphysics" was as close as one could get while remaining intellectually respectable. Philosophers whose formal contributions were underpinned by metaphysical views kept those views hidden. The logician Kurt Gödel, for example, was secretly a Platonic-Kantian idealist.

By the late 1970s, however, the situation had changed somewhat. Sprigge said in *The Vindication of Absolute Idealism* that "the philosopher who steps forward as a speculative metaphysician need no longer feel that his attempt to reach a view of the nature of things by methods distinctively philosophical will be dismissed in advance by most fellow philosophers as an enterprise of its very nature doomed to vacuity." As the antimetaphysical methodologies exhausted discussion of the relevant topics,

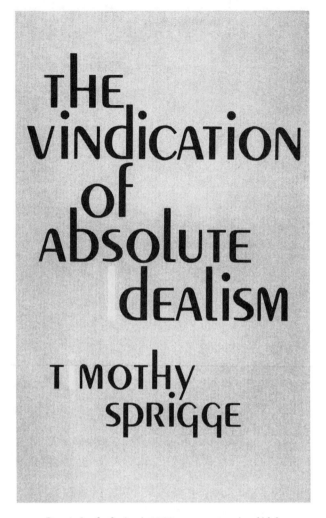

Dust jacket for Sprigge's 1983 magnum opus, in which he
combines the nonmainstream metaphysical positions
of panpsychism and absolute idealism
(Collection of Leemon B. McHenry)

some philosophers sensed that the field was succumbing to fatigue and atrophy. Moreover, the arrival of computers brought about a renewal of interest in such traditional metaphysical topics as the nature of consciousness, the mind-body problem, free will, and personal identity.

Sprigge's opportunity to develop his metaphysical views was enhanced by his appointment in 1979 to the distinguished chair of logic and metaphysics at the University of Edinburgh; previous occupants of the position included Norman Kemp Smith and W. H. Walsh. The Scottish capital maintained some independence in philosophical thought, especially in the history of philosophy and metaphysics; Whitehead, the Gifford Lecturer at Edinburgh in 1928, had in *The Principle of Relativity, with Applications to Physical Science* (1922) described the city as "the capital of British metaphysics, haunted by the shade of [David] Hume," and according to Sprigge, "the very air of the university and city of Edinburgh are the

breath of life to a metaphysician." At the university the metaphysical systems of Plato, René Descartes, Georg Wilhelm Friedrich Hegel, and Bradley were balanced against the antimetaphysical philosophies of Hume, Russell, Ludwig Wittgenstein, and Ayer.

For Sprigge, metaphysical inquiry begins with consciousness in its purely subjective features. His inaugural lecture at Edinburgh, "The Importance of Subjectivity," published in 1982, is one of the clearest accounts of his approach. In knowing oneself as a center of consciousness, he says, one knows the inherent nature of a concrete reality, and through empathy one can achieve knowledge of other sentient creatures. This kind of knowledge is to be contrasted with knowledge of physical reality as it is presented to the senses or as its structure is conceptualized in the abstract terms of science and mathematics. The former is direct acquaintance; the latter is description. Sprigge analogizes the scientific understanding of nature to a deaf person's understanding of a musical score:

> A congenitally deaf person, it would seem, might learn quite a lot about musical structures. He could surely learn to look at a score, most simply a piano score, and realise that the work inscribed there is a fugue, or that it changes from the major to the minor at a certain point, and so on. So he may learn an indefinite amount about structure of various sorts of music, or individual pieces, but have no idea of heard sound as the concrete way in which structure is realized.

Sprigge's emphasis on subjectivity is not intended as an attack on objectivity or on the importance of evidence and reasoning in the development and testing of scientific hypotheses or, for that matter, of metaphysical claims. His point is that the attempt to know reality merely as appearance or in terms of the structural features of matter fails to grasp the inherent reality of the world, or what it is like to be an entity in its full concreteness. Sprigge had pioneered this approach in the article "Final Causes" in 1971, but it was made famous by Thomas Nagel in 1974 in his paper "What Is It Like to Be a Bat?" While Nagel's application of the approach is limited to the case of the bat, in "The Distinctiveness of American Philosophy" (1980) Sprigge is concerned to draw a much wider conclusion for metaphysics: "if a philosopher would grasp reality in its concreteness, and arrive at a philosophic position adequate to such grasp, he must take the flow of his own experience as his paradigm example of the true pulse of existence, and continually check the results of his reasoning by reference back to it." This attempt, he says, resembles James's generalization of the main points of his psychological theory into his philosophy of radical empiricism and Whitehead's method in *Process and Reality: An Essay in*

Cosmology (1929). Whitehead's method is described by Sprigge as "metaphysical generalization from an initially psychological concept." Sprigge has identified the move from the private experience of consciousness to the realization of its implications for general understanding of reality as a distinctive mark of the classical American philosophers, and it has led him to panpsychism and the doctrine of the Absolute.

Sprigge systematically weaves together panpsychism and absolute idealism by a chain of arguments in his 1983 magnum opus, *The Vindication of Absolute Idealism*. The very title of the book was a challenge to contemporary philosophy, since the British mainstream regarded absolute idealism as an antiquated relic of earlier centuries that had been destroyed by Russell, Moore, and Ayer. Sprigge indicates that he is well aware that the consensus of philosophical opinion will regard his ideas as far-fetched or even absurd, but he is determined to demonstrate that Spinoza, Bradley, and Royce were right.

Sprigge's fundamental question in *The Vindication of Absolute Idealism* is couched in Kantian terms: What is the noumenal backing, or the "in itself," of the phenomena that are perceived as physical reality? After considering and rejecting several answers to this question—naive realism, subjective idealism, naive scientism, critical scientism, phenomenalism, phenomenalist instrumentalism, and physicalism—he arrives at the view that reality is consciousness manifested in various forms. More specifically, reality is composed of innumerable mutually interacting momentary centers of experience related to form enduring centers of experience such as one finds in oneself. The enduring centers, in turn, cumulate in the Absolute, which occurs as one grand epochal moment of the universe.

In opposition to the Kantian tradition, according to which the noumenal reality lying beyond appearances is completely unknowable, Sprigge argues that human beings have direct knowledge of noumenal reality in themselves and, through empathy, of the noumenal reality of other beings. The usual distinctions between organic and inorganic, living and nonliving, and humans and animals fail to have ultimate significance for such a panpsychist metaphysics. As Royce said in *The World and the Individual* (1899, 1901), "Where we see inorganic Nature seemingly dead, there is, in fact, conscious life, just as surely as there is any Being present in Nature at all." In Sprigge's view each "in itself" feels itself as a whole at each moment, but the aggregates may or may not themselves be sentient. Thus, a pebble on the beach, a mountain, or an artifact such as a computer consists of an aggregate of individually experiencing centers, but there is nothing that is the sentience of such a thing as a whole. For Sprigge the terms "consciousness" and "sentience" are synonyms, but he distinguishes between high-grade centers of experience

such as human consciousness and the low-grade centers of experience that constitute the greater part of nature. In the case of human beings, the continuity of the momentary centers is best described by James's phrase "the stream of consciousness." Although Sprigge does not undertake a classification of sentient wholes and parts, he notes that such an inquiry would be a valuable undertaking for a panpsychist philosopher of science.

Sprigge's view is a radical departure from the view that consciousness arose at a late stage in the evolution of life on the planet Earth, since he holds that consciousness of some sort has always been there. As W. V. Quine states this view in his *Theories and Things* (1981), "The propositions of biology and psychology are local generalizations about some terrestrial growths of our acquaintance." But the view runs into difficulties that a panpsychist seeks to overcome by positing sentience from the beginning. The great mystery for the physicalistic view is the two abrupt changes in the evolutionary process: the emergence of life from inanimate matter and, later, the emergence of consciousness from organic life. Panpsychism, as James and Whitehead saw, provides for smooth and continuous transitions rather than sudden breaks in nature. Sprigge argues that panpsychism also makes the mind-body relationship more intelligible.

One of Sprigge's central theses is that the momentary centers exist eternally in the Absolute. This theory brings together principles of absolute idealism, as developed by Bradley and Royce, with Santayana's views on time. Sprigge's most important writings on this topic include "Ideal Immortality" (1972); his presidential address to the Aristotelian Society, "The Unreality of Time" (1992); and various chapters in *Santayana: An Examination of His Philosophy, The Vindication of Absolute Idealism,* and *James and Bradley: American Truth and British Reality* (1993). According to "determinationism," as Sprigge calls his view, past, present, and future are all intrinsically present. One calls events "past" or "future" relative to one's own present, but there is nothing special about the moment that happens to be illuminated as "now"; in and of themselves, all events are "now." Determinationism is not to be confused with determinism, according to which one could, in principle, predict future events if one had adequate knowledge of the present and of the laws of nature. The determinist, that is, believes that future events will be causally determined by present events and are, therefore, inevitable, but they do not as yet exist. The determinationist, on the other hand, holds that future events, like those of the past and present, exist eternally.

The basis of the determinationist view is Santayana's argument that all statements or propositions about events in time must refer to a reality that makes them true or false. If a proposition about the past is

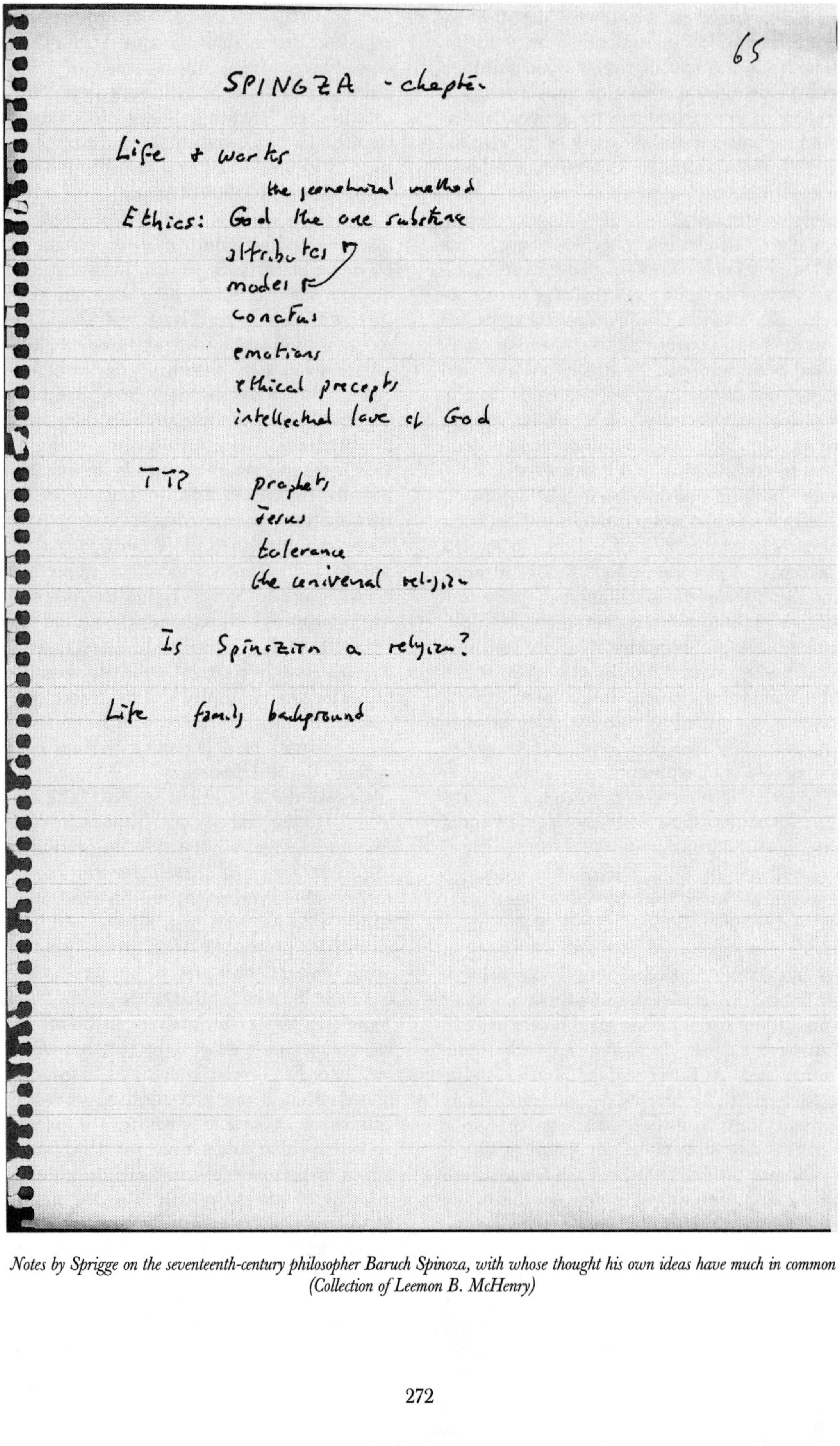

65

SPINOZA - chapter

Life & works
                the geometrical method
Ethics: God the one substance
        attributes ⇗
        modes ⇗
        conatus
        emotions
        ethical precepts
        intellectual love of God

    TTP   prophets
           Jesus
           tolerance
           the universal religion

        Is Spinozism a religion?

    Life   family background

Notes by Sprigge on the seventeenth-century philosopher Baruch Spinoza, with whose thought his own ideas have much in common
(Collection of Leemon B. McHenry)

true—for example, a proposition about the pain that King Harold felt when the arrow pierced his eye at the Battle of Hastings—it must be because there is some reality that makes it true. But Sprigge points out that if the past has become nothing, it is impossible to distinguish what *was* in the past from what *was not*. If an event has changed by becoming past, Sprigge asks in *The Vindication of Absolute Idealism,* then what is to prevent it from changing in other ways, as well? "Surely a past which might change does not supply that anchoring for historical truth we were seeking. Yet an untransformed past cannot have any quality of pastness; it must eternally be a realm of events each as much a fleeting present from its own point of view as is the feeling you have now, and only past as viewed from a perspective belonging to a different time." In other words, the referent of all propositions about the past is an object that is still a reality in itself.

If this argument about the intrinsic reality of the past is valid, then it follows that the same holds for all events subsequent to the one recognized as "now"; that is, one cannot consistently hold that the past is determinate in character but that the future is not. From the perspective of the Absolute, all events are present, as Spinoza said, sub specie aeternitatis (under the aspect of eternity), even though from the human perspective, which is *sub specie temporis* (under the aspect of time), the future appears to be open to manipulation. Metaphysically, then, time is unreal—or, at least, the human experience of time as perpetually perishing is an illusion. Nothing perishes; all events are eternally experienced as present in the Absolute consciousness.

Santayana saw that this view of time implied certain consequences for the ordinary sentiments of nostalgia, fear, and hope and for the concept of immortality. A Stoic or Spinozistic rationalism results from recognizing the metaphysical necessity of the eternal presence of each moment of time. The moment of one's death, for example, is just as fixed in the future as the moment of one's birth is fixed in the past, and nothing can alter this fact. But if this realization is disturbing to the common-sense notion of free will, there is some consolation in the recognition that one's life does not pass into nothingness at death. While there is no afterlife in the sense of a continued postmortem existence, one's life is eternally preserved—not merely in some deity's cosmic memory but, rather, as an actual eternal presence in the Absolute itself. The notion of consciousness absorbed in the eternal can overcome dread of death.

Sprigge contends in *The Vindication of Absolute Idealism* that the experience of the Absolute must be conceived as a kind of frozen specious present; from the point of view of the whole, all of the noumenal essences are interdependent in such a way that the whole of time is experienced as happening at once: "the best image of

the unitary totality of things is that of a vast symphony which experiences itself in one single specious present of colossal extent and complexity." Spinoza thought that a philosopher who arrived at this point of rapturous recognition of the unity of all things experienced "the intellectual love of God," in which such dualisms as God and nature, mental and physical, thought and emotion, and time and eternity lose their significance. Sprigge's view is virtually identical with Spinoza's.

Sprigge's metaphysical outlook, with its emphasis on sentient experience, is associated with an ethical theory that has both theoretical and practical aspects. He works out the theory in *The Rational Foundations of Ethics* (1988), but as early as 1979, in his essay "Metaphysics, Physicalism, and Animal Rights," he attempted to demonstrate that physicalistic accounts of reality can damage the moral sense. Insofar as any metaphysical construction is taken seriously today, he points out, the dominant movement has been toward materialism or physicalism; there has not been an attempt to relate this outlook explicitly to ethics, but the unconscious acceptance of it might lead to callous or cruel behavior of human beings toward one another, animals, and nature in general. Sprigge's metaphysics, on the contrary, implies that the consciousness of animals is essentially the same as that of humans, and he concludes that experimentation on animals is as objectionable as the similar treatment of human beings would be. Sprigge rejects Descartes's claim that animals do not possess "souls," or consciousness, and that what appears to be pain and suffering in such beings is, therefore, merely a mechanistic response. Although modern physicalism or behaviorism is far from Cartesian dualism, they provide theoretical backing for the state of mind in which one regards other sentient beings merely as objects in the phenomenal world that may be treated as means to one's own ends: "To equate consciousness with processes in the brain or alternatively with functional features or computer-type programmes currently guiding behaviour, or anything at all of that kind, however subtle its description, is necessarily to forget what consciousness is, and to treat it as merely a postulated detail in the world of presentation as extended by theory." Such accounts fail to recognize the most fundamental truth about others' reality and the moral obligation that results from it.

In *The Rational Foundation of Ethics* Sprigge advances a form of utilitarianism; in later works he calls it "way-of-life utilitarianism." Morally desirable actions are actions in the spirit of that way of life that is the best available in terms of maximizing pleasure and minimizing suffering for all those who are engaged in or affected by the way of life; morally obligatory actions are those that are part of the goodness of that way of life and that one should be blamed for not doing. Sprigge rejects Bentham's "hedonistic calculus," or quantitative weigh-

Sprigge before a monument to Spinoza in the Hague

ing of pleasures and pains. He also rejects the utilitarian cost/benefit analysis that can lead to the endorsement of intrinsically wrong actions because they promote the interests of the greatest number. It could be asked, however, whether Sprigge's metaphysics and ethics are, in fact, consistent: could one act in the manner he prescribes if determinationism is true? That is, if all moments of time are eternally present in the Absolute, how can one change one's behavior toward one's fellow human beings and animals for the better? A normative ethics implies freedom to act or forbear, but such freedom seems to be ruled out by determinationism. Also, holding human beings morally blameworthy for their actions would seem to make sense only if the Absolute were incomplete or evolving, but Sprigge denies that it is. Spinoza had a similar problem: his philosophy is meant to show the path to blessedness, or "the intellectual love of God," but whether one will achieve this state or not is entirely determined. It seems simply to be a matter of luck as to whether one will be set on the path of rational thought that leads to the state of blessedness.

In 1989 Sprigge retired from his position as professor of logic and metaphysics and became emeritus professor and endowment fellow. The change gave him more time for research and academic travel. He continued to teach on a part-time basis, including undergraduate lecture courses on metaphysics and ontology, Descartes, Spinoza, Santayana, James, and George Berkeley, and graduate seminars. In 1991 he served as president of the Aristotelian Society, and in 1993 he was elected a fellow of the Royal Society of Edinburgh. He has been a keynote speaker at conferences in the United States on the classical American philosophers, a regular lecturer to the Spinoza Society of the Netherlands, and a member of a group of British and Indian philosophers who meet in India to explore relations between Western and Indian thought. As a proponent of animal rights he has been involved in campaigns against animal experimentation and for the improvement of animal welfare and has served as chairman of the group Advocates for Animals. Throughout the 1980s and 1990s he participated in international conferences on the ethics of animal experimentation and the exploration of alternatives to the use of animals in medical research.

Sprigge has had a mixed reception from his peers, though some now-widespread ideas on such matters as counterfactuals, universals, and consciousness originated in *Facts, Words and Beliefs* and some of his other early works. He certainly won the respect and affection of scores of undergraduate and graduate students at Sussex and Edinburgh, even those who regarded his views as archaic and unfashionable. Some thought of him as Spinoza reincarnated in the twentieth century. He and one of his Ph.D. students were frequently seen walking between the David Hume Tower and Edinburgh's West End, so deeply engaged in discussing some philosophical issue that they seemed oblivious to the chilling gales blowing off the Firth of Forth; Edinburgh undergraduates called them "Don Quixote and Sancho Panza." Many students have been converted by Sprigge's arguments to animal rights and vegetarianism and a few to panpsychism.

References:

A. D. Naik, "Sprigge's Argument for Absolute Idealism," *Darshana International,* 31 (1992): 36–44;

Raymond N. Osei, "The Case for Agnostic Materialism," Ph.D. thesis, University of Liverpool, 1997;

Howard Robinson, "How to Give Analytical Rigour to 'Soupy Metaphysics,'" *Inquiry,* 40/41 (1997): 95–114.

Papers:

Timothy L. S. Sprigge's papers are in the Edinburgh University Library.

P. F. Strawson

(23 November 1919 –   )

Tadeusz Szubka
Catholic University of Lublin

BOOKS: *Introduction to Logical Theory* (London: Methuen, 1952; New York: Wiley, 1952);

Individuals: An Essay in Descriptive Metaphysics (London: Methuen, 1959; Garden City, N.Y.: Doubleday, 1963);

The Bounds of Sense: An Essay on Kant's "Critique of Pure Reason" (London: Methuen, 1966);

Meaning and Truth: An Inaugural Lecture Delivered before the University of Oxford on 5 November 1969 (Oxford: Clarendon Press, 1970);

Logico-Linguistic Papers (London: Methuen, 1971);

Freedom and Resentment, and Other Essays (London & New York: Methuen, 1974);

Subject and Predicate in Logic and Grammar (London: Methuen, 1974);

Skepticism and Naturalism: Some Varieties. The Woodbridge Lectures 1983 (New York: Columbia University Press, 1985; London: Methuen, 1985);

Analyse et Métaphysique: Une série de leçons donnée au Collège de France en mars 1985 (Paris: Vrin, 1985); revised and enlarged English version published as *Analysis and Metaphysics: An Introduction to Philosophy* (Oxford & New York: Oxford University Press, 1992);

Entity and Identity and Other Essays (Oxford & New York: Oxford University Press, 1997).

OTHER: "Construction and Analysis," in *The Revolution in Philosophy* (London: Macmillan, 1956; New York: St. Martin's Press, 1956), pp. 97–110;

"Metaphysics," by Strawson, H. Paul Grice, and David F. Pears, in *The Nature of Metaphysics,* edited by Pears (London: Macmillan, 1957; New York: St. Martin's Press, 1957), pp. 1–22;

"The Post-Linguistic Thaw," in *The British Imagination: A Critical Survey from* The Times Literary Supplement, edited by Arthur Crook (London: Cassell, 1961), pp. 168–174;

"Analyse, Science et Métaphysique," in *La Philosophie Analytique* (Paris: Editions de Minuit, 1962), pp. 105–118; original English version published as "Analysis, Science, and Metaphysics," in *The Lin-*

P. F. Strawson

guistic Turn: Recent Essays in Philosophical Method, edited by Richard M. Rorty (Chicago & London: University of Chicago Press, 1967), pp. 312–320;

"Carnap's Views on Constructed Systems versus Natural Languages in Analytic Philosophy," in *The Philosophy of Rudolf Carnap,* edited by Paul Arthur Schilpp, The Library of Living Philosophers, volume 11 (La Salle, Ill.: Open Court, 1963), pp. 503–518;

Philosophical Logic, edited by Strawson (London: Oxford University Press, 1967);

275

Studies in the Philosophy of Thought and Action: British Academy Lectures, edited by Strawson (London & New York: Oxford University Press, 1968);

"Does Knowledge Have Foundations?" in *Conocimiento y creencia: Actas del IV Simposio de Lógica y Filosofía de la Ciencia* (Valencia: Universidad de Valencia, 1974), pp. 99–110;

"Perception and Its Objects," in *Perception and Identity: Essays Presented to A. J. Ayer, with His Replies to Them,* edited by Graham F. Macdonald (London: Macmillan, 1979), pp. 41–60;

"Liberty and Necessity," in *Spinoza: His Thought and Work,* edited by Nathan Rotenstreich and Norma Schneider (Jerusalem: Israel Academy of Sciences and Humanities, 1983), pp. 120–129;

"Causation and Explanation," in *Essays on Davidson: Actions and Events,* edited by Bruce Vermazen and Merrill B. Hintikka (Oxford: Clarendon Press, 1985; New York: Oxford University Press; 1985), pp. 115–135;

"Sensibility, Understanding, and the Doctrine of Synthesis: Comments on Henrich and Guyer," in *Kant's Transcendental Deductions: The Three "Critiques" and the "Opus Postumum,"* edited by Eckhart Förster (Stanford, Cal.: Stanford University Press, 1989), pp. 69–77;

"Two Conceptions of Philosophy," in *Perspectives on Quine,* edited by Robert B. Barrett and Roger F. Gibson (Oxford & Cambridge, Mass.: Blackwell, 1990), pp. 310–318;

"Individuals," in *Philosophical Problems Today,* volume 1, edited by Guttorm Fløistad (London, Boston & Dordrecht, Netherlands: Kluwer, 1994), pp. 21–44;

"Knowing from Words," in *Knowing from Words: Western and Indian Philosophical Analysis of Understanding and Testimony,* edited by Bimal Krishna Matilal and Arindam Chakrabarti (London, Boston & Dordrecht, Netherlands: Kluwer, 1994), pp. 23–27;

"My Philosophy," in *The Philosophy of P. F. Strawson,* edited by Pranab Kumar Sen and Roop Rekha Verma (New Delhi: Indian Council of Philosophical Research, 1995), pp. 1–18;

"Intellectual Autobiography," in *The Philosophy of P. F. Strawson,* edited by Lewis E. Hahn, The Library of Living Philosophers, volume 26 (Chicago: Open Court, 1998), pp. 1–21;

"Entailment and Its Paradoxes," in *Realism: Responses and Reactions: Essays in Honour of Pranab Kumar Sen,* edited by D. P. Chattopadhyaya and others (New Delhi: Indian Council of Philosophical Research, 2000), pp. 22–31;

"What Have We Learned from Philosophy in the Twentieth Century?" in *Contemporary Philosophy,*

Proceedings of the Twentieth World Congress of Philosophy, volume 8, edited by Daniel O. Dahlstrom (Bowling Green, Ohio: Philosophy Documentation Center, Bowling Green State University, 2000), pp. 269–274.

SELECTED PERIODICAL PUBLICATIONS–
UNCOLLECTED: "Necessary Propositions and Entailment-Statements," *Mind,* 57 (1948): 184–200;

"Ethical Intuitionism," *Philosophy,* 24 (1949): 23–33;

"Truth," *Analysis,* 9 (1949): 83–97;

"A Reply to Mr. Sellars," *Philosophical Review,* 63 (1954): 216–231;

"A Logician's Landscape," *Philosophy,* 30 (1955): 229–237;

"In Defense of a Dogma," by Strawson and H. Paul Grice, *Philosophical Review,* 65 (1956): 141–158;

"Singular Terms, Ontology and Identity," *Mind,* 65 (1956): 433–454;

"Proper Names," *Proceedings of the Aristotelian Society,* supplementary volume, 31 (1957): 191–228;

"On Justifying Induction," *Philosophical Studies,* 9 (1958): 20–21;

"The 'Direction' of Non-Symmetrical Relations," *Crítica,* 6, nos. 16–17 (1972): 3–13;

"Different Conceptions of Analytical Philosophy," *Tijdschrift voor Filosofie,* 35 (1973): 800–834;

"Semantics, Logic and Ontology," *Neue Hefte für Philosophie,* 8 (1975): 1–13;

"Knowledge and Truth," *Indian Philosophical Quarterly,* 3 (1975–1976): 273–282;

"Scruton and Wright on Anti-Realism Etc.," *Proceedings of the Aristotelian Society,* 77 (1976–1977): 15–21;

"La logique philosophique," *Critique,* 36 (1980): 830–838;

Review of Grice, *Studies in the Way of Words, Synthese,* 84 (1990): 153–161;

"Comments on Some Aspects of Peter Unger's *Identity, Consciousness and Value,*" *Philosophy and Phenomenological Research,* 52 (1992): 145–148;

"Echoes of Kant," *TLS: The Times Literary Supplement* (3 July 1992): 12–13;

"The Incoherence of Empiricism," *Proceedings of the Aristotelian Society,* 66, supplementary volume (1992): 139–143.

P. F. Strawson is one of the best-known and most influential British philosophers of the post–World War II era. Although he concedes that there are several legitimate conceptions of philosophy, his strong conviction is that the analytic approach is the most fruitful one, and all of his work exemplifies it. Within the analytic tradition Strawson is usually associated with the movement known as Oxford ordinary language philosophy, Oxford analytic philosophy, or, simply, Oxford philosophy. The members of this loosely structured movement, which also includes J. L. Austin, H. Paul Grice, and Gilbert Ryle, maintain that philosophers should pay special attention to the use in ordinary language of philosophically relevant expressions. Strawson's early work in the philosophy of language reflects this idea, but he soon realized that focusing on ordinary linguistic usage takes too much for granted and does not reveal the relationships between the most basic concepts. Those limitations are especially evident in metaphysics, the aim of which is to investigate the fundamental and most general features of the conceptual scheme in terms of which human beings think about reality. Accordingly, in his later work Strawson shows how linguistic analysis may be supplemented by other methods or models of philosophical analysis. In particular, he suggests that analytic philosophers adopt some elements of Immanuel Kant's transcendental method in the *Kritik der reinen Vernunft* (1781; revised, 1787; translated as *Critique of Pure Reason*, 1855), which he considers the greatest single work in modern Western philosophy. By that suggestion Strawson contributed not only to the radical transformation of Oxford analytic philosophy but also to the revival of interest among analytic philosophers in metaphysics and in Kant's philosophy.

Although Kant's example has persuaded Strawson that philosophy should be systematic in character, he has never attempted to construct a unified system embodying a comprehensive philosophical doctrine. His aim has been the more modest one of addressing a set of interrelated philosophical issues and illuminating them in various ways. One prominent topic, however, consistently recurs in his writing: reference and predication and their metaphysical underpinnings in the distinction between particulars and universals. In addition to that thematic unity, a pervasive feature of Strawson's approach to philosophical problems is a deep mistrust of "reductive naturalism" and "scientism." That is, he refuses to accept the idea, defended most forcefully by the American philosopher W. V. Quine, that the natural sciences provide a complete account of the universe and that philosophy is continuous with science. According to Strawson, there is more to the universe than natural scientists are willing to admit, and philosophy is an autonomous discipline, though, strictly speaking, it does not have a special subject matter of its own.

At the beginning of his academic career Strawson collaborated closely with Grice, who had a major impact on his early work. He has also been influenced by both the general approach and the particular views of Austin, Ryle, G. E. Moore, and Ludwig Wittgenstein, and his philosophy owes a great deal to critical exchanges and discussions with A. J. Ayer, Bertrand Russell, Wilfrid Sellars, and, especially, Quine. Of the great philosophers of the past, the influence of Kant on Strawson's work is unrivaled; nevertheless, one may also discern in it ideas generally associated with Aristotle and David Hume. A succinct account of Strawson's philosophical views and life may be found his article "Individuals" in *Philosophical Problems Today* (1994), edited by Guttorm Fløistad; in his essay "My Philosophy" in *The Philosophy of P. F. Strawson* (1995), edited by Pranab Kumar Sen and Roop Rekha Verma; and in his "Intellectual Autobiography" in the Library of Living Philosophers volume devoted to him (1998).

Peter Frederick Strawson was born on 23 November 1919 in the London suburb of Ealing to Cyril Walter and Nellie Dora Jewell Strawson, both of whom were schoolteachers. He received his secondary education at Christ's College in Finchley, where he developed a strong interest in grammar and English literature. He won an open scholarship in English to St. John's College of the University of Oxford and enrolled there in October 1937; instead of English, however, he studied philosophy, politics, and economics. Of those subjects he was especially attracted by philosophy, in which his principal tutor was John D. Mabbott. He also received instruction from Grice, the other philosophy tutor at St. John's. The tutorials with Grice usually lasted much longer than the customary one hour, and Strawson acknowledges in his "Intellectual Autobiography" that from Grice he "learned more of the difficulty and possibilities of philosophical argument than from anyone else."

When he completed his undergraduate studies in the summer of 1940, Strawson was drafted into the Royal Artillery and sent for training to a territorial searchlight battery in Sussex. In 1942 he was transferred to the Royal Electrical and Mechanical Engineers. Although he admits that his military career was in no way distinguished, he rose to the rank of captain. In 1945 he married Grace Hall Martin, whom he later renamed Ann. They have four children: Julia Katharine; John Galen, who is also a philosopher; Robert Neville; and Virginia Ann.

Strawson left the army in 1946 and, with the support of his former tutor Mabbott, was appointed assistant lecturer in philosophy at the University College of North Wales, Bangor. In 1947 he won the prestigious John Locke Prize of the University of Oxford. Ryle, who was one of the examiners, recommended Strawson for the post of philosophy tutor at Oxford's University College. Strawson was appointed to the position in 1947 and remained in it for the next two decades.

In 1949 and 1950 Strawson published two papers, both titled simply "Truth." In the first paper, published in the journal *Analysis,* he takes issue with the semantic theory of truth proposed by the Polish mathematician and logician Alfred Tarski. According to that theory, to say that a statement is true is to make a statement about the original statement (in more technical terms, to say that a sentence of a given language is true amounts to ascribing to that sentence the semantic property of truth). Strawson rejects this claim on the grounds that it misconstrues the way the word *true* is actually used. More faithful to that use is the redundancy account of truth that was first formulated by the University of Cambridge philosopher and mathematician Frank P. Ramsey. According to this account, to say that a statement is true is not to make any further statement but is just to make the same statement; hence, the introductory phrase "it is true that" and the predicate "is true" are redundant and do not express any property of the original statement. Strawson modifies the redundancy account by saying that *true* is frequently used to express agreement with what someone else has said; the word, then, has mainly a "confirmatory" or "admissive" role.

In the second paper, originally published in the supplementary volume of *Proceedings of the Aristotelian Society* and collected in his *Logico-Linguistic Papers* (1971), Strawson defends his modified redundancy account, which is sometimes called the "performative theory" to distinguish it from Ramsey's pure redundancy theory, and argues against the correspondence theory of truth as reformulated by Austin. The traditional correspondence theory of truth says that a statement is true if it corresponds to a fact or state of affairs; a standard objection to it is that it is hard to make sense of the idea of correspondence. Trying to provide an unobjectionable version of the theory, Austin said that for a large class of statements, to say of a given statement that it is true is to say that a certain speech episode is related in virtue of some linguistic conventions to something in the world. Strawson thinks that Austin failed to achieve his aim, since he did not make sufficiently clear what the relation is and what its terms are. Strawson concludes that the correspondence theory requires not reformulation or purification but elimination. In his later writings Strawson qualified that harsh judgment of the theory, though he continued to insist that whatever is credible in it is nothing more than platitudes or trivialities; taken by themselves, they cannot be considered a theory but merely a starting point for a genuine, substantial account of truth.

In 1950 Strawson published "On Referring" in the journal *Mind;* it quickly received the status of a classic of analytical philosophy and remains one of his best-known papers. In the article, which is collected in his *Logico-Linguistic Papers,* Strawson criticizes the Theory of Descriptions, which was proposed by Russell in 1905. Russell's theory, regarded by many as a paradigm of analytic philosophy, was devised to solve the puzzle of sentences, such as "The present king of France is bald," that are meaningful but about which one cannot decide whether they are true or false. It seems that "The present king of France is bald" would be true if the present king of France were bald and false if he were not bald. But since there is no present king of France, the subject of the sentence fails to refer to anything, and so one is unable to decide whether the sentence is true or false. Russell's solution is that while the sentence is grammatically of the subject-predicate form, logically it is of the existential form. That is, the sentence actually is a conjunction of three assertions: there is a present king of France; there is no more than one present king of France; and there is nothing that is both the present king of France and not bald. Since the first of these assertions is false, the sentence is false.

Strawson disagrees both with Russell's analysis and with his conclusion. He maintains that one should distinguish between a sentence and the use of that sentence, as well as between what one asserts by using a sentence and what one implies or presupposes by using it. Those distinctions enable one to appreciate that the same sentence with the same meaning may be used in different contexts to assert different things. In some contexts what is asserted is true, and in others it is false. There may be, however, still other contexts in which using the sentence commits one to a false presupposition; and the falsity of the presupposition prevents one from making an assertion that is either true or false. If one makes the statement "The present king of France is bald" today, then one is falsely presupposing that there is a person who is the present king of France; hence, one fails to make an assertion that is either true or false.

In his early writings Strawson pays much attention to what people are naturally inclined to say in various ordinary contexts and to the ways in which they use certain philosophically relevant expressions. He insists that one should not assimilate the ordinary use of these expressions to the use of apparently similar expressions in systems of formal logic, since there are many crucial differences between ordinary discourse and logic. He identifies those differences in his first book, *Introduction to Logical Theory* (1952), in which he gives a nontechnical discussion of logical terms such as *inconsistency, contradiction,* and *entailment.* Strawson is especially concerned to show that the widely held identification of the truth-functional constants of the propositional calculus, such as *and, either . . . or,* and *if . . . then,* with the corresponding ordinary expressions is extremely misleading, despite "some degree of interpenetration of meanings" between the two sets of expressions. He concludes that "simple deductive relationships are not the only kind we have to consider if we wish to understand the logical workings of language. We have to think in many more dimensions than that of entailment and contradiction, and use many tools of analysis besides those which belong to formal logic."

In 1956 Strawson collaborated with Grice on "In Defense of a Dogma," a response to Quine's famous attack in his "Two Dogmas of Empiricism" (1951) on the distinction between analytic statements, such as "All bachelors are unmarried men," which are true by definition, and synthetic statements, such as "Some swans are white," which can be true or false depending on the facts. Strawson and Grice argue that the distinction is supported both by philosophical considerations and by ordinary linguistic usage. Moreover, they say, it is not true, as Quine claimed, that the distinction cannot be properly clarified; there are many informal ways to elucidate it that Quine simply overlooks.

This article, together with his earlier publications, established Strawson as one of the ablest exponents of Oxford analytic philosophy. Nevertheless, he soon noticed the limitations of some of the tenets of that movement. In "Construction and Analysis" (1956) he maintains that philosophy is not merely the elucidation of the ordinary uses of expressions so as to remove conceptual confusions; it also has an explanatory function:

> For fully to understand our conceptual equipment, it is not enough to know, to be able to say, how it works. We want to know also *why* it works as it does. To ask this is to ask to be shown how the nature of our thinking is rooted in the nature of the world and in our own natures. This is not an impossible inquiry; for it is quite possible to imagine our experience being different in fundamental ways, and then to consider how our conceptual apparatus might naturally be adjusted to accommodate these differences. In seeing this, we see also how our concepts, as they are, are rooted in the world, as it is.

Strawson implements this conception of philosophy in his second book, *Individuals: An Essay in Descriptive Metaphysics* (1959). It grew out of lectures he had delivered at Oxford in 1954–1955 and out of an uncompleted collaboration with Grice on predication and the Aristotelian categories. Strawson's most widely read and influential book, it is a work of what he calls "descriptive metaphysics": that is, its aim is to give an account of the actual structure of human thought about the world, as opposed to "revisionary metaphysics," which tries to replace that structure with a supposedly better one. The wide scope and extreme generality of metaphysical investigations, Strawson says, makes the

method of analysis of ordinary usage less useful here than in other branches of philosophy:

> Up to a point, the reliance upon a close examination of the actual use of words is the best, and indeed the only sure, way in philosophy. But the discriminations we can make, and the connections we can establish, in this way, are not general enough and not far-reaching enough to meet the full metaphysical demand for understanding. For when we ask how we use this or that expression, our answers, however revealing at a certain level, are apt to assume, and not to expose, those general elements of structure which the metaphysician wants revealed. The structure he seeks does not readily display itself on the surface of language, but lies submerged. He must abandon his only sure guide when the guide cannot take him as far as he wishes to go.

To establish the necessary connections that hold among various elements of the human conceptual structure, descriptive metaphysicians must use "transcendental arguments," reminiscent of Kant's, to show the conditions that make it possible to possess a given concept or have a certain experience. In *Individuals* Strawson establishes that a necessary condition of being able to ascribe mental states to oneself is the ability to identify mental states in others. Moreover, descriptive metaphysicians may engage in thought experiments to show that some basic features of the conceptual scheme are indispensable. For instance, the impossibility of imagining a completely auditory universe, that is, a universe containing only sounds, shows that the idea of spatiality (or, at least, an analogue of it) is an unavoidable feature of the human conceptual structure.

The most basic and pervasive procedural elements of the conceptual scheme in terms of which people think about the world include constantly identifying and reidentifying various particulars and ascribing properties or qualities to them. In Strawson's terminology, people make identifying reference to, and predicate various things of, particulars. The primary objects of that identifying reference are, for Strawson, material bodies and persons. He defines material bodies as three-dimensional objects enduring through time that have enough diversity, richness, and stability to constitute a unified spatiotemporal system in which all other particulars are located and identified. They may be contrasted with more or less fleeting events, processes, states, and conditions. Among the latter, one may also distinguish between those events, processes, states, and conditions that necessarily and conspicuously involve a material body and those that do not. "Thus a death is necessarily the death of some creature. But that a flash or a bang occurred does not entail that anything flashed or banged." That distinction turns out, however, not to be significant, since it is possible to show that events, processes, states, and conditions are metaphysically dependent on material bodies.

Along with material bodies, persons enjoy ontological or metaphysical priority. For Strawson, persons are entities to which one may properly ascribe both states of consciousness and bodily characteristics—that is, they have minds and bodies. Given the dominance of the Cartesian philosophical tradition, however, this statement may be misunderstood as claiming that the notion of a person is derivative from, and reducible to, the more basic notions of an immaterial mind and a material body. On the contrary, Strawson insists that the concept of person is primitive, which means "that it is not to be analysed in a certain way or ways."

The identification and reidentification of particulars and the ascription of various properties and qualities to them gives rise to the distinction on the ontological level between particulars and universals and on the linguistic level between reference and predication, or subject and predicate. Some philosophers have regarded the subject-predicate distinction as a purely grammatical one with no basis in reality, but Strawson accepts the distinction as real and seeks its explanation in the ontological distinction between particulars and universals. The association of grammatical subjects with particulars and predicates with universals may suggest that the only objects of reference are particulars; but Strawson asserts in *Individuals,* and emphasizes even more strongly in later publications, that universals—that is, general properties and abstract objects— may legitimately occur as subjects and, as a matter of fact, frequently do occur as such.

Individuals was widely and intensively discussed by analytic philosophers for more than two decades. A prominent question in these discussions was the cogency of the transcendental arguments formulated in the book, especially those directed against skepticism concerning the existence of unperceived material objects and of minds other than one's own. In his influential paper "Transcendental Arguments" (1968) Barry Stroud argues that Strawson is unable to refute those two kinds of skepticism without relying on a discredited version of the verification principle, according to which one can make sense only of those things one is able to know; in other words, meaningfulness entails knowability. If one gives up that principle, Stroud contends, transcendental arguments entitle one to conclude not that the world must be a certain way, but merely that human beings must think or believe that it is a certain way, given fundamental features of their conceptual scheme; and that is not enough to rebut skepticism. In other words, transcendental arguments can establish necessary connections between the elements of the human conceptual scheme but are unable to determine how that conceptual scheme is rooted in the world.

Whether or not they regard Strawson's arguments as successful, many philosophers have described *Individuals* as an impressive attempt to argue in a Kantian way for Aristotelian conclusions. Strawson himself, in an article titled "The Post-Linguistic Thaw" that he published anonymously in *The Times Literary Supplement* in 1960, says that the book is "a scaled-down Kantianism, pared of idealism on the one hand and a particular conception of physical science on the other."

Strawson's next book, *The Bounds of Sense: An Essay on Kant's "Critique of Pure Reason"* (1966), is an attempt to separate the sound and ingenious aspects of Kant's philosophy from the inconsistent and incoherent ones. Although the work deals with a prominent philosopher of the past, it is not a study in the history of ideas but a systematic philosophical treatise based on a close reading and interpretation of the *Critique of Pure Reason.* Strawson maintains that Kant is engaged in that work in a kind of descriptive metaphysics that may be called "the metaphysics of experience." The purpose of the metaphysics of experience is to identify and describe the necessary structural features of human experience— or, more ambitiously, of any conception of experience that can be made intelligible. In other words, its aim is to identify the structural elements that make any experience possible and without which experience simply does not make sense. Kant finds that the necessary features of experience include temporality; a degree of unity of experiences sufficient to allow a subject of those experiences to ascribe them to himself or herself; awareness of objects that appear to be independent of the subjective experience of them; the fact that the experienced objects are usually spatial; the fact that particular experiences and their objects are all members of one unified spatiotemporal framework; and the fact that the objects existing in space are governed by principles of permanence and causality. According to Strawson, some of those features are obviously necessary ingredients of any conception of experience; to show that all of the others are also necessary, he says, one would have to devise elaborate transcendental arguments. And one should not be skeptical about the possibility of constructing such arguments, he says, even though Kant's metaphysics of experience needs a radical purification from its entanglement in the mathematical and scientific conceptions of his time.

Kant claims that his metaphysics of experience accounts for why all attempts to propose metaphysical theories that go beyond the limits of experience—that is, all theories of transcendent, as opposed to transcendental, metaphysics—have failed. But while rejecting traditional forms of transcendent metaphysics, Strawson points out, Kant at the same time put forward a transcendent metaphysics of his own. Kant claims that one can know only how objects appear; one can know nothing about the objects as they are in themselves. For Strawson this doctrine, known as "transcendental idealism," is as misguided and empty as any other form of transcendent metaphysics and should be discarded.

The Bounds of Sense gave a new impetus to Kantian scholarship in Anglo-American philosophy. Discussions have concerned whether transcendental idealism is an essential part of Kant's system and whether Strawson's construal of it is the only admissible one. The cogency of Strawson's reformulation of Kant's transcendental arguments has also been put under close scrutiny. The book is Strawson's only major work on Kant, but he continued to lecture on Kant and publish papers on various aspects of Kant's philosophy.

In 1968 Strawson was elected to succeed Ryle as Waynflete Professor of Metaphysical Philosophy at Oxford, which meant he had to move from University College to Magdalen College. In his inaugural lecture on 5 November 1969, published as *Meaning and Truth* (1970), Strawson addresses the central question of the philosophy of language: the nature of linguistic meaning. He considers two widely held approaches to the question. The first is defended by philosophers he calls "the theorists of communication-intention." These philosophers hold that one cannot fully explicate the concept of meaning without referring to the intentions that speakers want to communicate. The other approach is endorsed by "the theorists of formal semantics"; they contend that meaning is constituted not by communicative intentions but by the system of syntactic and semantic rules that specify—in the case of declarative sentences, at least, which are the only kind that can be true or false—their truth conditions (that is, the circumstances or conditions under which those sentences are true). Putting aside the complicated issue of how to generalize that approach to nondeclarative sentences, Strawson finds the idea that truth conditions play a central role in the explication of meaning quite plausible. Its implementation, however, requires clarification of the notion of truth that it involves. Strawson suggests that one who utters a sentence makes a true statement if and only if things are as one states them to be. But it is obvious that what is involved here is not just a sentence and a set of rules specifying its truth conditions, but a sentence as uttered to make a statement—that is, a speech-act of the statement-making type. And that fact enables theorists of communication-intention to insist that it is impossible to specify the content of such speech acts without referring to the speaker's intention. Hence, Strawson admits that the approach endorsed by the theorists of formal semantics is not a genuine alter-

Cover for the 1992 revised and enlarged English version of lectures Strawson delivered in French at the Collège de France in 1985 (Bruccoli Clark Layman Archives)

native to a communication-intention theory of meaning but "leads us straight in to such a theory of meaning."

In *Subject and Predicate in Logic and Grammar* (1974) Strawson again explores the fundamental form of thought and speech, which, for him, is the subject-predicate form. The subject-predicate duality, he says, is ultimately based on the ontological distinction between particulars and universals. One encounters particulars in experience as falling under universals—that is, as possessing various qualities. Any human language must contain some semantically significant elements that can be, and usually are, combined in a specific way. The elements and their combinations may be represented by certain syntactical arrangements. The aim of what Strawson calls "perspicuous grammar" is to investigate those arrangements for various language types. Such a grammar can be pursued in a purely nonempirical, a priori way, but its results will shed light on actual languages. The perspicuousness of the grammar consists in "a guaranteed connection, clearly understood, between formal syntactic features, relations and classifications on the one hand and semantic interpretation on the other."

Subject and Predicate in Logic and Grammar was not as influential as Strawson's earlier books; indeed, it was almost ignored. Among the criticisms made by the few philosophers who undertook to discuss it in reviews and papers were that one cannot provide a noncircular account of the supposedly fundamental ontological distinction between particulars and universals; that singular predication is not basic to logic, since propositional logic does not distinguish among the parts of propositions, and predicate logic, which does so distinguish, is not concerned with singular predication but with entailments between generalized propositions; and that the project of a perspicuous grammar is a highly speculative enterprise. In spite of this reception, Strawson is fond of the book "as one might be of a neglected child," as he puts it in "My Philosophy."

Strawson was created a Knight Bachelor in 1977, entitling him to be called Sir Peter. In 1983 he delivered the prestigious Woodbridge Lectures at Columbia University in New York; they were published in book form as *Skepticism and Naturalism: Some Varieties* (1985). He addresses the question of whether it is possible to provide a justification of the conceptual scheme in terms of which people think about the world, the most crucial features of which he had tried to elucidate in his former publications. Skeptics put in doubt one's right to claim that the world actually is the way it is shown to be by one's conceptual scheme. That is, they say that one cannot claim to know, in the strict sense of the word *know,* that the world contains physical objects, or bodies, located in space and time, as well as human persons who possess both physical and mental characteristics; that the past is real and determinate; and that common inductive practices, in which generalizations are made on the basis of a small number of cases or future events are predicted on the basis of past ones, are generally reliable. Strawson maintains that such a radical skepticism cannot be refuted by rational arguments, but that that fact does not make skeptics winners in the debate with the defenders of the human conceptual scheme. The reason is that the commitments embedded in that scheme, though prerational, are natural and inescapable; they set "the natural limits within which, and only within which, the serious operations of reason, whether by way of questioning or of justifying beliefs, can take place."

Strawson does not claim that his way of rebutting skepticism is original. He points out that one can find it in the work of Hume, who emphasized that skeptical doubts, though intellectually stimulating and amusing,

are completely idle, since they are unable to undermine natural beliefs in the existence of bodies and the reliability of inductive generalizations and expectations. It is also conspicuous in Wittgenstein's later philosophy, which distinguishes between beliefs that are based on experience or supported by reasons and may be subject to further verification or falsification, on the one hand, and beliefs that constitute the framework that makes all procedures of empirical and rational justification possible, on the other hand. In a famous metaphor, Wittgenstein compares the propositions that are subject to justification to the water in a river and the background propositions that do not admit of justification to the bed or banks of the river. As the latter may shift over time, so the framework of background beliefs may undergo changes. Some elements of the framework are unchangeable, Strawson points out, since it is the scheme that embodies the human picture of the world– "a world of physical objects (bodies) in space and time including human observers capable of action and of acquiring and imparting knowledge (and error) both of themselves and each other and of whatever else is to be found in nature." But particular areas of the conceptual scheme do admit of modification. For instance, to achieve an "objective," "detached," or "impartial" point of view, one may refrain from applying moral predicates in describing human actions and suspend one's moral judgments and attitudes. One may also admit that one does not perceive things as they really are: the real natures of things and their properties are revealed by the natural sciences, and from that point of view things do not possess the usual sensible properties, such as color, odor, texture, and so on. But such modifications, which are often motivated by a reductive naturalism or scientism, are limited. They cannot be made once and for all; they are available only temporarily and without complete eradication of the ordinary standpoint, according to which human actions possess moral properties and things are as they are experienced to be under normal conditions. Strawson suggests that the conflict between the two different standpoints can easily be resolved by a "relativizing move": there is no one particular way that the world is, since it appears differently from different perspectives. The relativizing move is supported by the lack of any reason for maintaining that either the "objective" scientific standpoint or the ordinary perceptual and moral standpoint provides an adequate conception of the real nature of things.

Strawson's insistence that an ultimate external justification of the human conceptual scheme cannot be provided shows that transcendental arguments cannot be regarded as a way to refute skepticism. They should be taken, instead, as a useful tool in establishing and illuminating conceptual connections holding between various structural elements of the human conceptual scheme. They do not establish that the necessary condition of self-conscious experience is physical objects actually existing in space; they merely show that the necessary condition of self-conscious experience is that people believe that physical objects exist in space. Hence, Strawson agrees with Stroud's criticism that transcendental arguments cannot refute skepticism without relying on a discredited version of the verification principle.

Some of Strawson's followers and commentators have found that concession unacceptable; they say that in his later work Humean influences push out the Kantianism present in his earlier publications and declare, as Quassim Cassam does, that "it is with the latter that one must side." It is unclear, however, whether the tension between Kantianism and Humeanism is real or merely apparent. Some commentators argue for the latter interpretation on the grounds that the Kantianism of Strawson's earlier work is, as he himself has said, a "scaled-down" one and may be coherently combined with some Humean elements. If this interpretation is correct, Strawson's later work should be read as clarification and elaboration of his earlier ideas and an attempt to put them in a larger setting.

Almost every academic year from his election as Waynflete Professor of Metaphysical Philosophy until his retirement in 1987 Strawson delivered a series of introductory lectures on philosophy for Oxford undergraduates. He also gave some of these lectures at universities in other countries. In 1973 the first two lectures were combined under the title "Different Conceptions of Analytical Philosophy" and published in the Dutch journal *Tijdschrift voor Filosofie*. Strawson translated most of them into French and delivered them in 1985 at the Collège de France in Paris; they were published the same year as *Analyse et Métaphysique*. In 1992 he published a revised and enlarged version in English as *Analysis and Metaphysics: An Introduction to Philosophy*.

In spite of its subtitle, the book is too abstract and too demanding for beginners. It is, however, an excellent account of Strawson's metaphilosophical views—that is, his ideas about philosophy itself. He defends and elaborates his conception of philosophical analysis as the clarification and elucidation of certain concepts that people use in thinking about the world. The concepts on which philosophy focuses are highly general, irreducible, and indispensable or noncontingent, such as time, space, existence, identity, knowledge, and material object. Although often the main task of a particular philosopher is to remove misunderstandings and confusions concerning the use of such concepts, the central and primary task of analytic philosophy is the more systematic one of identifying and describing "a set

of general, pervasive, and ultimately irreducible concepts or concept-types which together form a structure—a structure which constitutes the framework of our ordinary thought and talk and which is presupposed by the various specialist or advanced disciplines that contribute, in their diverse ways, to our total picture of the world." The structure consists of concepts that are mutually dependent and interlocking, not of concepts that rest on a few basic and simple ones to which they may be reduced. Therefore, Strawson says, the proper model of systematic philosophical analysis is not the reductive one that was for a time widely accepted by the members of the analytic movement but the "connective model" of establishing the connections between various crucial elements of the human conceptual scheme and defining those elements in terms of their role in that scheme. A distinguishing feature of connective analysis is its liberal approach to the charge of circularity: circular analyses and definitions are acceptable, provided that the circle is wide and illuminating enough. Also, though he rejects the reductive model of analysis, Strawson maintains that one should look for concepts that are basic or fundamental to the human conceptual scheme. The order of priority among concepts may be recognized, he says, by noticing that the ability to operate with one set of concepts presupposes the ability to operate with another set, but not the other way around.

Christopher Peacocke, Strawson's immediate successor as Waynflete Professor of Metaphysical Philosophy, maintains that *Individuals* and *The Bounds of Sense* "now stand forth as major landmarks in twentieth-century philosophy." Strawson's influence was especially formative among the generation of Oxford philosophers that includes Cassam, Gareth Evans, John McDowell, and John Campbell. In "Things without the Mind—A Commentary upon Chapter Two of Strawson's *Individuals*," included in *Philosophical Subjects: Essays Presented to P. F. Strawson* (1980), edited by Zak Van Straaten, Evans explores the connections between the idea of an objective world and the idea of a spatial world and examines Strawson's thought experiment with an auditory universe. Although he is critical of some of the details of Strawson's arguments involved in that thought experiment, he agrees with Strawson's contention that the two ideas are closely connected and tries to support it with more-cogent reasons. In his posthumously published *The Varieties of Reference* (1982) Evans draws on Strawson's views on reference and identification; the editor of that book, McDowell, conjectures that if Evans had lived to write a preface to the work, he would have mentioned the extent to which Strawson shaped his ideas. In his own "Meaning, Communication, and Knowledge" (1998) McDowell criticizes Strawson's conception of meaning in terms of communicative intentions; but in his *Mind and World* (1994) he follows Strawson, and the Strawsonian interpretation of Kant, in his account of experience. In his *Self and World* (1997) Cassam focuses on Strawson's transcendental arguments for the claim that to be a self-conscious subject one must regard oneself as a bodily object among other bodily objects. Although he raises some doubts about the arguments and significantly modifies them, he admits that almost every page of the book has been influenced by Strawson's ideas. Campbell, in "The Role of Physical Objects in Spatial Thinking" (1993) and other publications, has confronted Strawson's a priori investigations of various dependencies among the crucial elements of the human conceptual scheme with the findings of empirical psychology.

Strawson's works have been widely read and discussed in the United States and Australia and have been translated into French, German, Japanese, Italian, Polish, and Spanish. His philosophy has been the subject of book-length monographs and collections of critical essays published in India, Israel, Italy, Poland, Spain, and Uruguay. In addition, Strawson was extremely successful as a teacher; one of his distinguished pupils, P. F. Snowdon, remarks in his contribution to the Library of Living Philosophers volume on Strawson that one could have no better training in philosophy "than to have had Strawson as a tutor."

P. F. Strawson is a philosopher's philosopher and has not been active in any other scholarly discipline or in public life. He admits, however, that his life has been immensely enriched by reading fiction, poetry, and history. In a 1989 interview with Edo Pivčević, he confessed that if he could have chosen his talents, he would have become a poet.

Interviews:

Bryan Magee, "Conversation with Peter Strawson," in his *Modern British Philosophy* (London: Secker & Warburg, 1971), pp. 115–130;

Edo Pivčević, "An Interview with Professor Sir Peter Strawson," *Cogito,* 3 (1989): 3–8; republished in *Key Philosophers in Conversation: The "Cogito" Interviews,* edited by Andrew Pyle (London: Routledge, 1999), pp. 36–43;

Maite Ezcurdia, Mark Sainsbury, and Martin Davies, *In Conversation: Professor Sir Peter Strawson* (London: Philosophy in Britain, 1994).

Bibliographies:

Roberta Corvi, "Bibliographia," in her *La filosofia di P. F. Strawson* (Milan: Vita e Pensiero, 1979), pp. 231–243;

"Select Bibliography," in *Philosophical Subjects: Essays Presented to P. F. Strawson,* edited by Zak Van Straaten (Oxford: Clarendon Press, 1980), pp. 297–300;

J. C. León Sánchez,"Bibliografía," in his *Análisis proposicional y Ontología: Estudio a través de Strawson y Geach* (Murcia, Spain: Publicationes de la Universidad de Murcia, 1984), pp. 209–231;

Tadeusz Szubka, "Bibliografia," in his *Metafizyka analityczna P. F. Strawsona* (Lublin: RW KUL, 1995), pp. 203–218;

"P. F. Strawson: A Select Bibliography," in *The Philosophy of P. F. Strawson,* edited by Pranab Kumar Sen and Roop Rekha Verma (New Delhi: Indian Council of Philosophical Research, 1995), pp. 437–445;

"Bibliography of P. F. Strawson," compiled by Strawson, in *The Philosophy of P. F. Strawson,* edited by Lewis E. Hahn, The Library of Living Philosophers, volume 26 (Chicago: Open Court, 1998), pp. 405–417.

References:

Henry E. Allison, *Kant's Transcendental Idealism: An Interpretation and Defense* (New Haven: Yale University Press, 1983);

A. J. Ayer, "The Concept of a Person," in his *The Concept of a Person and Other Essays* (London: Macmillan, 1963), pp. 82–128;

Thomas Baldwin, *Contemporary Philosophy: Philosophy in English since 1945* (Oxford: Oxford University Press, 2001), pp. 59–61, 172–176, 207–208;

Gustav Bergmann, "Strawson's Ontology," *Journal of Philosophy,* 57 (1960): 601–622; republished in his *Logic and Reality* (Madison: University of Wisconsin Press, 1964), pp. 171–192;

Clifford Brown, *Leibniz and Strawson: A New Essay in Descriptive Metaphysics* (Munich: Philosophia Verlag, 1990);

John Campbell, *Past, Space, and Self* (Cambridge, Mass.: MIT Press, 1994);

Campbell, "The Role of Physical Objects in Spatial Thinking," in *Spatial Representation: Problems in Philosophy and Psychology,* edited by Naomi Eilan, Rosaleen McCarthy, and Bill Brewer (Oxford: Blackwell, 1993), pp. 65–95;

Carlos E. Caorsi, ed., *Ensayos sobre Strawson* (Montevideo: Universidad de la República, 1992);

Quassim Cassam, *Self and World* (Oxford: Clarendon Press, 1997);

Roberta Corvi, *La filosofia di P. F. Strawson* (Milan: Vita e Pensiero, 1979);

Gareth Evans, *The Varieties of Reference,* edited by John McDowell (Oxford: Clarendon Press, 1982);

Wenceslao J. González, *La Teoría de la Referencia: Strawson y la Filosofía Analítica* (Salamanca: Ediciones Universidad de Salamanca, 1986);

Peter Hacker, "Strawson's Concept of a Person," *Proceedings of the Aristotelian Society,* 102 (2001): 21–40;

Lewis E. Hahn, ed., *The Philosophy of P. F. Strawson,* The Library of Living Philosophers, volume 26 (Chicago: Open Court, 1998);

Herbert Hochberg, "Strawson, Scepticism, and Metaphysics," *Theoria,* 42 (1976): 20–43;

Juan Carlos León Sánchez, *Análisis Proposicional y Ontología: Estudio a través de Strawson y Geach* (Murcia, Spain: Publicationes de la Universidad de Murcia, 1984);

C. B. Martin, "People," in *Contemporary Philosophy in Australia,* edited by Robert Brown and C. D. Rollins (London: Allen & Unwin, 1969), pp. 158–172;

John McDowell, "Meaning, Communication, and Knowledge," in his *Meaning, Knowledge, and Reality* (Cambridge, Mass.: Harvard University Press, 1998), pp. 29–50;

McDowell, *Mind and World* (Cambridge, Mass.: Harvard University Press, 1994; enlarged, 1996);

J. M. E. Moravcsik, "Strawson and Ontological Priority," in *Analytical Philosophy: Second Series,* edited by R. J. Butler (Oxford: Blackwell, 1968), pp. 106–119;

Moravcsik, "Strawson on Predication," *Journal of Philosophy,* 73 (1976): 329–348;

Christopher Peacocke, *Transcendental Arguments in the Theory of Content: An Inaugural Lecture Delivered before the University of Oxford on 16 May 1989* (Oxford: Clarendon Press, 1989);

Philosophia, special Strawson issue, 10 (1981);

Alvin Plantinga, "Things and Persons," *Review of Metaphysics,* 14 (1961): 493–519;

W. V. Quine, "Mr. Strawson on Logical Theory," *Mind,* 62 (1953): 433–451; republished in his *The Ways of Paradox and Other Essays,* revised and enlarged edition (Cambridge, Mass.: Harvard University Press, 1976), pp. 137–157;

Emanuele Riverso, *Riferimento e struttura: Il problema logico-analitico e l'opera di Strawson* (Rome: Armando, 1977);

Richard M. Rorty, "Strawson's Objectivity Argument," *Review of Metaphysics,* 24 (1970): 207–244;

Jay F. Rosenberg, "On Strawson: Sounds, Skepticism, and Necessity," *Philosophia,* 8 (1978): 405–419;

Wilfrid Sellars, "Presupposing," *Philosophical Review,* 63 (1954): 197–215;

Pranab Kumar Sen and Roop Rekha Verma, eds., *The Philosophy of P. F. Strawson* (New Delhi: Indian Council of Philosophical Research, 1995);

Robert Stern, ed., *Transcendental Arguments: Problems and Prospects* (Oxford: Clarendon Press, 2000);

Barry Stroud, "Transcendental Arguments" and "Kantian Argument, Conceptual Capacities, and Invulnerability," in his *Understanding Human Knowledge: Philosophical Essays* (Oxford: Oxford University Press, 1999), pp. 9–25, 155–176;

Tadeusz Szubka, "Connective Analysis and Basic Concepts," *Philosophia,* 26 (1998): 141–150;

Szubka, *Metafizyka analityczna P. F. Strawson* (Lublin: RW KUL, 1995);

Zak Van Straaten, ed., *Philosophical Subjects: Essays Presented to P. F. Strawson* (Oxford: Clarendon Press, 1980);

Bernard Williams, "Mr. Strawson on Individuals," *Philosophy,* 36 (1961): 309–332; republished in his *Problems of the Self: Philosophical Papers 1956–1972* (Cambridge: Cambridge University Press, 1973), pp. 101–126.

James Ward

(27 January 1843 – 4 March 1925)

Phillip Ferreira
Kutztown University of Pennsylvania

BOOKS: *The Relation of Physiology to Psychology: An Essay* (N.p.: Privately printed, 1875);

The Moral Sciences Tripos, The Student's Guide to the University of Cambridge, part 8, edited by J. R. Seeley (Cambridge: Cambridge University Press, 1891);

Naturalism and Agnosticism: The Gifford Lectures Delivered before the University of Aberdeen in the Years 1896–1898, 2 volumes (London & New York: Macmillan, 1899);

Philosophical Orientation and Scientific Standpoints (Berkeley: University of California Press, 1904);

The Realm of Ends; or, Pluralism and Theism: The Gifford Lectures in the University of St. Andrews in the Years 1907–1910 (Cambridge: Cambridge University Press, 1911; New York: Putnam, 1911);

Heredity and Memory: Being the Henry Sidgwick Memorial Lecture, Delivered at Newnham College, 9 November, 1912 (Cambridge: Cambridge University Press, 1913);

Psychological Principles (Cambridge: Cambridge University Press, 1918; New York: Putnam, 1919);

A Study of Kant (Cambridge: Cambridge University Press, 1922);

Psychology Applied to Education: A Series of Lectures on the Theory and Practice of Education, edited by G. Dawes Hickes (Cambridge: Cambridge University Press, 1926);

Essays in Philosophy: With a Memoir by Olwen Ward Campbell, edited by W. R. Sorley and G. F. Stout (Cambridge: Cambridge University Press, 1927).

OTHER: "Herbart," in *Encyclopædia Britannica,* ninth edition, volume 11 (Edinburgh: Black, 1880), pp. 718–720;

"Psychology," in *Encyclopædia Britannica,* ninth edition, volume 20 (Edinburgh: Black, 1886), pp. 37–85;

"Naturalism," in *Encyclopædia Britannica,* tenth edition, volume 31 (Edinburgh & London: Black, 1902), pp. 87–89;

James Ward (photograph by V. H. Mottram, 1911)

"Psychology," in *Encyclopædia Britannica,* tenth edition, volume 32 (Edinburgh & London: Black, 1902), pp. 54–70;

Henry Sidgwick, *Philosophy: Its Scope and Relations. An Introductory Course of Lectures,* edited by Ward (London: Macmillan, 1902; New York: Macmillan, 1902);

Sidgwick, *Lectures on the Philosophy of Kant, and Other Philosophical Lectures & Essays,* edited by Ward (London: Macmillan, 1905).

SELECTED PERIODICAL PUBLICATIONS–UNCOLLECTED: "Animal Locomotion," *Nature,* 9 (29 March 1874): 381–382; (9 April 1874): 440;

"An Attempt to Interpret Fechner's Law," *Mind,* 1 (1876): 452–466;

Review of G. H. Lewes's *Physical Basis of Mind, Academy* (16 March 1878); (20 April 1878);

"Observations on the Physiology of the Nervous System of the Crayfish," *Proceedings of the Royal Society of London,* 28 (6 March 1879): 379–383;

"Some Notes on the Physiology of the Nervous System of the Freshwater Crayfish (Astacus fluviatilis)," *Journal of Physiology,* 2 (1879): 214–227;

"Vitality of the Common Snail," *Nature,* 20 (14 August 1879): 363;

"Ueber die Auslosung von Reflexbewegungen durch eine Summe schwacher Reize," *Archiv f. (Anatomie u.) Physiologie* (1880): 72–91;

Review of Wilhelm Wundt, *Grundzüge der physiologischen Psychologie,* second edition, *Mind,* 6 (1881): 445–446;

"A General Analysis of Mind," *Journal of Speculative Philosophy,* 16 (1882): 366–385;

"Psychological Principles I: The Standpoint of Psychology," *Mind,* 8 (1883): 153–169;

"Psychological Principles II: Fundamental Facts and Conceptions," *Mind,* 8 (1883): 465–486;

"Objects and Their Interaction," *Journal of Speculative Philosophy,* 17 (1883): 169–179;

"Intellectual Training," *Journal of Education,* new series 5 (1883): 393–399;

"Psychological Principles III: Attention and the Field of Consciousness," *Mind,* 12 (1887): 45–67;

"Mr. F. H. Bradley's Analysis of Mind," *Mind,* 12 (1887): 564–575;

"The Psychological Theory of Extension," *Mind,* 14 (1889): 109–115;

"The Progress of Philosophy," *Mind,* 15 (1890): 213–233;

"Notes on Educational Values," *Journal of Education,* new series 12 (1 November 1890): 627–632;

"J. S. Mill's Science of Ethology," *International Journal of Ethics,* 1 (1891): 446–459;

Review of Edmund Husserl, *Philosophie der Arithmetik, Mind,* new series 1 (1892): 565–566;

Review of William James, *Text-book of Psychology, Mind,* new series 2 (1893): 54–82;

"'Modern' Psychology: A Reflexion," *Mind,* new series 2 (1893): 54–82;

"Assimilation and Association, I," *Mind,* new series 3 (1893): 347–362;

"Assimilation and Association, II," *Mind,* new series 3 (1894): 509–532;

Review of F. H. Bradley, *Appearance and Reality, Mind,* new series 3 (1894): 378–382;

"A Criticism of a Reply," *Mind,* new series 3 (1894): 142–143;

Review of Wundt, *Grundzüge der physologischen Psychologie,* fourth edition, *Mind,* new series 3 (1894): 277;

Review of *Arnoldi Geulincx opera philosophica,* edited by J. P. N. Land, *Mind,* new series 3 (1894): 277;

"Travestying Herbert Spencer," *Academy,* 57 (21 October 1899): 465;

"Reply to Mr. Herbert Spencer," *Fortnightly Review,* 73 (March 1900): 464–476;

"The Present Problem of General Psychology," *Philosophical Review,* 13 (1904): 603–621;

"A Note in Reply to Doctor Perry," *Journal of Philosophy, Psychology and Scientific Methods,* 1 (1904): 325;

"Mechanism and Morals: The World of Science and the World of History," *Hibbert Journal,* 4 (October 1905): 79–99;

"A Further Note on the Sensory Character of Black," *British Journal of Psychology,* 8 (1916): 212–221;

"Belief, Certainty, and Faith," *Indian Philosophical Review,* 1 (1918): 1–14;

"In the Beginning . . . ," *Proceedings of the Aristotelian Society,* 20 (1919): 1–24;

"Sense-Knowledge, I," *Mind,* new series 28 (1919): 257–274;

"Sense-Knowledge, II," *Mind,* new series 28 (1919): 447–462;

"Sense-Knowledge, III," *Mind,* new series 29 (1920): 129–144;

Review of Norman Kemp Smith, *Prolegomena to an Idealist Theory of Knowledge, Hibbert Journal,* 23 (1924): 175–183;

"Bradley's Doctrine of Experience," *Mind,* new series 34 (1925): 13–38;

"The Christian Idea of Faith and Eternal Life," *Hibbert Journal,* 23 (1925): 175–183;

"An Introduction to Philosophy," *Monist,* 36 (January 1926): 1–19.

Though his work is seldom discussed today, during his forty years of scholarly activity James Ward was one of the most formidable intellectual figures in the English-speaking world. At the height of his powers he held the chair in mental philosophy and logic at Cambridge University, and he is one of the few individuals to have twice delivered the prestigious Gifford Lectures. Ward was also one of the leading psychologists of his day; his views were seen by many as revolutionizing the field.

Ward was born in Hull, Yorkshire, on 27 January 1843, the first of three sons and six daughters of James and Hannah Ashton Ward, devout Calvinistic Congregationalists. His father was a Liverpool businessman who, though at times successful, was known for his speculative and risky ventures. Ward studied at the Liverpool Institute until age eleven, when his parents

*Ward and his wife, Mary, in their
garden during World War I*

decided that he should attend the Mostyn Home Academy in nearby Parkside. Graduates of Mostyn usually went on to Rugby School; but during Ward's second year his father's business failed, and the family was no longer able to afford the substantial Mostyn tuition.

The Wards moved to a more modest home in Waterloo, outside Liverpool. For the next two years Ward had no formal education but spent his days exploring the local landscape—he developed a keen interest in ornithology—and reading. In 1858 Ward prepared drawings of a mechanical pump that his father was developing. His parents were so impressed by the drawings that they decided that a career as an architect or an engineer was in order, and for the next four years Ward worked as an apprentice in a Liverpool architectural firm. Given his near obsession with political and theological debate, however, his parents began to think that law or the church would better suit him. At nineteen, while continuing to work at the architect's office, Ward began teaching at a local Sunday school. Ward's sister Olwen Ward Campbell says in the memoir included in Ward's *Essays in Philosophy* (1927), "we find the youth of nineteen exhorting the boys and girls in Sunday school to think of the Judgment, and reflect

upon the eternal fires." Financial help from family members and Ward's savings from his job at the architectural firm enabled him to enroll at Spring Hill College (later part of Harris Manchester College of the University of Oxford) in the fall of 1863 to study for the ministry. He achieved a first on his examinations in arts and theology in 1864. In 1866 he failed the Bachelor of Arts examination for the University of London, but he passed with honors on his second attempt later in the year.

During his fifth year at Spring Hill, Ward began to experience doubts about his Calvinist faith. His sermons were becoming increasingly complex and philosophical—so much so that his colleagues called them "essays" that required several readings to be understood. Ward began to wonder whether his turn of mind might make him unfit for the ministry. To test his commitment he applied for and won the Williams Scholarship, which allowed him to pursue advanced theological studies abroad. In the summer of 1869 he enrolled at the Dom Candidatten-Stift in Berlin. In addition to theological lectures Ward attended the more-philosophical courses taught by Isaak August Dorner and Friedrich Adolf Trendelenburg at the University of Berlin. After a term at the Dom Candidatten-Stift, Ward traveled to Göttingen to hear the lectures of Germany's most famous living philosopher, Rudolph Herman Lotze. Lotze showed Ward how such apparently disparate interests as natural science, philosophy, and religion could be successfully combined.

Ward returned to Spring Hill in August 1870. His letters to friends indicate that he was increasingly realizing that his inclinations lay not with religious but with scientific study. In a letter of 25 August 1870 Ward described his parishioners as "Narrow, ignorant, and old fashioned." Still, in October 1870 he accepted an invitation to go to Cambridge for a month to preach at the Emmanuel Congregational Chapel. Ward's sermons, which took as their theme "God is Love," were variously described as "shocking," "moving," and "unintelligible." Nevertheless, he was offered a permanent position, and in January 1871 he embarked on what he always regarded as the most miserable undertaking of his life. With each passing day Ward found himself less able to sympathize with his parishioners; many of the parishioners, in turn, were intolerant of Ward's intellectualized preaching, viewing his increasingly philosophical outlook as unorthodox if not heretical. Ward resigned in March 1872, abandoning any thought of a career as a clergyman, and enrolled at the University of Cambridge.

Despite his success at Spring Hill and the B.A. from the University of London, Ward was admitted to Cambridge only as a "non-collegiate" student: he could attend lectures, but he had no college affiliation. While he was drawn to philosophy–particularly the lectures of Henry Sidgwick–he wanted to complete the University of London bachelor of science degree that he had begun in 1866. He had passed the first round of examinations in 1868, but a second still had to be written. Admission to Trinity College was what Ward most desired, however, and his energies were directed almost entirely to preparing to compete for a scholarship to the college. In 1873 he came in first among the competitors. He was ill when he went to London in the fall to take the bachelor of science examination, and he was unsuccessful; by this time, however, the degree was of little significance to him. In 1874 he took a first in the Cambridge moral sciences tripos. That same year he published two papers on animal locomotion in the journal *Nature*.

Early in 1875 Ward's father's business failed again. Campbell says that a "public scandal was only narrowly averted" when Ward and his surviving brother, Arthur, agreed to pay their father's creditors a substantial sum every year. Ward and his brother also undertook to contribute to the support of their parents, but only after the senior Ward signed a document promising never again to pursue any business venture without the prior approval of both sons.

With his strained financial resources, Ward could continue his studies at Cambridge only if he obtained a fellowship at Trinity College. Though competition for the position was strong–three of the candidates later became original fellows of the British Academy–Ward was elected to the fellowship in 1875.

In the fall of 1876 Ward went to Leipzig to study physiology in the laboratory of Carl Ludwig. His letters from this period show that his thoughts were once more turning to philosophy; writing to J. N. Keynes in February 1877, Ward said that he felt he had "done nothing" and that his time in Leipzig was "the most intellectually stagnant" period of his adult life. In May 1877 he returned to Cambridge. He began studying the philosophies of René Descartes and John Locke, wrote several book reviews, published a summary of his Leipzig research, and engaged in some complex experiments on crayfish in the laboratories of Michael Foster. He also presented a series of lectures on general psychology, modern philosophy, and the philosophy of education to a group of female students. He became a member of Cambridge's famous discussion society, the Apostles, and of the Chit-Chat club. He also became a regular participant in the activities of other Cambridge societies: the Eranus and Ambarum groups, the Synthetic Society, and the Moral Science and Natural Science Clubs. Although he was increasingly absorbed by philosophical matters, he maintained his contacts with

colleagues in the natural sciences, such as Foster, Donald McAllister, and Frank Balfour. In 1879 his articles on his crayfish experiments in the *Proceedings of the Royal Society of London* and *The Journal of Physiology* drew the approving notice of the eminent biologist Thomas Henry Huxley. Foster said that it was physiology's loss that Ward had been "spoiled by philosophy."

In 1879 Ward was an examiner for the tripos examinations at Newnham College. He incorrectly added up the marks of a student named Mary Martin, who had actually earned a first. The blunder, which was quickly discovered by Martin and the other examiners, gave Ward the opportunity to converse with the woman who later became his wife.

In 1880 Ward contributed to the *Encylopædia Britannica* an article on Johann Friedrich Herbart that became required reading for anyone attempting to penetrate the German philosopher's thought. That same year Sidgwick persuaded Ward to apply for the chair in philosophy at Aberdeen University. His application was unsuccessful, but in 1881 he was elected to a lectureship in moral science at Cambridge. Though not a prestigious chair, it kept him at the heart of the English-speaking philosophical world and provided him with an income that enabled him to meet his considerable financial obligations.

Between 1880 and early 1882 Ward was absorbed in psychological research. In the spring of 1882 he contracted typhoid fever and returned to the family home in Waterloo, where he was nursed by one of his sisters. Though still weak, he was able to return to Cambridge at the end of the summer and soon became even more active in college life by being elected a member of the Trinity Council. In 1883, still recuperating, he traveled to Spain with the anthropologist James George Frazer.

Ward and Martin were married in July 1884. They settled in a temporary residence, while Ward's mother-in-law arranged to have a house built for them in Selwyn Gardens, Cambridge. Ward, the former architect's apprentice, had strong views about the design of the house, and these seldom coincided with those of the architect hired by his wife's mother; Campbell reports that several "violent battles" erupted. In the end Ward's vision triumphed. The Wards resided in Selwyn Gardens for the next forty years, during which time they had a son and two daughters.

Volume twenty of the ninth edition of the *Encyclopædia Britannica* (1886) included Ward's entry "Psychology." Though he had been urged by colleagues to forego the *Britannica* piece in favor of a book, the article established him as the discipline's preeminent theorist in the English-speaking world. In philosophical terms, it is

PSYCHOLOGICAL

PRINCIPLES

BY

JAMES WARD

SC.D. (CANTAB.), HON. LL.D. (EDIN.), HON. D.SC. (OXON.)
FELLOW OF THE BRITISH ACADEMY
FOREIGN MEMBER OF THE NEW YORK ACADEMY
AND OF THE DANISH ROYAL SOCIETY
CORRESPONDENT OF THE FRENCH INSTITUTE
AND
PROFESSOR OF MENTAL PHILOSOPHY, CAMBRIDGE

BF
121
.W3

Cambridge:
at the University Press
1918

Title page for Ward's elaboration of the views he had put forth in his article "Psychology" in the Encyclopædia Britannica *in 1886, generally regarded as having dealt the deathblow to the empiricist theory of associationism (Thomas Cooper Library, University of South Carolina)*

important for its refutation of some of the basic doctrines of empiricist epistemology.

Three ideas are particularly important in Ward's article: the theory of "intellection," the critique of associationism, and the doctrine of the pure ego. The theory of intellection opposes the empiricist claim that experience is built up from atomistic sense-data. Ward says that all perceptions—or "presentations," as he calls them—occur within a larger experiential continuum according to the principles of differentiation, retentiveness, and assimilation. A visual image becomes interpreted as, for example, a rabbit by being placed in the context of the perceiver's total experience, which requires the perceiver to retain what has been experienced previously and to assimilate it to what is now being apprehended: part of what makes the presentation that of a rabbit is the perceiver's awareness that it is not, say, a cow, weasel, or chicken; and it is seen as *this* rabbit, as opposed to any other, only by being compared to other rabbits the perceiver has seen. One only appreciates the individuality of an object by placing it within the context of everything else one knows.

The associationist theory, of which Alexander Bain was then the leading exponent, holds that thought proceeds on the basis of mental associations or "psychological habits." As Ward states the theory: "Any presentations whatever, which are in consciousness together or in close succession, cohere in such a way that when one recurs it tends to revive the rest, such tendency increasing with the frequency of conjunction." For example, though nothing about the sight of snow, in itself, suggests the tactile sensation of coldness, repeated experiences of the sight of snow being accompanied by a feeling of coldness cause these two ideas to become psychologically bound together. Then, when one sees snow, the idea of the feeling of coldness immediately arises in one's awareness, even though no actual sensation of coldness may be present. Association also occurs, according to the theory, because of "natural similarities" between ideas: for example, the sight of sea water might call up the ideas of other kinds of water. For the proponents of associationism, all factual inferences are based on either the habits formed by repeated conjunctions of ideas, on the one hand, or natural similarities, on the other.

Ward has several objections to this doctrine. First, as already pointed out, there is no basis for the claim that experience begins with independent perceptual data that are subsequently associated with each other: reflection on one's most primitive experiences reveals a continuum or "field of consciousness" within which distinctions arise as the result of subsequent discrimination. Second, the notion of association by natural similarity is incoherent: one idea cannot "revive" another on the basis of similarity, because for the similarity of two ideas to be apprehended, both ideas would have to be in one's awareness at the same time; but if both ideas are already in the mind, neither can revive or "call up" the other. Third, the associationist notion of contiguous and sequential relations between mental phenomena is unintelligible. In regard to contiguous presentations, the theory is unable to explain why some selected portion of the experiential continuum should be associated with this other portion rather than that one. For example, in a succession of events ABCD, such as the words of a poem that has been memorized, the associationist is unable to explain why the experience of C recalls D but not B, even though by his own account the bond between B and C should be at least as strong as that between C and D.

The pure ego was one of Ward's most controversial ideas. According to Ward, the ultimate ground of consciousness is nonobjectifiable and without empirical content. While the biological and psychological aspects of the self are empirical phenomena, the foundation of all experience is a self or ego that holds together the experiential continuum without being an element within it. Without the pure ego, one's awareness would collapse, in Immanuel Kant's phrase, into a "rhapsody of sensation" and become unintelligible; such a state could not meaningfully be called "experience" at all.

According to Ward, the pure ego cannot be known directly; direct knowledge is reserved for empirical phenomena. The path to indirect knowledge of the pure ego advances through several stages. The first sense of self one possesses is a direct awareness of one's own body. Next comes an awareness of one's "social self," in which "the individual advances to a higher self-knowledge by comparing self within with what is first discernible in other persons without." One then goes on to recognize that one plays many social roles, with the self as "an actor that sustains or impersonates them all." Finally, one realizes that no combination of roles can exhaust the self. The self is, ultimately, a pure "presence" behind all roles and all empirical presentations.

In 1889 Ward received an honorary degree from Edinburgh University. That same year his sister Lucy, to whom he was devoted, died. Ward claimed virtually all of her possessions; for the rest of his life he preserved her correspondence and her course notes from the school where she taught.

Between 1896 and 1898 Ward delivered the Gifford Lectures at the University of Aberdeen; the published version of the lectures, *Naturalism and Agnosticism,* appeared in 1899. Ward begins by criticizing "naturalism," the claim that the world studied by the physical sciences is all that exists. According to Ward, this position, of which Herbert Spencer and W. K. Clifford were among the most prominent advocates, arises from a primitive human desire to see reality whole and complete, but it achieves this comprehensiveness only at the expense of substituting abstract intellectual "representations" for what one actually encounters in lived experience. The flaws of naturalism are most apparent, Ward says, in its account of evolution, which ignores the teleological—purposeful or goal-oriented—aspects of nature. Primitive biological organisms do not, of course, possess anything like the human experience of purpose; but the notion of evolutionary development makes no sense without an appeal to such teleological concepts as "aversion to pain," "attraction to pleasure," or "instinct toward survival." These notions, however, escape the grasp of the naturalistic metaphysics, so that in appeal-

ing to them—as it inevitably must—naturalism violates its own fundamental premises.

The naturalistic account is even more implausible, Ward says, in its approach to mental phenomena. In considering these matters naturalism has available only one theoretical option: epiphenomenalism, the doctrine that mental phenomena lack substantive being and are mere "shadows" of the physical order (that is, of the brain and nervous system). But epiphenomenalism is self-contradictory, because the correspondence it postulates between the physical and the psychic series is only intelligible as a causal relation; but to postulate such a relation is to attribute to the "epiphenomena" a reality that the theory denies.

When one becomes disillusioned with naturalism, the logical next step is dualism, which acknowledges the equal reality of matter and mind. It, too, however, is faced with insuperable difficulties. For example, if mind is a wholly immaterial and nonextended substance, how can it have boundaries and be differentiated from other minds? Or, more generally, if mind and matter are separate and opposite kinds of being, then how can the self-enclosed mind know that external matter exists at all?

This question is sometimes answered by saying that the existence of matter is inferred as the cause of appearances ("sensations" or "impressions") that seem to be forced on the mind. But even the proponents of this view admit that inferences about the external world may be radically mistaken. It might also be said that the idea of matter is "clearly and distinctly" apprehended and that, therefore, the existence of that which corresponds to this idea is self-evident. But what is self-evident to one person may not be so to another. A third view—one that rejects the idea that minds are self-enclosed—is that the mind apprehends matter directly, not through the mediation of "ideas." But this theory cannot account for how an individual mind could, in the face of such direct apprehension, be mistaken as to the nature of matter—as, clearly, is often the case.

Such considerations force one to embrace what Ward calls "spiritualistic monism," the position that mind and matter constitute a "duality in unity"; that is, they are inseparable and necessary correlates of one another. This position implies that the unity, causality, and regularity found in nature derive from the mind itself. The desire to see nature as unified stems from the felt unity of one's own being. Similarly, the belief that causality exists in nature derives from human beings' experience of themselves and others as causal agents. Finally, the idea of regularity, or behavior according to natural laws, in nature is based on the fact that human beings are governed by laws. Ward summarizes by saying that his "argument is that the material and mechanical are not fundamental, but that the teleological and spiritual underlie them and are presupposed by them." The final sentence of the book declares that "the realm of Nature turns out to be the realm of Ends"–an idea that dominated his thought for the next thirty years.

In 1897, largely through Sidgwick's efforts, a chair in mental philosophy and logic was established at Cambridge, and Ward was selected as the first occupant of the position. The professorship required that he give up his Trinity College fellowship, which meant a substantial reduction in his income; he would also lose the pension provided for retired fellows. But since the professorship would open doors in the international scholarly community and allow more time for writing, Ward accepted it.

In the summer of 1904 Ward undertook a lecture tour of the United States. He spoke at universities, delivered a lecture at the St. Louis World's Fair, and taught a course at the University of California at Berkeley. On his return from the United States, Ward was again invited to give the Gifford Lectures, this time at the University of St. Andrews. The lecture series began in 1907 and continued into 1910; it was published in 1911 as *The Realm of Ends; or, Pluralism and Theism*.

In his first series of Gifford Lectures, Ward had argued for a metaphysics of "spiritualistic monism" that makes mind, rather than matter, fundamental to any understanding of the universe. Agreeing with the Absolute Idealists–or "singularists," as he calls them–F. H. Bradley and Bernard Bosanquet that reality is, in the end, nothing other than experience, Ward presses forward with what he acknowledges is an anthropomorphic doctrine. One must begin with immediate experience and work outward; having done so, one will find that any aspect of the universe that could make a difference to one always exhibits the nature of mind.

Ward acknowledges his debt both to Kant and to Gottfried Wilhelm Leibniz in the development of this view. From Kant he took the idea that every phenomenal object must conform to the structure of mind, and that at the foundation of all experience lies a nonempirical ego. From Leibniz he took the notion of "continuity," the view that one must postulate, both above and below human beings, entities whose experience is in some respect continuous with human experience. While he does not claim that rocks and streams are "conscious" in a human sense, he does hold that their experiences are locatable on a scale of experience of which they occupy the lowest rungs. At the top would be beings who possess the human sort of consciousness, plus a great deal more. Though humans have no direct awareness of the existence of such higher beings, philosophy must not deny their possible–indeed, probable–reality. Spirit, Ward asserts, is the "basal order of the universe" and is manifested in every nook and cranny of this or any other possible world.

Despite the pervasive spirituality of the universe, not all entities can be called "individuals." An individual, for Ward, is a being that has as its primary characteristic a seeking after "self-conservation" and "continuance"–something inanimate objects lack. Self-conservation is activity whereby a thing seeks the "betterment of its condition." Each individual possesses a "nisus," an urge to realize a state of existence superior to its present one. The universe is populated by a vast number of individuals; although their actions have elements in common–they are all seeking to survive and to better their condition–they are radically different. Each has a unique nature, and, insofar as it remains isolated, it possesses urges that are found nowhere else; but through the continuous interaction of individuals a commonality of viewpoint emerges that constitutes such unity as the universe possesses. While the universe may be moving toward a perfect unity of all individuals, this end is not preordained or in any way guaranteed. Directly opposing the views of the nineteenth-century German idealist philosopher Georg Wilhelm Friedrich Hegel and his British followers, Ward argues that the universe should not be seen as the self-differentiation of a primitive One or Absolute. While no evolutionary development can be undone once it has been realized, neither the precise nature of the development nor the fact that it would happen at all could have been predicted prior to its occurrence. Ward says, "From the standpoint of the many"–that is, of his own view, which he now calls "spiritualist pluralism" rather than "spiritualistic monism"–"we have no ground for assuming a Creator who does everything but only a Creator whose creatures create in turn. The real world must be the joint result of God and man (including by this term other finite intelligences both higher and lower), unless we are to deny the reality of that in us which leads to the idea of God at all."

The St. Andrews Gifford Lectures were highly successful, but the preparation and delivery of them took a toll on Ward. Campbell says only that he suffered from a "distressing ailment" that should have been treated earlier, but he wanted to complete the lectures first. In the fall of 1910 he entered a London hospital for an operation that he thought he might not survive, but he fully recovered.

In 1918 Ward finally published the book-length treatment of his psychological views that his colleagues had urged him to do in 1885. He considered *Psychological Principles* his magnum opus; but, though it was widely praised, it was really just a fuller statement of the views that he had put forward in the *Encyclopædia*

Britannica article. The impact of the book was thus not nearly as great as that of the article had been.

Elaborating his theory of "intellection," Ward says in *Psychological Principles* that the "differentiation"— the particularity and individuality—of a presentation is the result of psychological processes of "retention" and "assimilation"; in the absence of such processes, presentations would not only not be individual but also would be devoid of all significance. Since an act of "intellectual synthesis" must occur for individual presentations to arise at all, they possess intellectually generated content through and through; accordingly, Ward calls them "cognitions." Cognitions are relational: one apprehends a perceived object as a flower by placing it within a larger context of experience so that one recognizes that it is not a river, a tree, a rock, and so on. Even the most primitive conscious perceptions are relational and, therefore, have conceptual content.

Though Ward insists that all consciously experienced presentations are cognitive in nature and that there is "no sharp distinction" between sense and understanding, or percept and concept, he also says that conceptual content is not an intrinsic element of the sensuously given; and he goes on to put forth a distinction between "individual experience" and "intersubjective discourse." Individual experience, according to Ward, is a wholly subjective awareness that is dominated by the contents of an immediate presentation; it confines one's attention to the sensuous "here and now." Intersubjective discourse, by contrast, arises through the use of language and is the result of communication with others. Only through intersubjective discourse, Ward argues, can a finite individual escape his or her self-enclosed, sensuous existence: "How do individual subjects thus get beyond the immanence of 'immediacy' with which all experience begins? 'By a process of reasoning.' . . . Yes, but psychologically there is a prior process; for it is at least true in fact, whether necessarily true or not, that such reasoning is the result of social institutions, which obviously presuppose and rest upon individual experience." While Ward maintains that one cannot consciously apprehend a concept-free series of sensuous presentations, and that the shared ideas of intersubjective experience are of real objects and events—what would be experienced by "disembodied subjects"—he sees concept formation as contingent, not as necessitated by sensuous presentations themselves. Though influenced by Kant, Ward is unwilling to acknowledge the existence of a priori concepts, such as Kant's "categories of the understanding," that are innate in the mind and constitutive of experience: "Psychology again may claim to have shewn that in fact these categories are the result

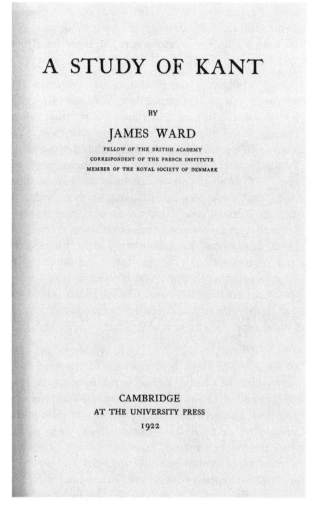

A STUDY OF KANT

BY

JAMES WARD

FELLOW OF THE BRITISH ACADEMY
CORRESPONDENT OF THE FRENCH INSTITUTE
MEMBER OF THE ROYAL SOCIETY OF DENMARK

CAMBRIDGE
AT THE UNIVERSITY PRESS
1922

Title page for the book on the German philosopher Immanuel Kant written by Ward in preparation for his 1922 Hertz Lecture to the British Academy (University of Rochester)

of that reflective self-consciousness to which social intercourse first gives rise."

Some critics—most notably, Ward's own follower G. F. Stout—argued that Ward's discussion of presentational immediacy suggests that there is nothing of a conceptual nature in primitive individual experience. But, they asked, if that is the case—if there is no continuity between primitive percept and developed concept—when universal concepts arise in intersubjective discourse, whence do they come? Are they created out of nothing? If not, they must have been in the presentational immediacy of each subject's sensuous experience from the beginning. Even his most careful students sometimes disagreed as to Ward's considered view on this matter. Those of an idealist persuasion argued that, while Ward's manner of expression is often unclear, he allows that the primitive conceptual content of all subsequent conceptualizations exists in presentational immediacy prior to its explicit manifestation in intersubjective discourse. Pragmatists, on the other hand, thought that he asserted the radically contingent nature of all concepts that arise within the intersubjective, or social, phase of experience.

In addition to the presentational component of experience, one must acknowledge, Ward says, the presence–and the profound importance for psychology–of "feeling" and "attention." Presentation, attention, and feeling, while conceptually distinguishable, are but actually inseparable elements within "one concrete state of mind." All presentations are attended to–that is, they always exist for a pure ego that situates them within a larger experiential nexus–and are accompanied by feeling. Feeling is the fundamental attraction or aversion–like or dislike–that one feels toward a presentation or series of presentations. (Though feeling and attention are not presentations, they may be transformed into such through an act of self-reflection.) What Ward calls "conative" activity is the goal-directed behavior that arises out of presentation, attention, and feeling.

Ward's *A Study of Kant* (1922), written in preparation for his 1922 Hertz Lecture to the British Academy, throws some light on his position in regard to the conceptual content of experience. For Kant, the intuitions of space and time and the twelve categories of the understanding are necessary and universal: any creature to which one might attribute "experience" must have that experience in a spatial/temporal framework and perceive the objects of experience as ordered by the categories; for example, objects must be seen as standing in causal relations to other objects, and the various properties of objects must be seen as inhering in underlying substances. But Ward sees the claim that the categories possess a primitive logical status as the principal weakness of Kant's philosophy. For Ward, the categories of the understanding are mere conceptual "filters" through which the contents of sensation are processed. They are not the "condition of any possible experience" but rather the result of "trans-subjective intercourse." He says of the Kantian categories, "their origin will prove not to be logomorphic–to coin a term–but anthropomorphic, not a logical form but a subjective 'analogy.'"

Walking home from his office one night in the winter of 1924–1925, Ward was struck by a car and suffered a concussion; he was unable to lecture for most of the following term. He also suffered from a persistent fatigue that was diagnosed as heart trouble. On 3 March he had a lively discussion about William Shakespeare with his elder daughter; the next day he died. A memorial service was held at Trinity Chapel on 8 March.

James Ward's influence on later thought is difficult to assess. He is generally regarded as having dealt the deathblow to associationism in his *Encyclopædia Britannica* article. According to many of his interpreters, his main philosophical achievement was his powerful rebuttal of the naturalism of Spencer and Clifford, but by the time of his death his arguments against these earlier forms of naturalism were being used by pragmatists such as the American philosopher John Dewey in support of their own naturalistic positions. Absent from their writings was Ward's idea that the refutation of crass naturalism was a vindication of a spiritualistic philosophy. In psychology the individual whom Ward most influenced was Stout; but Stout's views, though they anticipate much in Gestalt theory, resemble more closely those of the nineteenth-century idealists. With the demise of Stout, most of what Ward believed to be important in his own psychology was lost.

References:

C. D. Broad, "The Local Historical Background of Contemporary Cambridge Philosophy," in *British Philosophy in the Mid-Century: A Cambridge Symposium,* edited by C. A. Mace (London: Allen & Unwin, 1957; New York: Humanities Press, 1966), pp. 13–61;

G. W. Cunningham, "James Ward," in his *The Idealist Argument in Recent British and American Philosophy* (New York & London: Century, 1933), pp. 169–199;

D. W. Hamlyn, "Bradley, Ward, and Stout," in *Historical Roots of Contemporary Psychology,* edited by Benjamin B. Wolman (New York: Harper & Row, 1968), pp. 298–320;

Monist, special Ward issue, 36, no. 1 (1926);

Andrew Howson Murray, *The Philosophy of James Ward* (Cambridge: Cambridge University Press, 1937);

John Passmore, "Personality and the Absolute," in his *A Hundred Years of Philosophy* (London: Duckworth, 1957), pp. 81–85;

G. F. Stout, *Mind and Matter* (Cambridge: Cambridge University Press, 1931).

William Whewell

(24 May 1794 – 6 March 1866)

Edrie Sobstyl
University of Oregon at Eugene

BOOKS: *An Elementary Treatise on Mechanics* (Cambridge: Printed by J. Smith for J. Deighton, 1819);

A Treatise on Dynamics, Containing a Considerable Collection of Mechanical Problems (Cambridge: Printed for J. Deighton, 1823; revised and enlarged, 1834);

An Essay on Mineralogical Classification and Nomenclature: With Tables of the Orders and Species of Minerals (Cambridge: Printed by J. Smith, Printer to the University, 1828);

Architectural Notes on German Churches, with Remarks on the Origin of Gothic Architecture (Cambridge: Printed by J. Smith for J. & J. J. Deighton and sold by Longman, Rees, Orme, Brown & Green, 1830; revised and enlarged as *Architectural Notes on German Churches: A New Edition. To Which Is Now Added, Notes Written During an Architectural Tour in Picardy and Normandy* (Cambridge: Printed at the Pitt Press by John Smith for J. & J. J. Deighton, sold in London by Longman, W. Pickering & J. Weale, 1835);

Mathematical Exposition of Some of the Leading Doctrines in Mr. Ricardo's "Principles of Political Economy and Taxation" (Cambridge: Printed by J. Smith, 1831);

Analytical Statics: A Supplement to the Fourth Edition of An Elementary Treatise on Mechanics (Cambridge: Printed for J. & J. J. Deighton, 1833);

Astronomy and General Physics Considered with Reference to Natural Theology, Bridgewater Treatises, no. 3 (London: Pickering, 1833);

Remarks on Some Parts of Mr. Thirlwall's Letter on the Admission of Dissenters to Academical Degrees (Cambridge: Printed at the Pitt Press by John Smith for J. & J. J. Deighton, and Rivingtons, London, 1834);

Thoughts on the Study of Mathematics as Part of a Liberal Education (Cambridge & London: Printed at the Pitt Press by J. Smith for J. & J. J. Deighton and Whittaker & Arnot, 1835; revised and enlarged, 1836);

Newton and Flamsteed: Remarks on an Article in No. CIX. of the Quarterly Review (Cambridge, 1836; revised and enlarged, 1836);

William Whewell; engraving by E. U. Eddis, 1835

Answer to a Critique of the History of the Inductive Sciences (Cambridge, 1837);

History of the Inductive Sciences, from the Earliest to the Present Time, 3 volumes (London: Parker, 1837; revised and enlarged, 1847; revised and enlarged again, 1857; New York: Appleton, 1858);

On the Foundations of Morals: Four Sermons Preached before the University of Cambridge, November, 1837 (Cambridge: Cambridge University Press, 1837; New York: French, 1839);

295

On the Principles of English University Education (London: Parker, 1837; Cambridge: J. & J. J. Deighton, 1837; revised and enlarged, 1838);

The Doctrine of Limits with Its Applications; Namely, Conic Sections, the First Three Sections of Newton, the Differential Calculus: A Portion of a Course of University Education (Cambridge: J. & J. J. Deighton, 1838; London: Parker, 1838);

Trinity College Commemoration Sermon Preached in the College Chapel, December 15, 1838 (Cambridge: J. Smith, 1838);

The Philosophy of the Inductive Sciences, Founded upon Their History, 2 volumes (London: Parker, 1840; revised and enlarged, 1847); republished in three volumes as *History of Scientific Ideas: Being the First Part of the Philosophy of the Inductive Sciences* (London: Parker, 1858); *Novum Organon Renovatum: Being the Second Part of the Philosophy of the Inductive Sciences* (London: Parker, 1858); and *On the Philosophy of Discovery, Chapters Historical and Critical: Including the Completion of the Third Edition of the Philosophy of the Inductive Sciences* (London: Parker, 1860);

Demonstration That All Matter Is Heavy (Cambridge, 1841);

The Mechanics of Engineering, Intended for Use in Universities and in Colleges of Engineers (Cambridge: Parker, 1841);

Of a Liberal Education in General, and with Particular Reference to the Leading Studies of the University of Cambridge (London: Parker, 1845);

Elements of Morality, Including Polity, 2 volumes (London: Parker, 1845; New York: Harper, 1845);

Indications of the Creator: Extracts, Bearing upon Theology, from the History and the Philosophy of the Inductive Sciences (London: Parker, 1845);

Lectures on Systematic Morality Delivered in Lent Term, 1846 (London: Parker, 1846);

Sermons Preached in the Chapel of Trinity College, Cambridge (London: Parker, 1847; Cambridge: J. & J. J. Deighton, 1847);

Of Induction, with Especial Reference to Mr. J. Stuart Mill's System of Logic (London: Parker, 1849);

Lectures on the History of Moral Philosophy in England (London: Parker, 1852); revised and enlarged as *Additional Lectures on the History of Moral Philosophy in England* (Cambridge: Deighton, Bell, 1862);

Of the Plurality of Worlds: An Essay (London: Parker, 1853); revised and enlarged as *Of the Plurality of Worlds: An Essay; Also a Dialogue on the Same Subject* (London: Parker, 1854; Boston: Gould & Lincoln, 1854; revised and enlarged edition, edited by Michael Ruse, Chicago: University of Chicago Press, 2001);

Six Lectures on Political Economy, Delivered at Cambridge in Michaelmas Term, 1861 (Cambridge: Cambridge University Press, 1862).

Collection: *Selected Writings on the History of Science*, edited by Yehuda Elkana (Chicago: University of Chicago Press, 1984).

OTHER: Johann Wolfgang von Goethe, *Herman and Dorothea*, translated by Whewell (London, 1839);

Friedrich Schiller, *The Knight of Toggenburg*, translated by Whewell (Shelford, 1842);

Verse Translations from the German: Including Bürger's Lenore, Schiller's Song of the Bell, and Other Poems, translated by Whewell (London: Murray, 1847);

English Hexameter Translations from Schiller, Göthe, Homer, Callinus, and Meleager, edited by Whewell (London: Murray, 1847);

Richard Jones, *Literary Remains: Consisting of Lectures and Tracts on Political Economy, of the Late Rev. Richard Jones*, edited by Whewell (London: Murray, 1859);

"Barrow and His Academical Times," in volume 2 of *The Theological Works of Isaac Barrow, D.D.*, 9 volumes, edited by Alexander Napier (Cambridge: Cambridge University Press, 1859);

The Platonic Dialogues for English Readers, 3 volumes, translated by Whewell (Cambridge & London: Macmillan, 1859–1861);

The Mathematical Works of Isaac Barrow, edited by Whewell (Cambridge: Cambridge University Press, 1860);

"On the Influence of the History of Science upon Intellectual Education," in *The Culture Demanded by Modern Life*, edited by E. L. Youmans (New York, 1867), pp. 225–251;

"Of the Transformations of Hypotheses in the History of Science," in *Science before Darwin: A Nineteenth Century Anthology*, edited by Howard Mumford Jones and I. Bernard Cohen (London: Deutsch, 1963).

William Whewell is best known for coining the word *scientist*. When his name appears at all in standard histories of science, it is usually to note this linguistic contribution or his impact on his alma mater and professional home, the University of Cambridge; seldom is his broader influence on the philosophy of science discussed. Indeed, a marked hostility toward Whewell's work has been the rule. The historian of science George Sarton complained in 1936 that "nothing illustrates better the backwardness of our studies than the fact that Whewell's book was still commanding the respect of many thoughtful readers at the beginning of the century." It is puzzling that someone who was so influential and even feared in his own time could excite such contempt and then so easily vanish from the intellectual landscape. While Whewell's scientific findings were not significant, his philosophical writings anticipate many modern themes. The American pragmatist Charles Saunders Peirce was one of few noted philosophers of the early twentieth century to study Whewell's work, and even he emphasized scattered insights rather than attempting to recover Whewell's full-scale system. That system is reemerging as scholarship on Whewell increases; but given the sheer number of pages Whewell wrote and the diversity of his subjects, from original poetry and tracts on economics and morality to translations of works by Plato and Johann Wolfgang von Goethe, plus his florid Victorian prose, it is likely that the best understanding of his work will be achieved by focusing on more-limited aspects of his thought.

Whewell was born in Lancaster, Lancashire, on 24 May 1794, the eldest child of John Whewell, a master carpenter, and Elizabeth Bennison Whewell. The parish priest and some of the elite members of Lancaster society persuaded his father that Whewell's intelligence merited cultivation, and he was sent to the Heversham grammar school in Westmoreland for two years. There he was proficient in mathematics and showed a fine appreciation of the classics, including Greek and Latin, and architecture. He wrote poetry then and throughout his life. His later efforts at educational reform can be read as a vindication of his own diverse interests as those most befitting a gentleman scholar.

While at Heversham, Whewell qualified for an exhibition, or scholarship, to attend the University of Cambridge, although he had to raise money to supplement the award by public subscription. Later he was held up as an example of the class blindness of the British educational system, although, as the son of a master carpenter who owned property, Whewell was hardly the "poor scholar" or "underprivileged prodigy" that he was made out to be. His image as a humble lad who rose to prominence through hard work and natural inclination no doubt fed his widely noted vanity but also became a source of criticism.

Whewell entered Trinity College at Cambridge in October 1812. His classmates and near-contemporaries included Julius Hare, John Herschel, Connop Thirlwall, Richard Sheepshanks, Charles Babbage, George Peacock, and George Biddle Airy. Hare, Herschel, and Thirlwall remained especially close to Whewell; Adam Sedgwick, who had graduated in 1808 and been elected to a fellowship two years before Whewell arrived at Trinity, also became an influential friend and colleague. These men went on to spearhead sev-

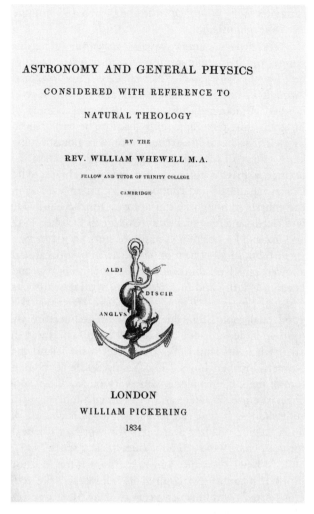

ASTRONOMY AND GENERAL PHYSICS
CONSIDERED WITH REFERENCE TO
NATURAL THEOLOGY

BY THE

REV. WILLIAM WHEWELL M.A.
FELLOW AND TUTOR OF TRINITY COLLEGE
CAMBRIDGE

LONDON
WILLIAM PICKERING
1834

Title page for the third edition of Whewell's 1833 Bridgewater Treatise, in which he argues that science points to the existence of a divine designer of the universe (from Whewell's Selected Writings on the History of Science, *edited by Yehuda Elkana [1984])*

eral learned societies, and some led the drive to reform English education and religion. Connop and Thirlwall are noteworthy as organizers of the Apostles, a discussion group at Cambridge that was influenced by the Romantic poet Samuel Taylor Coleridge's criticisms of Jeremy Bentham's utilitarianism and of William Paley's natural theology. Alfred Tennyson was among the members of the group. While Whewell shared their rejection of utilitarianism and eventually came to admire Coleridge and William Wordsworth, another favorite of the Apostles, he was always an advocate of natural theology, although not of that of Paley. Partly under Sedgwick's influence, Whewell was hostile to Paley's utilitarian moral philosophy for having torn "the notion of obligation loose from the idea of duty" and for positing usefulness as the standard for human behavior. This approach to morality debased humanity, Whewell thought.

Whewell's letters reveal a warm, generous nature, but his reputation for arrogance arose early in his Cambridge career. Nevertheless, his progress through Trinity was distinguished, and he won several honors. He narrowly missed taking the top honors of his graduating class, apparently because he had assured himself that his nearest competitor was not studying hard enough. After receiving his B.A. in 1816 he became a private tutor, as did many graduates who lacked the means and connections to pursue careers in the church, although he did not care for the work. He was elected a fellow of Trinity College in October 1817 and accepted a position as assistant tutor in mathematics in 1818. In 1819 he took his M.A., in part because it allowed him free admission to the public library, and began a lengthy and lucrative career writing textbooks with *An Elementary Treatise on Mechanics*. He traveled a good deal, nourishing his interest in architecture by touring cathedrals, but his life was nearly cut short in 1819 when his ship sank. He wrote to his friend the Reverend Robert Jones, "The Nancy is safe at the bottom of the Channel along with every ounce of our luggage. We are safe here and quite unencumbered with superfluities. If you can lend each of us a change of linen . . . you will be rewarded in this world or the next for your charity to such poor shipwrecked souls."

Whewell advanced from assistant tutor to tutor in 1823. Cambridge required its fellows to take religious orders within seven years of their M.A. degrees or lose their fellowships; Whewell waited until the last moment, becoming ordained deacon in 1825. His sermons were extremely popular. He became professor of mineralogy in 1828. In 1831 Whewell and some of his former schoolmates established the British Association for the Advancement of Science. During his lifetime Whewell was elected to or given honorary membership in some two dozen scientific societies throughout Europe.

The first of Whewell's works to attract notice from the public and his colleagues in science was his Bridgewater Treatise, *Astronomy and General Physics Considered with Reference to Natural Theology* (1833). The series was the legacy of Francis Henry Egerton, the eighth Earl of Bridgewater, who, on his death in 1829, had left £8,000 to commission a series of works showing "the Power, Wisdom, and Goodness of God, as manifested in Creation." The goal of the project was to affirm the liberal Anglican doctrine of natural theology–that is, the idea that nature is orderly, teleological, law-governed, benevolent, and uniform. By discovering general laws, the natural theologian revealed evidence of design in nature, reinforcing Christian belief in a divine designer.

The steadily mounting results of science could thus be encouraged without reservation because, if properly achieved, they posed no threat to revealed religion. Natural theologians were fond of saying that the book of nature and the book of Scripture had the same author, although a few favored a literal interpretation of Genesis. The Bridgewater Treatises provide a thorough summary of natural theology and form part of the backdrop against which several scientific controversies of the mid nineteenth century took place. Spirited, often vitriolic disputes about the origins of the earth, the occurrence of geological catastrophes such as the Great Flood, and the possibility of evolution pitted the natural theologians against both more-conservative and more-liberal forces. Davies Gilbert, president of the Royal Society, chose the authors of the treatises with the advice of the archbishop of Canterbury and the bishop of London. Critics of the series were dissatisfied with the way in which the commissions were assigned, but it is hard to see how Davies could have carried out Bridgewater's bequest without choosing clergymen and their allies to participate. The series was lavishly printed and expensive. With the authors' backgrounds and the religious content, these features provided grist for critics in the radical press, who derided them as the "Bilgewater Treatises" destined for the showy, vapid libraries of the upper classes. Whewell's four-hundred-page volume was the first to appear, in March 1833, and it was by far the most popular, remaining in print through seven editions. (In 1837 the mathematician Babbage, the creator of the first "calculating engine," or digital computer, published *The Ninth Bridgewater Treatise: A Fragment* on his own initiative, fearing that Whewell had shown too little enthusiasm for science.)

The central argument of *Astronomy and General Physics* is that the Earth is the central part of God's creation and humanity the most exalted creature on Earth. Nature has been created to fit the needs of all its inhabitants, especially humans, and something of the divine purpose can be read in what is found in nature. Meteorological evidence such as the cycles of the seasons and the composition of the atmosphere show an excellent fit between nature and the needs of earth's inhabitants that could not have come about by accident. There is no physical necessity for the heavens and Earth to be as they are, so, obviously, divine intention must be the explanation: "One of the great uses to which the vegetable wealth of the earth is applied, is the support of man, whom it provides with goods and clothing; and the adaptation of tribes of indigenous vegetables to every climate has, we cannot but believe, a reference to the intention that the human race should be diffused over the whole globe." The proper aim of the physical sciences is the discovery of mathematically expressible descriptive and unifying laws, and the human mind, as a creation of God, is as fitted to make such discoveries as the climate is to the growth of crops for human nourishment.

Whewell divides scientists into "plodders" and "geniuses," depending on their tendency toward deduction or induction, respectively; the "inductive mind"—the mind that does not merely collect facts but makes hypotheses about them, all the while showing "a habit of considering the world as the work of God"—is the source of the most well-grounded scientific knowledge. Whewell's emphasis on the intellectual and moral character of individual scientists is, perhaps, his most significant contribution to the philosophy of science, although his critics did not agree.

The most famous of Whewell's works are *History of the Inductive Sciences, from the Earliest to the Present Time,* published in three volumes in 1837, and *The Philosophy of the Inductive Sciences, Founded upon Their History,* published in two volumes three years later. Together, these two works represent the core of Whewell's position on science. Between the publication of the two works, in 1838, Whewell was named Knightsbridge Professor of Moral Philosophy at Cambridge.

History of the Inductive Sciences, from the Earliest to the Present Time appeared at the end of a difficult period in Whewell's own investigations. He had received worldwide data on the tides from friends, missionaries, foreign governments, and imperial corporations and had analyzed them. He received the Royal Medal from the Royal Society for his work in 1837; but the project taught him how demanding original investigation is, and he remained dissatisfied with the results. His frustration heightened his consciousness of the need to comment on how science ought to be done, as he wrote to his friend Herschel in the midst of the work on the tides: "I . . . only grieve at the small chance there is of my ever making those original discoveries and advances in the science which give a man the right and power to regulate its external clothing." He wrote *History of the Inductive Sciences, from the Earliest to the Present Time* for his compatriots in science, basing it on his conviction, surprisingly novel at that time, that "to learn the best methods of discovering truth" one had to look at how "truths, now universally recognized, have already been discovered." Whewell assumed that a unifying methodological principle underlay all the sciences, and that although it might not have reached the same stage in each science, it would emerge eventually in all of them.

The 1,500-page opus was generally well received, and it remains a passable account of the history of science from the Greeks through the Arabs to Whewell's contemporaries. Subsequent editions tried valiantly to stay abreast of developments. It is no simple recounting of history, as Whewell's principal biographer, Isaac Todhunter, notes: "The special characteristic of the *History of the Inductive Sciences* is the distribution of each course into various decisive Epochs, each Epoch having its Prelude and Sequel: this the author claims as a novelty, and justly regards as of great value. The prominent parts of each science are well selected, and the whole is written with a vigour of language and a felicity of illustration rare in the treatment of such abstruse subjects." The preludes and sequels connect the various epochs together into a well-unified chronology. One sees clearly from one section to the next how the questions and discoveries of previous epochs were modified and developed to bring about new questions and new results in subsequent ones. Whewell maintains that the story of scientific growth is one of gradual accumulation of knowledge, building not only on past advances but also on past errors. His picture of science as a work in progress clearly influenced Peirce and resonates strongly today. Whewell, like Hans Reichenbach and Karl Popper after him, thinks that the courage to guess incorrectly and to give up one's conjectures is the mark of a good scientist. His pedagogical ideas were consistent with this notion, since he thought it was vital for students to learn about their predecessors' accomplishments and failures in equal measure. The ability to take risks could not be taught, he believed—there was no "art of discovery"—but morally good people would be good speculators in science. This view incited the indignation of Whewell's fellows, who thought it outlandish to suggest evaluating the moral character of someone such as Euclid or Isaac Newton as part of an assessment of his work.

Whewell praises inductive over deductive thought, holding that "induction involves something which elevates and ennobles, while deduction is groveling and servile." He has no use for the naive brand of inductivism advocated by Francis Bacon, in which conclusions are "read off" from lists of observations like temperatures from thermometers. Most of the instances Whewell uses to illustrate the inductive nature of good science fail to support his claims, however: to the modern reader—and even to many of his contemporaries—they look like deductions. He differs from the traditional Baconian position that facts exist independently of theories and can be collected "objectively"—that is, without hypotheses; he insists that the distinction between fact and theory is neither simple nor absolute but that the two always blend into one another to varying degrees. He holds that the mind is an active contributor to the process of making observations into facts and using them to confirm or disconfirm hypotheses, rather than the passive recorder it is claimed to be by

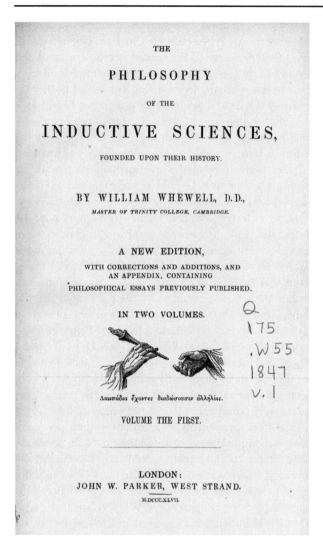

THE

PHILOSOPHY

OF THE

INDUCTIVE SCIENCES,

FOUNDED UPON THEIR HISTORY.

BY WILLIAM WHEWELL, D.D.,
MASTER OF TRINITY COLLEGE, CAMBRIDGE.

A NEW EDITION,
WITH CORRECTIONS AND ADDITIONS, AND
AN APPENDIX, CONTAINING
PHILOSOPHICAL ESSAYS PREVIOUSLY PUBLISHED.

IN TWO VOLUMES.

Λαμπάδια ἔχοντες διαδώσουσιν ἀλλήλοις.

VOLUME THE FIRST.

LONDON:
JOHN W. PARKER, WEST STRAND.
M.DCCC.XLVII.

Title page for the first volume of the revised edition of Whewell's
attempt to persuade his colleagues and the public to appreciate
the practical and moral value of science (Thomas Cooper
Library, University of South Carolina)

both Baconian empiricism and Cartesian rationalism—
all the more reason for scientists to possess the kind of
mind that can perform this task creatively and with
sagacity. Whewell offers the evidence of comparative
anatomy to support Georges Cuvier's teleological
explanation of morphology, according to which organisms have the structures that they do because they are
part of "an intelligible scheme and discoverable end, in
the organization of animals." Charles Darwin's theory
of evolution by natural selection was still nearly twenty
years from publication, but Cuvier was already in disfa-
vor by this time—as Whewell's critics were quick to
point out. More-recent critics of the *History of the Inductive Sciences* add that the work has been little cited and is
riddled with elementary errors such as getting dates
wrong by as much as two centuries.

In the dedication to *The Philosophy of the Inductive
Sciences* Whewell tells his friend Sedgwick that the book
is the "moral of the story" that Sedgwick had found
lacking in the *History of the Inductive Sciences* and is almost
as long as that story itself. The work is 1,400 pages in
length, with no index; written hastily, it does not hang
together well. While many of Whewell's critics admired
the breadth of *History of the Inductive Sciences,* they could
not accept the premises of *The Philosophy of the Inductive
Sciences,* and the quasi Kantianism of the work gained
no disciples.

Science was on the cusp of emerging as a respectable profession during Whewell's lifetime, but it was
still a small enterprise dominated by churchmen and
aristocrats and in need of justification and defense.
Knowledge was increasingly seen both in England and
on the Continent as a factor in social unrest. Whewell
wanted to place the authority of science on the firmest
ground possible. He was convinced that while science
and the church could remain allied, science and politics
must not mix. (Whewell threatened to quit when the
British Association for the Advancement of Science
began debating issues such as the disestablishment of
the Church of Scotland and the new Poor Law, "for
what kind of an institution do we become, if we allow
ourselves to be made an annual ambulatory meeting for
agitating in assemblies when both *eminent* and *notorious*
men address a miscellaneous crowd on the sorest and
angriest subjects which occur among the topics of the
day?") Whewell wanted his university colleagues and
the public to appreciate the practical and moral value of
science. It is curious, however, that he expected *The Philosophy of the Inductive Sciences* to help them do so.

Whewell's epistemology is ambitious but, ultimately, incoherent. He freely admits his debt to
Immanuel Kant and to Scottish common sense philosophy—both acknowledgments were hazardous, since his
English audience regarded German philosophy as a
"mere jargon of unmeaning words" and Scots as
"obscure and wearisome." Yet, Whewell is not just trying to persuade his English readers of the merits of
Kant. As usual, he thinks that his forebears were important but that he can do better. While he agrees with
Kant that ideas such as space, time, and cause are not
derived from experience but are conditions for experience, he denies that all the ideas of science are valid a
priori, rather than discovered through observation and
equipment. Rather than make Kant's move to the "transcendental" to justify knowledge, Whewell turns to
experience. In this respect he occupies an enigmatic
middle ground between Kantianism and traditional
empiricism, both of which struggled to make sense of
the relationship between individual experiences and
universal generalizations. Perhaps Whewell hoped that

his reliance on the gradual imitation of necessity and the moral worth of individual minds would provide the missing glue that both camps needed.

Whewell begins with what he calls "Fundamental Ideas." (He is fond of capitalizing crucial words and phrases, so his readers must remember that *Ideas* is a technical term, while *ideas* is not; but he is not consistent in this usage.) These ideas are part of the activity of the mind in seeking knowledge; they make perception, and meaningful expression of that perception, possible; and each science matures as it develops the Fundamental Ideas that organize its observations. The task of science is to discover necessary truths by joining experiences with Fundamental Ideas. Observed facts are transformed into necessary truths slowly, intuitively, and through careful application of "Conceptions" to clear and certain facts. Here is where the acumen of the scientist comes in: the scientist must be capable of introducing clear, precise Conceptions about observed facts into hypotheses and must have the kind of mental discipline necessary for intuiting necessary truths from them.

Each science, then, will contain a mixed stock of empirical generalizations and necessary truths, with established sciences such as optics and astronomy having a preponderance of necessary truths. One will not know in advance which of the empirical generalizations are likely to yield necessary truth, and there is no mechanical method for making the latter out of the former. On this point, perhaps, Whewell differs most from the empiricist and rationalist traditions. Both Bacon and René Descartes attempted to establish epistemologies of habit that would allow anyone, in principle, to discover and certify knowledge. Whewell turns against this egalitarian tide and makes science depend on the capacity of rare, ingenious, well-trained individuals to apprehend facts clearly and distinctly—and sometimes to misapprehend them—and to derive necessity from them.

Whewell's theory of induction is a difficult one. Progress in science consists in an increasingly comprehensive system of ever more universal and necessary natural laws that are the products of induction—that is, inference from particular instances. He thinks that the chain of inductive generalization can be modeled both observationally and historically as an "Inductive Table," and he includes detailed tables for the sciences of optics and astronomy. The table for optics begins with such low-level generalizations about light as "rays falling on water" and "rays passing through water and glass," observed by Euclid and Ptolemy, upward through higher-level claims about angles of refraction, polarization by crystals, and so on, until Newton's mature optics appears at the top. Just before the highest

level of generalization is reached, Whewell makes the cryptic comment, "The Laws of these Phenomena were never discussed till Theory had indicated them." But if the tables are constructed correctly, the support offered by the evidence for the conclusions at each successive level should be readily apparent just by looking, in much the same way that the conclusion of a syllogism is deductively obvious. (Whewell asked the noted logician Augustus DeMorgan for an opinion on his work, and when DeMorgan reacted negatively to the inductive tables, Whewell responded, with characteristic hubris, "I do not wonder at your denying these devices a place in Logic, and you will think me heretical and profane, if I say, *so much the worse for Logic*.") Good inductions for scientific purposes are those that exhibit "consilience" and simplicity—that is, different classes of facts should be explained by the same inductive hypothesis, and the hypothesis should be inclusive, or, in Whewell's term, should "colligate" more concepts than alternative hypotheses. The best inductions, also, can be used to generate novel predictions and can be expressed mathematically.

Up to this point, except for the peculiarity of the inductive tables, Whewell's position on induction is not especially eccentric. Where he departs from tradition is in the psychological part of his thesis. The process by which inductive generalizations are reached is not one of description or aggregation, as it was for his opponent John Stuart Mill, but of deliberate cognition. The mind intuits connections between observations because they have been organized and properly "colligated" with clear conceptions imposed by creative, disciplined, truth-seeking scientists over long periods. This kind of attention is a special one, but it is not "magical"; it is fallible and proceeds by trial and error. Thus, Whewell is presenting something like a logic of discovery rather than a logic of justification; but his detractors rejected it as leaving too much to ingenuity and luck.

Scientist was not the only term of Whewellian coinage: he writes at length in *The Philosophy of the Inductive Sciences* about the need for clear terminology in a well-organized, productive science, and he is responsible, directly or indirectly, for *physicist, uniformitarianism, ion, anode,* and *cathode.* In a letter to Charles Lyell, Whewell the neologist and advocate of clarity wrote, "I am glad you are trying to concinnate your nomenclature. I will tell you the result of my speculations thereupon. The termination *synchronous* seems to me to be long, harsh, and inappropriate."

On 12 October 1841 Whewell married Cordelia Marshall, of a wealthy Leeds industrial family. While on his honeymoon, he received the news of his impending appointment as master of Trinity. He extended his influence on Cambridge even further in the coming

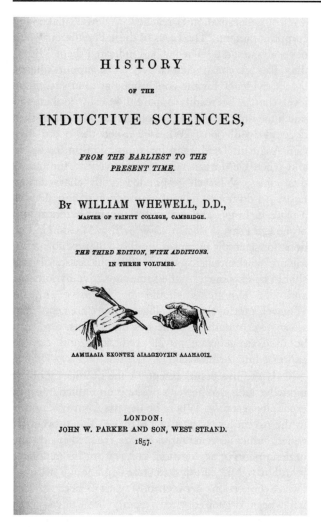

HISTORY

OF THE

INDUCTIVE SCIENCES,

*FROM THE EARLIEST TO THE
PRESENT TIME.*

BY WILLIAM WHEWELL, D.D.,

MASTER OF TRINITY COLLEGE, CAMBRIDGE.

THE THIRD EDITION, WITH ADDITIONS.
IN THREE VOLUMES.

ΛΑΜΠΑΔΙΑ ΕΧΟΝΤΕΣ ΔΙΑΔΩΣΟΥΣΙΝ ΑΛΛΗΛΟΙΣ.

LONDON:
JOHN W. PARKER AND SON, WEST STRAND.
1857.

*Title page for the second revision of Whewell's account of science from
the ancient Greeks through the Arabs to his own time (from Whewell's*
Selected Writings on the History of Science,
edited by Yehuda Elkana [1984])

years: he was appointed vice chancellor of the university for the academic years 1842–1843 and 1856–1857. His hard personality became fully entrenched after he rose to the position of master. Lyell complained that Whewell treated university students like children, demanding absolute obedience and deference. The moral philosopher Henry Sidgwick, who was a young don under Whewell, complained of his autocratic demeanor and imposition of confused and dogmatic rules. The importance of submission and reverence for the "old order" is a prevalent theme in Whewell's behavior and work, especially his writings on educational reform. As master of Trinity, a Crown appointment that Whewell would probably not have received had it been an elected position, he could bring the college's curriculum in line with his pedagogical ideals. He

thought that the faculties of language and reason are definitively human, and that the task of education is not to fill the student with information but to form the mind in a way that maximizes its humanity; the object of a liberal education, he wrote in *Of a Liberal Education in General, and with Particular Reference to the Leading Studies of the University of Cambridge* (1845), "is to make men truly men." This goal requires the inculcation of proper habits, and training in mathematics is the principal, although not the only, means of acquiring such habits.

Even the inhabitants of the town of Cambridge bore the brunt of Whewell's forceful persona. Albert Pell, a wealthy American who attended the university in the 1840s, relates the tale of a group of Trinity dons summoned to resolve a student dispute. "A townsman ventured the attempt of thrusting Whewell aside, whereupon that wondrous example of stature and wisdom took the rapscallion by the coat-collar into an angle of the church opposite and pummelled him unmercifully—a warning to us undergraduates that we had better take ourselves off, which we did." For the most part, according to Sheldon Rothblatt, people thought Whewell arrogant, snobbish, "arbitrary, unconciliatory and sometimes excessively rude."

Whewell published two more works of natural theology: *Indications of the Creator: Extracts, Bearing upon Theology, from the History and the Philosophy of the Inductive Sciences* (1845) and *Of the Plurality of Worlds* (1853). The former was intended as a brief but definitive response to Robert Chambers's *Vestiges of the Natural History of Creation* (1844), which stirred up a great deal of proevolutionary sentiment but was on weak grounds scientifically and was roundly rejected with Whewell's help. *Of the Plurality of Worlds* is a more substantial work, running to hundreds of pages. It is Whewell's only anonymous publication, but everyone knew who the author was. While the work delighted his readers, especially the religious ones, the book is so complex and detailed, and his arrogance was by then so legendary, that one waggish reviewer wrote that it was

A book meant to show
That throughout all infinity
There's nothing so grand
As the Master of Trinity.

Whewell's wife died on 18 December 1855 after a long illness; Whewell's tender side is revealed in a collection of elegiac poems he had privately printed. On 1 July 1858 he married Everina Frances Affleck, née Ellis, the widow of a baronet.

Darwin and Whewell had been acquainted while Darwin was a student at Cambridge, and the two maintained cordial relations. When his *On the Origin of Species by Means of Natural Selection, Or, the Preservation of Favoured Races in the Struggle for Life* appeared in 1859, Darwin paid homage to Whewell's reputation as the leading advocate of scientific method by placing a passage from Whewell's Bridgewater volume, along with a quotation from Bacon, on the frontispiece. In spite of the honor, Whewell was unpersuaded by Darwin's book and wrote to tell him so. While the fastidious scholar Whewell openly admired the detail that Darwin had marshaled to support his theory, he nevertheless exercised his privilege as college master to keep the work off the shelves of the Trinity Library for several years.

Whewell's administrative obligations as master of Trinity and as vice chancellor left him little time to write giant multivolume books. He did continue to engage his critics in print, and he still published diversely, if not at as great length. He increasingly turned his efforts to moral philosophy and educational reform, and his views on both began to seem more and more conservative as times changed around him.

Whewell's second wife, who had continued to be known as Lady Affleck, died in 1865. On 24 February 1866 Whewell was injured in a fall from a horse. He died on 6 March and was buried in the Trinity College Chapel near the statue of Bacon that he had given to the college. In his will he endowed the Whewell Chair for the study of international law at Cambridge. Herschel wrote his obituary for the *Proceedings of the Royal Society.*

Biographies:

Isaac Todhunter, *William Whewell, D.D.: Master of Trinity College, Cambridge; An Account of His Writings with Selections from His Literary and Scientific Correspondence,* 2 volumes (London: Macmillan, 1876);

Janet Stair Douglas, *The Life and Selections from the Correspondence of William Whewell, D.D.* (London: Kegan Paul, 1881);

Walter F. Cannon, "William Whewell, F.R.S.: Contributions to Science and Learning," *Notes and Records of the Royal Society of London,* 19 (1964): 176–191;

Robert Robson, "William Whewell, F.R.S., Academic Life," *Notes and Records of the Royal Society of London,* 19 (1964): 168–176;

Menachem Fisch and Simon Schaffer, eds., *William Whewell: A Composite Portrait* (Oxford: Oxford University Press, 1991).

References:

Robert E. Butts, ed., *William Whewell's Theory of Scientific Method* (Indianapolis: Hackett, 1989);

Adrian Desmond, *The Politics of Evolution: Morphology, Medicine, and Reform in Radical London* (Chicago: University of Chicago Press, 1989);

Martha McMackin Garland, *Cambridge before Darwin: The Ideal of a Liberal Education 1800–1860* (Cambridge: Cambridge University Press, 1980);

A. W. Heathcote, "William Whewell's Philosophy of Science," *British Journal for the History of Science,* 4 (1954): 302–314;

Jack Morrell and Arnold Thackray, *Gentlemen of Science: Early Years of the British Association for the Advancement of Science* (Oxford: Clarendon Press, 1981);

Sheldon Rothblatt, *The Revolution of the Dons: Cambridge and Society in Victorian England* (Cambridge: Cambridge University Press, 1968);

Michael Ruse, "William Whewell and the Argument from Design," *Monist,* 60 (1977): 244–268;

Richard Yeo, *Defining Science: William Whewell, Natural Knowledge, and Public Debate in Early Victorian Britain* (Cambridge: Cambridge University Press, 1993);

Yeo, "William Whewell, Natural Theology and the Philosophy of Science in Mid Nineteenth Century Britain," *Annals of Science,* 36 (1979): 493–516.

Papers:

William Whewell's papers and correspondence are collected at the Wren Library of Trinity College, Cambridge. His correspondence with John Herschel can be found in Herschel's papers at the Royal Society of London.

Alfred North Whitehead

(15 February 1861 – 30 December 1947)

Leemon B. McHenry
Loyola Marymount University and California State University, Northridge

BOOKS: *A Treatise on Universal Algebra, with Applications* (Cambridge: Cambridge University Press, 1898);

The Axioms of Projective Geometry, Cambridge Tracts in Mathematics and Mathematical Physics, no. 4 (Cambridge: Cambridge University Press, 1906; New York: Hafner, 1960);

The Axioms of Descriptive Geometry, Cambridge Tracts in Mathematics and Mathematical Physics, no. 5 (Cambridge: Cambridge University Press, 1907; New York: Hafner, 1960);

Principia Mathematica, 3 volumes, by Whitehead and Bertrand Russell (Cambridge: Cambridge University Press, 1910–1913);

An Introduction to Mathematics, Home University Library of Modern Knowledge, no. 15 (London: Williams & Norgate, 1911; New York: Holt, 1911);

The Organisation of Thought, Educational and Scientific (London: Williams & Norgate, 1917; Philadelphia: Lippincott, 1917);

An Enquiry Concerning the Principles of Natural Knowledge (Cambridge: Cambridge University Press, 1919; revised, 1925);

The Concept of Nature: The Tarner Lectures Delivered in Trinity College, November, 1919 (Cambridge: Cambridge University Press, 1920);

The Principle of Relativity, with Applications to Physical Science (Cambridge: Cambridge University Press, 1922);

The Rhythm of Education: An Address Delivered to the Training College Association (London: Christophers, 1922);

Science and the Modern World: Lowell Lectures, 1925 (New York: Macmillan, 1925; Cambridge: Cambridge University Press, 1926);

Religion in the Making: Lowell Lectures, 1926 (New York: Macmillan, 1926; Cambridge: Cambridge University Press, 1927);

Symbolism: Its Meaning and Effect (New York: Macmillan, 1927; London: Cambridge University Press, 1928);

Alfred North Whitehead

The Aims of Education and Other Essays (New York: Macmillan, 1929; London: Williams & Norgate, 1929);

The Function of Reason (Princeton: Princeton University Press, 1929);

Process and Reality: An Essay in Cosmology. Gifford Lectures Delivered in the University of Edinburgh during the Session 1927–28 (New York: Macmillan, 1929; Cambridge: Cambridge University Press, 1929);

Adventures of Ideas (New York: Macmillan, 1933; Cambridge: Cambridge University Press, 1933);

Nature and Life (Chicago: University of Chicago Press, 1934; Cambridge: Cambridge University Press 1934);

Modes of Thought: Six Lectures Delivered in Wellesley College, Massachusetts, and Two Lectures in the University of Chicago (New York: Macmillan, 1938; Cambridge: Cambridge University Press, 1938);

Essays in Science and Philosophy (New York: Philosophical Library, 1947; London & New York: Rider, 1948);

Alfred North Whitehead: An Anthology, edited by F. S. C. Northrop and Mason W. Gross (New York: Macmillan, 1953)–includes "On Mathematical Concepts of the Material World," pp. 7–82;

Dialogues of Alfred North Whitehead, edited by Lucien Price (Boston: Little, Brown, 1954; London: Reinhardt, 1954).

Collection: *The Wit and Wisdom of Alfred North Whitehead,* edited by A. H. Johnson (Boston: Beacon, 1947).

OTHER: "The First Physical Synthesis," in *Science and Civilization,* edited by F. S. Marvin (London & New York: Oxford University Press, 1923), pp. 161–178;

"Time," in *Proceedings of the Sixth International Congress of Philosophy, Harvard University, Cambridge, Massachusetts, United States of America, September 13, 14, 15, 16, 17, 1926,* edited by Edgar S. Brightman (New York: Longmans, Green, 1927), pp. 59–64;

"Autobiographical Notes," "Mathematics and the Good," and "Immortality," in *The Philosophy of Alfred North Whitehead,* edited by Paul Arthur Schilpp, The Library of Living Philosophers, volume 3 (Evanston, Ill. & Chicago: Northwestern University Press, 1941), pp. 1–14, 666–700.

SELECTED PERIODICAL PUBLICATIONS–
UNCOLLECTED: "The Geodesic Geometry of Surfaces in Non-Euclidean Space," *Proceedings of the London Mathematical Society,* 29 (1897–1898): 275–324;

"Memoir on the Algebra of Symbolic Logic," *American Journal of Mathematics,* 23 (1901): 139–165, 297–316;

"On Cardinal Numbers," *American Journal of Mathematics,* 24 (1902): 367–394;

"The Logic of Relations, Logical Substitution Groups, and Cardinal Numbers," *American Journal of Mathematics,* 26 (1903): 157–178;

"The Philosophy of Mathematics," *Science Progress in the Twentieth Century,* 5 (October 1910): 234–239;

"Einstein's Theory: An Alternative Suggestion," *Times Educational Supplement,* 12 February 1920, p. 83;

"Discussion: The Idealistic Interpretation of Einstein's Theory," by Whitehead, H. Wildon Carr, T. P. Nunn, and Dorothy Wrinch, and "The Philosophical Aspects of the Principle of Relativity," *Proceedings of the Aristotelian Society,* 22 (1921–1922): 123–138, 215–223;

"Symposium–The Problem of Simultaneity: Is There a Paradox in the Principle of Relativity in Regard to the Relation of Time Measured to Time Lived?" by Whitehead, Carr, and R. H. Sampson, *Proceedings of the Aristotelian Society, Supplement 3* (1923): 34–41;

"Principia Mathematica," *Mind,* 35 (1926): 130;

"Indication, Classes, Numbers, Validation," *Mind,* 43 (1934): 281–297.

Alfred North Whitehead is acknowledged as one of the intellectual giants of the twentieth century. A Cambridge University–trained mathematician, he collaborated with Bertrand Russell on the epoch-making *Principia Mathematica* (1910–1913), gaining a prominent place in the history of logic. His critical evaluation of Albert Einstein and his attempt to advance his own form of relativity theory earned him a high reputation in the philosophy of physics. Finally, after becoming a professor of philosophy at Harvard University, Whitehead produced one of the most original and powerful systems of metaphysics since that of Georg Wilhelm Friedrich Hegel in the early nineteenth century. His biographer, Victor Lowe, says that Whitehead was a man of kindness, wisdom, and perfectly disciplined vigor. Russell reports that undergraduates affectionately nicknamed him "the Cherub" at Cambridge; at Harvard he was known as a benign sage who had great personal influence on his students.

Against the dominant trend of increasingly narrow specialization that characterized academic philosophy in the twentieth century, Whitehead attempted to produce a comprehensive system that would unify the sciences and provide a common basis for all areas of inquiry. The distrust of speculative philosophy established by logical positivism early in the century and the sheer difficulty of understanding his thought have, however, combined to keep Whitehead outside the mainstream of contemporary philosophy. His influence has been greatest on the disciplines of process philosophy and process theology, both of which he is regarded

Whitehead's parents, Alfred and Sarah Buckmaster Whitehead

as having founded. Renegade physicists and biologists have also advanced his ideas as alternatives to prevailing orthodoxy.

The Latin inscription in commemoration of Whitehead's life in the Trinity College Chapel, University of Cambridge, says in part, "just as he was a citizen of two countries, so he seems to have lived three lifespans: first as an authority in mathematics, second in physics, and third in metaphysics." Rather than a succession of interests, however, Whitehead's thought is best characterized as a developing unity. In each of the three phases he refutes a traditional notion—the quantitative conception of mathematics, scientific materialism, and the British empiricist notion of experience—and then advances his own novel contribution. Whitehead's thought radiated outward to ever increasing generalities from his initial concerns in mathematics and logic; ideas developed in an earlier phase carry over into a later one in which their significance is fully realized. Whitehead's exposition of technical details is always combined with a wealth of humanistic learning and a brilliance of expression.

Whitehead was born on 15 February 1861 in Ramsgate on the Isle of Thanet, Kent, to Alfred Whitehead, the vicar of St. Peter's Parish, and Sarah Buckmaster Whitehead. The family home was filled with relics of the past, some of them from Roman castles and Norman churches. The Angles, Saxons, and Jutes had landed on these very beaches in the fifth century; St. Augustine of Canterbury, the future archbishop, had landed there in 597 and had preached his first sermon to the pagan subjects of King Ethelbert a mile or so inland. The Straits of Dover and the Thames estuary also had a turbulent history, filling Whitehead's youthful imagination with invading Roman forces, William the Conqueror, and the ships of the Tudors and the Stuarts.

Whitehead was educated at home by his father until 1875, when he began studying classics, history, and mathematics at Sherborne, an ancient school in Dorsetshire. He recounts in his "Education of an Englishman" (1926) that he was taught by masters who had read the classics with sufficient zeal to convert them to the principles of Athenian democracy and Roman tyrannicide. The romance of the English countryside, the strong characters he knew in his boyhood, and the deep sense of history inspired by his surroundings made a lasting impression on Whitehead and influenced his later philosophical thought.

In 1880 Whitehead enrolled at Trinity College, Cambridge. He wrote his fellowship dissertation in 1884 on James Clerk Maxwell's *Treatise on Electricity and*

Magnetism (1873). Although the focus of Whitehead's studies was applied mathematics, Cambridge provided a wide range of educational opportunities. Most valuable in regard to his later career in philosophy was his election to an elite discussion club, the Cambridge Conversazione Society, commonly known as "the Apostles," during his first year as a fellow of Trinity. Most of the sessions were philosophical in nature, and the members, active and honorary, included a long list of distinguished thinkers of one of the university's most illustrious periods. The philosophers Russell, Henry Sidgwick, James Ward, and J. M. E. McTaggart were involved in the society during Whitehead's time; other regular participants included mathematicians, scientists, classical scholars, poets, statesmen, judges, educators, and historians.

On 16 December 1890 Whitehead married Evelyn Wade. The academic year 1882–1883–"the Year of the Forty Brides"–had been the first in which Cambridge dons were allowed to marry without either giving up their fellowships or taking holy orders. The Whiteheads contributed to the baby boom that followed with three children: Thomas North, born in 1891; Jessie, born in 1894; and Eric Alfred, born in 1898. Whitehead said that Evelyn taught him that beauty is the aim of existence, inspiring the emphasis on creativity and aesthetic experience that marks the last phase of his career as a philosopher.

As a lecturer in mathematics Whitehead was interested in the various systems of symbolic reasoning allied to ordinary algebra, such as Sir William Hamilton's theory of quaternions, Hermann Grassman's calculus of extension, and George Boole's algebra of logic. His study of these systems led to his first book, *A Treatise on Universal Algebra, with Applications* (1898). His purpose in the work is to investigate several new systems of algebra–he calls them "extraordinary algebras"–and plead for their recognition as legitimate forms of mathematics. The new algebras, he argues, are capable of unification in a universal algebra, provided that mathematics is redefined as the development of all types of formal, necessary, deductive reasoning instead of being restricted to its traditional definition as the science of discrete and continuous magnitude. He accepts a multiplicity of mathematical systems that may have no relationship to number or quantity and seeks a ground of unity for them in some common interpretation.

To justify including the new algebras as legitimate systems of mathematics, Whitehead adopts the traditional method of interpreting them through an extension of geometry. Specifically, he attempts to demonstrate the unity of mathematical systems by means of a generalized idea of space that arises as an abstraction from geometry. This mathematical space is populated by a "manifold of elements," or abstract objects. In this way Whitehead seeks to ground the algebras in ontology: formulas and symbols refer to mathematical reality.

A Treatise on Universal Algebra failed to influence the course of mathematics in any significant way; mathematicians complained that it was "too philosophical." The work did, however, lead to Whitehead's election to the Royal Society of London in 1903; more importantly, it was a crucial step toward his collaboration with Russell on *Principia Mathematica.*

Russell had been Whitehead's most brilliant student in mathematics at Trinity. Unlike Whitehead, however, he chose to specialize in philosophy rather than mathematics. At first he was influenced by the Hegelian metaphysics dominant at Cambridge in the late 1890s, but when he read Hegel's remarks on the philosophy of mathematics, he began what he called his "Revolt into Pluralism." After abandoning Hegel, Russell turned his attention to the work of German mathematicians such as K. W. T. Weierstrass, Richard Dedekind, Georg Cantor, and Gottlob Frege on the principles of mathematics. He believed that they had swept away great quantities of confused metaphysics that obstructed clear thinking in the subject.

At the Second International Congress of Mathematics in Paris in 1900 Whitehead and Russell met Giuseppe Peano, whose five axioms for the arithmetic of natural numbers showed that a rigorous foundation could be laid down for the most fundamental part of mathematics. He also persuaded them that the technical adaptability of his system of symbolic notation was far superior to any other. Russell adopted Peano's symbolism and applied it to the logic of relations. When he persuaded Whitehead that the method could greatly facilitate the latter's work, a partnership was established that lasted for ten years. The projected second volumes of Whitehead's *A Treatise on Universal Algebra* and Russell's *The Principles of Mathematics* (1903) were abandoned in favor of the three volumes of *Principia Mathematica,* published in 1910, 1912, and 1913; a fourth volume, on the foundations of geometry, was to have been written by Whitehead alone but was never completed.

In the *Principia Mathematica* Whitehead and Russell attempted to deduce all of mathematics from logic. A centerpiece of the project was the then newly developed logic of relations, which, Russell claimed, "gave thought wings." Its main advantage was that the technique allowed for all sorts of distinctions of order and sense for quantitative differences–for example, transitive and asymmetrical relations.

In *Principia Mathematica* Whitehead and Russell were attempting a project that had been a dream of

Evelyn Wade Whitehead in 1892

of classes of classes, the formation of classes of relations, and the calculus of relations to the definitions of all of the concepts employed in mathematics.

While work on *Principia Mathematica* was proceeding, Whitehead applied its techniques to the natural sciences in his Royal Society "memoir" of 1906, "On Mathematical Concepts of the Material World." His plan in this complex paper is to initiate the "mathematical investigation of various possible ways of conceiving the nature of the material world." He considers five such conceptions, ranging from the worldview of classical physics to a cosmology that closely resembles the one he later advanced in *Process and Reality: An Essay in Cosmology* (1929), in the light of a set of definitions that apply to an "essential relation" and a set of primitive entities chosen for each view. He adds to each conception a set of axioms that state relationships between the essential relation and the primitive entities, then deduces theorems from the axioms.

By 1910 Whitehead and his wife had grown tired of life in small-town Cambridge. Whitehead resigned his position at Trinity College, and, although he had no position waiting for him, the family moved to London. In 1911 Whitehead took a position as lecturer in applied mathematics at University College London and was promoted to reader in geometry. In 1914 he became professor of applied mathematics and dean of the faculty of science at the Imperial College of Science and Technology in London. The death of his son Eric in World War I had a profound effect on his theology: he decided that nothing is lost from the finite world in the everlasting nature of God. Whitehead dedicated *An Enquiry Concerning the Principles of Natural Knowledge* (1919) to his son, writing: "The music of his life was without discord, perfect in its beauty."

Although Whitehead's interests were always philosophical regardless of the formal subject of his investigations, he claims in his "Autobiographical Notes" in *The Philosophy of Alfred North Whitehead* (1941) that his philosophical writing really began in London toward the end of the war when he became a frequent contributor of papers to the Aristotelian Society. At this time, he says, he also became involved in the problems relating to higher education in a modern industrial civilization. The idea of a university was being extended beyond the Oxford and Cambridge models to allow for the education of people from all social classes.

During this period Whitehead gained prominence as a philosopher of physics with the publication of the trio *An Enquiry Concerning the Principles of Natural Knowledge, The Concept of Nature* (1919), and *The Principle of Relativity, with Applications to Physical Science* (1922). With minor differences, all three books develop the same view. Observing the breakdown of Newtonian physics

many champions of pure rationality: to show that the entire edifice of mathematical science (arithmetic, algebra, geometry, calculus, and so on) can be derived by deductive inference from logic–an enterprise that is known as "the logicist thesis." They begin with primitive logical concepts, such as "elementary proposition," "propositional function," "negation," and "disjunction," that cannot be defined but must be intuited. From these concepts they develop basic propositions, which they adopt as formal axioms–"tautology," "addition," "permutation," the "associative principle," and the "principle of summation." They go on to provide a detailed treatment of symbolic logic, formulated first in terms of propositions and propositional functions and then in terms of a formal theory of classes and relations. The key concepts of Peano's axioms–"number," "successor," and "zero"–are not primitive in *Principia Mathematica;* they are defined in terms of classes and the primitive logical ideas. Volume one eventually develops a purely logical theory of cardinal and ordinal numbers. The three volumes of the work move from the calculus of elementary propositions through the calculus of general propositions, the calculus of classes, the formation

with the revolution initiated by Einstein and the early quantum physicists, Whitehead sought a new conception of the physical world that would reconcile these diverse developments and set physics back on strong empirical foundations. All of his previous work in mathematics, physics, and philosophy comes together in this original system of nature, in which events, rather than material substances, become the basic particulars.

The least technical exposition of Whitehead's philosophy of natural science is that given in *The Concept of Nature,* originally delivered as the Tarner Lectures at Cambridge in 1919. The invitation to give the lectures provided Whitehead with the opportunity to communicate the ideas of *An Enquiry Concerning the Principles of Natural Knowledge* (which, he says, was "thought out and written amid the sounds of guns–guns of Kitchener's army training on Salisbury Plain, guns on the Somme echoing faintly across the Sussex coast; some few parts composed to pass times of expectation during air-raids over London, punctuated by the sounds of bombs and the answer of artillery, with argument clipped by the whirr of aeroplanes" of World War I) to a wider audience. His central task is the attempt to unify the natural sciences under one concept. In *The Principle of Relativity, with Applications to Physical Science* he calls this enterprise "pan-physics."

Whitehead begins the lectures with a criticism of the concept of nature that underlies Newtonian physics. He argues that this view has been passed on from century to century by what seems to have been the authority of science, but, in reality, it has only been thrust upon scientific thinking by a naive common sense. Whitehead finds that the doctrine has its origin in a misconception that began with the Greeks: matter has been conceived as a metaphysical substratum for the properties that are perceived; it has thereby become disconnected from the complex of immediate fact and survives only as an abstraction of thought. Thus, natural science–physics in particular–has lost its empirical footing.

After critiquing the traditional concept of matter, Whitehead argues against its attendant doctrine, which he calls "the bifurcation of nature." This doctrine holds that nature is partitioned into two systems of reality: a world of phenomenal appearances in the mind and a world of material objects that are the inferred causes of the appearances. According to this view, which was espoused in one form or another in the seventeenth century by René Descartes and John Locke and in the eighteenth century by Immanuel Kant, the reality of matter is never known but only conjectured, while the reality of appearances is known but remains purely mental, like that of a dream. Whitehead proposes, instead, to view nature as one system of relations; on this view there is no apparent nature, only nature as known in perceptual knowledge.

At the beginning of *An Enquiry Concerning the Principles of Natural Knowledge* Whitehead says: "Modern speculative physics with its revolutionary theories concerning the natures of matter and of electricity has made urgent the question, What are the ultimate data of science?" In *Science and the Modern World: Lowell Lectures, 1925* (1925) he says that "the field is now open for the introduction of some new doctrine . . . which may take the place of the materialism with which, since the seventeenth century, science has saddled philosophy." The "new doctrine," advanced in *An Enquiry Concerning the Principles of Natural Knowledge,* is that "the ultimate facts of nature, in terms of which all physical and biological explanation must be expressed, are events connected by their spatio-temporal relations, and that these relations are in the main reducible to the property of events that they can contain (or extend over) other events which are parts of them."

Thus, for panphysics, events are the primary constituents of reality. Whitehead had suggested this direction for science as early as "On Mathematical Concepts of the Material World," and with the dematerialization of nature implied by the concept of vibratory energy in field theory, the event was the most likely candidate for the basis of nature. One cannot "go behind" events to find anything more basic or substantial; endurance and stability in nature must be explained in terms of events of varying duration. Ordinary objects of perception, for example, are merely monotonous events; the difference between these entities and those that are ordinarily called "events" is one of time span. Events happen once and do not repeat themselves. Properties in events do happen again and retain their identity through time. Whitehead calls these entities "objects," which he says have "ingression" in events. Ingression is the relation of objects to events. This repetition of objects makes science possible: the discovery of the laws of nature is predicated on the fact that certain objects repeat themselves in a fairly stable fashion.

Whitehead distinguishes three kinds of objects: "sense-objects," such as individual colors, sounds, and scents; "perceptual objects," which are the ordinary macroscopic bodies of perceptual experience; and "scientific objects," such as electrons and molecules. Sense-objects are the empirical building blocks that are compounded in various ways to form perceptual objects. Scientific objects, on the other hand, are never observed directly but are conceived as necessary for the physicist's task of obtaining a simple expression of the character of events. Scientific objects are crucial to physical measurement: they are the things in nature to which scientific formulas refer.

Evelyn Whitehead with the Whiteheads' children,
T. North, Jessie, and Eric, in 1899

The apparatus of events and objects is put forward to correspond to a difference that is evident in perceptual knowledge; it is not an attempt to advance yet another metaphysical dualism to replace the phenomenon/material object bifurcation. According to Whitehead's theory of natural knowledge, all that is known of nature is in nature itself; he refuses to admit what he calls "psychic additions" as a causal result of the motions of matter. As he says in *The Concept of Nature,* "the red glow of the sunset should be as much part of nature as are the molecules and electric waves by which men of science would explain the phenomenon."

Aside from what is immediately discerned in the perceptual field, Whitehead recognizes distant entities that are undiscriminated as to quality (for example, the back side of the moon before it was observed by space probes or Apollo astronauts) but must be included to complete the spatial relations of that which is perceived. These entities make up what he calls the "discernible" and include the relata of events within ordinary objects of perception (for example, the inside of a tennis ball) and the complex system of relations beyond the solar system. Whitehead's doctrine of "significance" holds that the discerned (what is directly experienced) is part of the broader field of the discernible (what would be experienced if one were in the right situation or had the right technology); that is, nature is a system of overlapping events. The most thorough exposition of the doctrine of significance is

in a lecture, "The Relatedness of Nature," that Whitehead delivered before the Royal Society of Edinburgh in 1922 and republished as chapter 2 of *The Principle of Relativity, with Applications to Physical Science.*

Whitehead uses the logic of *Principia Mathematica* throughout the exposition of his panphysics, but nowhere is its application more evident than in his procedure for defining the elements of space and time on the basis of the fundamental relation of extension. The "Method of Extensive Abstraction" is a technical instrument that takes one gradually from the "rough" world of immediate experience to the "smooth" world of mathematical physics. Russell, who was enthusiastic about Whitehead's invention, saw extensive abstraction as a way to apply Occam's Razor, or the principle of parsimony—a bias toward simplicity in the construction of theories—to physics: one need not assume that "points," "lines," "planes," and "instants" are additional entities in nature; instead, they can be viewed as abstractions or ideals of pure thought that are derived from the harmonious texture of immediate experience.

In *The Concept of Nature* Whitehead begins his exposition of the procedure with the "specious present," duration of immediate perception that can be individuated into smaller events but not down to timeless instants. This event is defined as a set of events related as whole and part, either spatially or temporally or both. The relation of "extending over" (the relation of whole and part) is transitive, asymmetrical, and compact or dense. His next step is to define an "abstractive set" by two conditions: first, of any two of its events, one encloses the other; and second, there is no event that is a common part of every event of the set. Hence, each set is composed of an infinite series of successively smaller events that converge without arriving at a final event. Abstractive sets are now conceived in terms of classes and types of classes such that sets that diminish in all three dimensions are distinguished from those that diminish in one or two dimensions only; thus, sets that are needed to define points are separated from those that are needed to define lines and planes. The "abstractive element"—point, line, plane, and so forth— is defined as the class of all equivalent abstractive sets of the same type. The abstractive element, therefore, replaces the notion of a point or instant as an entity radically different from anything known in one's experience of the physical world; it is understood as an ideal limit of diminution of extensions. The merit of defining the geometrical entities in this manner is that they are viewed as logical functions of extension, instead of as actual particulars in nature; yet, they do the same mathematical work that is required for physics. For example, the physicist's use of concepts such as "force at a point" or "configuration at an instant" is now understood in terms of ideal entities derived from converging series of extensive regions.

While teaching at the Imperial College, Whitehead devoted a great deal of attention to the revolutionary theories of Einstein. The theory of events was Whitehead's response to the rethinking of space, time, and matter required by the Special Theory of Relativity. He was aware, however, of serious problems in the foundations of relativity theory. As he says in *The Principle of Relativity, with Applications to Physical Science*, "the worst homage we can pay to genius is to accept uncritically formulations of truths which we owe to it."

Aside from the extremely difficult mathematical treatment of relativity in *The Principle of Relativity, with Applications to Physical Science*, Whitehead also delivered three papers on the topic to the Aristotelian Society in 1922 and 1923: "The Philosophical Aspects of the Principle of Relativity," "The Idealistic Interpretation of Einstein's Theory," and "The Problem of Simultaneity: Is There a Paradox in the Principle of Relativity in Regard to the Relation of Time Measured to Time Lived?" Another short piece, "Einstein's Theory: An Alternative Suggestion," in the *Times* (London) *Educational Supplement* in 1920 is the clearest statement for the general reader of his disagreement with Einstein.

Whitehead's theory of relativity is based on the theory of extended spatiotemporal events developed in *An Enquiry Concerning the Principles of Natural Knowledge*. Arguing that Einstein's theory was constructed on an empirical foundation that was too narrowly restricted to laboratory operations, Whitehead bases his own theory on the fundamental fact of observation: durations, which are events with finite temporal and infinite spatial extension. Durations are parallel when any two of them are extended over by a third; otherwise, they are nonparallel. Families of parallel durations and their parallel moments constitute the succession of time in any one system; time is the abstraction of parallel moments from the sense of passage within parallel durations. There are an indefinite number of families of parallel durations constituting different time-systems.

Whitehead now brings in the concept of "cogredience" as the basis of motion and rest in his theory of relativity. Cogredience is the extension of a finite event throughout a duration. If the duration is the content of the "specious present" of an observer, a cogredient event is part of this content that lasts through the whole duration and does not change its position relative to the percipient during the specious present. The event can be a particular body that occupies successive positions in one time-system. A body is at rest for an observer whose specious present includes the body within the permanent space of that time-system. But relative to the space of another time-system, the body is moving in a straight line. Motion and rest depend on the time-system that is fundamental for the observation.

By means of a complex system of "event-particles," "routes," "stations," and "point-tracks," Whitehead works out the details of the stratified time-systems from which he defines motion and rest. The most important idea is that the whole of space-time is derived from events; its structure is simply the underlying order of extension, of which physics investigates the contingent relations and geometry expresses the uniform relatedness. The uniform structure of space-time, constructed on the basis of alternative time-systems, marks Whitehead's most distinctive contrast with Einstein, who believed that the structure of space-time varies with its contents because of peculiarities in the distribution of matter throughout the universe; the presence of matter distorts the uniform space-time structure and results in a curved space-time. But in Whitehead's view, this conclusion depends on acceptance of the traditional concept of matter. Once space is defined in terms of objects ingredient in events, the space-time of perception is conceived as continuously uniform with the more refined space-time of scientific objects. Whitehead further argues that since Einstein's theory depends on operational procedures involving the transmission of light signals, measurement depends on the contingencies of the physical field. But in that case, there can be no conditions that remain the same for operations of measurement.

In spite of Whitehead's disagreements with Einstein, he accepts the latter's fundamental principle of the fusion of space and time into a four-dimensional structure. But this view undergoes radical revision in Whitehead's later works.

When Whitehead was nearing retirement in 1924, he received an invitation to become a professor of philosophy at Harvard University. The department had included William James, Josiah Royce, Ralph Perry, and George Santayana in its "Golden Age" between 1869 to 1912. But after several retirements, great thinkers were being sought to restore the department's standing. Whitehead's reputation as the co-author of *Principia Mathematica* and as a philosopher of physics made him an ideal candidate. He accepted the invitation with the understanding that his teaching would provide him the opportunity to develop his original ideas on logic, philosophy of science, and metaphysics, rather than being required to expound and criticize the views of other philosophers. His outstanding students at Harvard and at its associated school for women, Radcliffe College, included W. V. Quine, Victor Lowe, Paul Weiss, Raphael Demos, Susanne K. Langer, and Dorothy Emmet. Quine, a logician who wrote his doctoral dissertation under Whitehead, recorded in his autobiography that he "retained a vivid

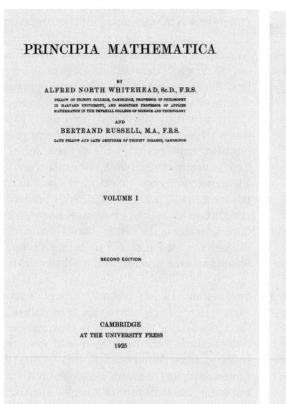

*Title and interior pages from the first volume of Whitehead and Bertrand Russell's groundbreaking attempt
to reduce mathematics to logic. The other two volumes appeared in 1912 and 1913
(Trinity College, University of Cambridge).*

sense of being in the presence of the great." Many others echoed this sentiment.

At Harvard, Whitehead's philosophical system reached completion; but there were hints prior to this period that foreshadowed the metaphysics that he developed between 1925 and 1929. In a note to the second edition (1925) of *An Enquiry Concerning the Principles of Natural Knowledge,* he says that "the true doctrine that 'process' is the fundamental idea, was not in my mind with sufficient emphasis" at the time he wrote the first edition. In his mature thought, "process" replaces "extension"; the holistic conception of events in his philosophy of natural science is developed into a pluralistic temporal atomism; and the geometrical and primarily spatial thinking of his earlier preoccupation with relativity gives way to a theory that, as he says, "takes time seriously." Whitehead's "metaphysical phase" was an extemely productive period, with the publication of *Science and the Modern World, Religion in the Making: Lowell Lectures, 1926* (1926), *Symbolism: Its Meaning and Effect* (1927), *The Function of Reason* (1929), and his magnum opus, *Process and Reality,* all occurring within four years.

The ideas in these works, he said, had accumulated in his mind for decades.

Science and the Modern World, originally delivered as the Lowell Lectures in Boston in 1925, marked Whitehead's debut on the American intellectual scene. His most popular book, it attracted scores of students to his lectures and seminars at Harvard. In this work Whitehead begins to sketch the view of nature that he calls "the philosophy of organism." Continuing his attack on scientific materialism, he shows how the presuppositions of the philosopher-scientists of the seventeenth century were challenged by the Romantic poets of the nineteenth century, such as William Wordsworth, Percy Bysshe Shelley, and Alfred Tennyson: for them, conceiving reality as mere matter in motion presented a picture of the universe that was at odds with everything people valued in their experience of nature. In the past three centuries, he points out, the cosmology derived from science has asserted itself at the expense of those that might be derived from ethics, aesthetics, and religion. Whitehead's new system of nature attempts to synthesize the revolutionary developments in modern physics and biology with the insights of the Romantic poets, thereby achieving the harmony of facts and values that is denied by the bifurcation of nature.

Some of the most fundamental concepts of Whitehead's metaphysics first appear in *Science and the Modern World*. Aware of the inadequacy of the traditional modes of thought embedded in ordinary language to express his vision of reality as process, he introduced neologisms such as "actual occasion," "prehension," and "eternal object." This terminology, he thought, would allow him to surpass the substance-property metaphysics and begin afresh; but it has led to the perception that his views are obscure. Even Russell confessed in his *Portraits from Memory, and Other Essays* (1956) that there was much in Whitehead's philosophy that he never succeeded in understanding.

Whitehead had speculated in *The Concept of Nature* that "this alliance of the passage of mind and the passage of nature arises from their both sharing in some ultimate character of passage which dominates all being." His concept of the "actual occasion" accomplishes this fusion of mind and nature and replaces his earlier notion of an event. Actual occasions are unities that synthesize their relations to other occasions in the process of becoming; an example of an actual occasion is a moment of human experience. Whitehead explains in *Science and the Modern World* that he arrived at the concept via modern science—in particular, biology and physics—and reflection on the experience of value. He was seeking a fundamental ontological unit that makes sense of the evolution of organisms, electromagnetic energy, and the higher phases of human consciousness. In a 7 March 1928 letter to his son North he said: "I am trying to evolve one way of speaking which applies equally to physics, physiology, psychology, and to our aesthetic experiences. The ordinary philosophic abstractions won't do this." Whitehead's method is to identify the most concrete entities first and then explain more-abstract things as derived from them. His "fallacy of misplaced concreteness" criticizes other philosophers for mistaking the abstract—such as "mind" and "matter"—for the concrete.

A "prehension" is the emergence of a particular pattern as grasped in the unity of an actual occasion. Events in nature are centers of activity in active relations with all the other events in their environment. At this point in Whitehead's thinking, the concept of prehension explains the interdependence of nature by showing how every occasion is internally related to every other occasion in the universe. This view is the reverse of materialism, according to which every bit of matter has a "simple location" in space and time and is independent from and externally related to every other. The idea of an energy field, such as an electro-

magnetic field, in which each part simultaneously influences and is influenced by every other part, appears to be the model from which Whitehead is working in rejecting simple location and advancing the prehension in its place.

Just as "actual occasion" replaces "event" in *Science and the Modern World*, so "eternal object" replaces "object." Eternal objects are endless in variety but include mathematical and geometrical forms, relations, colors, sounds, tastes, and emotions. They are virtually anything that is recognized in the concrete process again and again. Eternal objects are related to the concrete process by "ingression," and those of a particular type are related to each other in a complex hierarchy of grades from simple to increasingly complex. This complex system of relations provides the metaphysical foundation for mathematics Whitehead sought in the concept of a mathematical space in *A Treatise on Universal Algebra*. One should not view Whitehead's hierarchies of eternal objects as a Platonic "heaven": he eschewed the term "universals" so as not to suggest any association with Plato's transcendent Forms. For Whitehead all of reality is grounded in actuality; apart from the process of actual occasions there is absolutely nothing. Finally, all eternal objects are envisaged in what Whitehead calls the "Primordial Nature of God."

Whitehead's opportunity to refine the metaphysical ideas of *Science and the Modern World* came with an invitation to deliver the prestigious Gifford Lectures in Natural Theology at the University of Edinburgh; his predecessors in this lectureship included James, Bernard Bosanquet, Henri Bergson, and Arthur Stanley Eddington. He originally chose the title "The Concept of Organism" for the ten lectures but replaced it with "Process and Reality" when he delivered them in June 1928. According to Lowe, for his early lectures Whitehead had an audience as large as Eddington's; but as he presented his baffling system of metaphysics, the number dwindled to half a dozen—including the two sponsoring professors, Norman Kemp Smith and A. E. Taylor. One professor, E. T. Whittaker, remarked that had he not known Whitehead personally, he would have suspected that the person on stage was an impostor, making up his talk as he went along. Presented orally, the new metaphysics was bound to be unintelligible; the technical detail in the book version that appeared in 1929, *Process and Reality*, gives some indication of what the Edinburgh audience faced.

In an essay titled "Process and Reality," written for the celebration of his seventieth birthday at Harvard, Whitehead says: "Almost all of *Process and Reality* can be read as an attempt to analyse perishing on the same level as Aristotle's analysis of becoming. The notion of prehension of the past means that the past is

First page of a letter from Whitehead to the philosopher Norman Kemp Smith of the University of Edinburgh
(Edinburgh University Library)

an element which perishes and thereby remains an element in the state beyond, and thus is objectified. That is the whole notion." As Whitehead moved from the novel but rudimentary ideas expressed in *Science and the Modern World* to the final position articulated in *Process and Reality,* he focused on the temporal process of becoming and perishing of actual occasions.

The actual occasion can be understood as a metaphysical generalization of a psychological concept. Whitehead notes that there is no experience of an instant of time. Rather, one experiences a duration, a specious present, in which the present moment emerges from the immediate past and flows into the immediate future. Each actual occasion comes into being all at once, not in bits and pieces. All of the actual occasions that comprise nature come into being in a fraction of a second and contribute their novel syntheses to the future as they perish. Whitehead calls this merging of the past into the present "concrescence."

Whitehead believes that the puzzle of the connectedness of nature is solved by appealing to the texture of life that is always right before one. The final actualities are all alike: they are natural units of process—of becoming and perishing. But compared to the infinite multitude of actualities in nature, the ones that make up human consciousness are highly specialized instances. This position—that all of reality is, on some level, sentient—is sometimes called "panpsychism," though Whitehead never used this term to characterize his metaphysics; he preferred "the philosophy of organism." This view that all of nature is alive dethrones physics from its place in the hierarchy of the sciences and puts biology in its place as the fundamental science.

Whitehead criticizes the British Empiricists for concentrating on elements of experience that are clear and distinct, such as David Hume's "impressions" and "ideas." Whitehead contends that these aspects of perception, which he designates "presentational immediacy," are secondary to the more fundamental feelings of passage revealed in what he calls "causal efficacy." Where presentational immediacy supplies the details of sensation, causal efficacy provides continuity to experience; it so pervades experience that one hardly takes notice of it. It is the massive presence of the past in the process of merging into the present. Evolution has given human beings acute receptors in the form of highly developed sense organs, and so people naturally focus on the clear and distinct sensations of presentational immediacy. But in the absence of such sensations they encounter a more fundamental reality as throbs of experience blending into one another. The dim consciousness of half-sleep, the thumping of one's heartbeat, and the visceral feelings of well-being all suggest continuous becoming in the mode of causal efficacy.

The functioning together of presentational immediacy and causal efficacy in ordinary human perception is what Whitehead calls "symbolic reference."

Perception in the mode of causal efficacy points to the primacy of prehension as the master principle in Whitehead's metaphysics. The original idea is now modified: a prehension is an asymmetrical relation between the past and the present. The present actual occasion is dependent on the past and is, therefore, internally related to the data that it "prehends." But the past actual occasions are independent of any activity in their future and so are externally related to later occasions. The creative advance of nature is, thus, a one-way dependence.

All actualities are more or less creative via prehensive activity; each is an "artist" that creates itself from its own subjective aim. In the beginning of the concrescent process an actual occasion inherits the eternal objects that are given from the past. If the occasion has a "dominance in its physical pole," there is simply a brute inheritance of the same data presented by the immediate past. Occasions of this sort make up the things that are identified in perception as inert matter or low-level organisms. But as occasions become more and more sophisticated in higher-level organisms or in consciousness, there is more opportunity for originality. Such an occasion has what Whitehead calls "dominance in its mental pole": it actively selects data that are compatible with its aim for its present self-creation. These are positive prehensions; the act of excluding incompatible data is a negative prehension. In this way Whitehead explains novelty, or how something new is added to the universe—a new virus, a new species of plant or animal, or a new movement in art, music, literature, or philosophy.

Whitehead's theory of extension in *Process and Reality* explains how the microscopic actual occasions form the basis for the enduring things of perceptual experience—rocks, plants, animals, planets, stars, galaxies, and so forth. The main problem is to explain why the individuals rather than the multitudes of actual occasions are perceived. Whitehead makes the transition from the microscopic to the macroscopic world with his notion of transmutation, whereby occasions in any one physical body are prehended as a unity: when one perceives a macroscopic entity, one prehends an aggregate of many occasions as one final unity. Whitehead calls such an aggregate of occasions a "nexus" (the plural is "nexūs").

Sense perceptions are often vague and confused. They omit any discrimination of the fundamental activities within nature, even though, via symbolic reference, they pick out the broad outlines of order in actual occasions. The properties one is able to per-

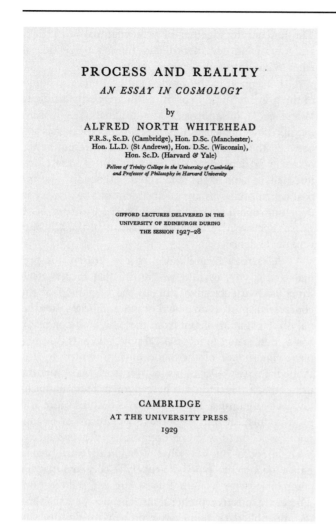

PROCESS AND REALITY

AN ESSAY IN COSMOLOGY

by

ALFRED NORTH WHITEHEAD

F.R.S., Sc.D. (Cambridge), Hon. D.Sc. (Manchester).
Hon. LL.D. (St Andrews), Hon. D.Sc. (Wisconsin),
Hon. Sc.D. (Harvard & Yale)

*Fellow of Trinity College in the University of Cambridge
and Professor of Philosophy in Harvard University*

GIFFORD LECTURES DELIVERED IN THE
UNIVERSITY OF EDINBURGH DURING
THE SESSION 1927–28

CAMBRIDGE
AT THE UNIVERSITY PRESS
1929

*Title page for the principal work in which Whitehead
elaborates his "philosophy of organism" (Trinity
College Library, University of Cambridge)*

ceive in any particular body approximate, more or less, the type of order that dominates among the members of that nexus.

Whitehead's concept of a "society" is central to his theory of how actual occasions are grouped together. A society is a nexus of social order in which the constituent actual occasions must positively prehend those eternal objects that not only define the society in question but also ensure its continued survival. A society is not simply an aggregate of mutually contemporary occasions but consists of multiple lines of inheritance. Societies are simple or vastly complex. The simplest ones are those with "personal order," in which the members are ordered serially. In more complex ones there are societies within societies within societies. A cell, for example, would be a complex structured society in the sense that it harbors the existence of lower, more specialized societies—molecules, atoms,

electrons, and so on. This concept applies to societies of highly general order that constitute the system of space-time and the geometry that reigns in this particular cosmic epoch.

Most societies encountered in ordinary perception are "democracies" in the sense that their subordinate societies function together without a central, unified mentality. This sort of society would include certain cell colonies, plants, ecosystems, and most lower forms of many-celled animals. Higher animals, however, have a dominant living nexus of personal order. In the case of the vertebrate animals, the nexus of occasions with a dominance of the mental pole arises out of the complex nervous system, which is a system of occasions that form neuron cells. In the case of human beings, the final route of actual occasions constituting consciousness is a dominant nexus of purely temporal, single-line inheritance. In this manner Whitehead explains consciousness as made up of something similar to the basic stuff of reality; that is, consciousness emerges in degrees of complexity from a rudimentary sentience that pervades the whole of nature. This view contrasts sharply with the dualistic approach, which sees mind and matter as two different but interacting substances, and with the materialistic approach, which recognizes only matter and its properties.

Process and Reality culminates in a natural theology. As Whitehead attempts to reconcile "ideal opposites" of permanence and transience, he advances a nontraditional theism consistent with his view of the natural world as process. In some of his most poetic prose, he describes what he calls the most general formulation of the religious problem: "whether the process of the temporal world passes into the formation of other actualities, bound together in an order in which novelty does not mean loss." The world craves novelty; yet, it is "haunted by the terror at the loss of the past," for the present never embodies the past in its totality. Such is the experience of the joy of birth and the sorrow of death in the world. But for Whitehead, loss from the temporal process does not mean annihilation from the universe: God saves the world as it passes into the immediacy of his everlasting consciousness.

Whitehead argues that traditional religion has misconceived the nature of God by imagining him as an imperial ruler, a ruthless moralist, or an unmoved mover. But Christianity is, at least, correct in its conception of a God who loves and finds the reward of love in the immediate present. Bringing this vision of God into harmony with the principles of his system of metaphysics, Whitehead makes his most radical deviation from traditional theism by proposing that God is in process with the world. God is an "actual entity," rather than an actual occasion, because God does not perish in the temporal process as actual occasions do but is an ever-lasting concrescence. Furthermore, just as actual occasions have mental and physical poles, God, too, has a twofold nature as primordial and consequent. As primordial, God is conceptual and atemporal. In this aspect he is the conceptual valuation of the wealth of eternal objects. And as the keeper of the potentials, God is the beginning of feelings in the world by providing the lure for their realization. God is, therefore, immanent in each occasion, supplying it with its initial subjective aim and instilling in it the desire for such perfection as is possible in its situation. As consequent, God is physical and temporal. He is the unbiased reception of the temporal universe, regardless of whether the occasion has met the desire for perfection. God, however, is devoid of negative prehensions.

Given this conception of God, each occasion is individually free to accept or reject God's ideal. Either way, it will be preserved in God's consequent side as a cosmic memory of the universe. No actual occasion achieves subjective or "personal" immortality, however, since actual occasions lose subjectivity once they perish. Thus, the physical and transient side of the universe passes into the mental, permanent side of deity through the consequent nature of God. The many become one by reaching a final completion and harmonization in God's everlasting concrescence. The world responds to God's aim, and God, in turn, responds to the world's processes, weaving them into a great aesthetic harmony that is preserved forever. *Process and Reality* ends: "In this way, the insistent craving is justified—the insistent craving that zest for existence be refreshed by the ever-present, unfading importance of our immediate actions, which perish and yet live for evermore."

As opposed to traditional theism, in which God is conceived as an eternal being whose nature is deduced according to the logic of perfection (omnipotence, omniscience, impassibility, immutability, incorporeality, and so on), Whitehead's God changes with the universe and has no knowledge of specific events in the future. This God also has no power to force his will on the universe or to prevent the destructiveness of human evil or natural disasters. Instead, God operates by gentle persuasion in acting as the lure for the good. Neither God nor the world ever reaches a state of static completion.

Whitehead himself recognized at least one serious problem in his conception of God: since God is always evolving, there is no determinate entity to function as an "object" for the actual occasions of the temporal world. According to Whitehead's metaphysical principles, two contemporary actual occasions cannot prehend each other. Thus, since God is always present, he cannot influence any other occasion. So it

seems that Whitehead's God is meant to be the chief exemplification of his metaphysical principles; yet, at the same time, God violates those principles in important respects.

In 1931 the Austrian logician Kurt Gödel published the paper "Über formal unentscheidbare Sätze der *Principia Mathematica* und verwandter Systeme" (On Formally Undecidable Sentences of the *Principia Mathematica* and Systems), in which he presented his famous incompleteness theorem. Gödel showed that the project of the *Principia Mathematica,* and all similar projects, are doomed to failure, because it is impossible in principle to set up a logically consistent system of propositions that does not imply some propositions that the system is unable either to prove or disprove; that is, the system can be either consistent or complete, but not both. Whitehead himself had anticipated the trouble in *Process and Reality,* saying that "even in mathematics the statement of the ultimate logical principles is beset with difficulties, as yet insuperable." *Principia Mathematica* nonetheless remains a monument of exact thought and holds an unquestioned place in the development of symbolic logic.

After *Process and Reality,* Whitehead wrote two more important books: *Adventures of Ideas* (1933) and *Modes of Thought: Six Lectures Delivered in Wellesley College, Massachusetts, and Two Lectures in the University of Chicago* (1938). The first is an exploration of the role of metaphysical ideas in the history of European civilization; Whitehead undertakes to show that civilization advances by balancing the penetrating new idea against the stability of tradition. In this process "The pure conservative is fighting against the essence of the universe." The second book is "a free examination of some ultimate notions, as they occur naturally in daily life." One chapter, "Nature and Life," which had been published as an independent book in 1934, provides an explanation of the philosophy of organism in nontechnical terms.

Whitehead gave his last lecture at Harvard on 8 May 1936. He continued to accept invitations to lecture and deliver addresses in the years that followed his retirement, which gave him and Evelyn an opportunity to travel widely in the United States. He received honorary degrees from Harvard, Yale, McGill, Wisconsin, Manchester, and St. Andrews Universities and the Butler Medal from Columbia University. He had been elected to the British Academy in 1931 and was awarded the Order of Merit—one of the highest honors the British Crown can bestow on an individual for personal achievement—in 1945. He died on 30 December 1947.

Whitehead came to the profession of philosophy relatively late, after spending most of his career working on problems in mathematics, symbolic logic, and mathematical physics. This situation had advantages and disadvantages. A discipline is often enhanced by cross-fertilization, and the ideas Whitehead contributed came from someone who had not been rigidly trained in a particular school of philosophy and was not so absorbed in a specific set of abstractions that they formed an intellectual straitjacket. His command of the technical disciplines of logic and mathematics provided a rigorous basis on which to construct a comprehensive theory of reality, and as a creative thinker he was able to produce strikingly original insights—especially in *Process and Reality*. But some professional philosophers fault Whitehead for not providing arguments in the usual manner, which consists of taking up the positions of others and offering refutations of them. Instead, his style is almost purely expository, as if he were elucidating the position of another philosopher or deducing theorems from axioms and definitions. When Whitehead does deal with figures from the history of philosophy, he draws liberally from their ideas so as to show analogies with his own position. Thus, he often says that an idea of his approximates the position of Plato, Aristotle, Locke, George Berkeley, James, Bergson, or F. H. Bradley. His characterizations of those positions are not always historically accurate; it often seems that Whitehead is reading too much into the doctrines of other thinkers and thereby making their affinity with his own thought closer than it actually is. It is likely that he was influenced not so much by earlier philosophers as by ideas in the fields he knew best—mathematics, physics, and biology.

An obvious omission in Whitehead's system is moral philosophy. At no point did he attempt to work out an ethical theory, and he does not discuss moral problems in detail in any of his works. When Whitehead does deal with values, it is always in the context of a metaphysical theory. Truth, beauty, and goodness are ideals toward which persons should strive; but whether they are manifest in human experience or not, they are always present in the experience of God, who provides the lure for their realization.

In the twentieth century, philosophy was dominated by the analytical approach in Britain and the United States and by existentialism and phenomenology on the Continent. Whitehead's thought appealed to many who were unswayed by the dominant trends. Yet, some of those who have been most influenced by Whitehead have fostered the notion that he was a sort of guru and have thereby inadvertently contributed to his isolation from the mainstream. Finally, the prominent place of theology in his thought has made it all the more difficult for the predominantly secular modern philosophic milieu to appreciate the rest of his ideas. As

the British philosopher Anthony Quinton put it in "The Right Stuff," his 5 December 1985 review of Lowe's biography, "Outside the sequestered province of the cult, Whitehead is regarded with a measure of baffled reverence, mingled with suspicion." Alfred North Whitehead attempted to produce a comprehensive metaphysics when the current fashion dictated that it was impossible to do so; but he was also respected for his command of the techniques of logic and mathematics. The problem is that he wanted to say in highly precise terms that reality is ultimately vague.

Bibliographies:

Gene Reeves and David Ray Griffin, "A Bibliography of Secondary Literature on Alfred North Whitehead," *Process Studies,* 1 (Winter 1971), pp. 2–77;

Barry Woodbridge, *Alfred North Whitehead: A Primary-Secondary Bibliography* (Bowling Green, Ohio: Philosophy Documentation Center, 1977).

Biography:

Victor Lowe, *Alfred North Whitehead: The Man and His Work,* 2 volumes, volume 2 edited by J. B. Schneewind (Baltimore: Johns Hopkins University Press, 1985, 1990).

References:

William Christian, *An Interpretation of Whitehead's Metaphysics* (New Haven: Yale University Press, 1959);

John B. Cobb Jr., *A Christian Natural Theology, Based on the Thought of Alfred North Whitehead* (Philadelphia: Westminster Press, 1965);

Cobb and David Ray Griffin, *Process Theology: An Introductory Exposition* (Philadelphia: Westminster Press, 1976);

Murray Code, *Order and Organism: Steps to a Whiteheadian Philosophy of Mathematics and the Natural Sciences* (Albany: State University of New York Press, 1984);

C. R. Eisendrath, *The Unifying Moment: The Psychological Philosophy of William James and Alfred North Whitehead* (Cambridge, Mass.: Harvard University Press, 1971);

Dorothy Emmet, *Whitehead's Philosophy of Organism* (London: Macmillan, 1932);

Lewis S. Ford, *The Emergence of Whitehead's Metaphysics* (Albany: State University of New York Press, 1984);

Ford and George L. Kline, eds., *Explorations in Whitehead's Philosophy* (New York: Fordham University Press, 1983);

Kurt Gödel, "Über formal unentscheidbare Sätze der *Principia Mathematica* und verwandter Systeme,"

Monatshefte für Mathematik und Physik, 37 (1931): 349–360;

David Ray Griffin, *God, Power and Evil: A Process Theodicy* (Philadelphia: Westminster Press, 1976);

David L. Hall, *The Civilization of Experience: A Whiteheadian Theory of Culture* (New York: Fordham University Press, 1973);

Charles Hartshorne, *Whitehead's Philosophy: Selected Essays, 1935–1970* (Lincoln: University of Nebraska Press, 1972);

Thomas E. Hosinski, *Stubborn Fact and Creative Advance: An Introduction to the Metaphysics of Alfred North Whitehead* (Lanham, Md.: Rowman & Littlefield, 1993);

Judith A. Jones, *Intensity: An Essay in Whiteheadian Ontology* (Nashville: Vanderbilt University Press, 1998);

Kline, ed., *Alfred North Whitehead: Essays on His Philosophy* (Englewood Cliffs, N.J.: Prentice-Hall, 1963);

John W. Lango, *Whitehead's Ontology* (Albany: State University of New York Press, 1972);

Nathaniel Lawrence, *Whitehead's Philosophical Development* (Berkeley: University of California Press, 1956);

Ivor Leclerc, *Whitehead's Metaphysics* (London: Allen & Unwin, 1958);

Leclerc, ed., *The Relevance of Whitehead* (New York: Macmillan, 1961);

Victor Lowe, *Understanding Whitehead* (Baltimore: Johns Hopkins University Press, 1962);

George R. Lucas Jr., *The Rehabilitation of Whitehead* (Albany: State University of New York Press, 1989);

Wolfe Mays, *The Philosophy of Whitehead* (London: Allen & Unwin, 1959);

Leemon B. McHenry, *Whitehead and Bradley: A Comparative Analysis* (Albany: State University of New York Press, 1992);

Jorge Luis Nobo, *Whitehead's Metaphysics of Extension and Solidarity* (Albany: State University of New York Press, 1986);

Robert M. Palter, *Whitehead's Philosophy of Science* (Chicago: University of Chicago Press, 1960);

Ann L. Plamondon, *Whitehead's Organic Philosophy of Science* (Albany: State University of New York Press, 1979);

Lucien Price, *Dialogues of Alfred North Whitehead* (Boston: Little, Brown, 1954);

W. V. Quine, *The Time of My Life: An Autobiography* (Cambridge, Mass.: MIT Press, 1985);

Nicholas Rescher, *Process Metaphysics* (Albany: State University of New York Press, 1996);

Paul Arthur Schilpp, ed., *The Philosophy of Alfred North Whitehead,* The Library of Living Philosophers, volume 3 (Evanston, Ill.: Northwestern University Press, 1941);

Paul F. Schmidt, *Perception and Cosmology in Whitehead's Philosophy* (New Brunswick, N.J.: Rutgers University Press, 1967);

Donald W. Sherburne, *A Whiteheadian Aesthetic* (New Haven: Yale University Press, 1961);

Sherburne, ed., *A Key to Whitehead's* Process and Reality (New York: Macmillan, 1966);

Santiago Sia, *God in Process Thought* (Dordrecht, Netherlands: Nijhoff, 1985);

Barry Whitney, *Evil and the Process God* (New York: Edwin Mellen Press, 1985);

Forrest Wood, *Whiteheadian Thought as the Basis for a Philosophy of Religion* (Lanham, Md.: University Press of America, 1986).

Papers:

The Alfred North Whitehead Collection in the Milton S. Eisenhower Library at Johns Hopkins University in Baltimore is the major repository of Whitehead's documents, books, and letters. Other important collections are at the Center for Process Studies in Claremont, California; the Bertrand Russell Archives at McMaster University in Hamilton, Ontario; and the Documentation Center on Process Thought at the Katholieke Universitiet Leuven in Louvain, Belgium.

Ludwig Wittgenstein

(26 April 1889 – 29 April 1951)

Robert Deans
University of East Anglia

and

Rupert Read
University of East Anglia

BOOKS: *Tractatus Logico-Philosophicus,* translated by C. K. Ogden and Frank Ramsey, introduction by Bertrand Russell (London: Kegan Paul, Trench, Trübner, 1922; New York: Harcourt, Brace, 1922);

Wörterbuch für Volksschulen (Vienna: Hölder-Pichler-Tempsky, 1926);

Philosophical Investigations, translated by G. E. M. Anscombe (Oxford: Blackwell, 1953; New York: Macmillan, 1953);

Remarks on the Foundations of Mathematics, edited by Anscombe, Georg Henrik von Wright, and Rush Rhees, translated by Anscombe (Oxford: Blackwell, 1956; New York: Macmillan, 1956);

Preliminary Studies for the "Philosophical Investigations," Generally Known as The Blue and Brown Books (Oxford: Blackwell, 1958; New York: Harper, 1958);

Notebooks, 1914–1916, edited by von Wright and Anscombe, translated by Anscombe (New York: Harper, 1961; Oxford: Blackwell, 1961);

Lectures and Conversations on Aesthetics, Psychology and Religious Belief, compiled from notes taken by Rhees, Yorick Smythies, and James Taylor, edited by Cyril Barrett (Oxford: Blackwell, 1966; Berkeley: University of California Press, 1966);

Zettel, edited by Anscombe and von Wright, translated by Anscombe (Oxford: Blackwell, 1967; Berkeley: University of California Press, 1967);

On Certainty, edited by Anscombe and von Wright, translated by Anscombe and Denis Paul (Oxford: Blackwell, 1969; New York: Harper, 1969);

Prototractatus: An Early Version of Tractatus Logico-Philosophicus, edited by von Wright, B. F. McGuinness, and T. Nyberg, translated by McGuinness and D. F. Pears (London: Routledge

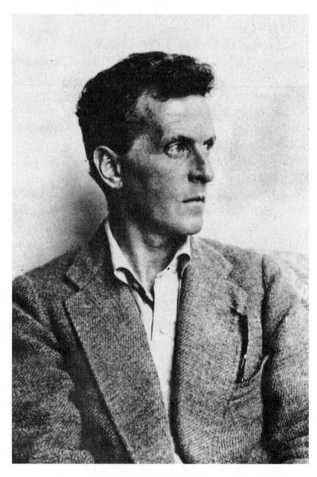

Ludwig Wittgenstein

& Kegan Paul, 1971; Ithaca, N.Y.: Cornell University Press, 1971);

Philosophical Grammar, edited by Rhees, translated by Anthony Kenny (Oxford: Blackwell, 1974; Berkeley: University of California Press, 1974);

Philosophical Remarks, edited by Rhees, translated by Raymond Hargreaves and Roger White (Oxford: Blackwell, 1975; Chicago: University of Chicago Press, 1975);

Wittgenstein's Lectures on the Foundations of Mathematics, Cambridge, 1939: From the Notes of R. G. Bosanquet, Norman Malcolm, Rush Rhees and Yorick Smythies, edited by Cora Diamond (Hassocks, U.K.: Harvester Press, 1976; Ithaca, N.Y.: Cornell University Press, 1976);

Remarks on Colour, edited by Anscombe, translated by Linda L. McAlister and Margaret Schättle (Oxford: Blackwell, 1977; Berkeley: University of California Press, 1977);

Wittgenstein's Lectures, Cambridge, 1932–1935: From the Notes of Alice Ambrose and Margaret Macdonald, edited by Alice Ambrose (Oxford: Blackwell, 1979; Totowa, N.J.: Rowman & Littlefield, 1979);

Culture and Value, edited by von Wright and Heikki Nyman, translated by Peter Winch (Oxford & Cambridge, Mass.: Blackwell, 1980);

Wittgenstein's Lectures, Cambridge, 1930–1932: From the Notes of John King and Desmond Lee, edited by Desmond Lee (Totowa, N.J.: Rowman & Littlefield, 1980; Oxford: Blackwell, 1980);

Remarks on the Philosophy of Psychology, 2 volumes, edited by Anscombe and von Wright, translated by Anscombe (Chicago: University of Chicago Press, 1980; Oxford: Blackwell, 1980);

Last Writings on the Philosophy of Psychology, 2 volumes, edited by von Wright and Nyman, translated by C. G. Luckhardt and Maximilian A. E. Aue (Chicago: University of Chicago Press, 1982, 1992; Oxford: Blackwell, 1982, 1992)–comprises volume 1, *Preliminary Studies for Part II of "Philosophical Investigations"* (1982), and volume 2, *The Inner and the Outer* (1992);

Wittgenstein's Lectures on Philosophical Psychology, 1946–47, edited by P. T. Geach (Chicago: University of Chicago Press, 1988; Brighton, U.K.: Harvester, 1988);

Philosophical Occasions, 1912–1951, edited by James Klagge and Alfred Nordmann (Cambridge & Indianapolis: Hackett, 1993);

Ludwig Wittgenstein: Wiener Ausgabe, 9 volumes published, edited by Michael Nedo (Vienna & New York: Springer, 1993–);

Wittgenstein's "Nachlass": The Bergen Electronic Edition, CD-ROM, 4 volumes (Oxford & New York: Oxford University Press, 1998–2001).

Editions: *Tractatus Logico-Philosophicus,* translated by D. F. Pears and B. F. McGuinness (New York: Humanities Press, 1961; London: Routledge & Kegan Paul, 1961);

Wörterbuch für Volksschulen, edited by Adolf Hübner-Werner and Elisabeth Leinfellner (Vienna: Hölder-Pichler-Tempsky, 1977).

Ludwig Wittgenstein is regarded as one of the leading analytic philosophers of the twentieth century. He is usually credited with instigating not one revolution in philosophical method but two. Until recently it was common to divide his work into two distinct periods. According to this division, the early period culminated in the publication in 1921 of the *Tractatus Logico-Philosophicus,* which he completed during active service in World War I, while the later period culminated in the 1953 publication of the *Philosophical Investigations,* which he composed between 1936 and 1948. Each greatly influenced the subsequent direction of analytic philosophy. The primary influence of the *Tractatus Logico-Philosophicus* was initially on the development of logical positivism in Europe in the 1920s and 1930s and, following the immigration of many of the principal members of the Vienna Circle to the United States, on the development of pragmatism. Its influence in the United Kingdom was confined in the interwar years to a small group of philosophers at the University of Cambridge, where Wittgenstein had studied prior to the outbreak of World War I. The main influence of the *Philosophical Investigations* in the 1950s and 1960s was initially on the development of ordinary-language philosophy, which was centered at the University of Oxford but which extended throughout the English-speaking world.

Critics generally agree that the philosophy of the "later Wittgenstein" is more relevant to modern discussions of language, mind, and society than that of the "early Wittgenstein." Philosophers who describe their own work as being influenced by him typically want to use the insights and methods they find in the later work. Those who do not describe themselves as Wittgensteinians also accept the superiority of the later work, even if they do not agree with it. But the sharp division of his work into these two periods has proved contentious.

Ludwig Josef Johann Wittgenstein was born on 26 April 1889 into one of the wealthiest families in the Austro-Hungarian Empire. The family was of Jewish descent; following the Napoleonic decree of 1808, which required Jews to use a Gentile surname, Wittgenstein's paternal great-grandfather, Moses Maier, had adopted the family name Wittgenstein. Ludwig Wittgenstein's grandfather, Herman Christian Wittgenstein, converted to Protestantism just before his marriage in 1839. Wittgenstein's father, Karl, was born in Gohlis, a suburb of Leipzig, in 1847; in 1850 the family moved to Austria, where Herman Christian built a highly profitable real-estate business. The children followed their

Wittgenstein in 1891

father's advice and married into the ranks of the Viennese Protestant establishment.

After running away from home several times, as far away as New York, Karl was allowed to pursue a career in engineering instead of following his brothers into real-estate management. He made a fortune in the iron and steel industry. In 1873 he married Leopoldine Kalmus, a Catholic; they had eight children: Hermine, Hans, Kurt, Rudolf, Margarete, Helene, Paul, and Ludwig. The children were baptized Catholic and raised as members of the high bourgeoisie; Karl had declined to become part of the aristocracy by adding "von" to his name. Nonetheless, his immense wealth enabled the family to live in the style of the aristocracy. Their home in the Alleegasse in Vienna was palatial; they also owned a large country estate, the Hochreit, where they spent the summers. Karl and Leopoldine both had a passion and talent for music; Leopoldine was an exceptionally gifted pianist. The children were similarly creatively endowed. After his retirement in 1898, Karl became a patron of the arts. The Wittgensteins were thus at the center of Viennese social, cultural, and intellectual life. Many famous musicians and artists of the day were regular visitors at their home.

Karl Wittgenstein decided that his sons should enter his business empire; they were not to be sent to school, where they might acquire bad habits, but were to be educated privately. Thus, Ludwig Wittgenstein was educated at home by tutors, according to a strict curriculum devised by his father, until he was fourteen.

Only the oldest brother, Kurt, the least gifted of the family, actually followed his father's plan, eventually becoming a company director. Hans might have become a great composer or concert musician; unable to pursue his own choice of career, he, like his father before him, ran away to New York. In 1902 he disappeared from a boat in Chesapeake Bay. Following his presumed suicide, the strict paternal regime was relaxed. Paul and Ludwig were sent to a state school and allowed to pursue their own futures. Ludwig was enrolled at the Staatsoberrealschule in Linz, Upper Austria, in 1903. The school was chosen because it specialized in modern subjects; thus, Wittgenstein received a less classical but more practical education than he might have elsewhere. The relaxation of their father's rules enjoyed by Ludwig and Paul, however, came too late for Rudolf: he, like Kurt, had rebelled against his father's wishes, but he had gone to Berlin to seek a career in the theater. In 1904 he killed himself by taking cyanide.

At Linz, Wittgenstein demonstrated an aptitude for mechanics and theoretical physics and was interested in the work of the physicist Heinrich Hertz. He expressed a desire to study physics in Vienna under Ludwig Boltzmann, who was an authority on Hertz. Boltzmann, however, committed suicide in 1906, the same year Wittgenstein graduated from the Staatsoberrealschule.

With his father's encouragement, Wittgenstein decided to become an engineer. In October 1906 he enrolled as a student of mechanical engineering at the Technische Hochschule in Berlin. There he took a particular interest in flying objects, especially hot-air balloons. He remained at the Technische Hochschule until the spring of 1908. Then, on his father's advice, he went to England to pursue theoretical and applied studies in aeronautics at the College of Technology in Manchester. He spent the summer term at the Kite Flying Upper Atmosphere Station in Glossop, conducting experiments on the stabilization and steering of flying objects. The experiments convinced him of the need for some kind of aeronautical engine, and he conceived the idea of using reaction jets on top of a propeller blade. This notion led him to investigate the design of propellers, which required a thorough grasp of mathematical principles. He soon became fascinated by pure mathematics, and his inquiry into the foundations of mathematics led him to works on philosophical logic by Gottlob Frege and Bertrand Russell. In 1911 Wittgenstein visited Frege in Jena; Frege advised him to study the "new logic" under Russell at the University of Cambridge.

At the beginning of 1912 Wittgenstein was admitted to Trinity College of Cambridge and registered in the university, first as an undergraduate and later as an "advanced student." At the end of the first term he was still unsure whether he wanted to devote his life to engineering or to philosophy. He went to Russell for advice; Russell asked him to write a vacation essay, on the basis of which Russell urged him to give up aeronautics and devote himself to logic. Wittgenstein studied at Cambridge for the three terms of 1912 and the first two terms of 1913, quickly establishing himself as Russell's equal and collaborating with Russell on logical problems.

The decade before World War I was a period of exceptional intellectual activity at Cambridge. It was the era of Russell, G. E. Moore, and Alfred North Whitehead. Among Wittgenstein's acquaintances at Cambridge were the mathematician G. H. Hardy, the logician W. E. Johnston, and the economist John Maynard Keynes.

Wittgenstein's eccentricity and intensity of character were well known among his peers at Cambridge. In the fall of 1913 he built a hut in a remote part of Norway where he could study uninterrupted. There he wrote two short but seminal pieces, "Notes on Logic" in 1913 and "Notes Dictated to Moore" in 1914. The pieces are of great significance in tracing the development of Wittgenstein's thinking, particularly how it was diverging from Russell's. Both are included as appendices to Wittgenstein's *Notebooks, 1914–1916,* published posthumously in 1961.

Wittgenstein saw active service in World War I on the eastern and southern fronts and was decorated several times for bravery, becoming a lieutenant in 1918. His brother Kurt committed suicide the same year, after troops under his command refused to obey his orders. In October 1918, on the collapse of the Austro-Hungarian army, Wittgenstein was taken prisoner by the Italians. He spent most of his captivity near Monte Cassino, Italy.

When he was captured, Wittgenstein had in his rucksack the manuscript for a book titled *Logisch-philosophische Abhandlung;* it is better known by the Latin title suggested by Moore for its 1922 English translation, *Tractatus Logico-Philosophicus,* which is generally shortened to *Tractatus.* Wittgenstein's surviving notebooks from the war period include entries from 22 August 1914 to 10 January 1917. They show Wittgenstein's preoccupation with problems of logic and representation and a growing concern with problems of

Wittgenstein at age nine

ethics, the will, solipsism, and the meaning of life. In the entries Wittgenstein is clearly trying to see how the two sets of problems might be related. It is unfortunate that his later notebooks have not survived, for these early journal entries have been used to suggest an interpretation of how Wittgenstein resolved these matters that may not be a reliable guide to how the *Tractatus* is intended to be read.

Grounds for this concern are to be found in an earlier version of the *Tractatus* that has survived; known as the *Prototractatus,* it dates to the summer of 1918 and was published in 1971. It shows the fluidity of Wittgenstein's thinking at this time: he was still incorporating new material into the text and rearranging sections. These changes suggest a development in Wittgenstein's thinking that the earlier notebooks fail to capture. What had been presented in the early journal entries as two sets of related problems concerning the relationship of language to the objectivity of facts and subjectivity of values seem, by the time the *Tractatus* reached its final form, to have ceased to be regarded as problems requiring solution at all.

Released in August 1919, Wittgenstein returned to Vienna. His first act was to dispose of the fortune he

Wittgenstein's sister Margarete; painting by Gustav Klimt, 1905 (from Ray Monk, Ludwig Wittgenstein: The Duty of Genius, *1990)*

had inherited on his father's death in 1913; he gave it all to his surviving brothers and sisters.

In the *Tractatus* Wittgenstein remarks that he has solved the problems of philosophy and that nothing remains to be said on the matter. Therefore, in September 1919 he decided to become a primary schoolteacher and enrolled at the Teachers Training Institute in Vienna. He was also trying to find a publisher for the *Tractatus,* but without success. In December 1919 he met with Russell at The Hague to discuss the publi-

cation of the work. Russell wrote an introduction for it, which Wittgenstein thought seriously misrepresented his ideas. Continuing to encounter difficulties in finding a publisher, Wittgenstein finally left the publication of the *Tractatus* to Russell. In 1920 Wittgenstein became a schoolteacher in Trattenbach, Austria. The book was published in German in the journal *Annalen der Naturphilosophie,* edited by Wilhelm Ostwald, in 1921 and in English translation, with parallel German text and Russell's introduction, in 1922. That year Wittgenstein moved to a school in Puchberg-am-Schneeberg, Austria.

While working as a village schoolteacher, Wittgenstein was frequently visited by the logician and mathematician Frank P. Ramsey, who had assisted C. K. Ogden in the translation of the *Tractatus.* Ramsey kept Wittgenstein in touch with philosophical developments at Cambridge. Wittgenstein was also contacted in 1924 by Moritz Schlick, who wrote for permission to visit him in Puchberg with a group of students and colleagues; this discussion group later developed into the Vienna Circle. By the time Schlick's letter reached Wittgenstein, however, he was no longer living in Puchberg but had begun teaching in Otterthal, Austria.

In Otterthal, Wittgenstein wrote *Wörterbuch für Volksschulen* (Dictionary for Elementary Schools), which was intended to help the pupils recognize the confusion caused by various grammatical uses of words. It was published in 1926. That year Wittgenstein came into conflict with the education authorities after some parents complained about the harshness of his teaching methods. Although he was cleared of any wrongdoing, he decided to give up teaching. During the spring and summer of 1926 he worked as an undergardener in the monastery of the Brothers of Mercy in the village of Hutteldorf, near Vienna. For the next two years he collaborated with the architect Paul Englemann in designing a house for his sister Margarete.

In April 1926 Schlick had tried to visit Wittgenstein in Otterthal, unaware that he had resigned his teaching post and left the city. Only in February of the following year did Wittgenstein, at Margarete's urging, finally meet with Schlick. Soon afterward he was introduced to other members of the Vienna Circle. He continued to meet with the group until the end of 1928 to discuss the *Tractatus,* which was highly influential among logical positivists such as the members of the Vienna Circle. Wittgenstein, however, thought that they did not understand his work, and they thought it was too metaphysical.

In March 1928 Wittgenstein was persuaded by two members of the Vienna Circle, Friedrich Waismann and Herbert Feigl, to attend a lecture by the Dutch mathematician L. E. J. Brouwer on the subject of mathematics, science, and language. Brouwer's "intu-itionism" aroused Wittgenstein's indignation. Work on his sister's house was completed in the fall, and Wittgenstein decided to take a vacation in England; for health reasons, the trip was postponed until January 1929. The visit resulted in Wittgenstein's returning to Cambridge to study philosophy. He submitted the *Tractatus* as his Ph.D. dissertation and became a fellow of Trinity College in 1930.

Much of this period was occupied by Wittgenstein actively and rapidly considering possible alterations to the *Tractatus* "system." He tried treating the *Tractatus* at first as if it were the kind of book that his readers—especially the logical positivists—had said it was and seeing how it could be corrected if viewed on that basis. For instance, he experimented with "verificationist" views a good deal.

In the early 1930s Wittgenstein dictated—unusually for him, in English—the notes that became known as the Blue and Brown Books because of the color of the covers of the notebooks in which Wittgenstein's comments were recorded. The Blue Book is particularly important, because Wittgenstein circulated it among some of his students. The Brown Book is the first of Wittgenstein's works clearly to anticipate the opening of the major work of the later part of his career, the *Philosophical Investigations*. Both books are much more ordinary in their prose style than the *Philosophical Investigations*.

After toying with various formats for his writings, at the end of the 1930s Wittgenstein embarked on writing the *Philosophical Investigations*, composing sparse and yet elaborately intertwining sets of meandering remarks that do not respect traditional philosophical subject-matter boundaries. In 1939 he was appointed professor of philosophy at Cambridge.

Wittgenstein considered World War II an inappropriate time to work publicly in philosophy; instead, he served in various parts of England as a medical orderly. He also worked in Newcastle as a technician for the Medical Research Council's Clinical Research Unit, which was engaged in defining clinically the condition known as "wound shock." Meanwhile, he continued to write the *Philosophical Investigations*. In the preface to the work, written in 1945, Wittgenstein says that he is making his remarks public "with doubtful feelings. It is not impossible that it should fall to the lot of this work, in its poverty and in the darkness of this time, to bring light into one brain or another—but, of course, it is not likely."

The years 1945 to 1947 were the only period during which Wittgenstein served actively as professor of philosophy at Cambridge. He found the intellectual environment there "poisonous" and destructive of the possibility of doing good honest work. The contents of most of his lectures during this period were recorded and have been published. After his retirement in 1947, Wittgenstein spent most of his time in Ireland reworking the *Philosophical Investigations*.

At the invitation of his former student Norman Malcolm, Wittgenstein traveled to the United States in July 1949. He stayed with Malcolm in Ithaca, New York, and met regularly with Malcolm and other philosophers at Cornell University. Soon after the beginning of the autumn term Wittgenstein fell ill. He returned to England in October and was diagnosed with prostate cancer in November. He traveled to Vienna in December and returned to London in March 1950. At the beginning of April he went to stay with another former student, Georg Henrik von Wright, who had succeeded him as professor of philosophy at Cambridge. At the end of April he went to stay with yet another former pupil, G. E. M. Anscombe, in Oxford. In October he went to Norway for a vacation. In January 1951 he returned to Cambridge and moved in with his doctor, as he needed constant medical attention. He died on 29 April, working almost until his final day principally on the notes that were published in 1969 as *On Certainty*. Apart from the *Tractatus* and a couple of minor short pieces, all of Wittgenstein's works were published posthumously.

After several decades of relative unanimity concerning the interpretation of Wittgenstein's work, in 2002 it is no longer possible to speak of a settled reading. The consensus that previously existed did have its differences, but they were contained within an agreed-on framework as to how to approach his work. This consensus is referred to as the "standard interpretation" of Wittgenstein. The core of the standard interpretation is that in his later work Wittgenstein explicitly rejects beliefs he held in his early work. This rejection is usually expressed in terms of a movement away from a "dogmatic" conception of philosophy in the *Tractatus* toward a "therapeutic" conception in the *Philosophical Investigations*. A dogmatic conception is characterized by the promulgation of a doctrine, while a therapeutic conception is characterized by the demonstration of a method. The standard interpretation maintains that the movement from the dogmatic to the therapeutic is consistent with Wittgenstein's having substantive philosophical commitments, albeit fundamentally different ones, in both works.

Recently, a revisionist challenge to the standard interpretation has emerged. The revisionist interpretation, which has been designated "resolutism," maintains that in the *Tractatus* Wittgenstein was already committed to the rejection of dogmatic philosophy and the advocacy of therapeutic philosophy; what primarily dis-

Wittgenstein circa 1907

therapeutic philosophy. The revisionist interpretation does not just claim that the *Tractatus* is a work of therapeutic philosophy in the same way that the standard interpretation regards the *Philosophical Investigations* to be a work of therapeutic philosophy; it also claims that in both works Wittgenstein had a conception of therapeutic philosophy that is radically different from the one that is attributed to him by the standard interpretation. Consequently, the revisionist interpretation calls for a complete reassessment of Wittgenstein's entire corpus, since if the *Tractatus* has been misunderstood by the standard interpretation, then, because of the relationship between the two works, the standard interpretation has also misunderstood the comparisons and contrasts that can properly be made between the *Tractatus* and the *Philosophical Investigations*.

The standard interpretation holds that both the "early Wittgenstein" and the "later Wittgenstein" are preoccupied with philosophical problems concerning the foundations of language, such as how words get their meanings and how propositions get their sense; how the limits of sense-bearing discourse are to be determined; and how, in particular cases, it is to be shown that these limits have been transgressed. Central to the standard interpretation, however, is the thesis that the solutions Wittgenstein gives to these problems in the *Tractatus* are explicitly rejected in the *Philosophical Investigations* and diametrically opposed by the answers he gives to them in the later work.

The standard interpretation of the *Tractatus* does not consist of a single reading. All of the readings, however, accept the possibility of a perspective from which one could explain and describe how words and propositions are able to represent objects and states of affairs in the world. How this logical possibility is conceived distinguishes the two principal variants of the standard interpretation, known in the literature as "positivism" and "ineffabilism." The positivist reading influenced the initial reception of the *Tractatus;* it has given way to the ineffabilist reading, which now predominates among advocates of the standard interpretation and was the orthodox reading until challenged by the recent revisionist interpretation. Positivism regards the *Tractatus* as having been motivated by a form of "antirealism": that is, he is endorsing the view that the world contains nothing more than can be known through scientific investigation and that nothing can be said about the nature of any reality that may lie beyond this limit. The only perspective on reality that is available is from within language itself; all one can do to give a true account of how language is connected to the world is to analyze the logical syntax and linguistic conventions that constitute language.

tinguishes that work from the *Philosophical Investigations* is the technique that Wittgenstein uses to achieve his purpose. Furthermore, the revisionist interpretation claims that Wittgenstein's intention in both works is to express no philosophical commitments whatsoever. The research being conducted under the revisionist interpretation has been focused on reevaluating the method and aim of the *Tractatus* and their relationship to the method and aim of the *Philosophical Investigations*.

Wittgenstein says in the preface to the *Philosophical Investigations* that his new thoughts in that work can only be seen in the right light "by contrast with and against the background of my old way of thinking." If the revisionist interpretation is correct in claiming that by the time Wittgenstein wrote the *Tractatus* he already had a fundamentally therapeutic conception of philosophy, then this comment raises not only the issue of the relationship between the two works but also, and more important, the issue of what Wittgenstein means by

Ineffabilism, on the other hand, regards the *Tractatus* as motivated by a form of realism: that is, the view that the world does contain more than can be known through scientific investigation and that something can be shown, rather than said, about the reality that lies beyond this limit. Ineffabilists do not believe that Wittgenstein thinks that an analysis of the logical syntax and linguistic conventions constitutive of language is all there is to giving a true account of how language is connected to the world. They maintain that Wittgenstein thought that it is possible to get outside of language; while they acknowledge that language cannot be used self-referentially to state how the world must necessarily be, they hold that the use of language shows something about the nature of this necessity. Both readings, therefore, agree that in the *Tractatus* Wittgenstein was engaged in what he himself later described as "dogmatic philosophy."

In contrast to the "scientism" of positivism and the "mysticism" of ineffabilism, the revisionist interpretation evokes proposition 6.54 of the *Tractatus,* in which Wittgenstein says that his propositions are nonsensical and that the reader must use them as a ladder to climb up beyond them and then throw away the ladder. Revisionists do not deny that the *Tractatus* can be read as the positivists and ineffabilists do, but they regard these readings as stages in an unfolding dialectic—as, metaphorically, rungs of a ladder that is to be climbed and then thrown away—and they are committed to seeing the process through to its end. In contrast to the standard interpretation, revisionism does not regard the *Tractatus* as motivated by either antirealism or realism. It does not accept that it is possible to imagine a perspective from which one can survey how language is connected to the world, either from an internal or an external point of view. Revisionists believe that both positivists and ineffabilists commit the fallacy of thinking that if something can be said, it must be imaginable. Revisionism suggests that Wittgenstein's aim in the *Tractatus* is that the reader come to realize that not everything that can be said is imaginable—that is, that apparently sense-bearing propositions about how language is or is not connected to the world are nonsense. It regards the possibilities of either an internal or an external point of view on how language connects to the world as equally unintelligible and as symptomatic of the philosophical illness that the *Tractatus* itself diagnosed and attempted to cure.

The standard and the revisionist interpretations agree that the *Tractatus* has a "Frame," which consists of what the text says about itself, and a "Body," which consists of what it says about other matters. Whether a section belongs to the Frame is determined by its function in the text, not its location; thus, while the preface

and the closing propositions 6.53 to 7 undoubtedly constitute a major part of the Frame, other sections in the text are also included.

Wittgenstein begins the preface:

> This book will perhaps only be understood by those who have themselves already thought the thoughts which are expressed in it—or similar thoughts. It is therefore not a textbook. Its object would be attained if it afforded pleasure to one who read it with understanding.

Wittgenstein is saying that the *Tractatus* will only be understood by those who have been attracted to or perplexed by the philosophical problems it addresses. If they do understand it, they will delight in seeing how these problems are not problems, after all. It is for this reason that he says that the *Tractatus* is not a textbook. As the original German word "*Lehrbuch,*" from the verb *lehren* (to teach) makes clear, a textbook is intended to teach something. In contrast, the purpose of the *Tractatus* is to give pleasure to someone who recognizes in it the expression of thoughts that he or she has already had.

But the work has the appearance of a textbook. In addition to the preface it consists of seven major propositions, each followed by a series of subordinate propositions designated by the same whole number plus one to four decimals meant to indicate the relative importance and relationship of the respective propositions.

Both the standard and the revisionist interpretations are aware of the tension between what Wittgenstein says the *Tractatus* is and what it appears to be. Upholders of the standard interpretation conclude that Wittgenstein either has failed to carry out his intention or is being duplicitous, for the *Tractatus* betrays its philosophical commitments to antirealism (according to the positivists) or realism (according to the ineffabilists). They claim that despite what Wittgenstein says in the preface, the *Tractatus* gives a philosophical account of the foundations of language—that it is an investigation into how language is able to represent the world and into the limits of sense-bearing discourse. In contrast, revisionists take seriously Wittgenstein's claim that the *Tractatus* is not a textbook and try to read the text with that understanding. This program requires them to make a convincing case that Wittgenstein deliberately used a style of writing in the *Tractatus* that the reader would expect to find in a philosophical treatise in order to make evident that what has been read is not to be regarded as teaching anything.

The preface continues:

> The book deals with the problems of philosophy and shows, as I believe, that the method of formulating these problems rests on the misunderstanding of the

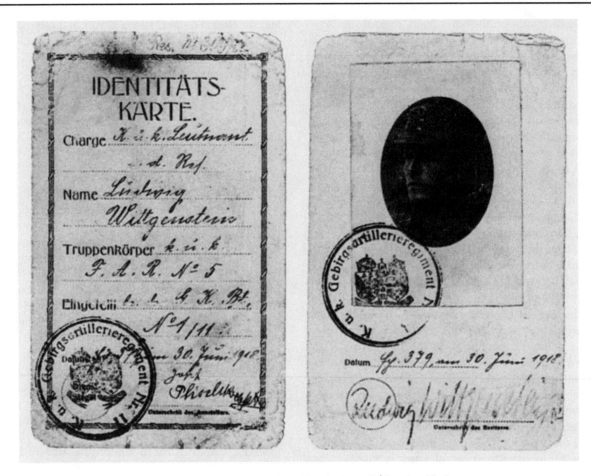

Wittgenstein's World War I military identification card (from Ray Monk,
Ludwig Wittgenstein: The Duty of Genius, *1990)*

logic of our language. Its whole meaning could be summed somewhat as follows: What can be said at all can be said clearly; and whereof one cannot speak thereof one must be silent.

The standard interpretation holds that Wittgenstein provides answers to philosophical problems—answers that can be true or false—and that, therefore, the *Tractatus* is a work of dogmatic philosophy. The revisionist interpretation claims that Wittgenstein shows, instead, that these "problems" are not real problems at all; therefore, the *Tractatus* is a work of therapeutic philosophy.

Both positivists and ineffabilists see an endorsement of their respective positions in Wittgenstein's comment that the "whole meaning" of the *Tractatus* is "somewhat" summarized as "what can be said at all can be said clearly" and "whereof one cannot speak thereof one must be silent." Positivists emphasize the first clause, ineffabilists the second. In contrast, revisionists argue that the literary style of the *Tractatus* is an essential part of how Wittgenstein intends to establish how "misunderstanding of the logic of our language" causes

philosophical problems. That is, the form of the *Tractatus* cannot be dismissed as incidental to the thoughts that it expresses; these thoughts are not expressible in a more conventional way.

Wittgenstein goes on:

The book will, therefore, draw a limit to thinking, or rather—not to thinking, but to the expression of thoughts; for, in order to draw a limit to thinking, we should have to be able to think both sides of this limit (we should therefore have to be able to think what cannot be thought).

According to revisionists, Wittgenstein is here expressing the impossibility of attempting to draw a limit to thought, for to do so both sides of the limit would have to be thinkable—that is, one would have to be able to think what cannot be thought. For a thought to be a thought at all, it must be thinkable; and if a thought is thinkable, it cannot be illogical. In other words, there is no such thing as illogical thought.

The preface continues:

> The limit can, therefore, only be drawn in language
> and what lies on the other side of the limit will be sim-
> ply nonsense.

Since thoughts are expressed in language, an investigation of the limits of thought necessarily becomes an
investigation of the expression of thoughts in language.
In contrast to the impossibility of illogical thought,
Wittgenstein suggests the possibility of a limit being
drawn in language to the expression of thoughts. Thus,
while it is impossible to think illogically, it is possible to
speak nonsense. A limit to the expression of thoughts
will, therefore, separate propositions that make sense
from those that do not. A nonsensical proposition that
means something is just as unintelligible as an illogical
thought that means something. Wittgenstein characterizes all such attempts as "simply nonsense."

At the end of the preface Wittgenstein says:

> If this work has a value it consists in two things.
> First that in it thoughts are expressed, [and] the *truth* of
> the thoughts communicated here seems to me unassail-
> able and definitive. I am, therefore, of the opinion that
> the problems have in essentials been finally solved.
> And if I am not mistaken in this, then the value of this
> work secondly consists in the fact that it shows how lit-
> tle has been done when these problems have been
> solved.

The standard interpretation maintains that the "true
thoughts" that the *Tractatus* expresses constitute a philosophical account of the foundations of language that
solves the problems of philosophy; these true thoughts
are the antirealist or realist assumptions that underlie
the positivist and ineffabilist readings, respectively. In
contrast, those who hold the revisionist interpretation
argue that the true thoughts to which Wittgenstein
refers are that there is no such thing as a philosophical
account of the foundations of language. The standard
interpretation of Wittgenstein's remark that the *Tractatus* shows how little has been done when the problems
of philosophy have been solved is that it is an expression of modesty on his part after the hubris of claiming
that he has solved the problems. The revisionist interpretation is that it is an expression of Wittgenstein's
concern that "the logic of our language" will continue
to give rise to philosophical problems.

The standard and the revisionist interpretations
agree that the *Tractatus* makes an important distinction
between signs and symbols. A sign is perceptible to the
senses; it has external properties that can be investi-
gated independently of any propositional context. A
symbol, by contrast, has internal properties that are

possibilities of occurrence within a propositional context. Signs become symbols by being put to use in language; it is the symbol—the sign in use—that is the
bearer of meaning.

At this point opinions diverge between the two
interpretations, and the difference between them goes
to the heart of how each understands the *Tractatus*. The
upholders of the standard interpretation take as the criteria for making or failing to make sense whether a
proposition consists of meaningful words and, if it does,
whether the words are combined in accordance with
the rules of logical syntax. Revisionists argue that the
standard interpretation has begged the question of what
it is for a word to be meaningful. On the basis of the
sign/symbol distinction, they suggest that two different
kinds of nonsense appear to be possible: "mere" nonsense results when there is a string of signs in which no
symbol can be perceived and that has no discernible
logical syntax; "substantial" nonsense occurs when a
string of signs does symbolize but has a logically flawed
syntax because of a clash in the logical category of its
symbols. This distinction enables revisionists to make a
further distinction between two related conceptions of
nonsense: the "substantial" conception of nonsense,
which holds that there are two logically distinct kinds of
nonsense—substantial nonsense and mere nonsense;
and the "austere" conception of nonsense, which holds
that there is only mere nonsense. Revisionists find
nothing controversial in the first criterion. A proposition, to be a proposition at all, can only consist of meaningful words—although this statement says nothing
about what makes a word meaningful.

Positivists, ineffabilists, and revisionists would
regard as falling under the first criterion strings such as:

(1) "vjtebk hueht oisavw kiwnc jolre ggfxzze
dpoe" (produced by random keystrokes).
(2) "that ashamed proceed might apartment created mean-minded by father summit" (a random
selection of words from Emily Brontë's *Wuthering
Heights* [1847]).
(3) "'Twas brillig, and the slithy toves did gyre
and gimble in the wabe" (the first line of "Jabber-
wocky" from Lewis Carroll's *Through the Looking-
Glass and What Alice Found There* [1871]).

The standard interpretation would regard as falling
under the second criterion strings such as:

(4) "Caesar is a prime number" (an expression
that vexed Frege and Rudolf Carnap).
(5) "There are objects" (an expression that vexed
Wittgenstein).

The standard interpretation sees (4) and (5) as nonsense because they put an item of one logical category
where an item of another logical category belongs: in
(4) a proper name is found where a number is required;

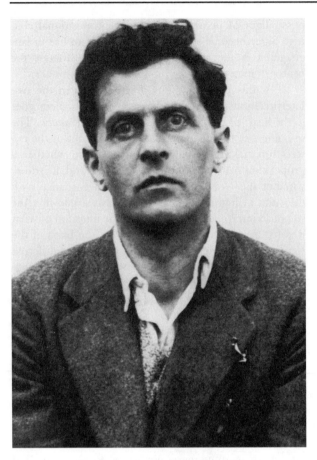

Wittgenstein in 1929, the year he returned to the
University of Cambridge from Austria

in (5) a formal concept is found where a material concept is required. According to the standard interpretation, such strings fail to make sense because they violate the rules of logical syntax. Both positivists and ineffabilists, therefore, have a substantial conception of nonsense. The difference between them is that while both would regard (4) and (5) as meaningless, ineffabilists would say that even though nothing has been "said," something might still be "shown" by the assertion of such a meaningless string.

Positivists and ineffabilists believe that the sense of a proposition depends on how the meanings of its individual words combine. Consequently, they claim that it is possible to distinguish, a priori, a proposition that makes sense from one that does not by using logical analysis to check whether a proposition violates the rules of logical syntax. Positivists and ineffabilists think that they know what the impermissible combinations of symbols in (4) and (5) are trying but failing to say; they, therefore, think that they can find both sides of the limit between sense and nonsense thinkable. Thus, they admit the possibility of illogical thought.

In contrast, revisionism has an austere conception of nonsense. The only kind of nonsense, mere nonsense, results from a string of signs in which no symbol can be perceived and that has no discernible logical syntax. When nonsense results, the problem is not that some signs are incapable of having a meaning or that some signs have been given the wrong meaning; the problem is that no meaning has been given to some of the signs. Revisionists believe that a sense can be given to any combination of signs by finding a proper context, although doing so may require some imagination.

Consequently, revisionists do not think that the sense of a proposition depends on the meanings of the words that compose it. Rather, it is the language user who succeeds or fails in making sense—who succeeds or fails in perceiving the symbol in the sign. Revisionists maintain that the sense of a proposition has to be known before it can be logically segmented into its parts. Hence, the meaning of a word cannot be independent of the proposition in which it is used. It is, therefore, context, not compositionality, that has precedence in determining how a proposition is to be logically segmented. Propositions succeed or fail to make sense through their comparison with other significant propositions of the language. Significant propositions have classifiable similarities and dissimilarities; they share logical form. What determines the logical segmentation of a proposition, according to revisionists, is the inferential relations that obtain between the thought that the proposition attempts to express and other thoughts. The logical segmentation of a proposition into its constitutive expressions cannot be done simply by reference to the syntax of the language to which such expressions belong. Revisionists, therefore, do not think that it is possible, using logical analysis, to distinguish a priori a proposition that makes sense from one that does not.

Faced with such strings as (1) to (5), revisionists can only look to the context of use to see if they share a logical form with other significant propositions of the language and, if such a form can be found, whether a meaning can be given to each of the expressions in the proposition to determine its sense. If it is not possible to discern any inferential relations between the thought that the proposition attempts to express and other thoughts, then the conclusion is not that the proposition is an example of illogical thought but that it is no thought at all. This judgment, however, does not end the matter. The proposition could be reformed so that another attempt to understand it can be made, or it could be withdrawn in recognition that one is attempting to mean something by the words that, in that context of use, they cannot mean. Revisionists argue that what cannot be done is to dismiss the proposition as nonsense solely on the basis of an examination of the string, for to do so is to claim the same kind of privileged a priori insight that is a feature of positivism and ineffabilism.

Misunderstanding "the logic of our language" is, according to Wittgenstein, the cause of philosophical problems. In later sections of the *Tractatus* that are also regarded as part of the Frame he says more about the status of such problems and how they are to be resolved:

[4.003] Most of the propositions and questions to be found in philosophical works are not false but nonsensical. Consequently we cannot give any answer to questions of this kind, but can only point out that they are nonsensical. Most of the propositions and questions of philosophers arise from our failure to understand the logic of our language.

And it is not surprising that the deepest problems are in fact *not* problems at all.

The problems with which philosophical works are concerned are shown not to be problems at all through logical analysis. Just what "logical analysis" amounts to, however, depends on whether the determination of sense and nonsense is understood according to the standard or the revisionist interpretation.

Wittgenstein continues:

[4.112] The object of philosophy is the logical clarification of thoughts.

Philosophy is not a theory but an activity.

A philosophical work consists essentially of elucidations.

The result of philosophy is not a number of "philosophical propositions," but to make propositions clear.

Philosophy should make clear and delimit sharply the thoughts which otherwise are, as it were, opaque and blurred.

At issue between the interpretations of Wittgenstein is how philosophy is to go about this task of achieving clarity. The standard interpretation regards clarity as the outcome of a theoretical inquiry into how language is able to represent the world and into the limits of sense-bearing discourse. In contrast, revisionists think that clarity results from a practical inquiry into whether symbols can be perceived in a particular combination of signs.

The standard interpretation finds in the *Tractatus* a series of arguments concerning the foundations of language. It sees the work as divided into two major parts: the major propositions 1, 2, and 3 and their subordinate propositions, which are regarded as an investigation into metaphysics; and the major propositions 4, 5, 6, and 7 and their subordinate propositions, which are

considered an investigation into "the logic of our language." The first part is held to be the basis for the second: that is, the metaphysics describes the necessary conditions that must obtain if language is to be able to represent the world. The metaphysical part of the book says that the world is all that is the case, that what is the case is facts, that facts are the existence of "states of affairs," and that a state of affairs is a combination of objects; the logical part says that objects are represented by names, that a combination of names is an elementary proposition, that an elementary proposition represents states of affairs, that propositions are truth-functions of elementary propositions, and that language is the totality of all propositions. The two parts are connected by the transition from an initial conception of a thought as "a logical picture of facts" to a conception of a thought as "a proposition with a sense." Thought, that is, moves from a passive to an active mode—from registering what is the case, given the metaphysical structure of the world, to asserting what is the case, given the logical structure of language.

The standard interpretation finds in the *Tractatus* a "picture theory of meaning" and "logical atomism." The picture theory of meaning holds that an isomorphism exists between the objects and states of affairs in the world, on the one hand, and their representation by the names and elementary propositions of language, on the other hand; language is able to represent the world because it has the same form as the world. Words are given meaning through a psychological act of correlating names with objects. This correlation occurs when thought moves from its passive to its active mode. Logical atomism holds that the world ultimately consists of simple objects and simple names, neither of which can be broken down into further constituents. Logical analysis is the task of rewriting and reducing the propositions of ordinary language into these simple constituents by determining the elementary propositions that represent states of affairs and then determining the names that represent objects.

Further according to the standard interpretation, the *Tractatus* categorizes discourse into three domains: the factual, which consists of the propositions of natural science; the syntactical, which comprises the propositions of logic; and the mystical, which includes all other propositions. The propositions of natural science *say* how things stand in the world, and, if they are true, they also *show* how things stand; the propositions of logic say nothing about how things stand in the world and show that they say nothing, for they are either tautologies (necessarily true) or contradictions (necessarily false); mystical propositions say and show nothing. Consequently, the propositions of natural science are

*Wittgenstein in the Fellows' Garden of Trinity College, Cambridge, in 1939
(photograph by Norman Malcolm)*

sense bearing; the propositions of logic are senseless; and mystical propositions are nonsense.

The positivist reading of the *Tractatus* is characterized by the contention that it is possible to *state* the logical structure of sentences and the relationship between language and the world *directly,* but only from within an antirealist framework. Ineffabilists contend that it is possible to *show* the logical structure of sentences and the relationship between language and the world *indirectly,* but only from within a realist framework. The problem for both positivism and for ineffabilism, according to the revisionists, is that insofar as Wittgenstein uses the "say/show" distinction, the propositions of logic are senseless. A further problem for ineffabilism, according to the revisionists, is that it maintains that mystical propositions, which include those of aesthetics, ethics, and religion, can show something about the source and nature of transcendent value. Insofar as Wittgenstein uses the "say/show" distinction, however, these propositions are nonsense. The revisionists conclude that neither positivism nor ineffabi-

lism reflects how Wittgenstein uses the "say/show" distinction in the *Tractatus*.

Revisionists maintain that neither the picture theory of meaning nor logical atomism is supported by the text. They agree that the threefold categorization of domains of discourse and the "say/show" distinction are to be found in the *Tractatus* but deny that these ideas are meant to express any doctrine. Instead, revisionists regard these remarks as "transitional," that is, as moves in a still-unfolding dialectic, the purpose of which is to call into question the possibility of making such a priori determinations about the foundations of language. In other words, these apparent doctrines are present in the text as targets of criticism, not as philosophical commitments on Wittgenstein's part.

Wittgenstein goes on to take up the issue of limits that he raised in the preface, saying of philosophy:

[4.114] It must set limits to what can be thought; and, in doing so, to what cannot be thought.

It must set limits to what cannot be thought by working outwards through what can be thought.

[4.115] It will signify what cannot be said, by presenting clearly what can be said.

[4.116] Everything that can be thought at all can be thought clearly. Everything that can be put into words can be put clearly.

Wittgenstein is saying that the setting of limits between what can and cannot be thought and between what can and cannot be said can only be done from within language, that is, "by working outwards through what can be thought." In the *Tractatus* a thought can equally be considered as "a logical picture of facts" or as "a proposition with a sense," depending on whether it is articulated in language. What these limits establish is that whatever makes sense does so just because it can be thought and said clearly, whereas whatever does not is simply nonsense. The notion of a nonsensical proposition that means something is just as unintelligible as an illogical thought that means something. Upholders of the standard interpretation understand these comments as part of a theoretical inquiry that enables a demarcation to be made between sense and nonsense, while revisionists understand them as part of a practical inquiry, the purpose of which is to get clear about one's thinking. For revisionists there can be no limits of the kind envisaged by positivism and ineffabilism, as there is no perspective from which one could make such an a priori demarcation.

In proposition 6.53, which is also regarded as part of the Frame, Wittgenstein says,

The right method of philosophy would be this. To say nothing except what can be said, *i.e.* the propositions of natural science, *i.e.* something that has nothing to do with philosophy: and then always, when someone else wished to say something metaphysical, to demonstrate to him that he had given no meaning to certain signs in his propositions. This method would be unsatisfying to the other–he would not have the feeling that we were teaching him philosophy–but it would be the only strictly correct method.

The issue between the standard and revisionist interpretations in regard to this passage is how Wittgenstein intends that it be demonstrated that no meaning has been given to certain signs in a proposition. For upholders of the standard interpretation a proposition is nonsense not because some of its words have no meaning but because of the meanings that the words have. They have a substantial conception of nonsense and see nonsense as arising from an impermissible combination of symbols. For revisionists nonsense results when the

speaker fails to give a meaning to certain signs in a proposition. They have an austere conception of nonsense that sees nonsense as arising not from the meanings the signs have but rather from an absence of meaning. Revisionists claim that upholders of the standard interpretations fail to follow the sign/symbol distinction that Wittgenstein makes in the *Tractatus*.

The dissatisfaction with the "right method" experienced by "the other" comes from the inability of the method to make sense of metaphysical propositions and, therefore, to answer metaphysical questions. The *Tractatus* itself does not adopt the right method, for there is no interlocutor to ask and answer questions. Instead, Wittgenstein uses the literary style of the text to achieve the same purpose. This requires that the reader find his or her own voice echoed in the propositions of the *Tractatus*. This voice may be positivist, ineffabilist, revisionist, or a multiple one as the reader engages dialectically with the text.

Wittgenstein continues:

[6.54] My propositions are elucidatory in this way: he who understands me finally recognizes them as senseless, when he has climbed out through them, on them, over them. (He must so to speak throw away the ladder, after he has climbed up on it.)
He must surmount these propositions; then he sees the world rightly.

According to revisionists, the 1961 D. F. Pears and B. F. McGuinness translation is more accurate in its rendering of the beginning of this proposition than is the Ogden and Ramsey version: "My propositions serve as elucidations in the following way: anyone who understands me eventually recognizes them as nonsensical. . . ."

It is not immediately clear which propositions Wittgenstein is talking about, let alone how such nonsensical propositions are elucidatory. The standard interpretation claims that in the *Tractatus* Wittgenstein categorizes all propositions according to whether they belong to the factual domain and are sense bearing, to the syntactical realm and are senseless, or to the mystical domain and are nonsense. The dilemma for the standard interpretation, according to revisionists, is: into what category do the propositions of the *Tractatus* fall? They are neither factual nor syntactical. If they are nonsensical, then what is the status of the categorization of propositions into three domains of discourse? Revisionists contend that the standard interpretation is left with an unresolvable paradox: it claims that Wittgenstein, despite what he may say in the Frame, ends up contradicting himself, for the *Tractatus*, as a work of philosophy, includes both philosophical propositions and theory. The revisionists claim that they avoid the para-

Wittgenstein shortly before his death

dox by regarding this categorization as a target of criticism and not as a philosophical commitment. Revisionists are, therefore, able to accept Wittgenstein's propositions as nonsensical.

Wittgenstein's comments in a letter to Ogden on how the latter translated 6.54 assist in clarifying the purpose of such nonsensical propositions:

> Here you misunderstand my meaning entirely. I didn't mean to use "elucidate" intransitively: what I meant to say was: My propositions elucidate–whatever they do elucidate–in this way: etc.
>
> Similarly I might have said "My propositions clarify in this way . . ." meaning "My propositions clarify whatever they do clarify–say, the propositions of natural science–in this way: . . ." Here clarify is not used intransitively although the object is not mentioned.
>
> You may put it thus: "My propositions elucidate philosophic matters in this way: . . ." This is something like the right meaning. Or "My propositions are elucidations in this way: . . ." but this I suppose is bad. If

nothing better is suggested and my first way of putting it really won't do add "philosophic matters" as above.

The revisionist interpretation of these remarks is that according to Wittgenstein, a philosophical work consists essentially, but not entirely, of elucidations, the purpose of which is to clarify "philosophical matters." It does so by showing that certain propositions that one thinks have philosophical significance are nonsensical and that this nonsensicality is caused by a failure to give meaning to certain signs in the proposition, not by the meaning such signs have. The *Tractatus* elucidates philosophical matters by attempting to make sense of its propositions; through the failure of this attempt the reader comes to realize that such propositions are nonsensical. The upholders of the standard interpretation claim that Wittgenstein, despite what he may say in the Frame, contradicts himself, for they think that it is possible to understand the propositions of the *Tractatus*. Revisionists stress that the reader is meant to understand Wittgenstein's authorial intentions, not his propositions.

The metaphor of climbing the ladder, according to revisionists, points to the need for the reader's active engagement with and participation in the text. Wittgenstein has been understood when the reader can finally acknowledge that the *Tractatus* uses nonsensical propositions to elucidate philosophical matters. The "deep problems" with which dogmatic philosophy concerns itself are then found not to be problems, after all; the questions that seem to have been raised are found not to be questions; the answers that have been given are found not to be false but nonsensical. Revisionists insist that caution must be taken here, however, for the propositions of the *Tractatus* cannot simply be dismissed as nonsense on the basis of a general condemnation of metaphysics, as if nonsense were a property of certain kinds of propositions. To do so, the revisionists say, is to fall back into a substantial conception of nonsense. Instead, the nonsense has to be exposed. Getting clear about one's thinking requires that the reader work through the details of the particular philosophical problems raised by the text. The task for the reader is, accordingly, twofold: first, to find out just how it is that a sense is failing to be given, that some of the signs are not signifying, that one is trying to mean by one's words what those words cannot mean in that context of use; and second, to discover what sense could be given to these propositions in some other context. Revisionists argue that the aim of the *Tractatus* is for the reader to realize that in the context of metaphysics its propositions are nonsense and in nonmetaphysical contexts its propositions are trivial or self-evident.

Upholders of the standard interpretation maintain that the ladder that is to be climbed takes the reader somewhere. The ladder offers a perspective, whether from an "internal" or an "external" point of view or within an antirealist or realist framework, from which it is possible to survey how language is connected to the world. According to revisionism, the reader climbs the ladder as part of a dialectic that ultimately discards the notion that such a perspective could even be imagined. In a final act of liberation, revisionism "throws the ladder away." Revisionism regards positivism and ineffabilism as mistaking the rungs of the ladder for the ladder itself and then hanging onto it when it should be thrown away. What, then, is left of the Frame? According to revisionists, its purpose is to enable the reader to get into focus the "philosophic matters" that the *Tractatus* is elucidating. If nonsense is being used to elucidate nonsense, then, revisionists maintain, nothing should remain when the ladder is thrown away.

Revisionists, however, regard the *Tractatus* as a flawed expression of Wittgenstein's commitment to a therapeutic conception of philosophy. Wittgenstein was himself critical of aspects of his work. In the preface to the *Philosophical Investigations* he says, "I have been forced to recognize grave mistakes in what I wrote in that first book." Revisionists locate these "grave mistakes" in the failure of the Frame to "decompose organically" with the rest of the text. To the extent that these "grave mistakes" remain, the appearance is given that there is, after all, a theoretical substructure underpinning the *Tractatus* that is expressive of philosophical commitments that can be held onto when the ladder is thrown away. Revisionists believe that the standard interpretation fails to understand these "grave mistakes" precisely because it fails to understand the aim and method of the *Tractatus*.

Wittgenstein ends the *Tractatus* with his famous proposition 7: "Whereof one cannot speak, thereof one must be silent." Or, as the Pears and McGuinness translation puts it: "What we cannot speak about we must pass over in silence."

Positivists and ineffabilists read 6.54 and 7.0 in a way that enables them to hold onto their respective theoretical commitments. Positivists exclude from what must be discarded their belief that language can be used to state the logical structure of sentences and the relationship between language and the world directly. Ineffabilists exclude their belief that language can be used to show the logical structure of sentences and the relationship between language and the world indirectly. Revisionists regard the theoretical commitments to which positivists and ineffabilists cling as precisely those that the *Tractatus* is calling the reader to throw away. They

conclude that "what we cannot speak about" refers back to the philosophical matters that the reader has, through a process of elucidation, come to recognize as nonsense. Silence is the only response to the realization that in a specific context of use the particular combination of words that one wants to say cannot mean what one wants them to mean. It prohibits nothing else. Paraphrased, it says nothing more than "what we cannot speak about we cannot speak about." It is, therefore, as empty and as meaningless as any tautology.

The disagreement between the standard and revisionist interpretations of the *Tractatus* concerns the conception of philosophy that motivated the "early Wittgenstein." Positivists and ineffabilists believe that he was motivated by a dogmatic conception; consequently, they find in the *Tractatus* a philosophical account of the foundations of language, although they differ as to the details of this account. In contrast, revisionists believe that he was motivated by a therapeutic conception of philosophy and do not find a philosophical account of the foundations of language; instead, they find a demonstration that there is no such thing as the giving of such an account. Revisionism does not question the truth of positivism and ineffabilism but their intelligibility.

If revisionism is correct, then not only the standard interpretation of the *Tractatus* but also that of the *Philosophical Investigations* is undermined. Both stand or fall together, as both regard Wittgenstein as having given philosophical accounts of the foundations of language in both works. The established orthodoxy, ineffabilism, regards the account in the *Tractatus* as a realist one and the account in the *Philosophical Investigations* as antirealist. The dichotomy between realism and antirealism is expressed in a series of contrasts, with the first term in each opposition referring to the *Tractatus* and the second to the *Philosophical Investigations:* a truth-conditional semantics versus an assertibility-conditions semantics; a correspondence theory of truth versus a coherence theory of truth; a picture theory of meaning versus a use theory of meaning; language as a monolith versus language as a motley; logical pictures as structures versus language games as conventions; logical analysis versus grammatical investigation; logic as calculus versus grammar as rules; nonsense as resulting from violations of logical syntax versus nonsense as resulting from violations of grammar; an external standard of correctness versus an internal standard of correctness; and a dogmatic conception of philosophy versus a therapeutic conception. In contrast, revisionism rejects the realism-antirealism dichotomy that is central to the standard interpretation of the *Tractatus* and *Philosophical Investigations*.

Wittgenstein's grave in St. Giles Cemetery, Cambridge

various things that language can be used to do, of the "countless" kinds of activity ("language games") that can be performed with language; and second, the use of "objects of comparison" not just to remind readers of how language is used in particular contexts but also to demonstrate that no general and theoretical explanation can be given of the use of language. The second point undercuts the view of the standard interpretation that Wittgenstein is still giving a philosophical account of the foundations of language. The revisionists believe, in short, that the realism/antirealism dichotomy misunderstands both the continuities and the discontinuities between the two works. According to the revisionist interpretation, the intention of Wittgenstein in both the *Tractatus* and the *Philosophical Investigations* is to show that philosophical accounts of the foundations of language, whether realist or antirealist, are not possible. It, therefore, locates the continuity in Wittgenstein's ideas in his rejection of dogmatic philosophy. The revisionist interpretation maintains that both the early and later Wittgenstein think that there are no philosophical problems concerning language and, consequently, that philosophy has nothing to discover or to explain. The task of philosophy is neither in the *Tractatus* to provide a justification of "the logic of our language" nor in the *Philosophical Investigations* to provide a justification of the grammar of that language. Rather, its task is to dissolve the confusion and perplexity that gives rise to the mistaken belief that there could be such a thing as a philosophical account of the foundations of language to be given.

The standard interpretation takes the realist versus antirealist framework to be the contrast to which Wittgenstein is referring in the preface to the *Philosophical Investigations* when he says that his new thoughts can only be seen in the right light "by contrast with and against the background of my old way of thinking." But the revisionist interpretation holds that Wittgenstein is rejecting, in both the *Tractatus* and the *Philosophical Investigations,* a conception of philosophy according to which its task is the giving of philosophical accounts, and that, therefore, there is no realist/antirealist framework for the standard interpretation to hold onto. In that case, the revisionist interpretation maintains, the evidently significant differences in style and appearance between the *Tractatus* and the *Philosophical Investigations* must be understood in some different fashion. One relatively uncontroversial place to locate the difference between the two works is in the fact that the *Philosophical Investigations* emphasizes the complexity and diversity of actual linguistic practices and puts much less faith in the utility of any kind of symbolic notation than does the *Tractatus*. The issue, still being debated by the protagonists of

Both the standard and the revisionist interpretations accept that Wittgenstein's later work has greater philosophical significance than his earlier work. Concerning the early work, positivism and ineffabilism regard Wittgenstein as either being committed to a form of antirealism or a form of realism, respectively. The standard interpretation regards the later work as antirealist: it sees the later Wittgenstein as maintaining that an external point of view on linguistic practice is, perhaps regrettably, unavailable and that the inevitable consequence is the embracing of some form of idealism or relativism. But if revisionism is correct, such a position on the part of the later Wittgenstein would mean that he was backsliding from a therapeutic conception of philosophy in the *Tractatus* to a dogmatic conception of philosophy in the *Philosophical Investigations,* which would make his early work superior to his later work. Thus, according to the revisionist interpretation, there is no alternative to first determining how the *Tractatus* should be read. Only then, it claims, is it possible to understand what modifications Wittgenstein actually did make in the *Philosophical Investigations* to his previous way of thinking. Two of the main changes that revisionism points to are, first, a wider conception of the

the standard and revisionist interpretations, is just how Wittgenstein explicates this difference.

Historically, positivism dominated the reception of the *Tractatus* from its publication in 1921 until the early 1960s. During this period there were no book-length commentaries on the *Tractatus;* discussion was primarily confined to academic journals. The *Tractatus,* however, had a significant effect on the members of the Vienna Circle, particularly Rudolf Carnap, and influenced the subsequent development of logical positivism.

In 1959 the first book-length commentary on the *Tractatus* was published by Wittgenstein's former student G. E. M. Anscombe, who was one of his literary executors and the editor and translator of many of his works; her book was followed in the 1960s by commentaries by Erik Stenius, Alexander Maslow, Max Black, David Favrholdt, James Patrick Griffin, George Pitcher, and K. T. Fann. Collections of important papers were edited by Fann, Irving Copi and Robert W. Beard, and Peter Winch in the 1960s. These works rejected the stress that the positivists had placed on the notion of the "sayable," emphasizing, instead, that of the "showable" and thereby establishing the ineffabilist view. More book-length commentaries on the *Tractatus* appeared in the 1970s by Henry Le Roy Finch, James Bogen, Peter Michael Stephen Hacker, Anthony Kenny, Robert John Fogelin, and Derek E. Bolton, along with collections of papers edited by E. D. Klemke, Godfrey Vesey, and C. G. Luckhardt, that emphasized the differences between the early Wittgenstein and the later Wittgenstein that are essential to the positivist and ineffabilist views.

In the 1980s the ineffabilist view, which by then had the status of orthodoxy, was consolidated and refined by Kenny, Malcolm, Pears, J. N. Findlay, Merrill B. and Jaako Hintikka, and Gordon Baker. The first book-length commentaries on the *Tractatus* critical of the ineffabilist view were also published at this time by Robert J. Cavalier, Howard O. Mounce, Richard M. McDonough, Ben Worthington, and Peter Carruthers. In the 1990s dissatisfaction with the ineffabilist view brought further revisionist book-length commentaries on the *Tractatus* by Carruthers, Michael P. Hodge, Donald Peterson, Richard R. Brockhaus, Raymond Bradley, John W. Cook, Newton Garver, and Dale Jacquette. More-general and comparative assessments of Wittgenstein's early and late philosophy also appeared, written or edited by Glock, Hacker, Cook, David Bell and Neil Cooper, Michael Dummett, Hans Sluga and David G. Stern, William W. Tait, and Anat Biletzki and Anat Matar. The first book-length works sympathetic to the reso-

lutist view were published by Diamond, James Guetti, and John Koethe.

The fiftieth anniversary of Wittgenstein's death in 2001 occasioned several major international conferences to reassess the significance of his work. The two main topics of debate were the CD-ROM release of *Wittgenstein's "Nachlass": The Bergen Electronic Edition* (1998–2001) and the dispute between ineffabilists and resolutists. The growing recognition of the importance of the *Tractatus* to understanding Wittgenstein's philosophy has also been reflected in resolutist book-length commentaries by Ian Proops, Eli Friedlander, and Matthew B. Ostrow. Several works were published that offer general reassessments of Wittgenstein's entire philosophy; many of the papers in these collections are also resolutist. Authors or editors of these works include Glock, Alice Crary and Rupert Read, Avrum Stroll, Richard Gaskin, James Klagge, Eric H. Reck, Juliet Floyd and Sanford Shieh, and Timothy G. McCarthy and Sean C. Stidd.

Letters:

Letters to C. K. Ogden: Comments on the English Translation of the Tractatus Logico-Philosophicus, edited by Georg Henrik von Wright (Boston: Routledge & Kegan Paul, 1973; Oxford: Blackwell, 1973);

Letters to Russell, Keynes and Moore, edited by von Wright, translated by B. F. McGuinness (Ithaca, N.Y.: Cornell University Press, 1974; Oxford: Blackwell, 1974);

Cambridge Letters: Correspondence with Russell, Keynes, Moore, Ramsey and Sraffa, edited by McGuinness and von Wright (Oxford & Malden, Mass.: Blackwell, 1995).

Bibliographies:

Francis Lapointe, ed., *Ludwig Wittgenstein: A Comprehensive Bibliography* (Westport, Conn.: Greenwood Press, 1980);

V. A. Shanker and S. G. Shanker, *Ludwig Wittgenstein: Critical Assessments. A Wittgenstein Bibliography* (London: Croom Helm, 1986).

Biographies:

William Warren Bartley III, *Wittgenstein* (Philadelphia: Lippincott, 1973; London: Quartet, 1974);

Michael Nedo and Michele Ranchetti, eds., *Ludwig Wittgenstein: Sein Leben in Bildern und Texten* (Frankfurt am Main: Suhr Kamps, 1983);

B. F. McGuinness, *Wittgenstein: A Life. Young Ludwig (1889–1921)* (London: Duckworth, 1988);

Ray Monk, *Ludwig Wittgenstein: The Duty of Genius* (New York: Free Press, 1990).

References:

G. E. M. Anscombe, *An Introduction to Wittgenstein's* Tractatus (London: Hutchinson, 1959; New York: Harper & Row, 1963);

A. J. Ayer, *Language, Truth and Logic* (London: Gollancz, 1946);

Ayer, ed., *Logical Positivism* (New York: Free Press, 1959);

Gordon Baker, *Wittgenstein, Frege and the Vienna Circle* (Oxford: Blackwell, 1988; New York: Blackwell, 1988);

David Bell and Neil Cooper, eds., *The Analytic Tradition* (Oxford: Blackwell, 1990; Cambridge, Mass.: Blackwell, 1990);

Max Black, *A Companion to Wittgenstein's* Tractatus (Ithaca, N.Y.: Cornell University Press, 1964; Cambridge: Cambridge University Press, 1964);

Irving Block, ed., *Perspectives on the Philosophy of Wittgenstein* (Cambridge, Mass.: MIT Press, 1981; Oxford: Blackwell, 1981);

James Bogen, *Wittgenstein's Philosophy of Language: Some Aspects of Its Development* (London: Routledge & Kegan Paul, 1972; New York: Humanities Press, 1972);

Derek E. Bolton, *An Approach to Wittgenstein's Philosophy* (London: Macmillan, 1979; Atlantic Highlands, N.J.: Humanities Press, 1979);

Raymond Bradley, *The Nature of All Being: A Study of Wittgenstein's Modal Atomism* (Oxford: Oxford University Press, 1992; New York: Oxford University Press, 1992);

Richard R. Brockhaus, *Pulling Up the Ladder: The Metaphysical Roots of Wittgenstein's* Tractatus Logico-Philosophicus (La Salle, Ill.: Open Court, 1991);

Peter Carruthers, *The Metaphysics of the* Tractatus (New York: Cambridge University Press, 1990; Cambridge: Cambridge University Press, 1990);

Carruthers, *Tractarian Semantics: Finding Sense in Wittgenstein's* Tractatus (Oxford: Blackwell, 1989; Cambridge, Mass.: Blackwell, 1989);

Robert J. Cavalier, *Ludwig Wittgenstein's* Tractatus Logico-Philosophicus: *A Transcendental Critique of Ethics* (Washington, D.C.: University Press of America, 1980);

Stanley Cavell, *The Claim of Reason: Wittgenstein, Skepticism, Morality, and Tragedy* (Oxford: Oxford University Press, 1979; New York: Oxford University Press, 1979);

Cavell, *Must We Mean What We Say?* (Oxford: Oxford University Press, 1976; New York: Oxford University Press, 1976);

Ted Cohen, Paul Guyer, and Hilary Putnam, *Pursuits of Reason: Essays in Honor of Stanley Cavell* (Lubbock, Tex.: Texas Tech University Press, 1993);

James Conant, "Must We Show What We Cannot Say?" in *The Senses of Stanley Cavell,* edited by Richard Fleming and Michael Payne (Cranbury, N.J.: Associated University Presses, 1989), pp. 242–283;

Conant, "Putting Two and Two Together: Kierkegaard, Wittgenstein, and the Point of View for Their Work as Authors," in *Philosophy and the Grammar of Religious Belief,* edited by Timothy Tessin and Mario von der Ruhr (New York: Macmillan, 1995; London: Macmillan, 1995), pp. 248–331;

Conant, "The Search for Logically Alien Thought: Descartes, Kant, Frege and the *Tractatus*," *Philosophical Topics,* 20 (1991): 115–180;

Conant, "Throwing Away the Top of the Ladder," *Yale Review,* 79 (1991): 328–364;

Conant, "Wittgenstein on Meaning and Use," *Philosophical Investigations,* 21 (1998): 222–250;

John W. Cook, *Wittgenstein, Empiricism, and Language* (New York: Oxford University Press, 1999; Oxford: Oxford University Press, 1999);

Cook, *Wittgenstein's Metaphysics* (New York & Cambridge: Cambridge University Press, 1994);

Irving M. Copi and Robert W. Beard, eds., *Essays on Wittgenstein's* Tractatus (New York: Macmillan, 1966; London: Routledge & Kegan Paul, 1966);

Alice Crary and Rupert Read, eds., *The New Wittgenstein* (New York & London: Routledge, 2000);

Cora Diamond, *The Realistic Spirit: Wittgenstein, Philosophy and the Mind* (Cambridge, Mass.: MIT Press, 1991);

Michael Dummett, *Origins of Analytical Philosophy* (London: Duckworth, 1993);

David Edmonds and John Eidinow, *Wittgenstein's Poker: The Story of a Ten-Minute Argument between Two Great Philosophers* (London: Faber & Faber, 2001; New York : Ecco, 2001);

K. T. Fann, *Wittgenstein's Conception of Philosophy* (Berkeley: University of California Press, 1969; Oxford: Blackwell, 1969);

Fann, ed., *Ludwig Wittgenstein: The Man and His Philosophy. An Anthology* (New York: Dell, 1967; Brighton, U.K.: Harvester Press, 1967);

David Favrholdt, *An Interpretation and Critique of Wittgenstein's* Tractatus (Copenhagen: Ejnar Munksgaard, 1964; New York: Humanities Press, 1964);

Henry Le Roy Finch, *Wittgenstein—the Early Philosophy* (New York: Humanities Press, 1971);

Finch, *Wittgenstein—the Later Philosophy* (Atlantic Highlands, N.J.: Humanities Press, 1977);

J. N. Findlay, *Wittgenstein: A Critique* (London & Boston: Routledge & Kegan Paul, 1984);

F. A. Flowers III, ed., *Portraits of Wittgenstein,* 4 volumes (Bristol & Sterling, Va.: Thoemmes Press, 1999);

Juliet Floyd and Sanford Shieh, eds., *Future Pasts: The Analytic Tradition in Twentieth-Century Philosophy* (Oxford & New York: Oxford University Press, 2001);

Robert John Fogelin, *Wittgenstein: The Arguments of the Philosophers* (London & Boston: Routledge & Kegan Paul, 1976);

Eli Friedlander, "Heidegger, Carnap and Wittgenstein: Much Ado about Nothing," in *The Story of Analytic Philosophy: Plot and Heroes,* edited by Anat Biletzki and Anat Matar (London & New York: Routledge, 1998), pp. 226–237;

Friedlander, *Signs of Sense: Reading Wittgenstein's* Tractatus (Cambridge, Mass.: Harvard University Press, 2001);

Michael Friedman, *Reconsidering Logical Positivism* (Cambridge & New York: Cambridge University Press, 1999);

Newton Garver, *This Complicated Form of Life: Essays on Wittgenstein* (La Salle, Ill.: Open Court, 1994);

Richard Gaskin, ed., *Grammar in Early Twentieth-Century Philosophy* (London & New York: Routledge, 2001);

Hans-Johann Glock, *A Wittgenstein Dictionary* (Oxford & Malden, Mass.: Blackwell, 1996);

Glock, ed., *The Rise of Analytic Philosophy* (Oxford & Malden, Mass.: Blackwell, 1967);

Glock, ed., *Wittgenstein: A Critical Reader* (Oxford & Malden, Mass.: Blackwell, 2001);

James Patrick Griffin, *Wittgenstein's Logical Atomism* (Oxford & New York: Oxford University Press, 1964);

James Guetti, *Wittgenstein and the Grammar of Literary Experience* (Athens: University of Georgia Press, 1993);

Peter Michael Steven Hacker, *Insight and Illusion: Themes in the Philosophy of Wittgenstein* (Oxford: Oxford University Press, 1972);

Hacker, *Wittgenstein's Place in Twentieth-Century Analytic Philosophy* (Oxford & Malden, Mass.: Blackwell, 1996);

Oswald Hanfling, *Logical Positivism* (Oxford: Blackwell, 1981);

Hanfling, ed., *Essential Readings in Logical Positivism* (Oxford: Blackwell, 1981);

Merrill B. Hintikka and Jaakko Hintikka, *Investigating Wittgenstein* (Oxford & New York: Blackwell, 1986);

Michael P. Hodge, *Transcendence and Wittgenstein's* Tractatus (Philadelphia: Temple University Press, 1990);

Dale Jacquette, *Wittgenstein's Thought in Transition* (West Lafayette, Ind.: Purdue University Press, 1998);

Allan Janik, *Wittgenstein's Vienna Revisited* (New Brunswick, N.J.: Transaction, 2001);

Janik and Stephen Toulmin, *Wittgenstein's Vienna* (New York: Simon & Schuster, 1973);

William M. Johnston, *The Austrian Mind: An Intellectual and Social History 1848–1938* (Berkeley: University of California Press, 1972);

Anthony Kenny, *The Legacy of Wittgenstein* (Oxford & New York: Blackwell, 1984);

Kenny, *Wittgenstein* (London: Allen Lane, 1973; Cambridge, Mass.: Harvard University Press, 1973);

James C. Klagge, ed., *Wittgenstein: Biography and Philosophy* (Cambridge & New York: Cambridge University Press, 2001);

E. D. Klemke, ed., *Essays on Wittgenstein* (Urbana: University of Illinois Press, 1971);

John Koethe, *The Continuity of Wittgenstein's Thought* (Ithaca, N.Y.: Cornell University Press, 1996);

Victor Kraft, *The Vienna Circle: The Origin of Neo-Positivism. A Chapter in the History of Recent Philosophy* (New York: Philosophical Library, 1953);

Michael Kremer, "Contextualism and Holism in the Early Wittgenstein: From *Prototractatus* to *Tractatus,*" *Philosophical Topics,* 25 (1997): 87–120;

Kremer, "The Purpose of Nonsense," *Nous,* 35 (2001): 39–73;

Saul Kripke, *Wittgenstein: On Rules and Private Language* (Oxford: Blackwell, 1982);

C. G. Luckhardt, ed., *Wittgenstein: Sources and Perspectives* (Ithaca, N.Y.: Cornell University Press, 1979);

Norman Malcolm, *Nothing Is Hidden: Wittgenstein's Criticism of His Early Thought* (Oxford & New York: Blackwell, 1986);

Alexander Maslow, *A Study in Wittgenstein's Tractatus* (Berkeley: University of California Press, 1961; Cambridge: Cambridge University Press, 1961);

Timothy G. McCarthy and Sean C. Stidd, eds., *Wittgenstein in America* (Oxford & New York: Oxford University Press, 2001);

Richard M. McDonough, *The Argument of the* Tractatus (Albany: State University of New York Press, 1986);

Marie McGinn, "Between Metaphysics and Nonsense: Elucidation in Wittgenstein's *Tractatus,*" *Philosophical Quarterly,* 49 (1999): 491–513;

Howard O. Mounce, "Critical Notice: *The New Wittgenstein,*" *Philosophical Investigations,* 24 (2001): 185–192;

Mounce, "Philosophy, Solipsism and Thought," *Philosophical Quarterly,* 47 (1997): 1–18;

Mounce, *Wittgenstein's* Tractatus: *An Introduction* (Chicago: University of Chicago Press, 1981; Oxford: Blackwell, 1981);

Matthew B. Ostrow, *Wittgenstein's* Tractatus: *A Dialectical Interpretation* (Cambridge & New York: Cambridge University Press, 2002);

D. F. Pears, *The False Prison: A Study of the Development of Wittgenstein's Philosophy,* 2 volumes (Oxford & New York: Oxford University Press, 1987, 1988);

Donald Peterson, *Wittgenstein's Early Philosophy: Three Sides of the Mirror* (Toronto: University of Toronto Press, 1990);

George Pitcher, *The Philosophy of Wittgenstein* (Englewood Cliffs, N.J.: Prentice-Hall, 1964);

Ian Proops, *Logic and Language in Wittgenstein's* Tractatus (New York: Garland, 2000);

Read, "Is 'What is time?' a Good Question to Ask?" *Philosophy,* 77 (2002): 193–209;

Eric H. Reck, ed., *From Frege to Wittgenstein: Perspectives on Early Analytic Philosophy* (Oxford & New York: Oxford University Press, 2001);

Lynette Reid, "Wittgenstein's Ladder: The *Tractatus* and Nonsense," *Philosophical Investigations,* 21 (1998): 97–151;

Thomas G. Ricketts, "Carnap: From Logical Syntax to Semantics," in *The Origins of Logical Empiricism,* edited by Ronald N. Giere and Alan W. Richardson (Minneapolis: University of Minnesota Press, 1996), pp. 231–250;

Ricketts, "Frege, the *Tractatus* and the Logocentric Predicament," *Nous,* 19 (1985): 3–14;

Ricketts, "Generality, Meaning and Sense in Frege," *Pacific Philosophical Quarterly,* 67 (1986): 172–195;

Ricketts, "Logic and Truth in Frege," *Proceedings of the Aristotelian Society,* 70, supplement (1996): 121–140;

Ricketts, "Objectivity and Objecthood: Frege's Metaphysics of Judgment," in *Frege Synthesized,* edited by L. Haaparanta and Jaako Hintikka (Dordrecht, Netherlands: Reidel, 1986), pp. 65–95;

Carl E. Schorske, *Fin De Siècle Vienna: Politics and Culture* (New York: Knopf, 1980);

V. A. Shanker and S. G. Shanker, eds., *Ludwig Wittgenstein: Critical Assessments,* 5 volumes (London: Croom Helm, 1986);

Hans Sluga and David G. Stern, eds., *The Cambridge Companion to Wittgenstein* (Cambridge & New York: Cambridge University Press, 1996);

Erik Stenius, *Wittgenstein's* Tractatus: *A Critical Exposition of the Main Lines of Thought* (Ithaca, N.Y.: Cornell University Press, 1960; Oxford: Blackwell, 1960);

Avrum Stroll, *Twentieth-Century Analytic Philosophy* (New York: Columbia University Press, 2000, pp. 45–86, 113–145);

William W. Tait, ed., *Early Analytic Philosophy: Frege, Russell, Wittgenstein* (La Salle, Ill.: Open Court, 1997);

Tessin and von der Ruhr, eds., *Philosophy and the Grammar of Religious Belief* (London & New York: Macmillan, 1995);

Godfrey Vesey, ed., *Understanding Wittgenstein* (Ithaca, N.Y.: Cornell University Press, 1974; London: Macmillan, 1974);

Friedrich Waismann, *Ludwig Wittgenstein and the "Vienna Circle"* (Oxford: Blackwell, 1979);

Julius R. Weinberg, *An Examination of Logical Positivism* (London: Routledge & Kegan Paul, 1936);

Joan Weiner, *Frege in Perspective* (Ithaca, N.Y.: Cornell University Press, 1990);

Weiner, "Theory and Elucidation: The End of the Age of Innocence," in *Future Pasts: The Analytic Tradition in Twentieth-Century Philosophy,* edited by Floyd and Shieh (Oxford & New York: Oxford University Press, 2001), pp. 43–65;

Weiner, "Understanding Frege's Project," in *The Cambridge Companion to Frege,* edited by Ricketts (Cambridge & New York: Cambridge University Press, forthcoming);

Peter Winch, ed., *Studies in the Philosophy of Wittgenstein* (London: Routledge & Kegan Paul, 1969; New York: Humanities Press, 1969);

Ben Worthington, *Self-Consciousness and Self-Reference: An Interpretation of Wittgenstein's* Tractatus (Aldershot, U.K. & Brookfield, Vt.: Avebury, 1988).

Papers:

The main center for textual scholarship on the works of Ludwig Wittgenstein is the Bergen Wittgenstein Archive at the University of Bergen in Norway. Important papers and documents are also held by the Wren Library of Trinity College, University of Cambridge; the Bodleian Library, University of Oxford; the Österreichische Nationalbiliothek in Vienna, Austria; the Cornell University Library; and Wittgenstein's literary executors, including Georg Henrik von Wright, one of Wittgenstein's last surviving students, in Finland.

Books for Further Reading

Adamson, Robert. *The Development of Modern Philosophy: With Other Lectures and Essays,* 2 volumes, edited by W. R. Sorley. Edinburgh: Blackwood, 1903.

Ayer, A. J. *Philosophy in the Twentieth Century.* London: Weidenfeld & Nicolson, 1982; New York: Random House, 1982.

Ayer, ed. *Logical Positivism.* London: Allen & Unwin / Glencoe, Ill.: Free Press, 1959.

Ayer and Raymond Winch, eds. *British Empirical Philosophers: Locke, Berkeley, Hume, Reid, and J. S. Mill.* London: Routledge & Kegan Paul, 1952.

Baggini, Julian, and Jeremy Stangroom, eds. *Brit Phil: Philosophers in Conversation.* London & New York: Routledge, 2002.

Benn, Alfred William. *The History of English Rationalism in the Nineteenth Century.* London: Longmans, Green, 1906.

Berman, David. *A History of Atheism in Britain: From Hobbes to Russell.* London & New York: Croom Helm, 1988.

Boucher, David, and Andrew Vincent. *British Idealism and Political Theory.* Edinburgh: Edinburgh University Press, 2000.

Canfield, John V., ed. *Philosophy of Meaning, Knowledge and Value in the Twentieth Century.* Routledge History of Philosophy, volume 10. London: Routledge, 1997.

Carré, Meyrick Heath. *Phases of Thought in England.* Oxford: Clarendon Press, 1949.

Coates, Philip Adrian. *A Sceptical Examination of Contemporary British Philosophy.* London: Brentano's, 1929.

Copleston, Frederick C. *Contemporary Philosophy: Studies of Logical Positivism and Existentialism,* revised edition. London: Search Press, 1965.

Copleston. *A History of Philosophy,* volume 8: *Bentham to Russell.* London: Burns & Oates, 1999.

Copleston. *Philosophers and Philosophies.* London: Search Press, 1976.

Davie, George Elder. *The Democratic Intellect: Scotland and Her Universities in the Nineteenth Century.* Edinburgh: Edinburgh University Press, 1961.

Easthope, Antony. *British Post-Structuralism since 1968.* London: Routledge, 1988.

Ferrier, James Frederick. *Scottish Philosophy: The Old and the New. A Statement.* Edinburgh: Sutherland & Knox, 1856.

Flynn, Philip. *Enlightened Scotland: A Study and Selection of Scottish Philosophical Prose from the Eighteenth and Early Nineteenth Centuries.* Edinburgh: Scottish Academic Press, 1992.

Garland, Martha McMackin. *Cambridge before Darwin: The Ideal of a Liberal Education 1800–1860.* Cambridge: Cambridge University Press, 1980.

Graham, William. *English Political Philosophy from Hobbes to Maine.* London: Arnold, 1899.

Grave, S. A. *The Scottish Philosophy of Common Sense.* Oxford: Clarendon Press, 1960.

Gross, Barry R. *Analytic Philosophy: An Historical Introduction.* New York: Pegasus, 1970.

Inge, William. *The Platonic Tradition in English Religious Thought.* New York: Longmans, Green, 1926.

Kenny, Anthony, ed. *Rationalism, Empiricism and Idealism: British Academy Lectures on the History of Philosophy.* Oxford: Clarendon Press, 1986.

Mace, C. A., ed. *British Philosophy in the Mid-Century: A Cambridge Symposium.* London: Allen & Unwin, 1957.

Magee, Bryan. *Men of Ideas: Some Creators of Contemporary Philosophy.* Oxford: Oxford University Press, 1982.

Magee. *Talking Philosophy: Dialogues with Fifteen Leading Philosophers.* Oxford: Oxford University Press, 2001.

Magee, ed. *Modern British Philosophy.* Oxford: Oxford University Press, 1986.

Masson, David. *Recent British Philosophy: A Review, with Criticisms; Including Some Comments on Mr. Mill's Answer to Sir William Hamilton.* London & Cambridge: Macmillan, 1865.

McCosh, James. *The Scottish Philosophy: Biographical, Expository, Critical: from Hutcheson to Hamilton.* London: Macmillan / New York: R. Carter, 1875.

Mehta, Ved. *Fly and the Fly-Bottle: Encounters with British Intellectuals.* London: Weidenfeld & Nicolson, 1963; New York: Columbia University Press, 1983.

Metz, Rudolf. *A Hundred Years of British Philosophy,* edited by J. R. Muirhead, translated by J. W. Harvey, T. E. Jessop, and Henry Sturt. London: Allen & Unwin / New York: Macmillan, 1938.

Morell, John Daniel. *On the Philosophical Tendencies of the Age: Being Four Lectures Delivered at Edinburgh and Glasgow in January 1848.* Bristol: Thoemmes Press, 1990.

Morrell, Jack, and Arnold Thackray. *Gentlemen of Science: Early Years of the British Association for the Advancement of Science.* Oxford: Clarendon Press, 1981.

Morris, George Sylvester. *British Thought and Thinkers: Introductory Studies, Critical, Biographical and Philosophical.* Chicago: S. C. Griggs, 1880.

Muirhead, John H. *The Platonic Tradition in Anglo-Saxon Philosophy: Studies in the History of Idealism in England and America.* London: Allen & Unwin / New York: Macmillan, 1931.

Mure, Geoffrey Reginald Gilchrist. *Retreat from Truth.* Oxford: Blackwell, 1958.

Nicholson, Peter P. *The Political Philosophy of the British Idealists: Selected Studies.* Cambridge: Cambridge University Press, 1990.

Olson, Richard. *Scottish Philosophy and British Physics, 1750–1880.* Princeton: Princeton University Press, 1975.

Passmore, John. *A Hundred Years of Philosophy,* second edition. London: Duckworth, 1978.

Passmore. *Recent Philosophers: A Supplement to* A Hundred Years of Philosophy. London: Duckworth, 1985; La Salle, Ill.: Open Court, 1992.

Paul, Leslie Allen. *The English Philosophers.* London: Faber & Faber, 1953.

Priest, Stephen. *The British Empiricists: Hobbes to Ayer.* London: Penguin, 1990.

Randall, John Herman. *The Career of Philosophy,* 2 volumes. New York: Columbia University Press, 1962.

Raphael, D. D. *The Moral Sense.* London: Oxford University Press, 1947.

Robinson, Daniel Sommer, ed. *The Story of Scottish Philosophy: A Compendium of Selections from the Writings of Nine Pre-eminent Scottish Philosophers, with Biobibliographical Essays.* New York: Exposition Press, 1961.

Rothblatt, Sheldon. *The Revolution of the Dons: Cambridge and Society in Victorian England.* Cambridge: Cambridge University Press, 1968.

Russell, Bertrand. *A History of Western Philosophy: And Its Connection with Political and Social Circumstances from the Earliest Times to the Present Day.* New York: Simon & Schuster, 1945.

Seth, Andrew. *Scottish Philosophy: A Comparison of the Scottish and German Answers to Hume.* Edinburgh: Blackwood, 1885.

Seth, James. *English Philosophers and Schools of Philosophy.* London: Dent, 1912.

Shanker, Stuart G., ed. *Philosophy in Britain Today.* London: Croom Helm, 1986.

Shanker, ed. *Philosophy of Science, Logic, and Mathematics in the Twentieth Century.* Routledge History of Philosophy, volume 9. London: Routledge, 1996.

Sidgwick, Henry. *Outlines of the History of Ethics for English Readers.* London & New York: Macmillan, 1886.

Sorley, William Ritchie. *A History of British Philosophy to 1900.* Cambridge: Cambridge University Press, 1965; Westport, Conn.: Greenwood Press, 1973.

Stegmüller, Wolfgang. *Main Currents in Contemporary German, British, and American Philosophy,* translated by Albert E. Blumberg. Dordrecht, Netherlands: Reidel, 1969.

Stephen, Leslie. *The English Utilitarians,* 3 volumes. Bristol: Thoemmes Press, 1991.

Sutton, John. *Philosophy and Memory Traces.* Cambridge: Cambridge University Press, 1998.

Tait, William W., ed. *Early Analytic Philosophy: Frege, Russell, Wittgenstein. Essays in Honor of Leonard Linsky.* Chicago: Open Court, 1997.

Urmson, J. O. *Philosophical Analysis: Its Development between the Two World Wars.* Oxford: Clarendon Press, 1966.

Vincent, Andrew, and Raymond Plant. *Philosophy, Politics and Citizenship: The Life and Thought of British Idealists.* Oxford: Blackwell, 1984.

Waithe, Mary Ellen, ed. *A History of Women Philosophers,* volumes 3 and 4. Dordrecht, Netherlands & Boston: Kluwer, 1991, 1995.

Warnock, G. J. *English Philosophy since 1900.* The Home University Library of Modern Knowledge, no. 234. London & New York: Oxford University Press, 1958.

Willey, Basil. *The English Moralists.* London: Chatto & Windus, 1964.

Williams, Bernard, and Alan Montefiore, eds. *British Analytical Philosophy.* London: Routledge & Kegan Paul, 1971.

Contributors

Kathy Behrendt . . . . *University of Oxford*

David Boucher . . . . *Cardiff University*

Keith Campbell . . . . *University of Sydney*

David Crossley . . . . *University of Saskatchewan*

Darlei Dall'Agnol . . . . *Federal University of Santa Catarina, Brazil*

Peter Dalton . . . . *Florida State University*

Robert Deans . . . . *University of East Anglia*

Elizabeth R. Eames . . . . *Southern Illinois University at Carbondale*

Pascal Engel. . . . . *University of Paris–Sorbonne*

Phillip Ferreira. . . . .*Kutztown University of Pennsylvania*

Nick Fotion . . . .*Emory University*

Gisella Gisolo . . . . *University of Florence, Italy*

Ann-Barbara Graff. . . . . *University of Toronto*

Richard Hartzman. . . . . *New York City*

Konstantin Kolenda. . . . . *Rice University*

W. J. Mander . . . .*Harris Manchester College, Oxford*

Lou J. Matz . . . .*University of the Pacific*

Nicholas Maxwell . . . . *University of London*

Leemon B. McHenry. . . *Loyola Marymount University* and *California State University, Northridge*

Ian Morton . . . . *Liverpool John Moores University*

Rupert Read . . . . *University of East Anglia*

Anita R. Rose . . . . *Converse College*

George W. Shields. . . . . *Kentucky State University*

Edrie Sobstyl . . . . *University of Oregon at Eugene*

Susan Spencer . . . . *University of Central Oklahoma*

William Sweet. . . . .*St. Francis Xavier University*

Tadeusz Szubka. . . . . *Catholic University of Lublin*

Colin Tyler . . . . *University of Hull*

Bernhard Weiss. . . . .*University of Wales, Lampeter*

Fred Wilson. . . . . *University of Toronto*

Cumulative Index

Dictionary of Literary Biography, Volumes 1-262
Dictionary of Literary Biography Yearbook, 1980-2001
Dictionary of Literary Biography Documentary Series, Volumes 1-19
Concise Dictionary of American Literary Biography, Volumes 1-7
Concise Dictionary of British Literary Biography, Volumes 1-8
Concise Dictionary of World Literary Biography, Volumes 1-4

Cumulative Index

DLB before number: *Dictionary of Literary Biography,* Volumes 1-262
Y before number: *Dictionary of Literary Biography Yearbook,* 1980-2001
DS before number: *Dictionary of Literary Biography Documentary Series,* Volumes 1-19
CDALB before number: *Concise Dictionary of American Literary Biography,* Volumes 1-7
CDBLB before number: *Concise Dictionary of British Literary Biography,* Volumes 1-8
CDWLB before number: *Concise Dictionary of World Literary Biography,* Volumes 1-4

B

Cumulative Index

N

Q

Smith, H. Allen 1907-1976 . . . . .DLB-11, 29

Smith, Harrison, and Robert Haas
    [publishing house] DLB-46

Smith, Harry B. 1860-1936 . . . . .DLB-187

Smith, Hazel Brannon 1914- DLB-127

Smith, Henry circa 1560-circa 1591 . . . . .DLB-136

Smith, Horatio (Horace) 1779-1849 . . . . . .DLB-116

Smith, Horatio (Horace) 1779-1849 and
    James Smith 1775-1839 . . . . .DLB-96

Smith, Iain Crichton 1928- DLB-40, 139

Smith, J. Allen 1860-1924 . . . . .DLB-47

Smith, J. Stilman, and Company DLB-49

Smith, Jessie Willcox 1863-1935 . . . . .DLB-188

Smith, John 1580-1631 . . . . .DLB-24, 30

Smith, John 1618-1652 . . . . .DLB-252

Smith, Josiah 1704-1781 . . . . .DLB-24

Smith, Ken 1938- DLB-40

Smith, Lee 1944- DLB-143; Y-83

Smith, Logan Pearsall 1865-1946. . . . . . . .DLB-98

Smith, Margaret Bayard 1778-1844 . . . . . .DLB-248

Smith, Mark 1935- Y-82

Smith, Michael 1698-circa 1771 . . . . .DLB-31

Smith, Pauline 1882-1959 . . . . .DLB-225

Smith, Red 1905-1982 . . . . DLB-29, 171

Smith, Roswell 1829-1892 . . . . .DLB-79

Smith, Samuel Harrison 1772-1845 . . . . . . .DLB-43

Smith, Samuel Stanhope 1751-1819 . . . . . . .DLB-37

Smith, Sarah (see Stretton, Hesba)

Smith, Sarah Pogson 1774-1870 . . . . .DLB-200

Smith, Seba 1792-1868 . . . . .DLB-1, 11, 243

Smith, Stevie 1902-1971 . . . . .DLB-20

Smith, Sydney 1771-1845 . . . . .DLB-107

Smith, Sydney Goodsir 1915-1975 . . . . . . .DLB-27

Smith, Sir Thomas 1513-1577 . . . . .DLB-132

Smith, W. B., and Company DLB-49

Smith, W. H., and Son. DLB-106

Smith, Wendell 1914-1972 . . . . .DLB-171

Smith, William flourished 1595-1597. . . .DLB-136

Smith, William 1727-1803 . . . . .DLB-31

A General Idea of the College of Mirania
    (1753) [excerpts] DLB-31

Smith, William 1728-1793 . . . . .DLB-30

Smith, William Gardner 1927-1974 . . . . . . .DLB-76

Smith, William Henry 1808-1872 . . . . . . .DLB-159

Smith, William Jay 1918- DLB-5

Smithers, Leonard [publishing house] DLB-112

Smollett, Tobias
    1721-1771 . . . . .DLB-39, 104; CDBLB-2

Dedication, *Ferdinand Count
    Fathom* (1753) DLB-39

Preface to *Ferdinand Count Fathom* (1753) DLB-39

Preface to *Roderick Random* (1748) DLB-39

Smythe, Francis Sydney 1900-1949 . . . . . .DLB-195

Snelling, William Joseph 1804-1848 . . . . .DLB-202

Snellings, Rolland (see Touré, Askia Muhammad)

Snodgrass, W. D. 1926- DLB-5

Snow, C. P.
    1905-1980 . . . . .DLB-15, 77; DS-17; CDBLB-7

Snyder, Gary 1930- . . . DLB-5, 16, 165, 212, 237

Sobiloff, Hy 1912-1970. . . . . .DLB-48

The Society for Textual Scholarship and
    TEXT Y-87

The Society for the History of Authorship,
    Reading and Publishing Y-92

Söderberg, Hjalmar 1869-1941 . . . . .DLB-259

Södergran, Edith 1892-1923 . . . . .DLB-259

Soffici, Ardengo 1879-1964 . . . . .DLB-114

Sofola, 'Zulu 1938- DLB-157

Solano, Solita 1888-1975 . . . . .DLB-4

Soldati, Mario 1906-1999. . . . . .DLB-177

Šoljan, Antun 1932-1993 . . . . .DLB-181

Sollers, Philippe 1936- DLB-83

Sollogub, Vladimir Aleksandrovich
    1813-1882 . . . . .DLB-198

Sollors, Werner 1943- DBL-246

Solmi, Sergio 1899-1981 . . . . .DLB-114

Solomon, Carl 1928- DLB-16

Solway, David 1941- DLB-53

Solzhenitsyn and America Y-85

Somerville, Edith Œnone 1858-1949. . . . .DLB-135

Somov, Orest Mikhailovich
    1793-1833 . . . . .DLB-198

Sønderby, Knud 1909-1966 . . . . .DLB-214

Song, Cathy 1955- DLB-169

Sonnevi, Göran 1939- DLB-257

Sono Ayako 1931- DLB-182

Sontag, Susan 1933- DLB-2, 67

Sophocles 497/496 B.C.-406/405 B.C.
    . . . . DLB-176; CDWLB-1

Šopov, Aco 1923-1982. . . . . .DLB-181

Sørensen, Villy 1929- DLB-214

Sorensen, Virginia 1912-1991 . . . . .DLB-206

Sorge, Reinhard Johannes 1892-1916 . . . .DLB-118

Sorrentino, Gilbert 1929- DLB-5, 173; Y-80

Sotheby, James 1682-1742 . . . . .DLB-213

Sotheby, John 1740-1807 . . . . .DLB-213

Sotheby, Samuel 1771-1842 . . . . .DLB-213

Sotheby, Samuel Leigh 1805-1861. . . . . . .DLB-213

Sotheby, William 1757-1833. . . . . . . .DLB-93, 213

Soto, Gary 1952- DLB-82

Sources for the Study of Tudor and Stuart
    Drama DLB-62

Souster, Raymond 1921- DLB-88

The *South English Legendary* circa thirteenth-fifteenth
    centuries DLB-146

Southerland, Ellease 1943- DLB-33

Southern, Terry 1924-1995 . . . . .DLB-2

Southern Illinois University Press Y-95

Southern Writers Between the Wars DLB-9

Southerne, Thomas 1659-1746 . . . . .DLB-80

Southey, Caroline Anne Bowles
    1786-1854 . . . . .DLB-116

Southey, Robert 1774-1843 . . . . DLB-93, 107, 142

Southwell, Robert 1561?-1595. . . . . .DLB-167

Southworth, E. D. E. N. 1819-1899 . . . . .DLB-239

Sowande, Bode 1948- DLB-157

Sowle, Tace [publishing house] DLB-170

Soyfer, Jura 1912-1939 . . . . .DLB-124

Soyinka, Wole
    1934- DLB-125; Y-86, Y-87; CDWLB-3

Spacks, Barry 1931- DLB-105

Spalding, Frances 1950- DLB-155

Spark, Muriel 1918- DLB-15, 139; CDBLB-7

Sparke, Michael [publishing house] DLB-170

Sparks, Jared 1789-1866. . . . . .DLB-1, 30, 235

Sparshott, Francis 1926- DLB-60

Späth, Gerold 1939- DLB-75

Spatola, Adriano 1941-1988. . . . . .DLB-128

Spaziani, Maria Luisa 1924- DLB-128

Special Collections at the University of Colorado
    at Boulder Y-98

The Spectator 1828- DLB-110

Spedding, James 1808-1881 . . . . .DLB-144

Spee von Langenfeld, Friedrich
    1591-1635 . . . . .DLB-164

Speght, Rachel 1597-after 1630 . . . . .DLB-126

Speke, John Hanning 1827-1864 . . . . . . .DLB-166

Spellman, A. B. 1935- DLB-41

Spence, Catherine Helen 1825-1910 . . . . .DLB-230

Spence, Thomas 1750-1814 . . . . .DLB-158

Spencer, Anne 1882-1975. . . . . .DLB-51, 54

Spencer, Charles, third Earl of Sunderland
    1674-1722 . . . . .DLB-213

Spencer, Elizabeth 1921- DLB-6, 218

Spencer, George John, Second Earl Spencer
    1758-1834 . . . . .DLB-184

Spencer, Herbert 1820-1903 . . . . DLB-57, 262

    "The Philosophy of Style" (1852) DLB-57

Spencer, Scott 1945- Y-86

Spender, J. A. 1862-1942 . . . . .DLB-98

Spender, Stephen 1909-1995 . . .DLB-20; CDBLB-7

Spener, Philipp Jakob 1635-1705 . . . . . . .DLB-164

Spenser, Edmund
    circa 1552-1599 . . . . .DLB-167; CDBLB-1

Envoy from *The Shepheardes Calender* DLB-167

"The Generall Argument of the
    Whole Booke," from
    The Shepheardes Calender DLB-167

"A Letter of the Authors Expounding
    His Whole Intention in the Course
    of this Worke: Which for that It Giueth
    Great Light to the Reader, for the Better
    Vnderstanding Is Hereunto Annexed,"
    from *The Faerie Queene* (1590) DLB-167

"To His Booke," from
    The Shepheardes Calender (1579) DLB-167

"To the Most Excellent and Learned Both
    Orator and Poete, Mayster Gabriell Haruey,
    His Verie Special and Singular Good Frend
    E. K. Commendeth the Good Lyking of
    This His Labour, and the Patronage of
    the New Poete," from
    The Shepheardes Calender DLB-167

Sperr, Martin 1944- DLB-124

Truillier-Lacombe, Joseph-Patrice
1807-1863 . . . . DLB-99

Trumbo, Dalton 1905-1976 . . . . DLB-26

Trumbull, Benjamin 1735-1820 . . . . DLB-30

Trumbull, John 1750-1831 . . . . DLB-31

Trumbull, John 1756-1843 . . . . DLB-183

Truth, Sojourner 1797?-1883 . . . . DLB-239

Tscherning, Andreas 1611-1659 . . . . DLB-164

Tsubouchi, Shōyō 1859-1935 . . . . DLB-180

Tucholsky, Kurt 1890-1935 . . . . DLB-56

Tucker, Charlotte Maria
1821-1893 . . . . DLB-163, 190

Tucker, George 1775-1861 . . . . . . DLB-3, 30, 248

Tucker, James 1808?-1866? DLB-230

Tucker, Nathaniel Beverley
1784-1851 . . . . DLB-3, 248

Tucker, St. George 1752-1827 . . . . DLB-37

Tuckerman, Frederick Goddard
1821-1873 . . . . DLB-243

Tuckerman, Henry Theodore 1813-1871 . . DLB-64

Tumas, Juozas (see Vaizgantas)

Tunis, John R. 1889-1975 . . . . DLB-22, 171

Tunstall, Cuthbert 1474-1559 . . . . DLB-132

Tunström, Göran 1937-2000 . . . . DLB-257

Tuohy, Frank 1925- DLB-14, 139

Tupper, Martin F. 1810-1889 . . . . DLB-32

Tur, Evgeniia 1815-1892 . . . . DLB-238

Turbyfill, Mark 1896- DLB-45

Turco, Lewis 1934- Y-84

Turgenev, Aleksandr Ivanovich
1784-1845 . . . . DLB-198

Turgenev, Ivan Sergeevich 1818-1883 . . . DLB-238

Turnball, Alexander H. 1868-1918 . . . . . DLB-184

Turnbull, Andrew 1921-1970 . . . . DLB-103

Turnbull, Gael 1928- DLB-40

Turner, Arlin 1909-1980 . . . . DLB-103

Turner, Charles (Tennyson)
1808-1879 . . . . DLB-32

Turner, Ethel 1872-1958 . . . . DLB-230

Turner, Frederick 1943- DLB-40

Turner, Frederick Jackson
1861-1932 . . . . DLB-17, 186

Turner, Joseph Addison 1826-1868 . . . . . DLB-79

Turpin, Waters Edward 1910-1968 . . . . . DLB-51

Turrini, Peter 1944- DLB-124

Tutuola, Amos 1920-1997 . . DLB-125; CDWLB-3

Twain, Mark (see Clemens, Samuel Langhorne)

Tweedie, Ethel Brilliana circa 1860-1940 . . DLB-174

The 'Twenties and Berlin, by Alex Natan . DLB-66

Two Hundred Years of Rare Books and
Literary Collections at the
University of South Carolina Y-00

Twombly, Wells 1935-1977 . . . . DLB-241

Twysden, Sir Roger 1597-1672 . . . . DLB-213

Tyler, Anne
1941- DLB-6, 143; Y-82; CDALB-7

Tyler, Mary Palmer 1775-1866 . . . . DLB-200

Tyler, Moses Coit 1835-1900 . . . . DLB-47, 64

Tyler, Royall 1757-1826 . . . . DLB-37

Tylor, Edward Burnett 1832-1917 . . . . DLB-57

Tynan, Katharine 1861-1931 . . . . . DLB-153, 240

Tyndale, William circa 1494-1536 . . . . . DLB-132

U

Uchida, Yoshika 1921-1992 . . . . CDALB-7

Udall, Nicholas 1504-1556 . . . . DLB-62

Ugrêsić, Dubravka 1949- DLB-181

Uhland, Ludwig 1787-1862 . . . . DLB-90

Uhse, Bodo 1904-1963 . . . . DLB-69

Ujević, Augustin ("Tin") 1891-1955 . . . . . DLB-147

Ulenhart, Niclas flourished circa 1600 . . . DLB-164

Ulibarrí, Sabine R. 1919- DLB-82

Ulica, Jorge 1870-1926 . . . . DLB-82

Ulivi, Ferruccio 1912- DLB-196

Ulizio, B. George 1889-1969 . . . . DLB-140

Ulrich von Liechtenstein
circa 1200-circa 1275 . . . . DLB-138

Ulrich von Zatzikhoven
before 1194-after 1214 . . . . DLB-138

Ulysses, Reader's Edition Y-97

Unaipon, David 1872-1967 . . . . DLB-230

Unamuno, Miguel de 1864-1936 . . . . . . DLB-108

Under, Marie 1883-1980
. . . . DLB-220; CDWLB-4

Under the Microscope (1872), by
A. C. Swinburne DLB-35

Underhill, Evelyn
1875-1941 . . . . DLB-240

Ungaretti, Giuseppe 1888-1970 . . . . DLB-114

Unger, Friederike Helene 1741-1813 . . . . DLB-94

United States Book Company DLB-49

Universal Publishing and Distributing
Corporation DLB-46

The University of Iowa
Writers' Workshop
Golden Jubilee Y-86

University of Missouri Press Y-01

The University of South Carolina Press Y-94

University of Wales Press DLB-112

University Press of Florida Y-00

University Press of Kansas Y-98

University Press of Mississippi Y-99

"The Unknown Public" (1858), by
Wilkie Collins [excerpt] DLB-57

Uno, Chiyo 1897-1996 . . . . DLB-180

Unruh, Fritz von 1885-1970 . . . . DLB-56, 118

Unspeakable Practices II:
The Festival of Vanguard
Narrative at Brown University Y-93

Unsworth, Barry 1930- DLB-194

Unt, Mati 1944- DLB-232

The Unterberg Poetry Center of the
92nd Street Y Y-98

Unwin, T. Fisher [publishing house] DLB-106

Upchurch, Boyd B. (see Boyd, John)

Updike, John 1932-
. . . . DLB-2, 5, 143, 218, 227; Y-80, Y-82;
DS-3; CDALB-6

John Updike on the Internet Y-97

Upīts, Andrejs 1877-1970 . . . . DLB-220

Upton, Bertha 1849-1912 . . . . DLB-141

Upton, Charles 1948- DLB-16

Upton, Florence K. 1873-1922 . . . . DLB-141

Upward, Allen 1863-1926 . . . . DLB-36

Urban, Milo 1904-1982 . . . . DLB-215

Urista, Alberto Baltazar (see Alurista)

Urquhart, Fred 1912- DLB-139

Urrea, Luis Alberto 1955- DLB-209

Urzidil, Johannes 1896-1976 . . . . DLB-85

The Uses of Facsimile Y-90

Usk, Thomas died 1388 . . . . DLB-146

Uslar Pietri, Arturo 1906- DLB-113

Ussher, James 1581-1656 . . . . DLB-213

Ustinov, Peter 1921- DLB-13

Uttley, Alison 1884-1976 . . . . DLB-160

Uz, Johann Peter 1720-1796 . . . . DLB-97

V

Vac, Bertrand 1914- DLB-88

Vācietis, Ojārs 1933-1983 . . . . DLB-232

Vaičiulaitis, Antanas 1906-1992 . . . . DLB-220

Vaculík, Ludvík 1926- DLB-232

Vaičiūnaite, Judita 1937- DLB-232

Vail, Laurence 1891-1968 . . . . DLB-4

Vailland, Roger 1907-1965 . . . . DLB-83

Vaižgantas 1869-1933 . . . . DLB-220

Vajda, Ernest 1887-1954 . . . . DLB-44

Valdés, Gina 1943- DLB-122

Valdez, Luis Miguel 1940- DLB-122

Valduga, Patrizia 1953- DLB-128

Valente, José Angel 1929-2000 . . . . DLB-108

Valenzuela, Luisa 1938- . . . DLB-113; CDWLB-3

Valeri, Diego 1887-1976 . . . . DLB-128

Valerius Flaccus fl. circa A.D. 92 . . . . DLB-211

Valerius Maximus fl. circa A.D. 31 . . . . . DLB-211

Valéry, Paul 1871-1945 . . . . DLB-258

Valesio, Paolo 1939- DLB-196

Valgardson, W. D. 1939- DLB-60

Valle, Víctor Manuel 1950- DLB-122

Valle-Inclán, Ramón del 1866-1936 . . . . . DLB-134

Vallejo, Armando 1949- DLB-122

Vallès, Jules 1832-1885 . . . . DLB-123

Vallette, Marguerite Eymery (see Rachilde)

Valverde, José María 1926-1996 . . . . DLB-108

Van Allsburg, Chris 1949- DLB-61

Van Anda, Carr 1864-1945 . . . . DLB-25

van der Post, Laurens 1906-1996 . . . . . . DLB-204

Van Dine, S. S. (see Wright, Williard Huntington)

Van Doren, Mark 1894-1972 . . . . DLB-45

van Druten, John 1901-1957 . . . . DLB-10